D0761427

FEB 1998

DISCARD

OUTBOARD MOTOR AND INBOARD/OUTDRIVE

Wiring Diagrams
1956-1989

PROPERTY OF
THOUSAND OAKS LIBRARY
1401 E. Janss Road
Thousand Oaks, California

Published by
INTERTEC PUBLISHING CORPORATION
P.O. Box 12901, Overland Park, Kansas 66212

Copyright © 1990 Intertec Publishing Corporation

FIRST EDITION
First Printing June, 1990

Printed in U.S.A.

ISBN: 0-87288-388-4

Library of Congress: 90-055415

All rights reserved. Reproduction or use, without express permission, of editorial or pictorial content, in any manner, is prohibited. No patent liability is assumed with respect to the use of the information contained herein. While every precaution has been taken in the preparation of this book, the publisher assumes no responsibility for errors or omissions. Neither is any liability assumed for damages resulting from use of the information contained herein. Publication of the servicing information in this manual does not imply approval of the manufacturers of the products covered.

All instructions and diagrams have been checked for accuracy and ease of application; however, success and safety in working with tools depend to a great extent upon individual accuracy, skill and caution. For this reason the publishers are not able to guarantee the result of any procedure contained herein. Nor can they assume responsibility for any damage to property or injury to persons occasioned from the procedures. Persons engaging in the procedure do so entirely at their own risk.

Contents

Outboard Motor

Inboard/Outdrive

OUTBOARD MOTOR

CHRYSLER/FORCE

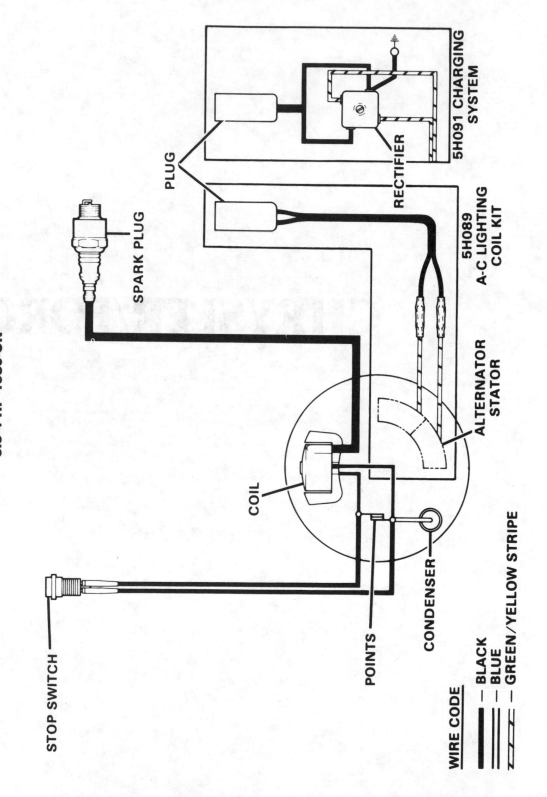

3.5-4 HP 1980-ON

SPARK PLUG

PLUG

RECTIFIER

5H091 CHARGING SYSTEM

5H089 A-C LIGHTING COIL KIT

ALTERNATOR STATOR

COIL

CONDENSER

POINTS

STOP SWITCH

GREEN/YELLOW STRIPE

WIRE CODE
— BLACK
— BLUE
— GREEN/YELLOW STRIPE

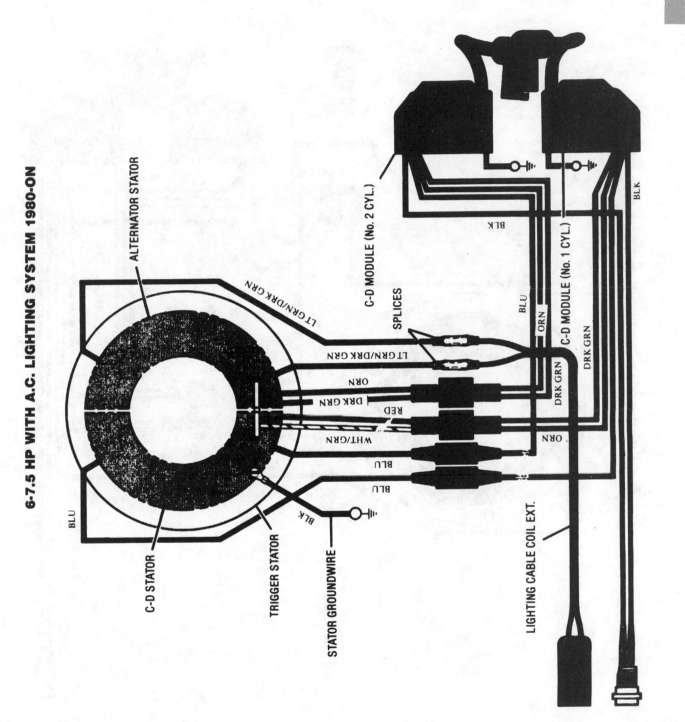

6-7.5 HP WITH A.C. LIGHTING SYSTEM 1980-ON

ALTERNATOR STATOR

C-D STATOR

TRIGGER STATOR

STATOR GROUNDWIRE

C-D MODULE (No. 2 CYL.)

SPLICES

C-D MODULE (No. 1 CYL.)

LIGHTING CABLE COIL EXT.

BLU
LT GRN/DRK GRN
LT GRN/DRK GRN
ORN
DRK GRN
RED
WHT/GRN
BLU
BLU
BLK
BLK
BLU
ORN
DRK GRN
DRK GRN
ORN
BLK

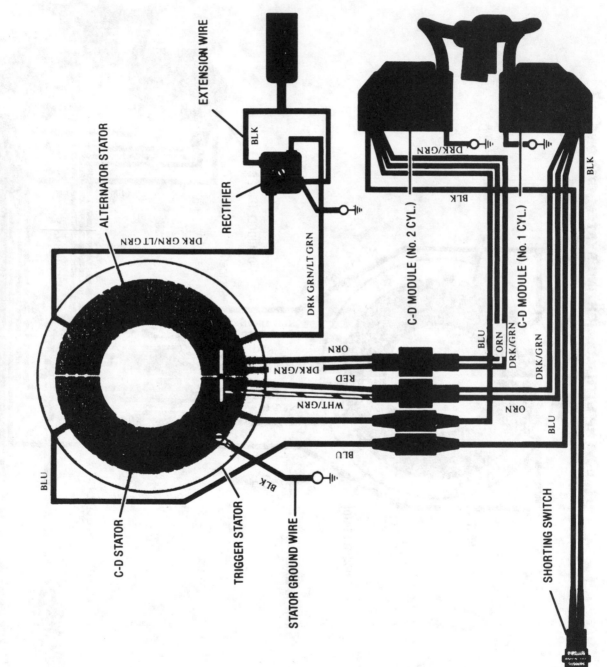

6-7.5 HP WITH D.C. BATTERY SYSTEM 1980-ON

6-8 HP ALTERNATOR CD IGNITION

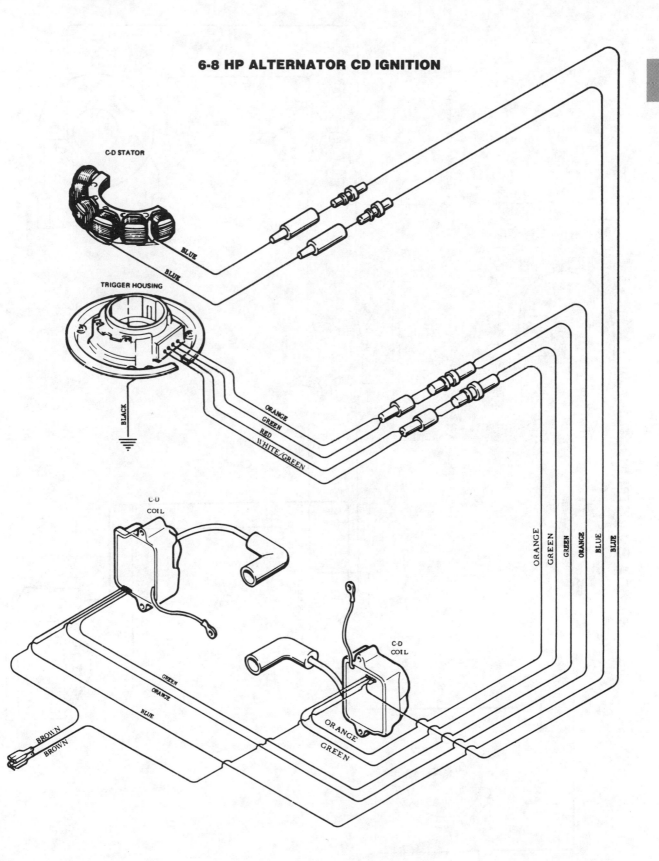

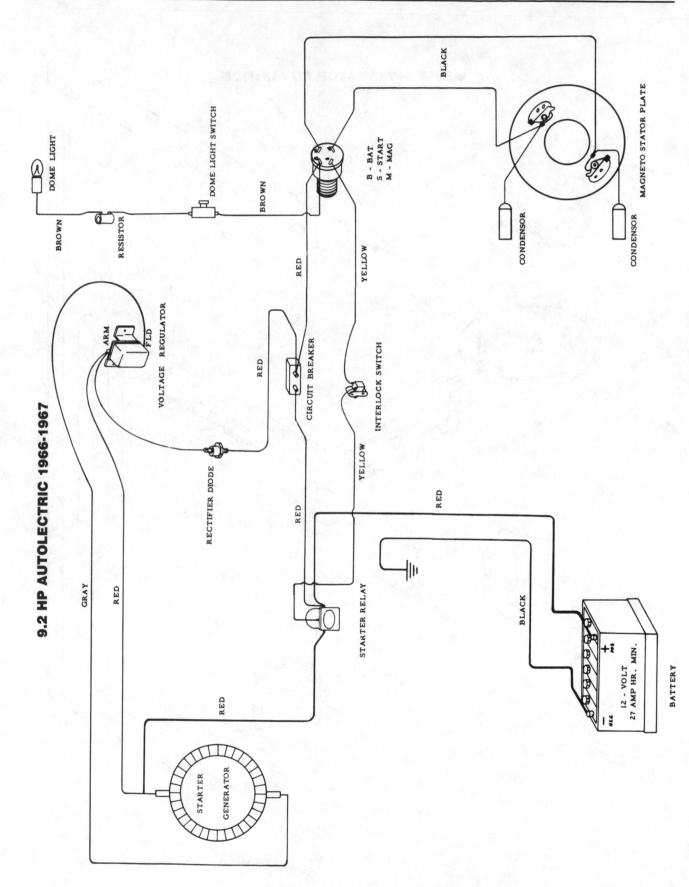

9.2 HP AUTOLECTRIC 1966-1967

9.9 HP AUTOLECTRIC 1968

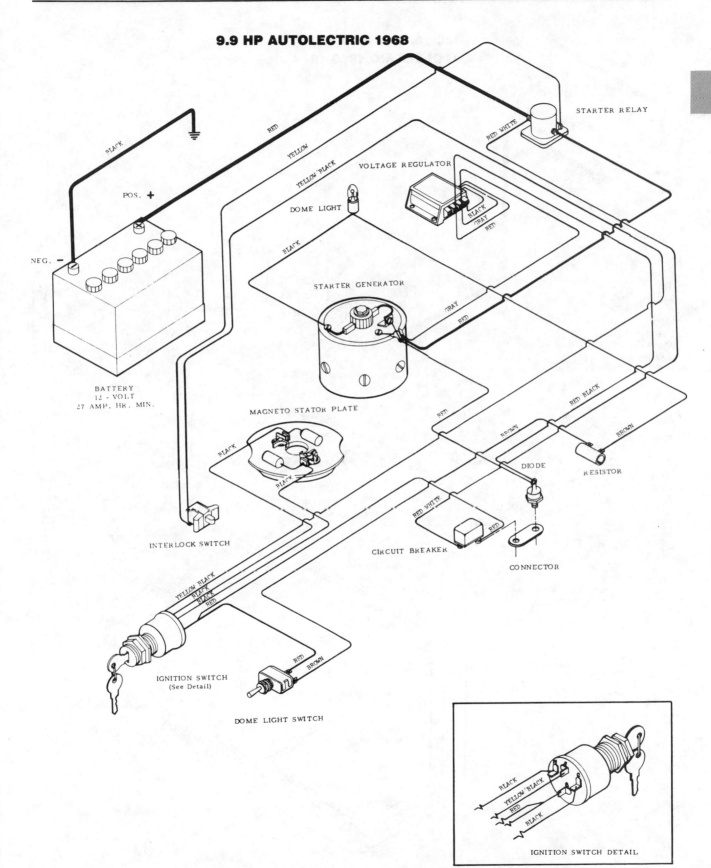

STARTER RELAY

RED WHITE

BLACK

RED

YELLOW

YELLOW BLACK

VOLTAGE REGULATOR

DOME LIGHT

BLACK
GRAY
RED

POS. +

BLACK

NEG. -

STARTER GENERATOR

GRAY   RED

RED

BATTERY
12 - VOLT
27 AMP. HR. MIN.

MAGNETO STATOR PLATE

RED

RED BLACK

BLACK

BROWN

BROWN

DIODE

RESISTOR

BLACK

RED WHITE

RED

INTERLOCK SWITCH

CIRCUIT BREAKER

CONNECTOR

YELLOW BLACK
BLACK
RED

IGNITION SWITCH
(See Detail)

RED   BROWN

DOME LIGHT SWITCH

BLACK
YELLOW BLACK
RED
BLACK

IGNITION SWITCH DETAIL

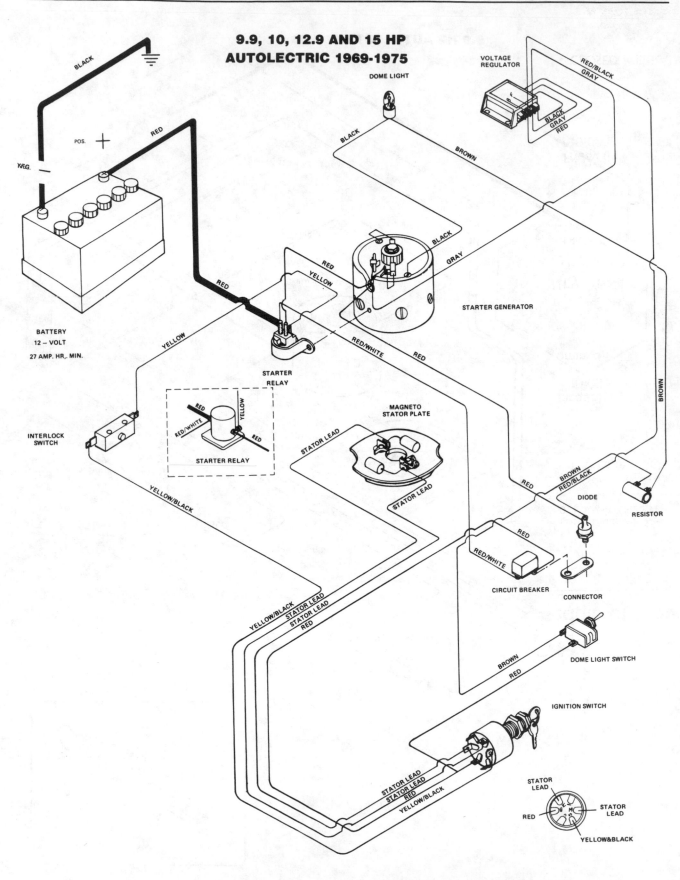

**9.9, 10, 12.9 AND 15 HP
AUTOLECTRIC 1969-1975**

1

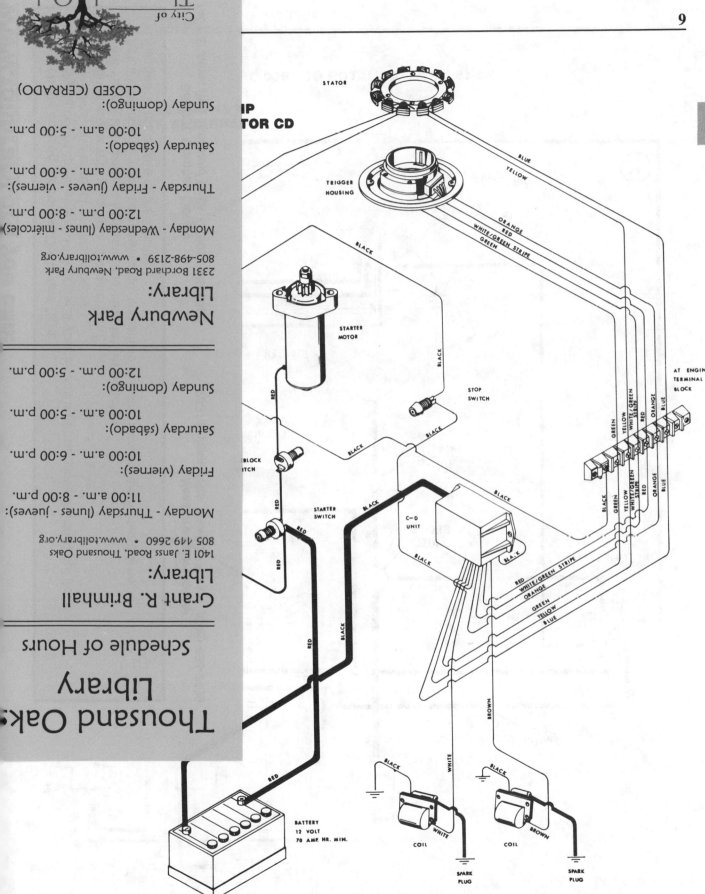

City of Thousand Oaks
LIBRARY

Thousand Oaks Library

Schedule of Hours

Grant R. Brimhall Library:
1401 E. Janss Road, Thousand Oaks • www.tolibrary.org
805 449 2660

Monday - Thursday (lunes - jueves):
11:00 a.m. - 8:00 p.m.
Friday (viernes):
10:00 a.m. - 6:00 p.m.
Saturday (sábado):
10:00 a.m. - 5:00 p.m.
Sunday (domingo):
12:00 p.m. - 5:00 p.m.

Newbury Park Library:
2331 Borchard Road, Newbury Park • www.tolibrary.org
805-498-2139

Monday - Wednesday (lunes - miércoles):
12:00 p.m. - 8:00 p.m.
Thursday - Friday (jueves - viernes):
10:00 a.m. - 6:00 p.m.
Saturday (sábado):
10:00 a.m. - 5:00 p.m.
Sunday (domingo):
CLOSED (CERRADO)

9.9-15 HP ALTERNATOR CD 1980-ON

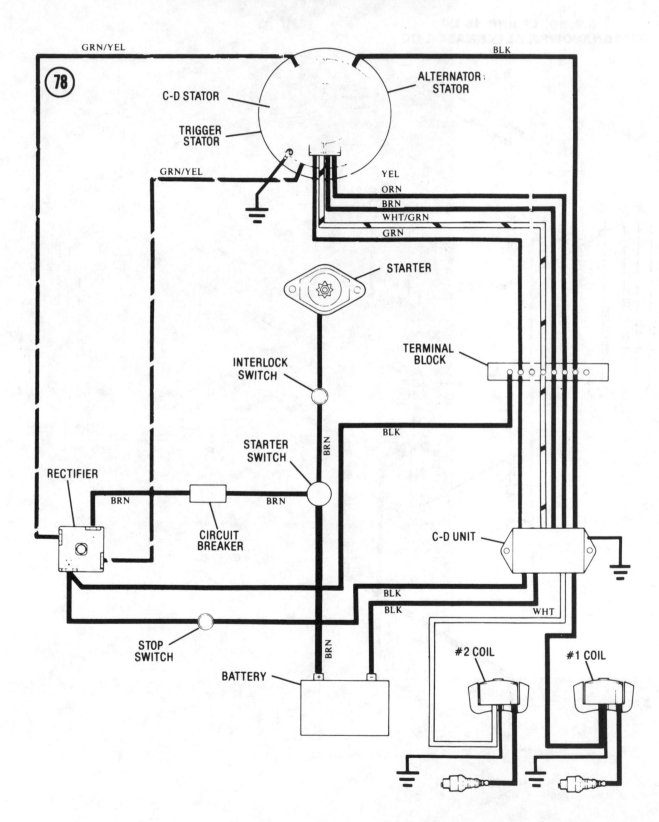

20 HP AUTOLECTRIC 1966-1967

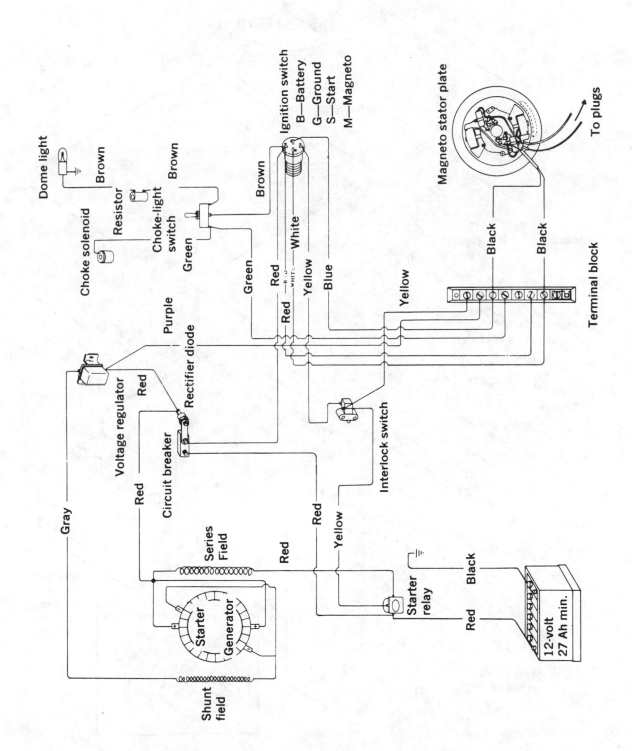

1

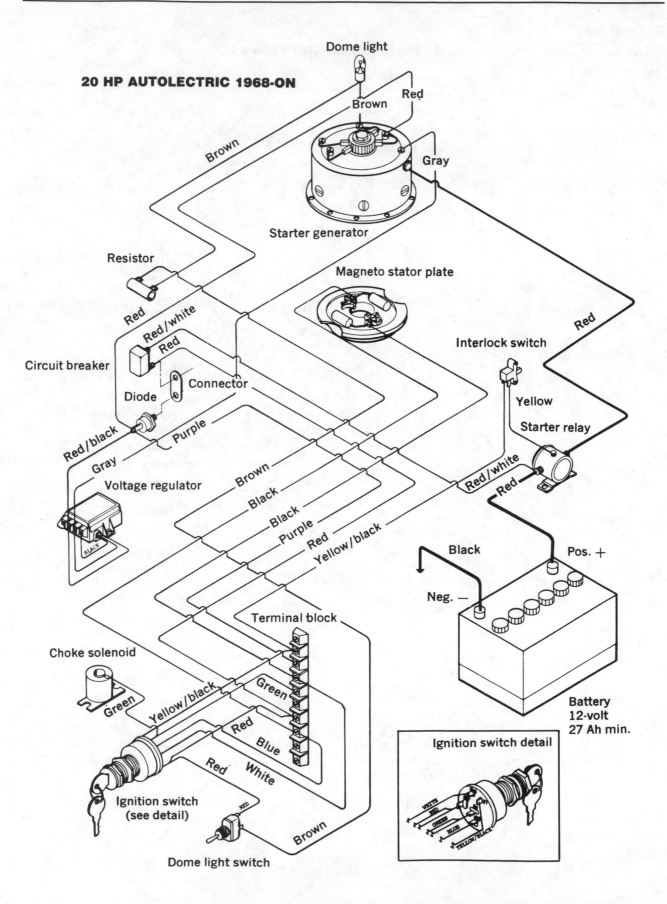

20 HP AUTOLECTRIC 1968-ON

Dome light

Red

Brown

Brown

Gray

Starter generator

Resistor

Magneto stator plate

Red

Red

Red/white

Interlock switch

Red

Circuit breaker

Connector

Diode

Yellow

Starter relay

Red/black

Purple

Gray

Red/white

Red

Voltage regulator

Brown

Black

Black

Purple

Red

Yellow/black

Black

Neg. —

Pos. +

Terminal block

Choke solenoid

Green

Green

Green

Yellow/black

Red

Blue

Red

White

Ignition switch
(see detail)

Battery
12-volt
27 Ah min.

Red

Ignition switch detail

Dome light switch

Brown

1

20 HP AUTOLECTRIC WITH REMOTE IGNITION SWITCH 1968-ON

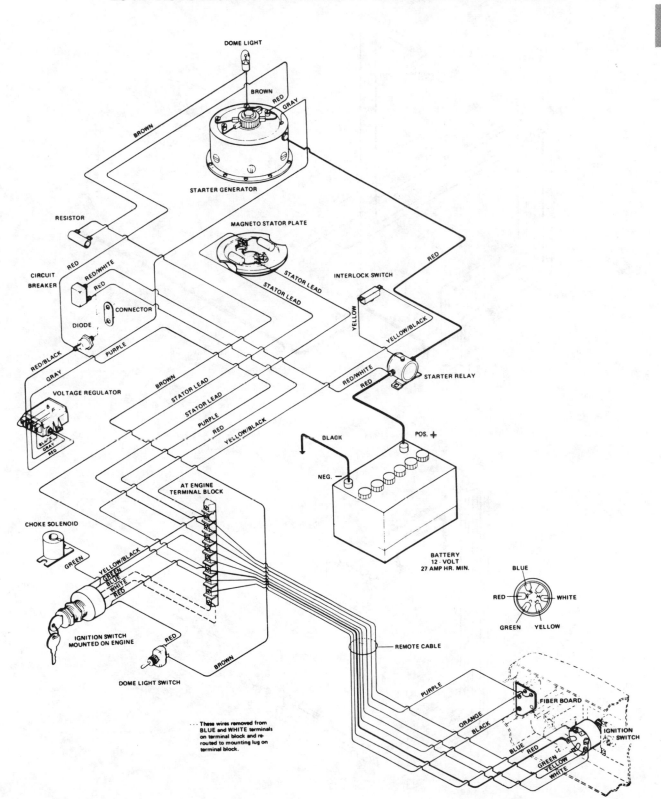

DOME LIGHT

BROWN
RED
GRAY

BROWN

STARTER GENERATOR

RESISTOR

MAGNETO STATOR PLATE

RED

CIRCUIT BREAKER

RED

RED/WHITE

CONNECTOR

STATOR LEAD

STATOR LEAD

INTERLOCK SWITCH

YELLOW

YELLOW/BLACK

DIODE

RED/BLACK

PURPLE

GRAY

VOLTAGE REGULATOR

BROWN

STATOR LEAD

STATOR LEAD

PURPLE

RED

YELLOW/BLACK

BLACK
GRAY
RED

RED/WHITE
RED

STARTER RELAY

BLACK

POS. +

NEG.

AT ENGINE TERMINAL BLOCK

CHOKE SOLENOID

GREEN

YELLOW/BLACK
GREEN
BLUE
WHITE
RED

BATTERY
12 · VOLT
27 AMP HR. MIN.

BLUE

RED — WHITE

GREEN   YELLOW

IGNITION SWITCH MOUNTED ON ENGINE

RED

REMOTE CABLE

BROWN

DOME LIGHT SWITCH

PURPLE

FIBER BOARD

ORANGE

BLACK

IGNITION SWITCH

BLUE RED

GREEN
YELLOW
WHITE

... These wires removed from BLUE and WHITE terminals on terminal block and re-routed to mounting lug on terminal block.

25-30 HP MAGNETO IGNITION

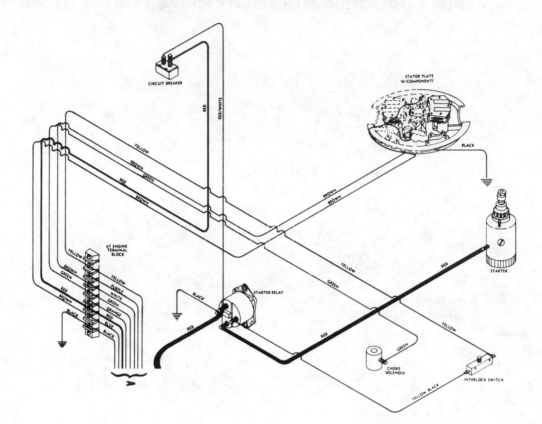

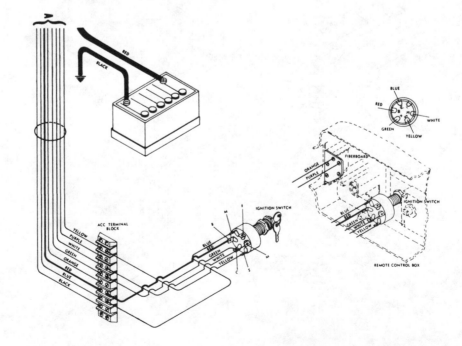

1980-ON 20 AND 30 HP, 1983-ON 35 HP (ELECTRIC START)

1

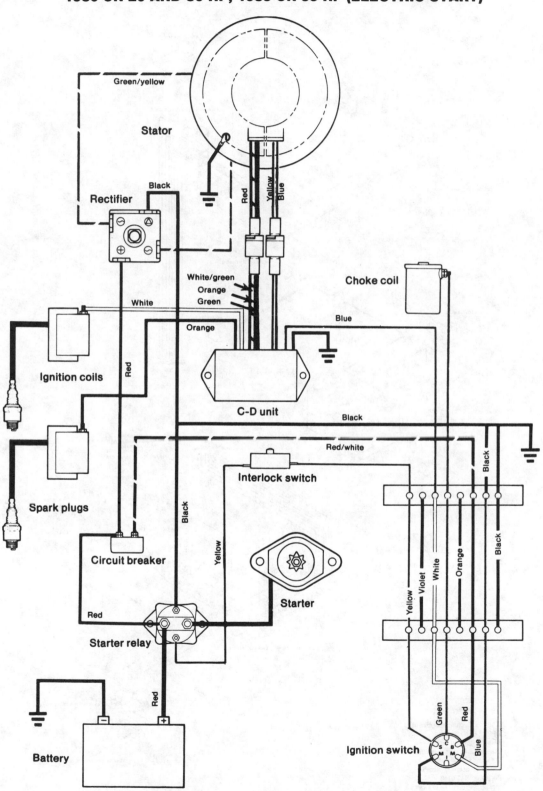

35, 45, 50 AND 55 HP MAGNETO IGNITION

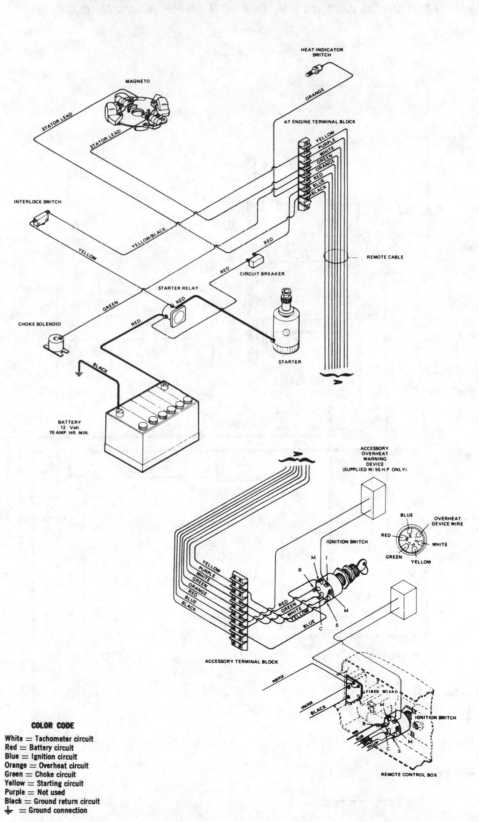

COLOR CODE

White = Tachometer circuit
Red = Battery circuit
Blue = Ignition circuit
Orange = Overheat circuit
Green = Choke circuit
Yellow = Starting circuit
Purple = Not used
Black = Ground return circuit
⏚ = Ground connection

35, 45, 50 AND 55 HP BATTERY IGNITION WITH ALTERNATOR

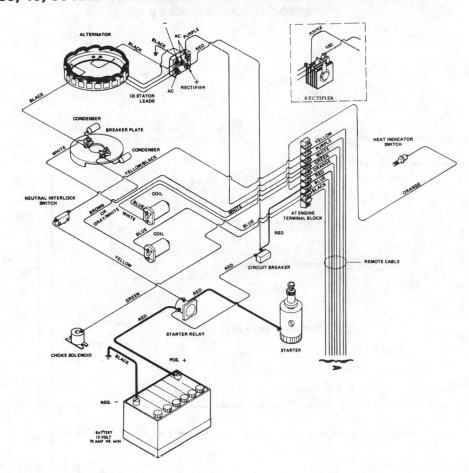

COLOR CODE

White = Tachometer circuit
Red = Battery circuit
Orange = Overheat circuit
Green = Choke circuit
Yellow = Starting circuit
Black = Ground return circuit
⏚ = Ground connection

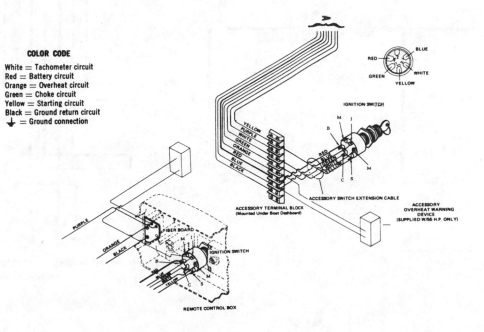

1980-ON 35, 45 AND 50 HP

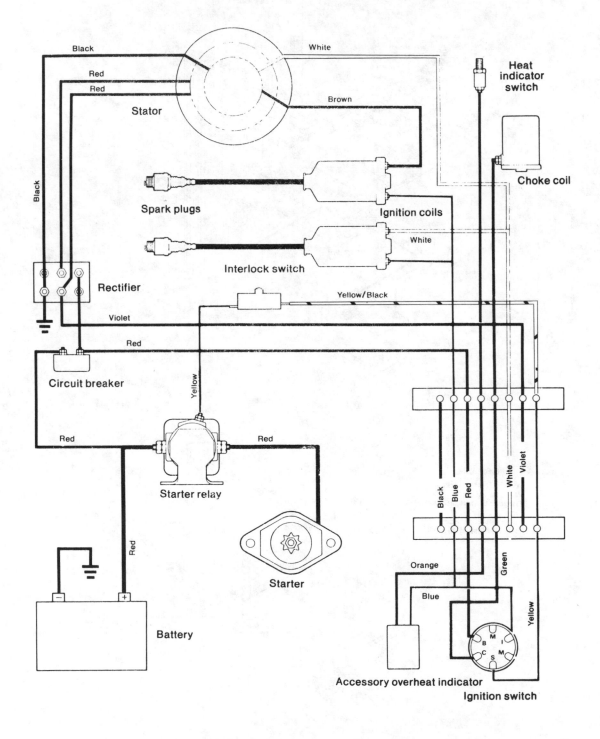

Black

White

Red

Red

Brown

Stator

Heat
indicator
switch

Black

Choke coil

Spark plugs

Ignition coils

White

Interlock switch

Rectifier

Yellow/Black

Violet

Red

Circuit breaker

Yellow

Starter relay

Red

Red

Red

Starter

Black

Blue

Red

White

Violet

Orange

Green

Blue

Yellow

Battery

Accessory overheat indicator

Ignition switch

1

55-65 HP MAGNAPOWER CD IGNITION

COIL NO. 1 CYLINDER

ALTERNATOR

HEAT INDICATOR SWITCH

BROWN

WHITE/BROWN

BLACK

SP. PLUG

SP. PLUG

GRAY

(3) STATOR LEADS

WHITE/GRAY

C-D UNIT

BLUE

WHITE

ORANGE

BROWN

WHITE/BROWN

BLACK

RECTIFIER

AC

AC

PURPLE

RED

+

YELLOW
PURPLE
WHITE
GREEN
ORANGE
RED
BLUE
BLACK

BREAKER PLATE

RED

AT ENGINE TERMINAL BLOCK

NEUTRAL INTERLOCK SWITCH

REMOTE ELECTRIC CABLE

YELLOW

YELLOW/BLACK

GREEN

CIRCUIT BREAKER

STARTER RELAY

RED

RED

RED

CHOKE SOLENOID

POS. +

STARTER

BLACK

NEG. –

BATTERY
12 - VOLT
70 Amp. Hr. Min.

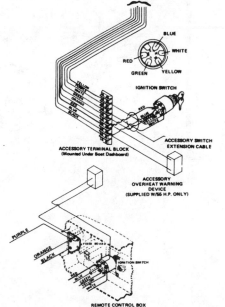

BLUE

RED

WHITE

GREEN

YELLOW

IGNITION SWITCH

ACCESSORY TERMINAL BLOCK
(Mounted Under Boat Dashboard)

ACCESSORY SWITCH EXTENSION CABLE

ACCESSORY OVERHEAT WARNING DEVICE
(SUPPLIED W/55 H.P. ONLY)

PURPLE

ORANGE

BLACK

IGNITION SWITCH

REMOTE CONTROL BOX

COLOR CODE

White = Tachometer circuit
Red = Battery circuit
Blue = Ignition circuit
Orange = Overheat circuit
Green = Choke circuit
Yellow = Starting circuit
Purple = Charge indicator circuit
Black = Ground return circuit
⏚ = Ground connection

1980-1981 55 HP

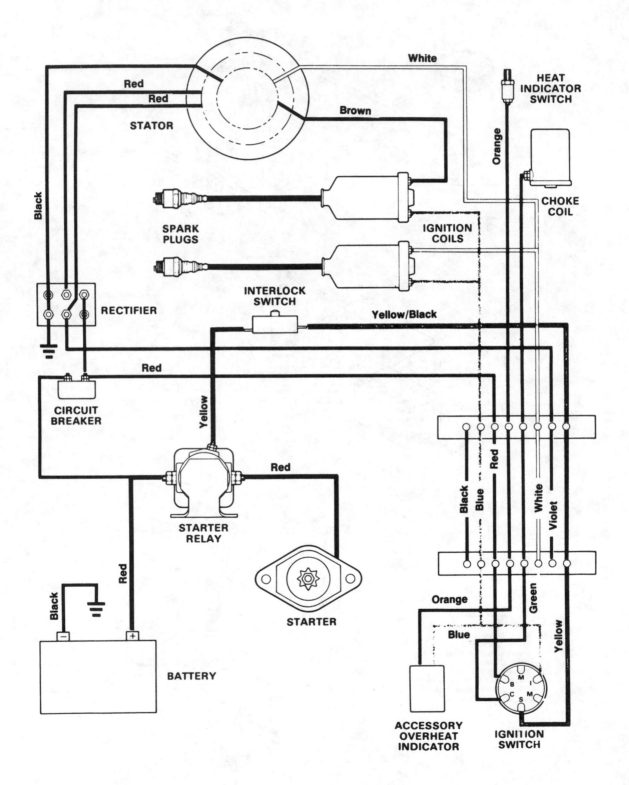

STATOR

White

HEAT INDICATOR SWITCH

Red

Red

Brown

Orange

CHOKE COIL

Black

SPARK PLUGS

IGNITION COILS

RECTIFIER

INTERLOCK SWITCH

Yellow/Black

Red

CIRCUIT BREAKER

Yellow

Black

Blue

Red

White

Violet

STARTER RELAY

Red

STARTER

Orange

Green

Yellow

Black

Red

Blue

BATTERY

ACCESSORY OVERHEAT INDICATOR

IGNITION SWITCH

1982-ON 55 HP

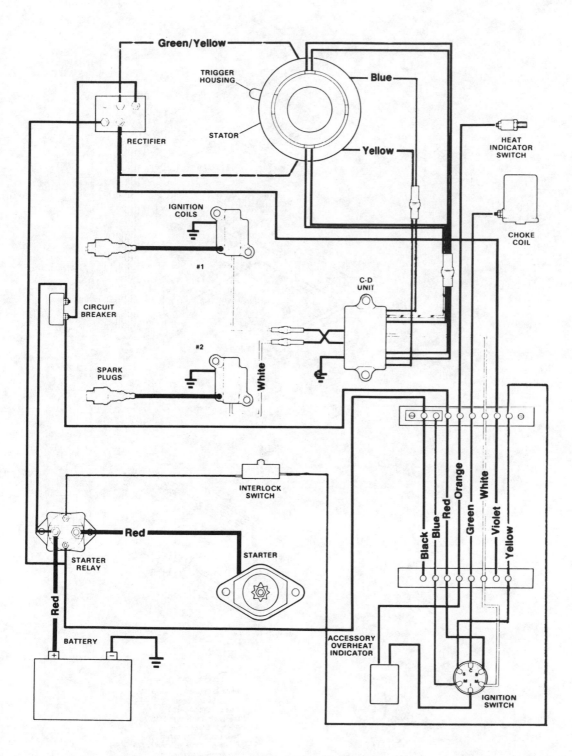

Green/Yellow

TRIGGER
HOUSING

Blue

STATOR

Yellow

HEAT
INDICATOR
SWITCH

RECTIFIER

CHOKE
COIL

IGNITION
COILS

#1

C-D
UNIT

CIRCUIT
BREAKER

#2

SPARK
PLUGS

White

INTERLOCK
SWITCH

Red

STARTER

STARTER
RELAY

Black
Blue
Red
Orange
Green
White
Violet
Yellow

Red

BATTERY

+   −

ACCESSORY
OVERHEAT
INDICATOR

IGNITION
SWITCH

75-105 HP BATTERY IGNITION WITH ALTERNATOR

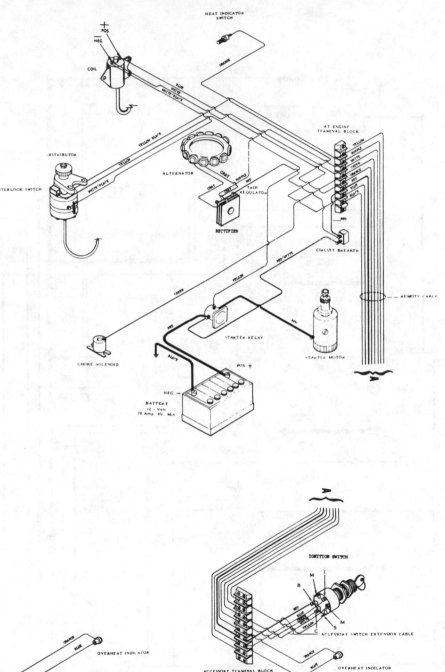

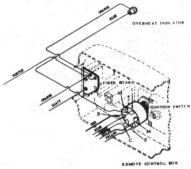

COLOR CODE

White = Tachometer circuit
Red = Battery circuit
Blue = Ignition circuit
Orange = Overheat circuit
Green = Choke circuit
Yellow = Starting circuit
Purple = Charge indicator circuit
Black = Ground return circuit
⏚ = Ground connection

70, 75, 85, 105, 120 AND 135 HP
MAGNAPOWER CD IGNITION (DELTA SYSTEM)

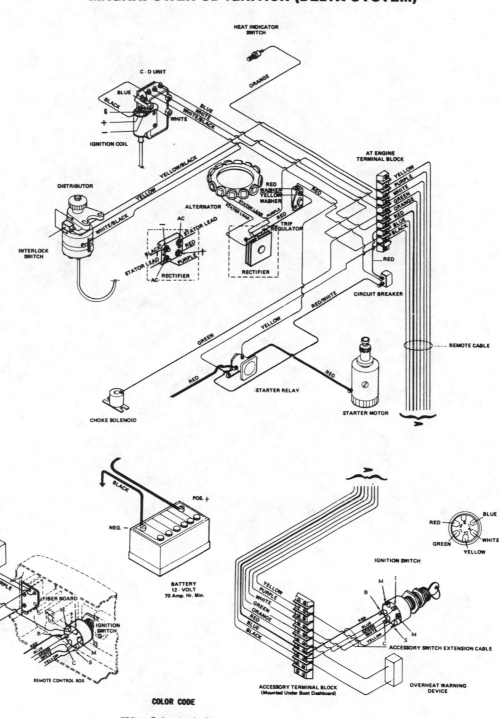

COLOR CODE

White = Tachometer circuit
Red = Battery circuit
Blue = Ignition circuit
Orange = Overheat circuit
Green = Choke circuit
Yellow = Starting circuit
Purple = Charge indicator circuit
Black = Ground return circuit
⏚ = Ground connection

70, 85, 105, 120 AND 135 HP
MAGNAPOWER CD IGNITION (MOTOROLA SYSTEM)

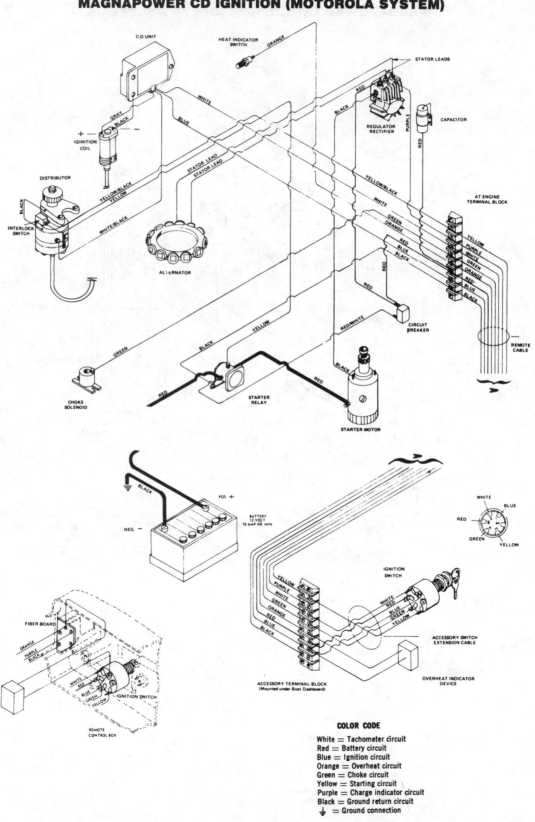

COLOR CODE

White = Tachometer circuit
Red = Battery circuit
Blue = Ignition circuit
Orange = Overheat circuit
Green = Choke circuit
Yellow = Starting circuit
Purple = Charge indicator circuit
Black = Ground return circuit
⏚ = Ground connection

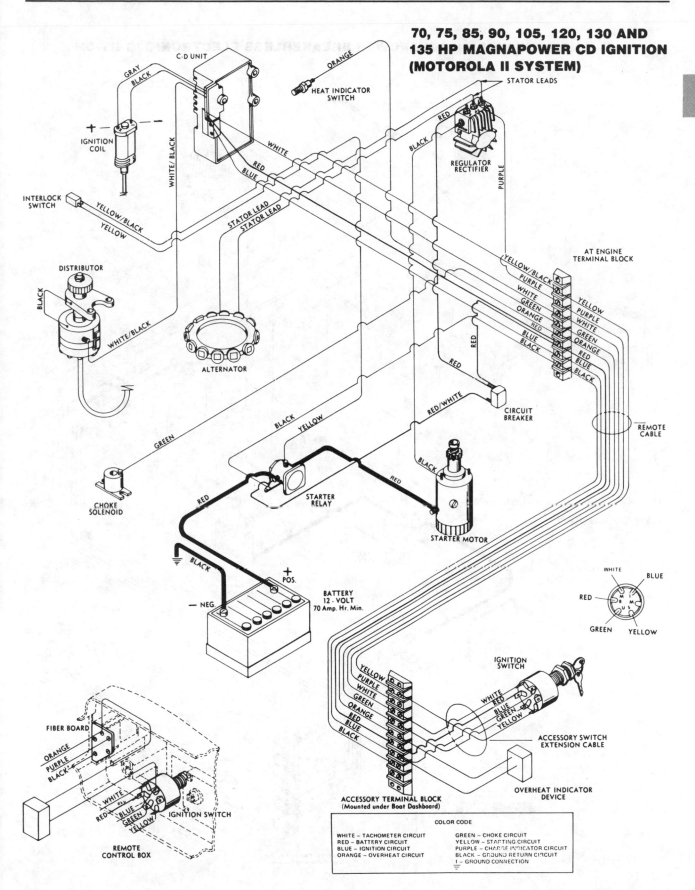

70, 75, 85, 90, 105, 120, 130 AND 135 HP MAGNAPOWER CD IGNITION (MOTOROLA II SYSTEM)

C-D UNIT

GRAY
BLACK
ORANGE

HEAT INDICATOR SWITCH

STATOR LEADS

IGNITION COIL

RED

WHITE/BLACK

WHITE

RED

BLUE

BLACK

REGULATOR RECTIFIER

PURPLE

INTERLOCK SWITCH

YELLOW/BLACK

YELLOW

STATOR LEAD

STATOR LEAD

AT ENGINE TERMINAL BLOCK

YELLOW/BLACK
PURPLE
WHITE
GREEN
ORANGE
RED
BLUE
BLACK

YELLOW
PURPLE
WHITE
GREEN
ORANGE
RED
BLUE
BLACK

DISTRIBUTOR

BLACK

WHITE/BLACK

ALTERNATOR

RED

RED

CIRCUIT BREAKER

REMOTE CABLE

GREEN

BLACK

YELLOW

RED/WHITE

RED

CHOKE SOLENOID

STARTER RELAY

BLACK

STARTER MOTOR

WHITE   BLUE

RED   M B U S   M

GREEN   YELLOW

BLACK

POS.

NEG.

BATTERY
12 - VOLT
70 Amp. Hr. Min.

YELLOW
PURPLE
WHITE
GREEN
ORANGE
RED
BLUE
BLACK

IGNITION SWITCH

WHITE
RED
BLUE
GREEN
YELLOW

ACCESSORY SWITCH EXTENSION CABLE

FIBER BOARD

ORANGE
PURPLE
BLACK

WHITE
RED
BLUE
GREEN
YELLOW

IGNITION SWITCH

ACCESSORY TERMINAL BLOCK
(Mounted under Boat Dashboard)

OVERHEAT INDICATOR DEVICE

REMOTE CONTROL BOX

COLOR CODE

WHITE – TACHOMETER CIRCUIT
RED – BATTERY CIRCUIT
BLUE – IGNITION CIRCUIT
ORANGE – OVERHEAT CIRCUIT

GREEN – CHOKE CIRCUIT
YELLOW – STARTING CIRCUIT
PURPLE – CHARGE INDICATOR CIRCUIT
BLACK – GROUND RETURN CIRCUIT
⏚ – GROUND CONNECTION

1

3- AND 4-CYLINDER MAGNAPOWER BREAKERLESS ELECTRONIC IGNITION

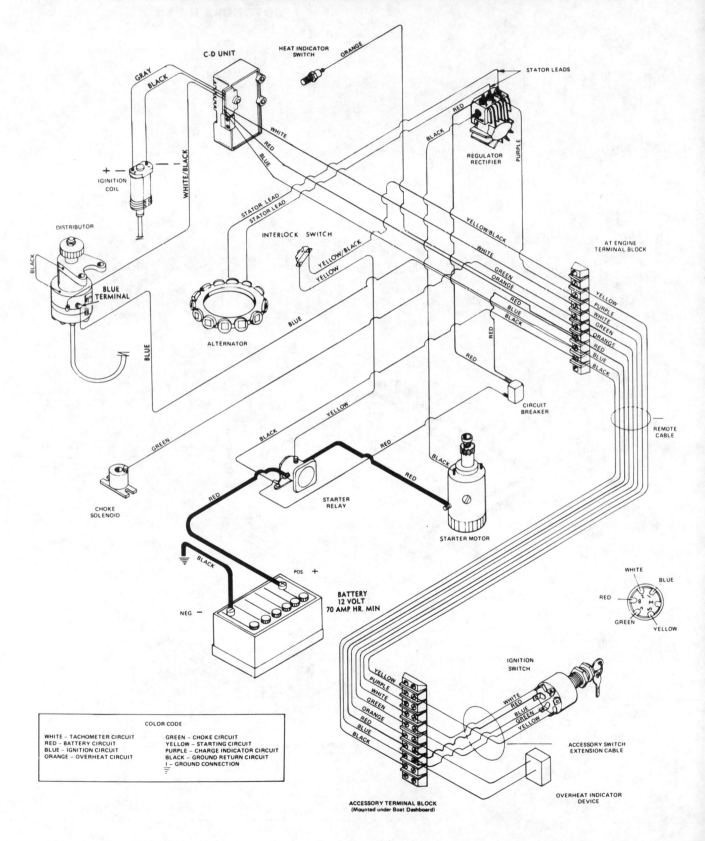

105, 120 AND 135 HP MAGNAPOWER II IGNITION

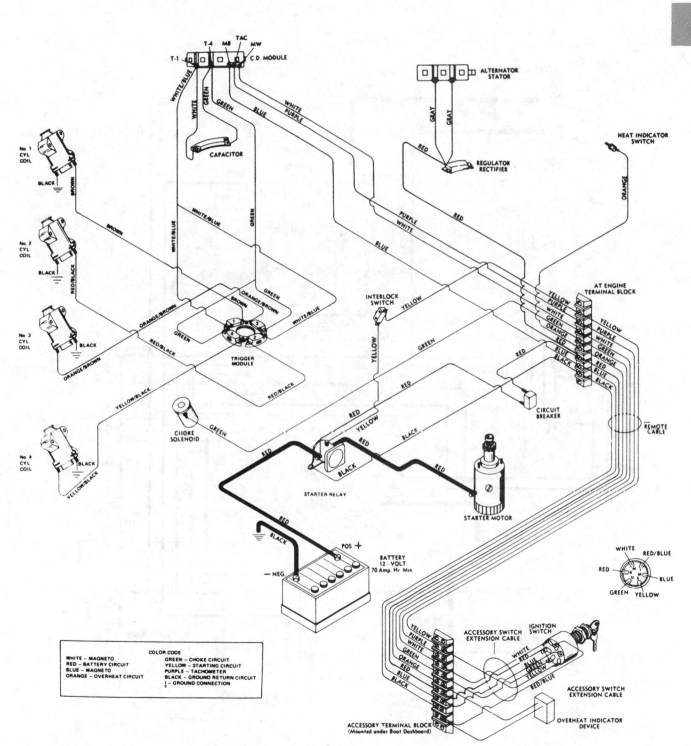

1

1980-ON 75 AND 85 HP (MOTOROLA)

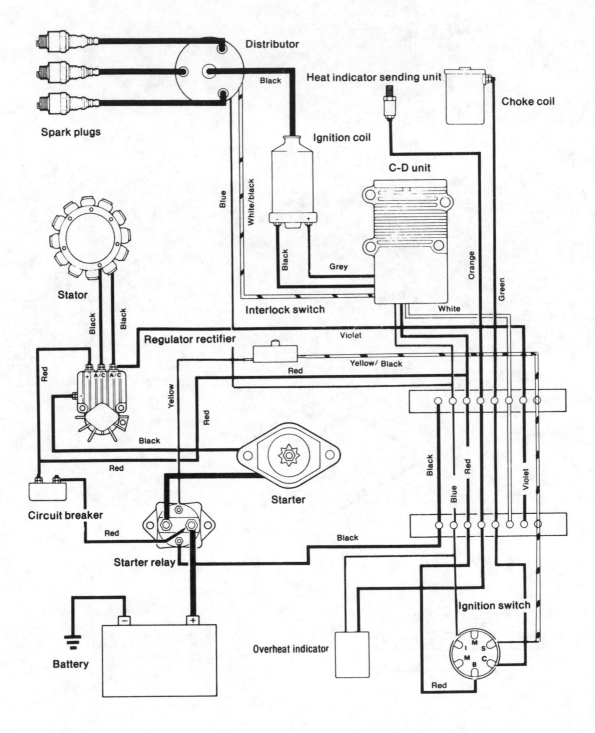

1983-ON 75 AND 85 HP (PRESTOLITE)

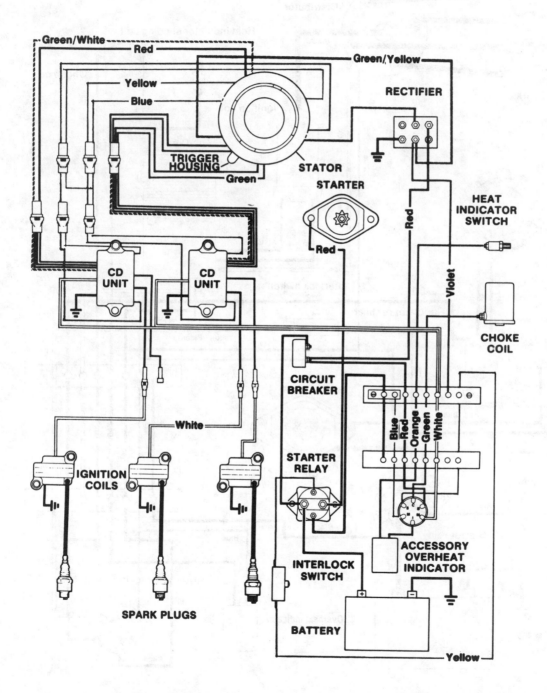

1980-ON 115 AND 140 HP (MOTOROLA)

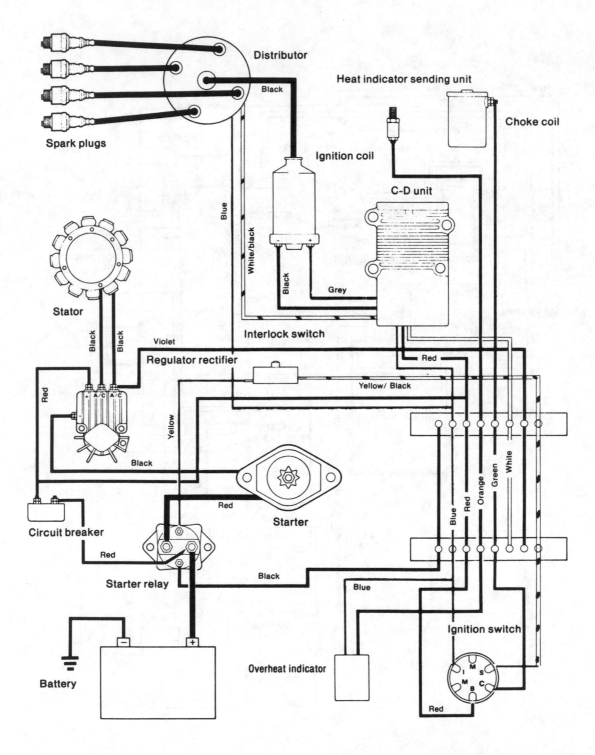

125 HP (PRESTOLITE)

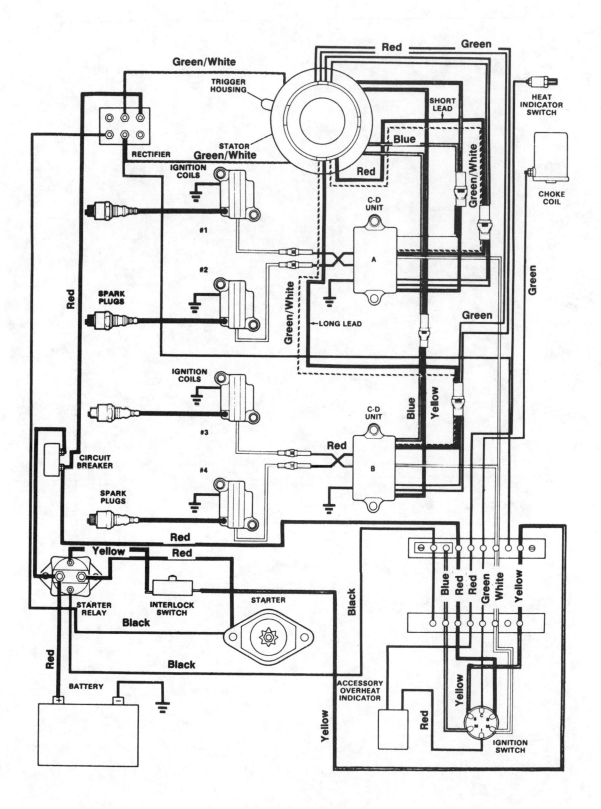

1

MARINER

RC MODEL WIRING DIAGRAM

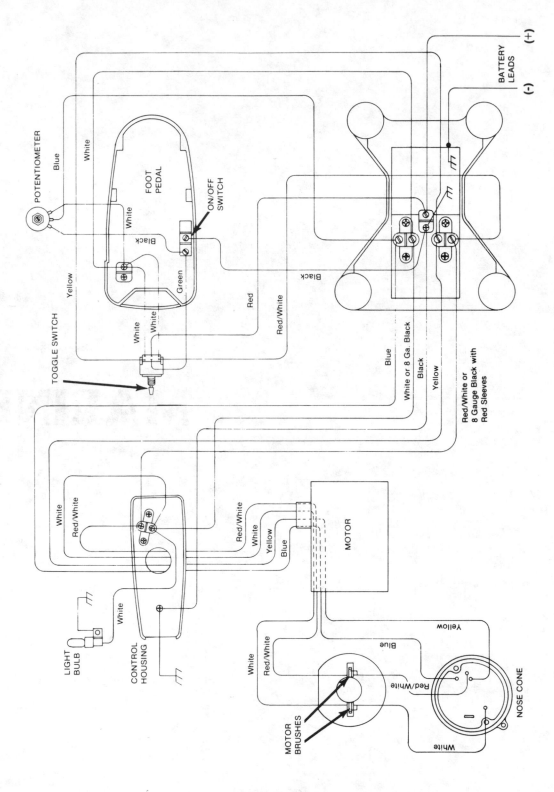

TM MODEL WIRING DIAGRAM

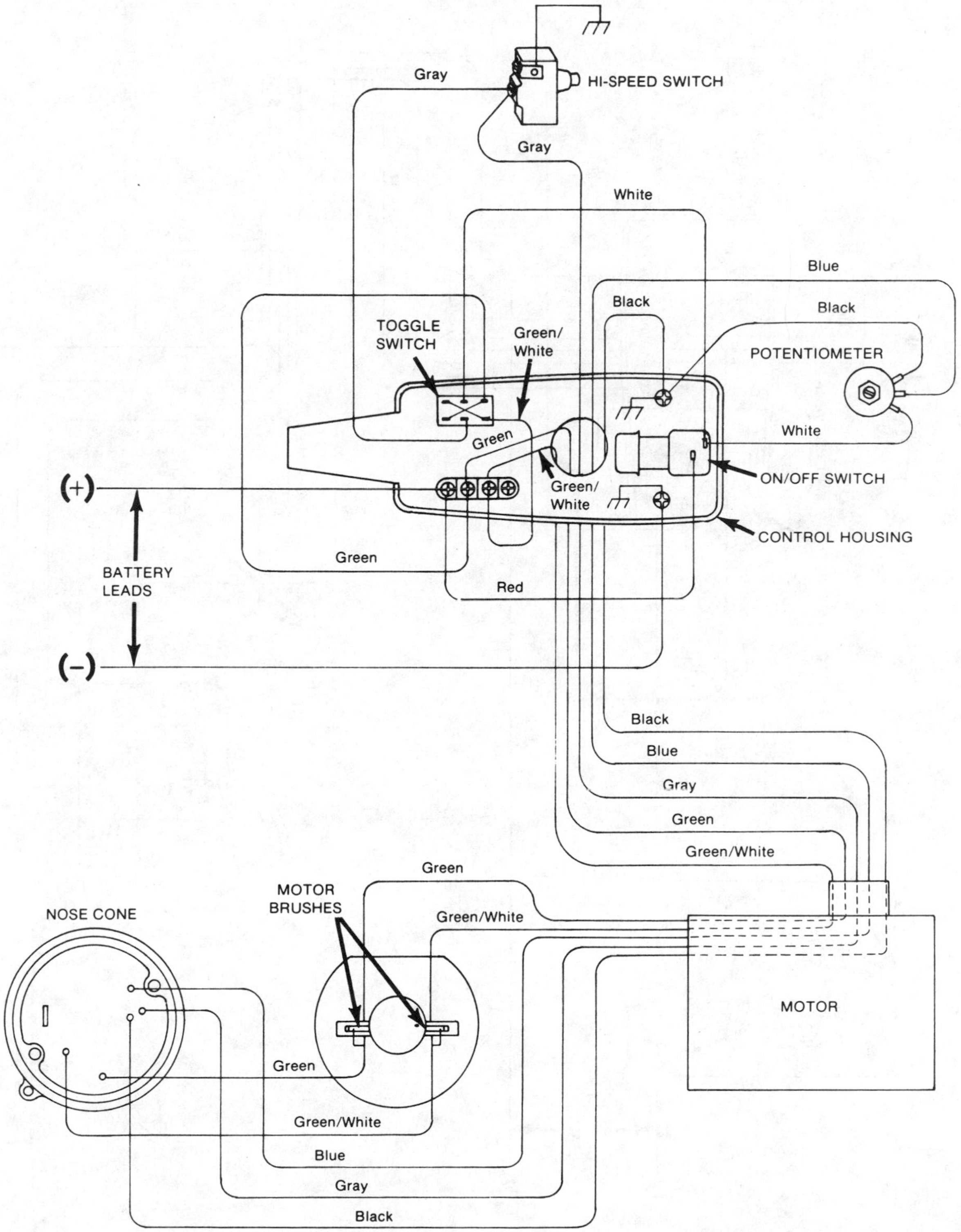

HI-SPEED SWITCH

Gray

Gray

White

Blue

Black

Black

TOGGLE
SWITCH

Green/
White

POTENTIOMETER

Green

Green/
White

White

ON/OFF SWITCH

(+)

CONTROL HOUSING

BATTERY
LEADS

Green

Red

(−)

Black

Blue

Gray

Green

Green/White

Green

MOTOR
BRUSHES

Green/White

NOSE CONE

MOTOR

Green

Green/White

Blue

Gray

Black

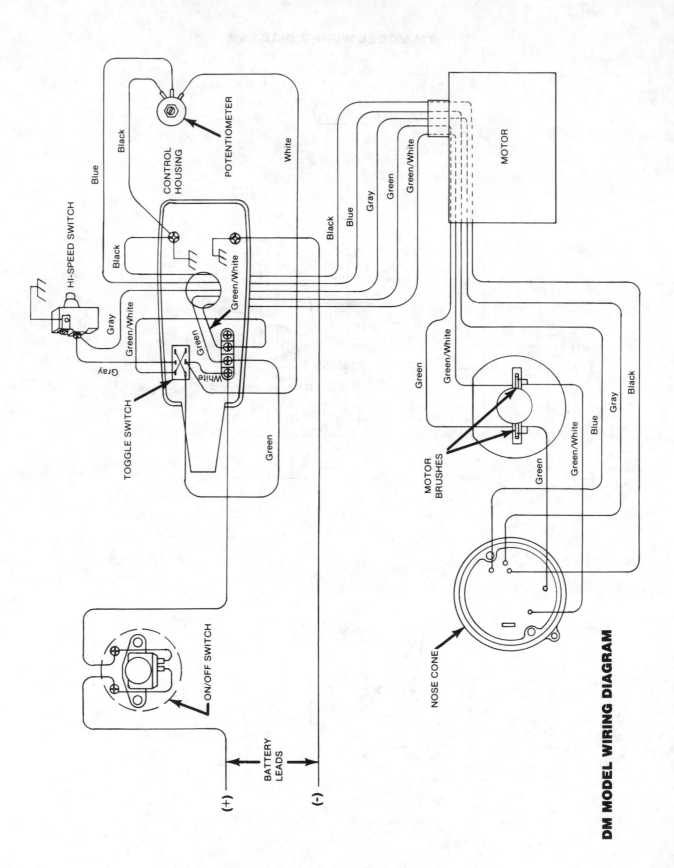

DM MODEL WIRING DIAGRAM

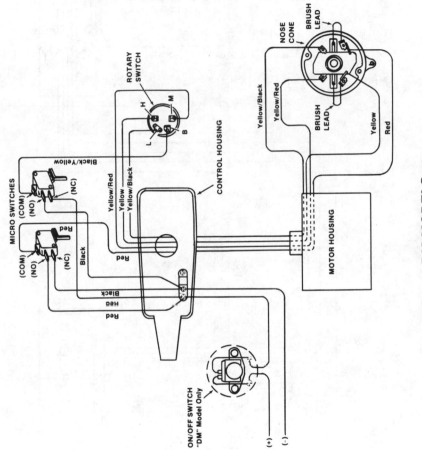

TM and DM MODELS (WITH VERTICAL MOUNTED MICRO SWITCHES)

ROTARY SWITCH

H

M

L

B

Black/Yellow

MICRO SWITCHES

(COM)

(NO)

(NC)

Red

(COM)

(NO)

(NC)

Red

Yellow/Red

Yellow

Yellow/Black

Black

Red

Red

Black

Red

Red

CONTROL HOUSING

Yellow/Black

Yellow/Red

BRUSH LEAD

BRUSH LEAD

NOSE CONE

Yellow

Red

MOTOR HOUSING

ON/OFF SWITCH "DM" Model Only

(+)

(−)

RC MODEL WIRING DIAGRAM

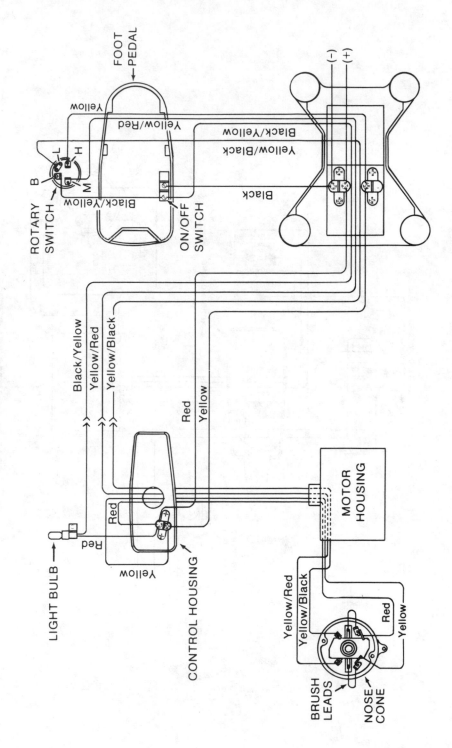

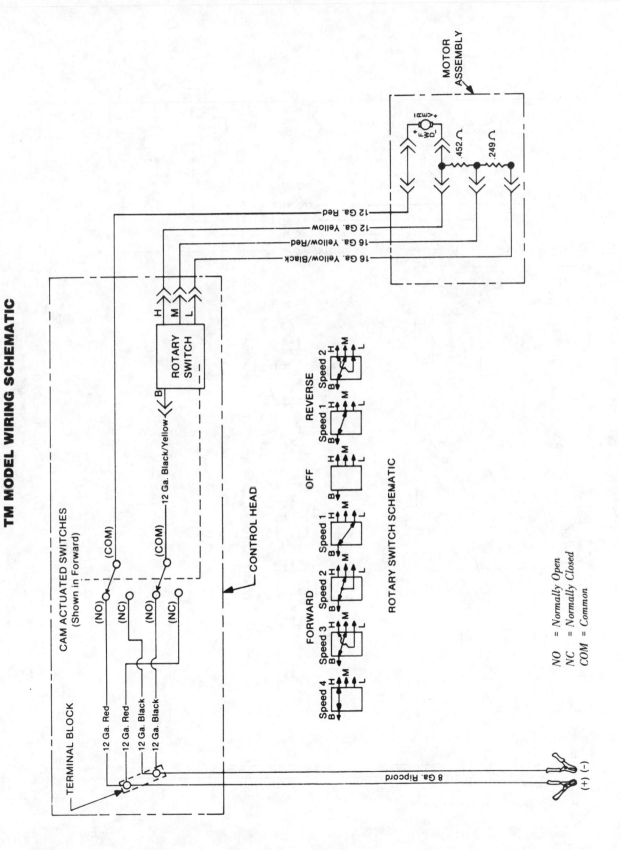

TM MODEL WIRING SCHEMATIC

MOTOR ASSEMBLY

.452 Ω
.249 Ω

12 Ga. Red
12 Ga. Yellow
16 Ga. Yellow/Red
16 Ga. Yellow/Black

ROTARY SWITCH

H
M
L
B

12 Ga. Black/Yellow

CONTROL HEAD

TERMINAL BLOCK

CAM ACTUATED SWITCHES
(Shown in Forward)

(COM)
(NO)
(NC)
(COM)
(NO)
(NC)

12 Ga. Red
12 Ga. Red
12 Ga. Black
12 Ga. Black

8 Ga. Ripcord

(+) (−)

ROTARY SWITCH SCHEMATIC

FORWARD

Speed 4
Speed 3
Speed 2
Speed 1

OFF

REVERSE

Speed 1
Speed 2

B H M L

NO = Normally Open
NC = Normally Closed
COM = Common

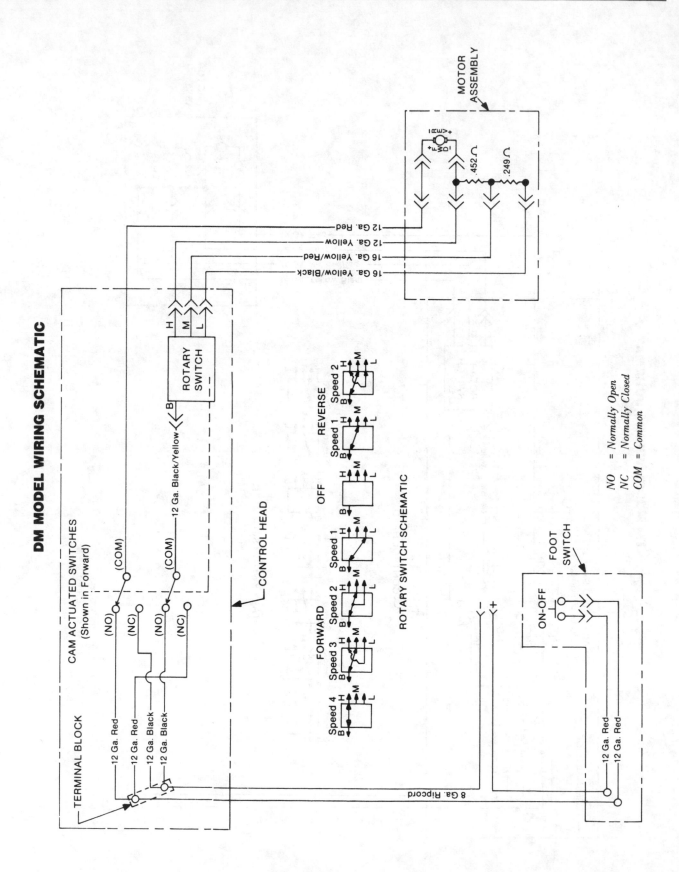

DM MODEL WIRING SCHEMATIC

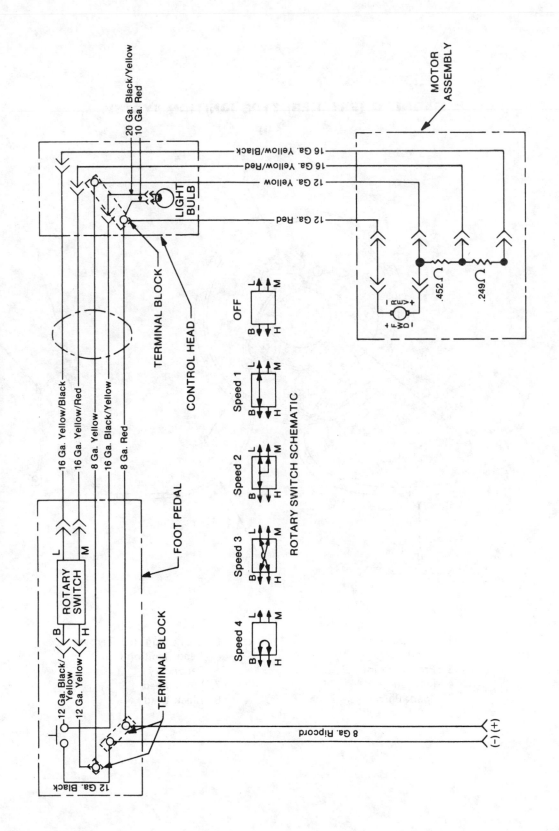

RC MODEL WIRING SCHEMATIC

MAGNETO (BREAKER) TYPE IGNITION SYSTEM
2 hp

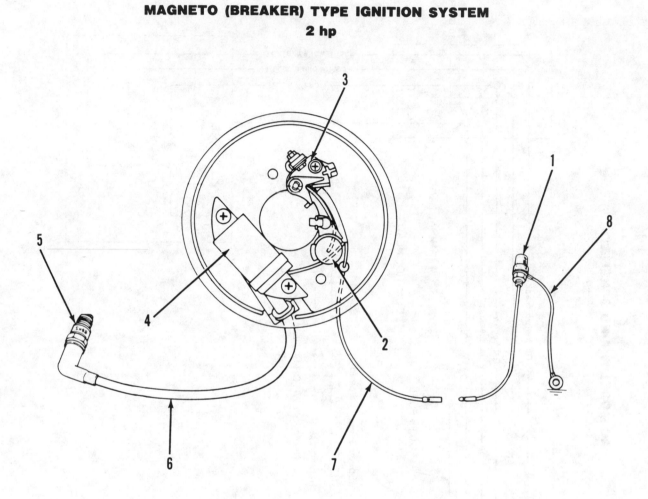

1. Stop Button
2. Condenser
3. Breaker Point
4. Ignition Coil
5. Spark Plug
6. Spark Plug High Tension Lead (Ignition Coil Secondary)
7. White Lead
8. Black Lead

CDI SYSTEMS SCHEMATIC DIAGRAM
4 hp

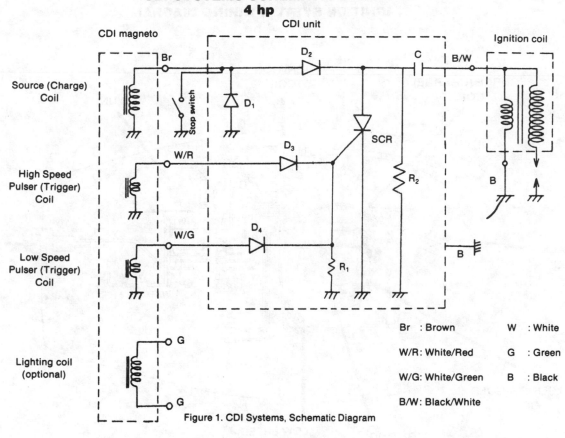

Figure 1. CDI Systems, Schematic Diagram

Br : Brown	W : White
W/R: White/Red	G : Green
W/G: White/Green	B : Black
B/W: Black/White	

RECTIFIER ASSEMBLY
4 hp

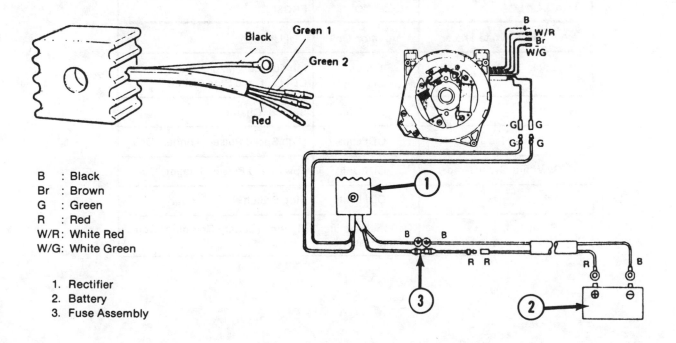

B : Black
Br : Brown
G : Green
R : Red
W/R: White Red
W/G: White Green

1. Rectifier
2. Battery
3. Fuse Assembly

2

IGNITION SYSTEM WIRING DIAGRAM
4 hp

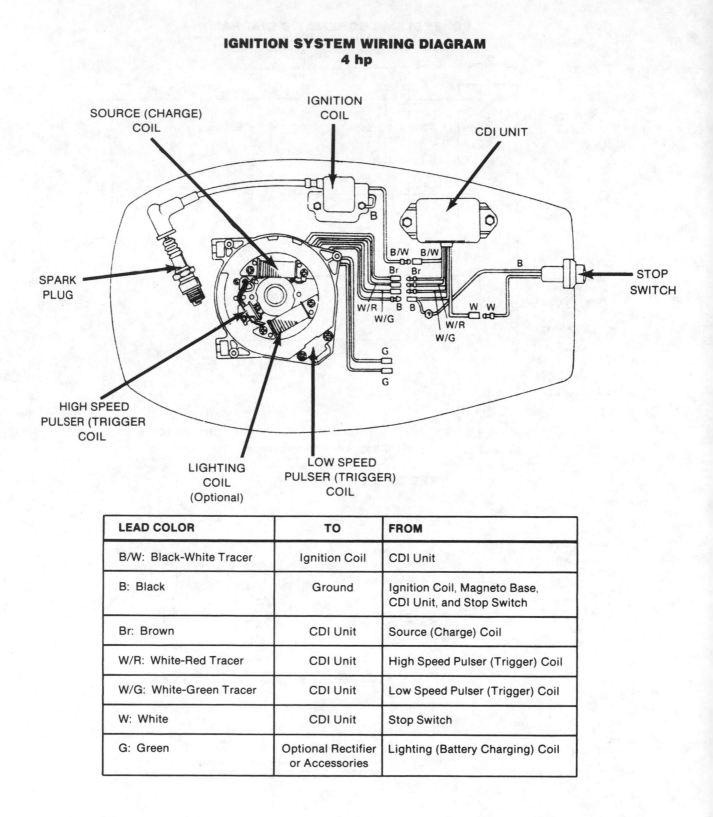

LEAD COLOR	TO	FROM
B/W: Black-White Tracer	Ignition Coil	CDI Unit
B: Black	Ground	Ignition Coil, Magneto Base, CDI Unit, and Stop Switch
Br: Brown	CDI Unit	Source (Charge) Coil
W/R: White-Red Tracer	CDI Unit	High Speed Pulser (Trigger) Coil
W/G: White-Green Tracer	CDI Unit	Low Speed Pulser (Trigger) Coil
W: White	CDI Unit	Stop Switch
G: Green	Optional Rectifier or Accessories	Lighting (Battery Charging) Coil

IGNITION SYSTEM
5 hp

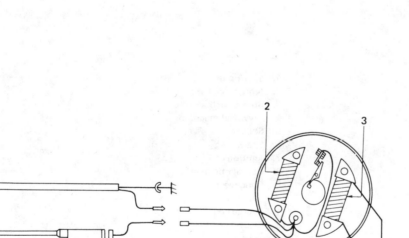

1. Ignition coil
2. Spark plug
3. Engine stop switch
4. Flywheel magneto
5. Contact breaker
6. Condenser
7. Ignition source coil
8. Lighting coil
9. Two-pole socket (Option)

1. Engine stop switch assembly
2. Ignition source coil
3. Lighting coil (option)
4. Ignition coil

2

IGNITION SYSTEM
8 hp

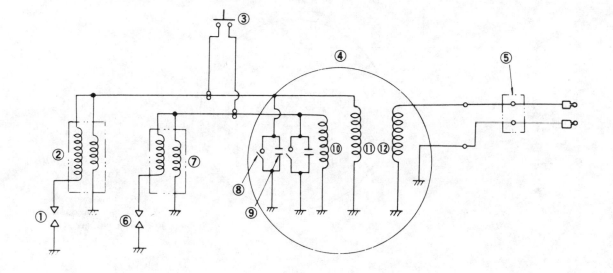

1. Spark plug
2. Ignition coil
3. Stop switch
4. Flywheel magneto
5. Socket
6. Spark plug
7. Ignition coil
8. Contact breaker
9. Condenser
10. Source coil
11. Source coil
12. Lighting coil

IGNITION SYSTEM
8 hp

1. First cylinder (Upper)
2. Stop switch ass'y
3. Second cylinder (Lower)
4. Ignition coil
5. Black
6. Gray
7. Socket
8. Ignition coil
9. Black
10. Orange
11. Source coil
12. Lighting coil

MAGNETO (BREAKER) TYPE IGNITION SYSTEM
8-9.9-15 hp

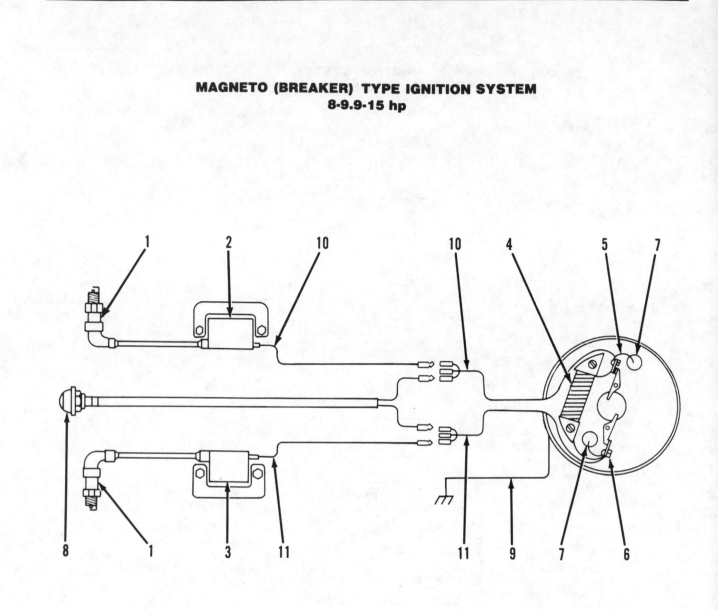

1. Spark Plug (2)
2. Secondary Ignition Coil -
   No. 1 Cylinder (Upper)
3. Secondary Ignition Coil -
   No. 2 Cylinder (Lower)
4. Primary Ignition Coil
5. Breaker Point - No. 1 Cylinder

6. Breaker Point - No. 2 Cylinder
7. Condenser
8. Stop Switch Assembly
9. Black Lead
10. Gray Lead
11. Orange Lead

STARTING AND IGNITION SYSTEM
8-9.9-15 hp

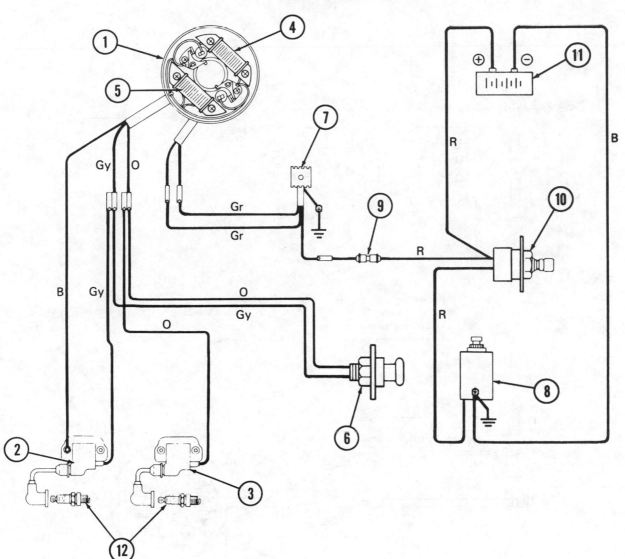

1. Flywheel magneto
2. Secondary Ignition Coil - No. 1 Cylinder (Top)
3. Secondary Ignition Coil - No. 2 Cylinder (Bottom)
4. Primary Ignition Coil
5. Lighting (Battery Changing) Coil
6. Stop Switch
7. Rectifier
8. Electric Starter Motor
9. Fuse
10. Start Switch
11. Battery
12. Spark Plug (2)

COLOR CODE LEGEND	
Gy	Gray
O	Orange
B	Black
R	Red
Gr	Green

IGNITION SYSTEM
15 hp

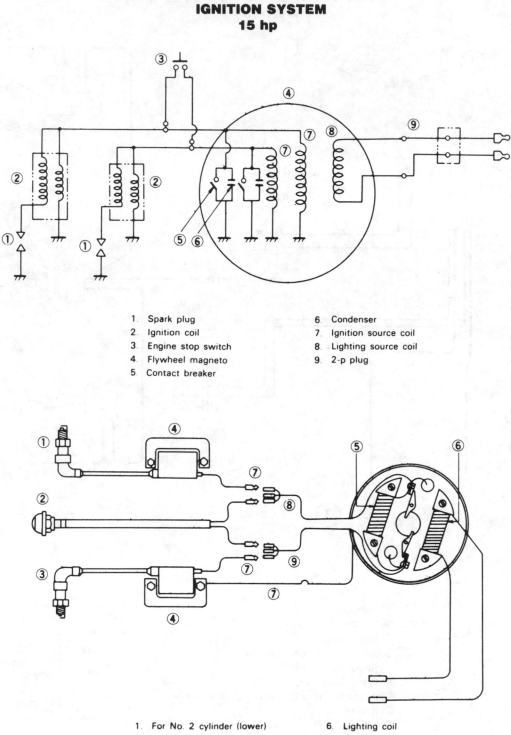

1. Spark plug
2. Ignition coil
3. Engine stop switch
4. Flywheel magneto
5. Contact breaker

6. Condenser
7. Ignition source coil
8. Lighting source coil
9. 2-p plug

1. For No. 2 cylinder (lower)
2. Engine stop switch assembly
3. For No. 1 cylinder (upper)
4. Ignition coil
5. Source coil

6. Lighting coil
7. Black
8. Orange
9. Gray

2

**CDI SYSTEM
20-25-30 hp**

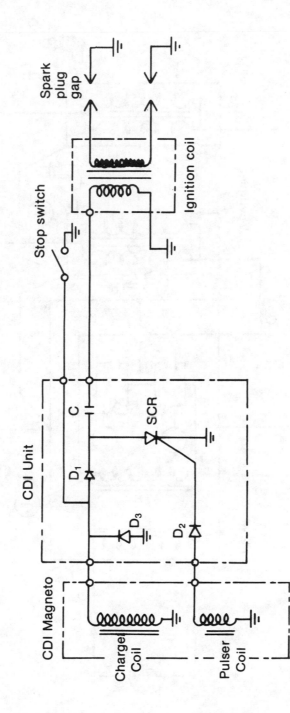

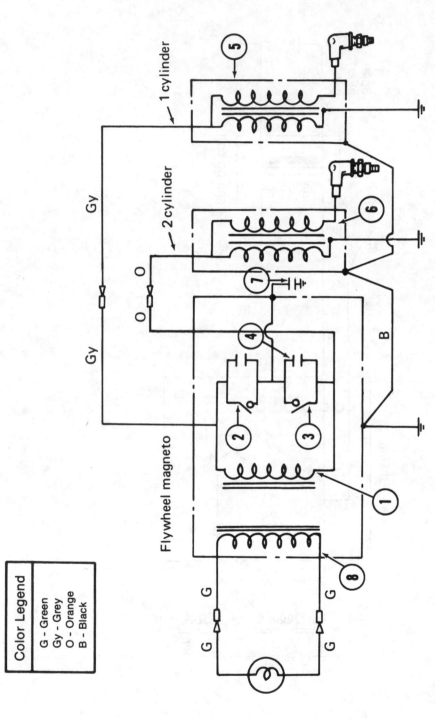

MODELS USING BENDIX TYPE MAGNETO SYSTEM
20-25-30 hp

Color Legend

G - Green
Gy - Grey
O - Orange
B - Black

1 cylinder

2 cylinder

Flywheel magneto

1. Primary Ignition Coil
2. Breaker Point - No. 1 Cylinder
3. Breaker Point - No. 2 Cylinder
4. Condensers (2)

5. Secondary Ignition Coil - No. 1 Cylinder
6. Secondary Ignition Coil - No. 2 Cylinder
7. Stop Switch.
8. Lighting Coil.

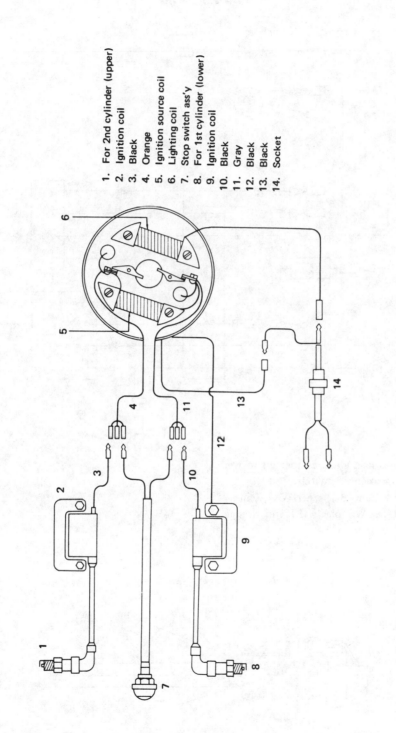

IGNITION SYSTEM
20-25-30 hp

1. For 2nd cylinder (upper)
2. Ignition coil
3. Black
4. Orange
5. Ignition source coil
6. Lighting coil
7. Stop switch ass'y
8. For 1st cylinder (lower)
9. Ignition coil
10. Black
11. Gray
12. Black
13. Black
14. Socket

2

CHARGING, IGNITION AND STARTING SYSTEMS
20-25-30 hp

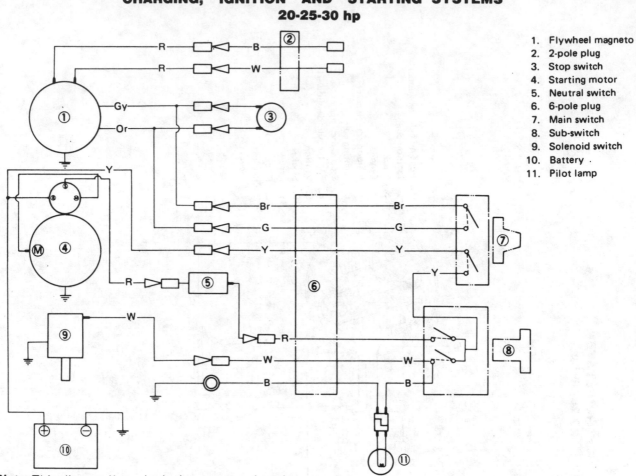

1. Flywheel magneto
2. 2-pole plug
3. Stop switch
4. Starting motor
5. Neutral switch
6. 6-pole plug
7. Main switch
8. Sub-switch
9. Solenoid switch
10. Battery
11. Pilot lamp

Note: This diagram shows lead wires connected to the starting motor and solenoid switch.

Wires are colored brown (Br), green (Gy), yellow (Y), red (R), white (W), black (B) and orange (Or).

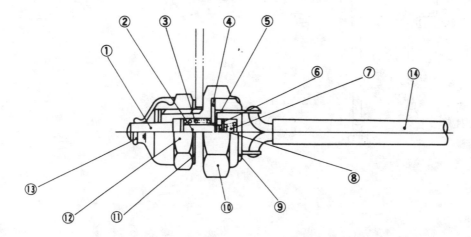

1. Shaft
2. Insulator
3. Spring
4. Washer
5. Terminal plate
6. Contact plate
7. Contact spring
8. Contact point
9. Base
10. Body
11. Gasket
12. Nut
13. Waterproof cover
14. Wire

MAGNETO IGNITION—ELECTRIC START SCHEMATIC
20-25-30 hp

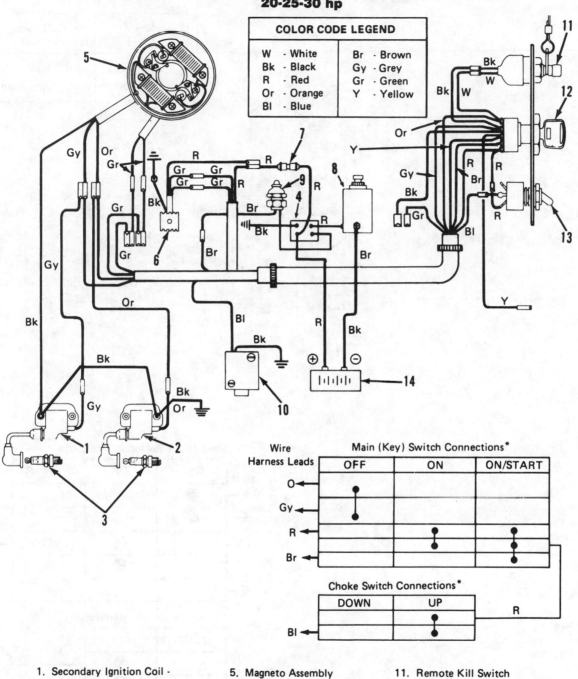

COLOR CODE LEGEND

W	- White	Br	- Brown
Bk	- Black	Gy	- Grey
R	- Red	Gr	- Green
Or	- Orange	Y	- Yellow
Bl	- Blue		

Main (Key) Switch Connections*

Wire Harness Leads	OFF	ON	ON/START
O	●		
Gy	●		
R		●	●
Br			●

Choke Switch Connections*

	DOWN	UP
Bl		●

R

1. Secondary Ignition Coil - No. 1 Cylinder (Top)
2. Secondary Ignition Coil - No. 2 Cylinder (Bottom)
3. Spark Plug (2)
4. Starter Solenoid
5. Magneto Assembly
6. Rectifier
7. Fuse
8. Electric Starter Motor
9. Neutral Start Switch
10. Choke Solenoid
11. Remote Kill Switch
12. Main (Key) Switch
13. Choke Switch
14. Battery

*Dots connected by the solid line(s) indicate those switch connections which are made (continuity between) when switch is in the specified position.

CDI, CHARGING AND STARTING SYSTEMS
20-25-30 hp

COLOR CODE	
W - White	Br - Brown
Bk - Black	Gr - Green
R - Red	Y - Yellow
Or - Orange	P - Pink
Bl - Blue	W/R - White/Red

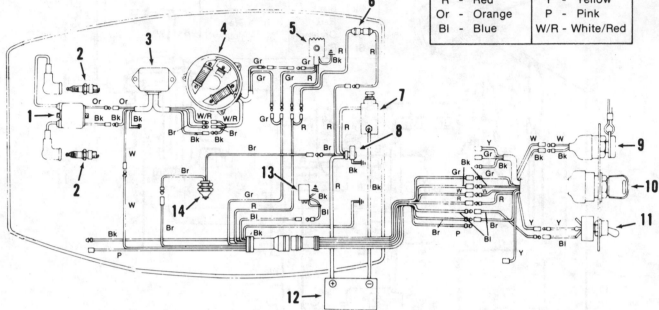

1. Secondary Ignition Coil
2. Spark Plug (2)
3. CDI Unit
4. CDI Magneto Assembly
5. Rectifier
6. Fuse Assembly
7. Starter Motor
8. Starter Motor Solenoid
9. Kill Switch
10. Main (Key) Switch
11. Choke Switch
12. Battery
13. Choke Solenoid
14. Neutral Start Switch

Main (Key) Switch Connections*

Wire Harness Leads	OFF	ON	ON/START
W ←	●		
Bk ←	●		
R ←		●	●
		●	●
Br ←			●

Choke Switch Connections*

	DOWN	UP
		●
Bl ←		●

*Dots connected by the solid line(s) indicate those switch connections (leads) which are made (continuity between) when switch is in specified position.

CDI TYPE SYSTEM
(IGNITION SCHEMATIC)
20-25-30 hp

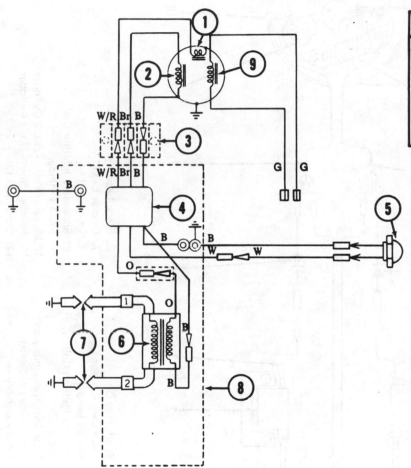

COLOR LEGEND

Bk - Black
Br - Brown
W/R - White/Red tracer
Or - Orange
W - White
G - Green

1. Magneto Pulser (Trigger) Coil
2. Magneto Charge (Source) Coil
3. Lead Terminal Holder
4. CDI Unit
5. Stop Switch Device
6. Ignition Coil
7. Spark Plug (2)
8. CDI Unit Base
9. Lighting Coil

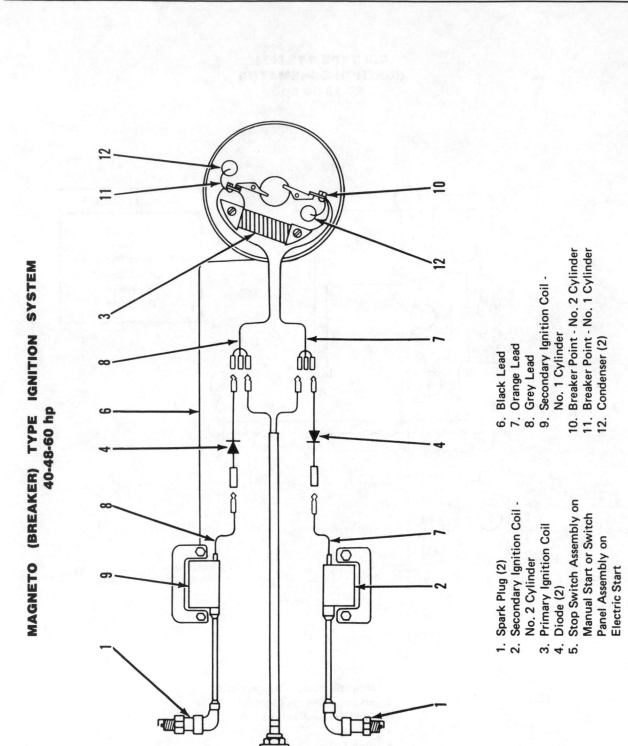

MAGNETO (BREAKER) TYPE IGNITION SYSTEM 40-48-60 hp

1. Spark Plug (2)
2. Secondary Ignition Coil - No. 2 Cylinder
3. Primary Ignition Coil
4. Diode (2)
5. Stop Switch Assembly on Manual Start or Switch Panel Assembly on Electric Start
6. Black Lead
7. Orange Lead
8. Grey Lead
9. Secondary Ignition Coil - No. 1 Cylinder
10. Breaker Point - No. 2 Cylinder
11. Breaker Point - No. 1 Cylinder
12. Condenser (2)

2

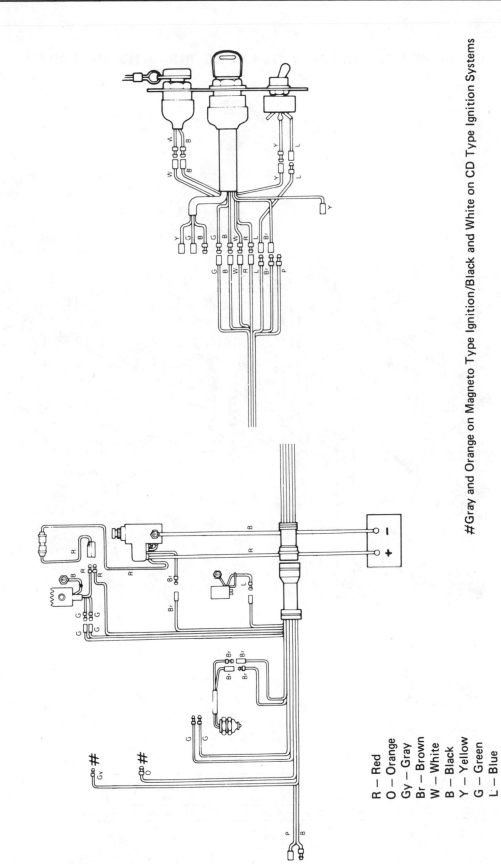

ELECTRIC START CIRCUIT SCHEMATIC
40-48-60 hp

#Gray and Orange on Magneto Type Ignition/Black and White on CD Type Ignition Systems

R – Red
O – Orange
Gy – Gray
Br – Brown
W – White
B – Black
Y – Yellow
G – Green
L – Blue

50 HP MANUAL START (SERIAL NO. INDICATED IN CHART)

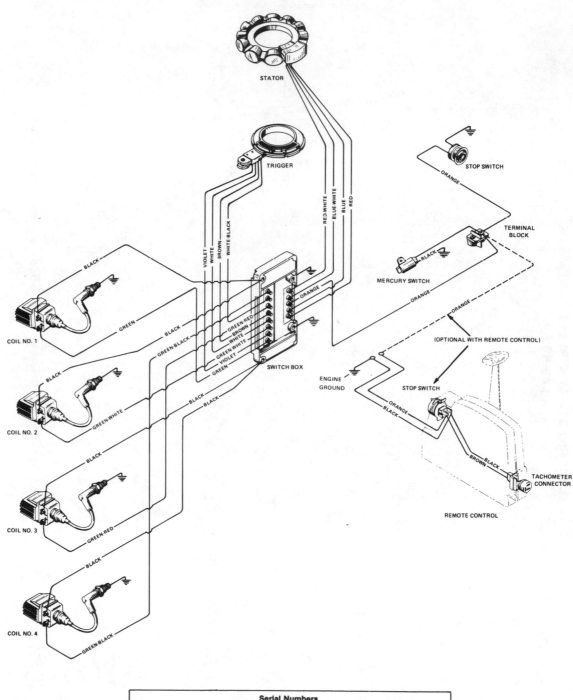

Serial Numbers			
U.S.A.	Canada	Australia	Europe
Below 5531630	Below 7143688	Below 8063985	Below 9248006

2

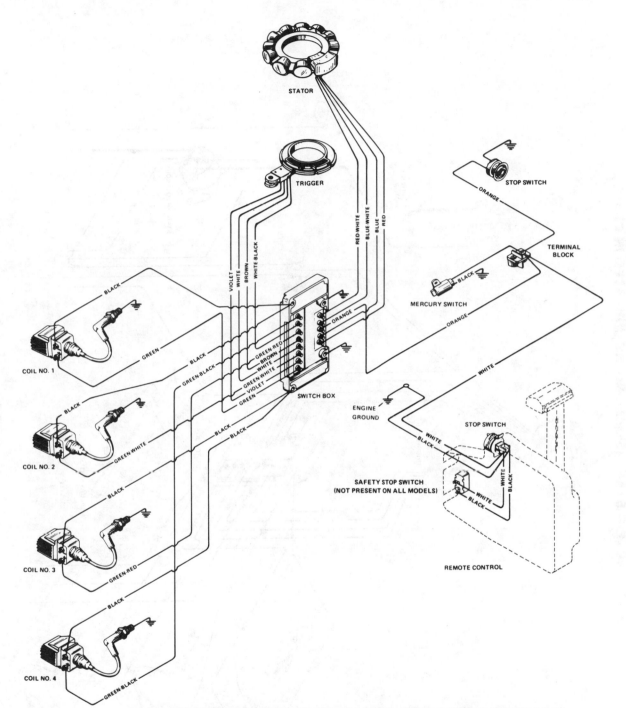

STATOR

TRIGGER

STOP SWITCH

ORANGE

TERMINAL BLOCK

RED-WHITE
BLUE-WHITE
BLUE
RED

BLACK

MERCURY SWITCH

ORANGE

VIOLET
WHITE
BROWN
WHITE-BLACK

BLACK

ORANGE

COIL NO. 1

GREEN

BLACK

BLACK

GREEN-BLACK

GREEN-RED
BROWN
WHITE
GREEN-WHITE
VIOLET
GREEN

SWITCH BOX

WHITE

BLACK

GREEN-WHITE

BLACK
BLACK

ENGINE GROUND

STOP SWITCH

WHITE

COIL NO. 2

BLACK

WHITE
BLACK

COIL NO. 3

BLACK

GREEN-RED

SAFETY STOP SWITCH
(NOT PRESENT ON ALL MODELS)

WHITE
BLACK

BLACK

BLACK

GREEN-BLACK

REMOTE CONTROL

COIL NO. 4

50 HP MANUAL START (SERIAL NO. INDICATED IN CHART)

Serial Numbers			
U.S.A.	**Canada**	**Australia**	**Europe**
Above 5531629	Above 7143687	Above 8063984	Above 9248005

50 HP ELECTRIC START (SERIAL NO. AS INDICATED IN CHART)

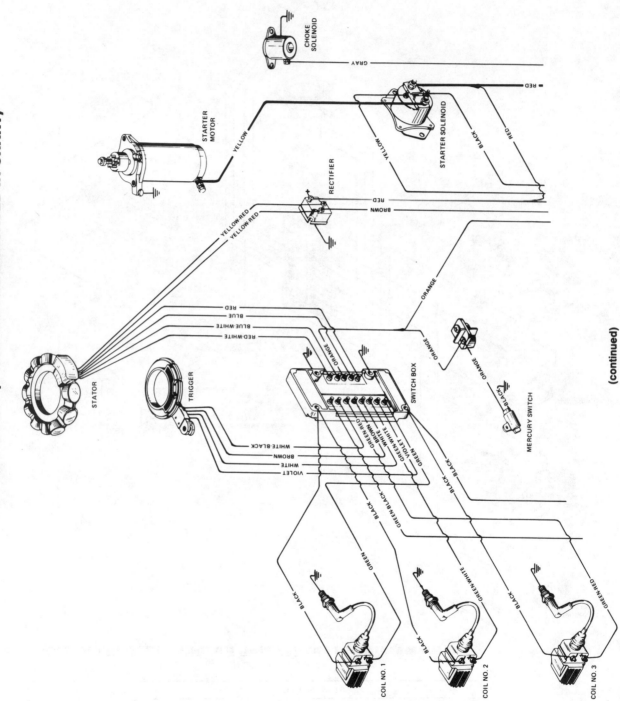

(continued)

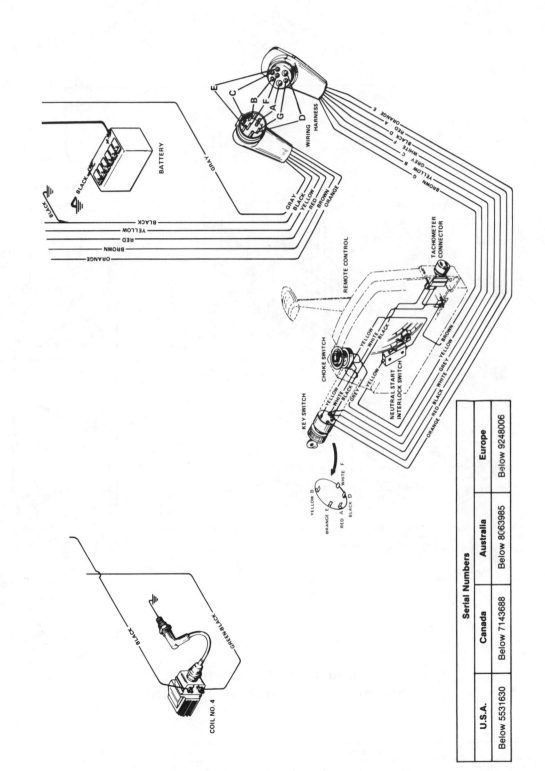

50 HP ELECTRIC START (SERIAL NO. AS INDICATED IN CHART) (continued)

2

Serial Numbers			
U.S.A.	Canada	Australia	Europe
Below 5531630	Below 7143688	Below 8063985	Below 9248006

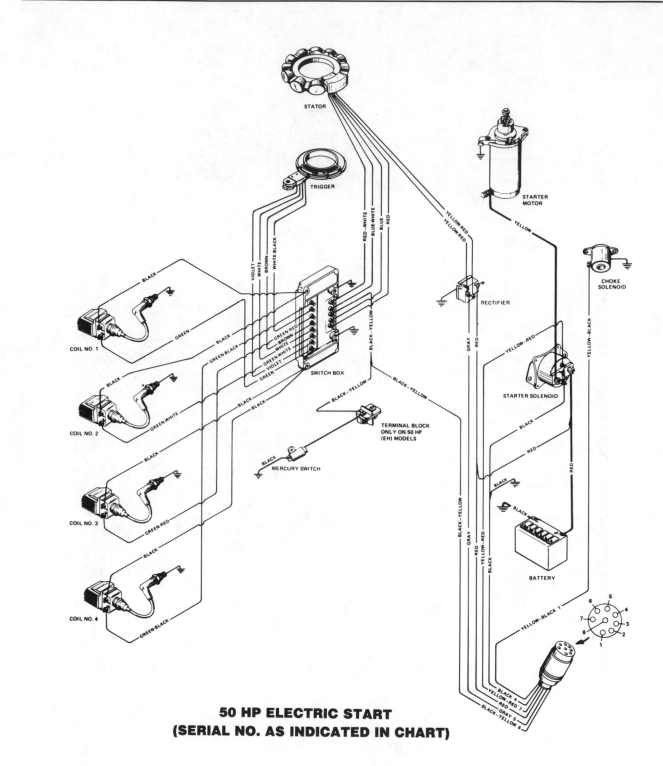

50 HP ELECTRIC START
(SERIAL NO. AS INDICATED IN CHART)

Serial Numbers			
U.S.A.	**Canada**	**Australia**	**Europe**
Above 5531629	Above 7143687	Above 8063984	Above 9248005

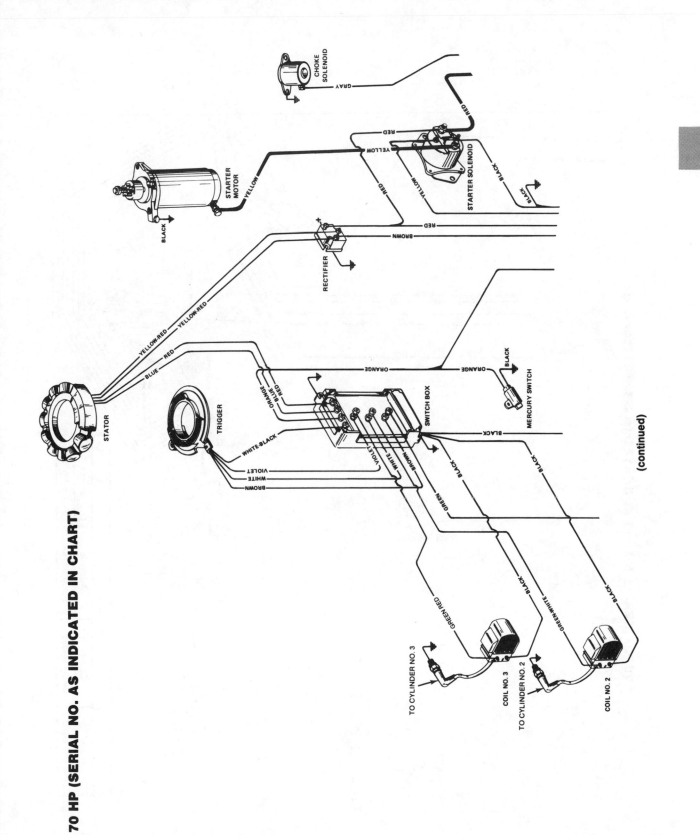

70 HP (SERIAL NO. AS INDICATED IN CHART)

(continued)

70 HP (SERIAL NO. AS INDICATED IN CHART) (continued)

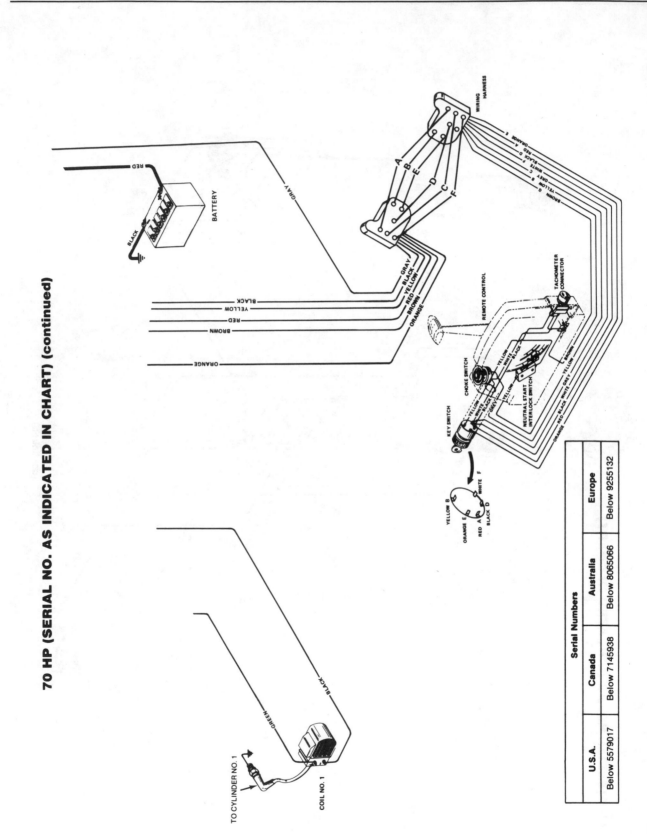

Serial Numbers			
U.S.A.	Canada	Australia	Europe
Below 5579017	Below 7145938	Below 8065066	Below 9255132

2

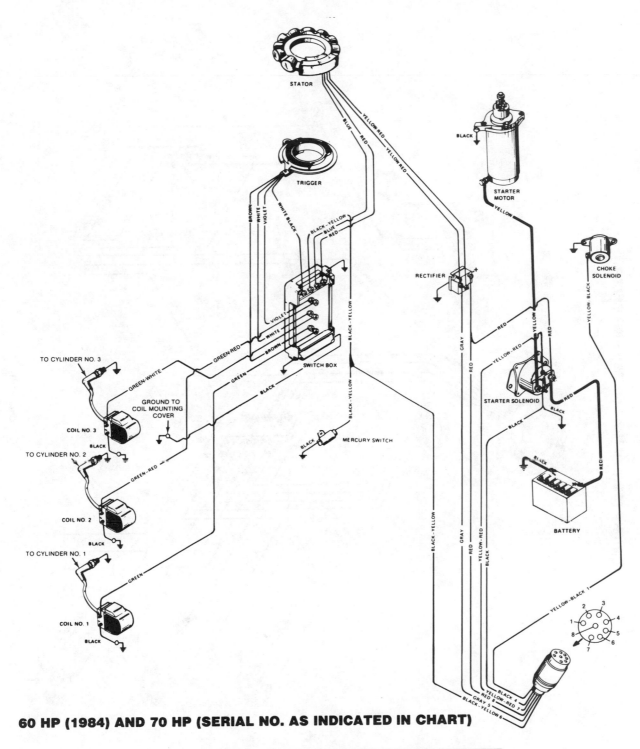

60 HP (1984) AND 70 HP (SERIAL NO. AS INDICATED IN CHART)

Serial Numbers			
U.S.A.	Canada	Australia	Europe
Above 5579016	Above 7145937	Above 8065065	Above 9255131

80 HP (SERIAL NO. 5582561 AND BELOW)

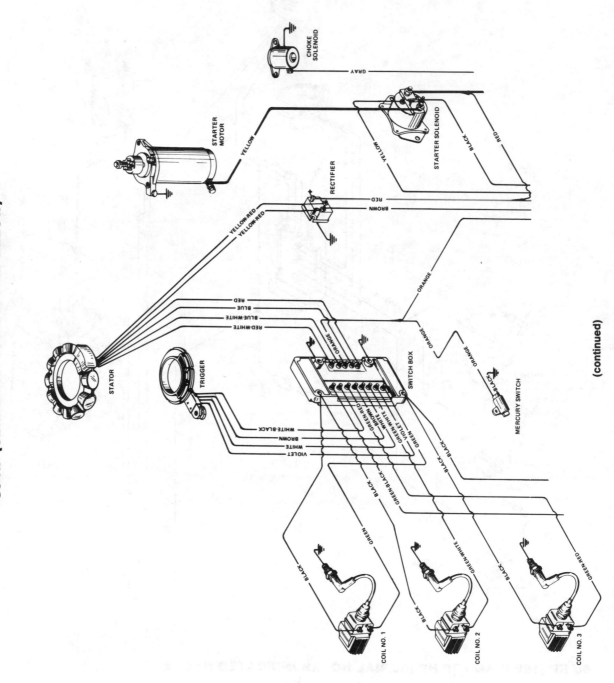

(continued)

80 HP (SERIAL NO. 5582561 AND BELOW) (continued)

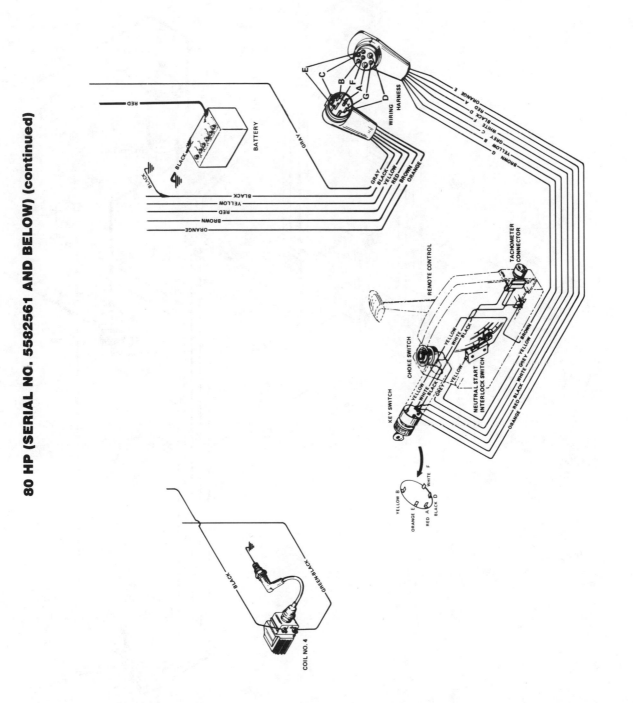

80 HP (SERIAL NO. 5582562 AND ABOVE)

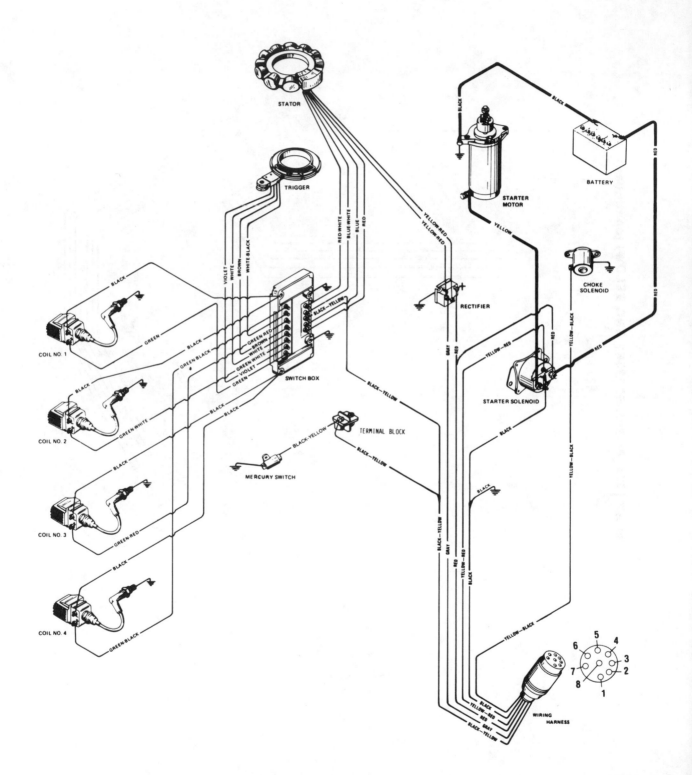

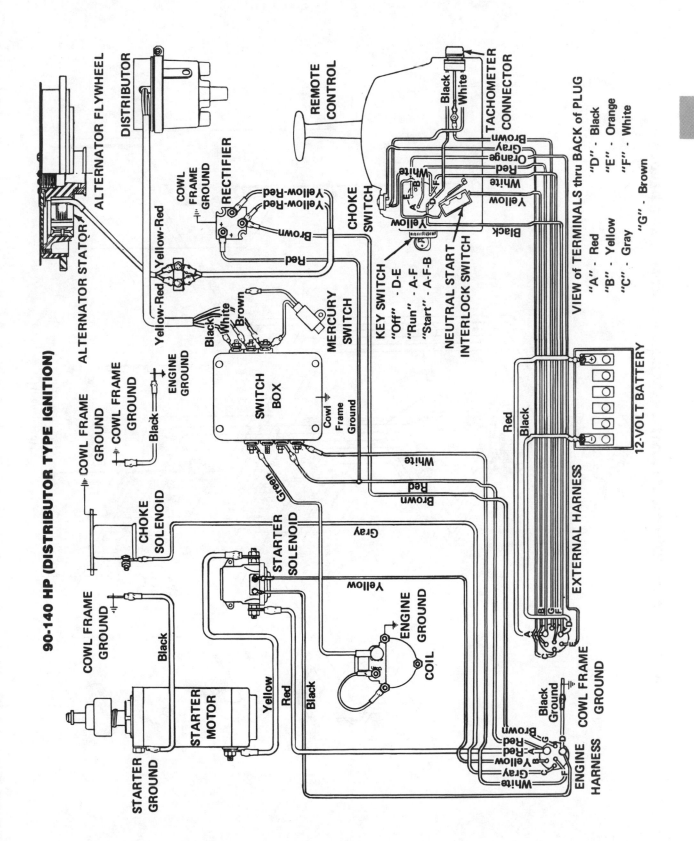

90-140 HP (DISTRIBUTOR TYPE IGNITION)

ALTERNATOR FLYWHEEL

DISTRIBUTOR

REMOTE CONTROL

TACHOMETER CONNECTOR

ALTERNATOR STATOR

RECTIFIER

COWL FRAME GROUND

Yellow-Red

Brown

Red

Yellow-Red Yellow-Red

CHOKE SWITCH

KEY SWITCH
"Off" - D-E
"Run" - A-F
"Start" - A-F-B

NEUTRAL START INTERLOCK SWITCH

Black
White
Brown
Gray
Orange
Red
White
Yellow
Yellow
Black

VIEW of TERMINALS thru BACK of PLUG

"A" - Red   "D" - Black
"B" - Yellow   "E" - Orange
"C" - Gray   "F" - White
              "G" - Brown

COWL FRAME GROUND

COWL FRAME GROUND

ENGINE GROUND

Black

Black
White
Brown

MERCURY SWITCH

Cowl Frame Ground

SWITCH BOX

COWL FRAME GROUND

Black

Green

White
Brown
Red

Gray

Red
Black

12-VOLT BATTERY

EXTERNAL HARNESS

CHOKE SOLENOID

STARTER SOLENOID

Yellow

ENGINE COIL GROUND

STARTER MOTOR

Yellow
Red
Black

ENGINE GROUND

STARTER GROUND

Black Ground

COWL FRAME GROUND

Brown
Red
Red
Yellow
Gray
White

ENGINE HARNESS

2

90, 115 AND 140 HP WITH ADI IGNITION (SERIAL NO. 5594656 AND BELOW)

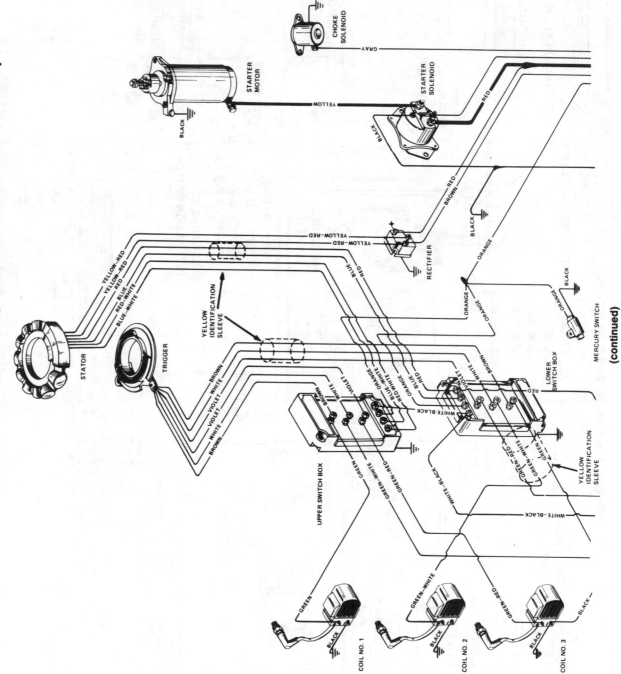

(continued)

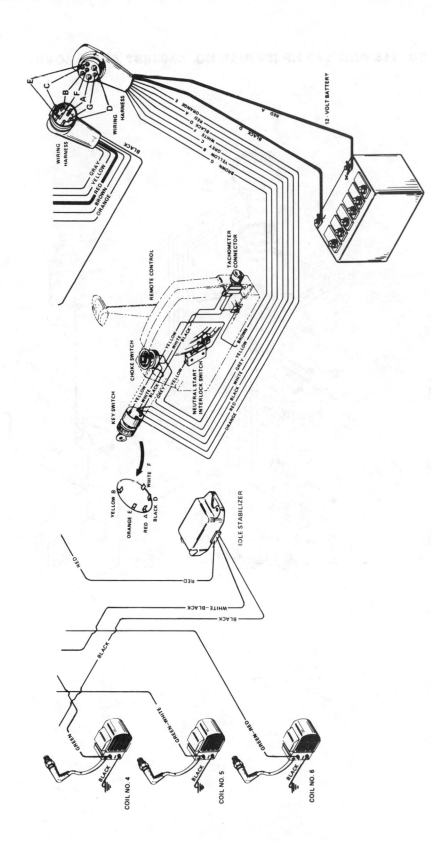

90, 115 AND 140 HP WITH ADI IGNITION (SERIAL NO. 5594656 AND BELOW) (continued)

2

90, 115 AND 140 HP (SERIAL NO. 5594657 AND ABOVE)

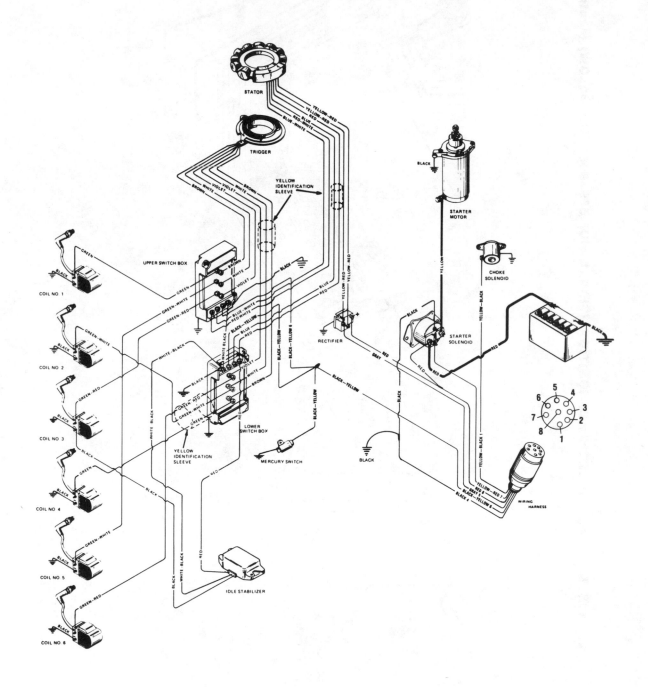

150 HP, 175 HP AND 200 HP V-6 MODELS WITH SERIAL NO. 5363918 AND BELOW (U.S.A.) OR 8061595 AND BELOW (AUSTRALIA)

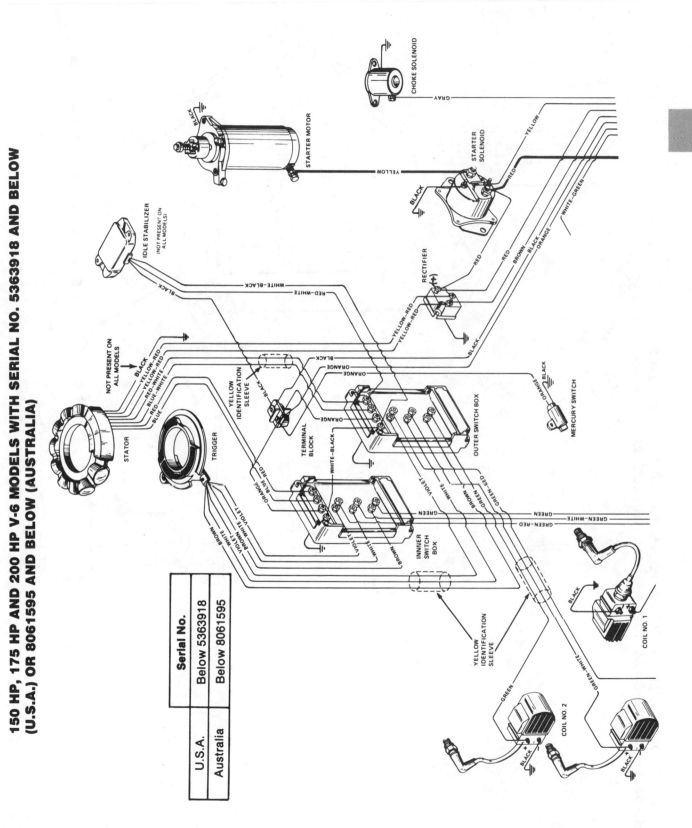

Serial No.	
U.S.A.	Below 5363918
Australia	Below 8061595

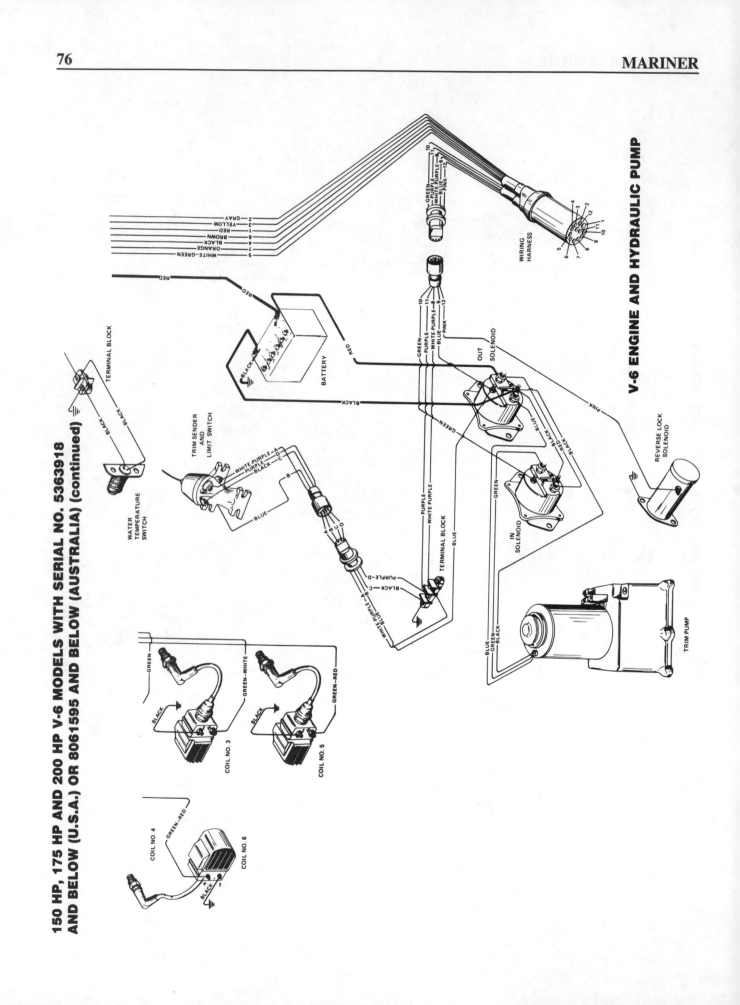

150 HP, 175 HP AND 200 HP V-6 MODELS WITH SERIAL NO. 5363918 AND BELOW (U.S.A.) OR 8061595 AND BELOW (AUSTRALIA) (continued)

V-6 ENGINE AND HYDRAULIC PUMP

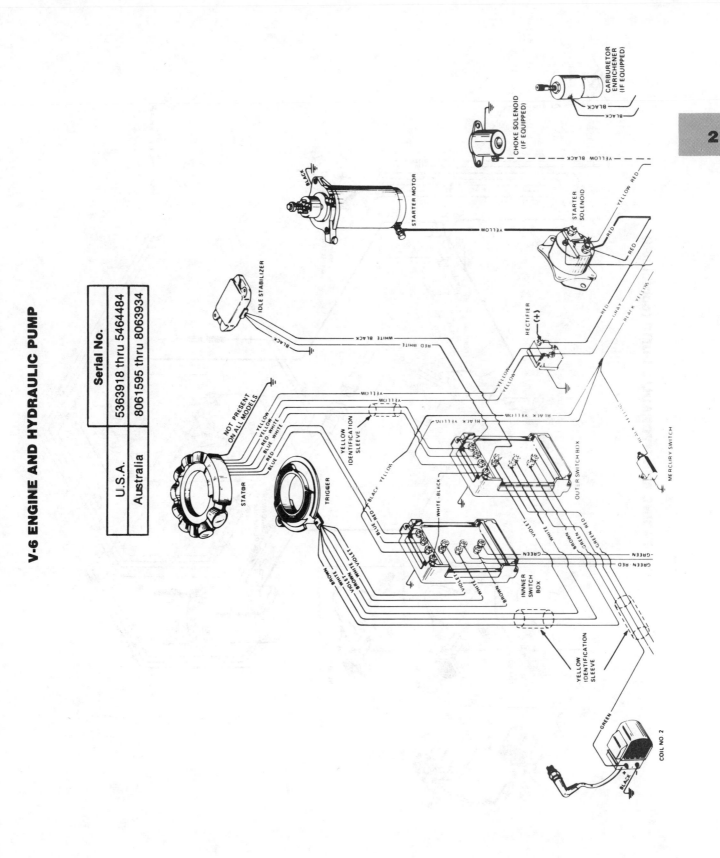

V-6 ENGINE AND HYDRAULIC PUMP

	Serial No.
U.S.A.	5363918 thru 5464484
Australia	8061595 thru 8063934

2

V-6 ENGINE AND HYDRAULIC PUMP (continued)

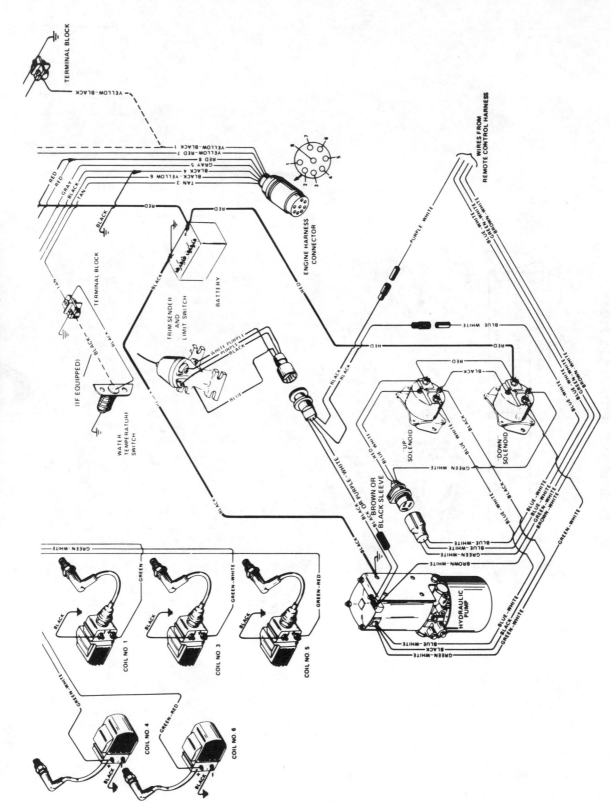

V-6 ENGINE SERIAL NO. 5464486 and UP (U.S.A.) OR 8063935 AND UP (AUSTRALIA)

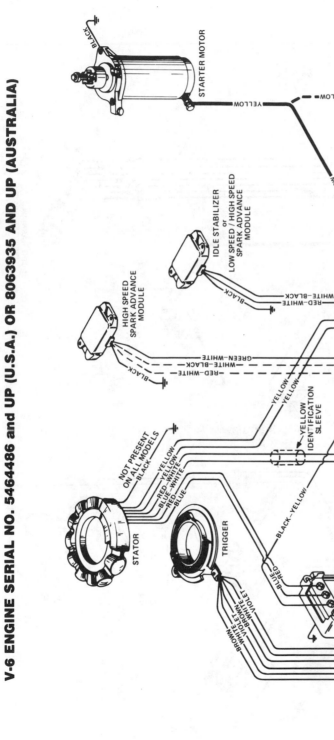

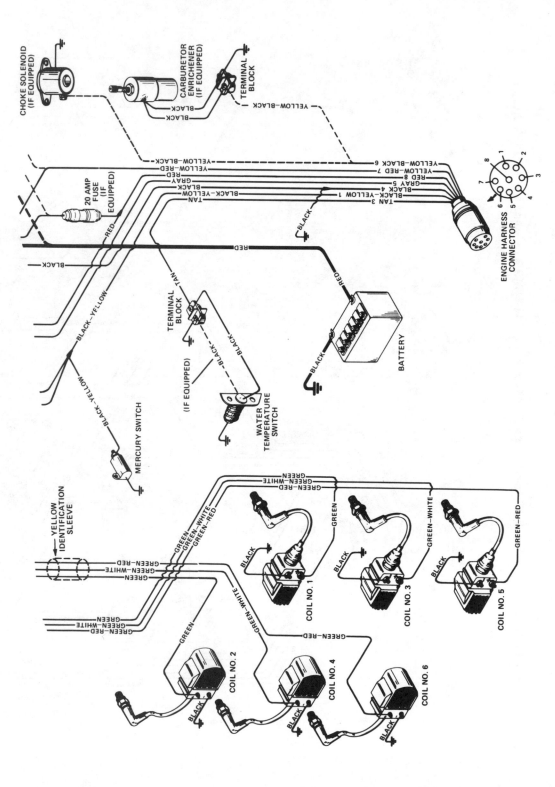

V-6 ENGINE SERIAL NO. 5464486 and UP (U.S.A.) OR 8063935 AND UP (AUSTRALIA) (continued)

HARNESS—50 HP WITH ELECTRIC START AND 70 HP (WITH PANEL CONTROL, SERIAL NO. AS INDICATED IN CHART) 50 HP 70 HP

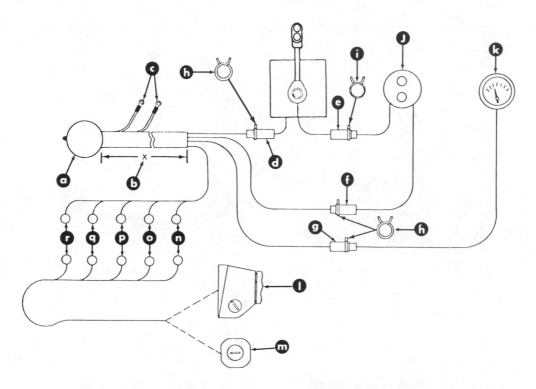

a. Extension harness (A-84-76954A10, 15, 20 and 40. For 65 HP and for 70 HP models, adaptor harness A-84-75291A2 is required.)
b. X = Length of harness in feet
c. Battery cables
d. 4-pin connector (Control to harness.)
e. 3-pin connector (Control to trailer/choke panel.)
f. 5-pin connector (Trailer/choke panel to harness.)
g. 4-pin connector (Harness to tachometer, if tachometer is not used, tape back and insulate connector wire connected to it.)
h. Spring-type clamp 13/16 in. (20.6 mm)
i. Spring-type clamp 3/4 in. (19.1 mm)
j. Trailer/ choke panel

k. Tachometer (optional)
l. Locking steering mount (A-66786A3)
m. Ignition switch panel (A-54211A2)
n. Black to black (Secure with screw and nut and insulate with rubber sleeve.)
o. Orange to orange (Secure with screw and nut and insulate with rubber sleeve.)
p. White to white (Secure with screw and nut and insulate with rubber sleeve.)
q. Yellow to yellow (Secure with screw and nut and insulate with rubber sleeve.)
r. Red to red/white (Secure with screw and nut and insulate with rubber sleeve.)

50 Hp Serial Numbers

USA	Canada	Australia	Europe
Below 5531630	Below 7143688	Below 8063985	Below 9248006

70 Hp Serial Numbers

USA	Canada	Australia	Europe
Above 5579016	Above 7145937	Above 8065065	Above 9255131

HARNESS—50 HP WITH ELECTRIC START AND 70 HP (WITH SINGLE ENGINE CONSOLE CONTROL, SERIAL NO. AS INDICATED IN CHART)

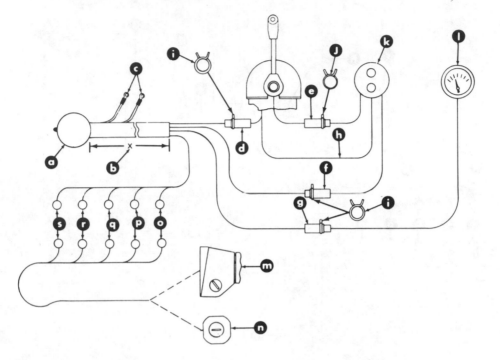

a. Extension harness (A-84-76954A10, 15, 20 and 40. For 65 HP and for 70 HP models, adaptor harness A-84-75291A2 is required.)
b. X = Length of harness in feet.
c. Battery leads
d. 4-pin connector (Control to harness.)
e. 3-pin connector (Control to trailer/choke panel.)
f. 5-pin connector (Trailer/choke panel to harness.)
g. 4-pin connector (Harness to tachometer, if tachometer is not used, tape back and insulate connector.)
h. White wire (Control to trailer/choke panel. Connect white wire to terminal on back side of panel that already has a white wire connected to it.)
i. Spring-type clamp 13/16 in. (20.6 mm)

j. Spring-type clamp 3/4 in. (19.1 mm)
k. Trailer/ choke panel
l. Tachometer (optional)
m. Locking steering mount (A-66786A3)
n. Ignition switch panel (A-54211A2)
o. Black to black (Secure with screw and nut and insulate with rubber sleeve.)
p. Orange to orange (Secure with screw and nut and insulate with rubber sleeve.)
q. White to white (Secure with screw and nut and insulate with rubber sleeve.)
r. Yellow to yellow (Secure with screw and nut and insulate with rubber sleeve.)
s. Red to red/white (Secure with screw and nut and insulate with rubber sleeve.)

50 Hp Serial Numbers

USA	Canada	Australia	Europe
Below 5531630	Below 7143688	Below 8063985	Below 9248006

70 Hp Serial Numbers

USA	Canada	Australia	Europe
Above 5579016	Above 7145937	Above 8065065	Above 9255131

HARNESS—80-140 HP (WITH PANEL CONTROL, SERIAL NO. 5582561 AND BELOW)

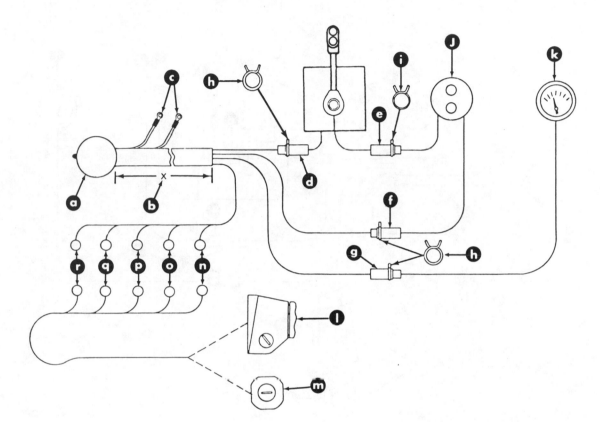

a. Wiring harness (Starboard and Port)
b. Screw-type clamps 1-5/8 in. (41.3 mm)
c. Tachometer
d. Trim indicator
e. 4-pin connector (Tachometer/trim indicator to harness.)
f. Choke/trailer panel (Rear view of panels.)
g. 5-pin connector (Choke/trailer panel to harness.)
h. Trim switch
i. 3-pin connector (Trim switch to choke/trailer panel.)
j. 4-pin connector (Control to harness.)
k. Ignition switch panel
l. Black to black (Secure with screw and nut and insulate with rubber sleeve.)

m. Orange to orange (Secure with screw and nut and insulate with rubber sleeve.)
n. White to white (Secure with screw and nut and insulate with rubber sleeve.)
o. Yellow to yellow (Secure with screw and nut and insulate with rubber sleeve.)
p. Red to red/white (Secure with screw and nut and insulate with rubber sleeve.)
q. White wire (Control to choke/trailer panel. Connect white wire to terminal on back side of panel that already has a white wire connected to it.)
r. Spring-type clamp (Secure wiring connections with clamp.)

HARNESS—80-140 HP (WITH SINGLE ENGINE CONSOLE CONTROL, SERIAL NO. 5582561 AND BELOW)

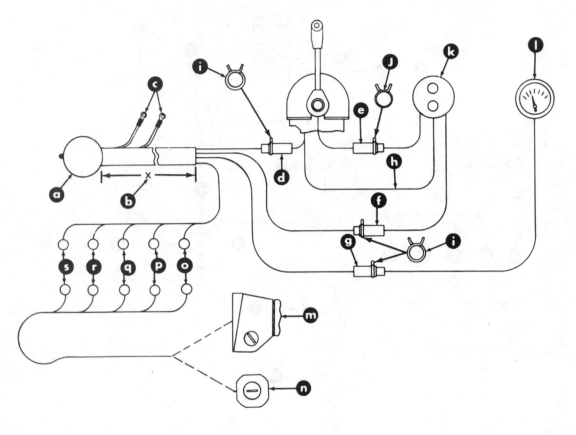

a. Extension harness (A-84-76954A10, 15, 20 and 40. For 70 HP models, adapter harness A-84-75291A2 is required.)
b. X = Length of harness in feet.
c. Battery leads
d. 4-pin connector (Control to harness.)
e. 3-pin connector (Control to trailer/choke panel.)
f. 5-pin connector (Trailer/choke panel to harness.)
g. 4-pin connector (Harness to tachometer, if tachometer is not used, tape back and insulate connector.)
h. White wire (Control to trailer/choke panel. Connect white wire to terminal on back side of panel that already has a white wire connected to it.)
i. Spring-type clamp 13/16 in. (20.6 mm)
j. Spring-type clamp 3/4 in. (19. 1 mm)

k. Trailer/choke panel
l. Tachometer (optional)
m. Locking steering mount (A-66786A3)
n. Ignition switch panel (A-54211A2)
o. Black to black (Secure with screw and nut and insulate with rubber sleeve.)
p. Orange to orange (Secure with screw and nut and insulate with rubber sleeve.)
q. White to white (Secure with screw and nut and insulate with rubber sleeve.)
r. Yellow to yellow (Secure with screw and nut and insulate with rubber sleeve.)
s. Red to red/white (Secure with screw and nut and insulate with rubber sleeve.)

HARNESS—V6 (WITH PANEL CONTROL) (SERIAL NO. AS INDICATED IN CHART)

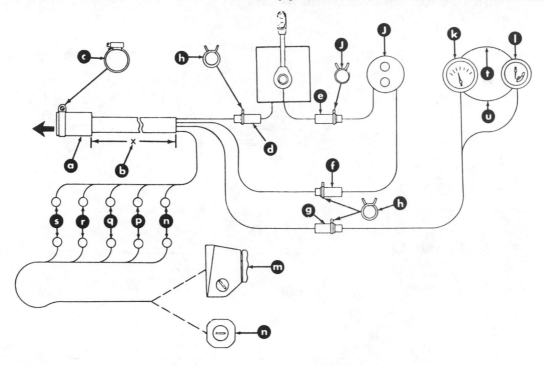

a. Extension harness (A-84-66005A10, A15, A20, A40)
b. X = Length of harness in feet.
c. Screw-type clamp 1-5/8 in. (43.3 mm)
d. 4-pin oonnector (Control to harness.)
e. 3-pin connector (Control to trailer/choke panel.)
f. 5-pin connector (Trailer/choke panel to harness.)
g. 4-pin connector (Harness to tachometer and trim indicator.)
h. Spring-type clamp 13/16 in. (20.6 mm)
i. Spring-type clamp 3/4 in. (19.1 mm)
j. Trailer/choke panel
k. Tachometer
l. Trim indicator

m. Locking steering mount (A-66786A3)
n. Ignition switch (A-54211A2)
o. Black to black (Secure with screw and nut and insulate with rubber sleeve.)
p. Orange to orange (Secure with screw and nut and insulate with rubber sleeve.)
q. White to white (Secure with screw and nut and insulate with rubber sleeve.)
r. Yellow to yellow (Secure with screw and nut and insulate with rubber sleeve.)
s. Red to red (Secure with screw and nut and insulate with rubber sleeve.)
t. Black jumper (Connect to ground on both gauges.)
u. White jumper (Connect to + 12V on both gauges.)

50 Hp Serial Numbers

USA	Canada	Australia	Europe
Below 5531630	Below 7143688	Below 8063985	Below 9248006

70 Hp Serial Numbers

USA	Canada	Australia	Europe
Below 5579017	Below 7145938	Below 8065066	Below 9255132

HARNESS—V6 (WITH SINGLE ENGINE CONSOLE CONTROL) (SERIAL NO. AS INDICATED IN CHART)

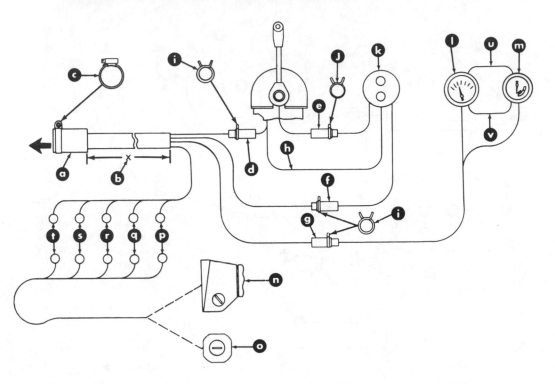

a. Extension harness (A-84-66005A10, A15, A20, A40)
b. X = Length of harness in feet.
c. Screw-type clamp 1-5/8 in. (43.3 mm)
d. 4-pin connector (Control to harness.)
e. 3-pin connector (Control to trailer/choke panel.)
f. 5-pin connector (Trailer/choke panel to harness.)
g. 4-pin connector (Harness to tachometer and trim indicator.)
h. White wire (Control to trailer/choke panel. Connect white wire to terminal on back side of panel that already has a wire connected to it.)
i. Spring-type clamp 13/16 in. (20.6 mm)
j. Spring-type clamp 3/4 in. (19.1 mm)
k. Trailer/choke panel
l. Tachometer

m. Trim indicator
n. Locking steering mount (A-66786A3)
o. Ignition switch (A-54211A2)
p. Black to black (Secure with screw and nut and insulate with rubber sleeve.)
q. Orange to orange (Secure with screw and nut and insulate with rubber sleeve.)
r. White to white (Secure with screw and nut and insulate with rubber sleeve.)
s. Yellow to yellow (Secure with screw and nut and insulate with rubber sleeve.)
t. Red to red (Secure with screw and nut and insulate with rubber sleeve.)
u. Black jumper (Connect to ground on both gauges.)
v. White jumper (Connect to + 12V on both gauges.)

50 Hp Serial Numbers

USA	Canada	Australia	Europe
Below 5531630	Below 7143688	Below 8063985	Below 9248006

70 Hp Serial Numbers

USA	Canada	Australia	Europe
Below 5579017	Below 7145938	Below 8065066	Below 9255132

HARNESS—V6 (WITH DUAL ENGINE CONSOLE CONTROL)

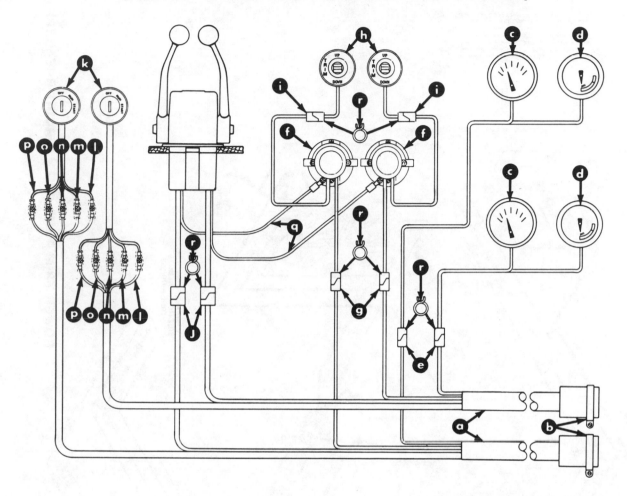

a. Wiring harnesses (Starboard and Port)
b. Screw-type clamps 1 5/8 in. (41.3 mm)
c. Tachometer
d. Trim indicator
e. 4-pin connector (Tachometer/trim indicator to harness.)
f. Choke/trailer panel (Rear view of panels.)
g. 5-pin connector (Choke/trailer panel to harness.)
h. Trim switch
i. 3-pin connector (Trim switch to choke/trailer panel.)
j. 4-pin connector (Control to harness.)
k. Ignition switch panel
l. Black to black (Secure with screw and nut and insulate with rubber sleeve.)

m. Orange to orange (Secure with screw and nut and insulate with rubber sleeve.)
n. White to white (Secure with screw and nut and insulate with rubber sleeve.)
o. Yellow to yellow (Secure with screw and nut and insulate with rubber sleeve.)
p. Red to red/white (Secure with screw and nut and insulate with rubber sleeve.)
q. White wire (Control to choke/trailer panel connect white wire to terminal on backside of panel that already has a white wire connected to it.)
r. Spring-type clamp (Secure wiring connections with clamp.)

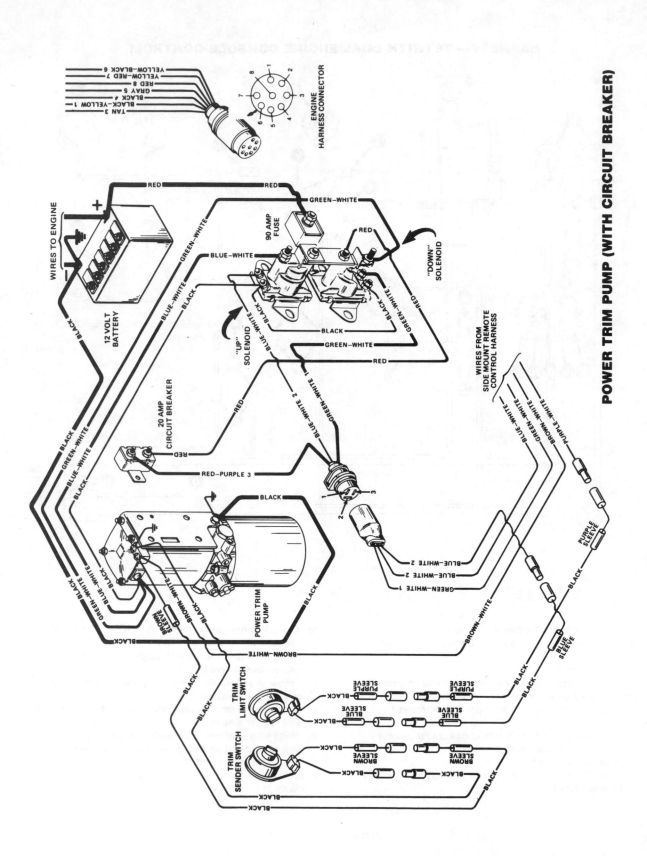

POWER TRIM PUMP (WITH CIRCUIT BREAKER)

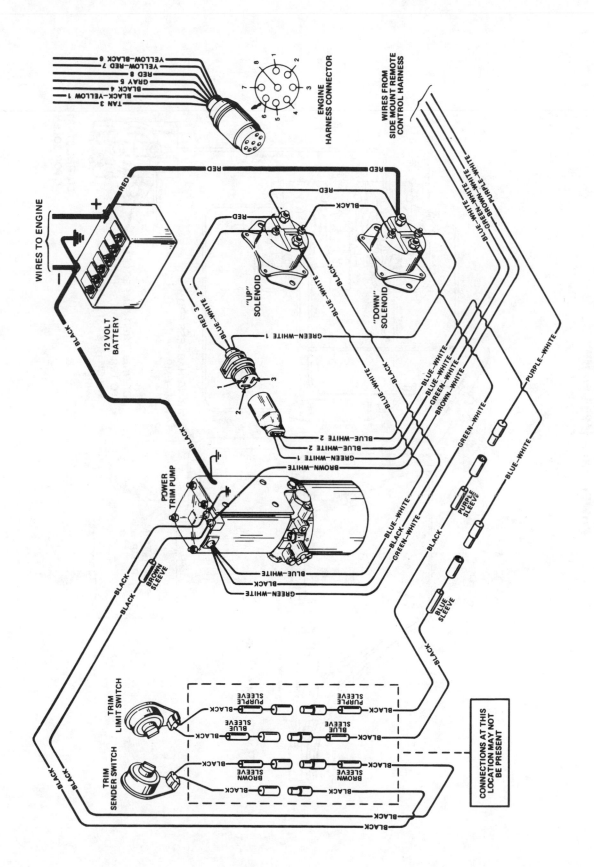

POWER TRIM PUMP (WITHOUT CIRCUIT BREAKER)

POWER TRIM (1984 80 HP)

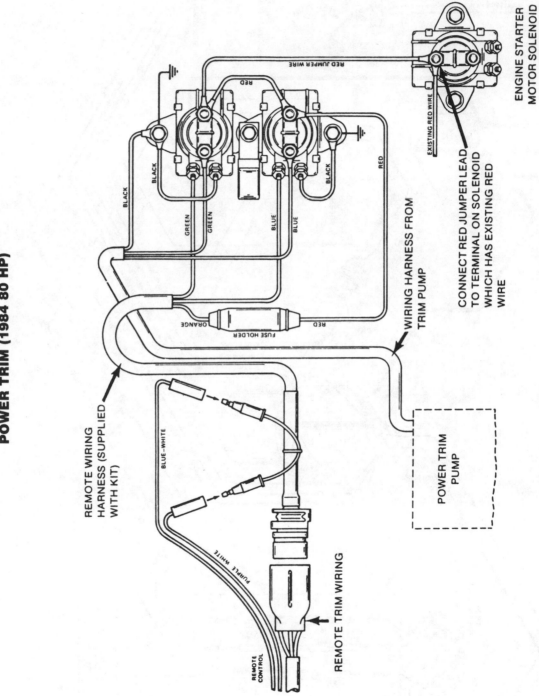

ENGINE STARTER MOTOR SOLENOID

CONNECT RED JUMPER LEAD TO TERMINAL ON SOLENOID WHICH HAS EXISTING RED WIRE

WIRING HARNESS FROM TRIM PUMP

RED JUMPER WIRE

EXISTING RED WIRE

RED

RED

BLACK

BLACK

GREEN

GREEN

BLUE

BLUE

BLACK

RED

ORANGE

FUSE HOLDER

REMOTE WIRING HARNESS (SUPPLIED WITH KIT)

POWER TRIM PUMP

BLUE—WHITE

PURPLE—WHITE

REMOTE TRIM WIRING

REMOTE CONTROL

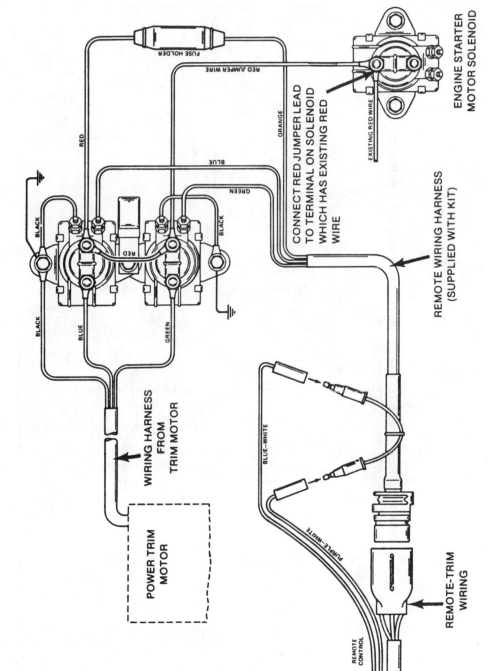

POWER TRIM (1984 90 AND 115 HP)

ENGINE STARTER
MOTOR SOLENOID

EXISTING RED WIRE

CONNECT RED JUMPER LEAD
TO TERMINAL ON SOLENOID
WHICH HAS EXISTING RED
WIRE

RED JUMPER WIRE

FUSE HOLDER

RED

ORANGE

BLUE

GREEN

BLACK

BLACK

RED

BLACK

BLUE

GREEN

REMOTE WIRING HARNESS
(SUPPLIED WITH KIT)

WIRING HARNESS
FROM
TRIM MOTOR

POWER TRIM
MOTOR

BLUE–WHITE

PURPLE–WHITE

REMOTE-TRIM
WIRING

REMOTE
CONTROL

2

POWER TRIM (1984 MODELS WITH COMMANDER SERIES SIDE MOUNT REMOTE CONTROL)

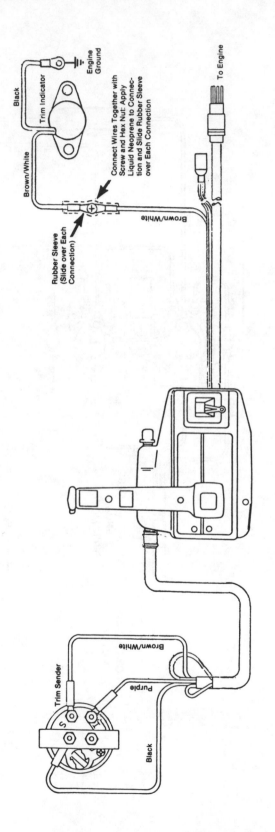

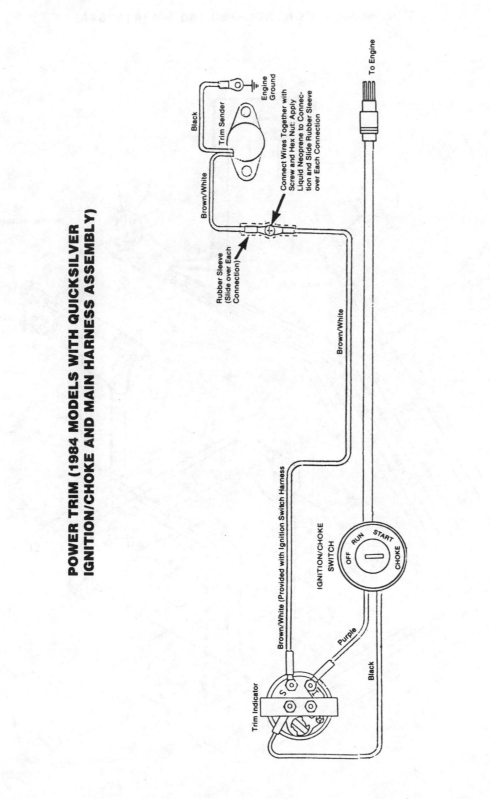

POWER TRIM (1984 MODELS WITH QUICKSILVER IGNITION/CHOKE AND MAIN HARNESS ASSEMBLY)

Engine Ground

Black

Trim Sender

Brown/White

Connect Wires Together with Screw and Hex Nut: Apply Liquid Neoprene to Connection and Slide Rubber Sleeve over Each Connection

To Engine

Rubber Sleeve (Slide over Each Connection)

Brown/White

Brown/White (Provided with Ignition Switch Harness

IGNITION/CHOKE SWITCH

OFF   RUN   START

CHOKE

Purple

Black

Trim Indicator

2

SIDE MOUNT CONTROL—50-140 HP (A76334A)

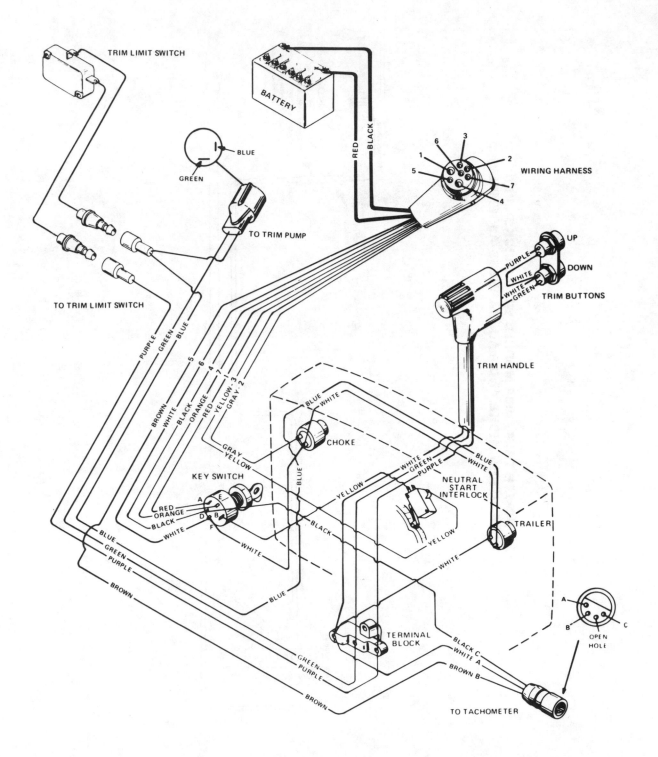

TRIM LIMIT SWITCH

BATTERY

BLUE

GREEN

TO TRIM PUMP

TO TRIM LIMIT SWITCH

RED

BLACK

WIRING HARNESS

UP

DOWN

PURPLE

WHITE

WHITE

GREEN

TRIM BUTTONS

TRIM HANDLE

PURPLE

GREEN

BLUE

BROWN

WHITE

BLACK

ORANGE

RED

YELLOW - 3

GRAY - 2

5

6

4

7

GRAY

YELLOW

BLUE

WHITE

CHOKE

BLUE

WHITE

GREEN

PURPLE

BLUE

WHITE

NEUTRAL
START
INTERLOCK

KEY SWITCH

YELLOW

RED

ORANGE

BLACK

WHITE

A   E

D   B

F

BLACK

YELLOW

TRAILER

WHITE

BLUE

GREEN

PURPLE

BROWN

WHITE

BLUE

A

B   C

OPEN
HOLE

GREEN

PURPLE

TERMINAL
BLOCK

BLACK C

WHITE A

BROWN

BROWN B

TO TACHOMETER

SIDE MOUNT CONTROL WITHOUT POWER TRIM—80-140 HP (A87953A, A87954A AND A87729A)

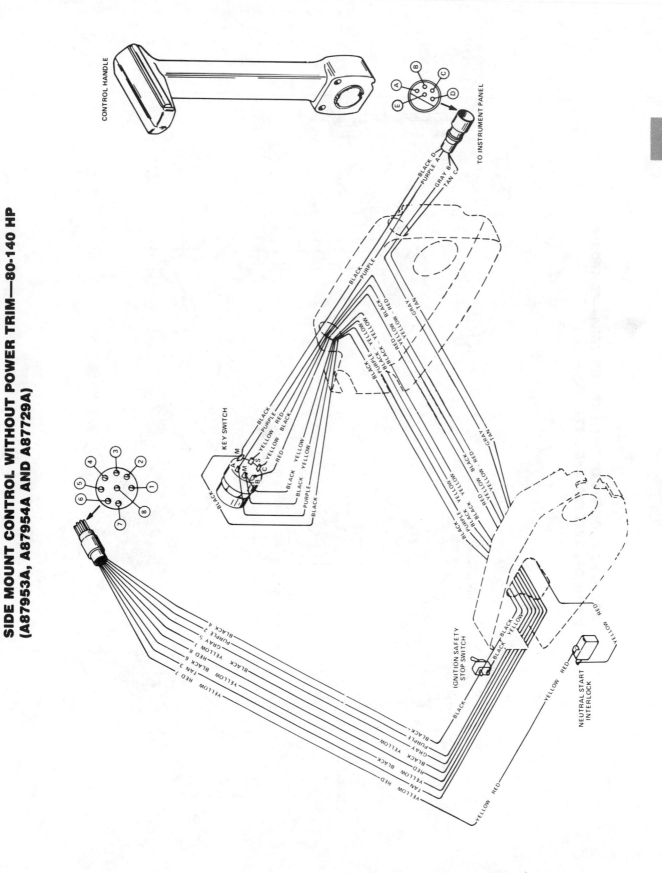

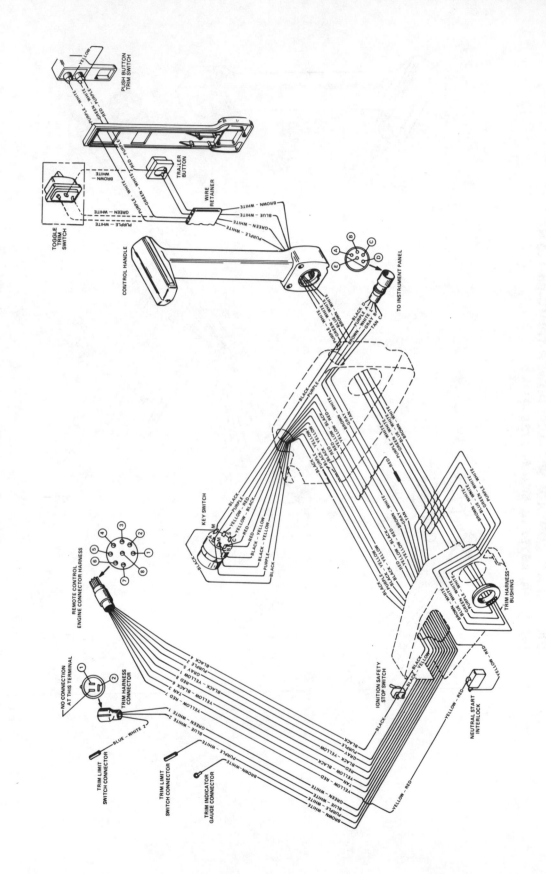

SIDE MOUNT CONTROL WITH POWER TRIM—80-140 HP (A85800A, A87273A AND A87317A)

REMOTE CONTROL—V6

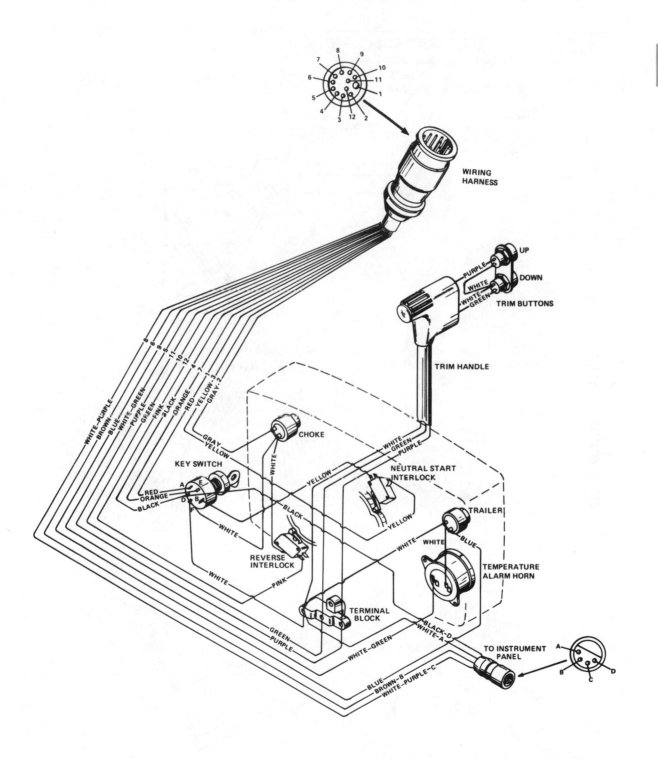

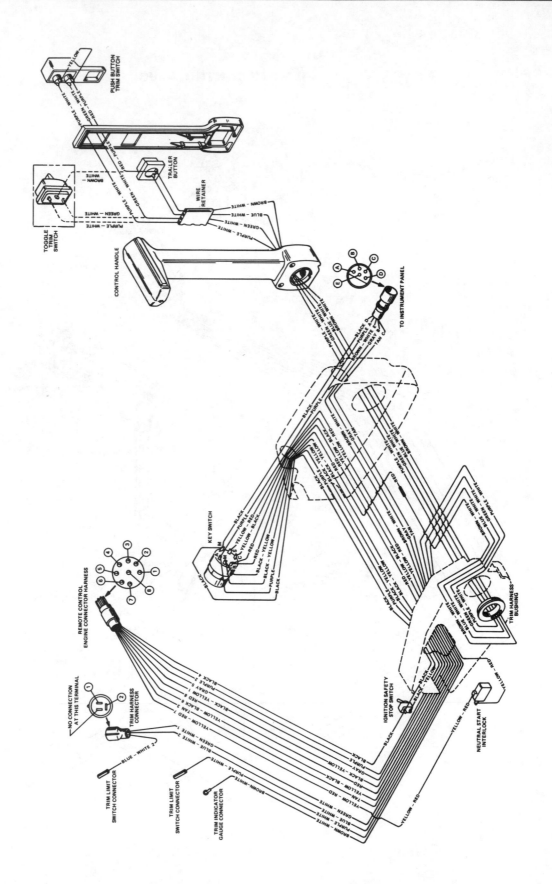

SIDE MOUNT CONTROL—V6 (DELUXE)

TRIM INDICATOR GAUGE (WITH LAMP WIRE)

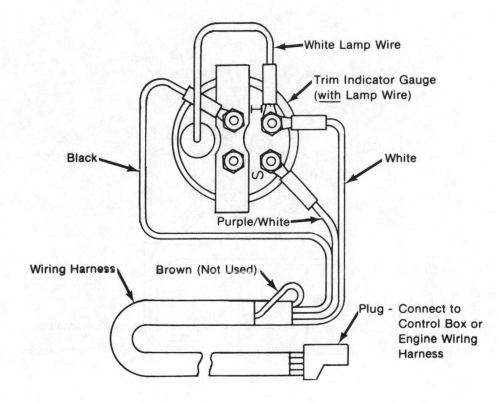

TRIM INDICATOR GAUGE (WITHOUT LAMP WIRE)

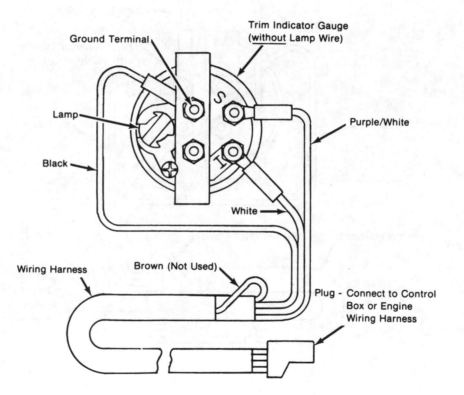

TRIM INDICATOR GAUGE AND ALARM HORN

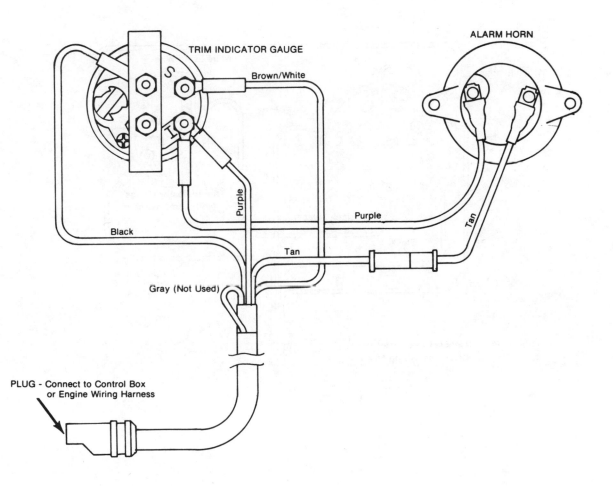

TRIM INDICATOR GAUGE AND TACHOMETER (WITH LAMP WIRE)

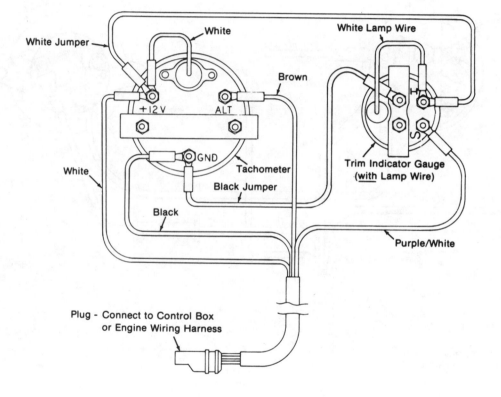

2

TRIM INDICATOR GAUGE AND TACHOMETER (WITHOUT LAMP WIRE)

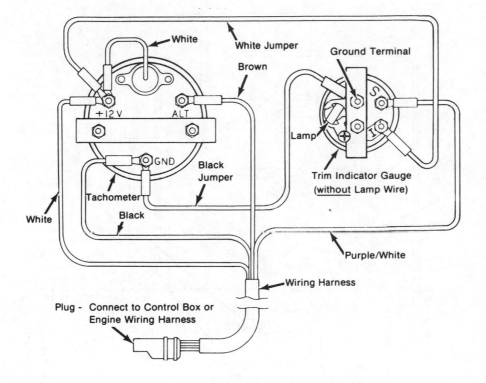

TACHOMETER (ADJUSTABLE DIAL), TRIM INDICATOR GAUGE AND ALARM HORN

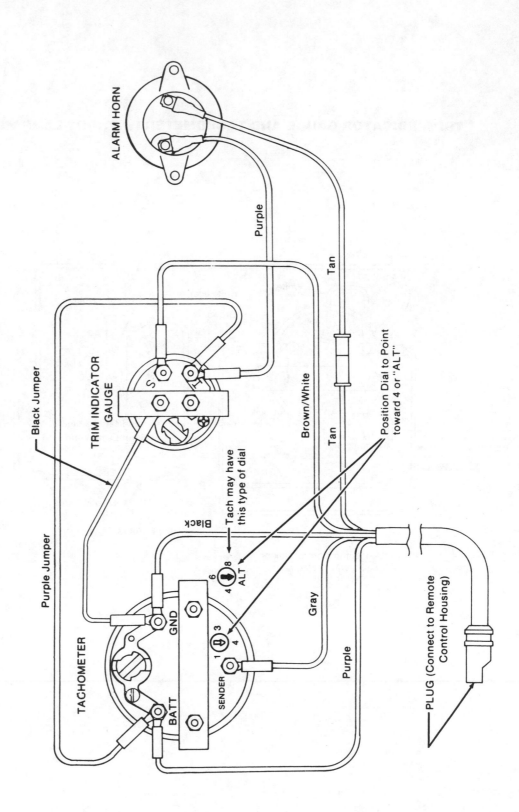

ALARM HORN

Purple

Tan

Black Jumper

TRIM INDICATOR GAUGE

Brown/White

Tan

Position Dial to Point toward 4 or "ALT"

Purple Jumper

Black

Tach may have this type of dial

TACHOMETER

GND

BATT

SENDER

Gray

Purple

PLUG (Connect to Remote Control Housing)

TACHOMETER (NON-ADJUSTABLE DIAL), TRIM INDICATOR GAUGE AND ALARM HORN

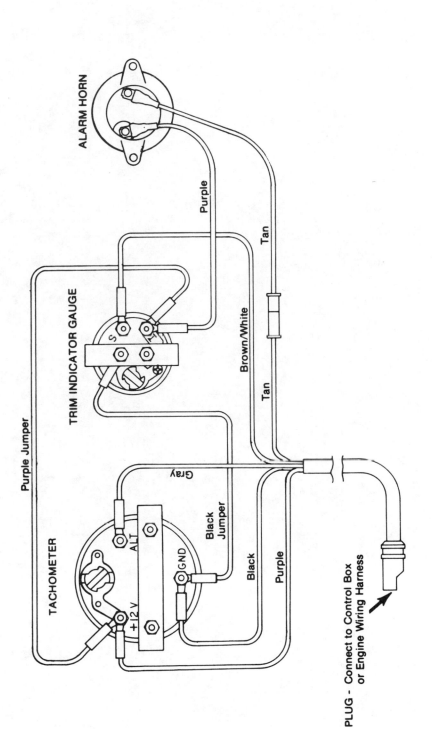

ALARM HORN

Purple

Tan

Brown/White

Tan

TRIM INDICATOR GAUGE

S

Purple Jumper

Gray

TACHOMETER

ALT

GND

Black Jumper

Black

Purple

+12 V

PLUG - Connect to Control Box or Engine Wiring Harness

MERCURY

MERC 200

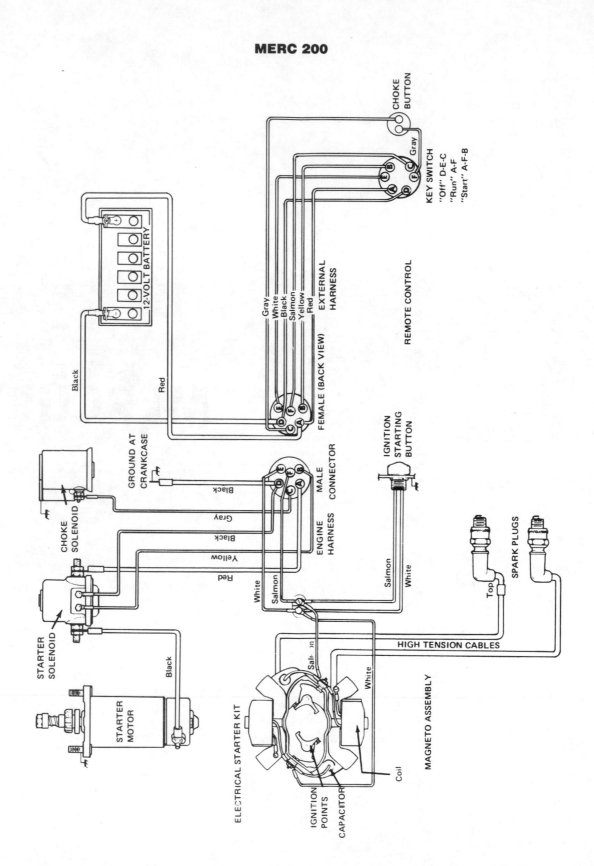

MERC 200 (1970-1971)

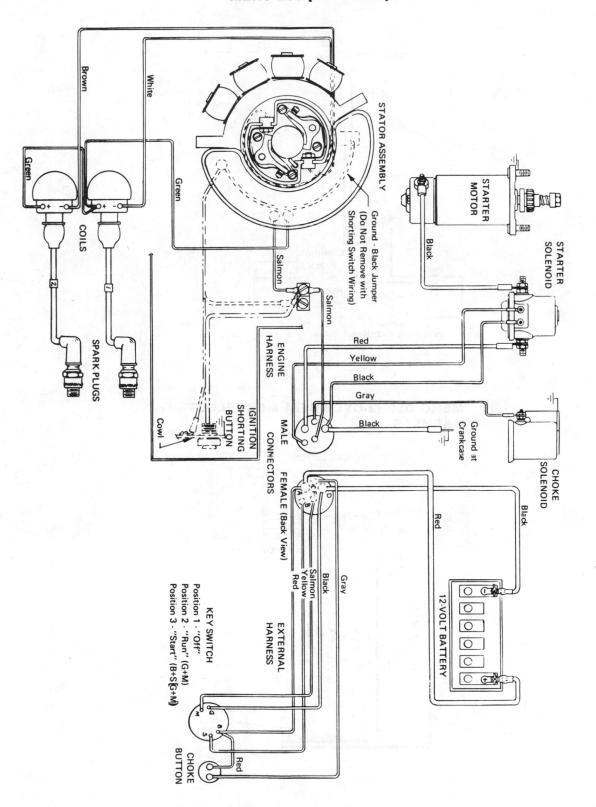

MERC 350 (2-CYLINDER) MERCELECTRIC

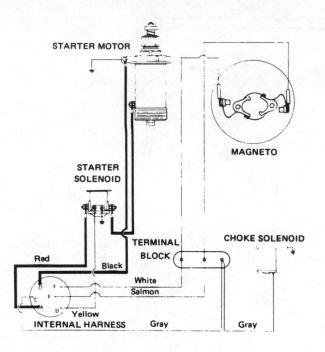

STARTER MOTOR

MAGNETO

STARTER
SOLENOID

CHOKE SOLENOID

TERMINAL
BLOCK

Red   Black

White

Salmon

Yellow

INTERNAL HARNESS   Gray   Gray

MERC 350 (2-CYLINDER) MERCELECTRIC HARNESS

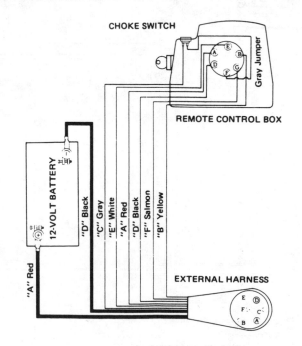

CHOKE SWITCH

Gray Jumper

REMOTE CONTROL BOX

12-VOLT BATTERY

"D" Black
"C" Gray
"E" White
"A" Red
"D" Black
"F" Salmon
"B" Yellow

"A" Red

EXTERNAL HARNESS

MERC 400

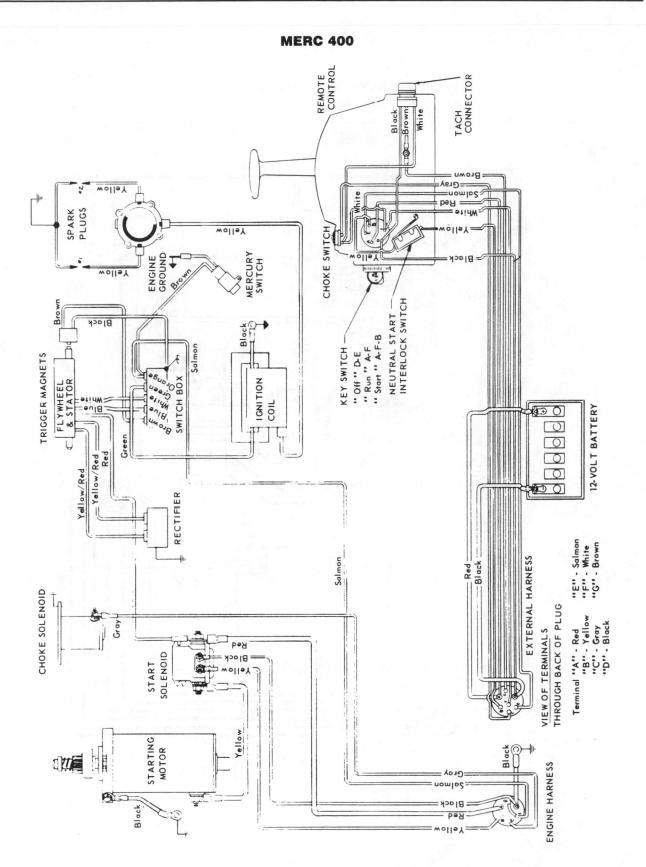

3

4-CYLINDER WITH KIEKHAEFER MERCURY MAGNETO

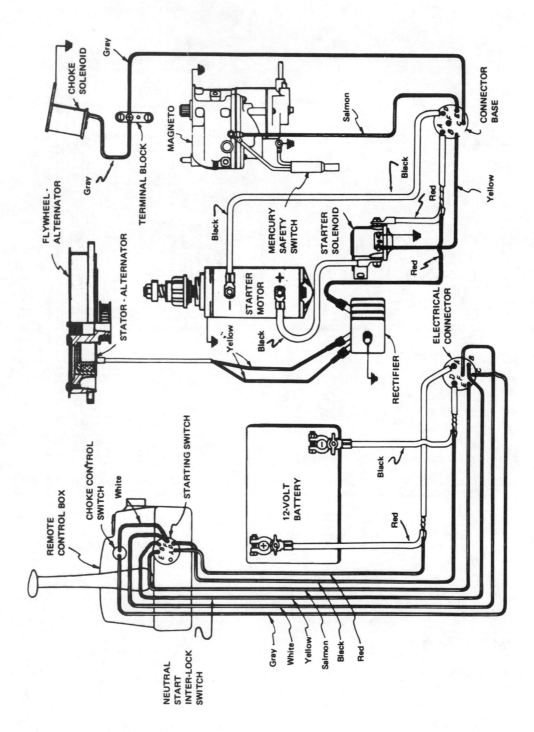

MERC 500 THUNDERBOLT IGNITION

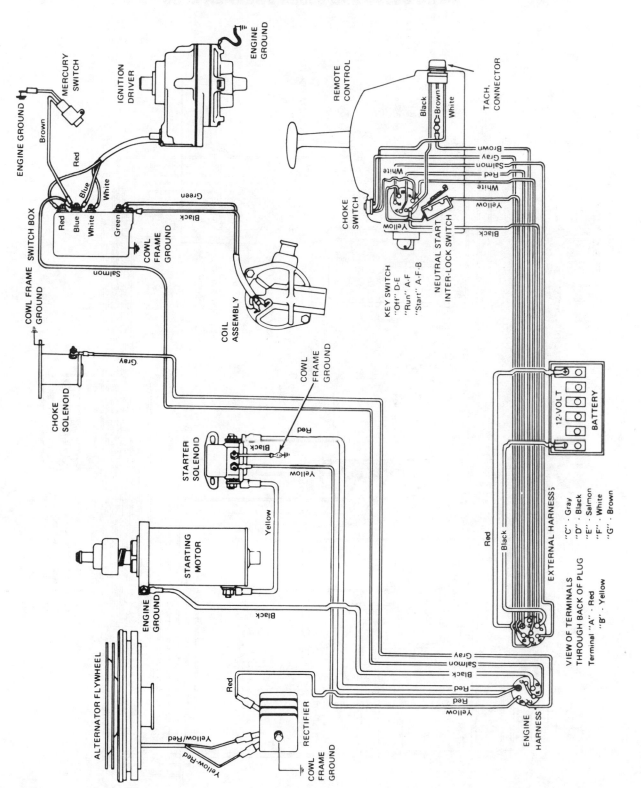

3

MERC 650SS AND 500SS BREAKER LESS

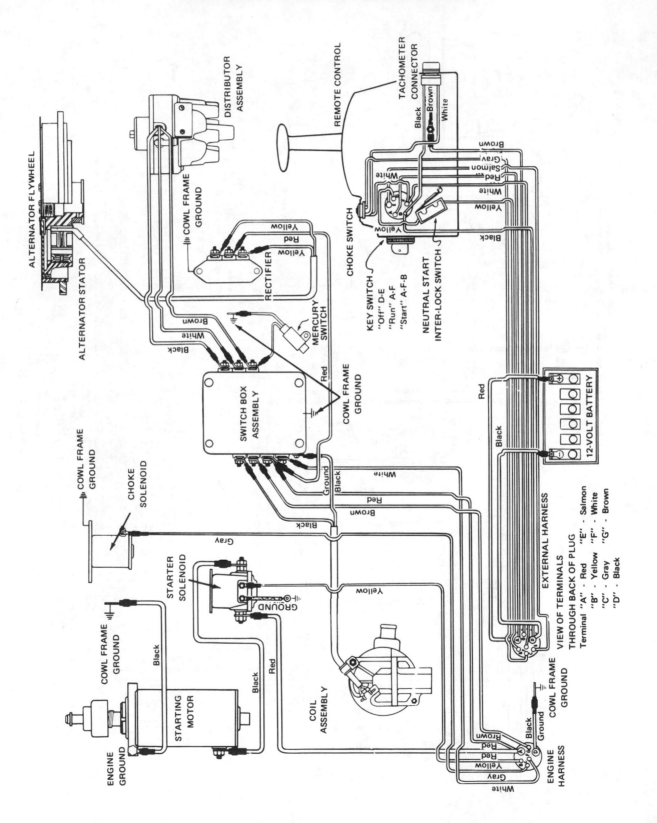

MERC 650S AND 500S BREAKER LESS WITH IGNITION DRIVER

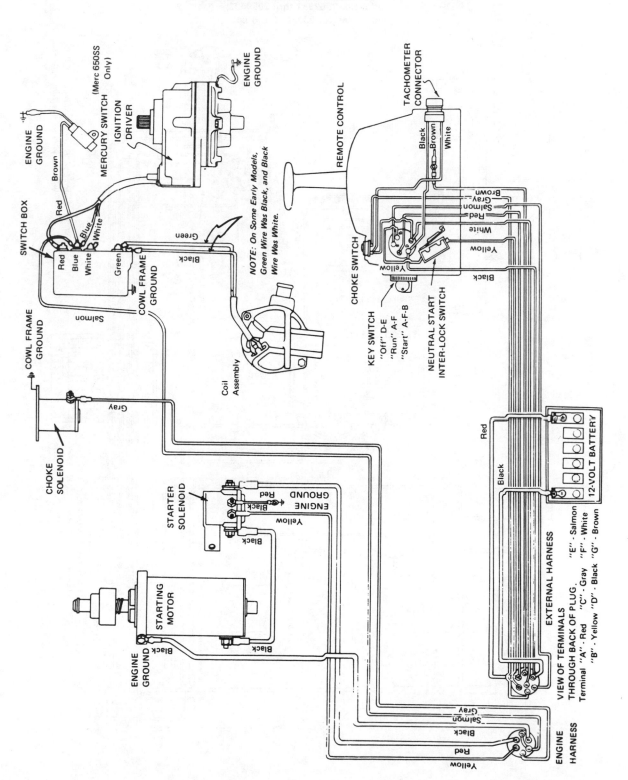

3

MERC 850-800*-650 (4-CYLINDER)
THUNDERBOLT IGNITION
(*Serial No. 2991033 and below;
Serial No. 3052381 thru 3059821;
and Serial No. 3307347 and up)

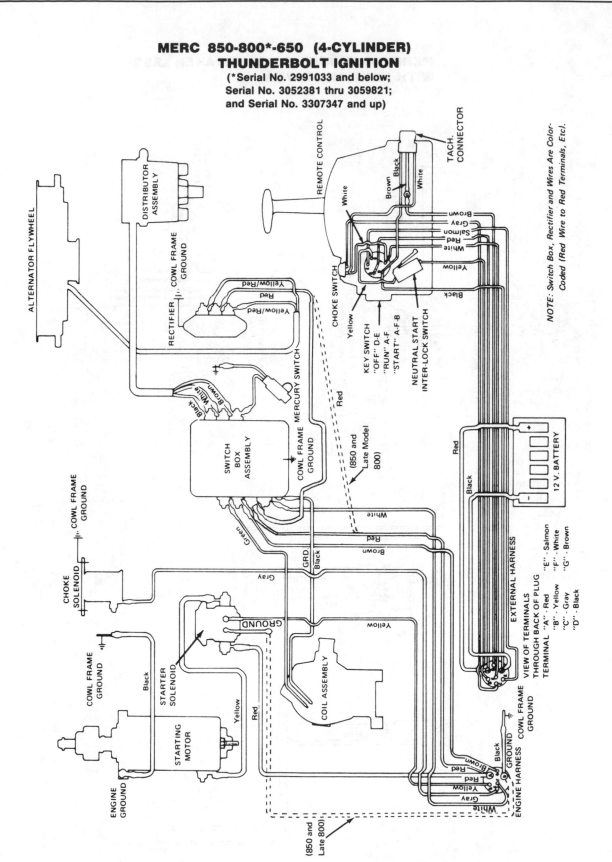

MERC 800 THUNDERBOLT IGNITION

ALTERNATOR FLYWHEEL

ALTERNATOR STATOR

ENGINE GROUND

DISTRIBUTOR ASSEMBLY

Cowl Frame Ground

Yellow/Red
Red
Yellow/Red
RECTIFIER

Black
Cowl Frame Ground

White

REMOTE CONTROL

Black
Brown
White
TACHOMETER CONNECTOR

White
Salmon
Red
Gray
Brown

White

Yellow
Yellow

Black

CHOKE SWITCH

KEY SWITCH
"Off" - D-E
"Run" - A-F
"Start" - A-F-B

NEUTRAL START INTER-LOCK SWITCH

Red

Black

12-VOLT BATTERY

MERCURY SWITCH

Grn Brn Blu Red
SWITCH BOX ASSEMBLY

COWL FRAME GROUND
Blue

COWL FRAME GROUND

Cowl Frame Ground

CHOKE SOLENOID

Blue

Gray

Brown

Red

White

EXTERNAL HARNESS

"D" - Black
"E" - Salmon
"F" - White
"G" - Brown

VIEW of TERMINALS THRU BACK of PLUG
Terminal "A" - Red
"B" - Yellow
"C" - Gray

Cowl Frame Ground

Black

STARTER SOLENOID

Yellow
Red
Black

Black

Green

IGNITION COIL

Yellow

STARTING MOTOR

Starter Ground

Cowl Frame Ground

Red
Red
Yellow
Gray
White
Brown
Black
Cowl Frame Ground

ENGINE HARNESS

3

MERC 1100SS AND 950SS

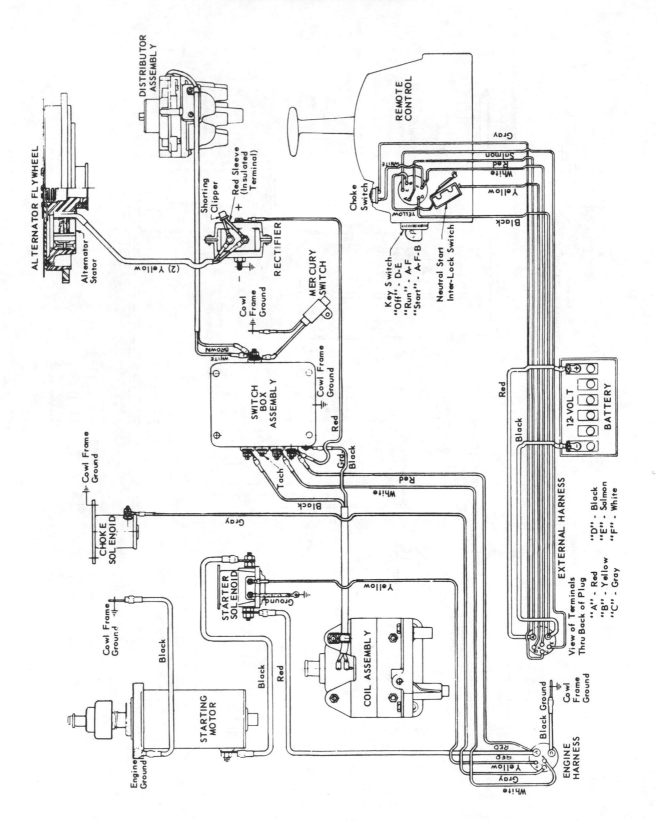

MERC 1100 AND 950

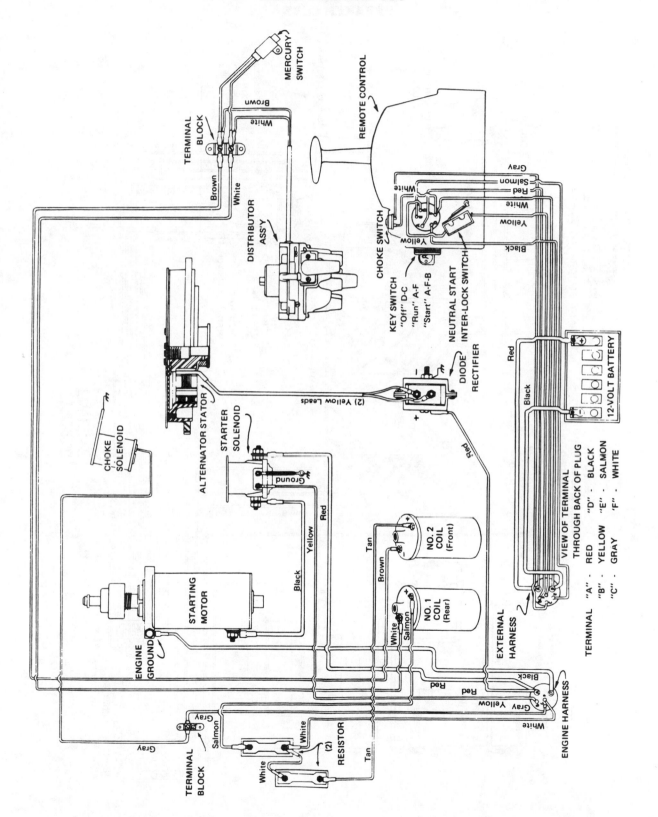

3

MERC 1250-1100-1000-950
BREAKER LESS

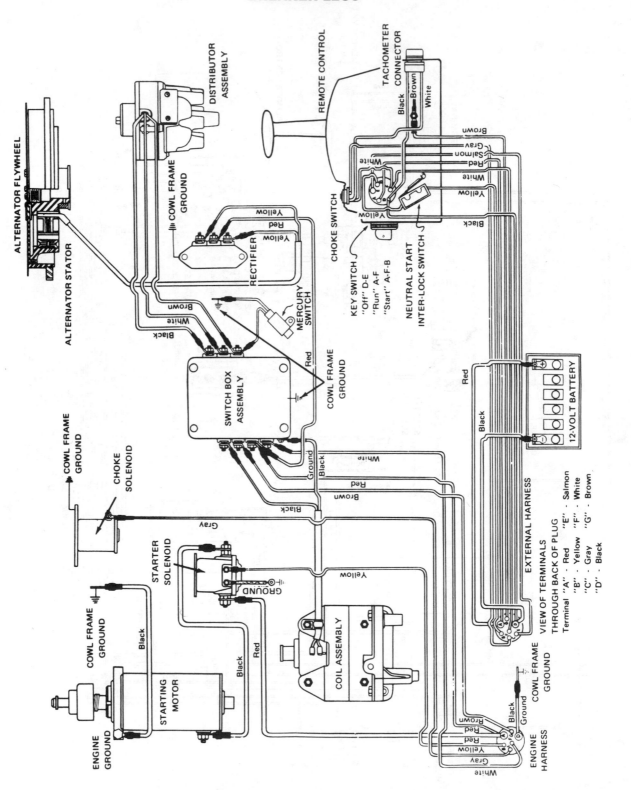

MERC 1500-1400-1350-1150
THUNDERBOLT IGNITION

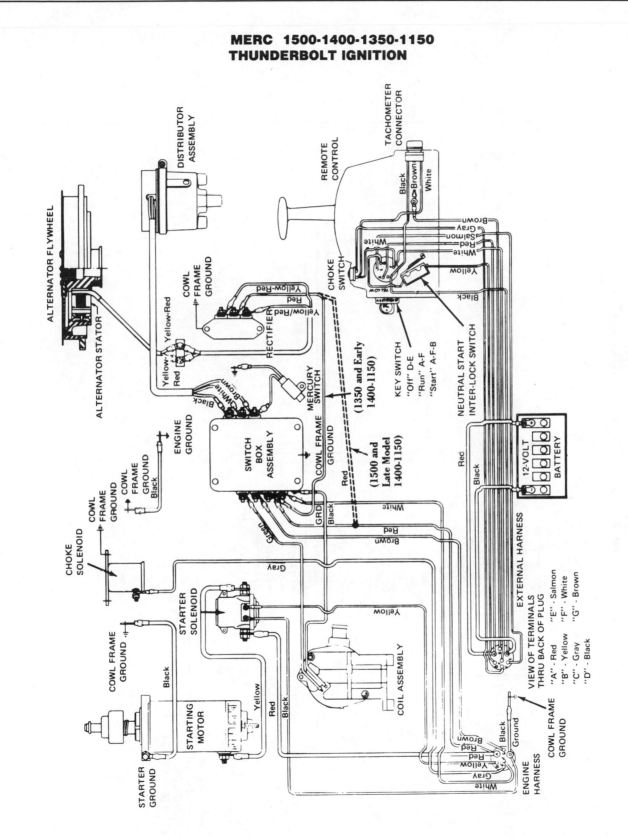

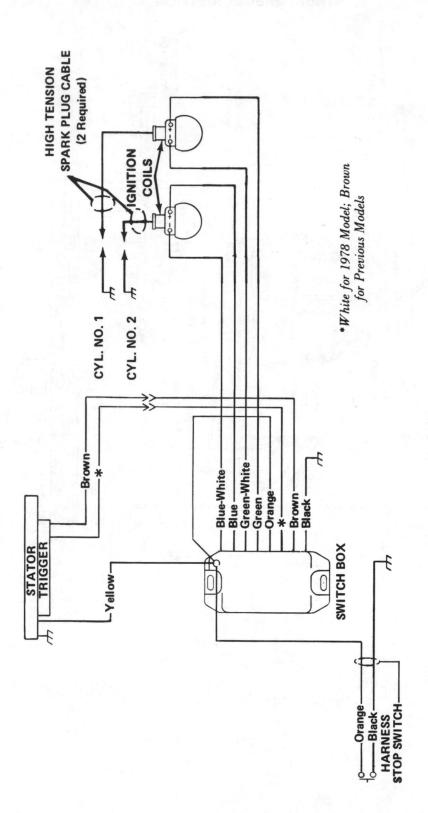

MERC 40 AND 4 HP (2-CYLINDER) MANUAL START

HIGH TENSION
SPARK PLUG CABLE
(2 Required)

IGNITION
COILS

CYL. NO. 1

CYL. NO. 2

*White for 1978 Model; Brown
for Previous Models

STATOR
TRIGGER

Brown

*

Yellow

Blue-White
Blue
Green-White
Green
Orange
*
Brown
Black

SWITCH BOX

Orange
Black
HARNESS
STOP SWITCH

**MERC 45, 4.5 AND 4 (1986-1987)
MANUAL START**

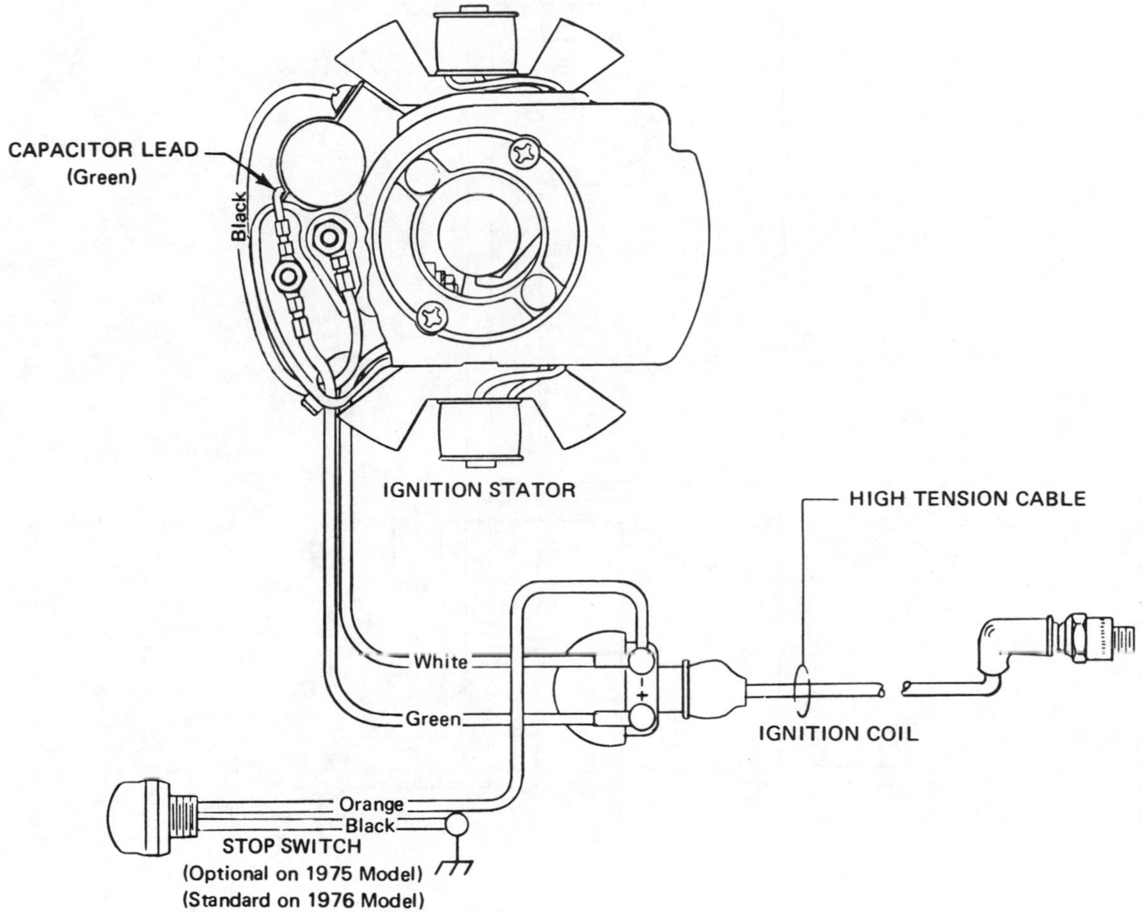

CAPACITOR LEAD
(Green)

Black

IGNITION STATOR

HIGH TENSION CABLE

White

Green

IGNITION COIL

Orange
Black
STOP SWITCH
(Optional on 1975 Model)
(Standard on 1976 Model)

3

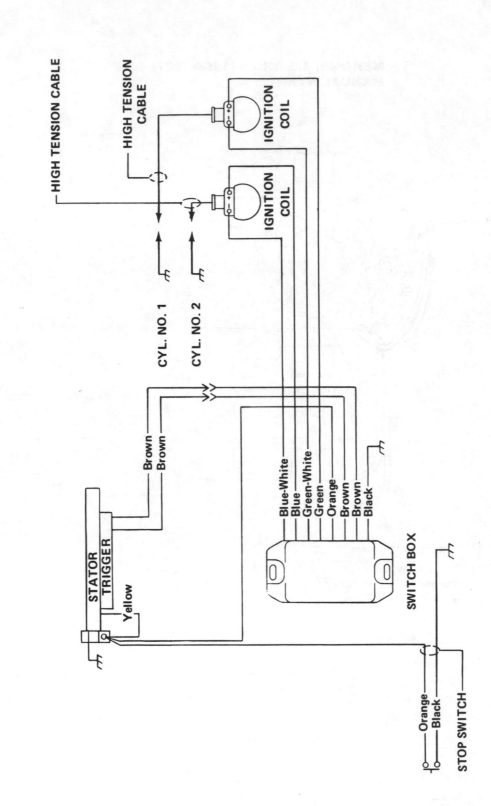

MERC 75 AND 110 (1975) MANUAL START

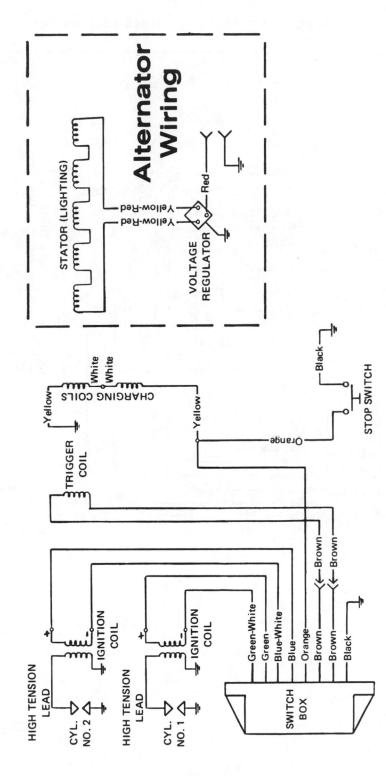

MERC 75 AND 110 (1976-77-78)
MANUAL START WITH ALTERNATOR

MERC 75-110 (1976-77-78) MANUAL START

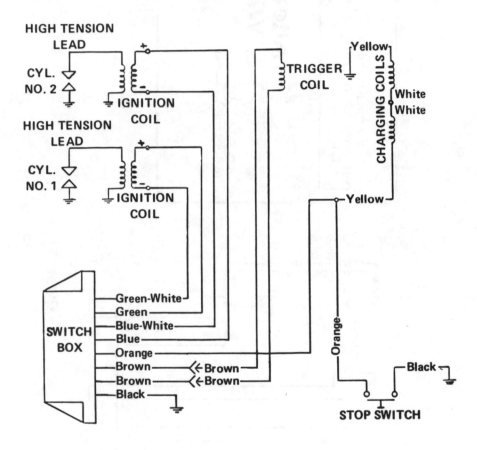

3

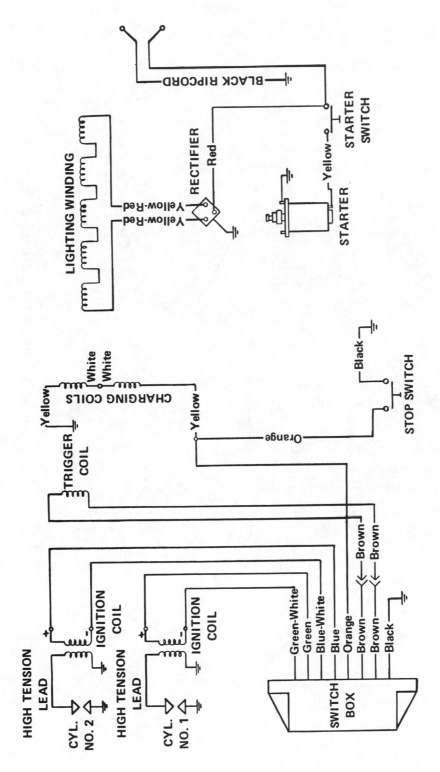

MERC 75-110 (1976-77-78) ELECTRIC START

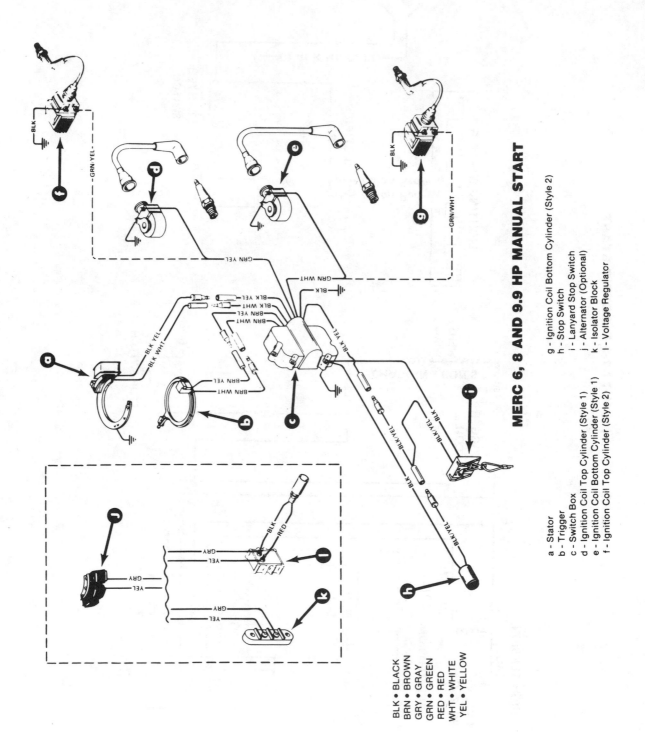

MERC 6, 8 AND 9.9 HP MANUAL START

a - Stator
b - Trigger
c - Switch Box
d - Ignition Coil Top Cylinder (Style 1)
e - Ignition Coil Bottom Cylinder (Style 1)
f - Ignition Coil Top Cylinder (Style 2)

g - Ignition Coil Bottom Cylinder (Style 2)
h - Stop Switch
i - Lanyard Stop Switch
j - Alternator (Optional)
k - Isolator Block
l - Voltage Regulator

BLK • BLACK
BRN • BROWN
GRY • GRAY
GRN • GREEN
RED • RED
WHT • WHITE
YEL • YELLOW

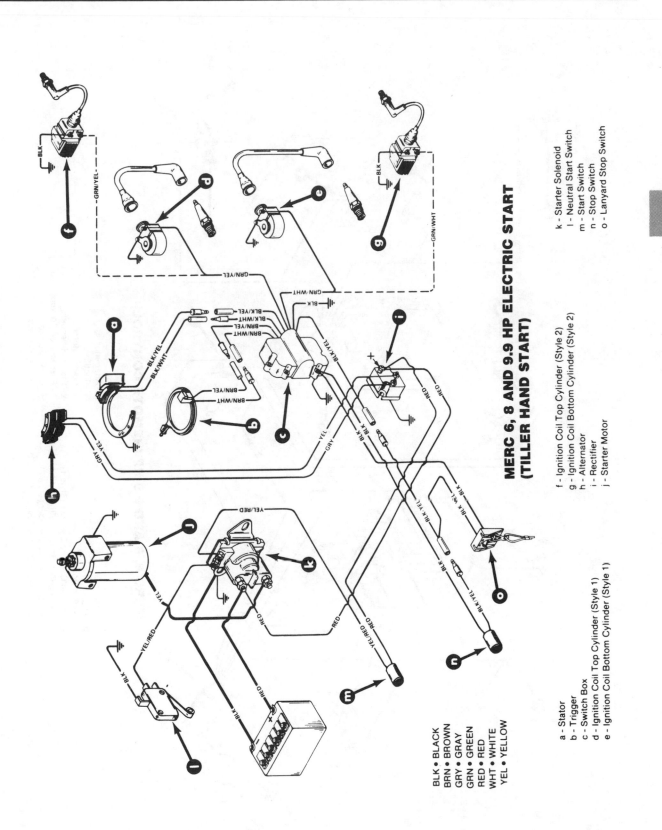

MERC 6, 8 AND 9.9 HP ELECTRIC START (TILLER HAND START)

a - Stator
b - Trigger
c - Switch Box
d - Ignition Coil Top Cylinder (Style 1)
e - Ignition Coil Bottom Cylinder (Style 1)

f - Ignition Coil Top Cylinder (Style 2)
g - Ignition Coil Bottom Cylinder (Style 2)
h - Alternator
i - Rectifier
j - Starter Motor

k - Starter Solenoid
l - Neutral Start Switch
m - Start Switch
n - Stop Switch
o - Lanyard Stop Switch

BLK • BLACK
BRN • BROWN
GRY • GRAY
GRN • GREEN
RED • RED
WHT • WHITE
YEL • YELLOW

3

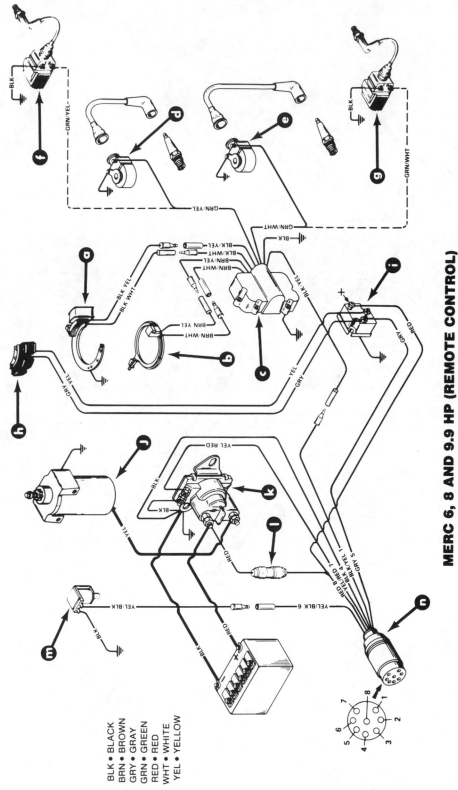

MERC 6, 8 AND 9.9 HP (REMOTE CONTROL)

a - Stator
b - Trigger
c - Switch Box
d - Ignition Coil Top Cylinder (Style 1)
e - Ignition Coil Bottom Cylinder (Style 1)
f - Ignition Coil Top Cylinder (Style 2)
g - Ignition Coil Bottom Cylinder (Style 2)

h - Alternator
i - Rectifier
j - Starter Motor
k - Starter Solenoid
l - Fuse Holder (20 Amp. Fuse)
m - Choke Solenoid
n - Wiring Harness

BLK • BLACK
BRN • BROWN
GRY • GRAY
GRN • GREEN
RED • RED
WHT • WHITE
YEL • YELLOW

MERC 200 (1975) ELECTRIC START

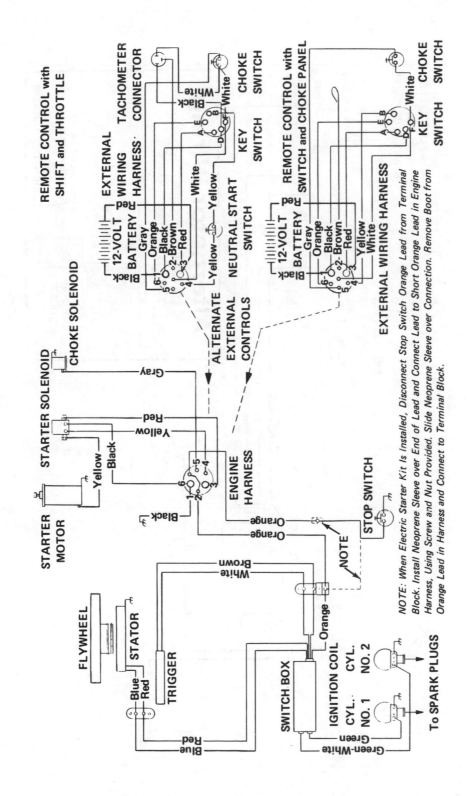

REMOTE CONTROL with SHIFT and THROTTLE

EXTERNAL WIRING HARNESS

TACHOMETER CONNECTOR

12-VOLT BATTERY

KEY SWITCH

CHOKE SWITCH

NEUTRAL START SWITCH

ALTERNATE EXTERNAL CONTROLS

REMOTE CONTROL with SWITCH and CHOKE PANEL

EXTERNAL WIRING HARNESS

KEY SWITCH

CHOKE SWITCH

CHOKE SOLENOID

STARTER SOLENOID

STARTER MOTOR

ENGINE HARNESS

STOP SWITCH

FLYWHEEL

STATOR

TRIGGER

SWITCH BOX

IGNITION COIL

CYL. NO. 1

CYL. NO. 2

To SPARK PLUGS

NOTE: When Electric Starter Kit Is Installed, Disconnect Stop Switch Orange Lead from Terminal Block. Install Neoprene Sleeve over End of Lead and Connect Lead to Short Orange Lead in Engine Harness, Using Screw and Nut Provided. Slide Neoprene Sleeve over Connection. Remove Boot from Orange Lead in Harness and Connect to Terminal Block.

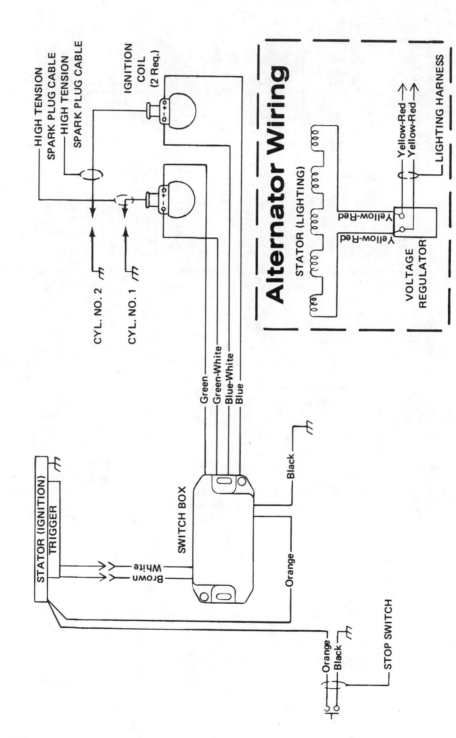

MERC 200 (1976-77-78) MANUAL START
WITH ALTERNATOR

MERC 200 (1976-77-78) ELECTRIC START

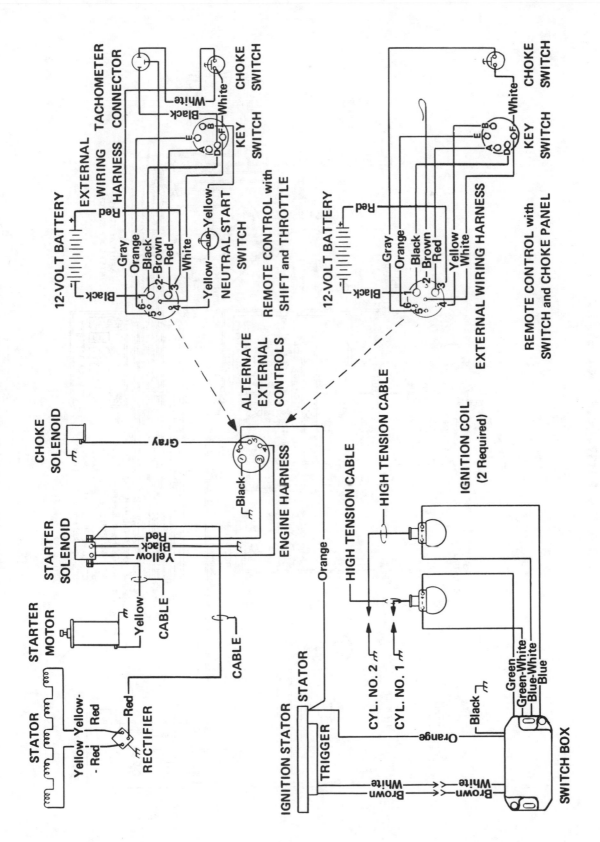

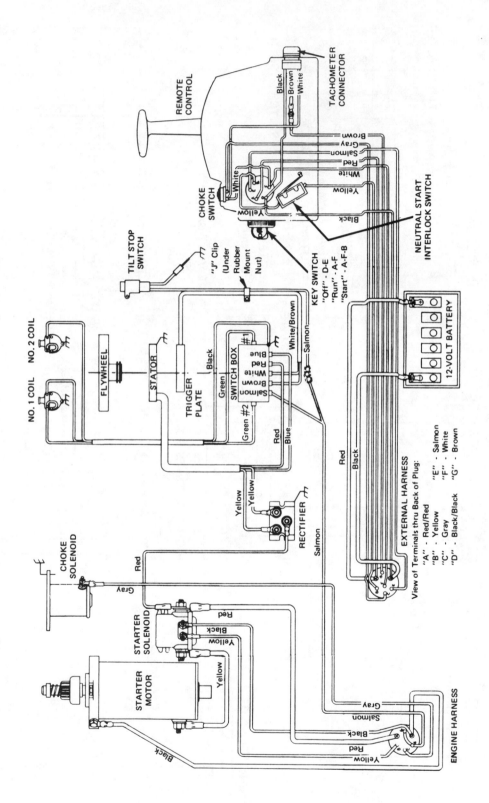

MERC 402 (1975) ELECTRIC START

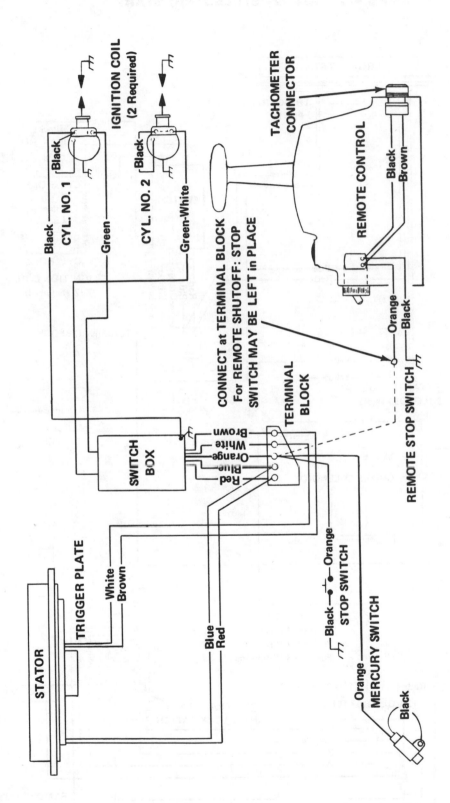

MERC 402 (1976-77-78) MANUAL START

MERC 402 (1976-77-78) ELECTRIC START

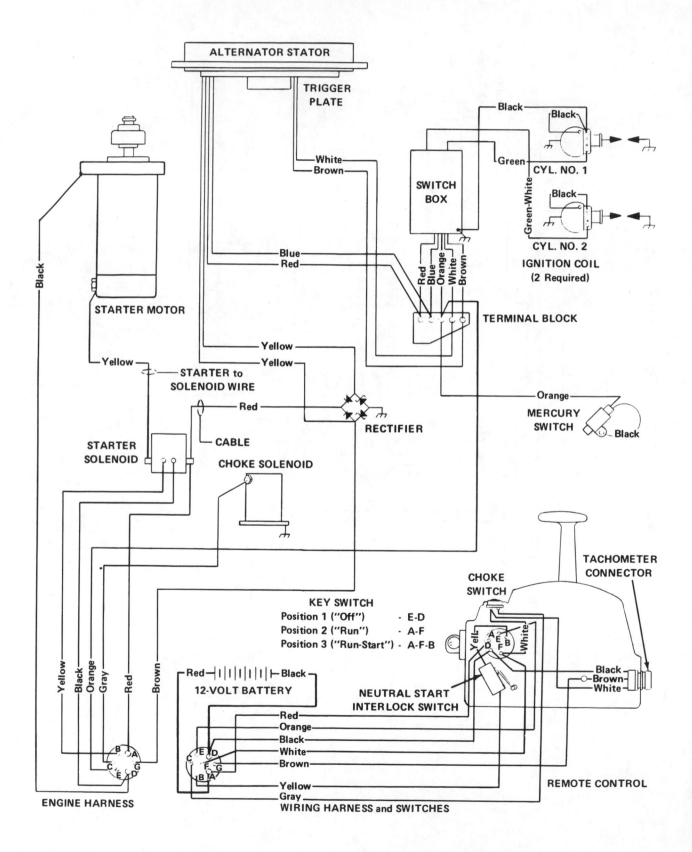

MERC 7.5 AND 9.8 HP MANUAL START

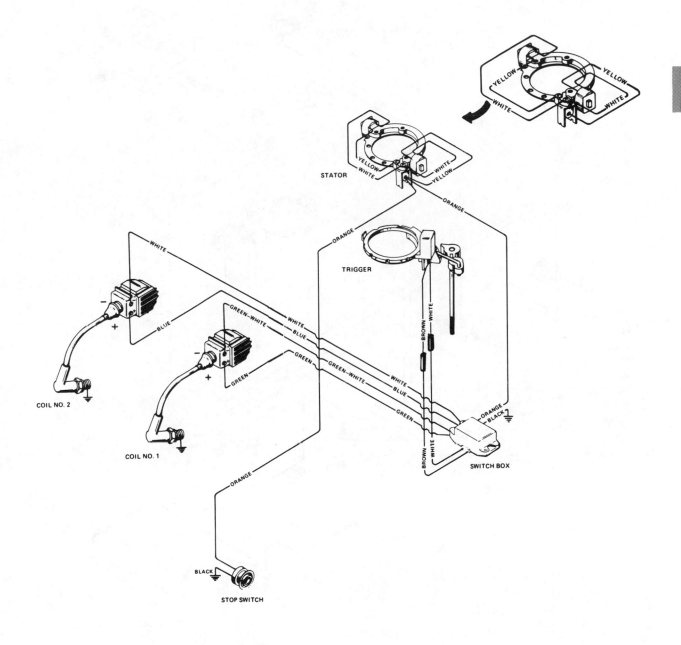

STATOR

TRIGGER

COIL NO. 2

COIL NO. 1

SWITCH BOX

STOP SWITCH

MERC 7.5 AND 9.8 HP ELECTRIC START

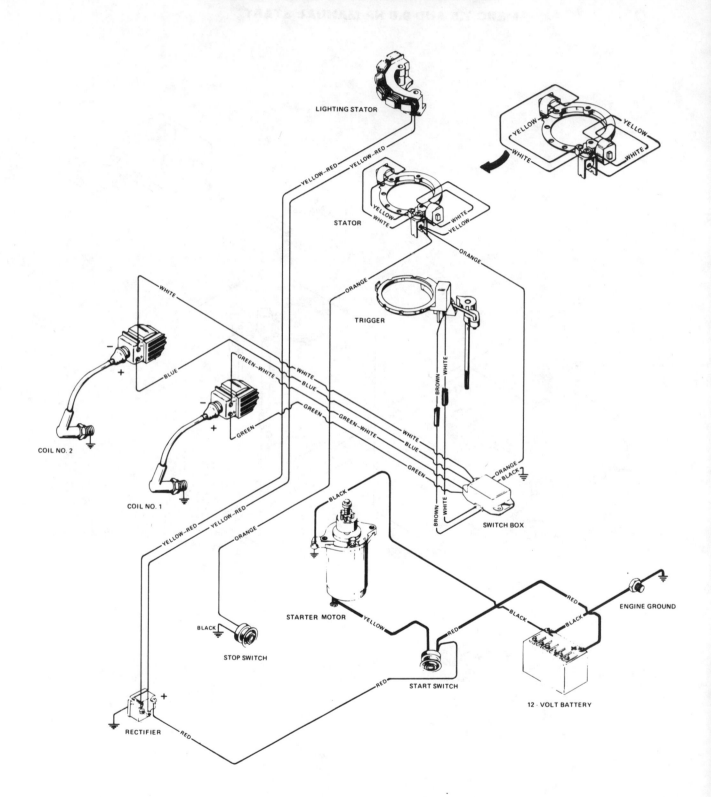

MERC 20 (PRIOR TO 1981)
HP MANUAL START

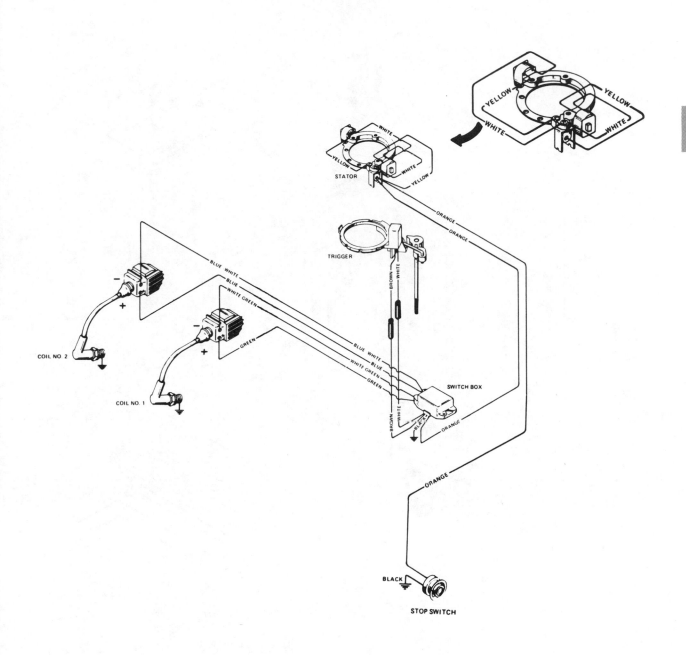

MERC 20 HP (PRIOR TO 1981)
ELECTRIC START

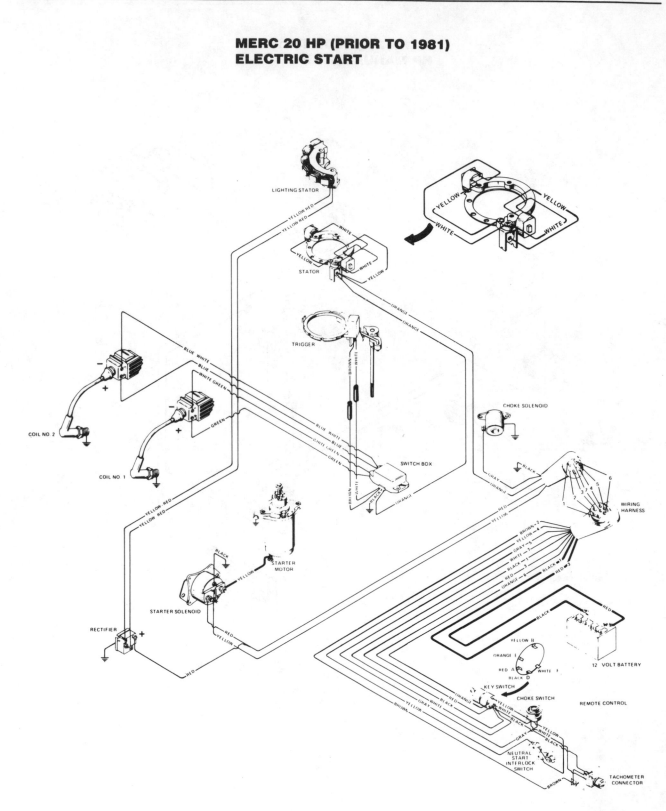

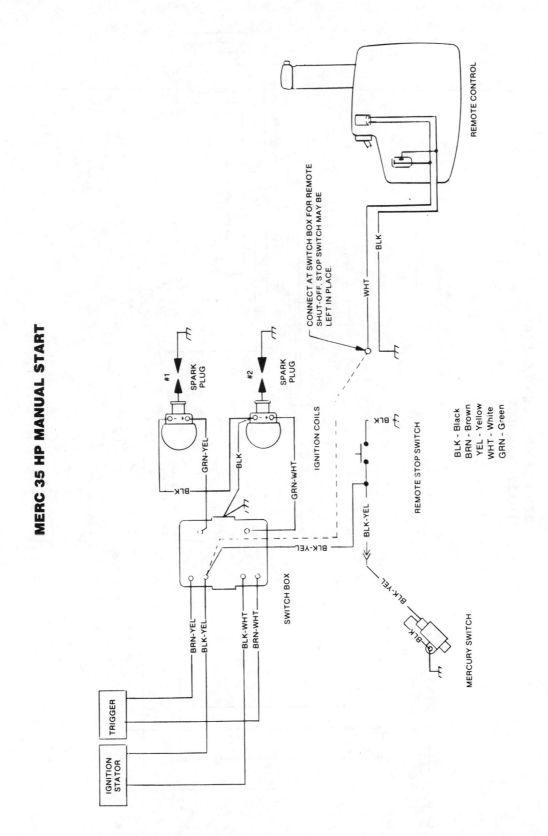

MERC 35 HP MANUAL START

REMOTE CONTROL

CONNECT AT SWITCH BOX FOR REMOTE SHUT-OFF. STOP SWITCH MAY BE LEFT IN PLACE.

WHT

BLK

#1 SPARK PLUG

#2 SPARK PLUG

IGNITION COILS

GRN-YEL

BLK

GRN-WHT

BLK

REMOTE STOP SWITCH

BLK - Black
BRN - Brown
YEL - Yellow
WHT - White
GRN - Green

BLK-YEL

BLK-YEL

BLK

MERCURY SWITCH

SWITCH BOX

BRN-YEL
BLK-YEL
BLK-WHT
BRN-WHT

TRIGGER

IGNITION STATOR

3

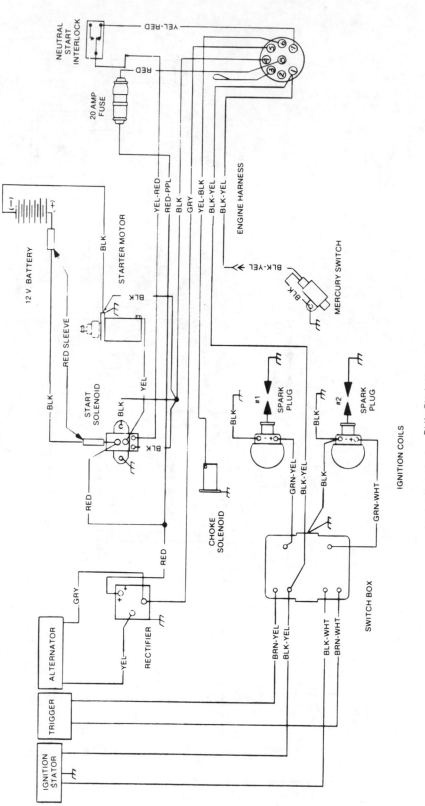

MERC 35 HP ELECTRIC START (TILLER HANDLE)

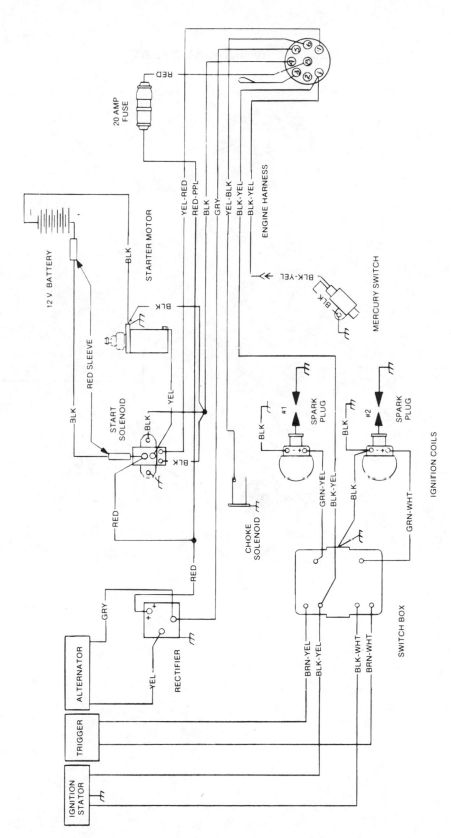

MERC 35 HP ELECTRIC START (REMOTE CONTROL)

BLK - Black
BRN - Brown
YEL - Yellow
WHT - White
GRN - Green
RED - Red
PPL - Purple
GRY - Gray

MERC 40 HP MANUAL START

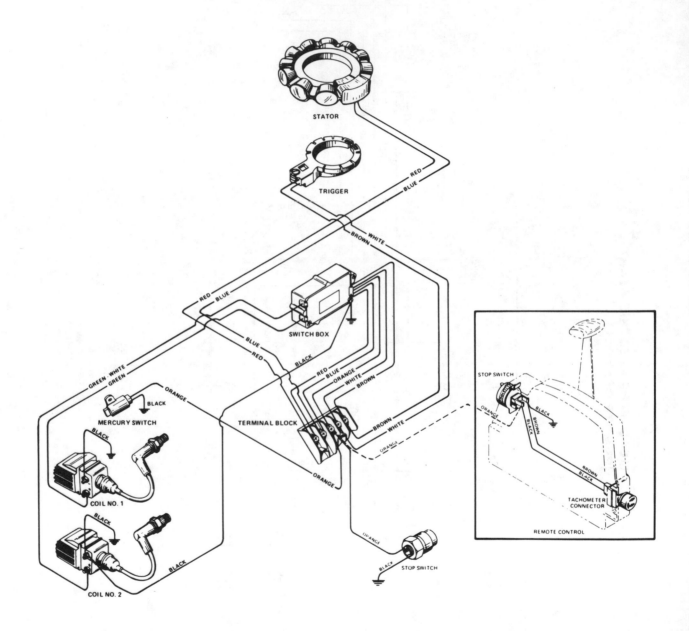

STATOR

TRIGGER

RED

BLUE

WHITE

BROWN

RED — BLUE

BLUE

RED

SWITCH BOX

BLACK

RED
BLUE
ORANGE
WHITE
BROWN

BROWN

WHITE

GREEN · WHITE
GREEN

ORANGE

BLACK

MERCURY SWITCH

TERMINAL BLOCK

ORANGE

BLACK

COIL NO. 1

BLACK

BLACK

COIL NO. 2

ORANGE

ORANGE

BLACK

STOP SWITCH

STOP SWITCH

ORANGE

BLACK

BLACK

BROWN

BROWN

BLACK

TACHOMETER
CONNECTOR

REMOTE CONTROL

MERC 40 HP ELECTRIC START

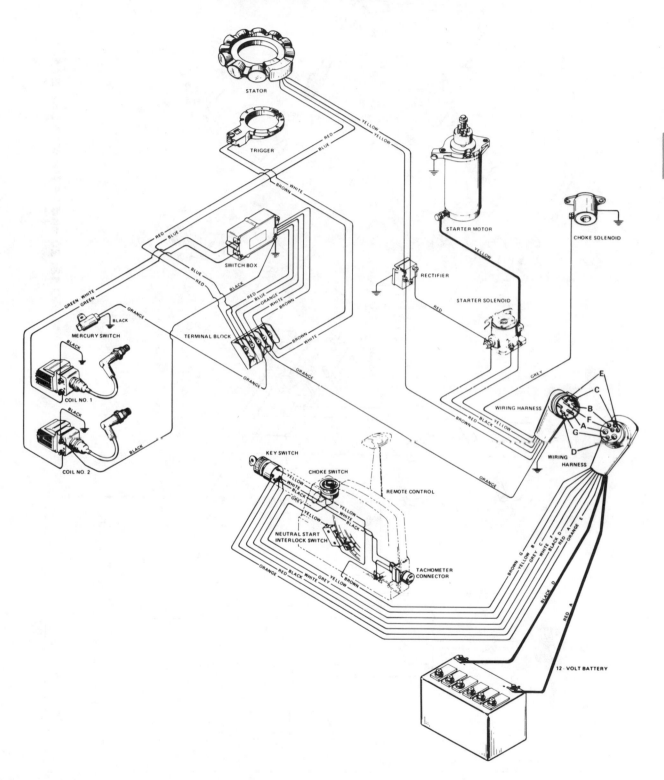

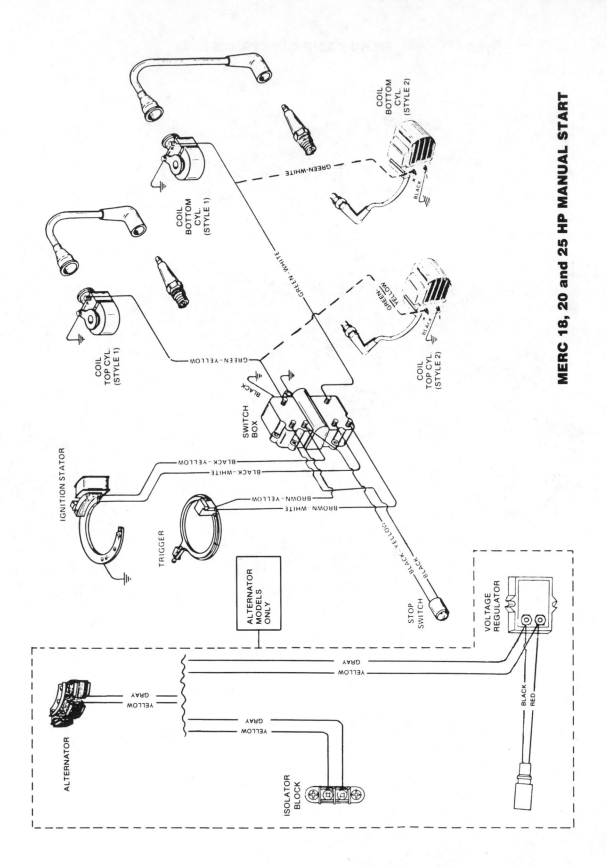

MERC 18, 20 and 25 HP MANUAL START

3

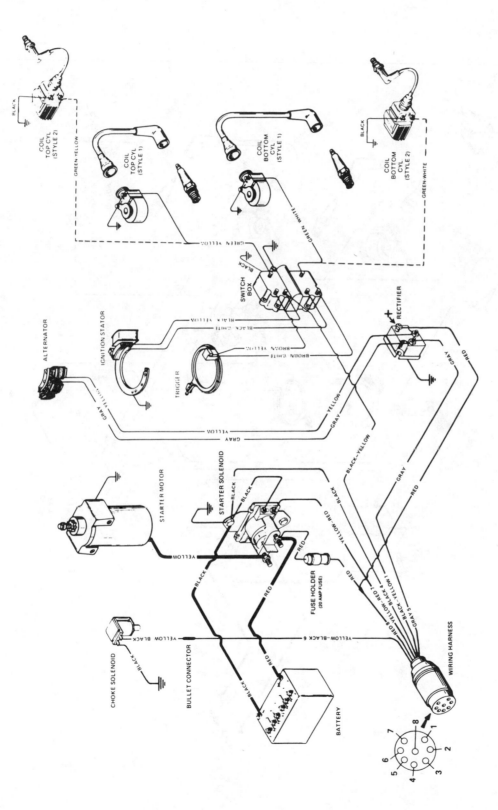

MERC 18, 20 AND 25 HP ELECTRIC START (REMOTE CONTROL)

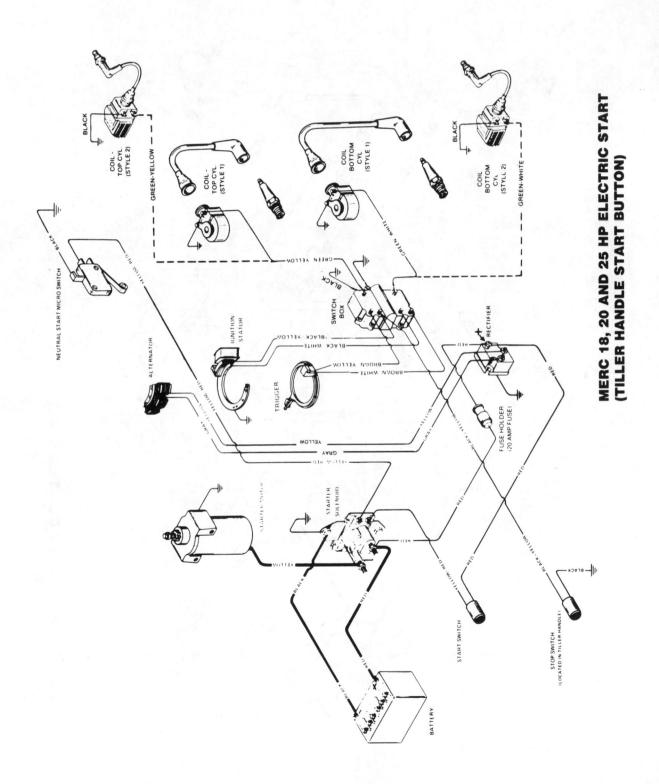

MERC 18, 20 AND 25 HP ELECTRIC START (TILLER HANDLE START BUTTON)

COIL - TOP CYL (STYLE 2)

BLACK

GREEN-YELLOW

COIL - TOP CYL (STYLE 1)

COIL BOTTOM CYL (STYLE 1)

BLACK

COIL BOTTOM CYL (STYLE 2)

GREEN-WHITE

GREEN WHITE

GREEN YELLOW

BLACK

NEUTRAL START MICRO SWITCH

BLACK

YELLOW RED

ALTERNATOR

IGNITION STATOR

SWITCH BOX

BLACK YELLOW

BLACK WHITE

BROWN YELLOW

BROWN WHITE

TRIGGER

GRAY YELLOW

GRAY

YELLOW

YELLOW

YELLOW WHITE

RECTIFIER

RED

FUSE HOLDER (20 AMP FUSE)

RED

RED

GRAY

WHITE

BLACK-YELLOW

RED

RED

STARTER SOLENOID

STARTER MOTOR

YELLOW

RED

YELLOW RED

RED

YELLOW RED

BLACK-YELLOW

BLACK

START SWITCH

STOP SWITCH (LOCATED IN TILLER HANDLE)

BLACK

RED

BLACK

BATTERY

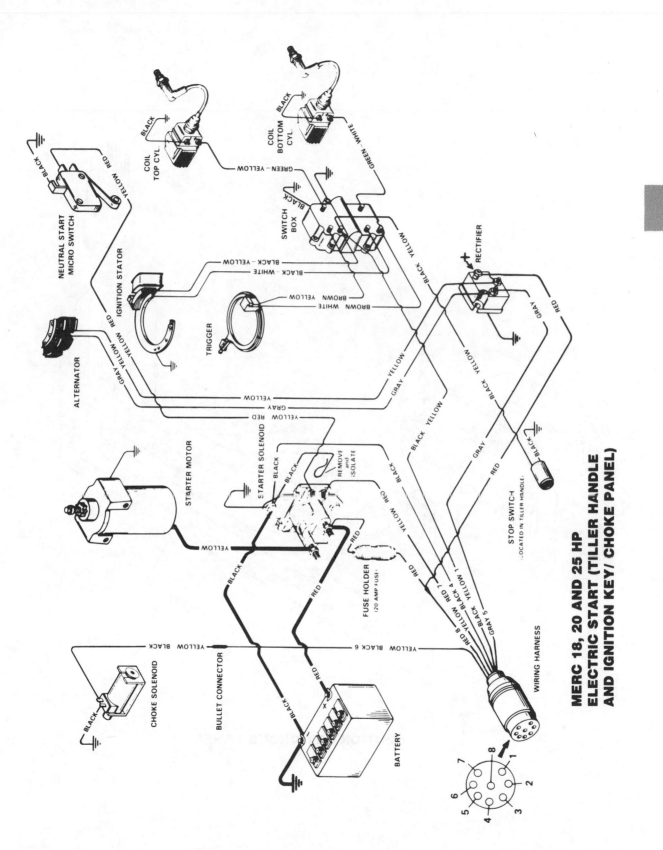

**MERC 18, 20 AND 25 HP
ELECTRIC START (TILLER HANDLE
AND IGNITION KEY/ CHOKE PANEL)**

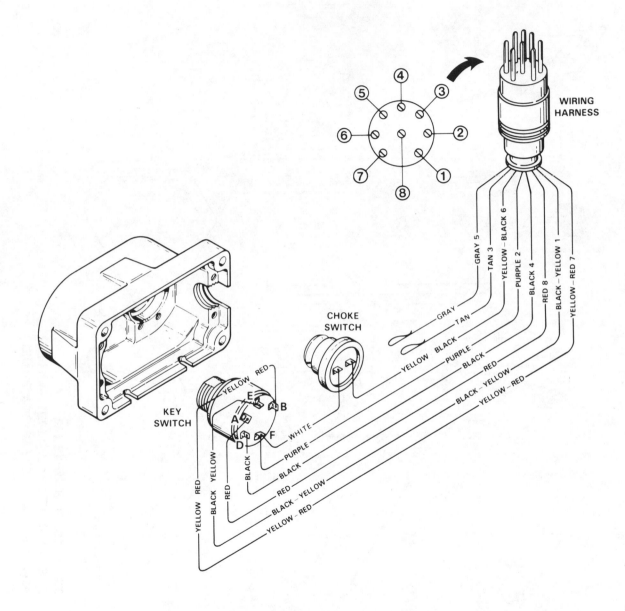

IGNITION KEY/CHOKE PANEL

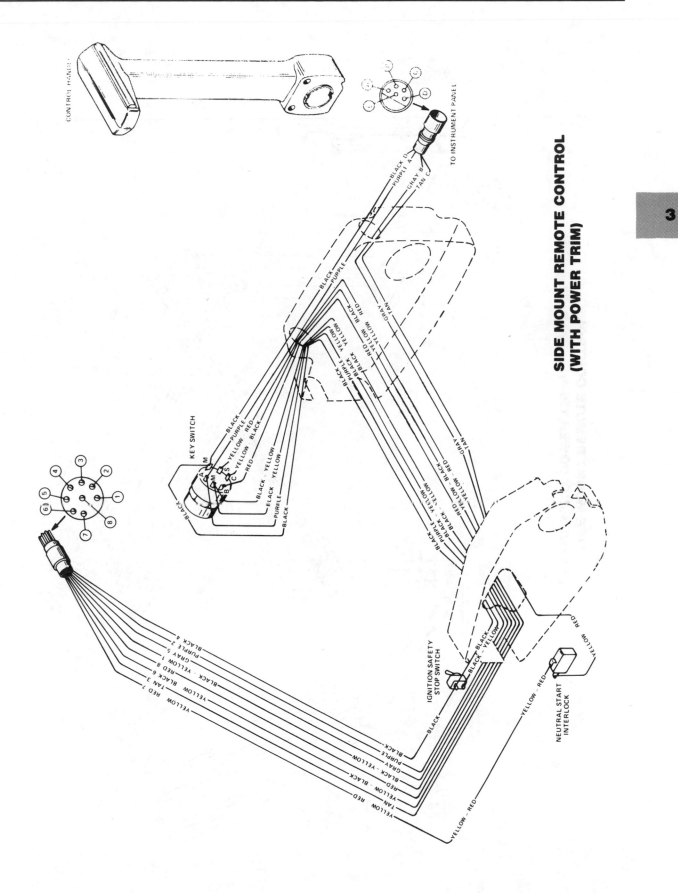

SIDE MOUNT REMOTE CONTROL
(WITH POWER TRIM)

3

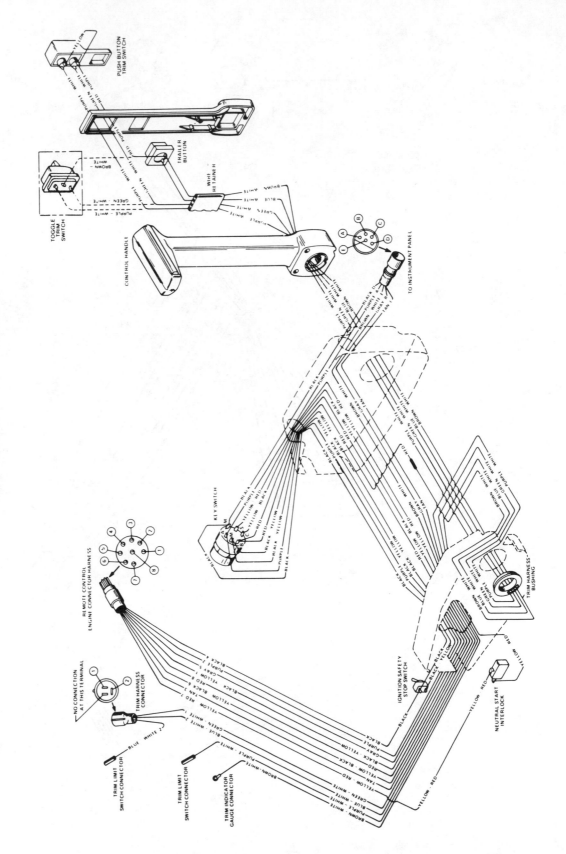

SIDE MOUNT REMOTE CONTROL (WITHOUT POWER TRIM)

"TM" AND "DM" MODELS (WITH ROTARY SWITCH AND HORIZONTAL MOUNTED MICRO SWITCHES)

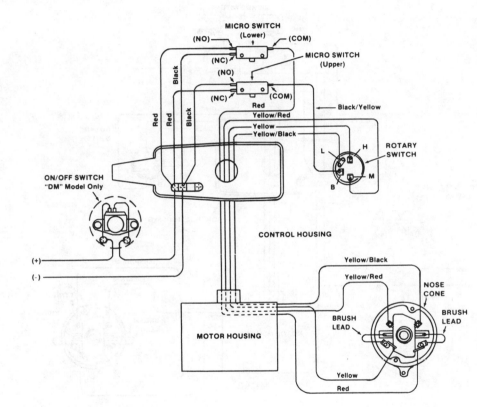

**"RC" MODEL (WITH ROTARY SWITCH
AND MICRO SWITCHES)**

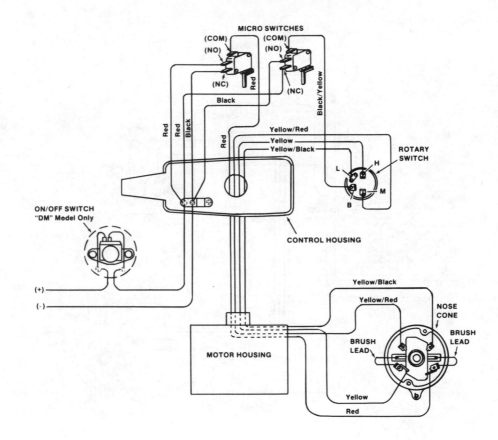

3

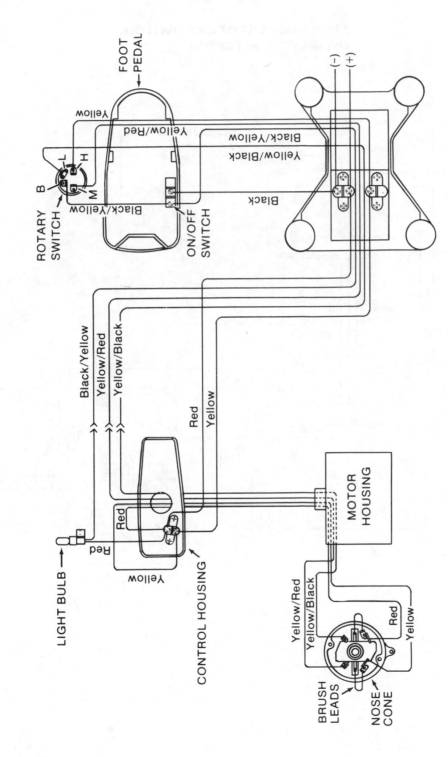

"TM" AND "DM" MODELS (WITH ROTARY SWITCH AND VERTICAL MOUNTED MICRO SWITCHES)

FOOT PEDAL

Yellow

Yellow/Red

Black/Yellow

Yellow/Black

Black

ROTARY SWITCH

L
H
B
M

Black/Yellow

ON/OFF SWITCH

(−) (+)

Black/Yellow
Yellow/Red
Yellow/Black

Red
Yellow

LIGHT BULB

Red

CONTROL HOUSING

Red

Yellow

MOTOR HOUSING

Yellow/Red
Yellow/Black
Red
Yellow

BRUSH LEADS

NOSE CONE

**"TM" MODEL (ROTARY SWITCH,
NO MICRO SWITCHES)**

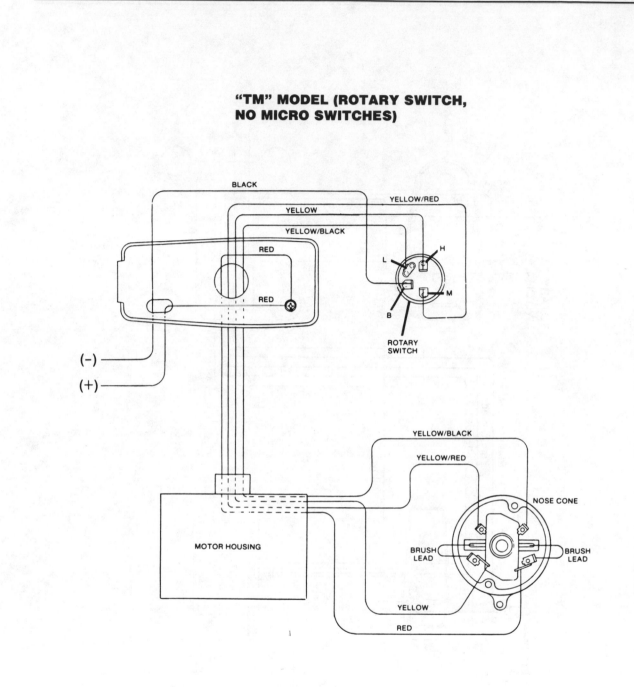

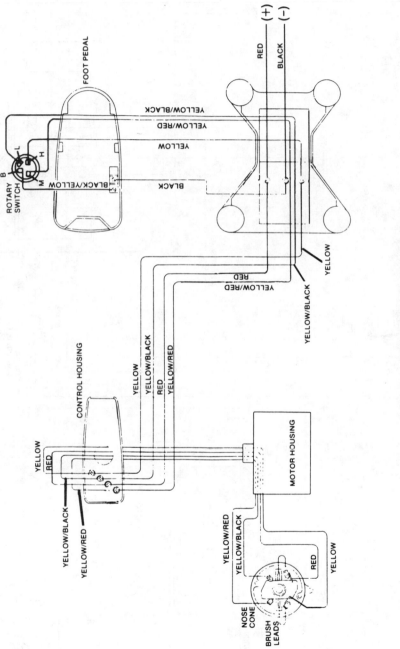

"RC MODEL (ROTARY SWITCH, NO MICRO SWITCHES)

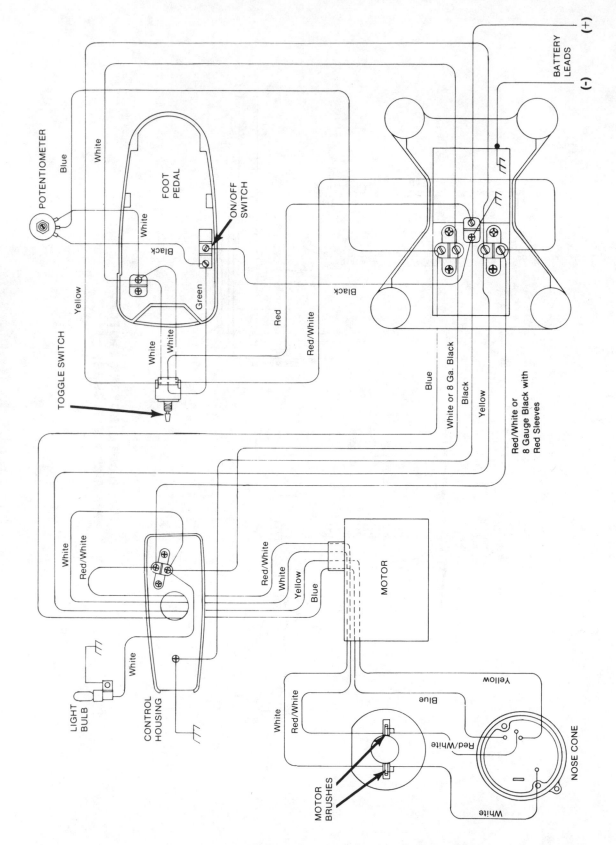

"RC" MODEL (WITH POTENTIOMETER)

POTENTIOMETER

Blue

White

FOOT PEDAL

White

ON/OFF SWITCH

Black

Yellow

Green

White

White

TOGGLE SWITCH

Red

Red/White

Black

BATTERY LEADS

(+)

(-)

Blue

White or 8 Ga. Black

Black

Yellow

Red/White or 8 Gauge Black with Red Sleeves

White

Red/White

Red/White

White

Yellow

Blue

MOTOR

LIGHT BULB

White

CONTROL HOUSING

White

Red/White

Blue

Yellow

Red/White

MOTOR BRUSHES

White

NOSE CONE

"TM" MODEL (WITH POTENTIOMETER)

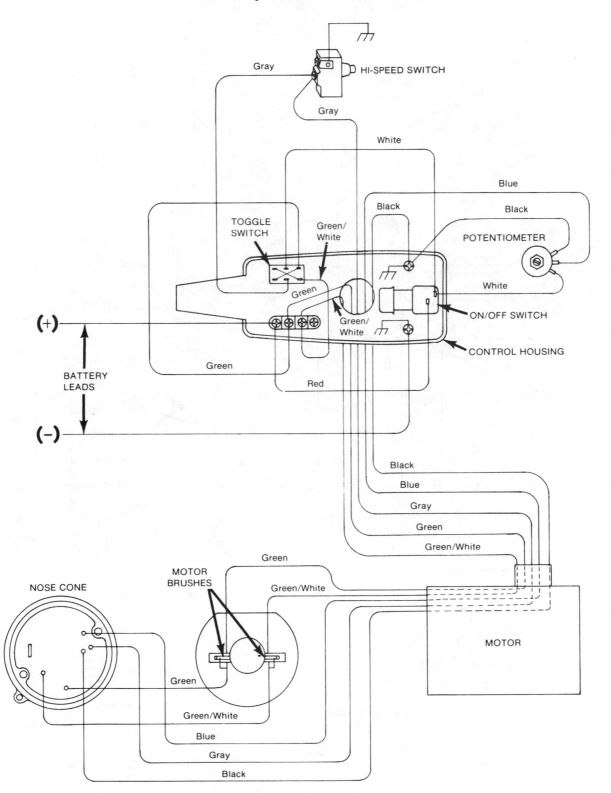

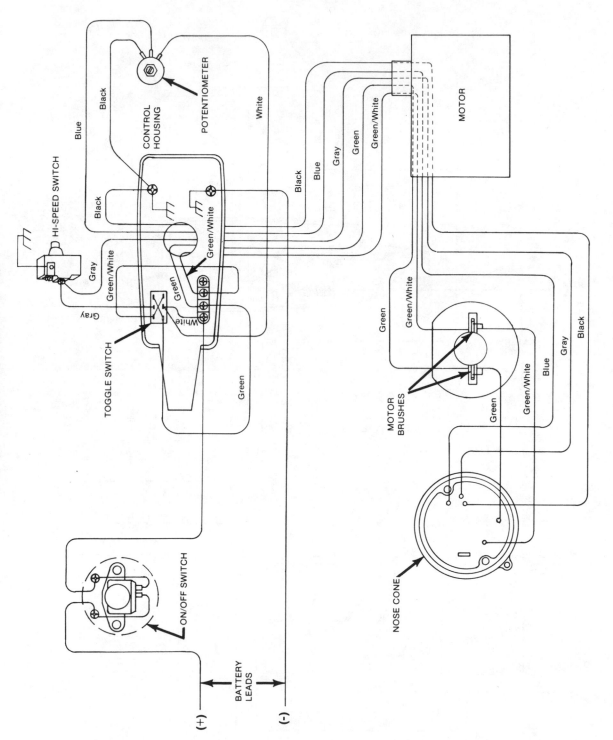

"DM" MODEL (WITH POTENTIOMETER)

CONTROL HOUSING

POTENTIOMETER

HI-SPEED SWITCH

TOGGLE SWITCH

ON/OFF SWITCH

BATTERY LEADS

(+)   (-)

MOTOR

MOTOR BRUSHES

NOSE CONE

MERC 500 THUNDERBOLT IGNITION THROUGH 1974

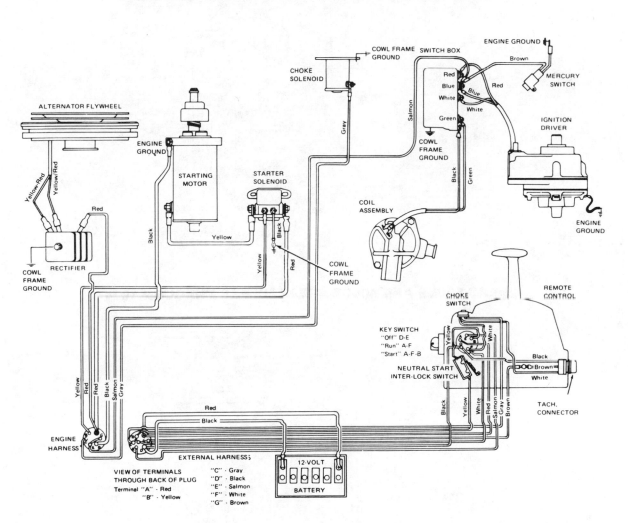

3

MERC 650S AND 500S BREAKERLESS WITH IGNITION DRIVER THROUGH 1974

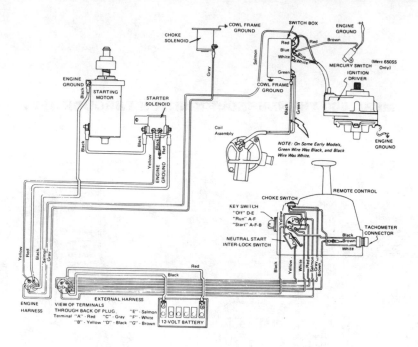

MERC 650SS AND 500SS BREAKERLESS THROUGH 1974

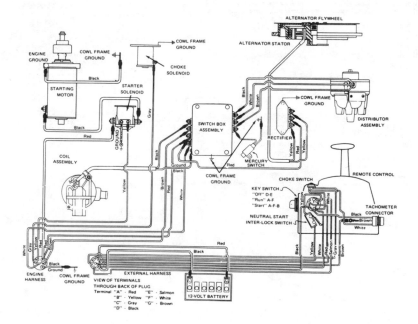

MERC 500 (1975) MANUAL START

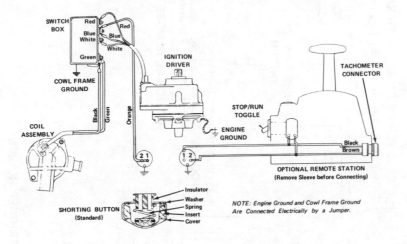

MERC 500 (1975) ELECTRIC START AD-CD IGNITION

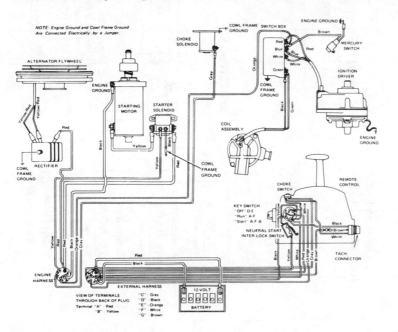

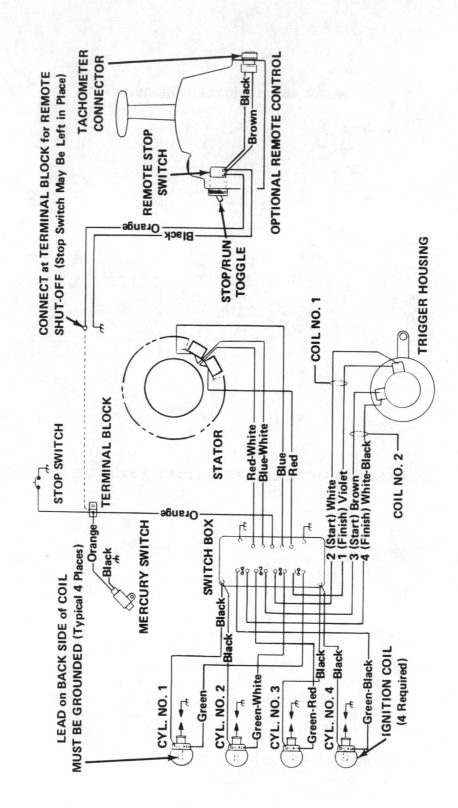

MERC 500 (1976-77-78) MANUAL START

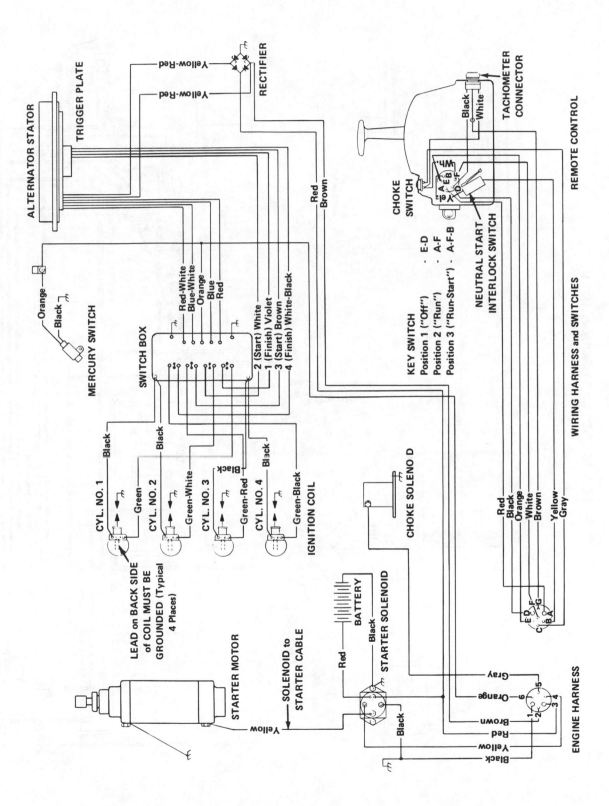

MERC 500 (1976-77-78) ELECTRIC START

3

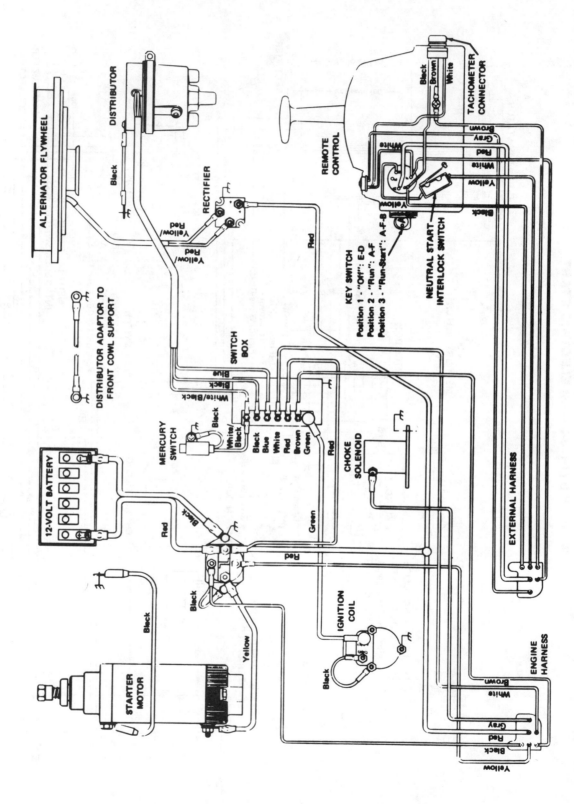

MERC 650 (3-CYL.) THROUGH 1974

ALTERNATOR FLYWHEEL

DISTRIBUTOR

Black

RECTIFIER

Yellow/Red

Yellow/Red

DISTRIBUTOR ADAPTOR TO FRONT COWL SUPPORT

SWITCH BOX

Blue

Black

White/Black

MERCURY SWITCH

Black

White/Black

Black
Blue
White
Red
Brown
Green

Red

CHOKE SOLENOID

Green

Red

12-VOLT BATTERY

Red

Black

Black

STARTER MOTOR

Yellow

IGNITION COIL

Black

REMOTE CONTROL

TACHOMETER CONNECTOR

Black
Brown
White

White
Gray
Brown
Red

White

Yellow

Yellow

Black

KEY SWITCH
Position 1 - "Off": E-D
Position 2 - "Run": A-F
Position 3 - "Run-Start": A-F-S

NEUTRAL START INTERLOCK SWITCH

EXTERNAL HARNESS

ENGINE HARNESS

Brown
White
Gray
Red
Black
Yellow

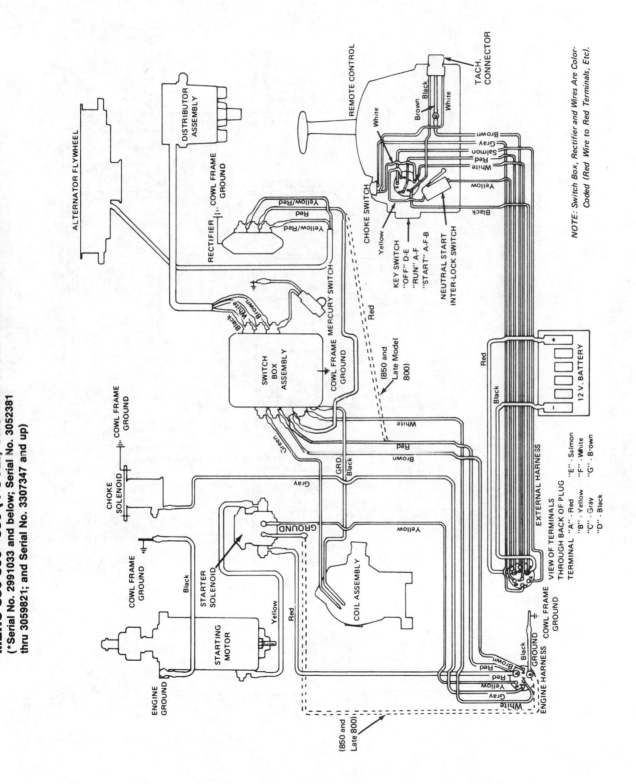

MERC 850-800*-650 (4-CYL.) THUNDERBOLT IGNITION THROUGH 1974
(*Serial No. 2991033 and below; Serial No. 3052381 thru 3059821; and Serial No. 3307347 and up)

ALTERNATOR FLYWHEEL

DISTRIBUTOR ASSEMBLY

RECTIFIER

COWL FRAME GROUND

Yellow/Red

Red

Yellow/Red

REMOTE CONTROL

TACH. CONNECTOR

White

Brown

Black

White

Brown

Gray

Salmon

Red

White

Yellow

Black

CHOKE SWITCH

KEY SWITCH
"OFF" D-E
"RUN" A-F
"START" A-F-B

NEUTRAL START INTER-LOCK SWITCH

Black

White

Brown

NOTE: Switch Box, Rectifier and Wires Are Color-Coded (Red Wire to Red Terminals, Etc).

SWITCH BOX ASSEMBLY

COWL FRAME MERCURY SWITCH GROUND

(850 and Late Model 800)

Red

CHOKE SOLENOID

COWL FRAME GROUND

Green

GRD.

Black

Gray

White

Red

Brown

Yellow

Red

Black

12 V. BATTERY

+

−

COWL FRAME GROUND

STARTER SOLENOID

Black

Yellow

Red

COIL ASSEMBLY

GROUND

Yellow

ENGINE GROUND

EXTERNAL HARNESS

VIEW OF TERMINALS THROUGH BACK OF PLUG

TERMINAL "A" - Red   "E" - Salmon
         "B" - Yellow   "F" - White
         "C" - Gray   "G" - B'rown
         "D" - Black

COWL FRAME GROUND

Black

Brown

Red

Red

Yellow

Gray

White

GROUND

ENGINE HARNESS

(850 and Late 800)

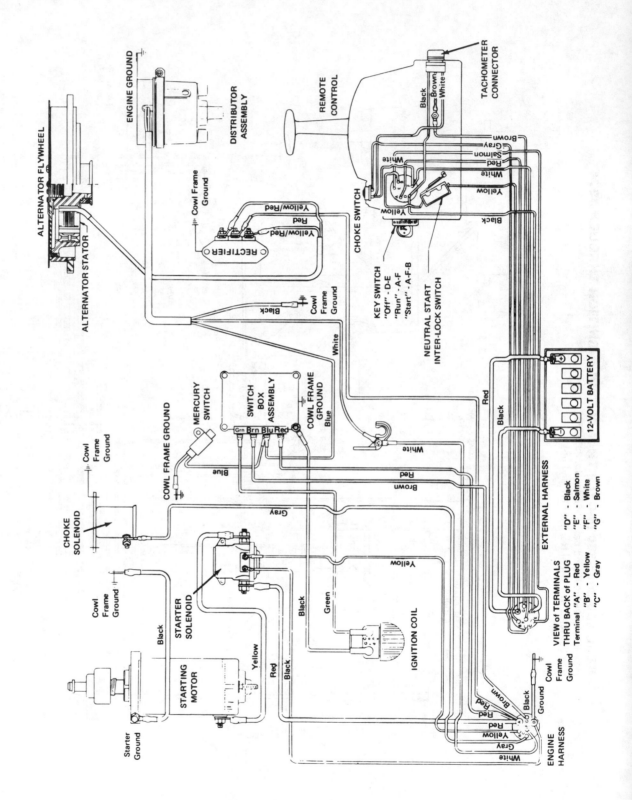

MERC 800 THUNDERBOLT IGNITION THROUGH 1974
(With Serial Nos. 2991034-3052380; 3059822-3307346)

ALTERNATOR FLYWHEEL

ALTERNATOR STATOR

ENGINE GROUND

DISTRIBUTOR ASSEMBLY

Cowl Frame Ground

RECTIFIER

Yellow/Red
Red
Yellow/Red

REMOTE CONTROL

Black Brown White

TACHOMETER CONNECTOR

CHOKE SWITCH

White
Red
Salmon
Gray
Brown

White
Yellow

KEY SWITCH
"Off" - D-E
"Run" - A-F
"Start" - A-F-B

NEUTRAL START
INTER-LOCK SWITCH

Yellow

Black

Black

Cowl Frame Ground

White

12-VOLT BATTERY

Red

Black

MERCURY SWITCH

SWITCH BOX ASSEMBLY

COWL FRAME GROUND
Blue

Grn Brn Blu Red

COWL FRAME GROUND

Blue

White

Red

Brown

Gray

EXTERNAL HARNESS

"D" - Black
"E" - Salmon
"F" - White
"G" - Brown

VIEW of TERMINALS
THRU BACK of PLUG
Terminal "A" - Red
"B" - Yellow
"C" - Gray

CHOKE SOLENOID

Cowl Frame Ground

Cowl Frame Ground

STARTER SOLENOID

Black

Yellow

Yellow

Black

Green

IGNITION COIL

Red

Black

STARTING MOTOR

Red

Starter Ground

Cowl Frame Ground

Red
Red
Brown
Black

Yellow
Gray
White

ENGINE HARNESS

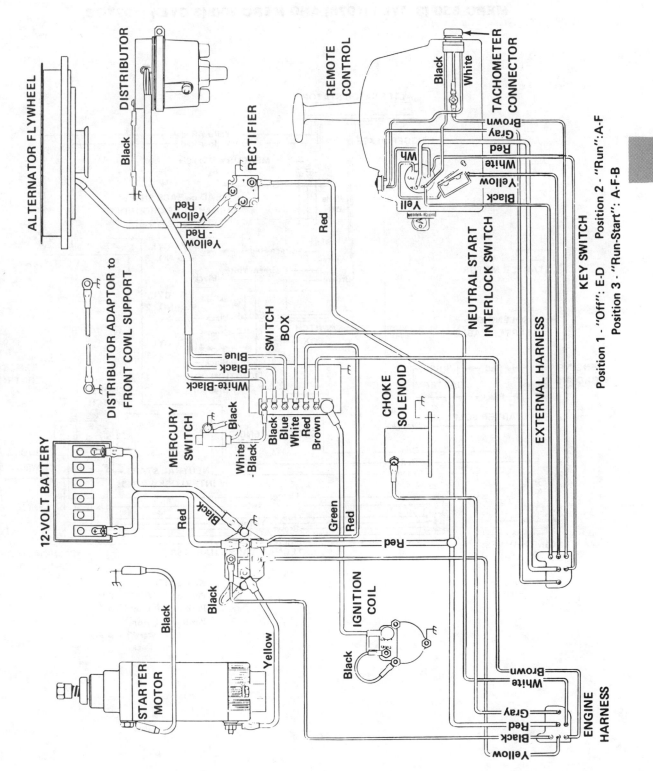

MERC 650 (3-CYL.) (1975) ELECTRIC START

ALTERNATOR FLYWHEEL

DISTRIBUTOR

RECTIFIER

REMOTE CONTROL

TACHOMETER CONNECTOR

Black
White

Brown
Gray
Red
White
Wh
Yellow
Black
Yell

KEY SWITCH

Position 1 - "Off": E-D   Position 2 - "Run":A-F
Position 3 - "Run-Start": A-F-B

Black

Yellow - Red
Yellow - Red

Red

DISTRIBUTOR ADAPTOR to
FRONT COWL SUPPORT

NEUTRAL START
INTERLOCK SWITCH

SWITCH BOX

Blue
Black
White-Black

MERCURY SWITCH

Black
White
- Black

Black
Blue
White
Red
Brown

CHOKE SOLENOID

EXTERNAL HARNESS

12-VOLT BATTERY

Red
Black

Black

Yellow

STARTER MOTOR

Green
Red

Red

IGNITION COIL

Black

White
Brown
Gray
Red
Black
Yellow

ENGINE HARNESS

MERC 650 (3 CYL.) (1976) AND MERC 700 (3-CYL.) (1977-78)

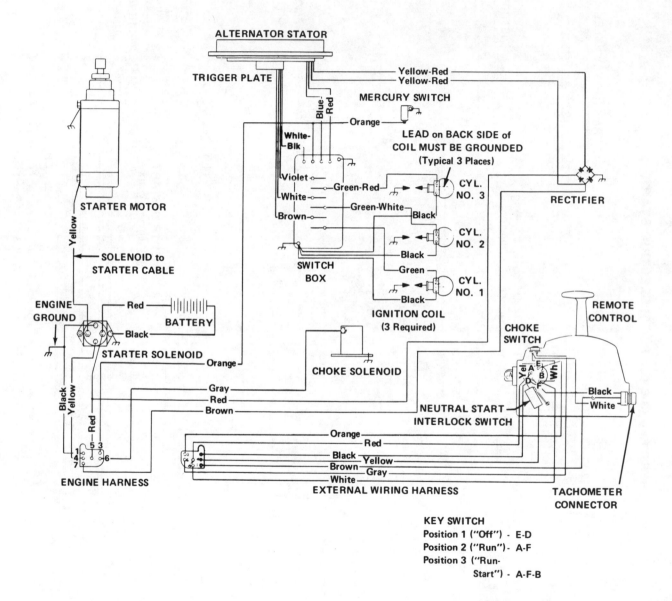

ALTERNATOR STATOR

TRIGGER PLATE

Yellow-Red
Yellow-Red

MERCURY SWITCH

Blue-Red

Orange

White-Blk

LEAD on BACK SIDE of
COIL MUST BE GROUNDED
(Typical 3 Places)

RECTIFIER

Violet

Green-Red

CYL. NO. 3

White

Green-White

Brown

Black

CYL. NO. 2

Black

SWITCH BOX

Green

CYL. NO. 1

Black

IGNITION COIL
(3 Required)

STARTER MOTOR

Yellow

SOLENOID to
STARTER CABLE

REMOTE CONTROL

CHOKE SWITCH

ENGINE GROUND

Red

Black

BATTERY

STARTER SOLENOID

Orange

CHOKE SOLENOID

Yel
A
E
B
D
Wh

Black
White

Gray
Red
Brown

NEUTRAL START
INTERLOCK SWITCH

Black
Yellow
Red

Orange
Red
Black
Yellow
Brown
Gray
White

1   5 3
4   6
7

ENGINE HARNESS

EXTERNAL WIRING HARNESS

TACHOMETER CONNECTOR

KEY SWITCH
Position 1 ("Off") - E-D
Position 2 ("Run")- A-F
Position 3 ("Run-
               Start") - A-F-B

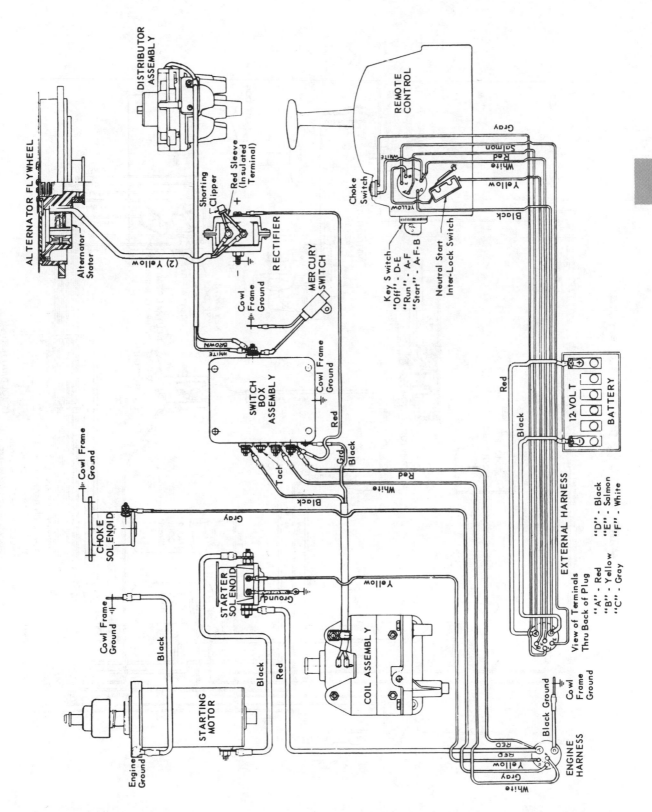

MERC 1100SS AND 950SS THROUGH 1974

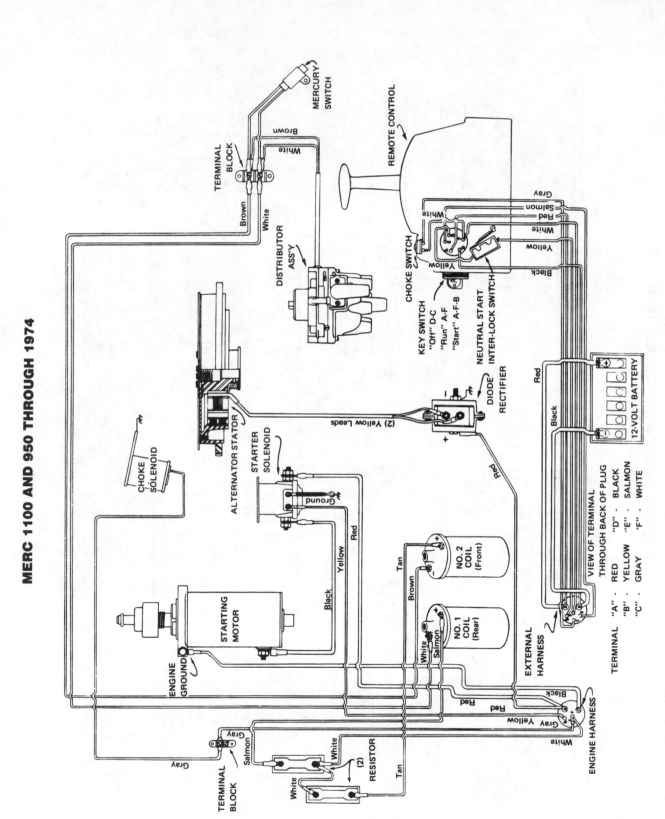

MERC 1100 AND 950 THROUGH 1974

3

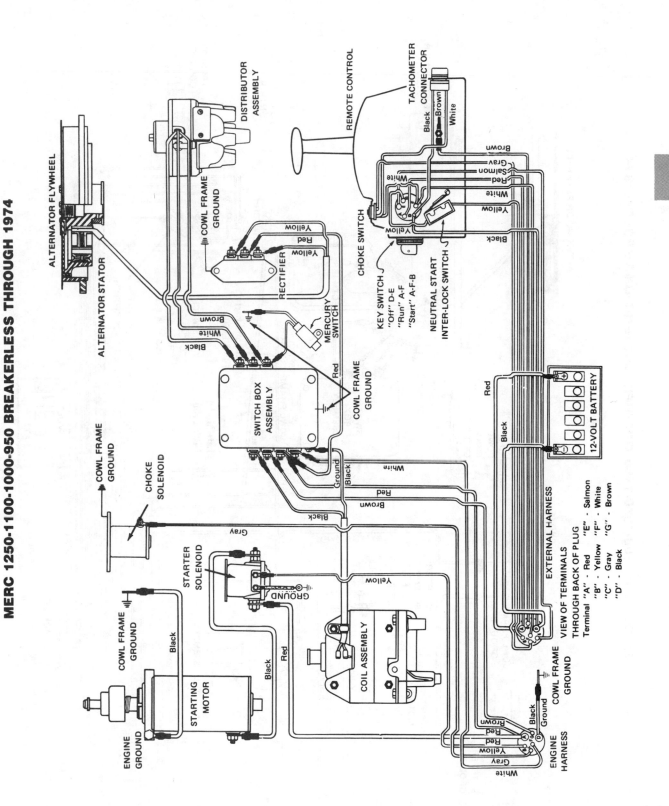

MERC 1250-1100-1000-950 BREAKERLESS THROUGH 1974

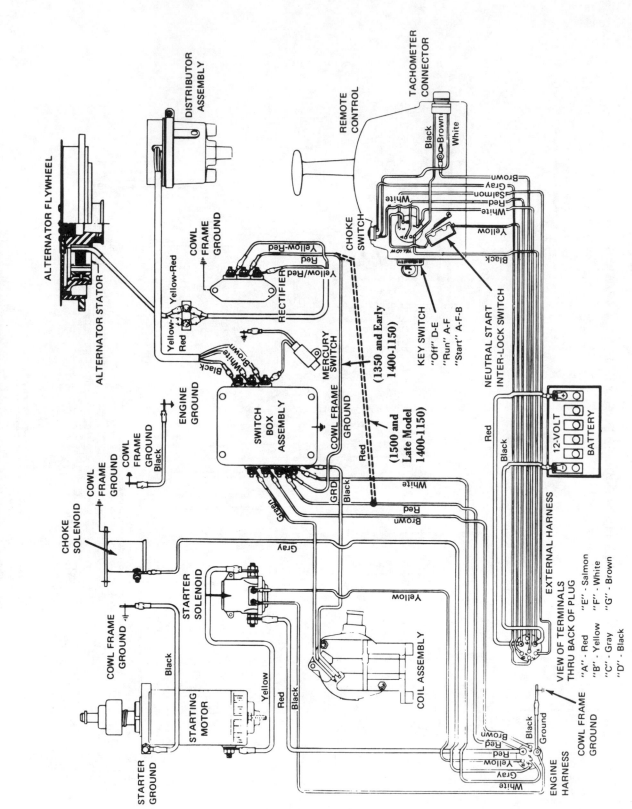

MERC 1500-1400-1350-1150 THUNDERBOLT IGNITION THROUGH 1974

ALTERNATOR FLYWHEEL

ALTERNATOR STATOR

DISTRIBUTOR ASSEMBLY

COWL FRAME GROUND

Yellow
Yellow-Red
Red

RECTIFIER

Yellow-Red
Red

Black
White
Brown

MERCURY SWITCH

SWITCH BOX ASSEMBLY

ENGINE GROUND

COWL FRAME GROUND

COWL FRAME GROUND
Black

CHOKE SOLENOID

COWL FRAME GROUND

STARTER GROUND

Black

STARTING MOTOR

Yellow

Red
Black

STARTER SOLENOID

Gray

Green

GRD

COWL FRAME GROUND

Black

White

Red

Brown

(1500 and Late Model 1400-1150)

(1350 and Early 1400-1150)

CHOKE SWITCH

REMOTE CONTROL

TACHOMETER CONNECTOR

Black
Brown
White

Brown
Gray
Salmon
Red
White
White

Yellow

YEL 60 W

Black

KEY SWITCH
"Off" D-E
"Run" A-F
"Start" A-F-B

NEUTRAL START INTER-LOCK SWITCH

Red

Red

Black

12-VOLT BATTERY

EXTERNAL HARNESS

COIL ASSEMBLY

Yellow

VIEW OF TERMINALS THRU BACK OF PLUG

"A" - Red   "E" - Salmon
"B" - Yellow   "F" - White
"C" - Gray   "G" - Brown
"D" - Black

COWL FRAME GROUND

Red
Yellow
Gray
Black
Brown
Ground
Black

White

ENGINE HARNESS

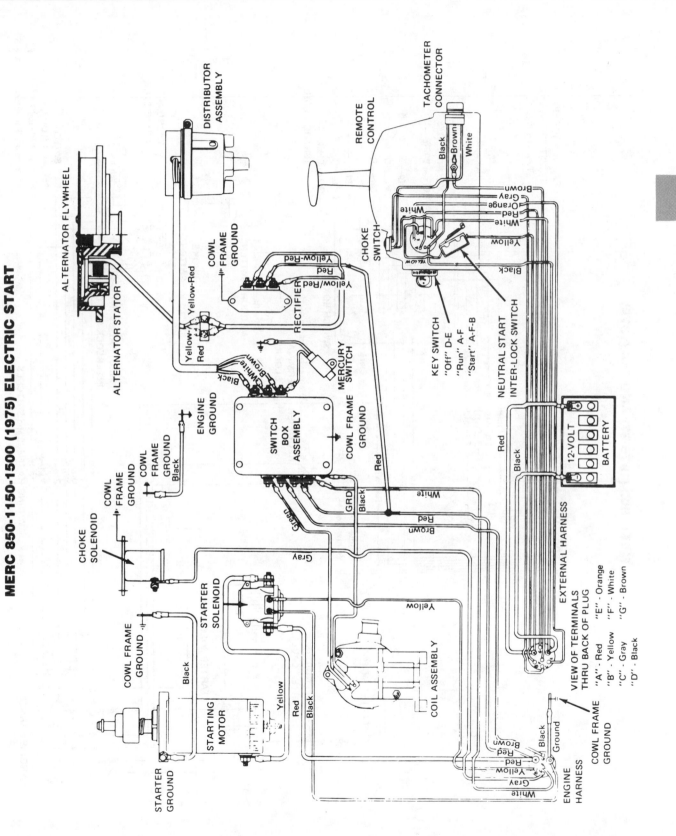

MERC 850-1150-1500 (1975) ELECTRIC START

ALTERNATOR FLYWHEEL

ALTERNATOR STATOR

DISTRIBUTOR ASSEMBLY

REMOTE CONTROL

TACHOMETER CONNECTOR

Black
Brown
White

Brown
Gray
Orange
Red
White

White

Yellow

Black

COWL FRAME GROUND

RECTIFIER

Yellow-Red
Red

Yellow/Red

Yellow-Red
Red

CHOKE SWITCH

KEY SWITCH
"Off" D-E
"Run" A-F
"Start" A-F-B

NEUTRAL START
INTER-LOCK SWITCH

YELLOW

White
Brown
Black

MERCURY SWITCH

ENGINE GROUND

COWL FRAME GROUND

COWL FRAME GROUND
Black

SWITCH BOX ASSEMBLY

COWL FRAME GROUND

Red

Red

Black

12-VOLT BATTERY

CHOKE SOLENOID

COWL FRAME GROUND

GRD
Green
Black
Red
Brown

White

EXTERNAL HARNESS

VIEW OF TERMINALS
THRU BACK OF PLUG

"A" - Red   "E" - Orange
"B" - Yellow   "F" - White
"C" - Gray   "G" - Brown
"D" - Black

STARTER SOLENOID

Gray

Yellow

COIL ASSEMBLY

COWL FRAME GROUND

Black

STARTING MOTOR

Yellow
Red
Black

Red
Brown
Black

Red
Yellow
Gray
White

Ground

ENGINE HARNESS

STARTER GROUND

3

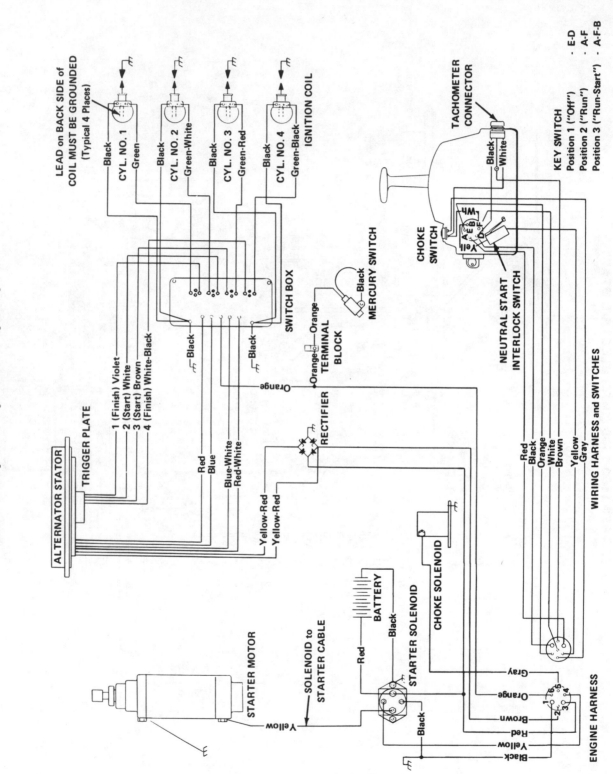

MERC 850 (1976-77) AND 800 (1978)

3

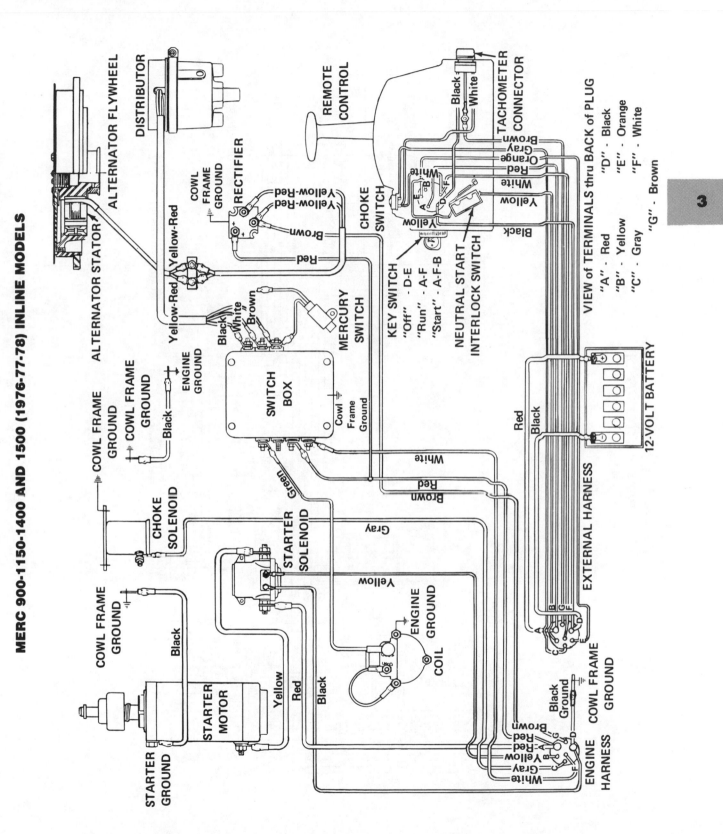

MERC 900-1150-1400 AND 1500 (1976-77-78) INLINE MODELS

ALTERNATOR FLYWHEEL

DISTRIBUTOR

REMOTE CONTROL

TACHOMETER CONNECTOR

Black
White

"D" - Black
"E" - Orange
"F" - White
"G" - Brown

"A" - Red
"B" - Yellow
"C" - Gray

VIEW of TERMINALS thru BACK of PLUG

ALTERNATOR STATOR

RECTIFIER

COWL FRAME GROUND

Yellow-Red

Brown

Red

CHOKE SWITCH

White

Yellow

Brown
Gray
Orange
Red
White

Yellow

Black

KEY SWITCH
"Off" - D-E
"Run" - A-F
"Start" - A-F-B

NEUTRAL START INTERLOCK SWITCH

Yellow-Red Yellow-Red

COWL FRAME GROUND

COWL FRAME GROUND

ENGINE GROUND

Black

Black
White
Brown

MERCURY SWITCH

SWITCH BOX

Cowl Frame Ground

12-VOLT BATTERY

CHOKE SOLENOID

COWL FRAME GROUND

Black

Green

STARTER SOLENOID

Gray

White

Red

Brown

Red
Black

Red
Black

EXTERNAL HARNESS

B
G
F

A
D

C
E

Yellow

ENGINE COIL GROUND

STARTER MOTOR

Yellow

Red

Black

STARTER GROUND

STARTER SOLENOID

Black
Ground

Brown
Red
Red
Yellow
Gray
White

G
D
A
B
C
F
E

COWL FRAME GROUND

ENGINE HARNESS

COWL FRAME GROUND

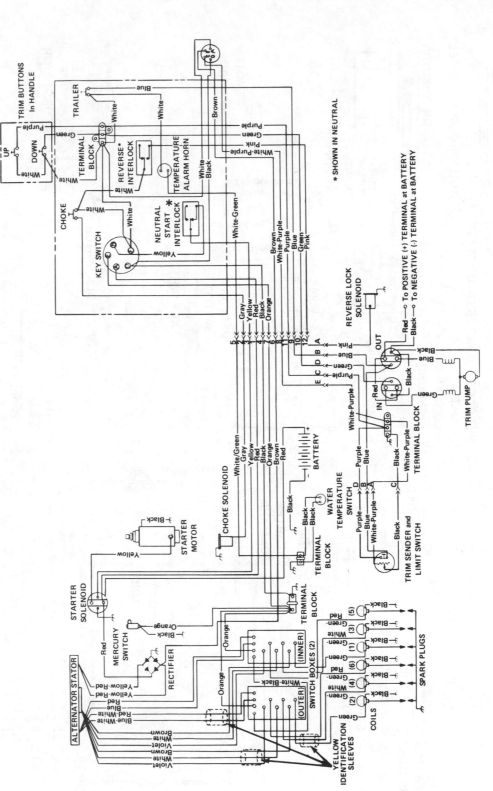

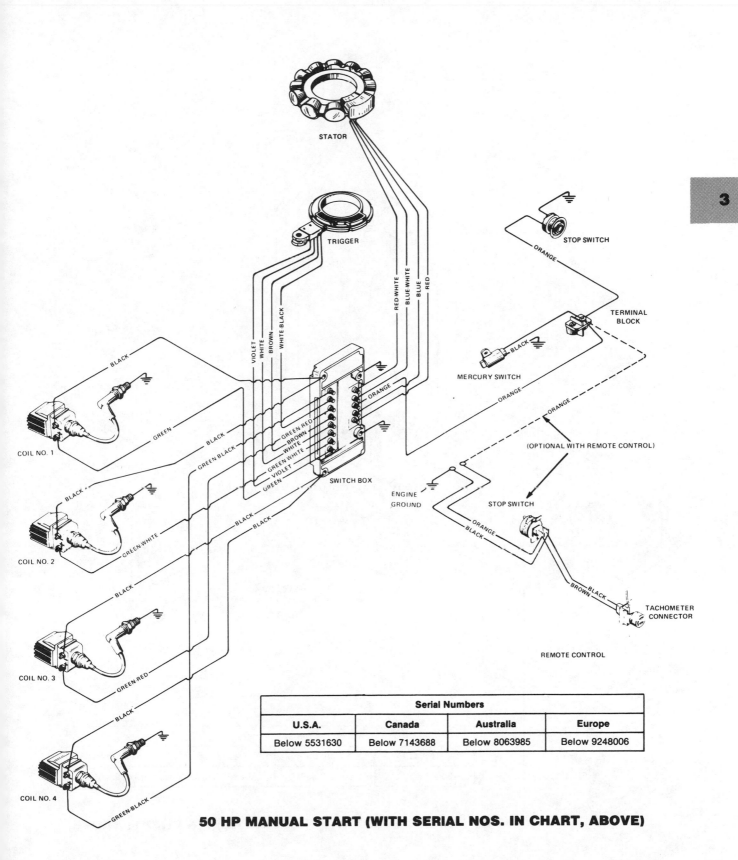

50 HP MANUAL START (WITH SERIAL NOS. IN CHART, ABOVE)

Serial Numbers			
U.S.A.	Canada	Australia	Europe
Below 5531630	Below 7143688	Below 8063985	Below 9248006

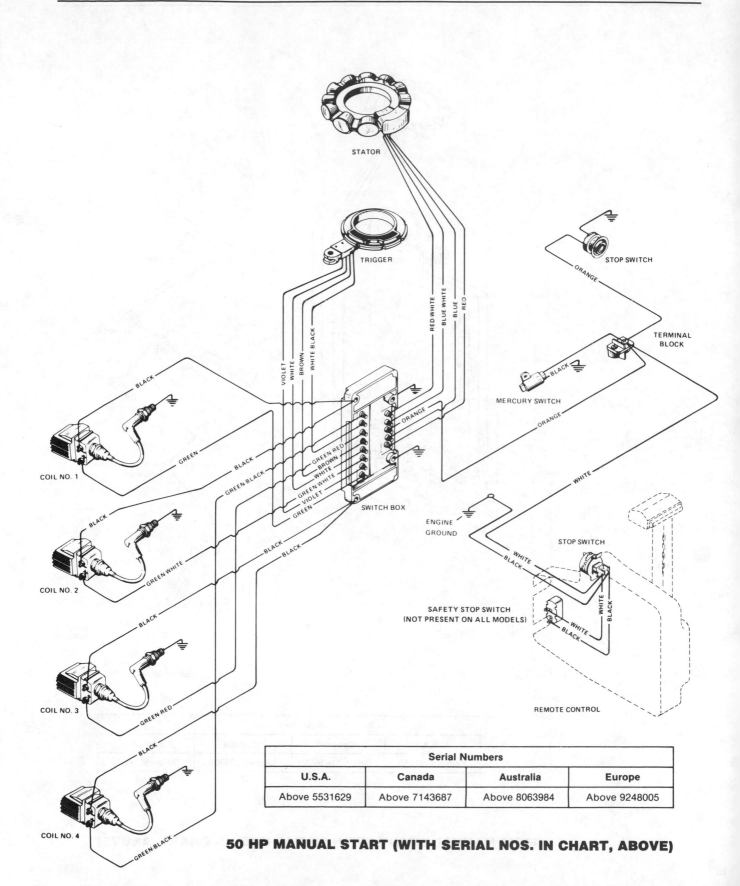

STATOR

TRIGGER

STOP SWITCH

RED WHITE

BLUE WHITE

BLUE

RED

ORANGE

TERMINAL BLOCK

BLACK

MERCURY SWITCH

VIOLET

WHITE

BROWN

WHITE BLACK

BLACK

ORANGE

ORANGE

COIL NO. 1

GREEN

BLACK

GREEN RED

BROWN

WHITE

GREEN WHITE

VIOLET

GREEN

SWITCH BOX

WHITE

BLACK

GREEN BLACK

ENGINE GROUND

STOP SWITCH

WHITE

BLACK

WHITE

COIL NO. 2

BLACK

GREEN WHITE

BLACK

BLACK

SAFETY STOP SWITCH
(NOT PRESENT ON ALL MODELS)

WHITE

BLACK

BLACK

COIL NO. 3

GREEN RED

REMOTE CONTROL

BLACK

COIL NO. 4

GREEN BLACK

Serial Numbers			
U.S.A.	**Canada**	**Australia**	**Europe**
Above 5531629	Above 7143687	Above 8063984	Above 9248005

50 HP MANUAL START (WITH SERIAL NOS. IN CHART, ABOVE)

3

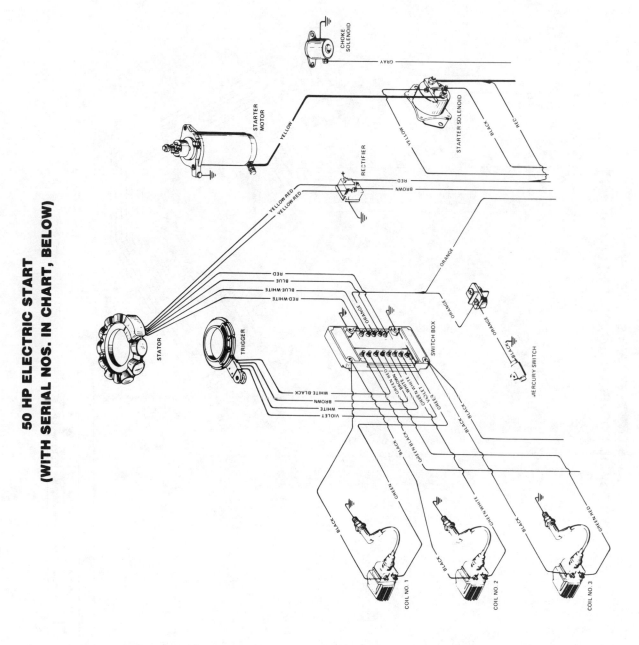

**50 HP ELECTRIC START
(WITH SERIAL NOS. IN CHART, BELOW)**

CHOKE SOLENOID

GRAY

STARTER MOTOR

YELLOW

STARTER SOLENOID

YELLOW

BLACK

RED

RECTIFIER

RED

BROWN

YELLOW RED

YELLOW RED

ORANGE

STATOR

TRIGGER

RED

BLUE

BLUE WHITE

RED WHITE

ORANGE

ORANGE

ORANGE

BLACK

MERCURY SWITCH

SWITCH BOX

BLACK WHITE

WHITE

GREEN RED

GREEN WHITE

VIOLET

GREEN

BLACK

BLACK BLACK

WHITE BLACK

BROWN

WHITE

VIOLET

GREEN BLACK

GREEN WHITE

BLACK

BLACK

GREEN RED

COIL NO. 1

COIL NO. 2

COIL NO. 3

50 HP ELECTRIC START
(WITH SERIAL NOS. IN CHART, BELOW) (continued)

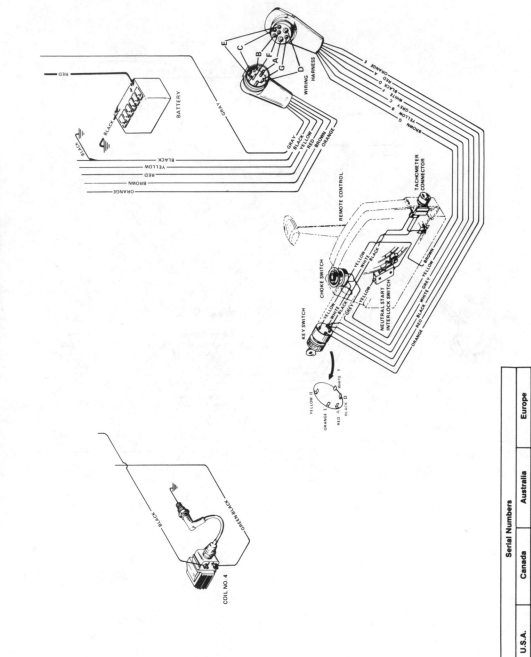

Serial Numbers			
U.S.A.	Canada	Australia	Europe
Below 5531630	Below 7143688	Below 8063985	Below 9248006

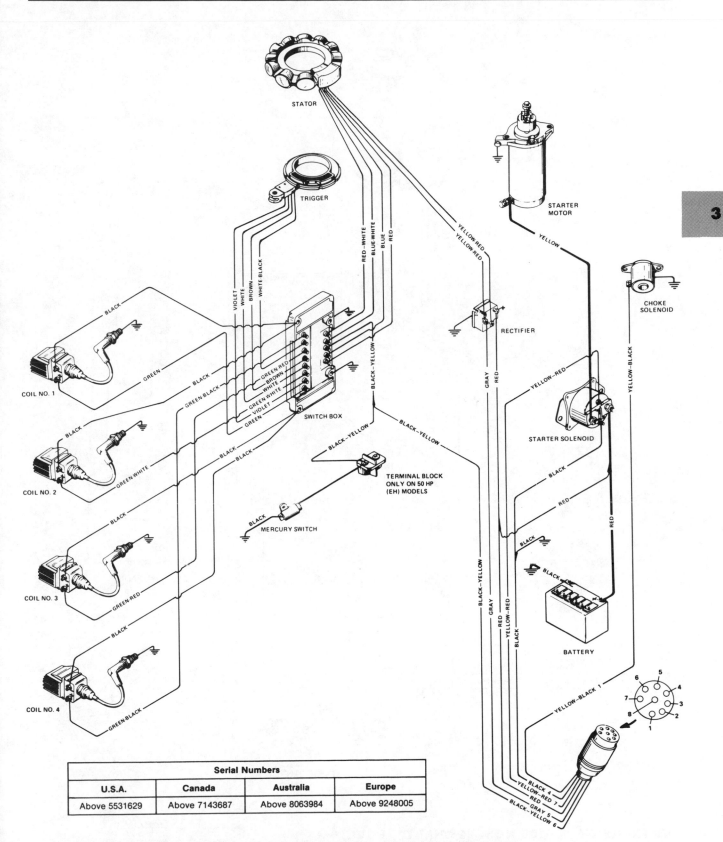

Serial Numbers			
U.S.A.	**Canada**	**Australia**	**Europe**
Above 5531629	Above 7143687	Above 8063984	Above 9248005

50 HP ELECTRIC START (WITH SERIAL NOS. IN CHART, ABOVE)

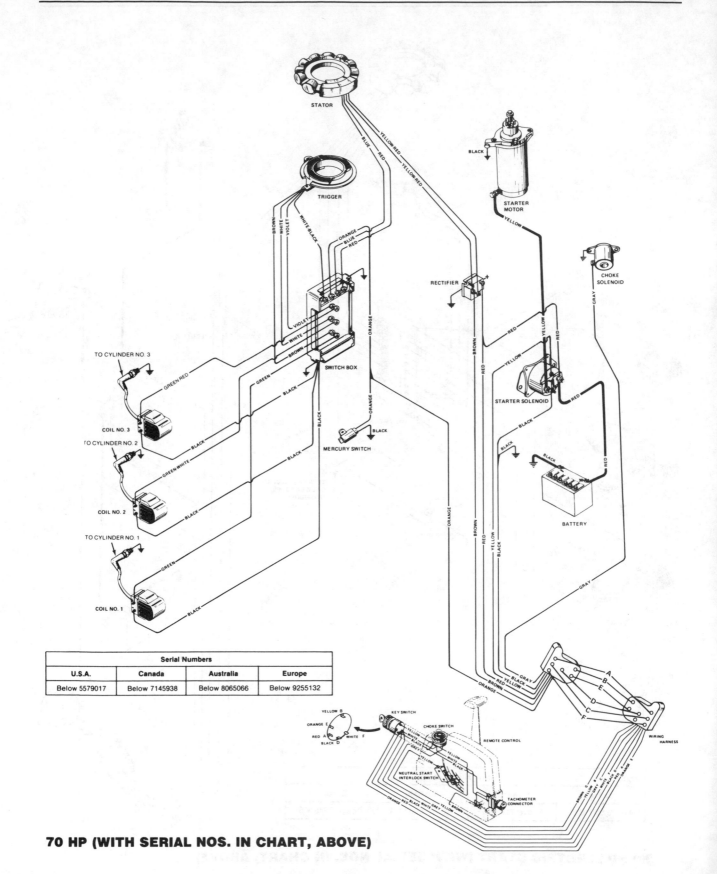

Serial Numbers			
U.S.A.	**Canada**	**Australia**	**Europe**
Below 5579017	Below 7145938	Below 8065066	Below 9255132

70 HP (WITH SERIAL NOS. IN CHART, ABOVE)

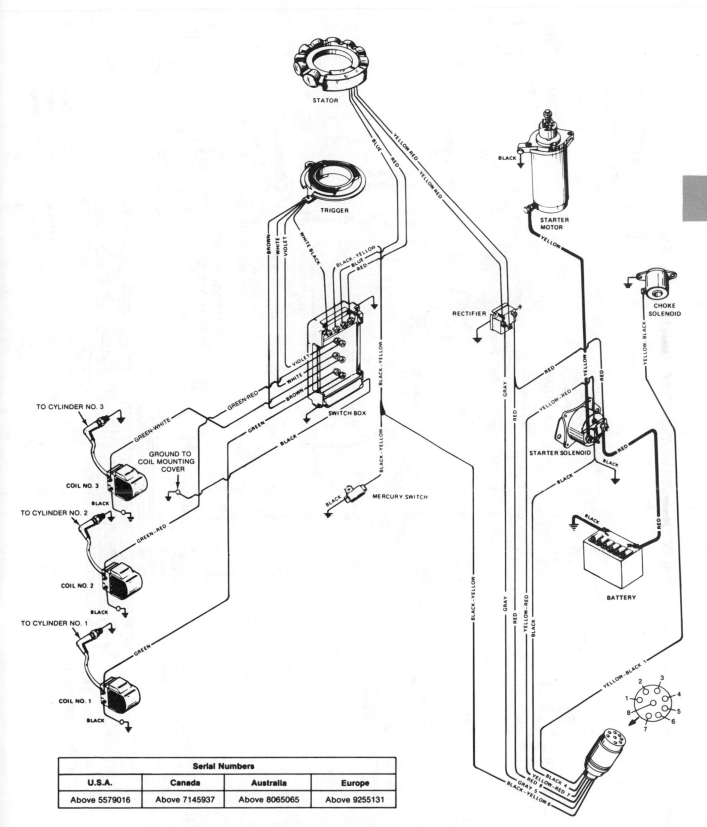

STATOR

TRIGGER

STARTER MOTOR

BLACK

YELLOW—RED

BLUE

RED

YELLOW—RED

BLACK

YELLOW

CHOKE SOLENOID

BROWN

WHITE

VIOLET

WHITE BLACK

BLACK—YELLOW

BLUE

RED

YELLOW—BLACK

RECTIFIER

TO CYLINDER NO. 3

GREEN-WHITE

GREEN-RED

GREEN

BLACK

BLACK—YELLOW

VIOLET

WHITE

BROWN

SWITCH BOX

RED

GRAY

RED

YELLOW

RED

YELLOW-RED

STARTER SOLENOID

BLACK

BLACK

RED

COIL NO. 3

GROUND TO COIL MOUNTING COVER

BLACK

TO CYLINDER NO. 2

GREEN-RED

BLACK

MERCURY SWITCH

BLACK

COIL NO. 2

BLACK

TO CYLINDER NO. 1

GREEN

BLACK

COIL NO. 1

BLACK

BATTERY

RED

BLACK—YELLOW

GRAY

RED

YELLOW-RED

BLACK

YELLOW-BLACK 1

2
1
8

3
4
5

7
6

BLACK 4
YELLOW-RED 7
GRAY 8
BLACK-YELLOW 6

Serial Numbers			
U.S.A.	Canada	Australia	Europe
Above 5579016	Above 7145937	Above 8065065	Above 9255131

70 HP (WITH SERIAL NOS. IN CHART, ABOVE)

3

90 HP THRU 150 HP (INLINE ENGINES) WITH DISTRIBUTOR TYPE IGNITION SYSTEM

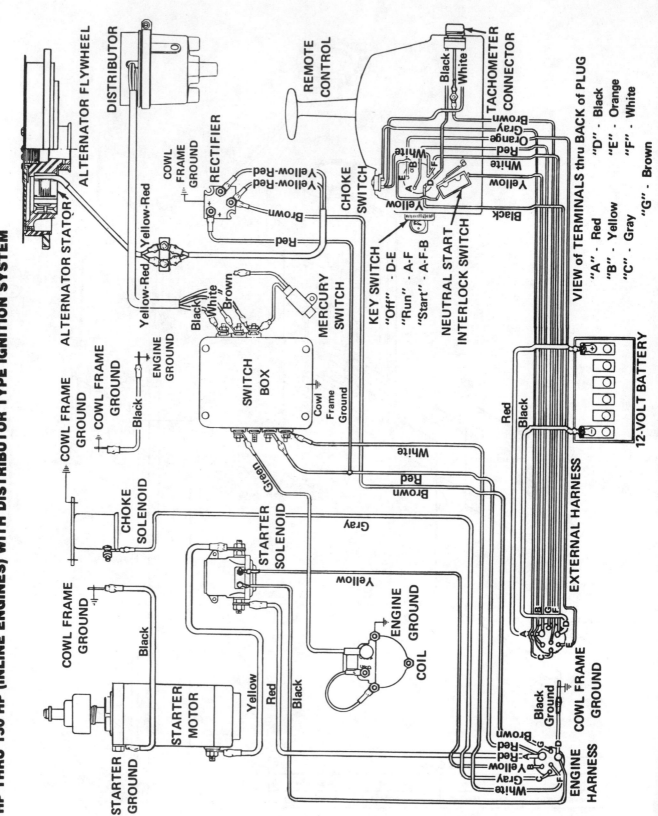

3

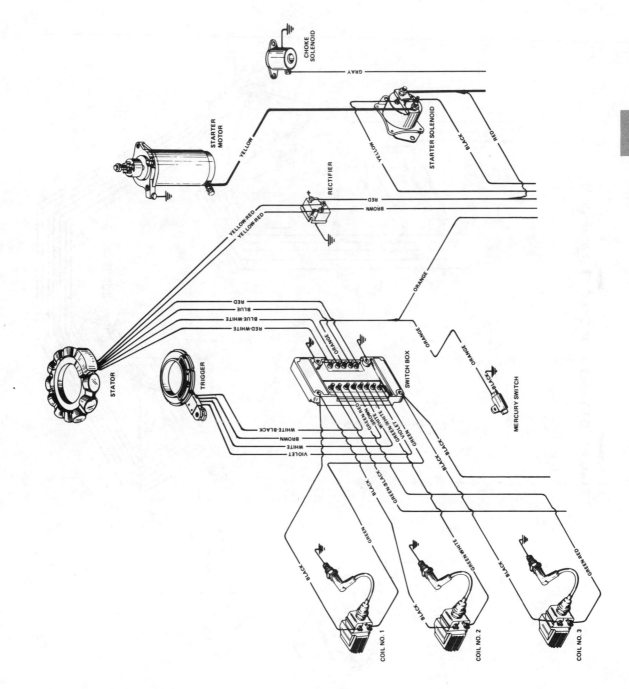

80 HP (SERIAL NO. 5582561 AND BELOW)

80 HP (SERIAL NO. 5582561 AND BELOW) (continued)

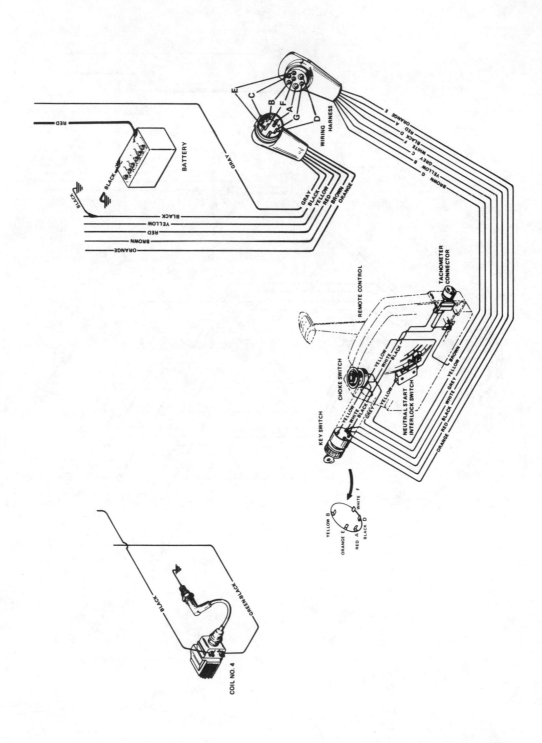

80 HP (SERIAL NO. 5582562 AND ABOVE)

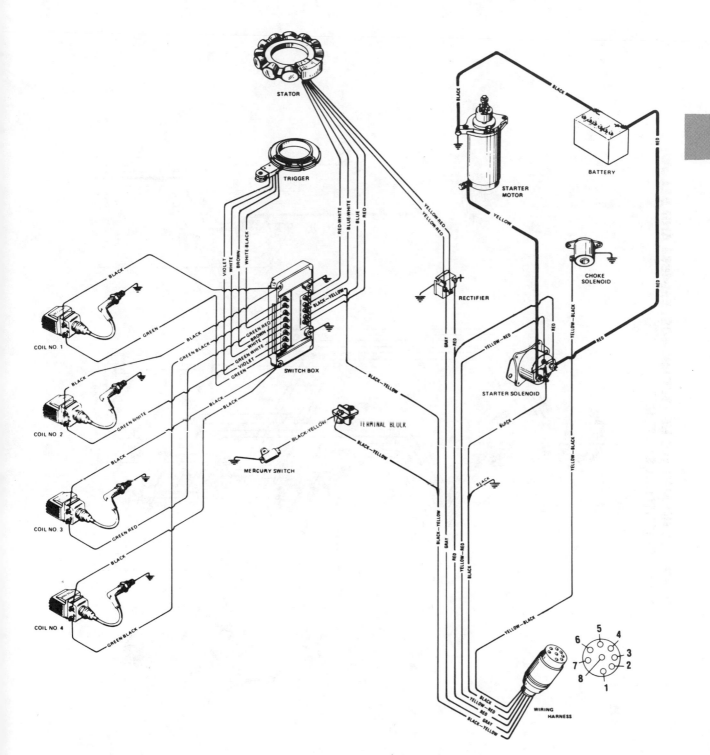

3

90 HP, 115 HP AND 140 HP (SERIAL NOS. 5594656 AND BELOW) WITH ADI IGNITION SYSTEM

CHOKE SOLENOID

GRAY

STARTER MOTOR

BLACK

YELLOW

STARTER SOLENOID

BLACK

RED

BROWN

RED

BLACK

ORANGE

YELLOW-RED

YELLOW-RED

RED-WHITE

YELLOW-RED

RED

BLUE

BLUE

RED

RECTIFIER

ORANGE

ORANGE

BLACK

ORANGE

MERCURY SWITCH

YELLOW IDENTIFICATION SLEEVE

STATOR

TRIGGER

YELLOW-RED
RED
BLUE
RED-WHITE

BROWN
WHITE
VIOLET
BROWN

VIOLET

WHITE

BROWN

BROWN

WHITE

ORANGE
BLUE
WHITE
ORANGE
WHITE-BLACK

BLUE
RED

WHITE
BROWN

VIOLET
WHITE
RED

UPPER SWITCH BOX

LOWER SWITCH BOX

WHITE-BLACK

YELLOW IDENTIFICATION SLEEVE

GREEN
GREEN-WHITE
GREEN-RED

GREEN-RED
GREEN-WHITE
GREEN

WHITE-BLACK

GREEN

GREEN-WHITE

GREEN-RED

BLACK

BLACK

BLACK

COIL NO. 1

COIL NO. 2

COIL NO. 3

90 HP, 115 HP AND 140 HP (SERIAL NOS. 5594656 AND BELOW) WITH ADI IGNITION SYSTEM (continued)

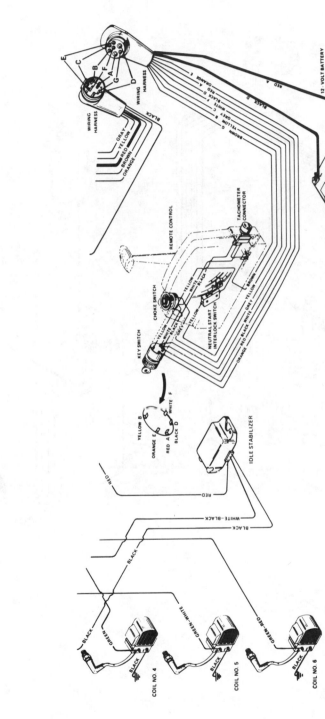

90 HP, 115 HP and 140 HP (SERIAL NOS. 5594657 AND ABOVE)

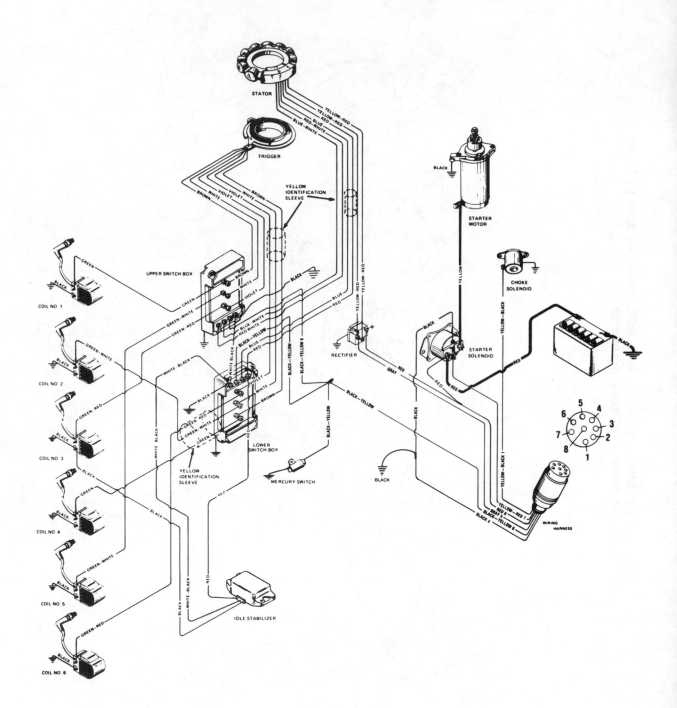

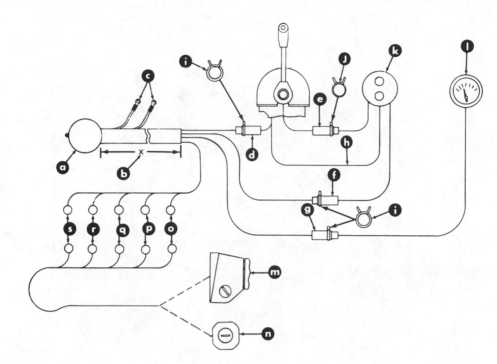

50-150 HP SINGLE ENGINE CONSOLE WIRING HARNESS

a. Extension harness (A-84-76954A10, 15, 20 and 40)
   (for 65 HP and for 70 HP models, adaptor
   harness A-84-75291A2 is required)

b. X = length of harness in feet

c. Battery leads

d. 4-pin connector (control to harness)

e. 3-pin connector (control to trailer/choke panel)

f. 5-pin connector (trailer/choke panel to harness)

g. 4-pin connector (harness to tachometer, if tachometer
   is not used, tape back and insulate
   connector)

h. White wire (control to trailer/choke panel) connect
   white wire to terminal on back side of
   panel that already has a white wire
   connected to it.

i. Spring-type clamp 13/16 in. (20.6 mm)

j. Spring-type clamp 3/4 in. (19.1 mm)

k. Trailer/choke panel

l. Tachometer (optional)

m. Locking steering mount (A-66786A3)

n. Ignition switch panel (A-54211A2)

o. Black to black (secure with screw and nut and
   insulate with rubber sleeve)

p. Orange to orange (secure with screw and nut and
   insulate with rubber sleeve)

q. White to white (secure with screw and nut and
   insulate with rubber sleeve)

r. Yellow to yellow (secure with screw and nut and
   insulate with rubber sleeve)

s. Red to red/white (secure with screw and nut and
   insulate with rubber sleeve)

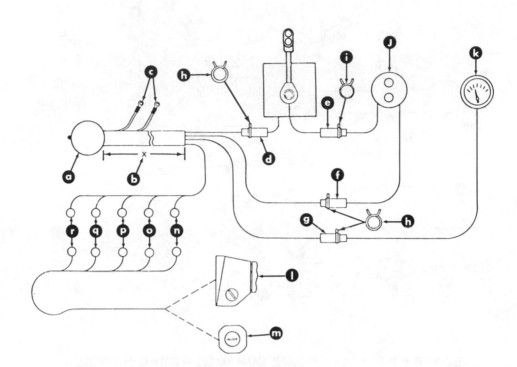

50-150 HP PANEL CONTROL WIRING HARNESS

a. Extension harness (A-84-76954A10, 15, 20 and 40)
   (for 65 HP and for 70 HP models, adaptor
   A-84-75291A2harness is required)

b. X = length of harness in feet

c. Battery cables

d. 4-pin connector (control to harness)

e. 3-pin connector (control to trailer/choke panel)

f. 5-pin connector (trailer/choke panel to harness)

g. 4-pin connector (harness to tachometer, if tachometer
   is not used, tape back and insulate
   connector wire connected to it.)

h. Spring-type clamp 13/16 in. (20.6 mm)

i. Spring-type clamp 3/4 in. (19.1 mm)

j. Trailer/ choke panel

k. Tachometer (optional)

l. Locking steering mount (A-66786A3)

m. Ignition switch panel (A-54211A2)

n. Black to black (secure with screw and nut and
   insulate with rubber sleeve)

o. Orange to orange (secure with screw and nut and
   insulate with rubber sleeve)

p. White to white (secure with screw and nut and
   insulate with rubber sleeve)

q. Yellow to yellow (secure with screw and nut and
   insulate with rubber sleeve)

r. Red to red/white (secure with screw and nut and
   insulate with rubber sleeve)

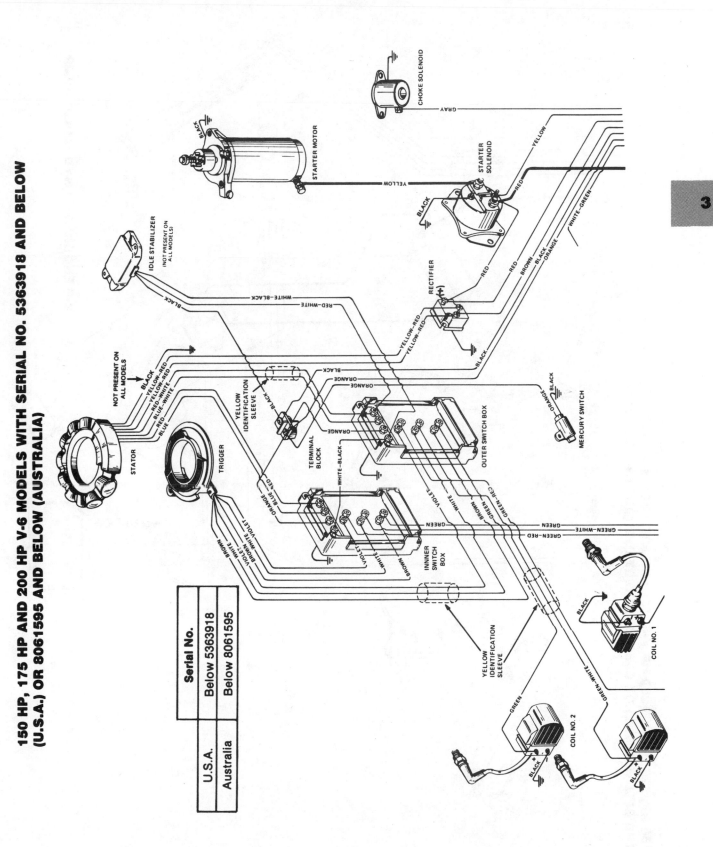

150 HP, 175 HP AND 200 HP V-6 MODELS WITH SERIAL NO. 5363918 AND BELOW (U.S.A.) OR 8061595 AND BELOW (AUSTRALIA)

Serial No.	
U.S.A.	Below 5363918
Australia	Below 8061595

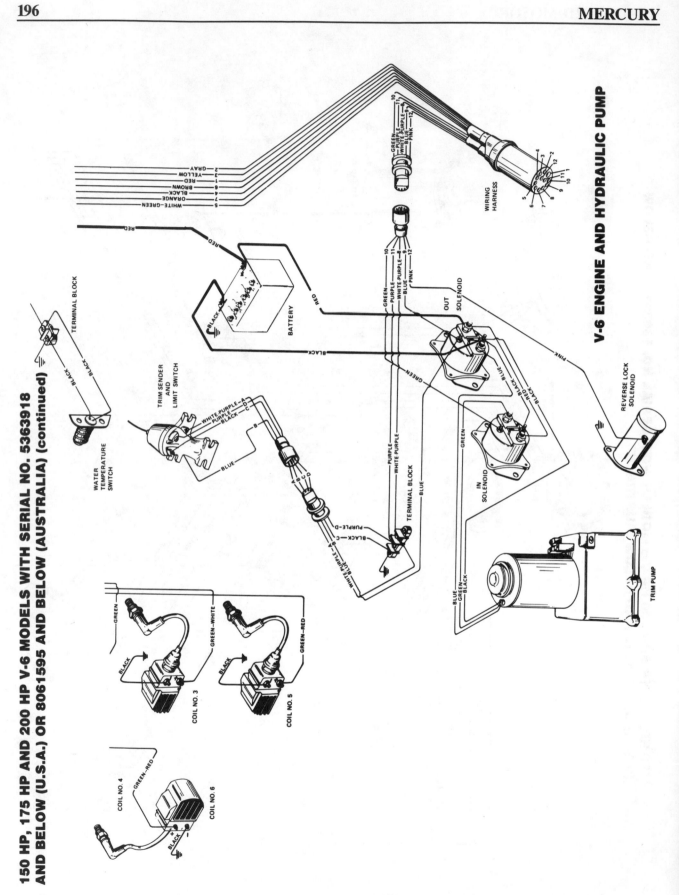

150 HP, 175 HP AND 200 HP V-6 MODELS WITH SERIAL NO. 5363918 AND BELOW (U.S.A.) OR 8061595 AND BELOW (AUSTRALIA) (continued)

V-6 ENGINE AND HYDRAULIC PUMP

V-6 ENGINE AND HYDRAULIC PUMP

Serial No.	
U.S.A.	5363918 thru 5464484
Australia	8061595 thru 8063934

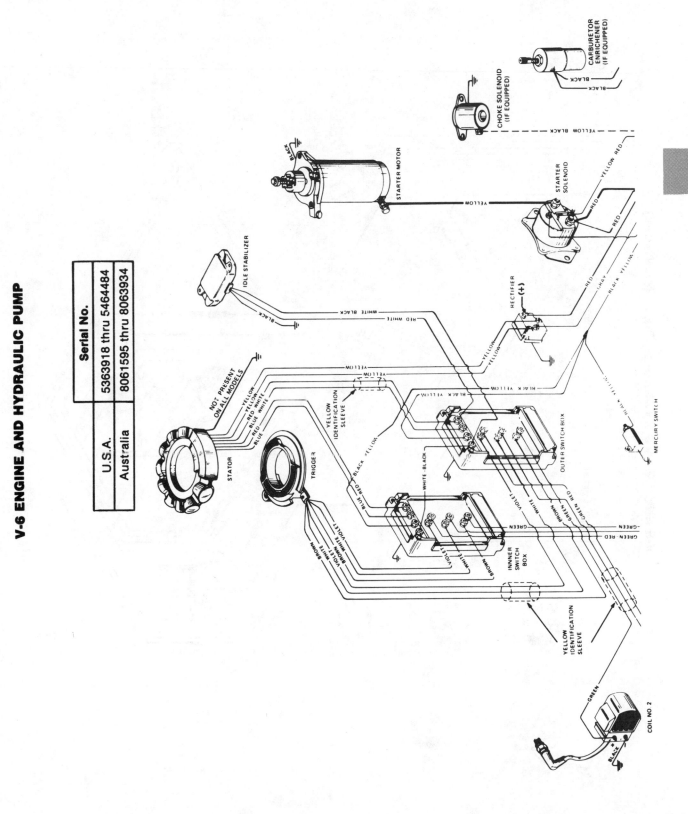

3

V-6 ENGINE AND HYDRAULIC PUMP (continued)

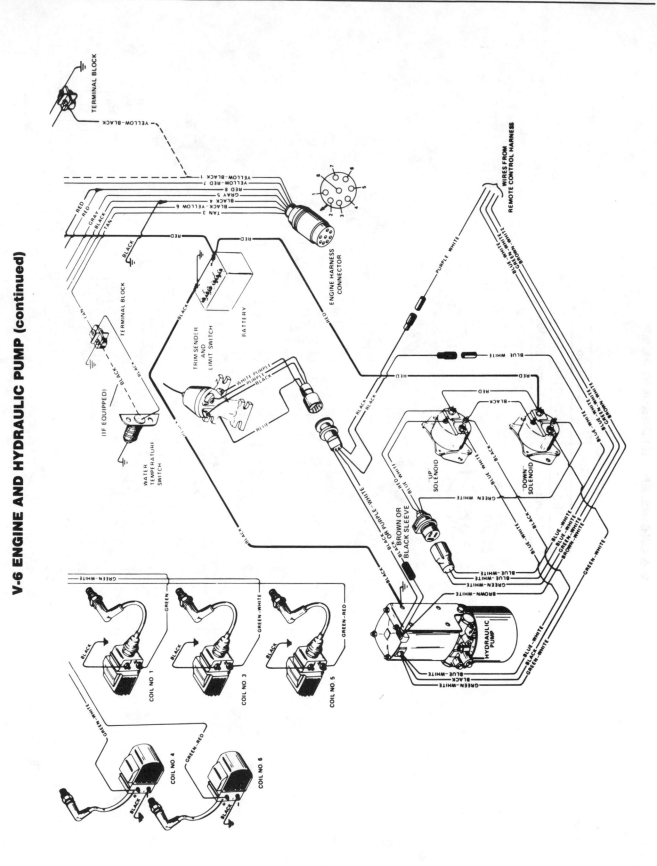

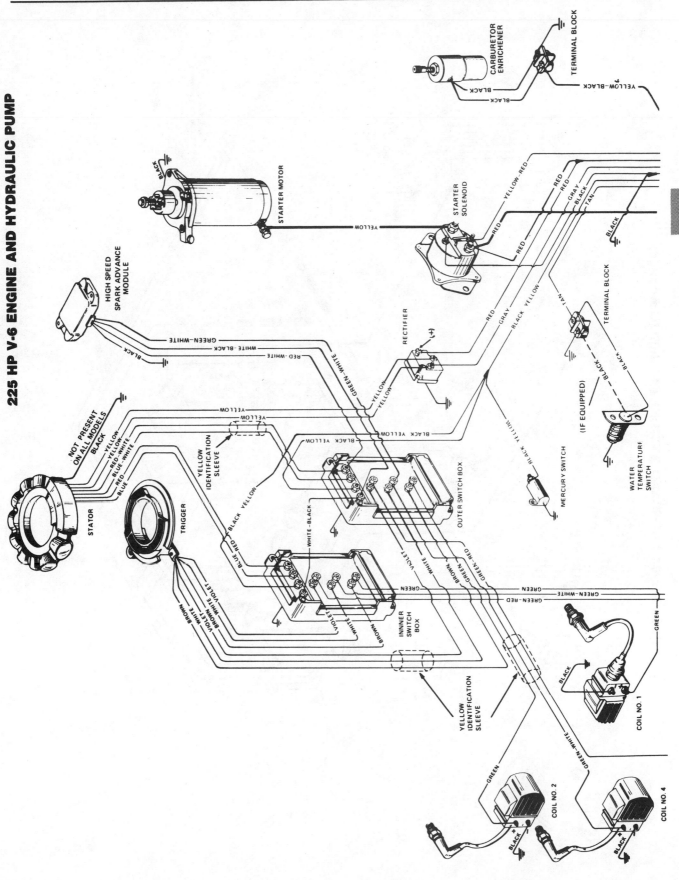

225 HP V-6 ENGINE AND HYDRAULIC PUMP

3

225 HP V-6 ENGINE AND HYDRAULIC PUMP (continued)

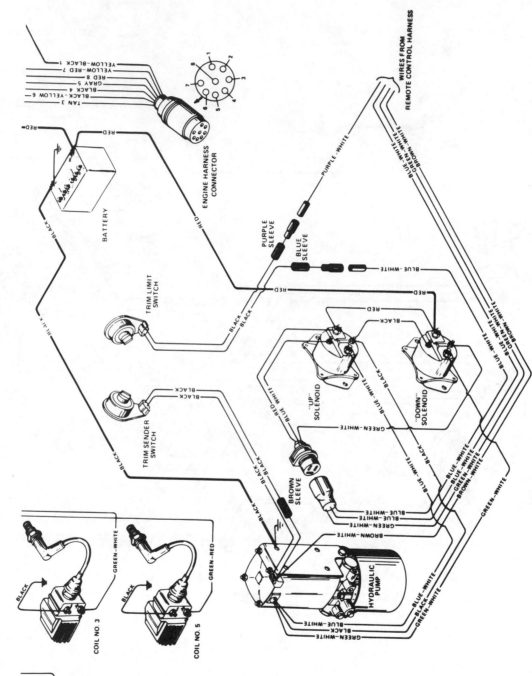

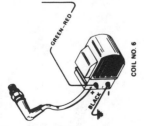

3

V-6 ENGINE SERIAL NO. 5464486 and UP (U.S.A.) OR 8063935 AND UP (AUSTRALIA)

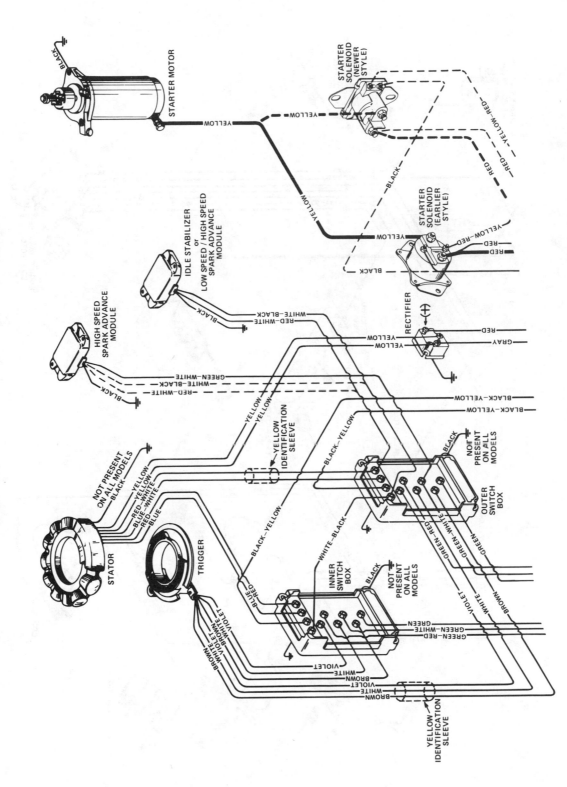

V-6 ENGINE SERIAL NO. 5464486 and UP (U.S.A.) OR 8063935 AND UP (AUSTRALIA) (continued)

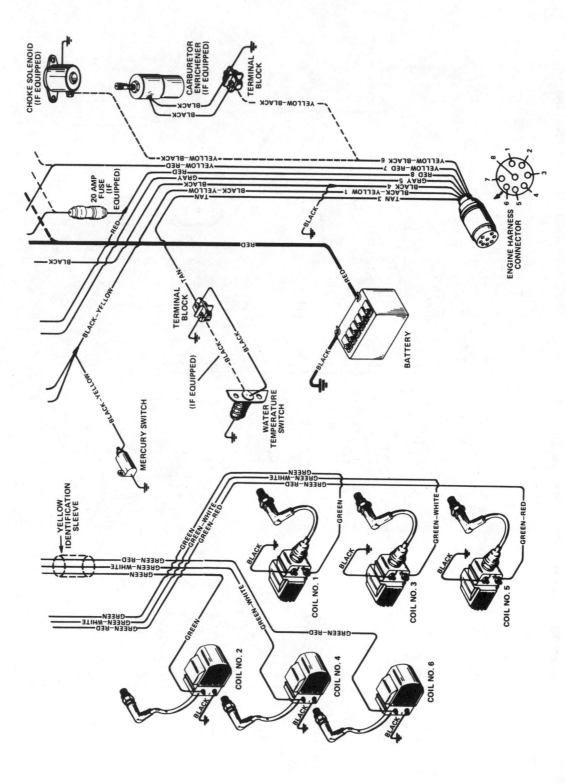

CHOKE SOLENOID (IF EQUIPPED)

CARBURETOR ENRICHENER (IF EQUIPPED)

TERMINAL BLOCK

BLACK
BLACK
YELLOW-BLACK

20 AMP FUSE (IF EQUIPPED)

YELLOW-BLACK
YELLOW-RED
RED
GRAY
BLACK
BLACK-YELLOW
TAN
RED

YELLOW-BLACK 6
YELLOW-RED 7
RED 8
GRAY 5
BLACK 4
BLACK-YELLOW 1
TAN 3

ENGINE HARNESS CONNECTOR

BLACK

RED

BLACK-YELLOW

BLACK

TERMINAL BLOCK

TAN

BLACK

BLACK

RED

BATTERY

BLACK

MERCURY SWITCH

BLACK-YELLOW

(IF EQUIPPED)

WATER TEMPERATURE SWITCH

YELLOW IDENTIFICATION SLEEVE

GREEN
GREEN-WHITE
GREEN-RED

GREEN-RED
GREEN-WHITE

GREEN
GREEN-WHITE
GREEN-RED

GREEN-RED
GREEN-WHITE
GREEN

BLACK

COIL NO. 1

BLACK

COIL NO. 3

GREEN

GREEN-WHITE

BLACK

GREEN-RED

COIL NO. 5

GREEN-WHITE

GREEN-RED

COIL NO. 2

GREEN-RED

COIL NO. 4

COIL NO. 6

BLACK

BLACK

BLACK

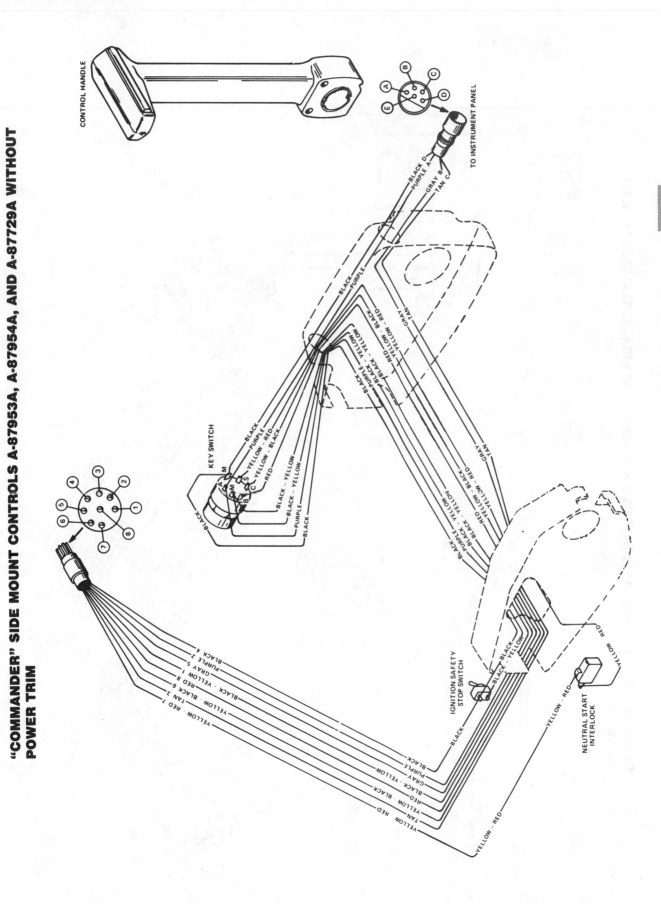

"COMMANDER" SIDE MOUNT CONTROLS A-87953A, A-87954A, AND A-87729A WITHOUT POWER TRIM

CONTROL HANDLE

TO INSTRUMENT PANEL

KEY SWITCH

IGNITION SAFETY STOP SWITCH

NEUTRAL START INTERLOCK

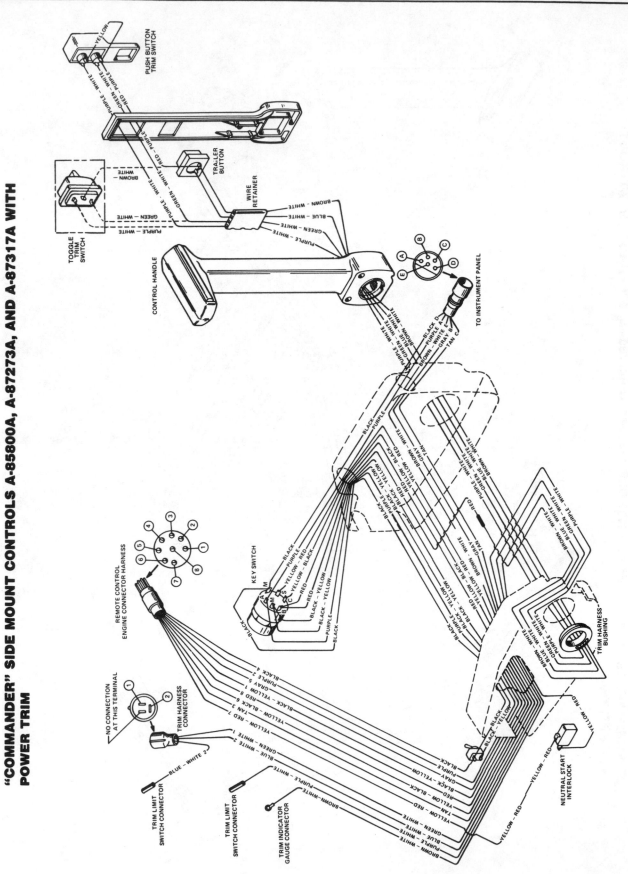

"COMMANDER" SIDE MOUNT CONTROLS A-85800A, A-87273A, AND A-87317A WITH POWER TRIM

"COMMANDER" SIDE MOUNT CONTROL A-76334A

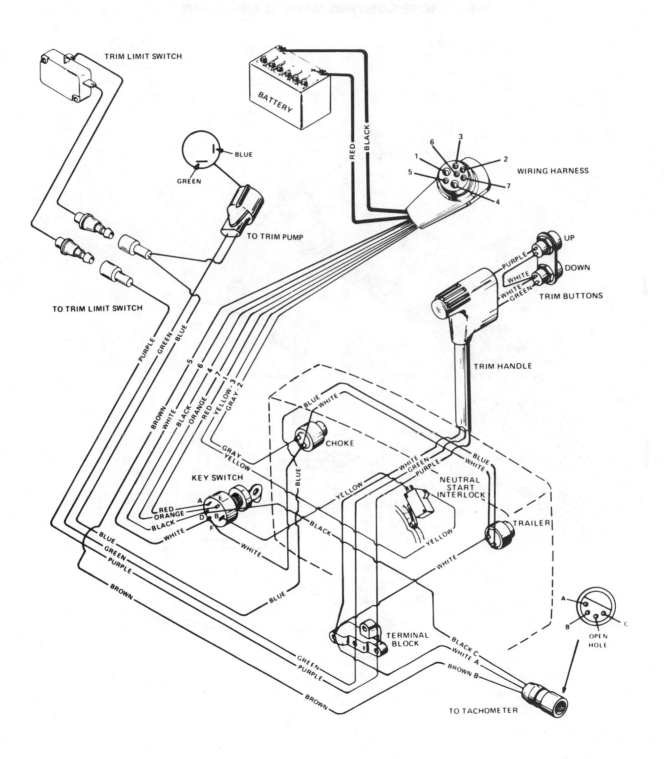

3

V-6 REMOTE CONTROL WITH ALARM HORN

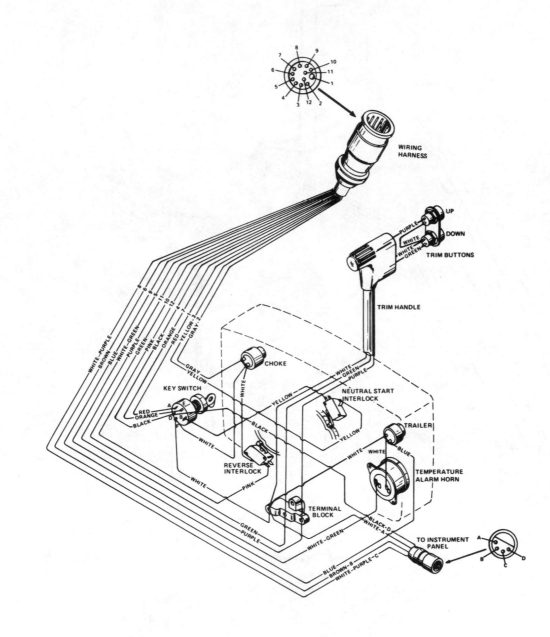

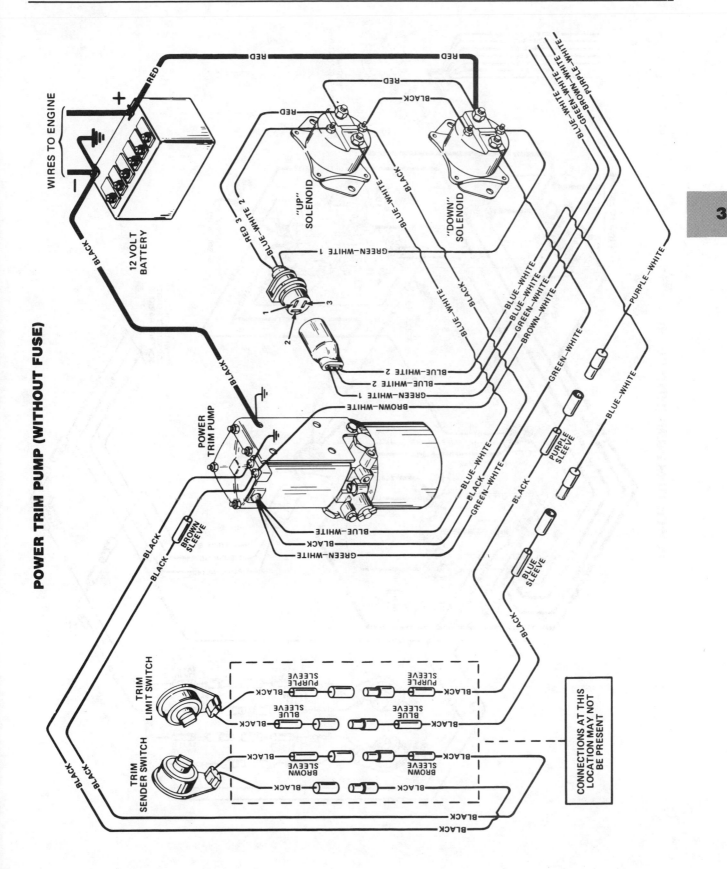

POWER TRIM PUMP (WITHOUT FUSE)

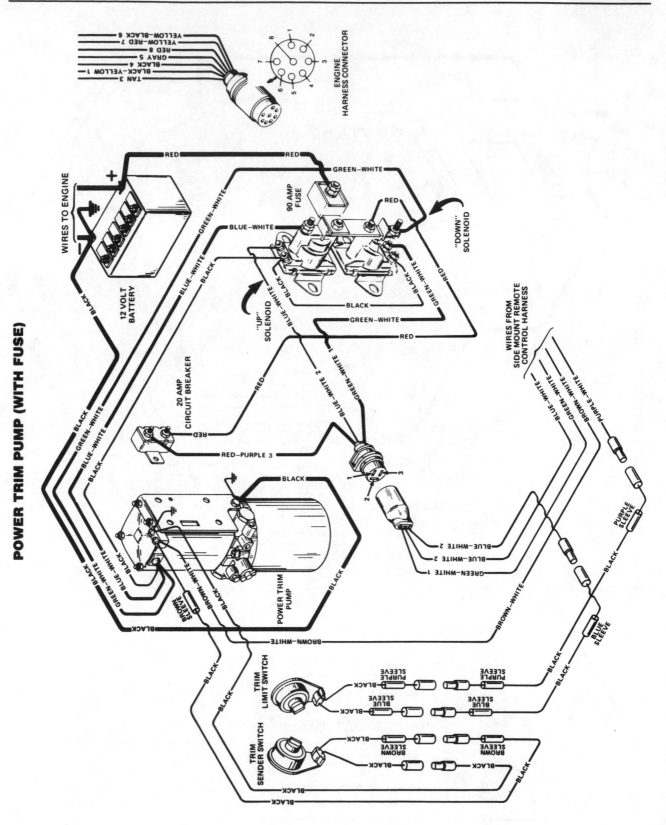

POWER TRIM PUMP (WITH FUSE)

HARNESS WIRING V-6 MODELS WITH PANEL CONTROL

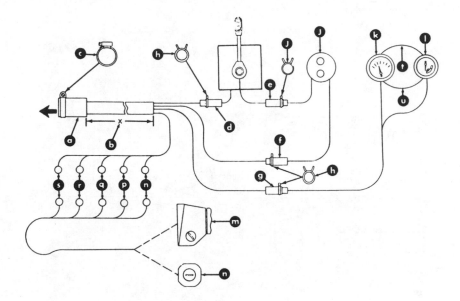

a. Extension harness
   (A-84-66005A10, A15, A20, A40)
b. X = Length of harness in feet
c. Screw-type clamp 1-5/8 in. (43.3 mm)
d. 4-pin connector (control harness)
e. 3-pin connector (control to trailer/choke panel)
f. 5-pin connector (trailer/choke panel to harness
g. 4-pin connector (harness to tachometer
   and trim indicator)
h. Spring-type clamp 13/16 in. (20.6 mm)
i. Spring-type clamp 3/4 in. (19.1 mm)
j. Trailer/choke panel
k. Tachometer
l. Trim indicator
m. Locking steering mount (A-66786A3)
n. Ignition switch (A-54211A2)
o. Black to black (secure with screw and nut and
   insulate with rubber sleeve)
p. Orange to orange (secure with screw and nut and
   insulate with rubber sleeve)
q. White to white (secure with screw and nut and
   insulate with rubber sleeve)
r. Yellow to yellow (secure with screw and nut and
   insulate with rubber sleeve)
s. Red to red (secure with screw and nut and
   insulate with rubber sleeve)
t. Black jumper (connect to ground on both gauges)
u. White jumper (connect to + 12V on both gauges)

HARNESS WIRING V-6 MODELS WITH SINGLE ENGINE CONSOLE CONTROL

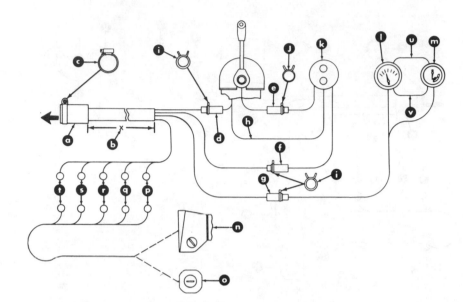

a. Extension harness (A-84-66005A10, A15, A20, A40)
b. X = Length of harness in feet
c. Screw-type clamp 1-5/8 in. (43.3 mm)
d. 4-pin connector (control harness)
e. 3-pin connector (control to trailer/choke panel)
f. 5-pin connector (trailer/choke panel to harness
g. 4-pin connector (harness to tachometer
   and trim indicator)
h. White wire (control to trailer/choke panel)
   connect white wire to terminal on back side
   of panel that already has a wire connected to it.
i. Spring-type clamp 13/16 in. (20.6 mm)
j. Spring-type clamp 3/4 in. (19.1 mm)
k. Trailer/choke panel
l. Tachometer
m. Trim indicator
n. Locking steering mount (A-66786A3)
o. Ignition switch (A-54211A2)
p. Black to black (secure with screw and nut and
   insulate with rubber sleeve)
q. Orange to orange (secure with screw and nut and
   insulate with rubber sleeve)
r. White to white (secure with screw and nut and
   insulate with rubber sleeve)
s. Yellow to yellow (secure with screw and nut and
   insulate with rubber sleeve)
t. Red to red (secure with screw and nut and insulate
   with rubber sleeve)
u. Black jumper (connect to ground on both gauges)
v White jumper (connect to + 12V on both gauges)

HARNESS WIRING V-6 MODELS WITH DUAL ENGINE CONSOLE CONTROL

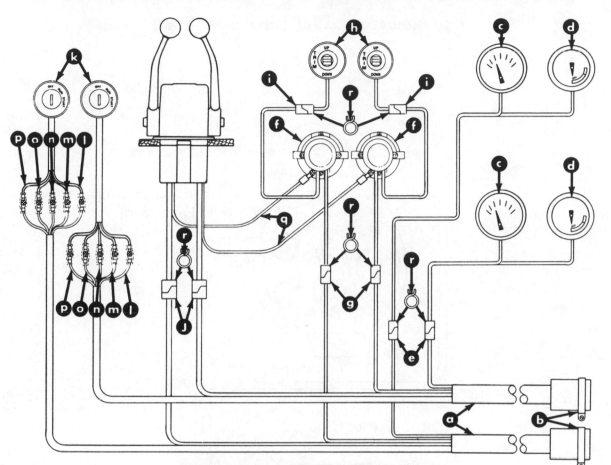

a. Wiring harness (starboard and port)
b. Screw-type clamps 1-5/8 in. (41.3 mm)
c. Tachometer
d. Trim indicator
e. 4-pin connector (tachometer/trim indicator to harness)
f. Choke/trailer panel (rear view of panels)
g. 5-pin connector (choke/trailer panel to harness)
h. Trim switch
i. 3-pin connector (trim switch to choke/trailer panel)
j. 4-pin connector (control harness)
k. Ignition switch panel
l. Black to black (secure with screw and nut and insulate with rubber sleeve)
m. Orange to orange (secure with screw and nut and insulate with rubber sleeve)
n. White to white (secure with screw and nut and insulate with rubber sleeve)
o. Yellow to yellow (secure with screw and nut and insulate with rubber sleeve)
p. Red to red/white (secure with screw and nut and insulate with rubber sleeve)
q. White wire (control to choke/trailer panel) connect white wire to terminal on back side of panel that already has a white wire connected to it.
r. Spring-type clamp (secure wiring connections with clamp)

TRIM INDICATOR GAUGE (WITH LAMP WIRE)

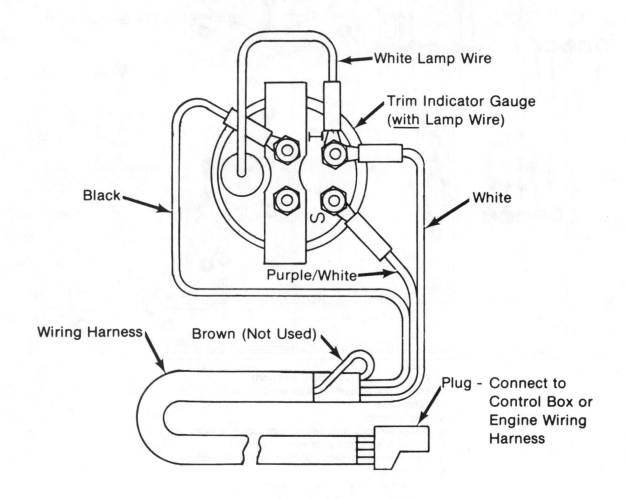

White Lamp Wire

Trim Indicator Gauge
(<u>with</u> Lamp Wire)

Black

White

Purple/White

Wiring Harness

Brown (Not Used)

Plug - Connect to
Control Box or
Engine Wiring
Harness

TRIM INDICATOR GAUGE (WITHOUT LAMP WIRE)

Ground Terminal

Trim Indicator Gauge
(without Lamp Wire)

Lamp

Purple/White

Black

White

Wiring Harness

Brown (Not Used)

Plug - Connect to Control
Box or Engine
Wiring Harness

3

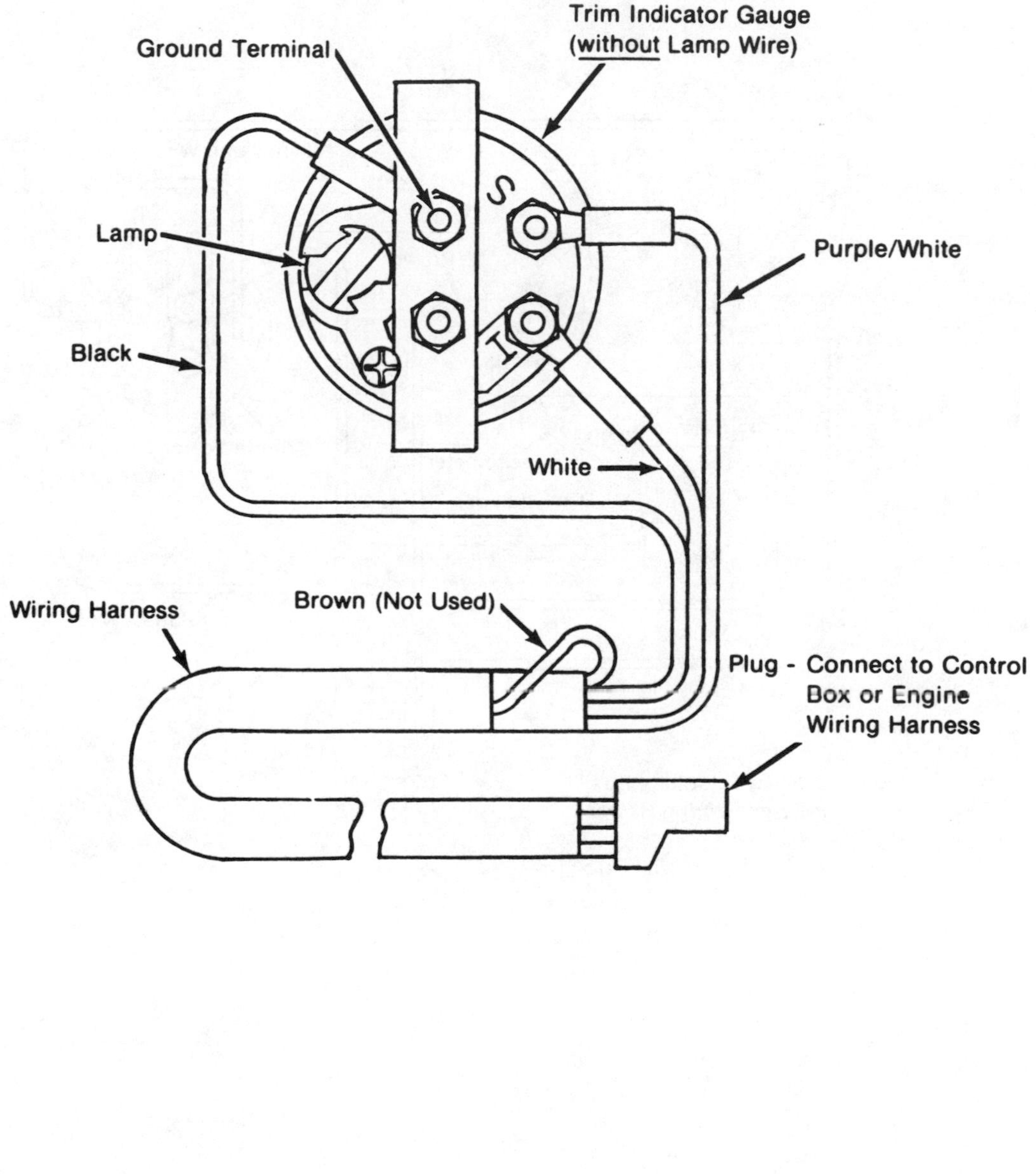

TACHOMETER WITH TRIM INDICATOR GAUGE (WITH LAMP WIRE)

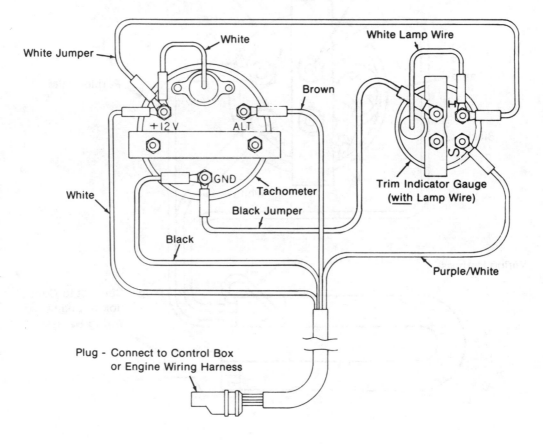

TACHOMETER WITH TRIM INDICATOR GAUGE (WITH LAMP WIRE)

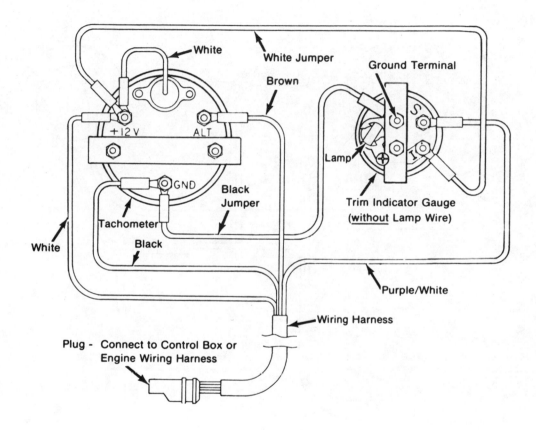

TRIM INDICATOR GAUGE AND ALARM HORN

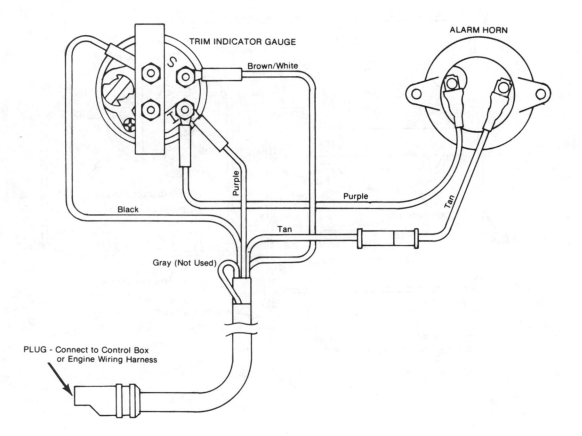

TACHOMETER (WITHOUT ADJUSTABLE DIAL), TRIM INDICATOR GAUGE AND ALARM HORN

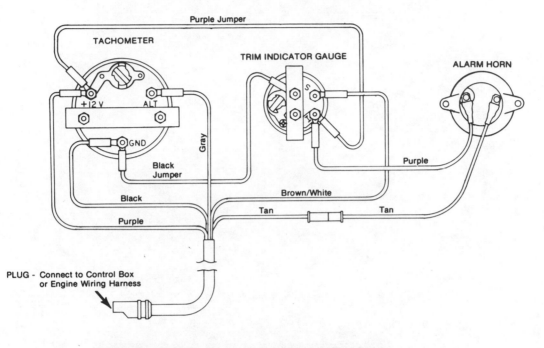

TACHOMETER (WITH ADJUSTABLE DIAL), TRIM INDICATOR GAUGE AND ALARM HORN

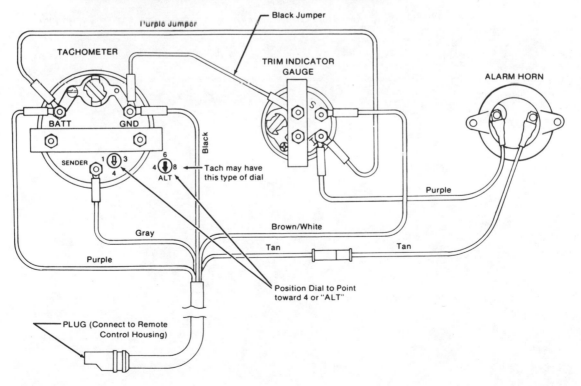

JOHNSON/EVINRUDE

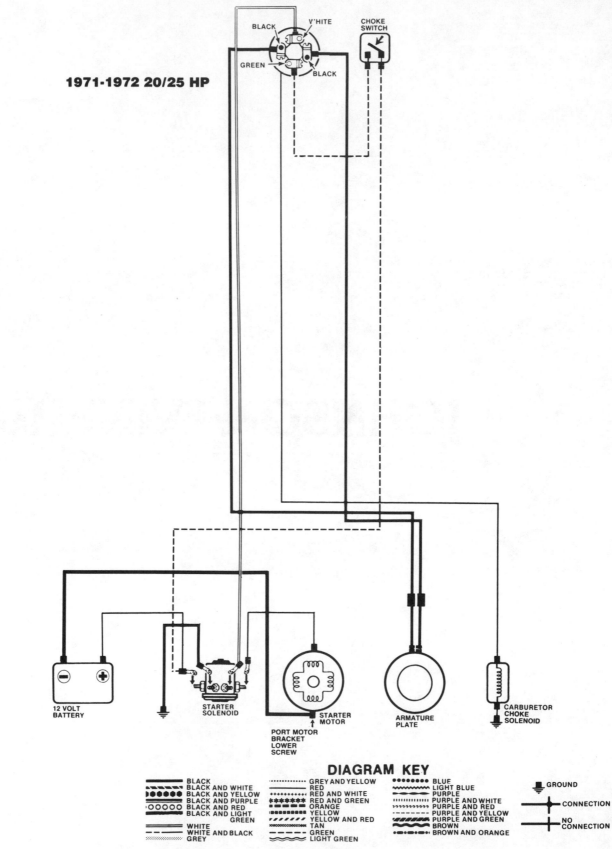

1971-1972 20/25 HP

BLACK   V'HITE

CHOKE
SWITCH

GREEN   BLACK

12 VOLT
BATTERY

STARTER
SOLENOID

PORT MOTOR
BRACKET
LOWER
SCREW

STARTER
MOTOR

ARMATURE
PLATE

CARBURETOR
CHOKE
SOLENOID

DIAGRAM KEY

BLACK	GREY AND YELLOW	BLUE
BLACK AND WHITE	RED	LIGHT BLUE
BLACK AND YELLOW	RED AND WHITE	PURPLE
BLACK AND PURPLE	RED AND GREEN	PURPLE AND WHITE
BLACK AND RED	ORANGE	PURPLE AND RED
BLACK AND LIGHT	YELLOW	PURPLE AND YELLOW
GREEN	YELLOW AND RED	PURPLE AND GREEN
WHITE	TAN	BROWN
WHITE AND BLACK	GREEN	BROWN AND ORANGE
GREY	LIGHT GREEN	

GROUND

CONNECTION

NO
CONNECTION

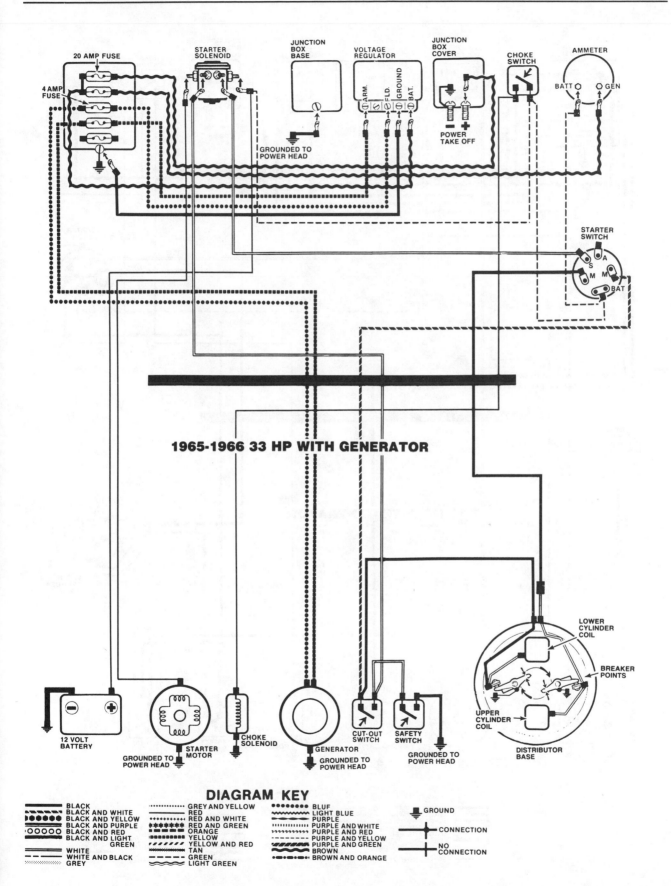

1965-1966 33 HP WITH GENERATOR

20 AMP FUSE

4 AMP FUSE

STARTER SOLENOID

JUNCTION BOX BASE

VOLTAGE REGULATOR

ARM. FLD. GROUND BAT.

JUNCTION BOX COVER

POWER TAKE OFF

CHOKE SWITCH

AMMETER

BATT GEN

GROUNDED TO POWER HEAD

STARTER SWITCH

A M M BAT S

12 VOLT BATTERY

GROUNDED TO POWER HEAD

STARTER MOTOR

CHOKE SOLENOID

GENERATOR

GROUNDED TO POWER HEAD

CUT-OUT SWITCH

SAFETY SWITCH

GROUNDED TO POWER HEAD

LOWER CYLINDER COIL

BREAKER POINTS

UPPER CYLINDER COIL

DISTRIBUTOR BASE

DIAGRAM KEY

BLACK	GREY AND YELLOW	BLUF
BLACK AND WHITE	RED	LIGHT BLUE
BLACK AND YELLOW	RED AND WHITE	PURPLE
BLACK AND PURPLE	RED AND GREEN	PURPLE AND WHITE
BLACK AND RED	ORANGE	PURPLE AND RED
BLACK AND LIGHT GREEN	YELLOW	PURPLE AND YELLOW
	YELLOW AND RED	PURPLE AND GREEN
WHITE	TAN	BROWN
WHITE AND BLACK	GREEN	BROWN AND ORANGE
GREY	LIGHT GREEN	

GROUND

CONNECTION

NO CONNECTION

4

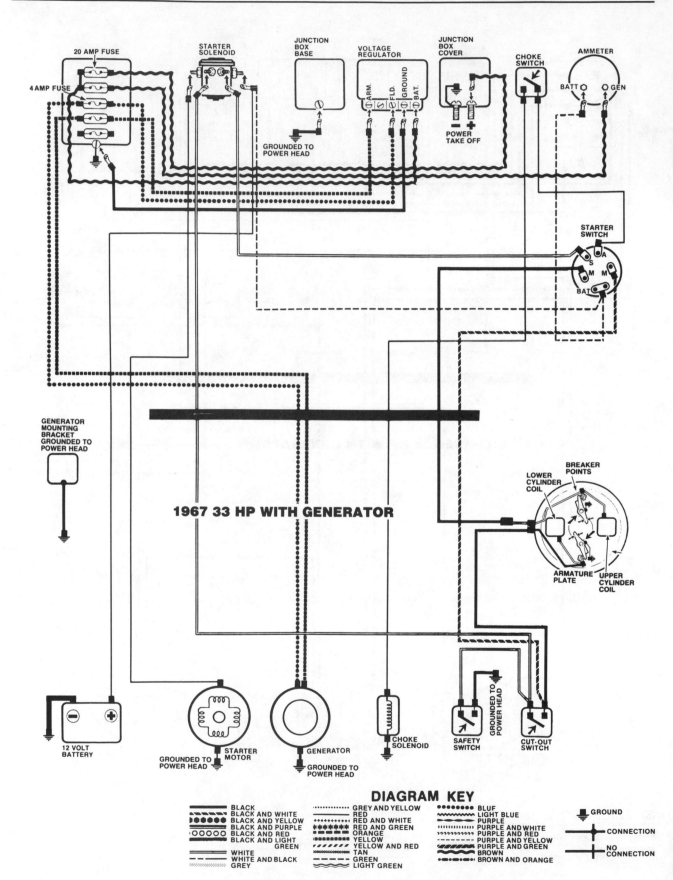

20 AMP FUSE

4 AMP FUSE

STARTER SOLENOID

JUNCTION BOX BASE

VOLTAGE REGULATOR

ARM. FLD. GROUND BAT.

JUNCTION BOX COVER

POWER TAKE OFF

CHOKE SWITCH

AMMETER

BATT GEN

GROUNDED TO POWER HEAD

STARTER SWITCH

S A
M M
BAT

GENERATOR MOUNTING BRACKET GROUNDED TO POWER HEAD

BREAKER POINTS

LOWER CYLINDER COIL

UPPER CYLINDER COIL

ARMATURE PLATE

1967 33 HP WITH GENERATOR

12 VOLT BATTERY

STARTER MOTOR

GROUNDED TO POWER HEAD

GENERATOR

GROUNDED TO POWER HEAD

CHOKE SOLENOID

SAFETY SWITCH

GROUNDED TO POWER HEAD

CUT-OUT SWITCH

DIAGRAM KEY

BLACK	GREY AND YELLOW	BLUE
BLACK AND WHITE	RED	LIGHT BLUE
BLACK AND YELLOW	RED AND WHITE	PURPLE
BLACK AND PURPLE	RED AND GREEN	PURPLE AND WHITE
BLACK AND RED	ORANGE	PURPLE AND RED
BLACK AND LIGHT GREEN	YELLOW	PURPLE AND YELLOW
	YELLOW AND RED	PURPLE AND GREEN
WHITE	TAN	BROWN
WHITE AND BLACK	GREEN	BROWN AND ORANGE
GREY	LIGHT GREEN	

GROUND

CONNECTION

NO CONNECTION

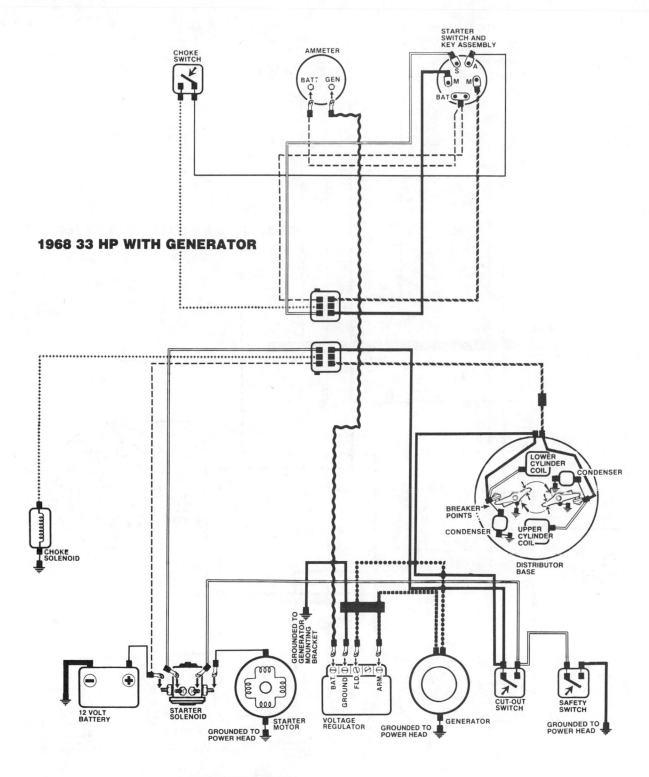

1968 33 HP WITH GENERATOR

CHOKE SWITCH

AMMETER

STARTER SWITCH AND KEY ASSEMBLY

CHOKE SOLENOID

LOWER CYLINDER COIL

CONDENSER

BREAKER POINTS

CONDENSER

UPPER CYLINDER COIL

DISTRIBUTOR BASE

12 VOLT BATTERY

STARTER SOLENOID

STARTER MOTOR
GROUNDED TO POWER HEAD

GROUNDED TO GENERATOR MOUNTING BRACKET

BAT.
GROUND
FLD.
ARM.

VOLTAGE REGULATOR

GENERATOR
GROUNDED TO POWER HEAD

CUT-OUT SWITCH

SAFETY SWITCH

GROUNDED TO POWER HEAD

DIAGRAM KEY

BLACK	GREY AND YELLOW	BLUE
BLACK AND WHITE	RED	LIGHT BLUE
BLACK AND YELLOW	RED AND WHITE	PURPLE
BLACK AND PURPLE	RED AND GREEN	PURPLE AND WHITE
BLACK AND RED	ORANGE	PURPLE AND RED
BLACK AND LIGHT GREEN	YELLOW	PURPLE AND YELLOW
	YELLOW AND RED	PURPLE AND GREEN
WHITE	TAN	BROWN
WHITE AND BLACK	GREEN	BROWN AND ORANGE
GREY	LIGHT GREEN	

GROUND

CONNECTION

NO CONNECTION

4

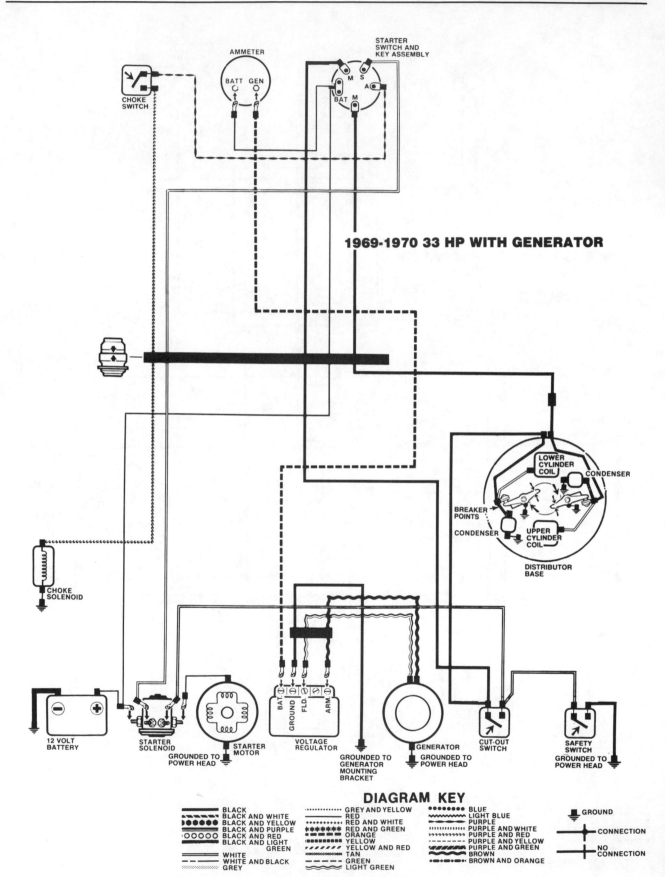

1969-1970 33 HP WITH GENERATOR

CHOKE SWITCH

AMMETER

BATT   GEN

STARTER SWITCH AND KEY ASSEMBLY

M   S

BAT   M   A

LOWER CYLINDER COIL

CONDENSER

BREAKER POINTS

CONDENSER

UPPER CYLINDER COIL

DISTRIBUTOR BASE

CHOKE SOLENOID

12 VOLT BATTERY

STARTER SOLENOID

GROUNDED TO POWER HEAD

STARTER MOTOR

BAT. GROUND FLD. ARM.

VOLTAGE REGULATOR

GROUNDED TO GENERATOR MOUNTING BRACKET

GENERATOR

GROUNDED TO POWER HEAD

CUT-OUT SWITCH

SAFETY SWITCH

GROUNDED TO POWER HEAD

DIAGRAM KEY

BLACK	GREY AND YELLOW	BLUE	GROUND
BLACK AND WHITE	RED	LIGHT BLUE	
BLACK AND YELLOW	RED AND WHITE	PURPLE	CONNECTION
BLACK AND PURPLE	RED AND GREEN	PURPLE AND WHITE	
BLACK AND RED	ORANGE	PURPLE AND RED	NO CONNECTION
BLACK AND LIGHT GREEN	YELLOW	PURPLE AND YELLOW	
	YELLOW AND RED	PURPLE AND GREEN	
WHITE	TAN	BROWN	
WHITE AND BLACK	GREEN	BROWN AND ORANGE	
GREY	LIGHT GREEN		

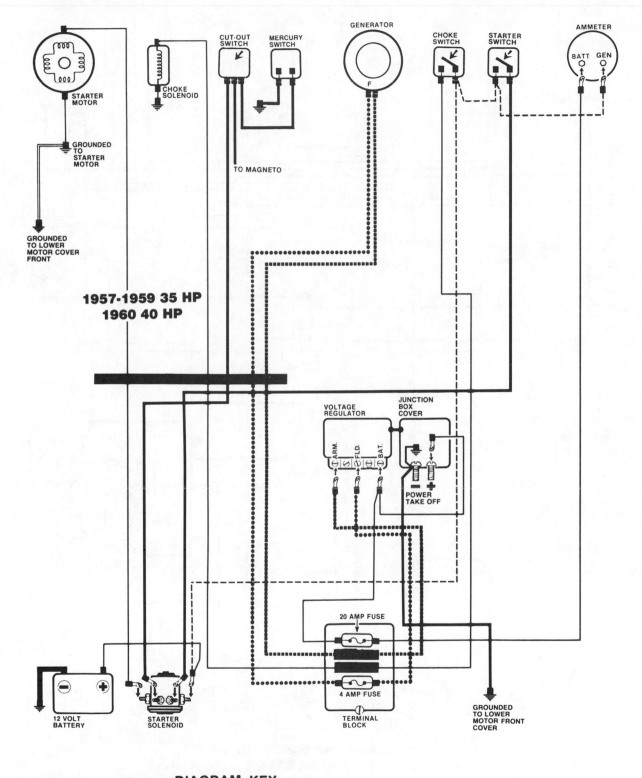

STARTER MOTOR

GROUNDED TO STARTER MOTOR

GROUNDED TO LOWER MOTOR COVER FRONT

CHOKE SOLENOID

CUT-OUT SWITCH

MERCURY SWITCH

TO MAGNETO

GENERATOR

F

CHOKE SWITCH

STARTER SWITCH

AMMETER

BATT   GEN

1957-1959 35 HP
1960 40 HP

VOLTAGE REGULATOR

ARM.   FLD.   BAT.

JUNCTION BOX COVER

POWER TAKE OFF

20 AMP FUSE

4 AMP FUSE

12 VOLT BATTERY

STARTER SOLENOID

TERMINAL BLOCK

GROUNDED TO LOWER MOTOR FRONT COVER

DIAGRAM KEY

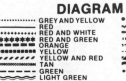

BLACK	
BLACK AND WHITE	
BLACK AND YELLOW	
BLACK AND PURPLE	
BLACK AND RED	
BLACK AND LIGHT GREEN	
WHITE	
WHITE AND BLACK	
GREY	

GREY AND YELLOW	
RED	
RED AND WHITE	
RED AND GREEN	
ORANGE	
YELLOW	
YELLOW AND RED	
TAN	
GREEN	
LIGHT GREEN	

BLUF	
LIGHT BLUE	
PURPLE	
PURPLE AND WHITE	
PURPLE AND RED	
PURPLE AND YELLOW	
PURPLE AND GREEN	
BROWN	
BROWN AND ORANGE	

GROUND

CONNECTION

NO CONNECTION

4

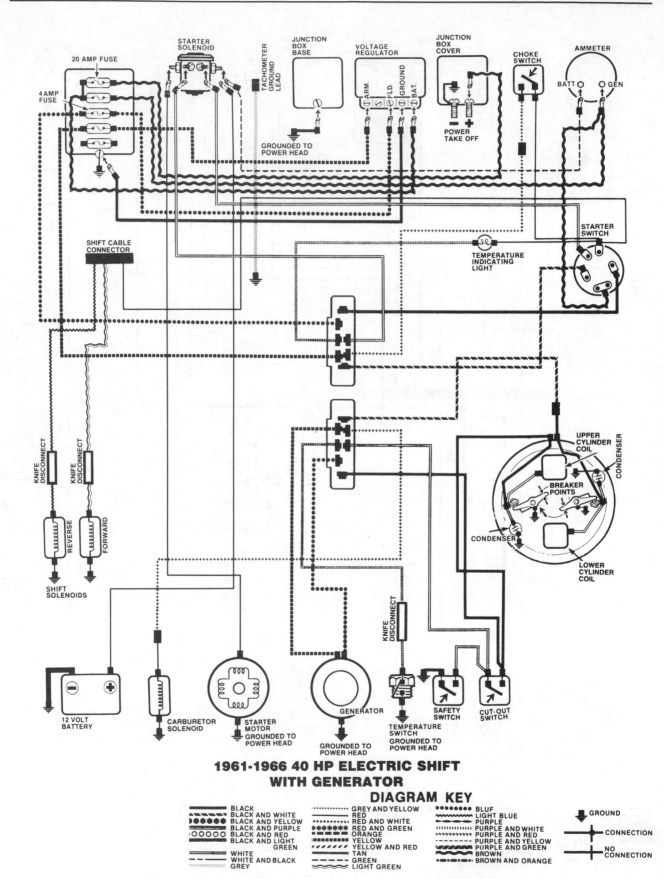

1961-1966 40 HP ELECTRIC SHIFT WITH GENERATOR

DIAGRAM KEY

BLACK	GREY AND YELLOW	BLUE
BLACK AND WHITE	RED	LIGHT BLUE
BLACK AND YELLOW	RED AND WHITE	PURPLE
BLACK AND PURPLE	RED AND GREEN	PURPLE AND WHITE
BLACK AND RED	ORANGE	PURPLE AND RED
BLACK AND LIGHT GREEN	YELLOW	PURPLE AND YELLOW
	YELLOW AND RED	PURPLE AND GREEN
WHITE	TAN	BROWN
WHITE AND BLACK	GREEN	BROWN AND ORANGE
GREY	LIGHT GREEN	

GROUND

CONNECTION

NO CONNECTION

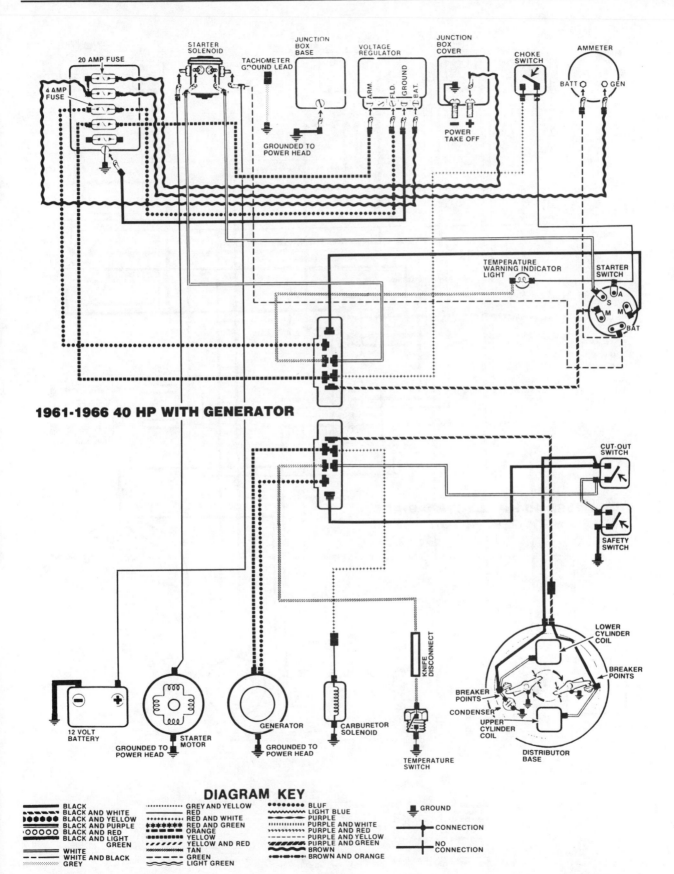

1961-1966 40 HP WITH GENERATOR

DIAGRAM KEY

BLACK	GREY AND YELLOW	BLUE	GROUND
BLACK AND WHITE	RED	LIGHT BLUE	
BLACK AND YELLOW	RED AND WHITE	PURPLE	
BLACK AND PURPLE	RED AND GREEN	PURPLE AND WHITE	CONNECTION
BLACK AND RED	ORANGE	PURPLE AND RED	
BLACK AND LIGHT GREEN	YELLOW	PURPLE AND YELLOW	
WHITE	YELLOW AND RED	PURPLE AND GREEN	NO CONNECTION
WHITE AND BLACK	TAN	BROWN	
GREY	GREEN	BROWN AND ORANGE	
	LIGHT GREEN		

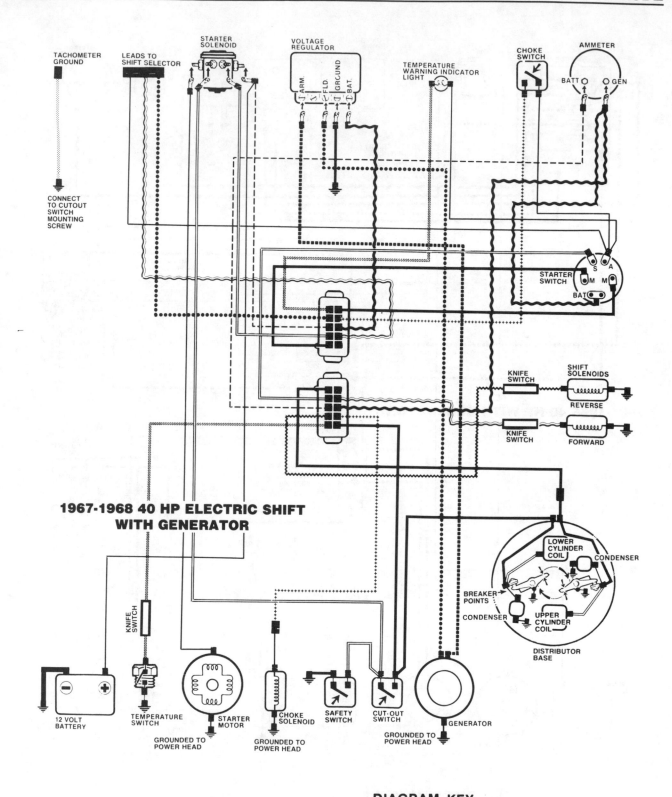

1967-1968 40 HP ELECTRIC SHIFT WITH GENERATOR

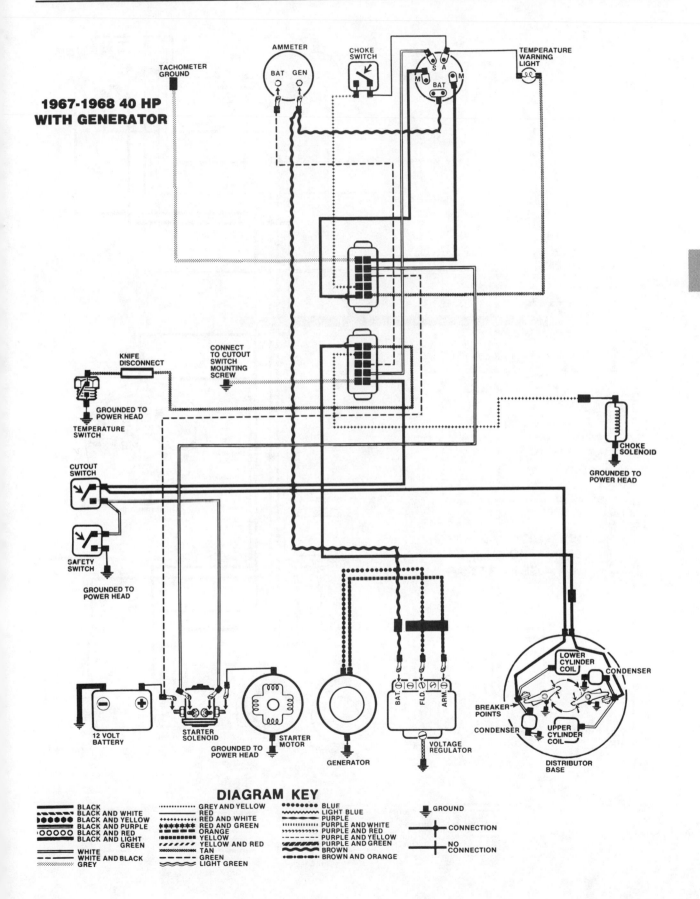

1967-1968 40 HP WITH GENERATOR

TACHOMETER GROUND

AMMETER
BAT   GEN

CHOKE SWITCH

S A
M   M
BAT

TEMPERATURE WARNING LIGHT

KNIFE DISCONNECT

CONNECT TO CUTOUT SWITCH MOUNTING SCREW

GROUNDED TO POWER HEAD

TEMPERATURE SWITCH

CHOKE SOLENOID

GROUNDED TO POWER HEAD

CUTOUT SWITCH

SAFETY SWITCH

GROUNDED TO POWER HEAD

12 VOLT BATTERY

STARTER SOLENOID

GROUNDED TO POWER HEAD

STARTER MOTOR

GENERATOR

BAT. FLD. ARM.

VOLTAGE REGULATOR

LOWER CYLINDER COIL

CONDENSER

BREAKER POINTS

CONDENSER

UPPER CYLINDER COIL

DISTRIBUTOR BASE

4

DIAGRAM KEY

BLACK	GREY AND YELLOW	BLUE
BLACK AND WHITE	RED	LIGHT BLUE
BLACK AND YELLOW	RED AND WHITE	PURPLE
BLACK AND PURPLE	RED AND GREEN	PURPLE AND WHITE
BLACK AND RED	ORANGE	PURPLE AND RED
BLACK AND LIGHT GREEN	YELLOW	PURPLE AND YELLOW
	YELLOW AND RED	PURPLE AND GREEN
WHITE	TAN	BROWN
WHITE AND BLACK	GREEN	BROWN AND ORANGE
GREY	LIGHT GREEN	

GROUND

CONNECTION

NO CONNECTION

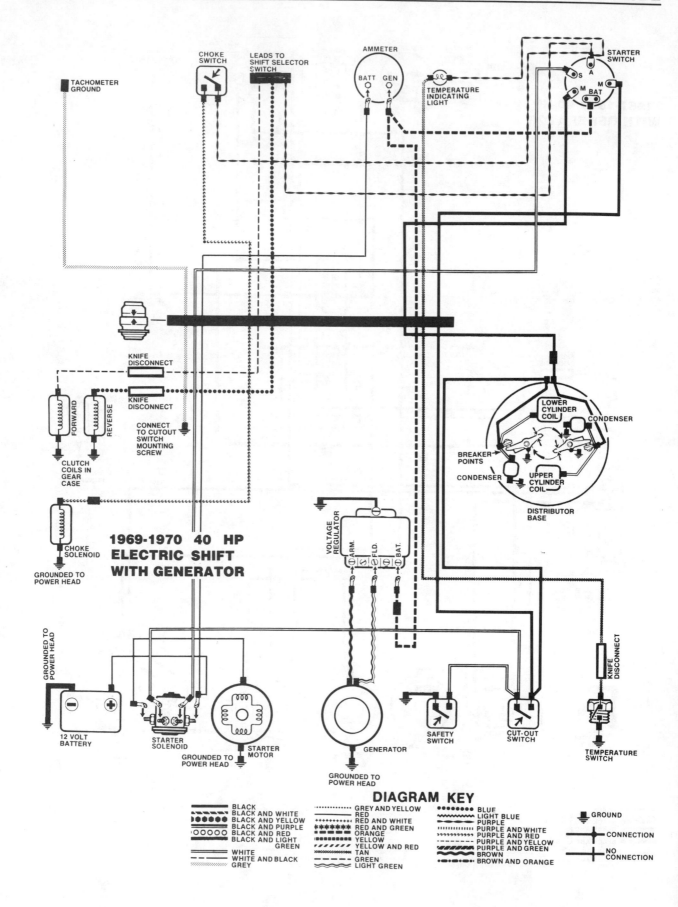

TACHOMETER GROUND

CHOKE SWITCH

LEADS TO SHIFT SELECTOR SWITCH

AMMETER

BATT GEN

TEMPERATURE INDICATING LIGHT

STARTER SWITCH

S   A

M   BAT

M

KNIFE DISCONNECT

KNIFE DISCONNECT

FORWARD

REVERSE

CONNECT TO CUTOUT SWITCH MOUNTING SCREW

CLUTCH COILS IN GEAR CASE

LOWER CYLINDER COIL

CONDENSER

BREAKER POINTS

CONDENSER

UPPER CYLINDER COIL

DISTRIBUTOR BASE

CHOKE SOLENOID

GROUNDED TO POWER HEAD

VOLTAGE REGULATOR

ARM.   FLD.   BAT.

**1969-1970 40 HP
ELECTRIC SHIFT
WITH GENERATOR**

GROUNDED TO POWER HEAD

12 VOLT BATTERY

STARTER SOLENOID

GROUNDED TO POWER HEAD

STARTER MOTOR

GENERATOR

GROUNDED TO POWER HEAD

SAFETY SWITCH

CUT-OUT SWITCH

KNIFE DISCONNECT

TEMPERATURE SWITCH

DIAGRAM KEY

BLACK	
BLACK AND WHITE	
BLACK AND YELLOW	
BLACK AND PURPLE	
BLACK AND RED	
BLACK AND LIGHT GREEN	
WHITE	
WHITE AND BLACK	
GREY	

GREY AND YELLOW	
RED	
RED AND WHITE	
RED AND GREEN	
ORANGE	
YELLOW	
YELLOW AND RED	
TAN	
GREEN	
LIGHT GREEN	

BLUE	
LIGHT BLUE	
PURPLE	
PURPLE AND WHITE	
PURPLE AND RED	
PURPLE AND YELLOW	
PURPLE AND GREEN	
BROWN	
BROWN AND ORANGE	

GROUND	
CONNECTION	
NO CONNECTION	

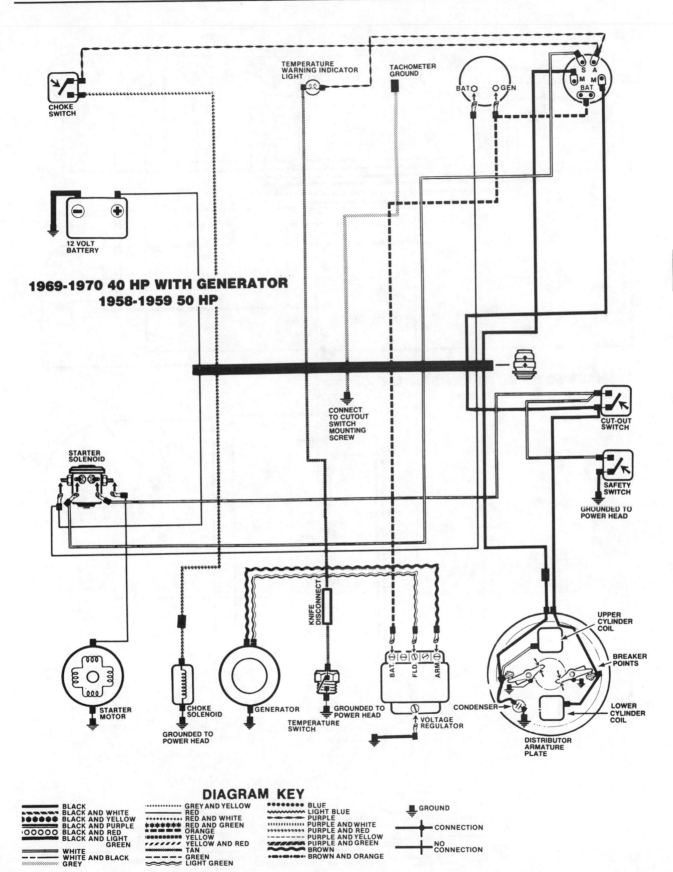

1969-1970 40 HP WITH GENERATOR
1958-1959 50 HP

TEMPERATURE WARNING INDICATOR LIGHT

TACHOMETER GROUND

CHOKE SWITCH

12 VOLT BATTERY

BAT   GEN

CONNECT TO CUTOUT SWITCH MOUNTING SCREW

CUT-OUT SWITCH

SAFETY SWITCH

GROUNDED TO POWER HEAD

STARTER SOLENOID

KNIFE DISCONNECT

UPPER CYLINDER COIL

BREAKER POINTS

STARTER MOTOR

CHOKE SOLENOID

GENERATOR

GROUNDED TO POWER HEAD
TEMPERATURE SWITCH

BAT.   FLD.   ARM.

VOLTAGE REGULATOR

CONDENSER

LOWER CYLINDER COIL

DISTRIBUTOR ARMATURE PLATE

GROUNDED TO POWER HEAD

DIAGRAM KEY

BLACK	GREY AND YELLOW
BLACK AND WHITE	RED
BLACK AND YELLOW	RED AND WHITE
BLACK AND PURPLE	RED AND GREEN
BLACK AND RED	ORANGE
BLACK AND LIGHT GREEN	YELLOW
	YELLOW AND RED
WHITE	TAN
WHITE AND BLACK	GREEN
GREY	LIGHT GREEN

BLUE	GROUND
LIGHT BLUE	
PURPLE	CONNECTION
PURPLE AND WHITE	
PURPLE AND RED	NO CONNECTION
PURPLE AND YELLOW	
PURPLE AND GREEN	
BROWN	
BROWN AND ORANGE	

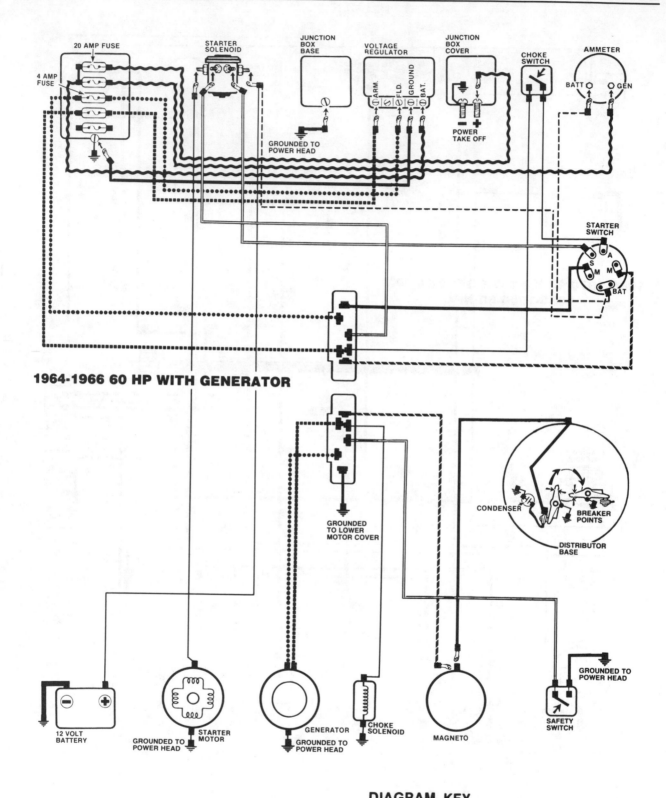

1964-1966 60 HP WITH GENERATOR

DIAGRAM KEY

BLACK	GREY AND YELLOW	BLUE	GROUND
BLACK AND WHITE	RED	LIGHT BLUE	
BLACK AND YELLOW	RED AND WHITE	PURPLE	CONNECTION
BLACK AND PURPLE	RED AND GREEN	PURPLE AND WHITE	
BLACK AND RED	ORANGE	PURPLE AND RED	NO
BLACK AND LIGHT GREEN	YELLOW	PURPLE AND YELLOW	CONNECTION
WHITE	YELLOW AND RED	PURPLE AND GREEN	
WHITE AND BLACK	TAN	BROWN	
GREY	GREEN	BROWN AND ORANGE	
	LIGHT GREEN		

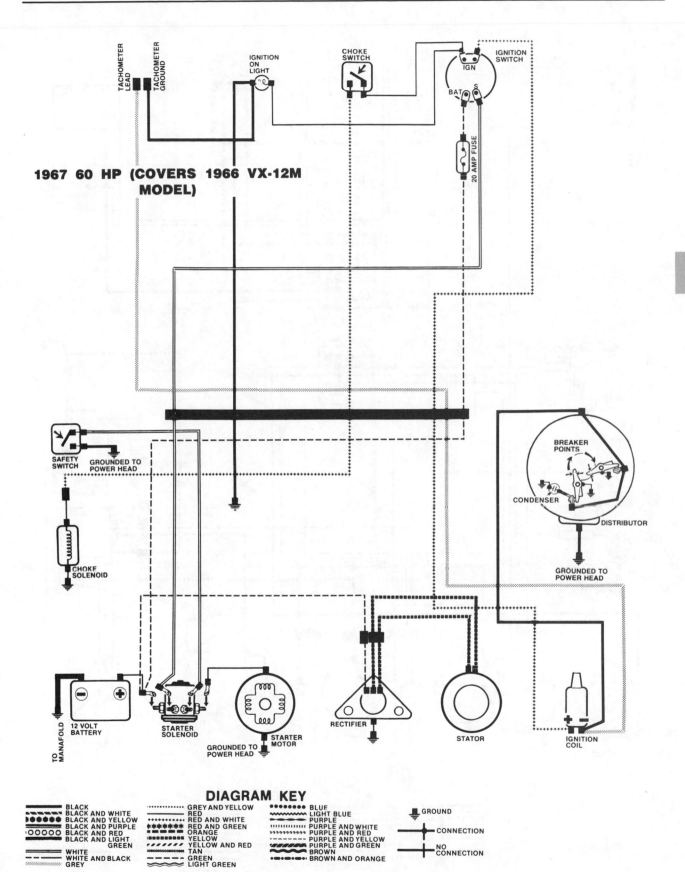

1967 60 HP (COVERS 1966 VX-12M MODEL)

DIAGRAM KEY

BLACK	GREY AND YELLOW	BLUE	GROUND
BLACK AND WHITE	RED	LIGHT BLUE	
BLACK AND YELLOW	RED AND WHITE	PURPLE	CONNECTION
BLACK AND PURPLE	RED AND GREEN	PURPLE AND WHITE	
BLACK AND RED	ORANGE	PURPLE AND RED	NO
BLACK AND LIGHT	YELLOW	PURPLE AND YELLOW	CONNECTION
GREEN	YELLOW AND RED	PURPLE AND GREEN	
WHITE	TAN	BROWN	
WHITE AND BLACK	GREEN	BROWN AND ORANGE	
GREY	LIGHT GREEN		

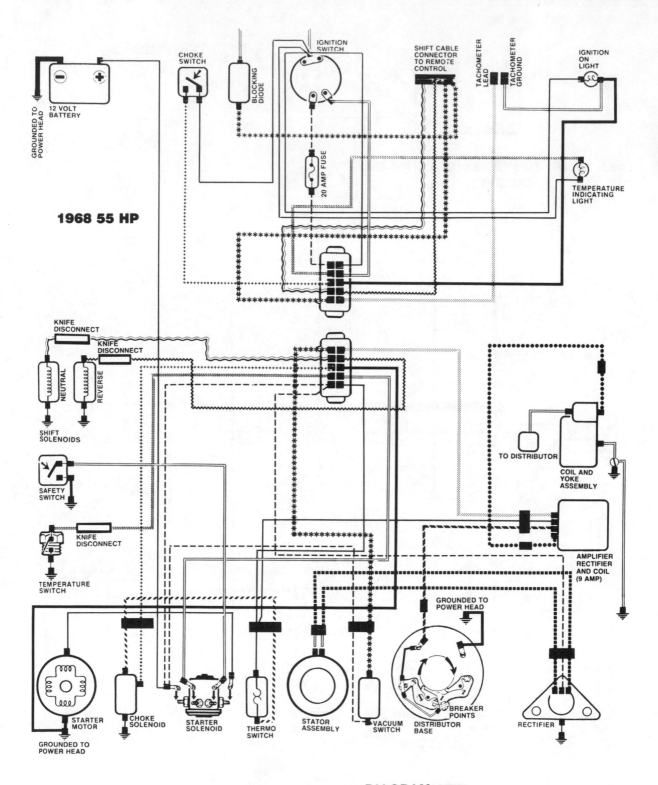

1968 55 HP

DIAGRAM KEY

BLACK	GREY AND YELLOW	BLUE	GROUND
BLACK AND WHITE	RED	LIGHT BLUE	
BLACK AND YELLOW	RED AND WHITE	PURPLE	CONNECTION
BLACK AND PURPLE	RED AND GREEN	PURPLE AND WHITE	
BLACK AND RED	ORANGE	PURPLE AND RED	NO
BLACK AND LIGHT GREEN	YELLOW	PURPLE AND YELLOW	CONNECTION
WHITE	YELLOW AND RED	PURPLE AND GREEN	
WHITE AND BLACK	TAN	BROWN	
GREY	GREEN	BROWN AND ORANGE	
	LIGHT GREEN		

1969 55 HP WITH ALTERNATOR

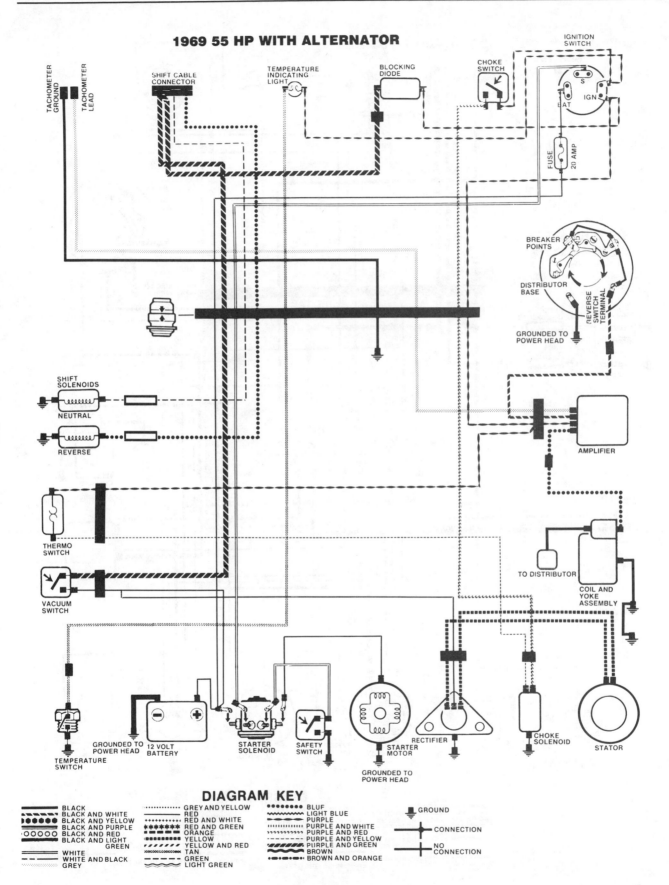

4

DIAGRAM KEY

BLACK	GREY AND YELLOW	BLUF	GROUND
BLACK AND WHITE	RED	LIGHT BLUE	
BLACK AND YELLOW	RED AND WHITE	PURPLE	
BLACK AND PURPLE	RED AND GREEN	PURPLE AND WHITE	CONNECTION
BLACK AND RED	ORANGE	PURPLE AND RED	
BLACK AND LIGHT GREEN	YELLOW	PURPLE AND YELLOW	
WHITE	YELLOW AND RED	PURPLE AND GREEN	NO
WHITE AND BLACK	TAN	BROWN	CONNECTION
GREY	GREEN	BROWN AND ORANGE	
	LIGHT GREEN		

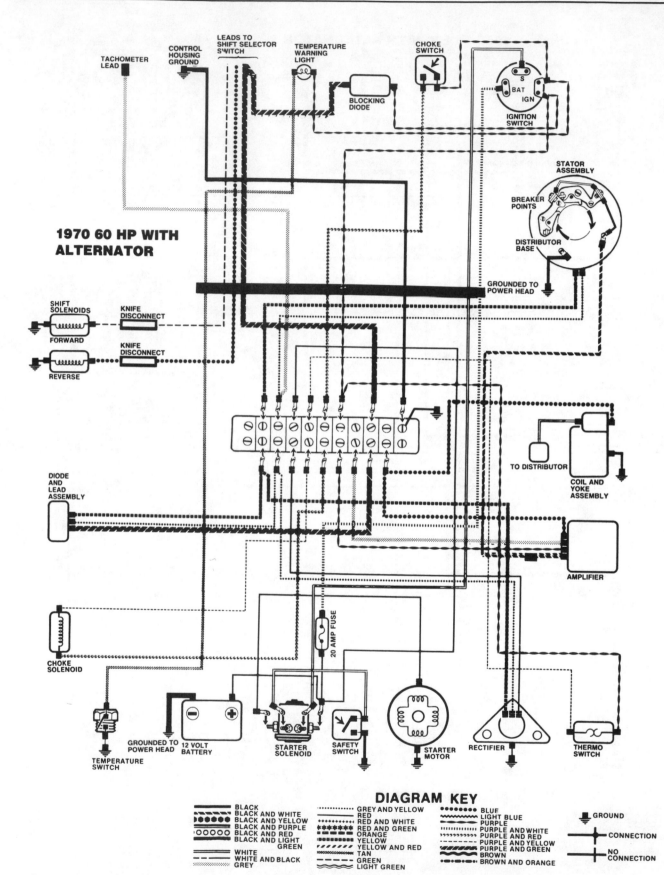

1970 60 HP WITH ALTERNATOR

TACHOMETER LEAD

CONTROL HOUSING GROUND

LEADS TO SHIFT SELECTOR SWITCH

TEMPERATURE WARNING LIGHT

CHOKE SWITCH

BLOCKING DIODE

S
BAT
IGN

IGNITION SWITCH

STATOR ASSEMBLY

BREAKER POINTS

DISTRIBUTOR BASE

GROUNDED TO POWER HEAD

SHIFT SOLENOIDS

KNIFE DISCONNECT

FORWARD

KNIFE DISCONNECT

REVERSE

DIODE AND LEAD ASSEMBLY

TO DISTRIBUTOR

COIL AND YOKE ASSEMBLY

AMPLIFIER

CHOKE SOLENOID

20 AMP FUSE

TEMPERATURE SWITCH

GROUNDED TO POWER HEAD

12 VOLT BATTERY

STARTER SOLENOID

SAFETY SWITCH

STARTER MOTOR

RECTIFIER

THERMO SWITCH

DIAGRAM KEY

BLACK	GREY AND YELLOW	BLUE
BLACK AND WHITE	RED	LIGHT BLUE
BLACK AND YELLOW	RED AND WHITE	PURPLE
BLACK AND PURPLE	RED AND GREEN	PURPLE AND WHITE
BLACK AND RED	ORANGE	PURPLE AND RED
BLACK AND LIGHT GREEN	YELLOW	PURPLE AND YELLOW
	YELLOW AND RED	PURPLE AND GREEN
WHITE	TAN	BROWN
WHITE AND BLACK	GREEN	BROWN AND ORANGE
GREY	LIGHT GREEN	

GROUND

CONNECTION

NO CONNECTION

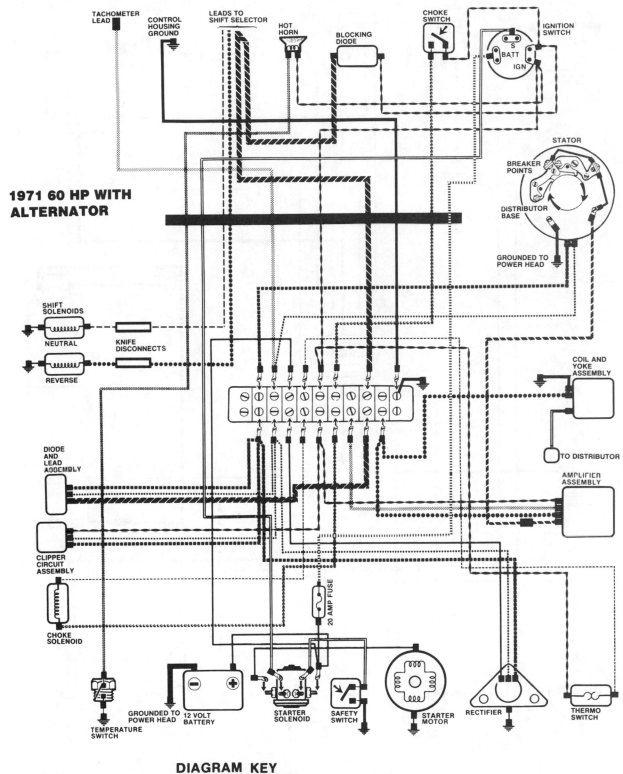

1971 60 HP WITH ALTERNATOR

TACHOMETER LEAD
CONTROL HOUSING GROUND
LEADS TO SHIFT SELECTOR
HOT HORN
BLOCKING DIODE
CHOKE SWITCH
IGNITION SWITCH
S
BATT
IGN

STATOR
BREAKER POINTS
DISTRIBUTOR BASE
GROUNDED TO POWER HEAD

SHIFT SOLENOIDS
NEUTRAL
REVERSE
KNIFE DISCONNECTS

COIL AND YOKE ASSEMBLY

TO DISTRIBUTOR

DIODE AND LEAD ASSEMBLY

AMPLIFIER ASSEMBLY

CLIPPER CIRCUIT ASSEMBLY

20 AMP FUSE

CHOKE SOLENOID

TEMPERATURE SWITCH

GROUNDED TO POWER HEAD
12 VOLT BATTERY
STARTER SOLENOID
SAFETY SWITCH
STARTER MOTOR
RECTIFIER
THERMO SWITCH

DIAGRAM KEY

BLACK	GREY AND YELLOW	BLUE
BLACK AND WHITE	RED	LIGHT BLUE
BLACK AND YELLOW	RED AND WHITE	PURPLE
BLACK AND PURPLE	RED AND GREEN	PURPLE AND WHITE
BLACK AND RED	ORANGE	PURPLE AND RED
BLACK AND LIGHT GREEN	YELLOW	PURPLE AND YELLOW
	YELLOW AND RED	PURPLE AND GREEN
WHITE	TAN	BROWN
WHITE AND BLACK	GREEN	BROWN AND ORANGE
GREY	LIGHT GREEN	

GROUND
CONNECTION
NO CONNECTION

4

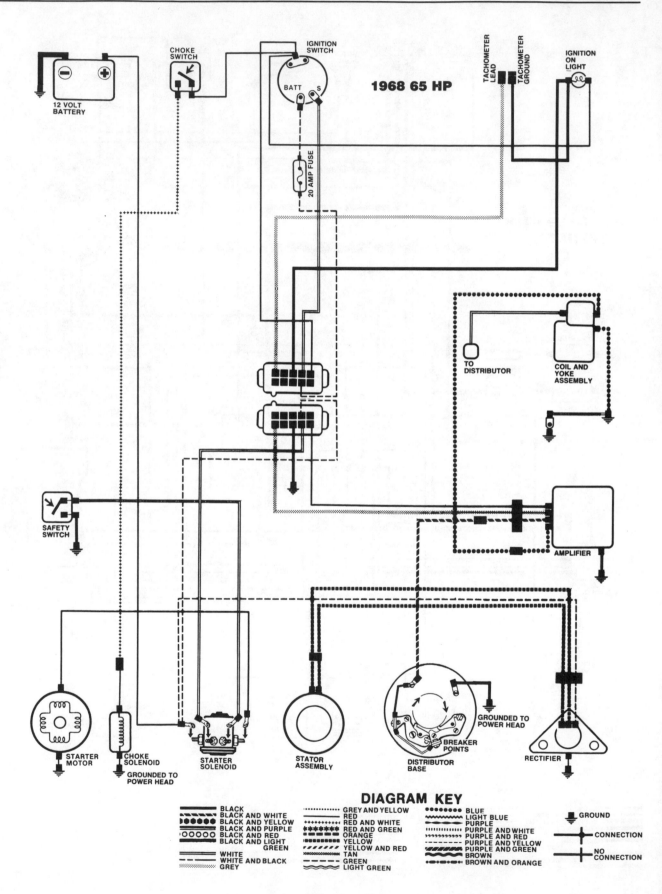

1968 65 HP

CHOKE SWITCH

IGNITION SWITCH

BATT   S

12 VOLT BATTERY

20 AMP FUSE

TACHOMETER LEAD

TACHOMETER GROUND

IGNITION ON LIGHT

TO DISTRIBUTOR

COIL AND YOKE ASSEMBLY

SAFETY SWITCH

AMPLIFIER

GROUNDED TO POWER HEAD

STARTER MOTOR

CHOKE SOLENOID

GROUNDED TO POWER HEAD

STARTER SOLENOID

STATOR ASSEMBLY

BREAKER POINTS

DISTRIBUTOR BASE

RECTIFIER

DIAGRAM KEY

BLACK	
BLACK AND WHITE	
BLACK AND YELLOW	
BLACK AND PURPLE	
BLACK AND RED	
BLACK AND LIGHT GREEN	
WHITE	
WHITE AND BLACK	
GREY	

GREY AND YELLOW	
RED	
RED AND WHITE	
RED AND GREEN	
ORANGE	
YELLOW	
YELLOW AND RED	
TAN	
GREEN	
LIGHT GREEN	

BLUE	
LIGHT BLUE	
PURPLE	
PURPLE AND WHITE	
PURPLE AND RED	
PURPLE AND YELLOW	
PURPLE AND GREEN	
BROWN	
BROWN AND ORANGE	

GROUND

CONNECTION

NO CONNECTION

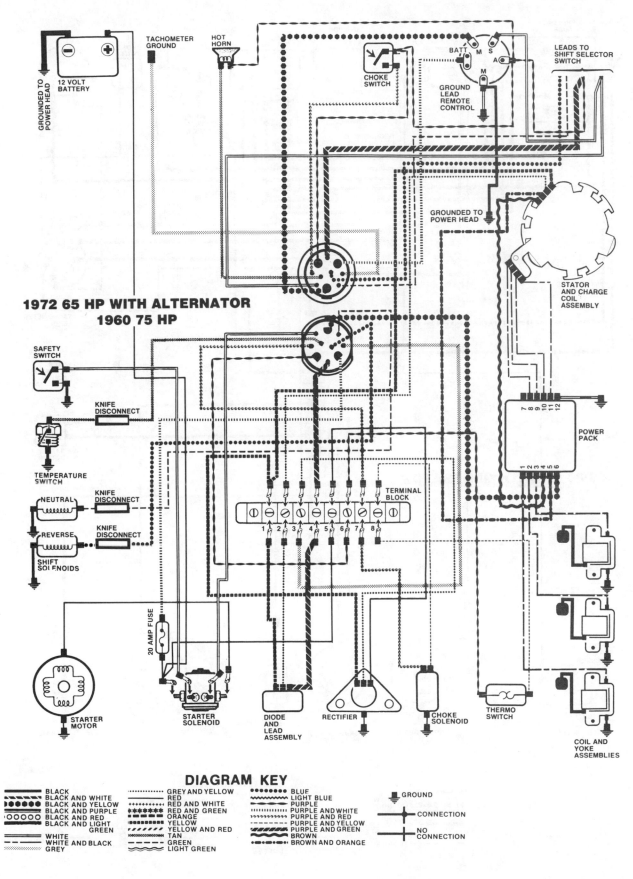

1972 65 HP WITH ALTERNATOR
1960 75 HP

DIAGRAM KEY

BLACK	GREY AND YELLOW	BLUE
BLACK AND WHITE	RED	LIGHT BLUE
BLACK AND YELLOW	RED AND WHITE	PURPLE
BLACK AND PURPLE	RED AND GREEN	PURPLE AND WHITE
BLACK AND RED	ORANGE	PURPLE AND RED
BLACK AND LIGHT GREEN	YELLOW	PURPLE AND YELLOW
	YELLOW AND RED	PURPLE AND GREEN
WHITE	TAN	BROWN
WHITE AND BLACK	GREEN	BROWN AND ORANGE
GREY	LIGHT GREEN	

GROUND

CONNECTION

NO CONNECTION

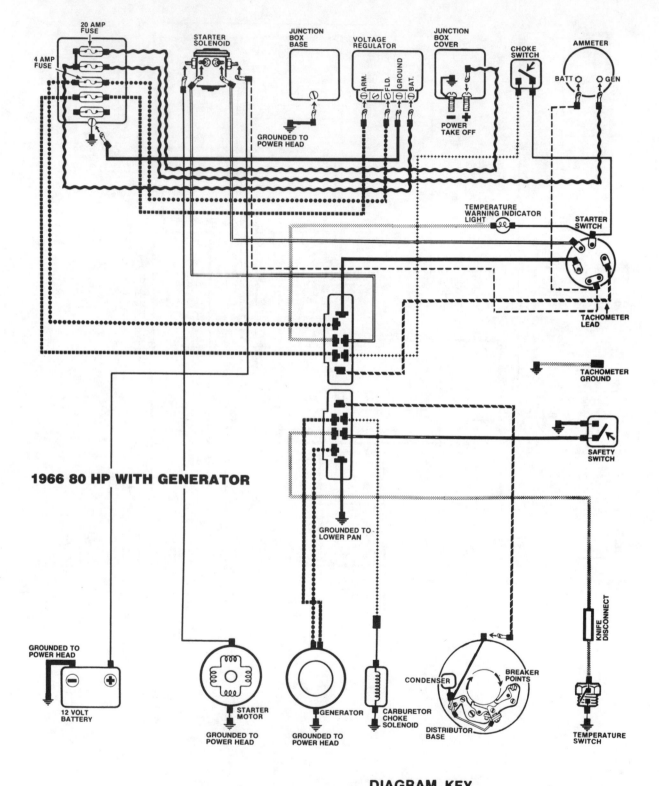

1966 80 HP WITH GENERATOR

DIAGRAM KEY

BLACK	GREY AND YELLOW	BLUE
BLACK AND WHITE	RED	LIGHT BLUE
BLACK AND YELLOW	RED AND WHITE	PURPLE
BLACK AND PURPLE	RED AND GREEN	PURPLE AND WHITE
BLACK AND RED	ORANGE	PURPLE AND RED
BLACK AND LIGHT GREEN	YELLOW	PURPLE AND YELLOW
	YELLOW AND RED	PURPLE AND GREEN
WHITE	TAN	BROWN
WHITE AND BLACK	GREEN	BROWN AND ORANGE
GREY	LIGHT GREEN	

GROUND
CONNECTION
NO CONNECTION

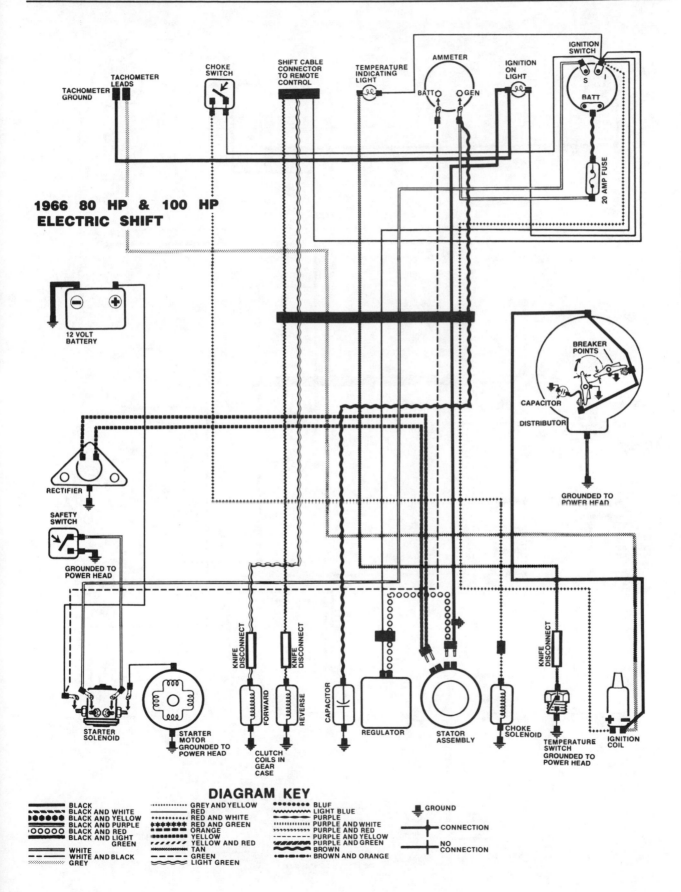

1966 80 HP & 100 HP ELECTRIC SHIFT

DIAGRAM KEY

BLACK	GREY AND YELLOW	BLUE
BLACK AND WHITE	RED	LIGHT BLUE
BLACK AND YELLOW	RED AND WHITE	PURPLE
BLACK AND PURPLE	RED AND GREEN	PURPLE AND WHITE
BLACK AND RED	ORANGE	PURPLE AND RED
BLACK AND LIGHT GREEN	YELLOW	PURPLE AND YELLOW
	YELLOW AND RED	PURPLE AND GREEN
WHITE	TAN	BROWN
WHITE AND BLACK	GREEN	BROWN AND ORANGE
GREY	LIGHT GREEN	

GROUND

CONNECTION

NO CONNECTION

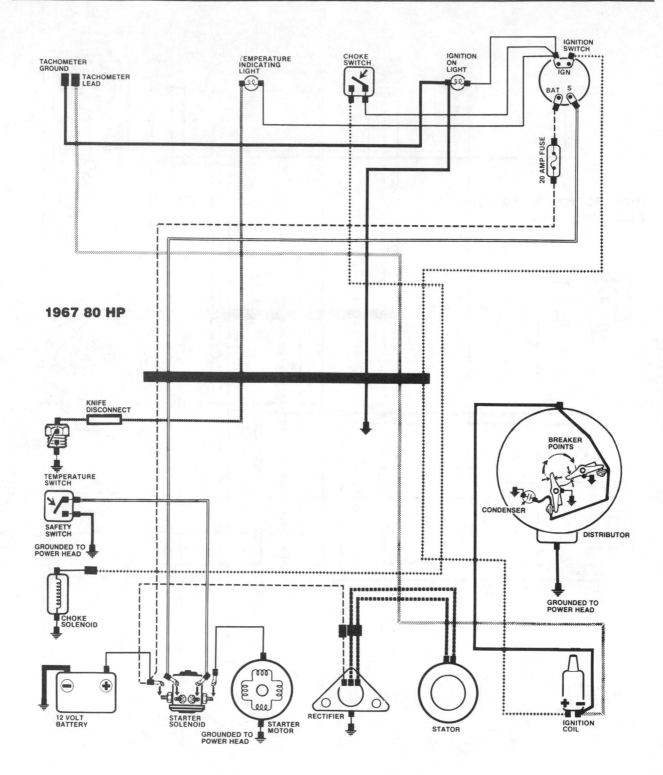

1967 80 HP

DIAGRAM KEY

	BLACK		GREY AND YELLOW		BLUF
	BLACK AND WHITE		RED		LIGHT BLUE
	BLACK AND YELLOW		RED AND WHITE		PURPLE
	BLACK AND PURPLE		RED AND GREEN		PURPLE AND WHITE
	BLACK AND RED		ORANGE		PURPLE AND RED
	BLACK AND LIGHT GREEN		YELLOW		PURPLE AND YELLOW
	WHITE		YELLOW AND RED		PURPLE AND GREEN
	WHITE AND BLACK		TAN		BROWN
	GREY		GREEN		BROWN AND ORANGE
			LIGHT GREEN		

GROUND

CONNECTION

NO CONNECTION

4

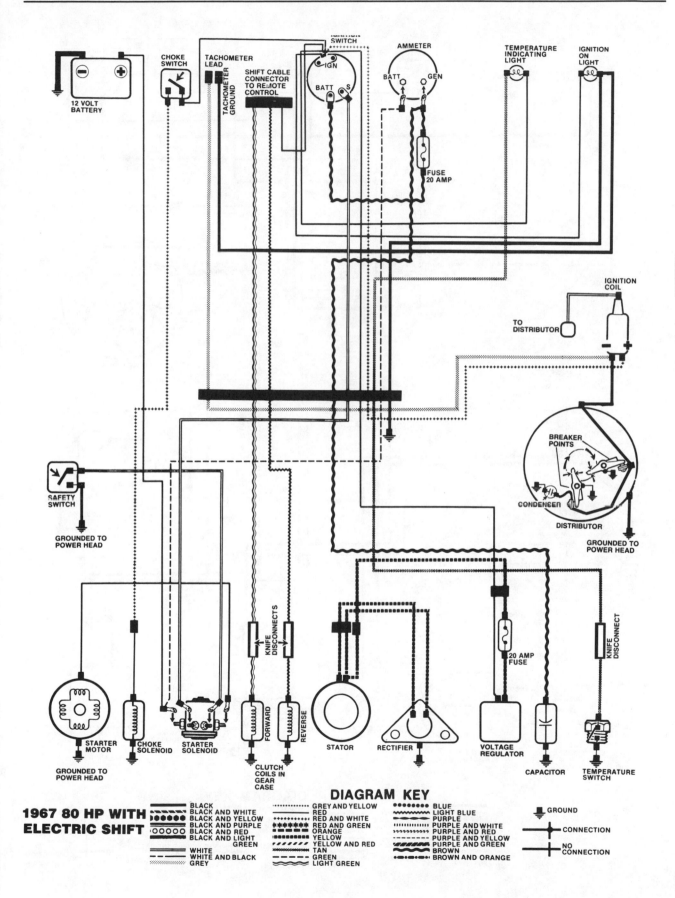

DIAGRAM KEY

1967 80 HP WITH ELECTRIC SHIFT

BLACK	GREY AND YELLOW	BLUE	GROUND
BLACK AND WHITE	RED	LIGHT BLUE	
BLACK AND YELLOW	RED AND WHITE	PURPLE	
BLACK AND PURPLE	RED AND GREEN	PURPLE AND WHITE	CONNECTION
BLACK AND RED	ORANGE	PURPLE AND RED	
BLACK AND LIGHT GREEN	YELLOW	PURPLE AND YELLOW	NO
WHITE	YELLOW AND RED	PURPLE AND GREEN	CONNECTION
WHITE AND BLACK	TAN	BROWN	
GREY	GREEN	BROWN AND ORANGE	
	LIGHT GREEN		

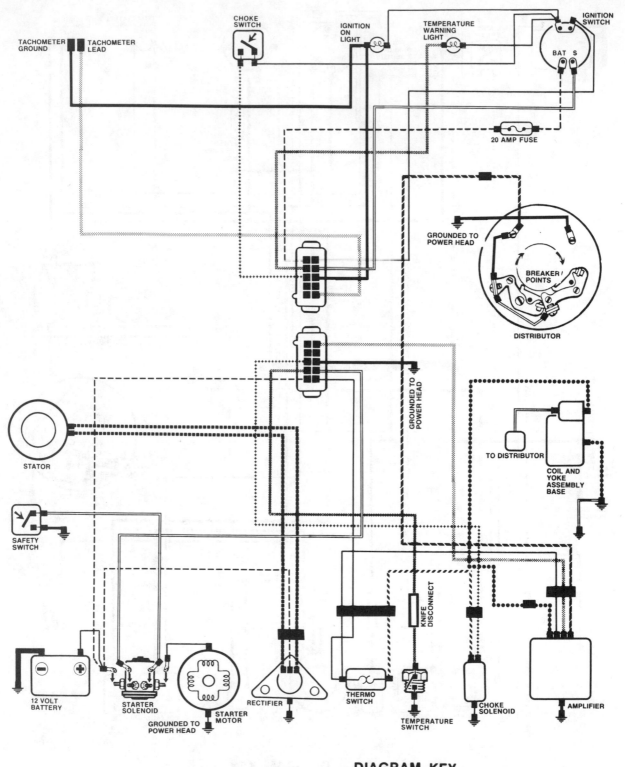

TACHOMETER GROUND   TACHOMETER LEAD

CHOKE SWITCH

IGNITION ON LIGHT

TEMPERATURE WARNING LIGHT

IGNITION SWITCH

BAT   S

20 AMP FUSE

GROUNDED TO POWER HEAD

BREAKER POINTS

DISTRIBUTOR

GROUNDED TO POWER HEAD

TO DISTRIBUTOR

COIL AND YOKE ASSEMBLY BASE

STATOR

SAFETY SWITCH

KNIFE DISCONNECT

12 VOLT BATTERY

STARTER SOLENOID

GROUNDED TO POWER HEAD

STARTER MOTOR

RECTIFIER

THERMO SWITCH

TEMPERATURE SWITCH

CHOKE SOLENOID

AMPLIFIER

1968 85 HP

DIAGRAM KEY

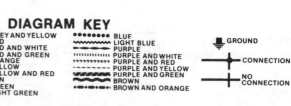

BLACK	GREY AND YELLOW	BLUE
BLACK AND WHITE	RED	LIGHT BLUE
BLACK AND YELLOW	RED AND WHITE	PURPLE
BLACK AND PURPLE	RED AND GREEN	PURPLE AND WHITE
BLACK AND RED	ORANGE	PURPLE AND RED
BLACK AND LIGHT GREEN	YELLOW	PURPLE AND YELLOW
	YELLOW AND RED	PURPLE AND GREEN
WHITE	TAN	BROWN
WHITE AND BLACK	GREEN	BROWN AND ORANGE
GREY	LIGHT GREEN	

GROUND

CONNECTION

NO CONNECTION

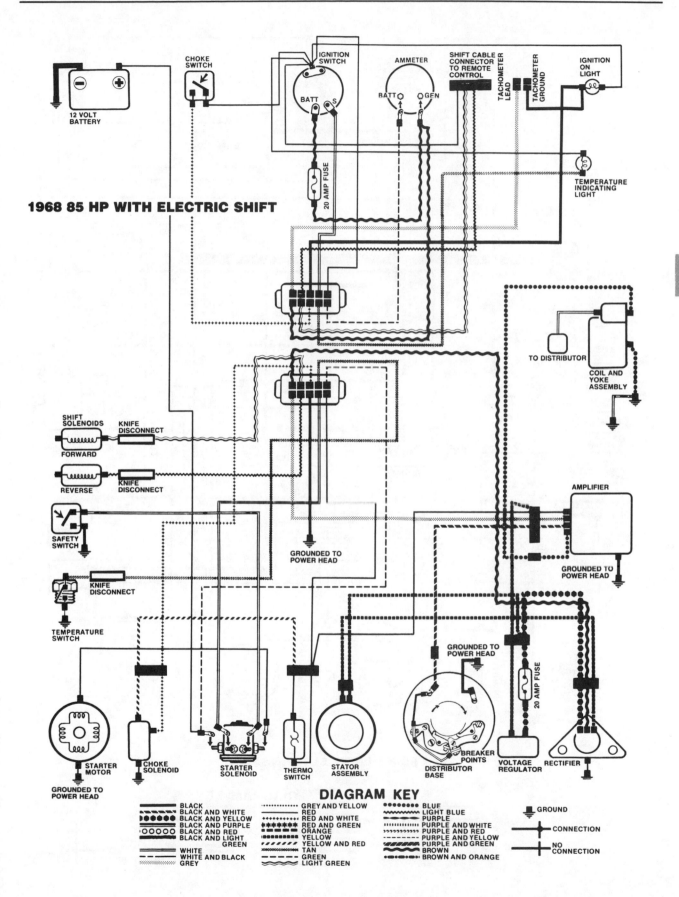

1968 85 HP WITH ELECTRIC SHIFT

DIAGRAM KEY

BLACK	GREY AND YELLOW	BLUE	GROUND
BLACK AND WHITE	RED	LIGHT BLUE	
BLACK AND YELLOW	RED AND WHITE	PURPLE	CONNECTION
BLACK AND PURPLE	RED AND GREEN	PURPLE AND WHITE	
BLACK AND RED	ORANGE	PURPLE AND RED	NO
BLACK AND LIGHT GREEN	YELLOW	PURPLE AND YELLOW	CONNECTION
WHITE	YELLOW AND RED	PURPLE AND GREEN	
WHITE AND BLACK	GREEN	BROWN	
GREY	LIGHT GREEN	BROWN AND ORANGE	

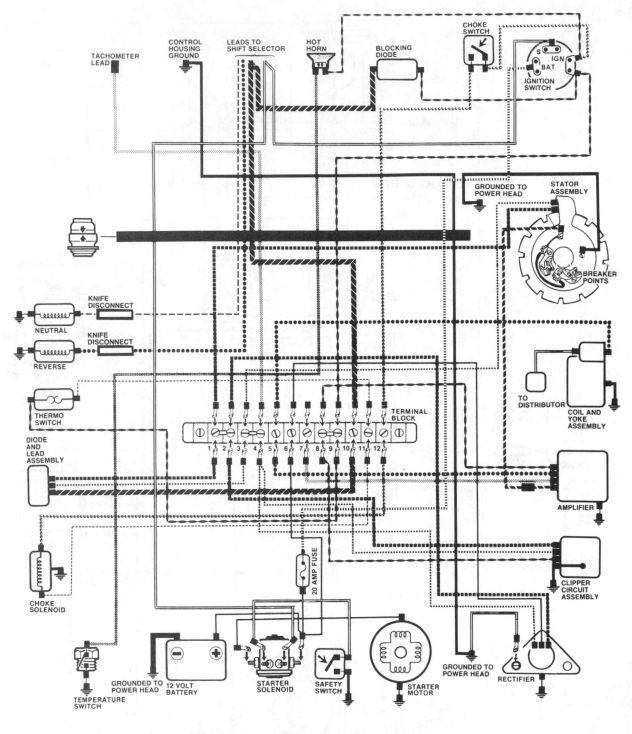

1972 85 HP WITH ALTERNATOR

DIAGRAM KEY

BLACK	GREY AND YELLOW	BLUE
BLACK AND WHITE	RED	LIGHT BLUE
BLACK AND YELLOW	RED AND WHITE	PURPLE
BLACK AND PURPLE	RED AND GREEN	PURPLE AND WHITE
BLACK AND RED	ORANGE	PURPLE AND RED
BLACK AND LIGHT GREEN	YELLOW	PURPLE AND YELLOW
	YELLOW AND RED	PURPLE AND GREEN
WHITE	TAN	BROWN
WHITE AND BLACK	GREEN	BROWN AND ORANGE
GREY	LIGHT GREEN	

GROUND
CONNECTION
NO CONNECTION

1969-1970 85 HP WITH ALTERNATOR

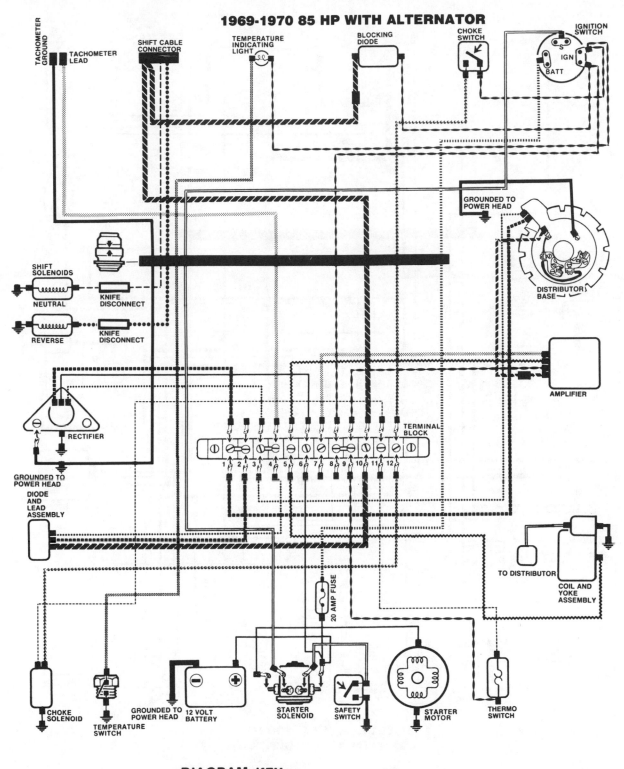

DIAGRAM KEY

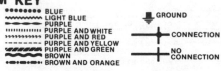

BLACK	GREY AND YELLOW	BLUE
BLACK AND WHITE	RED	LIGHT BLUE
BLACK AND YELLOW	RED AND WHITE	PURPLE
BLACK AND PURPLE	RED AND GREEN	PURPLE AND WHITE
BLACK AND RED	ORANGE	PURPLE AND RED
BLACK AND LIGHT GREEN	YELLOW	PURPLE AND YELLOW
	YELLOW AND RED	PURPLE AND GREEN
WHITE	GREEN	BROWN
WHITE AND BLACK	LIGHT GREEN	BROWN AND ORANGE
GREY		

GROUND

CONNECTION

NO CONNECTION

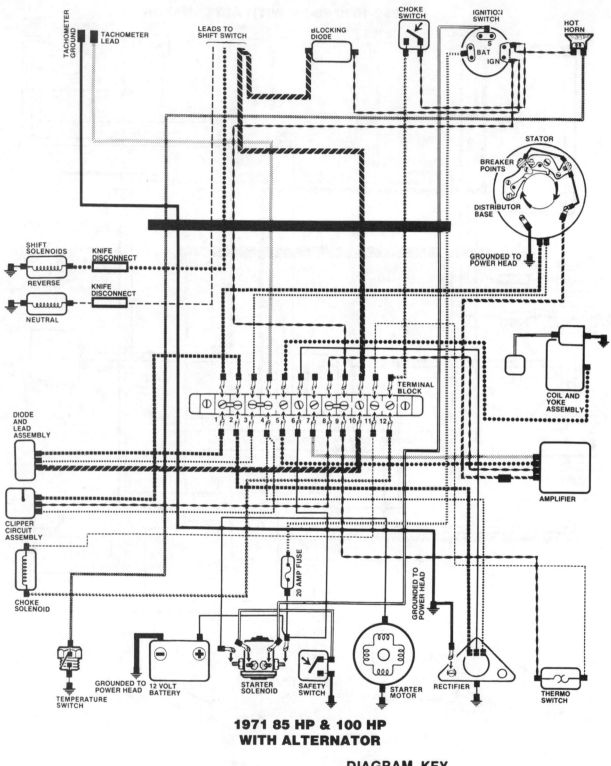

1971 85 HP & 100 HP
WITH ALTERNATOR

DIAGRAM KEY

1967 100 HP CD IGNITION

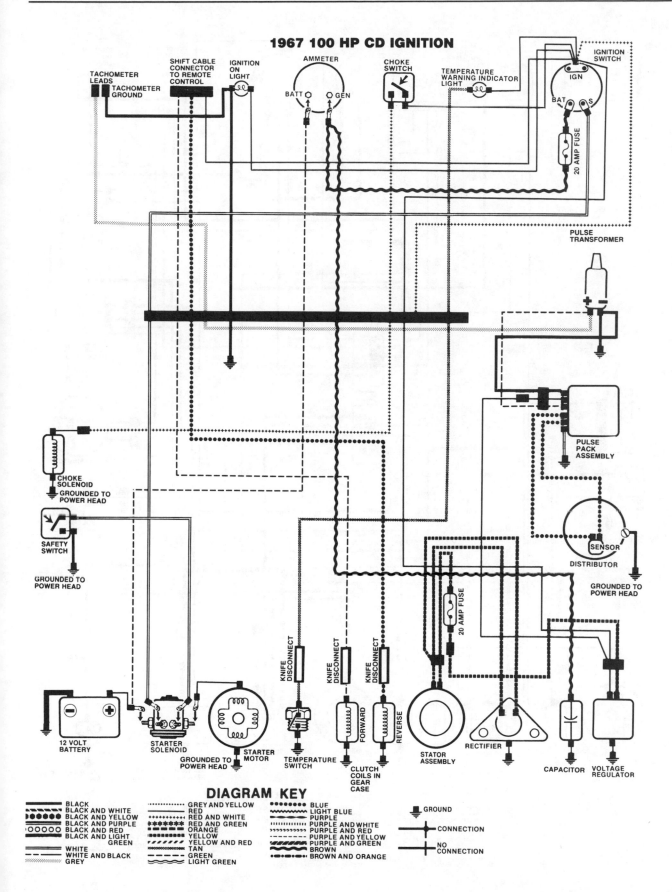

TACHOMETER LEADS
TACHOMETER GROUND
SHIFT CABLE CONNECTOR TO REMOTE CONTROL
IGNITION ON LIGHT
AMMETER
BATT
GEN
CHOKE SWITCH
TEMPERATURE WARNING INDICATOR LIGHT
IGNITION SWITCH
IGN
BAT
S
20 AMP FUSE
PULSE TRANSFORMER
PULSE PACK ASSEMBLY
CHOKE SOLENOID
GROUNDED TO POWER HEAD
SAFETY SWITCH
GROUNDED TO POWER HEAD
SENSOR
DISTRIBUTOR
GROUNDED TO POWER HEAD
20 AMP FUSE
KNIFE DISCONNECT
KNIFE DISCONNECT
KNIFE DISCONNECT
FORWARD
REVERSE
12 VOLT BATTERY
STARTER SOLENOID
GROUNDED TO POWER HEAD
STARTER MOTOR
TEMPERATURE SWITCH
CLUTCH COILS IN GEAR CASE
STATOR ASSEMBLY
RECTIFIER
CAPACITOR
VOLTAGE REGULATOR
DIAGRAM KEY
BLACK
BLACK AND WHITE
BLACK AND YELLOW
BLACK AND PURPLE
BLACK AND RED
BLACK AND LIGHT GREEN
WHITE
WHITE AND BLACK
GREY
GREY AND YELLOW
RED
RED AND WHITE
RED AND GREEN
ORANGE
YELLOW
YELLOW AND RED
TAN
GREEN
LIGHT GREEN
BLUE
LIGHT BLUE
PURPLE
PURPLE AND WHITE
PURPLE AND RED
PURPLE AND YELLOW
PURPLE AND GREEN
BROWN
BROWN AND ORANGE
GROUND
CONNECTION
NO CONNECTION

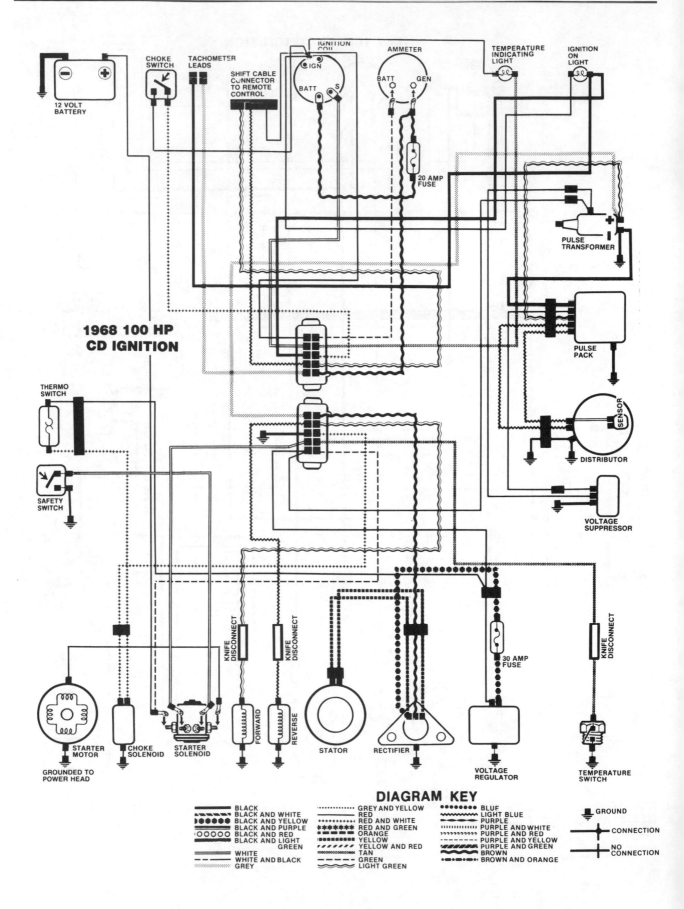

**1968 100 HP
CD IGNITION**

DIAGRAM KEY

BLACK	GREY AND YELLOW	BLUE
BLACK AND WHITE	RED	LIGHT BLUE
BLACK AND YELLOW	RED AND WHITE	PURPLE
BLACK AND PURPLE	RED AND GREEN	PURPLE AND WHITE
BLACK AND RED	ORANGE	PURPLE AND RED
BLACK AND LIGHT GREEN	YELLOW	PURPLE AND YELLOW
	YELLOW AND RED	PURPLE AND GREEN
WHITE	TAN	BROWN
WHITE AND BLACK	GREEN	BROWN AND ORANGE
GREY	LIGHT GREEN	

GROUND

CONNECTION

NO CONNECTION

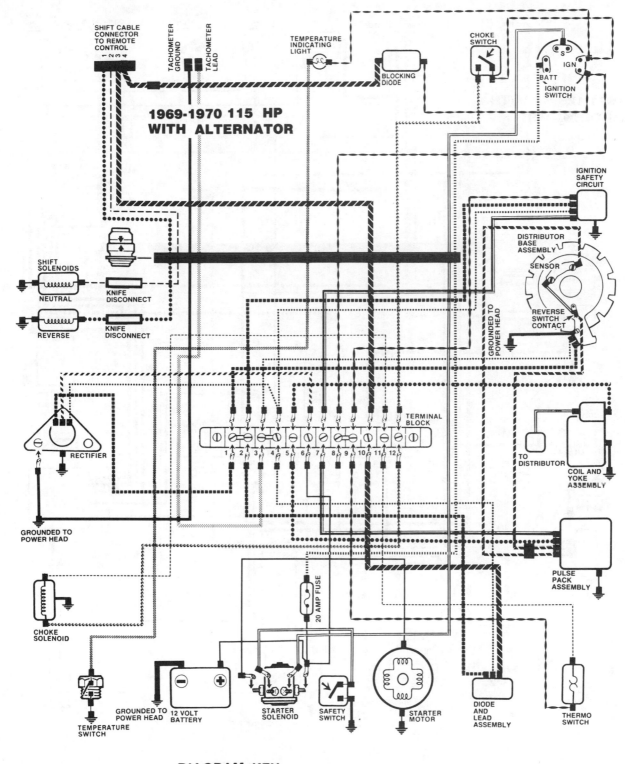

1969-1970 115 HP WITH ALTERNATOR

4

DIAGRAM KEY

BLACK
BLACK AND WHITE
BLACK AND YELLOW
BLACK AND PURPLE
BLACK AND RED
BLACK AND LIGHT GREEN
WHITE
WHITE AND BLACK
GREY

GREY AND YELLOW
RED
RED AND WHITE
ORANGE
YELLOW
YELLOW AND RED
TAN
GREEN
LIGHT GREEN

BLUE
LIGHT BLUE
PURPLE
PURPLE AND WHITE
PURPLE AND RED
PURPLE AND YELLOW
PURPLE AND GREEN
BROWN
BROWN AND ORANGE

GROUND
CONNECTION
NO CONNECTION

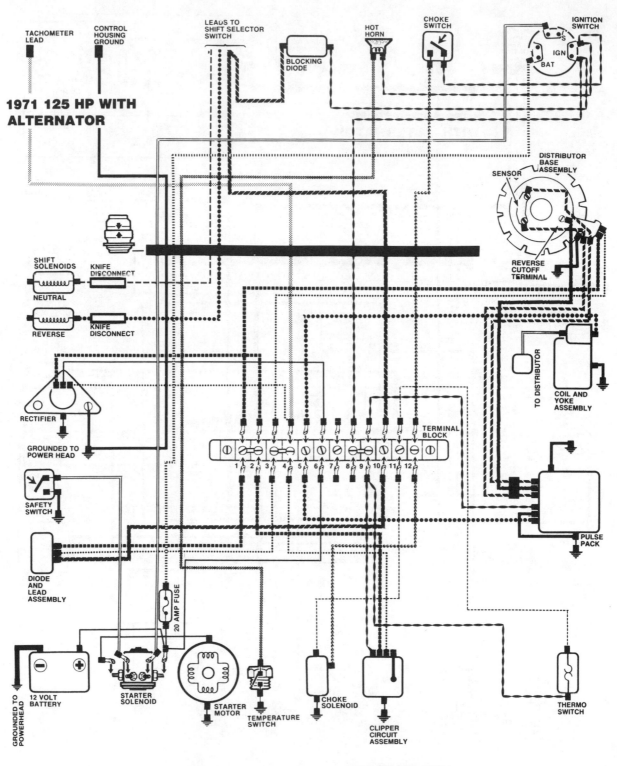

1971 125 HP WITH ALTERNATOR

TACHOMETER LEAD

CONTROL HOUSING GROUND

LEADS TO SHIFT SELECTOR SWITCH

BLOCKING DIODE

HOT HORN

CHOKE SWITCH

IGNITION SWITCH

DISTRIBUTOR BASE ASSEMBLY

SENSOR

REVERSE CUTOFF TERMINAL

SHIFT SOLENOIDS

KNIFE DISCONNECT

NEUTRAL

REVERSE

KNIFE DISCONNECT

TO DISTRIBUTOR

COIL AND YOKE ASSEMBLY

RECTIFIER

GROUNDED TO POWER HEAD

TERMINAL BLOCK

1 2 3 4 5 6 7 8 9 10 11 12

SAFETY SWITCH

PULSE PACK

DIODE AND LEAD ASSEMBLY

20 AMP FUSE

GROUNDED TO POWERHEAD

12 VOLT BATTERY

STARTER SOLENOID

STARTER MOTOR

TEMPERATURE SWITCH

CHOKE SOLENOID

CLIPPER CIRCUIT ASSEMBLY

THERMO SWITCH

DIAGRAM KEY

BLACK	GREY AND YELLOW	BLUE		GROUND
BLACK AND WHITE	RED	LIGHT BLUE		
BLACK AND YELLOW	RED AND WHITE	PURPLE		CONNECTION
BLACK AND PURPLE	RED AND GREEN	PURPLE AND WHITE		
BLACK AND RED	ORANGE	PURPLE AND RED		NO CONNECTION
BLACK AND LIGHT GREEN	YELLOW	PURPLE AND YELLOW		
	YELLOW AND RED	PURPLE AND GREEN		
WHITE	TAN	BROWN		
WHITE AND BLACK	GREEN	BROWN AND ORANGE		
GREY	LIGHT GREEN			

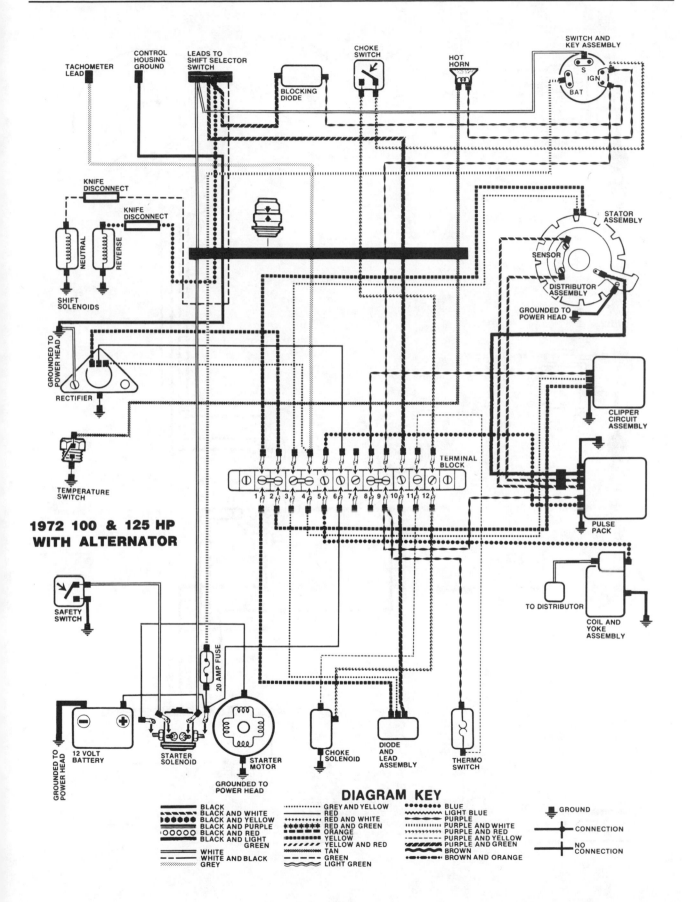

1972 100 & 125 HP WITH ALTERNATOR

DIAGRAM KEY

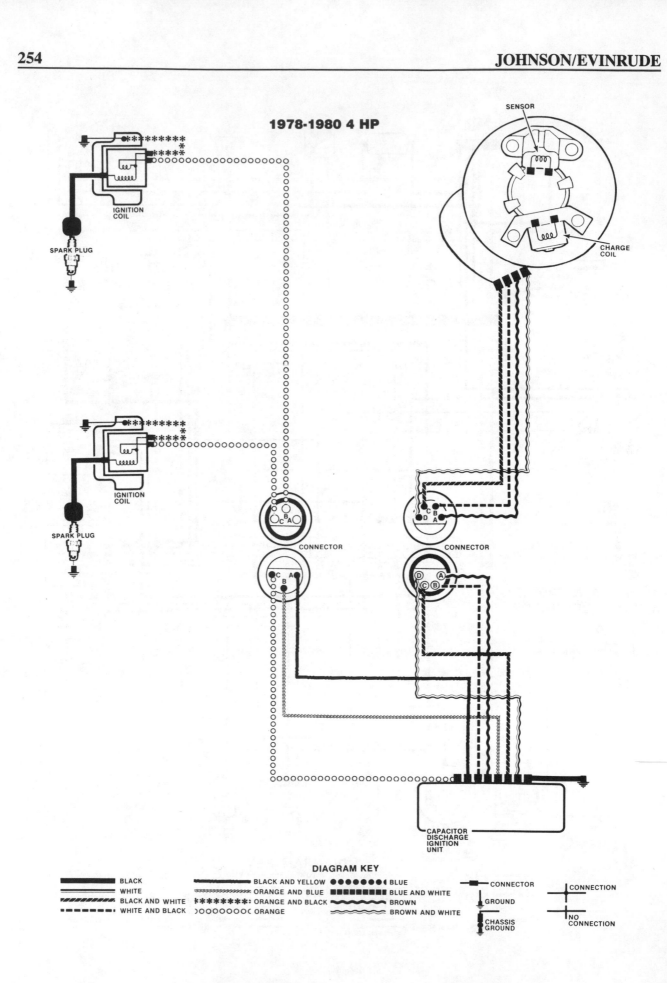

1978-1980 4 HP

DIAGRAM KEY

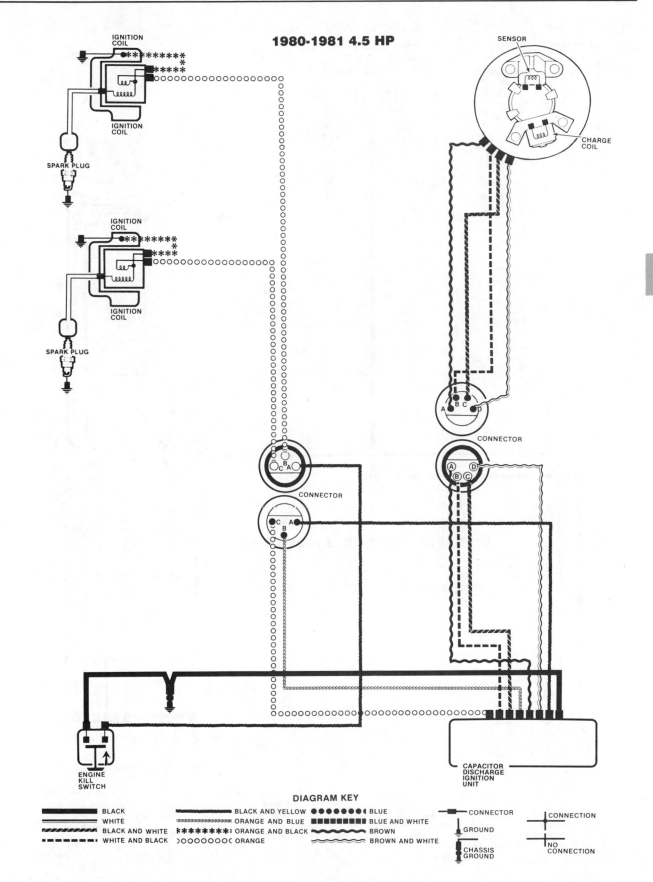

1980-1981 4.5 HP

IGNITION COIL

IGNITION COIL

SPARK PLUG

IGNITION COIL

IGNITION COIL

SPARK PLUG

SENSOR

CHARGE COIL

A B C D

CONNECTOR

C B A

CONNECTOR

A D
B C

C A
B

CONNECTOR

ENGINE KILL SWITCH

CAPACITOR DISCHARGE IGNITION UNIT

DIAGRAM KEY

BLACK	BLACK AND YELLOW	BLUE
WHITE	ORANGE AND BLUE	BLUE AND WHITE
BLACK AND WHITE	ORANGE AND BLACK	BROWN
WHITE AND BLACK	ORANGE	BROWN AND WHITE

CONNECTOR

GROUND

CHASSIS GROUND

CONNECTION

NO CONNECTION

4

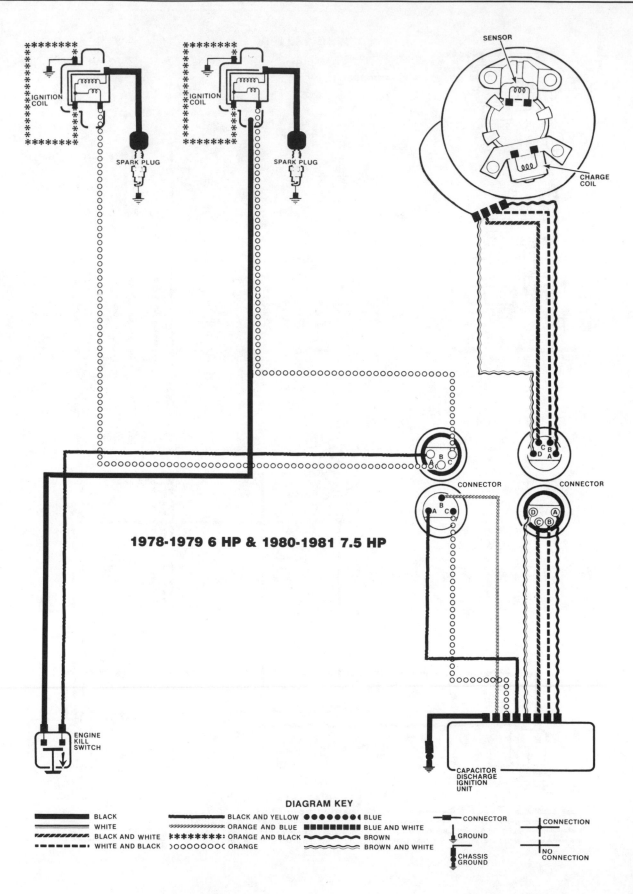

1978-1979 6 HP & 1980-1981 7.5 HP

SENSOR

CHARGE COIL

IGNITION COIL

IGNITION COIL

SPARK PLUG

SPARK PLUG

CONNECTOR

CONNECTOR

CONNECTOR

ENGINE KILL SWITCH

CAPACITOR DISCHARGE IGNITION UNIT

DIAGRAM KEY

BLACK	BLACK AND YELLOW	BLUE
WHITE	ORANGE AND BLUE	BLUE AND WHITE
BLACK AND WHITE	ORANGE AND BLACK	BROWN
WHITE AND BLACK	ORANGE	BROWN AND WHITE

CONNECTOR

GROUND

CHASSIS GROUND

CONNECTION

NO CONNECTION

1982-1984 4-35 HP MANUAL START

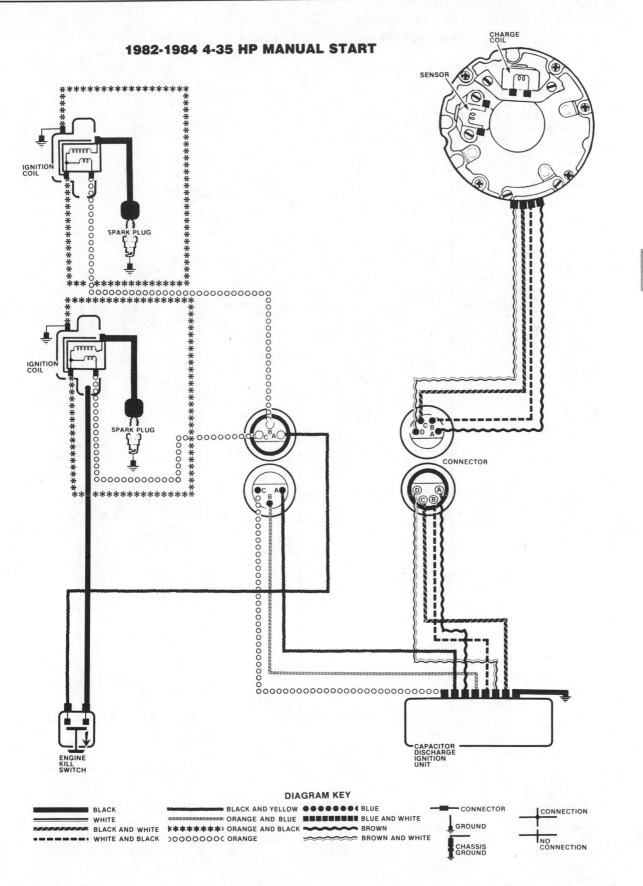

DIAGRAM KEY

▬▬▬ BLACK	∿∿∿ BLACK AND YELLOW	●●●●●● BLUE
═══ WHITE	≋≋≋ ORANGE AND BLUE	■■■■■ BLUE AND WHITE
▨▨▨ BLACK AND WHITE	✶✶✶✶ ORANGE AND BLACK	∿∿∿ BROWN
▬ ▬ ▬ WHITE AND BLACK	○○○○○ ORANGE	≈≈≈ BROWN AND WHITE

CONNECTOR

GROUND

CHASSIS GROUND

CONNECTION

NO CONNECTION

4

IGNITION COIL

SPARK PLUG

IGNITION COIL

SPARK PLUG

ENGINE KILL SWITCH

CHARGE COIL

SENSOR

CONNECTOR

CAPACITOR DISCHARGE IGNITION UNIT

1984 5-35 HP MANUAL START/AC LIGHTING

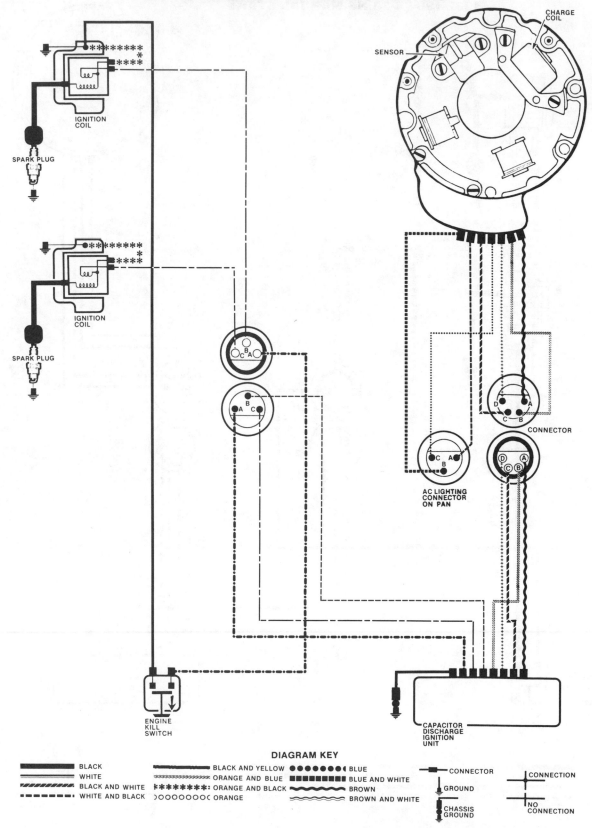

SENSOR

CHARGE COIL

IGNITION COIL

SPARK PLUG

IGNITION COIL

SPARK PLUG

CONNECTOR

AC LIGHTING CONNECTOR ON PAN

ENGINE KILL SWITCH

CAPACITOR DISCHARGE IGNITION UNIT

DIAGRAM KEY

BLACK	BLACK AND YELLOW	BLUE
WHITE	ORANGE AND BLUE	BLUE AND WHITE
BLACK AND WHITE	ORANGE AND BLACK	BROWN
WHITE AND BLACK	ORANGE	BROWN AND WHITE

CONNECTOR

GROUND

CHASSIS GROUND

CONNECTION

NO CONNECTION

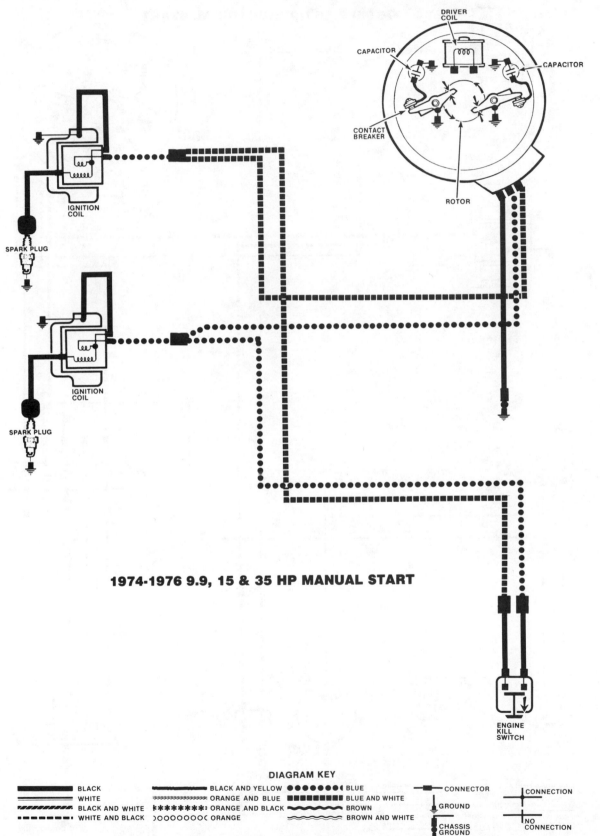

1974-1976 9.9, 15 & 35 HP MANUAL START

DIAGRAM KEY

BLACK	BLACK AND YELLOW	BLUE	CONNECTOR
WHITE	ORANGE AND BLUE	BLUE AND WHITE	CONNECTION
BLACK AND WHITE	ORANGE AND BLACK	BROWN	GROUND
WHITE AND BLACK	ORANGE	BROWN AND WHITE	CHASSIS GROUND
			NO CONNECTION

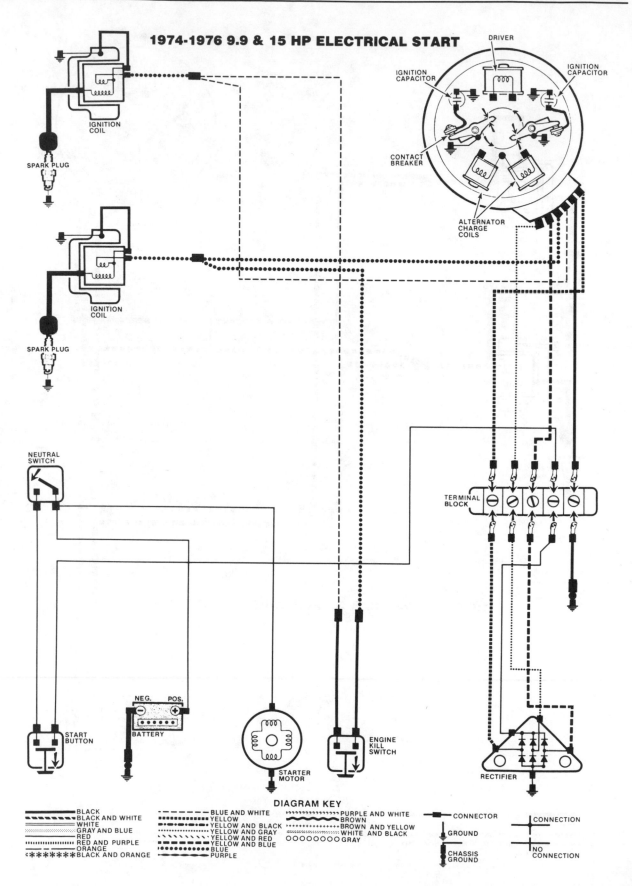

1974-1976 9.9 & 15 HP ELECTRICAL START

DRIVER

IGNITION CAPACITOR

IGNITION CAPACITOR

CONTACT BREAKER

ALTERNATOR CHARGE COILS

IGNITION COIL

SPARK PLUG

IGNITION COIL

SPARK PLUG

NEUTRAL SWITCH

TERMINAL BLOCK

START BUTTON

NEG.   POS.

BATTERY

STARTER MOTOR

ENGINE KILL SWITCH

RECTIFIER

DIAGRAM KEY

BLACK	BLUE AND WHITE
BLACK AND WHITE	YELLOW
WHITE	YELLOW AND BLACK
GRAY AND BLUE	YELLOW AND GRAY
RED	YELLOW AND RED
RED AND PURPLE	YELLOW AND BLUE
ORANGE	BLUE
BLACK AND ORANGE	PURPLE

PURPLE AND WHITE
BROWN
BROWN AND YELLOW
WHITE AND BLACK
GRAY

CONNECTOR

GROUND

CHASSIS GROUND

CONNECTION

NO CONNECTION

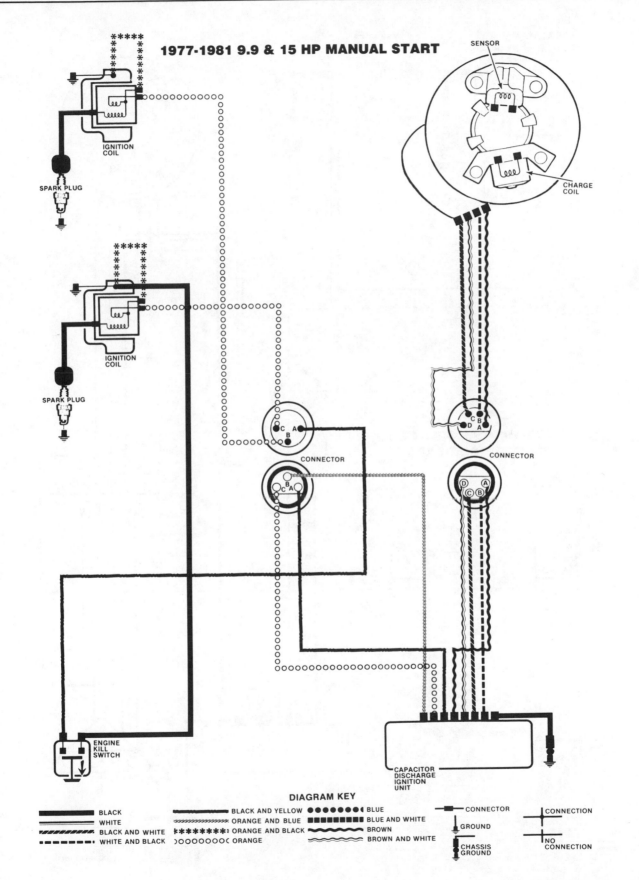

1977-1981 9.9 & 15 HP MANUAL START

SENSOR

CHARGE COIL

IGNITION COIL

SPARK PLUG

IGNITION COIL

SPARK PLUG

CONNECTOR

CONNECTOR

ENGINE KILL SWITCH

CAPACITOR DISCHARGE IGNITION UNIT

DIAGRAM KEY

BLACK	BLACK AND YELLOW	BLUE
WHITE	ORANGE AND BLUE	BLUE AND WHITE
BLACK AND WHITE	ORANGE AND BLACK	BROWN
WHITE AND BLACK	ORANGE	BROWN AND WHITE

CONNECTOR

GROUND

CHASSIS GROUND

CONNECTION

NO CONNECTION

4

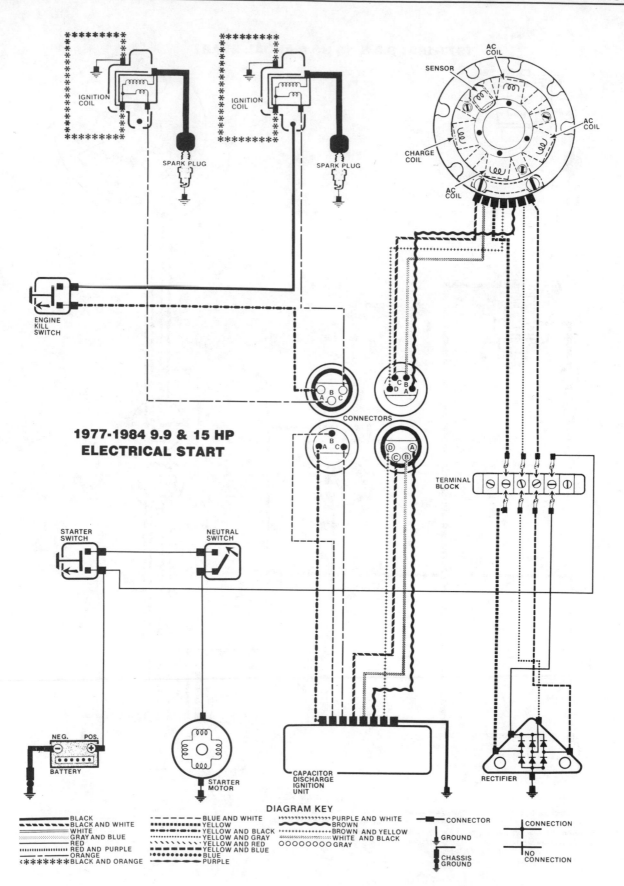

1977-1984 9.9 & 15 HP ELECTRICAL START

DIAGRAM KEY

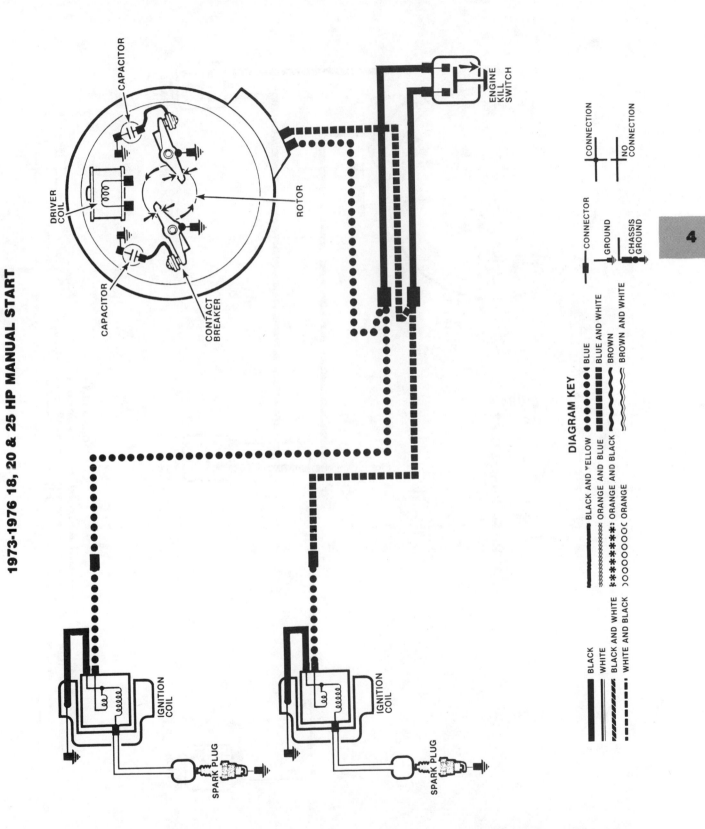

1973-1976 18, 20 & 25 HP MANUAL START

CAPACITOR

CAPACITOR

DRIVER COIL

CONTACT BREAKER

ROTOR

ENGINE KILL SWITCH

IGNITION COIL

IGNITION COIL

SPARK PLUG

SPARK PLUG

DIAGRAM KEY

BLACK

WHITE

BLACK AND WHITE

WHITE AND BLACK

BLACK AND YELLOW

ORANGE AND BLUE

ORANGE AND BLACK

ORANGE

BLUE

BLUE AND WHITE

BROWN

BROWN AND WHITE

CONNECTION

NO CONNECTION

CONNECTOR

GROUND

CHASSIS GROUND

4

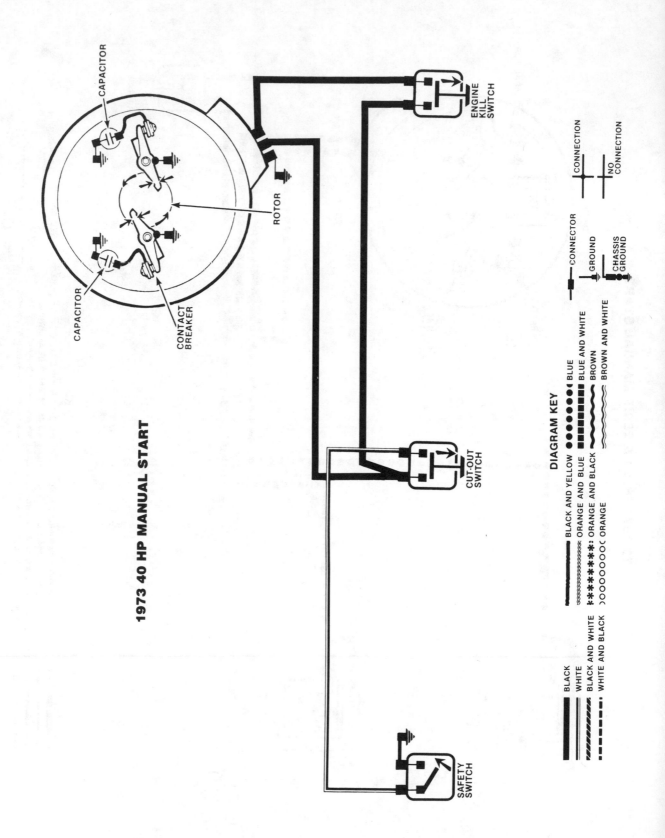

1973 40 HP MANUAL START

CAPACITOR

CAPACITOR

CONTACT BREAKER

ROTOR

ENGINE KILL SWITCH

CUT-OUT SWITCH

SAFETY SWITCH

DIAGRAM KEY

BLACK

WHITE

BLACK AND WHITE

WHITE AND BLACK

BLACK AND YELLOW

ORANGE AND BLUE

ORANGE AND BLACK

ORANGE

BLUE

BLUE AND WHITE

BROWN

BROWN AND WHITE

CONNECTION

NO CONNECTION

CONNECTOR

GROUND

CHASSIS GROUND

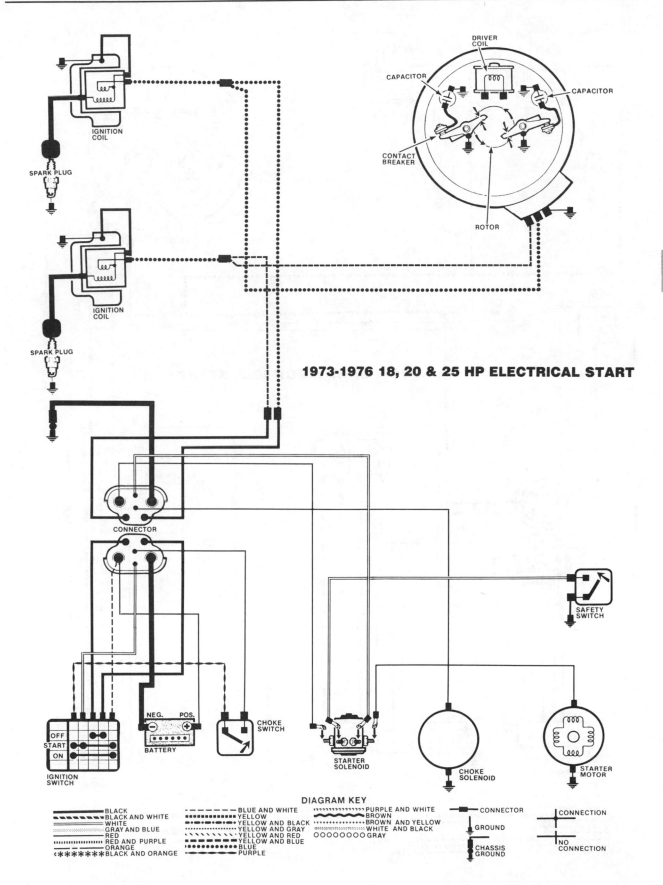

1973-1976 18, 20 & 25 HP ELECTRICAL START

4

SPARK PLUG

IGNITION COIL

SPARK PLUG

IGNITION COIL

DRIVER COIL

CAPACITOR

CAPACITOR

CONTACT BREAKER

ROTOR

CONNECTOR

SAFETY SWITCH

OFF
START
ON

IGNITION SWITCH

NEG. POS.

BATTERY

CHOKE SWITCH

STARTER SOLENOID

CHOKE SOLENOID

STARTER MOTOR

DIAGRAM KEY

BLACK	BLUE AND WHITE	PURPLE AND WHITE
BLACK AND WHITE	YELLOW	BROWN
WHITE	YELLOW AND BLACK	BROWN AND YELLOW
GRAY AND BLUE	YELLOW AND GRAY	WHITE AND BLACK
RED	YELLOW AND RED	GRAY
RED AND PURPLE	YELLOW AND BLUE	
ORANGE	BLUE	
BLACK AND ORANGE	PURPLE	

CONNECTOR

GROUND

CHASSIS GROUND

CONNECTION

NO CONNECTION

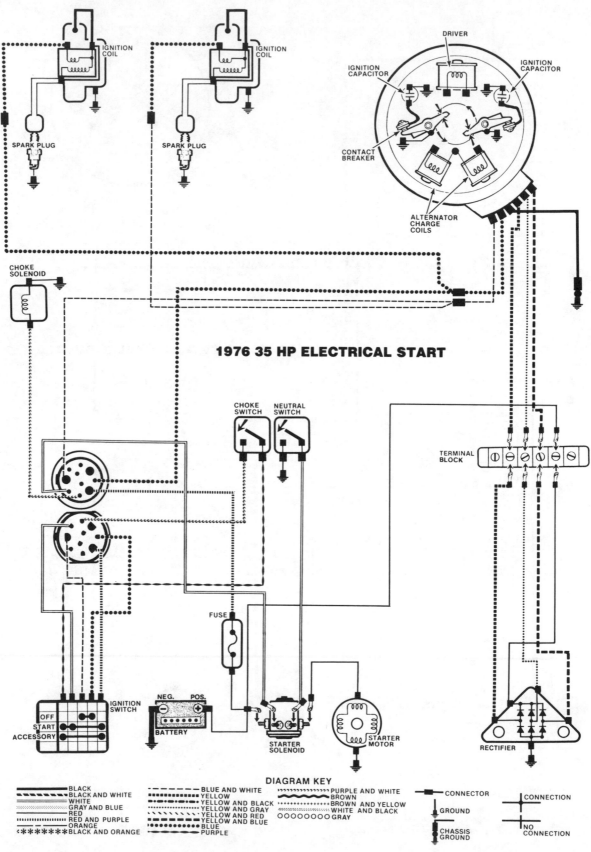

1976 35 HP ELECTRICAL START

DIAGRAM KEY

BLACK	BLUE AND WHITE	PURPLE AND WHITE	CONNECTOR
BLACK AND WHITE	YELLOW	BROWN	GROUND
WHITE	YELLOW AND BLACK	BROWN AND YELLOW	
GRAY AND BLUE	YELLOW AND GRAY	WHITE AND BLACK	CONNECTION
RED	YELLOW AND RED	GRAY	CHASSIS GROUND
RED AND PURPLE	YELLOW AND BLUE		NO CONNECTION
ORANGE	BLUE		
BLACK AND ORANGE	PURPLE		

1977-1981 25 HP MANUAL START

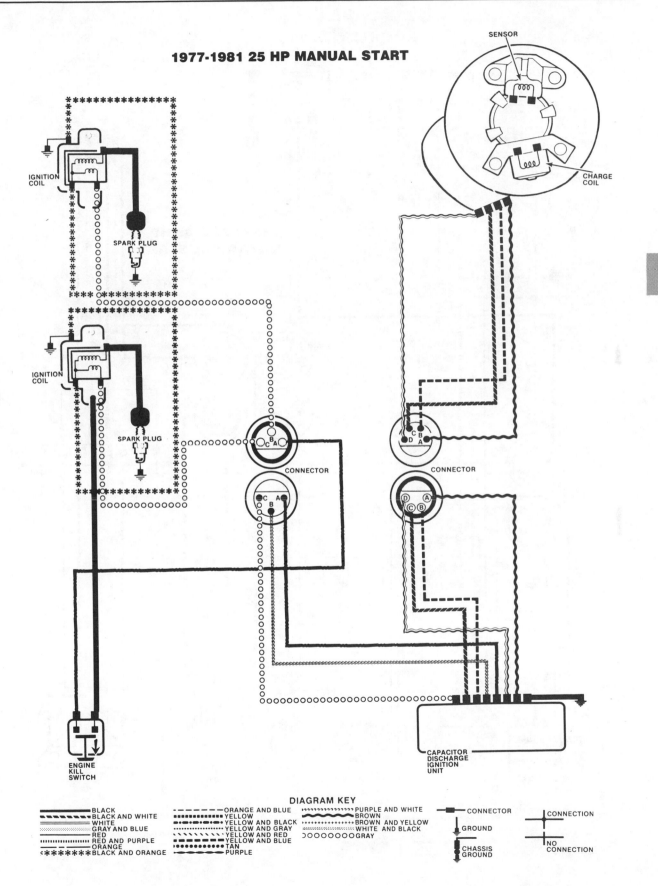

DIAGRAM KEY

──── BLACK	ORANGE AND BLUE	PURPLE AND WHITE	CONNECTOR	CONNECTION
BLACK AND WHITE	YELLOW	BROWN		
WHITE	YELLOW AND BLACK	BROWN AND YELLOW	GROUND	
GRAY AND BLUE	YELLOW AND GRAY	WHITE AND BLACK		NO
RED	YELLOW AND RED	GRAY	CHASSIS	CONNECTION
RED AND PURPLE	YELLOW AND BLUE		GROUND	
ORANGE	TAN			
BLACK AND ORANGE	PURPLE			

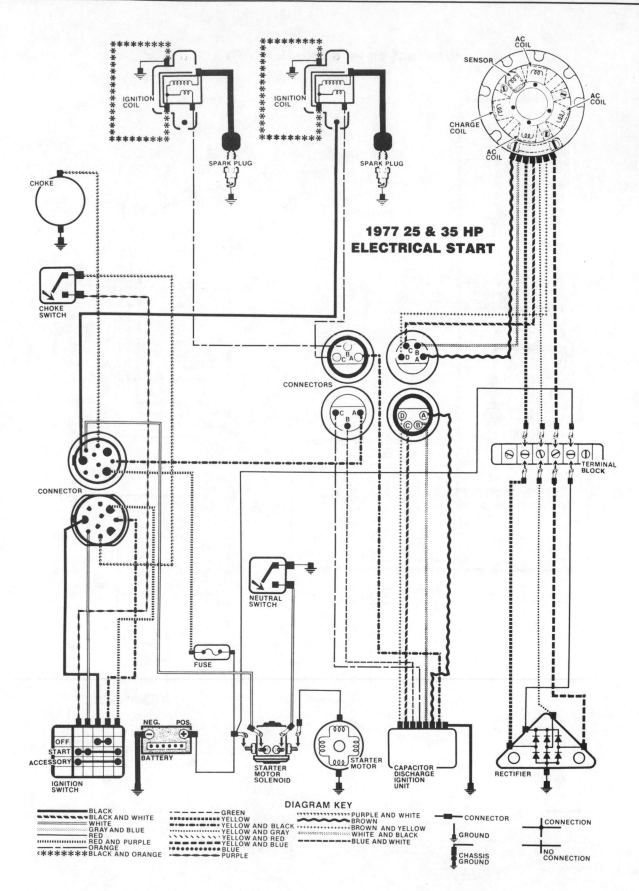

1977 25 & 35 HP ELECTRICAL START

DIAGRAM KEY

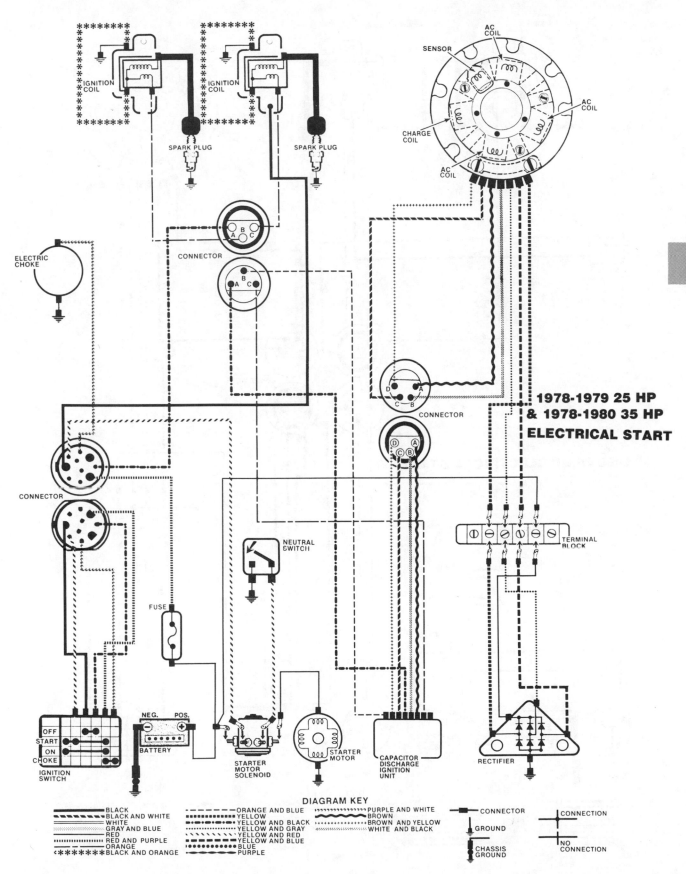

1978-1979 25 HP
& 1978-1980 35 HP
ELECTRICAL START

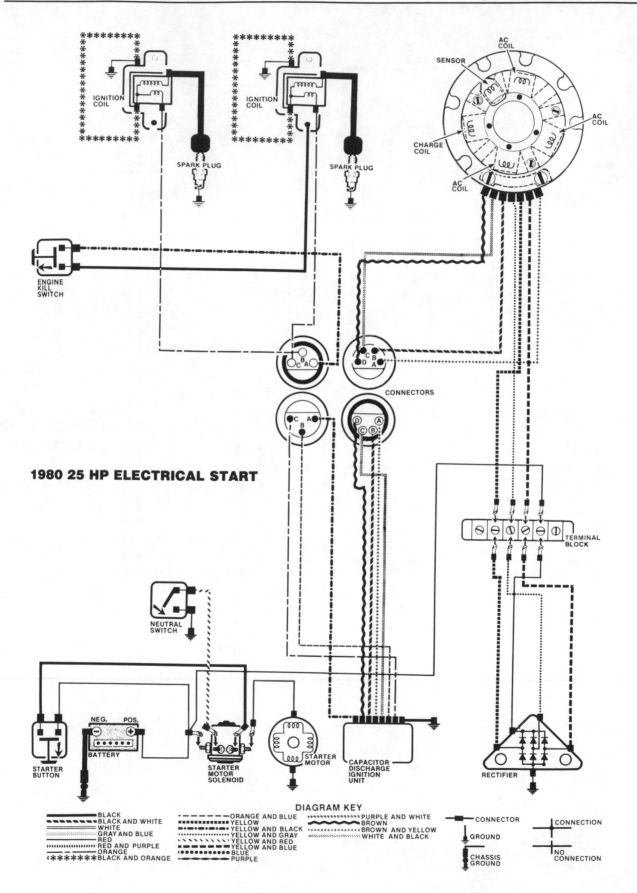

1980 25 HP ELECTRICAL START

DIAGRAM KEY

BLACK	ORANGE AND BLUE	PURPLE AND WHITE	CONNECTOR
BLACK AND WHITE	YELLOW	BROWN	GROUND
WHITE	YELLOW AND BLACK	BROWN AND YELLOW	CONNECTION
GRAY AND BLUE	YELLOW AND GRAY	WHITE AND BLACK	CHASSIS GROUND
RED	YELLOW AND RED		NO CONNECTION
RED AND PURPLE	YELLOW AND BLUE		
ORANGE	BLUE		
BLACK AND ORANGE	PURPLE		

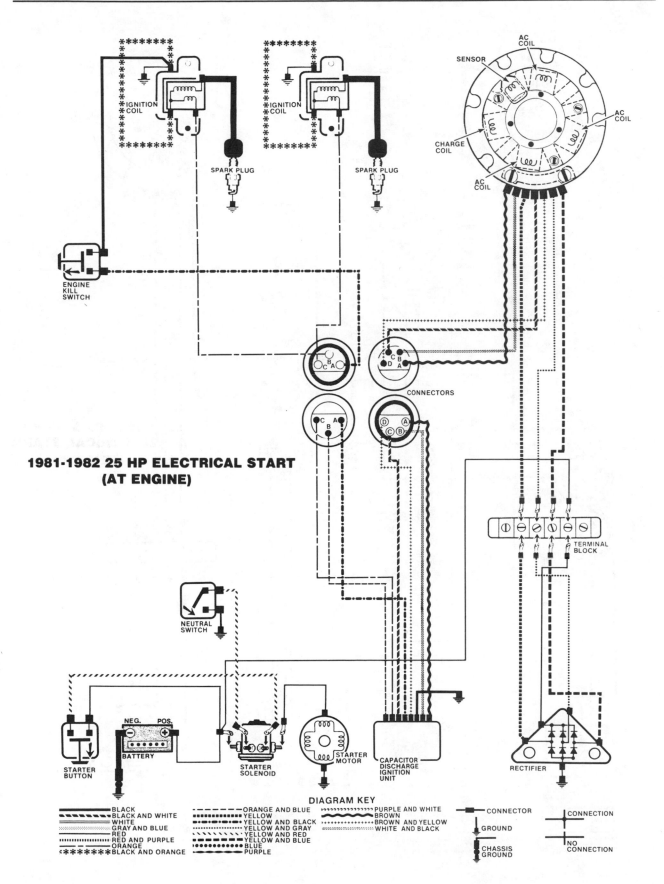

1981-1982 25 HP ELECTRICAL START (AT ENGINE)

DIAGRAM KEY

BLACK
BLACK AND WHITE
WHITE
GRAY AND BLUE
RED
RED AND PURPLE
ORANGE
BLACK AND ORANGE

ORANGE AND BLUE
YELLOW
YELLOW AND BLACK
YELLOW AND GRAY
YELLOW AND RED
YELLOW AND BLUE
BLUE
PURPLE

PURPLE AND WHITE
BROWN
BROWN AND YELLOW
WHITE AND BLACK

CONNECTOR
GROUND
CHASSIS GROUND

CONNECTION
NO CONNECTION

4

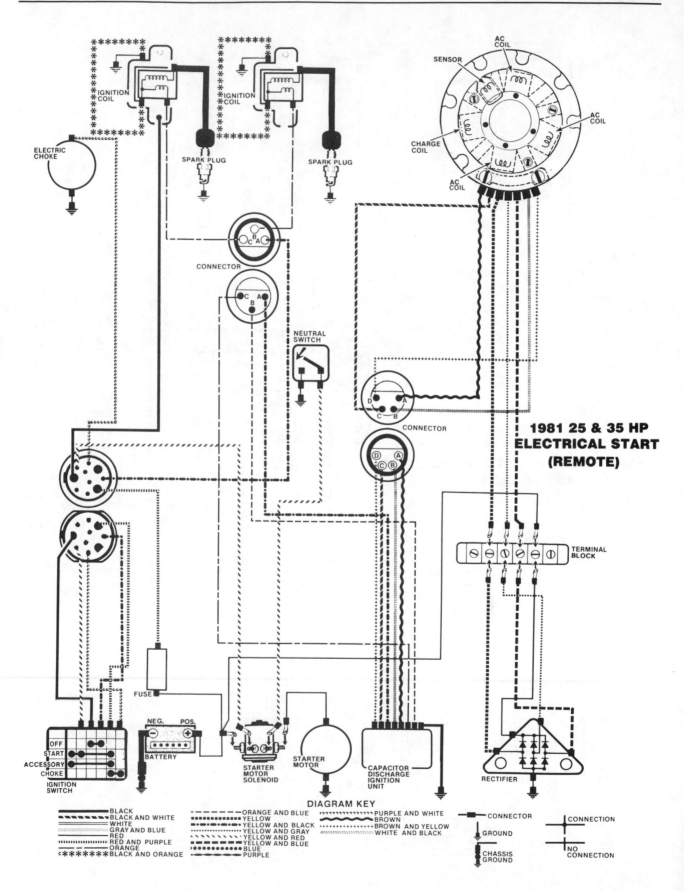

1981 25 & 35 HP
ELECTRICAL START
(REMOTE)

DIAGRAM KEY

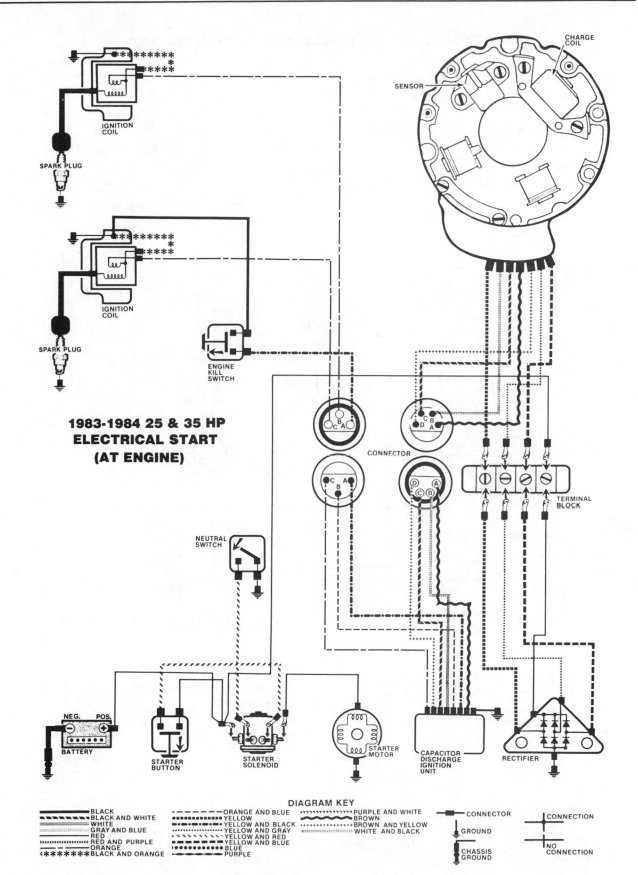

1983-1984 25 & 35 HP ELECTRICAL START (AT ENGINE)

DIAGRAM KEY

1982-1984 20, 25 & 35 HP ELECTRICAL START (REMOTE)

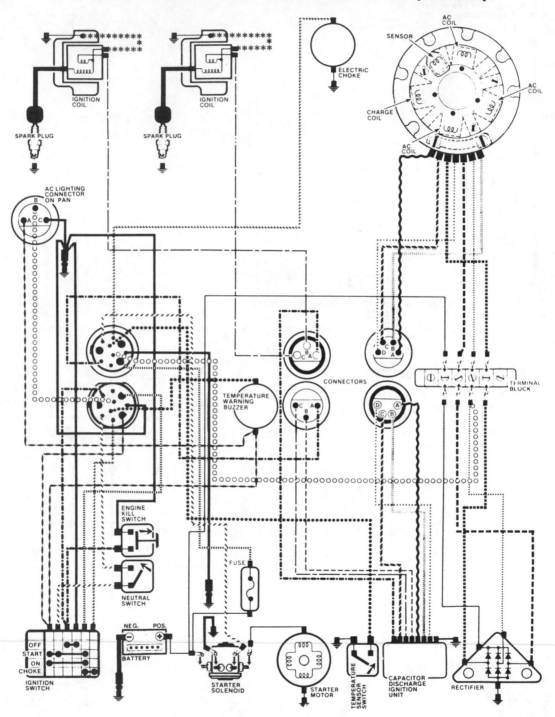

DIAGRAM KEY

———— BLACK	– – – – ORANGE AND BLUE
＝＝＝＝＝ BLACK AND WHITE	▪▪▪▪▪▪ YELLOW
———— WHITE	▪-▪-▪- YELLOW AND BLACK
▨▨▨▨▨ GRAY AND BLUE	////// YELLOW AND GRAY
———— RED	\\\\\\ YELLOW AND RED
▪▪▪▪▪▪ RED AND PURPLE	●●●●●● YELLOW AND BLUE
– – – – ORANGE	●●●●●● TAN
✱✱✱✱✱✱ BLACK AND ORANGE	———— PURPLE

‹‹‹‹‹ PURPLE AND WHITE	
∿∿∿∿ BROWN	
+++++ BROWN AND YELLOW	
♦♦♦♦♦ WHITE AND BLACK	
○○○○○○ GRAY	

▬■ CONNECTOR	┼ CONNECTION
▼ GROUND	
▮ CHASSIS GROUND	┴┬ NO CONNECTION

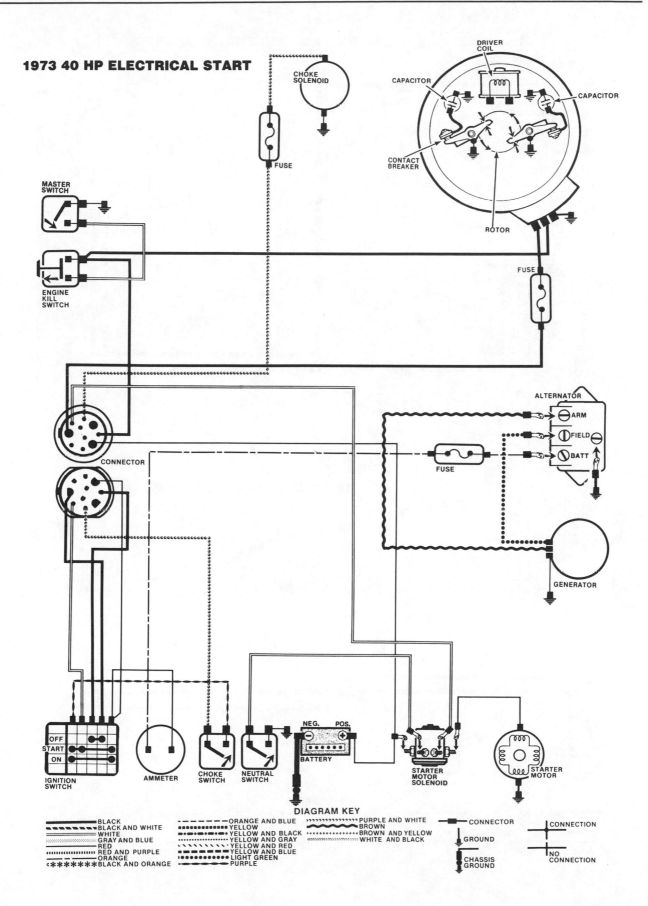

1973 40 HP ELECTRICAL START

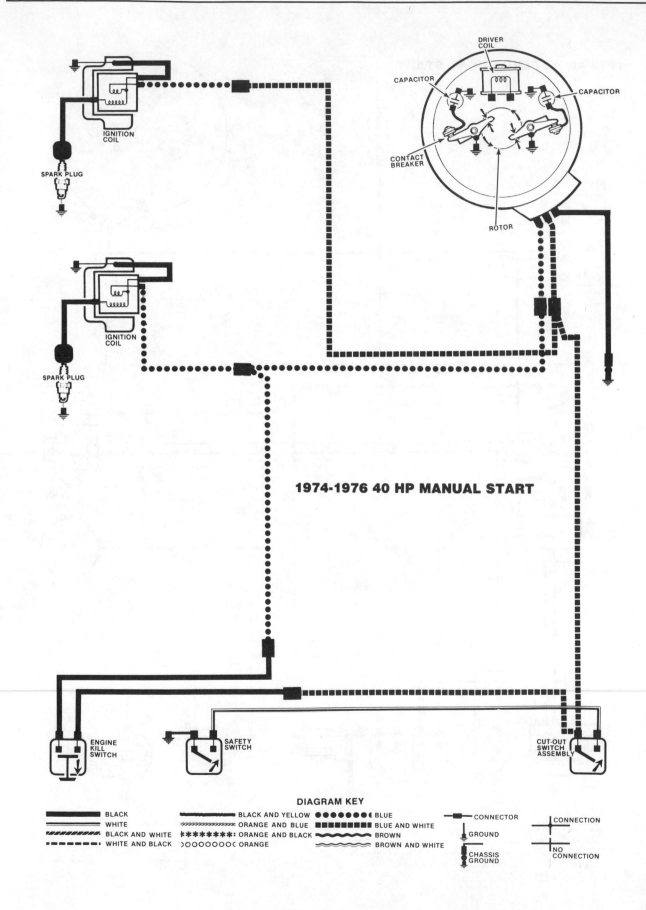

DRIVER COIL

CAPACITOR

CAPACITOR

CONTACT BREAKER

ROTOR

IGNITION COIL

SPARK PLUG

IGNITION COIL

SPARK PLUG

1974-1976 40 HP MANUAL START

ENGINE KILL SWITCH

SAFETY SWITCH

CUT-OUT SWITCH ASSEMBLY

DIAGRAM KEY

BLACK	BLACK AND YELLOW	BLUE
WHITE	ORANGE AND BLUE	BLUE AND WHITE
BLACK AND WHITE	ORANGE AND BLACK	BROWN
WHITE AND BLACK	ORANGE	BROWN AND WHITE

CONNECTOR

GROUND

CHASSIS GROUND

CONNECTION

NO CONNECTION

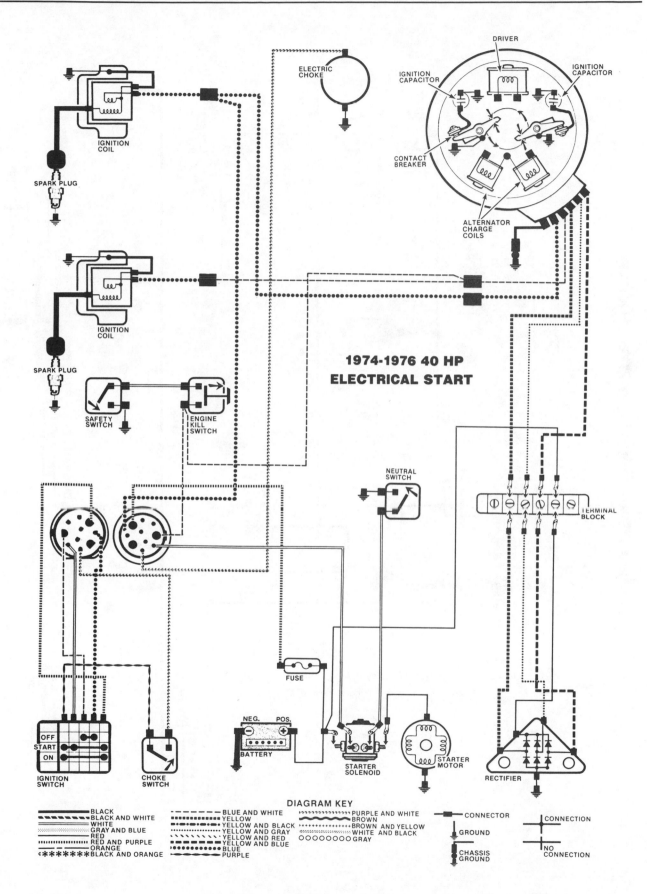

1974-1976 40 HP
ELECTRICAL START

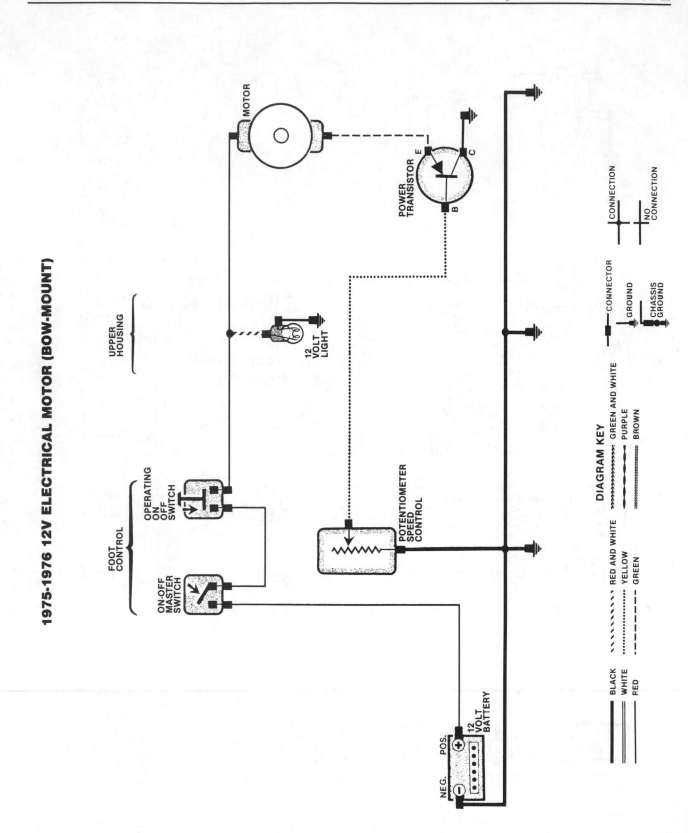

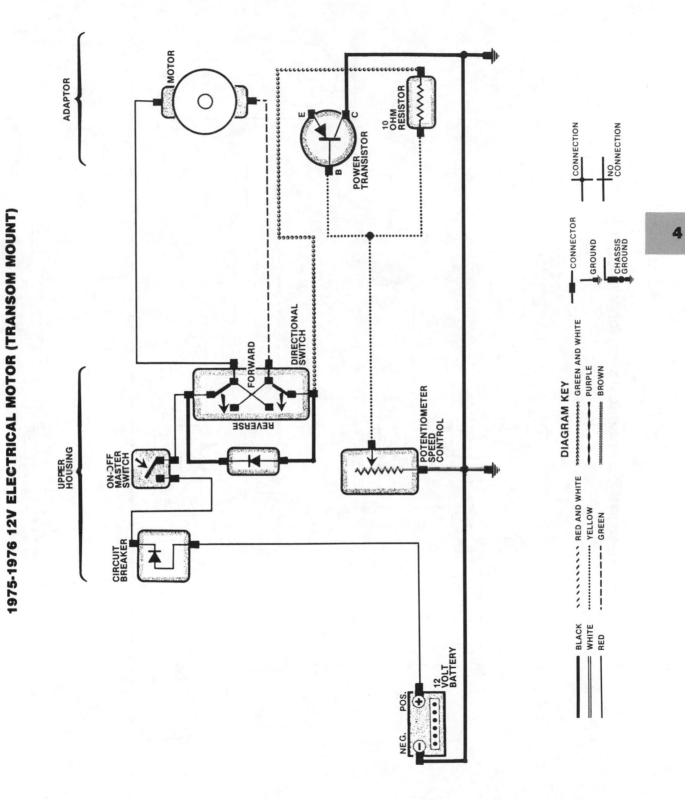

1975-1976 12V ELECTRICAL MOTOR (TRANSOM MOUNT)

ADAPTOR

MOTOR

POWER TRANSISTOR

10 OHM RESISTOR

E   C

B

UPPER HOUSING

FORWARD

DIRECTIONAL SWITCH

REVERSE

ON-OFF MASTER SWITCH

POTENTIOMETER SPEED CONTROL

CIRCUIT BREAKER

NEG.   POS.

12 VOLT BATTERY

DIAGRAM KEY

CONNECTION

NO CONNECTION

CONNECTOR

GROUND

CHASSIS GROUND

GREEN AND WHITE

PURPLE

BROWN

RED AND WHITE

YELLOW

GREEN

BLACK

WHITE

RED

4

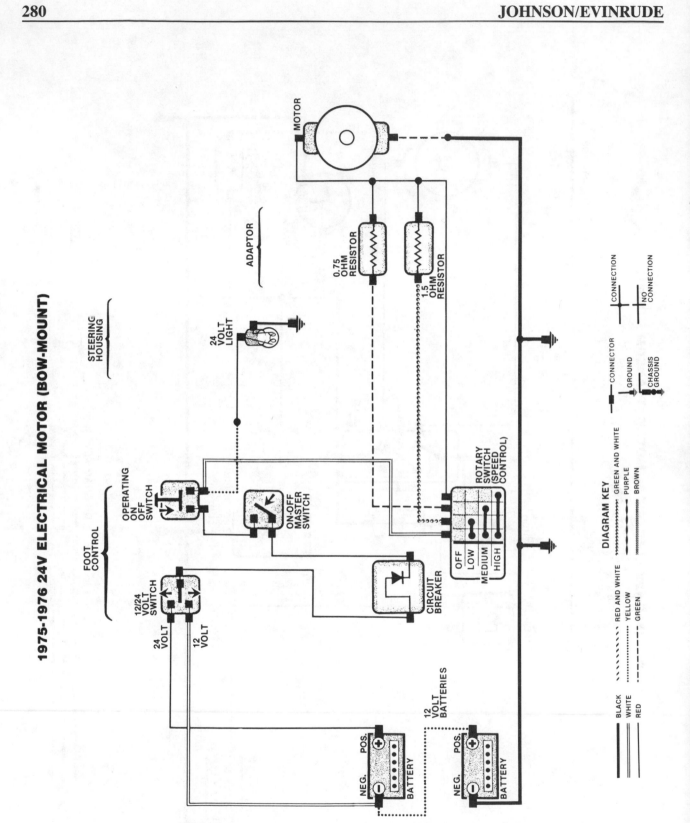

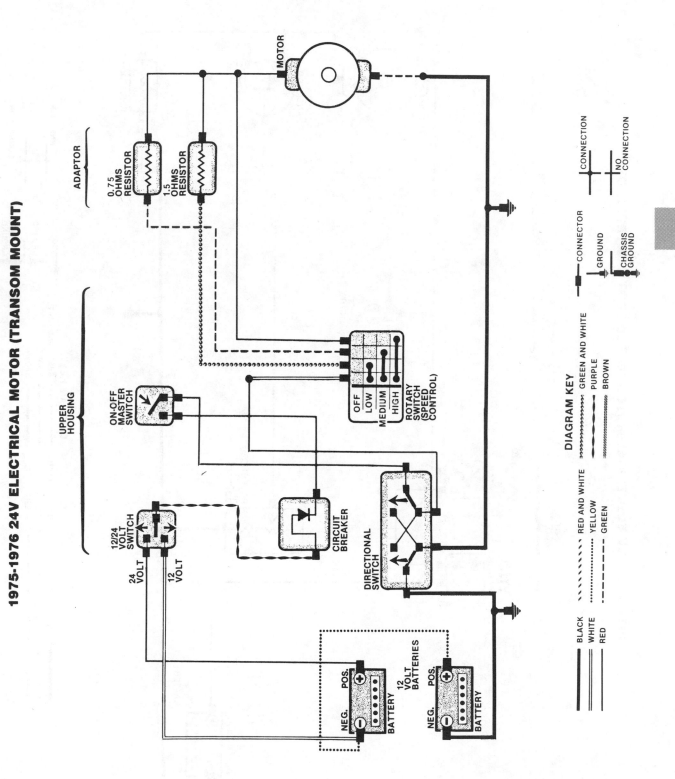

1975-1976 24V ELECTRICAL MOTOR (TRANSOM MOUNT)

ADAPTOR

0.75 OHMS RESISTOR

1.5 OHMS RESISTOR

MOTOR

CONNECTION

NO CONNECTION

CONNECTOR

GROUND

CHASSIS GROUND

UPPER HOUSING

ON-OFF MASTER SWITCH

OFF
LOW
MEDIUM
HIGH

ROTARY SWITCH (SPEED CONTROL)

12/24 VOLT SWITCH

24 VOLT

12 VOLT

CIRCUIT BREAKER

DIRECTIONAL SWITCH

DIAGRAM KEY

BLACK
WHITE
RED
RED AND WHITE
YELLOW
GREEN
GREEN AND WHITE
PURPLE
BROWN

4

BATTERY

12 VOLT BATTERIES

NEG. POS.

BATTERY

NEG. POS.

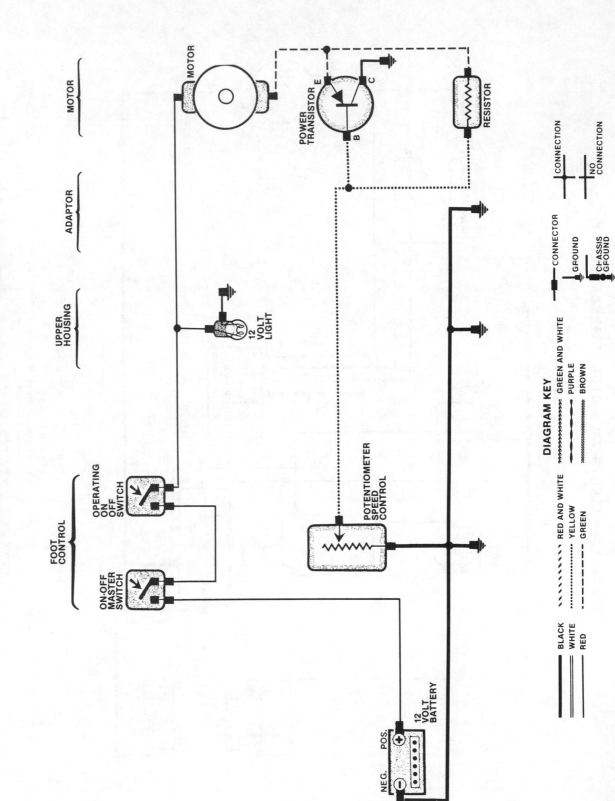

1977-1981 12V ELECTRICAL MOTOR (SPEED-FOOT CONTROLLED)

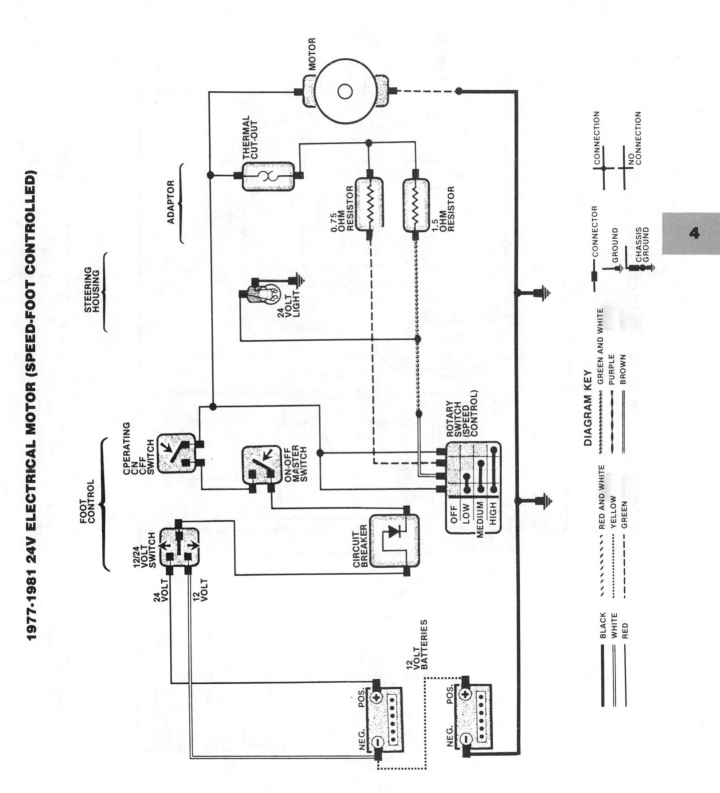

1977-1981 24V ELECTRICAL MOTOR (SPEED-FOOT CONTROLLED)

MOTOR

ADAPTOR

THERMAL CUT-OUT

STEERING HOUSING

0.75 OHM RESISTOR

1.5 OHM RESISTOR

24 VOLT LIGHT

OPERATING ON OFF SWITCH

ON-OFF MASTER SWITCH

ROTARY SWITCH (SPEED CONTROL)

OFF LOW MEDIUM HIGH

FOOT CONTROL

12/24 VOLT SWITCH

24 VOLT

12 VOLT

CIRCUIT BREAKER

12 VOLT BATTERIES

POS. NEG.

POS. NEG.

DIAGRAM KEY

CONNECTION

NO CONNECTION

CONNECTOR

GROUND

CHASSIS GROUND

GREEN AND WHITE

PURPLE

BROWN

RED AND WHITE

YELLOW

GREEN

BLACK

WHITE

RED

4

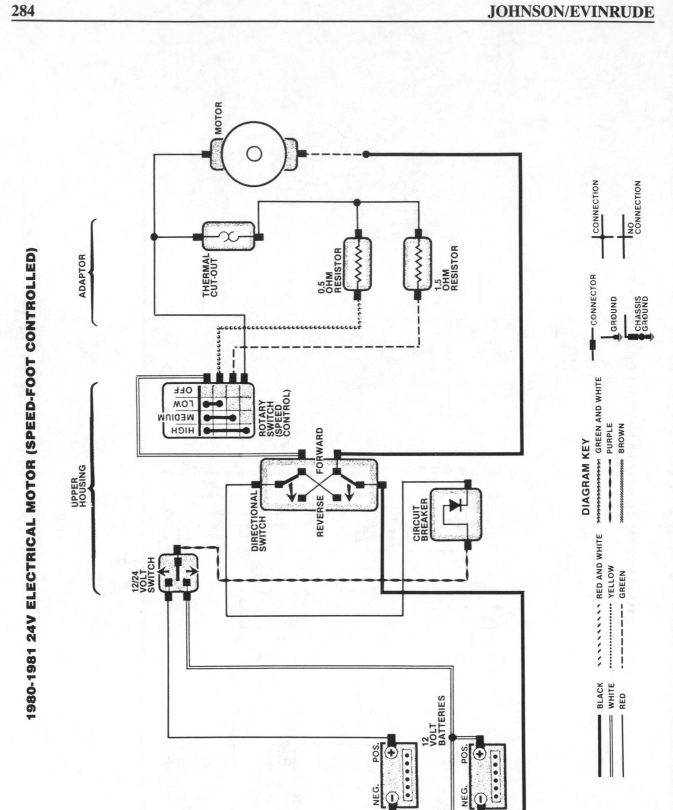

1980-1981 24V ELECTRICAL MOTOR (SPEED-FOOT CONTROLLED)

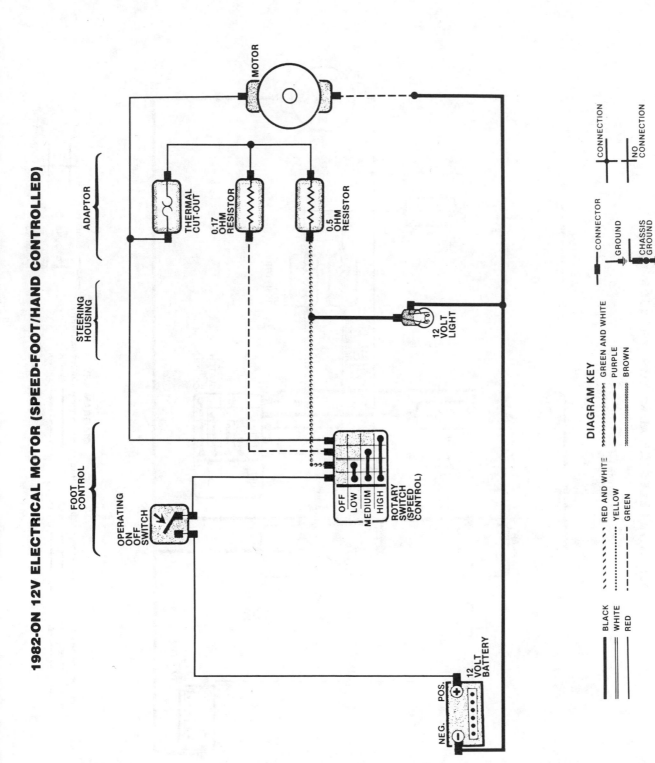

1982-ON 12V ELECTRICAL MOTOR (SPEED-FOOT/HAND CONTROLLED)

MOTOR

ADAPTOR

THERMAL CUT-OUT

0.17 OHM RESISTOR

0.5 OHM RESISTOR

STEERING HOUSING

12 VOLT LIGHT

FOOT CONTROL

OPERATING ON OFF SWITCH

OFF
LOW
MEDIUM
HIGH

ROTARY SWITCH (SPEED CONTROL)

12 VOLT BATTERY

NEG.
POS.

DIAGRAM KEY

CONNECTION

NO CONNECTION

CONNECTOR

GROUND

CHASSIS GROUND

BLACK

WHITE

RED

RED AND WHITE

YELLOW

GREEN

GREEN AND WHITE

PURPLE

BROWN

4

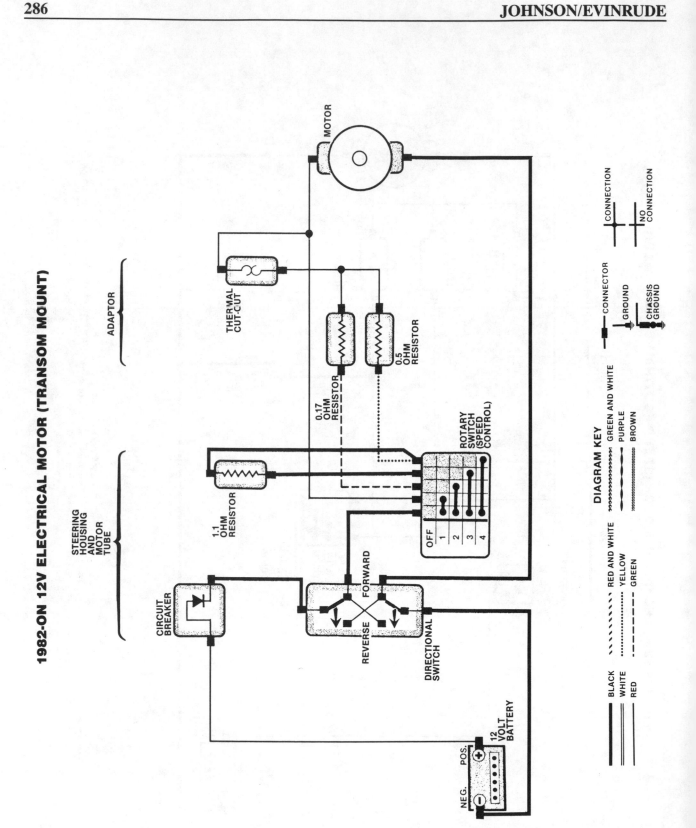

1982-ON 12V ELECTRICAL MOTOR (TRANSOM MOUNT)

MOTOR

ADAPTOR

THERMAL CUT-CUT

0.17 OHM RESISTOR

0.5 OHM RESISTOR

STEERING HOUSING AND MOTOR TUBE

1.1 OHM RESISTOR

ROTARY SWITCH (SPEED CONTROL)

OFF
1
2
3
4

CIRCUIT BREAKER

FORWARD

REVERSE

DIRECTIONAL SWITCH

NEG. POS.

12 VOLT BATTERY

DIAGRAM KEY

BLACK

WHITE

RED

RED AND WHITE

YELLOW

GREEN

GREEN AND WHITE

PURPLE

BROWN

CONNECTOR

GROUND

CHASSIS GROUND

CONNECTION

NO CONNECTION

1982-ON 12/24V ELECTRICAL MOTOR (SPEED-FOOT CONTROLLED)

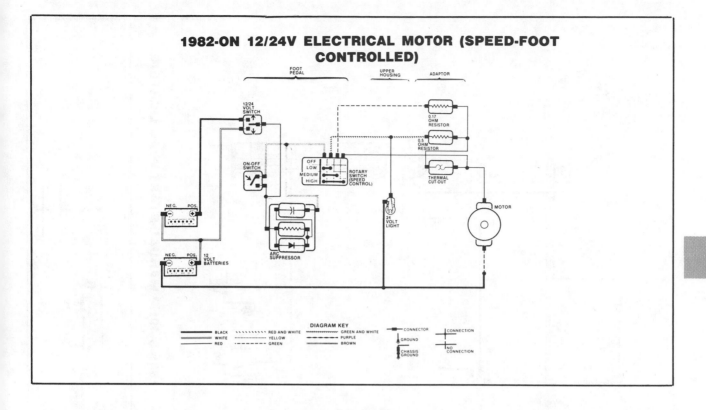

1982-ON 12/24V ELECTRICAL MOTOR (SPEED-HAND CONTROLLED)

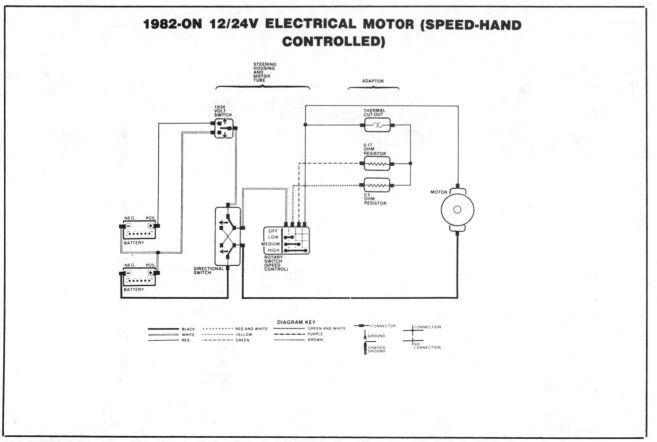

4

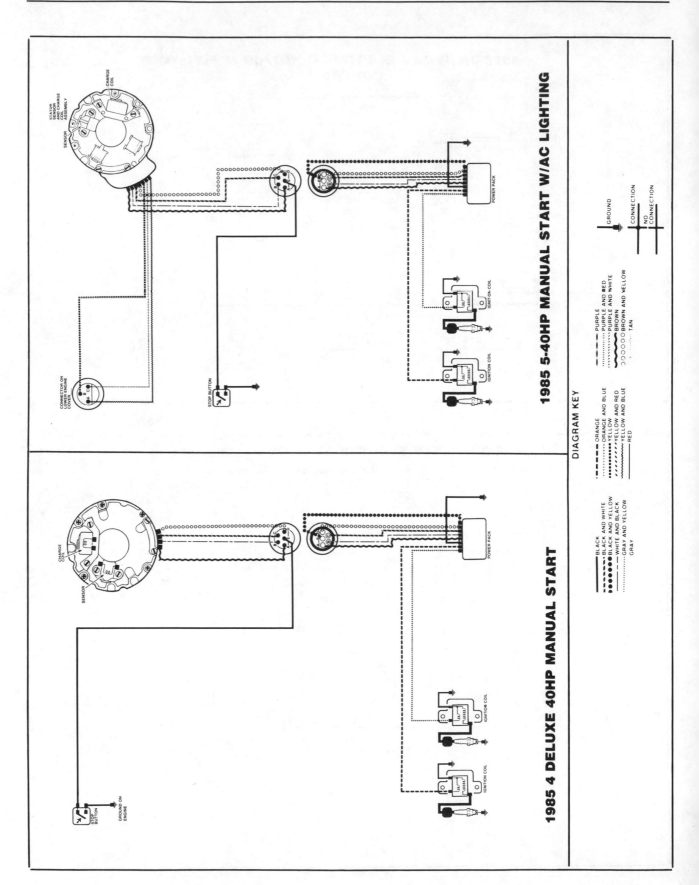

1985 5-40HP MANUAL START W/AC LIGHTING

1985 4 DELUXE 40HP MANUAL START

DIAGRAM KEY

BLACK
BLACK AND WHITE
BLACK AND YELLOW
WHITE AND BLACK
GRAY AND YELLOW
GRAY

ORANGE
ORANGE AND BLUE
YELLOW
YELLOW AND RED
YELLOW AND BLUE
RED

PURPLE AND RED
PURPLE AND WHITE
PURPLE AND WHITE
BROWN
BROWN AND YELLOW
TAN

GROUND

CONNECTION

NO
CONNECTION

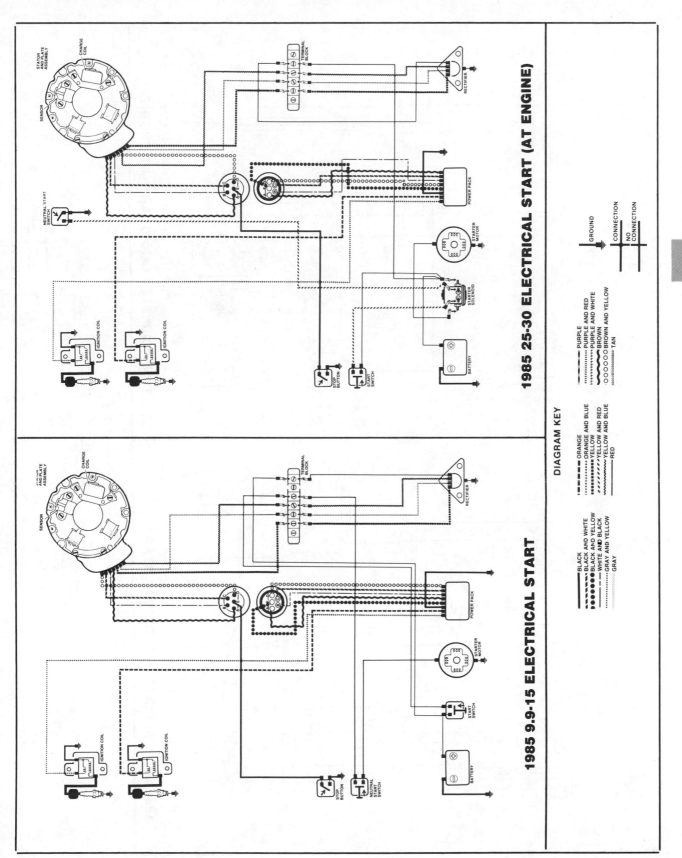

1985 25-30 ELECTRICAL START (AT ENGINE)

1985 9.9-15 ELECTRICAL START

DIAGRAM KEY

GROUND

CONNECTION

NO CONNECTION

4

BLACK
BLACK AND WHITE
BLACK AND YELLOW
WHITE AND BLACK
GRAY AND YELLOW
GRAY

ORANGE
ORANGE AND BLUE
YELLOW
YELLOW AND RED
YELLOW AND BLUE
RED

PURPLE
PURPLE AND RED
PURPLE AND WHITE
BROWN
BROWN AND YELLOW
TAN

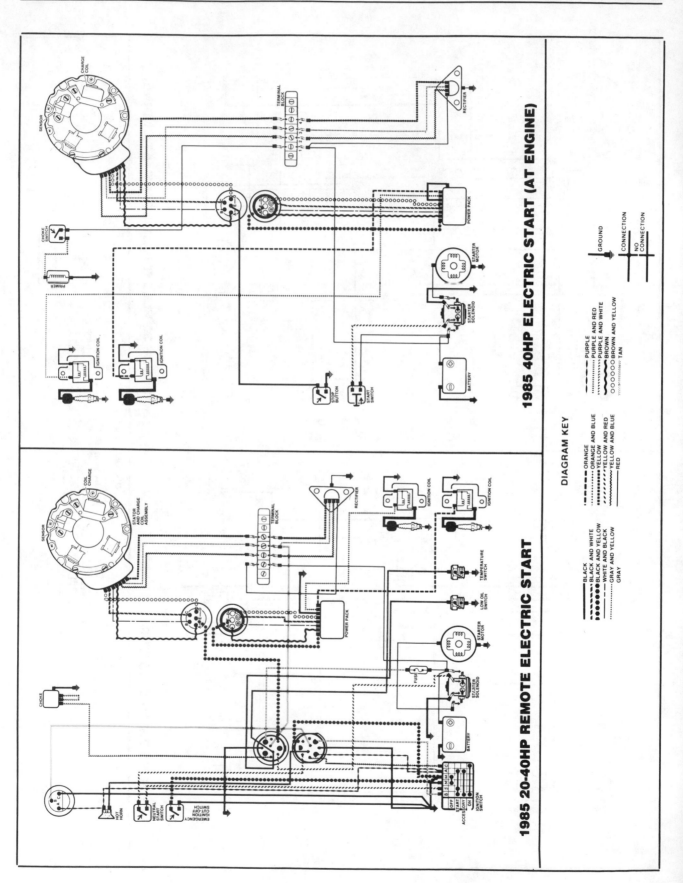

1985 40HP ELECTRIC START (AT ENGINE)

1985 20-40HP REMOTE ELECTRIC START

DIAGRAM KEY

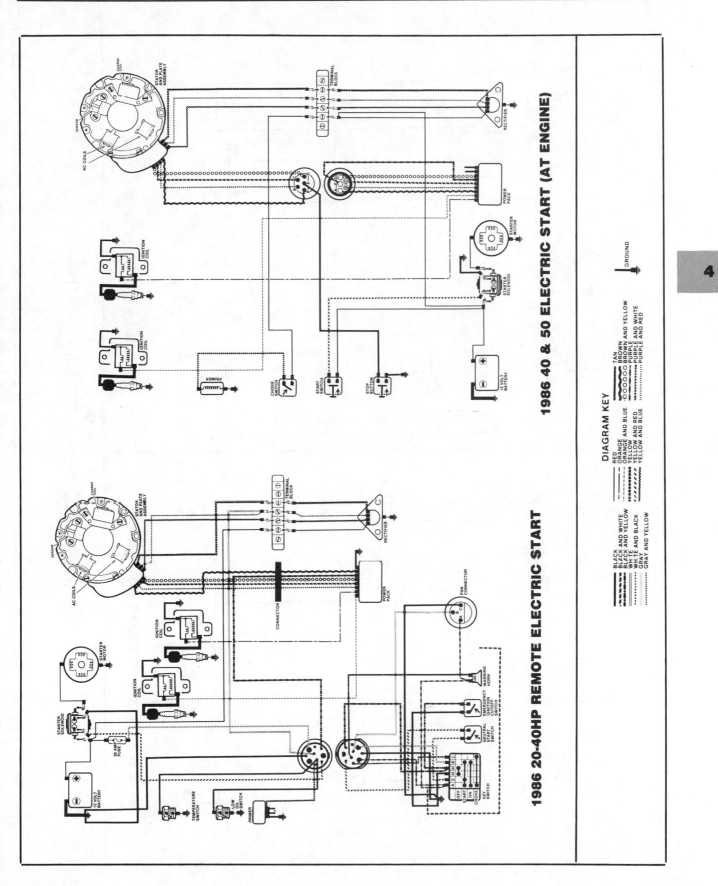

1986 40 & 50 ELECTRIC START (AT ENGINE)

1986 20-40HP REMOTE ELECTRIC START

DIAGRAM KEY

GROUND

4

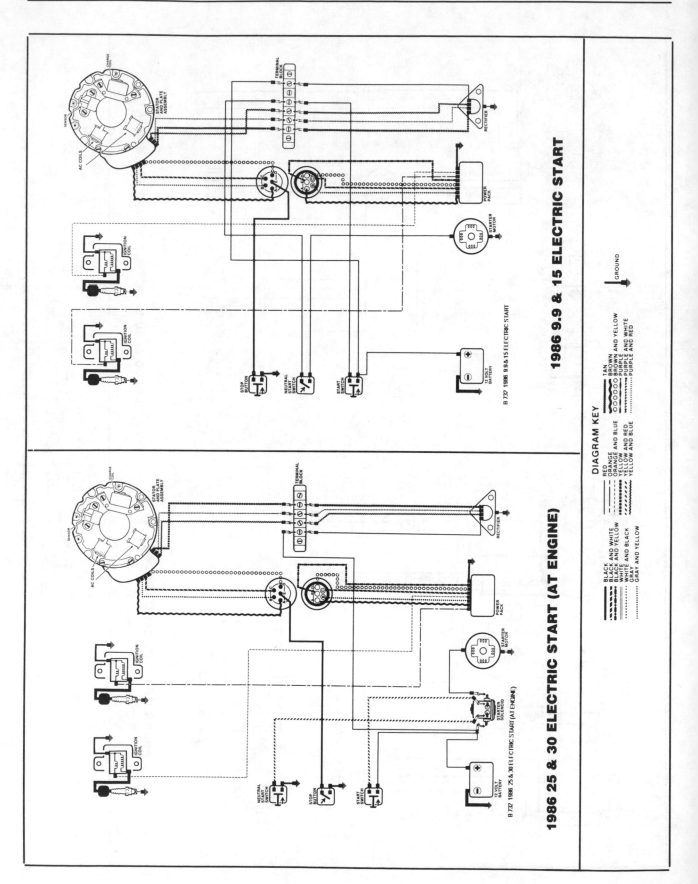

1986 9.9 & 15 ELECTRIC START

1986 25 & 30 ELECTRIC START (AT ENGINE)

DIAGRAM KEY

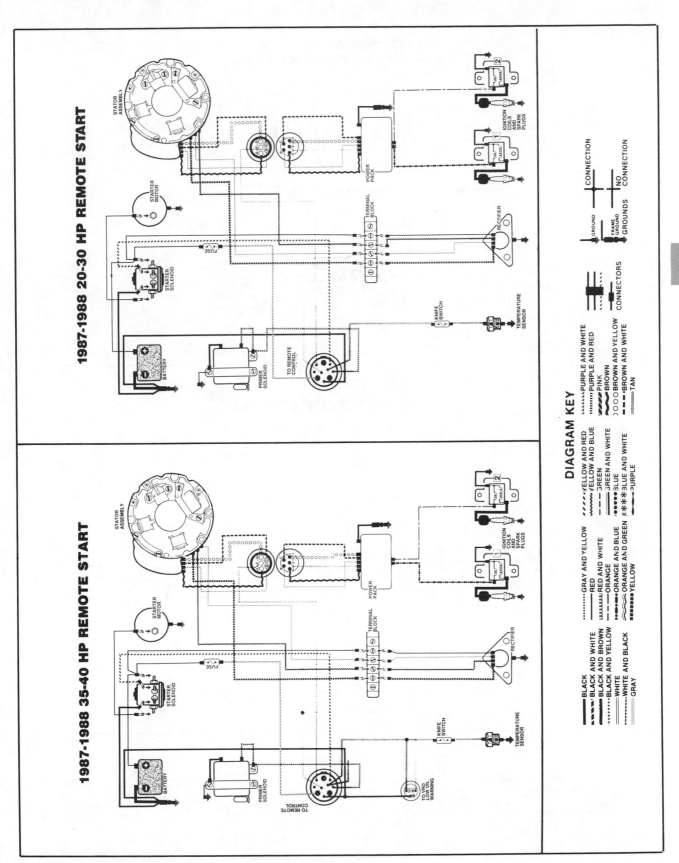

4

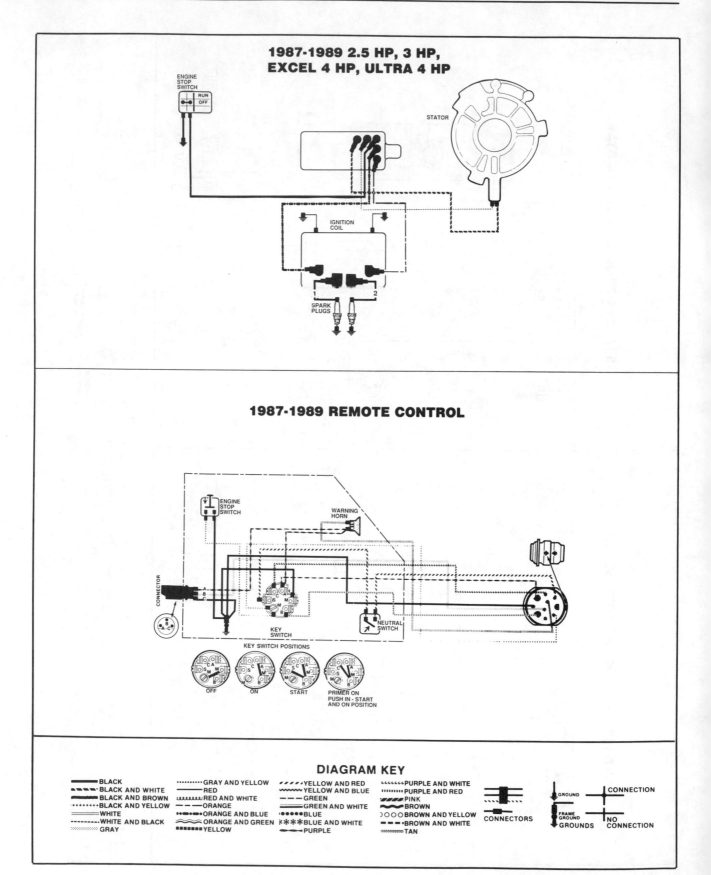

1987-1989 2.5 HP, 3 HP,
EXCEL 4 HP, ULTRA 4 HP

ENGINE
STOP
SWITCH

RUN
OFF

STATOR

IGNITION
COIL

SPARK
PLUGS

1987-1989 REMOTE CONTROL

ENGINE
STOP
SWITCH

WARNING
HORN

CONNECTOR

KEY
SWITCH

NEUTRAL
SWITCH

KEY SWITCH POSITIONS

OFF   ON   START   PRIMER ON
PUSH IN - START
AND ON POSITION

DIAGRAM KEY

BLACK	GRAY AND YELLOW	YELLOW AND RED	PURPLE AND WHITE
BLACK AND WHITE	RED	YELLOW AND BLUE	PURPLE AND RED
BLACK AND BROWN	RED AND WHITE	GREEN	PINK
BLACK AND YELLOW	ORANGE	GREEN AND WHITE	BROWN
WHITE	ORANGE AND BLUE	BLUE	BROWN AND YELLOW
WHITE AND BLACK	ORANGE AND GREEN	BLUE AND WHITE	BROWN AND WHITE
GRAY	YELLOW	PURPLE	TAN

CONNECTORS

GROUND

FRAME
GROUND
GROUNDS

CONNECTION

NO
CONNECTION

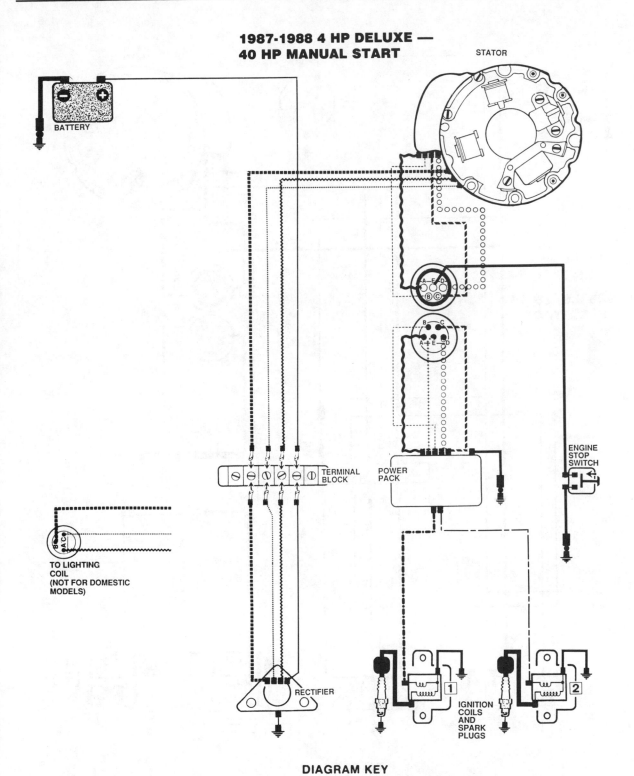

**1987-1988 4 HP DELUXE —
40 HP MANUAL START**

STATOR

BATTERY

TO LIGHTING
COIL
(NOT FOR DOMESTIC
MODELS)

TERMINAL
BLOCK

POWER
PACK

ENGINE
STOP
SWITCH

RECTIFIER

IGNITION
COILS
AND
SPARK
PLUGS

4

DIAGRAM KEY

BLACK	GRAY AND YELLOW	YELLOW AND RED	PURPLE AND WHITE
BLACK AND WHITE	RED	YELLOW AND BLUE	PURPLE AND RED
BLACK AND BROWN	RED AND WHITE	GREEN	PINK
BLACK AND YELLOW	ORANGE	GREEN AND WHITE	BROWN
WHITE	ORANGE AND BLUE	BLUE	BROWN AND YELLOW
WHITE AND BLACK	ORANGE AND GREEN	BLUE AND WHITE	BROWN AND WHITE
GRAY	YELLOW	PURPLE	TAN

CONNECTORS

GROUND   CONNECTION

FRAME
GROUND
GROUNDS   NO
                CONNECTION

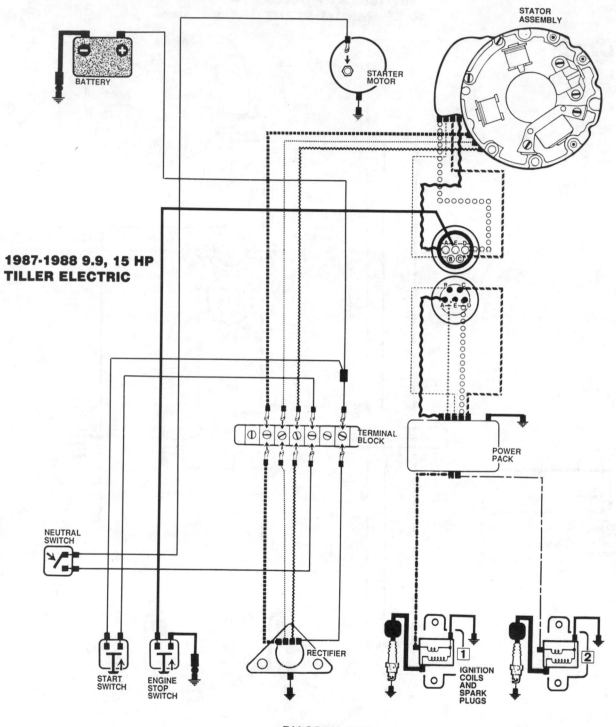

1987-1988 9.9, 15 HP TILLER ELECTRIC

STATOR ASSEMBLY

BATTERY

STARTER MOTOR

TERMINAL BLOCK

POWER PACK

NEUTRAL SWITCH

START SWITCH

ENGINE STOP SWITCH

RECTIFIER

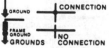

IGNITION COILS AND SPARK PLUGS

DIAGRAM KEY

BLACK	GRAY AND YELLOW	YELLOW AND RED	PURPLE AND WHITE
BLACK AND WHITE	RED	YELLOW AND BLUE	PURPLE AND RED
BLACK AND BROWN	RED AND WHITE	GREEN	PINK
BLACK AND YELLOW	ORANGE	GREEN AND WHITE	BROWN
WHITE	ORANGE AND BLUE	BLUE	BROWN AND YELLOW
WHITE AND BLACK	ORANGE AND GREEN	BLUE AND WHITE	BROWN AND WHITE
GRAY	YELLOW	PURPLE	TAN

CONNECTORS

GROUND

FRAME GROUND

GROUNDS

CONNECTION

NO CONNECTION

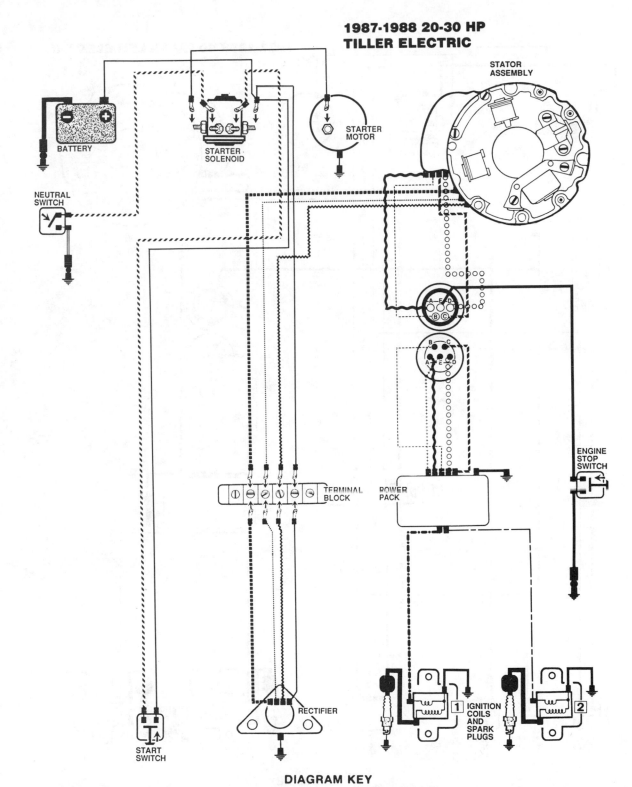

1987-1988 20-30 HP
TILLER ELECTRIC

STATOR ASSEMBLY

BATTERY

STARTER SOLENOID

STARTER MOTOR

NEUTRAL SWITCH

ENGINE STOP SWITCH

TERMINAL BLOCK

POWER PACK

START SWITCH

RECTIFIER

IGNITION COILS AND SPARK PLUGS

DIAGRAM KEY

BLACK	GRAY AND YELLOW	YELLOW AND RED	PURPLE AND WHITE		CONNECTION
BLACK AND WHITE	RED	YELLOW AND BLUE	PURPLE AND RED		
BLACK AND BROWN	RED AND WHITE	GREEN	PINK	GROUND	
BLACK AND YELLOW	ORANGE	GREEN AND WHITE	BROWN		
WHITE	ORANGE AND BLUE	BLUE	BROWN AND YELLOW	FRAME GROUND	NO
WHITE AND BLACK	ORANGE AND GREEN	BLUE AND WHITE	BROWN AND WHITE	GROUNDS	CONNECTION
GRAY	YELLOW	PURPLE	TAN	CONNECTORS	

4

1987-1988 40 HP TILLER ELECTRIC

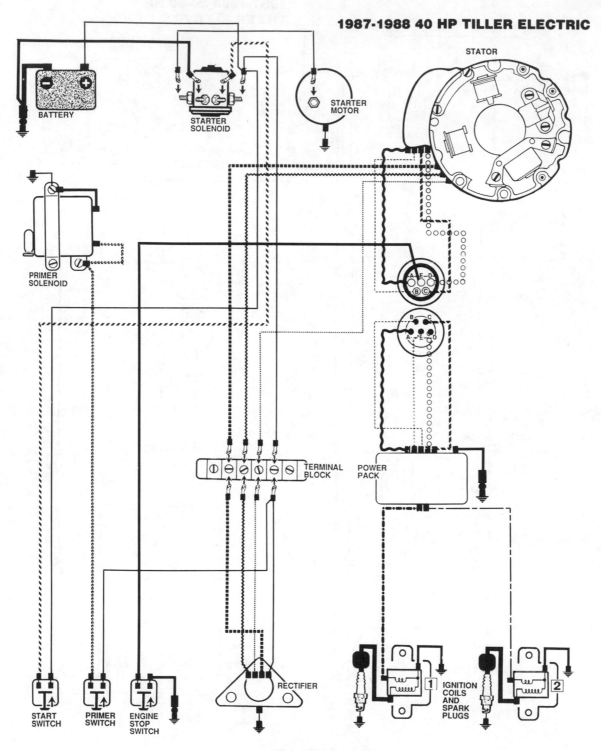

STATOR

BATTERY

STARTER SOLENOID

STARTER MOTOR

PRIMER SOLENOID

A E D
B C

B C
A D

TERMINAL BLOCK

POWER PACK

START SWITCH

PRIMER SWITCH

ENGINE STOP SWITCH

RECTIFIER

IGNITION COILS AND SPARK PLUGS

1

2

DIAGRAM KEY

BLACK	GRAY AND YELLOW	YELLOW AND RED	PURPLE AND WHITE
BLACK AND WHITE	RED	YELLOW AND BLUE	PURPLE AND RED
BLACK AND BROWN	RED AND WHITE	GREEN	PINK
BLACK AND YELLOW	ORANGE	GREEN AND WHITE	BROWN
WHITE	ORANGE AND BLUE	BLUE	BROWN AND YELLOW
WHITE AND BLACK	ORANGE AND GREEN	BLUE AND WHITE	BROWN AND WHITE
GRAY	YELLOW	PURPLE	TAN

GROUND

FRAME GROUND

GROUNDS

CONNECTION

NO CONNECTION

CONNECTORS

1989 MANUAL START WITH AC LIGHTING CONNECTOR

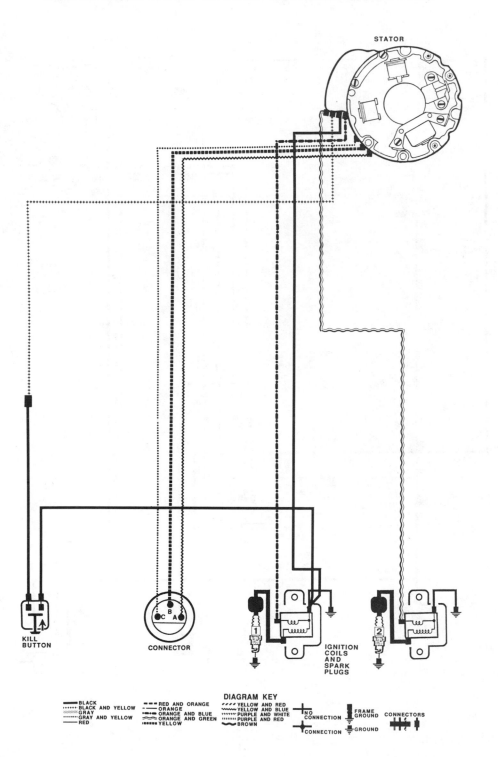

STATOR

KILL
BUTTON

CONNECTOR

IGNITION
COILS
AND
SPARK
PLUGS

DIAGRAM KEY

BLACK	RED AND ORANGE	YELLOW AND RED	NO CONNECTION
BLACK AND YELLOW	ORANGE	YELLOW AND BLUE	FRAME GROUND
GRAY	ORANGE AND BLUE	PURPLE AND WHITE	CONNECTORS
GRAY AND YELLOW	ORANGE AND GREEN	PURPLE AND RED	
RED	YELLOW	BROWN	CONNECTION GROUND

4

1989 4 DELUXE - 8 HP

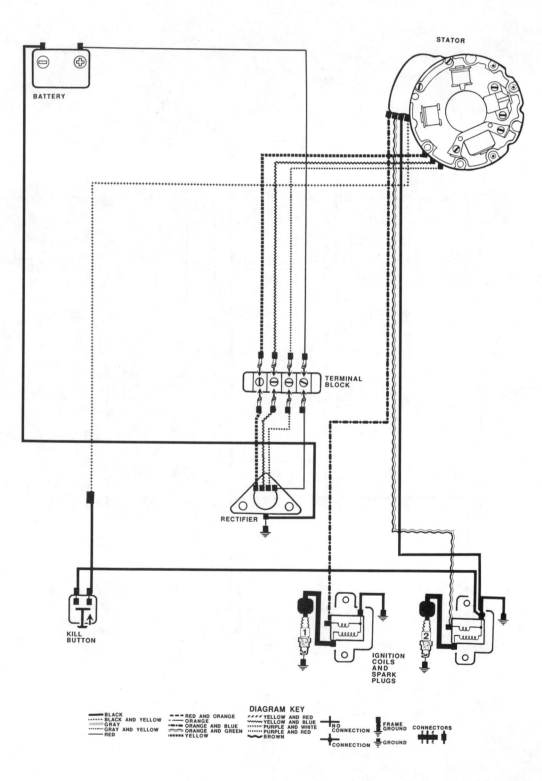

STATOR

BATTERY

TERMINAL BLOCK

RECTIFIER

KILL BUTTON

IGNITION COILS AND SPARK PLUGS

1

2

DIAGRAM KEY

BLACK
BLACK AND YELLOW
GRAY
GRAY AND YELLOW
RED

RED AND ORANGE
ORANGE
ORANGE AND BLUE
ORANGE AND GREEN
YELLOW

YELLOW AND RED
YELLOW AND BLUE
PURPLE AND WHITE
PURPLE AND RED
BROWN

NO CONNECTION

CONNECTION

FRAME GROUND

GROUND

CONNECTORS

1989 9.9-15 HP REMOTE START

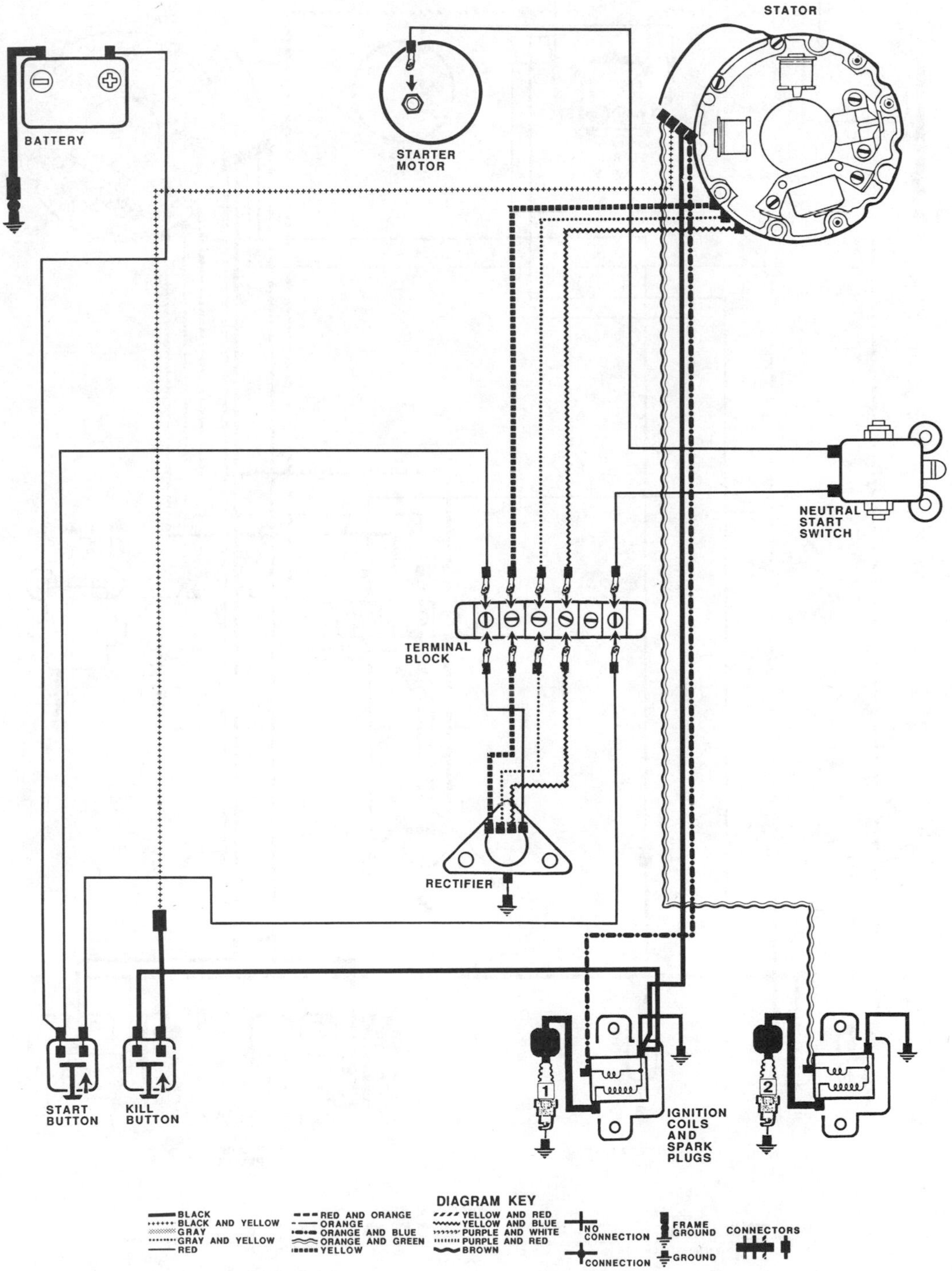

STATOR

BATTERY

STARTER
MOTOR

4

NEUTRAL
START
SWITCH

TERMINAL
BLOCK

RECTIFIER

START
BUTTON

KILL
BUTTON

IGNITION
COILS
AND
SPARK
PLUGS

1

2

DIAGRAM KEY

BLACK	RED AND ORANGE	YELLOW AND RED
BLACK AND YELLOW	ORANGE	YELLOW AND BLUE
GRAY	ORANGE AND BLUE	PURPLE AND WHITE
GRAY AND YELLOW	ORANGE AND GREEN	PURPLE AND RED
RED	YELLOW	BROWN

NO
CONNECTION

CONNECTION

FRAME
GROUND

GROUND

CONNECTORS

1989 20-30 HP TILLER ELECTRIC

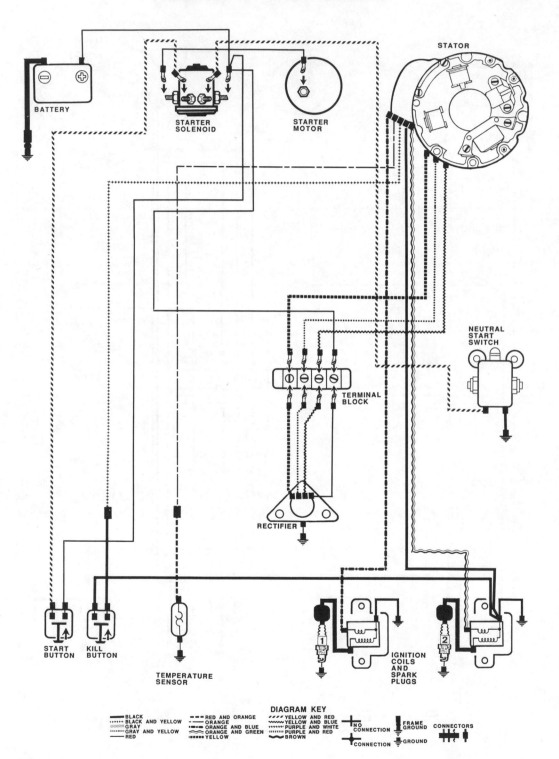

STATOR

BATTERY

STARTER
SOLENOID

STARTER
MOTOR

NEUTRAL
START
SWITCH

TERMINAL
BLOCK

RECTIFIER

START
BUTTON

KILL
BUTTON

TEMPERATURE
SENSOR

IGNITION
COILS
AND
SPARK
PLUGS

1

2

DIAGRAM KEY

BLACK	RED AND ORANGE	YELLOW AND RED
BLACK AND YELLOW	ORANGE	YELLOW AND BLUE
GRAY	ORANGE AND BLUE	PURPLE AND WHITE
GRAY AND YELLOW	ORANGE AND GREEN	PURPLE AND RED
RED	YELLOW	BROWN

NO
CONNECTION

FRAME
GROUND

CONNECTORS

CONNECTION

GROUND

1989 20-30 HP REMOTE START

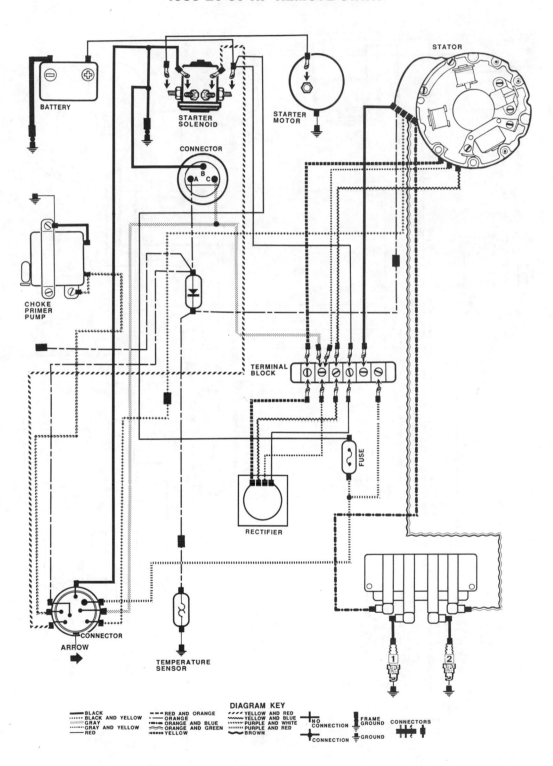

BATTERY

STARTER
SOLENOID

STARTER
MOTOR

STATOR

CONNECTOR

A B
C

CHOKE
PRIMER
PUMP

TERMINAL
BLOCK

FUSE

RECTIFIER

CONNECTOR

ARROW

TEMPERATURE
SENSOR

1   2

DIAGRAM KEY

BLACK
BLACK AND YELLOW
GRAY
GRAY AND YELLOW
RED
RED AND ORANGE
ORANGE
ORANGE AND BLUE
ORANGE AND GREEN
YELLOW
YELLOW AND RED
YELLOW AND BLUE
PURPLE AND WHITE
PURPLE AND RED
BROWN

NO
CONNECTION
CONNECTION

FRAME
GROUND
GROUND

CONNECTORS

4

1989 40 HP TILLER ELECTRIC

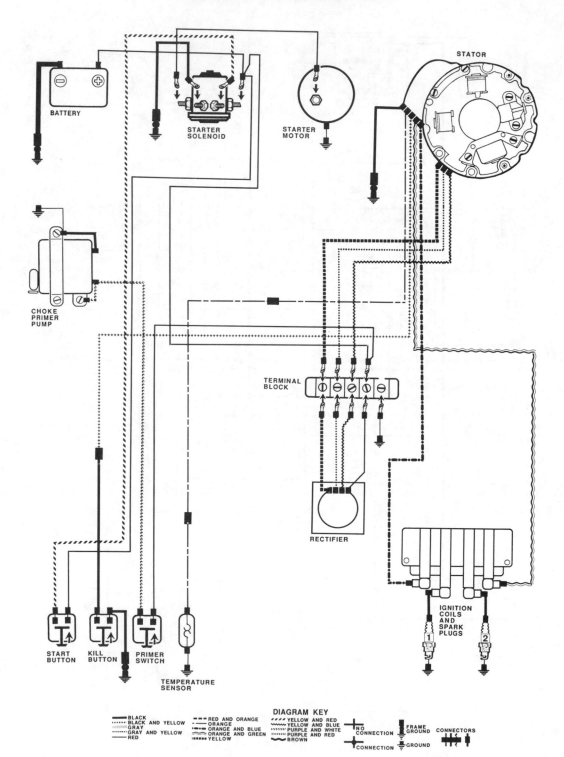

BATTERY

STARTER
SOLENOID

STARTER
MOTOR

STATOR

CHOKE
PRIMER
PUMP

TERMINAL
BLOCK

RECTIFIER

IGNITION
COILS
AND
SPARK
PLUGS

1   2

START
BUTTON

KILL
BUTTON

PRIMER
SWITCH

TEMPERATURE
SENSOR

DIAGRAM KEY

—— BLACK	--- RED AND ORANGE	//// YELLOW AND RED
····· BLACK AND YELLOW	— ORANGE	∿∿ YELLOW AND BLUE
▨▨▨ GRAY	—·— ORANGE AND BLUE	∿∿∿ PURPLE AND WHITE
— GRAY AND YELLOW	···· ORANGE AND GREEN	∿∿∿ PURPLE AND RED
— RED	▨▨▨ YELLOW	▨▨▨ BROWN

NO
CONNECTION

CONNECTION

FRAME
GROUND

GROUND

CONNECTORS

1989 40 HP REMOTE START

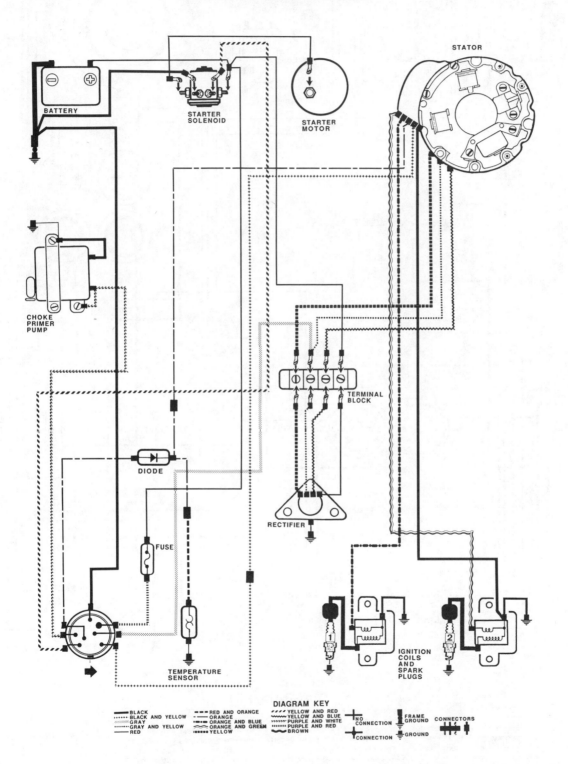

BATTERY

STARTER
SOLENOID

STARTER
MOTOR

STATOR

CHOKE
PRIMER
PUMP

TERMINAL
BLOCK

DIODE

RECTIFIER

FUSE

IGNITION
COILS
AND
SPARK
PLUGS

TEMPERATURE
SENSOR

DIAGRAM KEY

——— BLACK	– – – RED AND ORANGE	⁄⁄⁄⁄ YELLOW AND RED
········· BLACK AND YELLOW	—·— ORANGE	wwww YELLOW AND BLUE
········· GRAY	—··— ORANGE AND BLUE	········ PURPLE AND WHITE
········· GRAY AND YELLOW	——— ORANGE AND GREEN	········ PURPLE AND RED
——— RED	······ YELLOW	∿∿∿ BROWN

NO CONNECTION

CONNECTION

FRAME GROUND

GROUND

CONNECTORS

4

EVINRUDE 1982-1984 70 & 75 HP

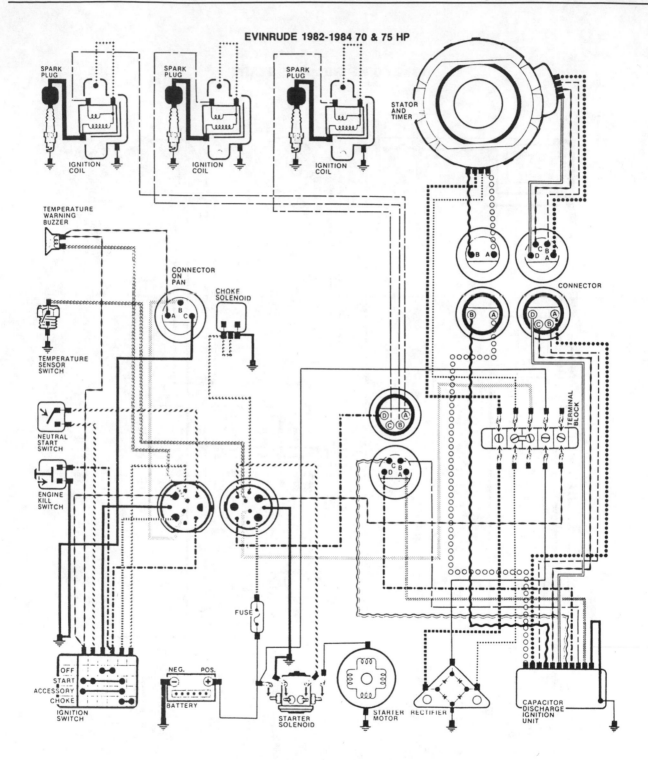

DIAGRAM KEY

———— BLACK	—— — RED	——— PURPLE
·–·–·– BLACK AND WHITE	– – – ORANGE	·········· PURPLE AND RED
••••••• BLACK AND ORANGE	———— ORANGE AND BLUE	··········· PURPLE AND WHITE
———— BLACK AND BROWN	～～～ ORANGE AND GREEN	～～～ BROWN
——— BLACK AND YELLOW	▬▬▬▬ YELLOW	⊃000000 BROWN AND YELLOW
———— WHITE	▬ ▬ ▬ YELLOW AND RED	———— BROWN AND WHITE
– – – – WHITE AND BLACK	∿∿∿∿ YELLOW AND PURPLE	≋≋≋≋ TAN
░░░░ GRAY	– – – GREEN	
·········· GRAY AND YELLOW	•••••••• BLUE	

⏚ GROUND

╪ CONNECTION

┼ NO CONNECTION

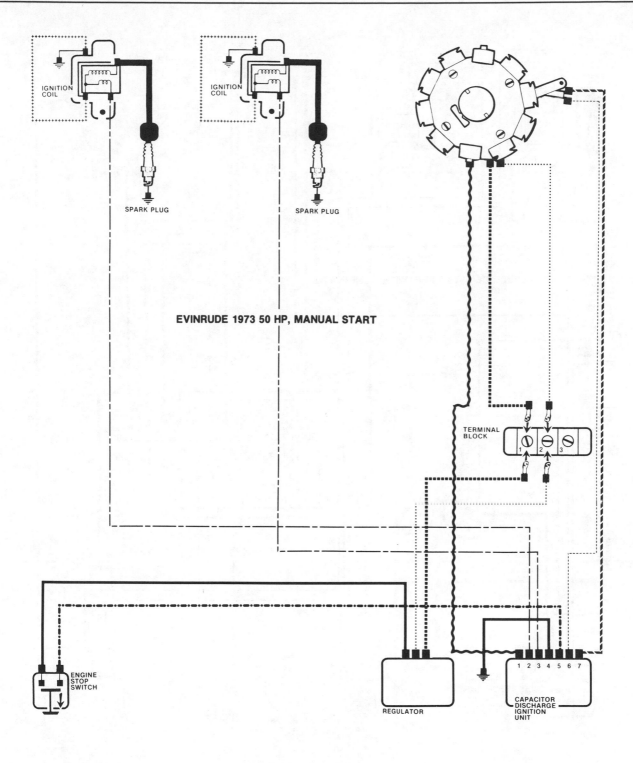

EVINRUDE 1973 50 HP, MANUAL START

DIAGRAM KEY

———— BLACK	———— RED	⌒⌒⌒ PURPLE
▬▬▬ BLACK AND WHITE	——— ORANGE	·············· PURPLE AND RED
+++++++++ BLACK AND ORANGE	▒▒▒▒ ORANGE AND BLUE	·············· PURPLE AND WHITE
════ BLACK AND BROWN	∿∿∿∿ ORANGE AND GREEN	∿∿∿ BROWN
▬·▬·▬· BLACK AND YELLOW	▬▬▬ YELLOW	⊃○○○○○ BROWN AND YELLOW
———— WHITE	///// YELLOW AND RED	▬▬ ▬▬ BROWN AND WHITE
- - - - WHITE AND BLACK	∿∿∿∿ YELLOW AND PURPLE	▨▨▨▨ TAN
▒▒▒▒ GRAY	- - - - GREEN	
············ GRAY AND YELLOW	●●●●●● BLUE	

⏚ GROUND

✛ CONNECTION

╋ NO CONNECTION

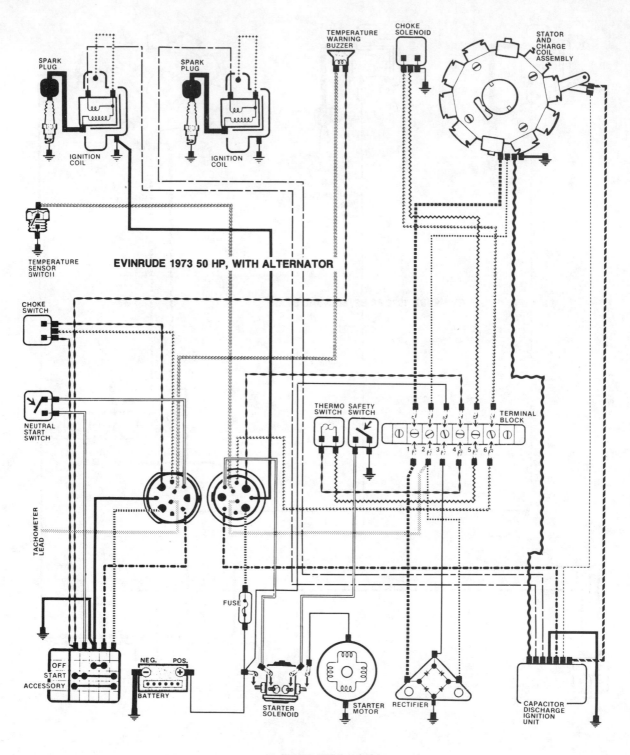

EVINRUDE 1973 50 HP, WITH ALTERNATOR

SPARK PLUG

SPARK PLUG

IGNITION COIL

IGNITION COIL

TEMPERATURE WARNING BUZZER

CHOKE SOLENOID

STATOR AND CHARGE COIL ASSEMBLY

TEMPERATURE SENSOR SWITCH

CHOKE SWITCH

NEUTRAL START SWITCH

THERMO SWITCH

SAFETY SWITCH

TERMINAL BLOCK

TACHOMETER LEAD

FUSE

OFF
START
ACCESSORY

NEG. POS.

BATTERY

STARTER SOLENOID

STARTER MOTOR

RECTIFIER

CAPACITOR DISCHARGE IGNITION UNIT

DIAGRAM KEY

BLACK	RED	PURPLE	GROUND
BLACK AND WHITE	ORANGE	PURPLE AND RED	
BLACK AND ORANGE	ORANGE AND BLUE	PURPLE AND WHITE	CONNECTION
BLACK AND BROWN	ORANGE AND GREEN	BROWN	
BLACK AND YELLOW	YELLOW	BROWN AND YELLOW	NO CONNECTION
WHITE	YELLOW AND RED	BROWN AND WHITE	
WHITE AND BLACK	YELLOW AND PURPLE	TAN	
GRAY	GREEN		
GRAY AND YELLOW	BLUE		

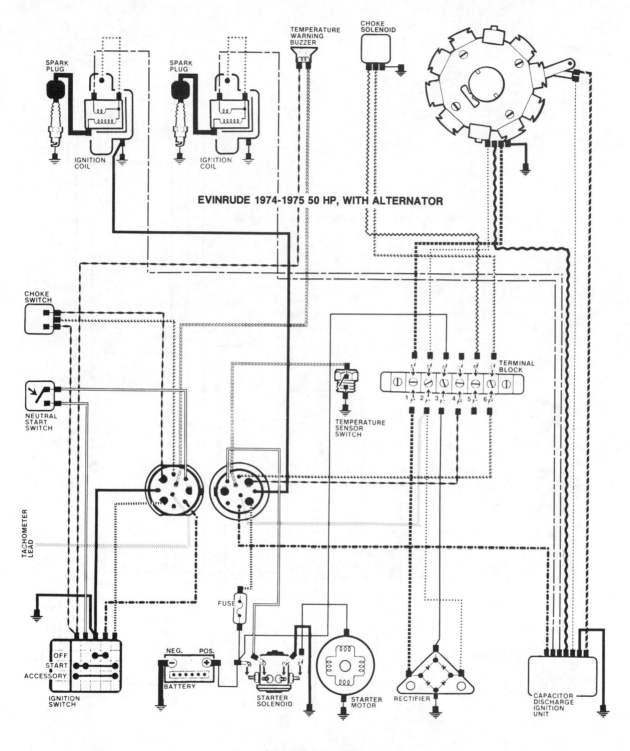

EVINRUDE 1974-1975 50 HP, WITH ALTERNATOR

4

DIAGRAM KEY

BLACK	RED	PURPLE		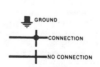 GROUND
BLACK AND WHITE	ORANGE	PURPLE AND RED		
BLACK AND ORANGE	ORANGE AND BLUE	PURPLE AND WHITE		CONNECTION
BLACK AND BROWN	ORANGE AND GREEN	BROWN		
BLACK AND YELLOW	YELLOW	BROWN AND YELLOW		NO CONNECTION
WHITE	YELLOW AND RED	BROWN AND WHITE		
WHITE AND BLACK	YELLOW AND PURPLE	TAN		
GRAY	GREEN			
GRAY AND YELLOW	BLUE			

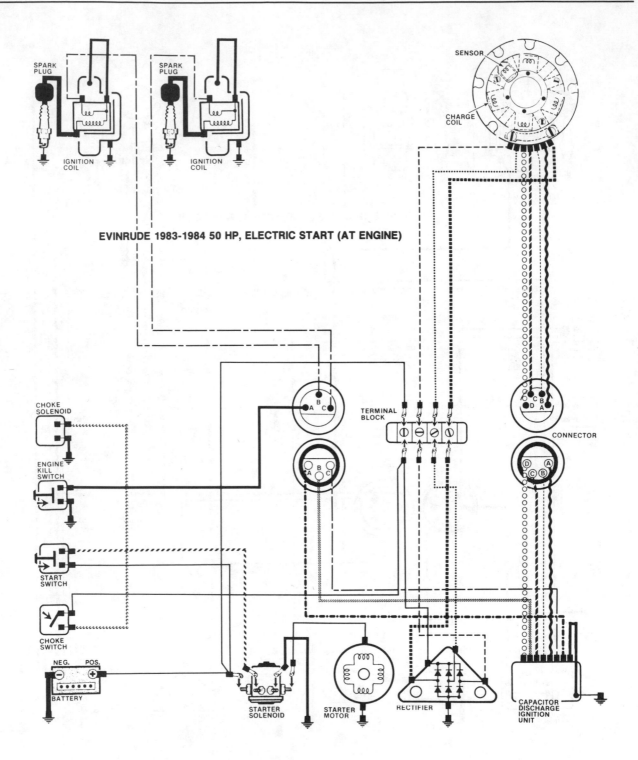

EVINRUDE 1983-1984 50 HP, ELECTRIC START (AT ENGINE)

DIAGRAM KEY

BLACK	RED	PURPLE
BLACK AND WHITE	ORANGE	PURPLE AND RED
BLACK AND ORANGE	ORANGE AND BLUE	PURPLE AND WHITE
BLACK AND BROWN	ORANGE AND GREEN	BROWN
BLACK AND YELLOW	YELLOW	BROWN AND YELLOW
WHITE	YELLOW AND RED	BROWN AND WHITE
WHITE AND BLACK	YELLOW AND PURPLE	TAN
GRAY	BLUE AND YELLOW	
GRAY AND YELLOW	BLUE	

GROUND

CONNECTION

NO CONNECTION

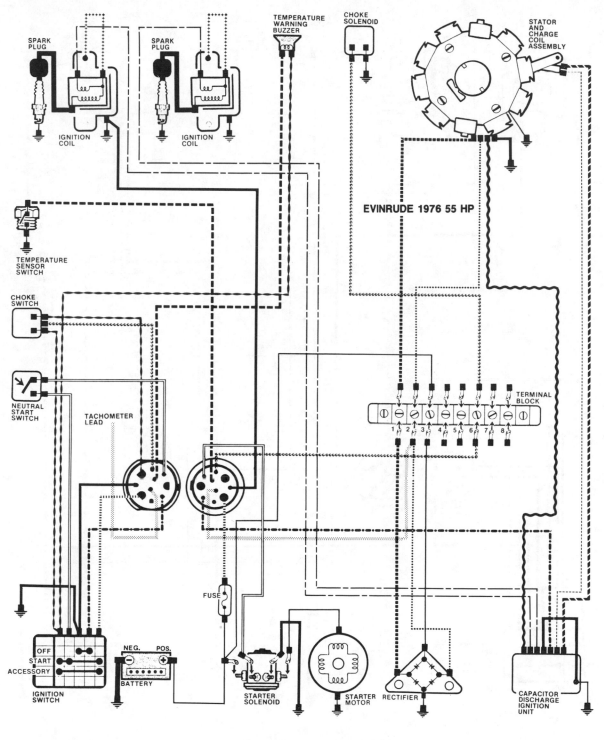

EVINRUDE 1976 55 HP

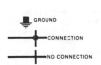

DIAGRAM KEY

BLACK	RED	PURPLE
BLACK AND WHITE	ORANGE	PURPLE AND RED
BLACK AND ORANGE	ORANGE AND BLUE	PURPLE AND WHITE
BLACK AND BROWN	ORANGE AND GREEN	BROWN
BLACK AND YELLOW	YELLOW	BROWN AND YELLOW
WHITE	YELLOW AND RED	TAN
WHITE AND BLACK	YELLOW AND PURPLE	
GRAY	BROWN AND ORANGE	GROUND
GRAY AND YELLOW	BLUE	CONNECTION
		NO CONNECTION

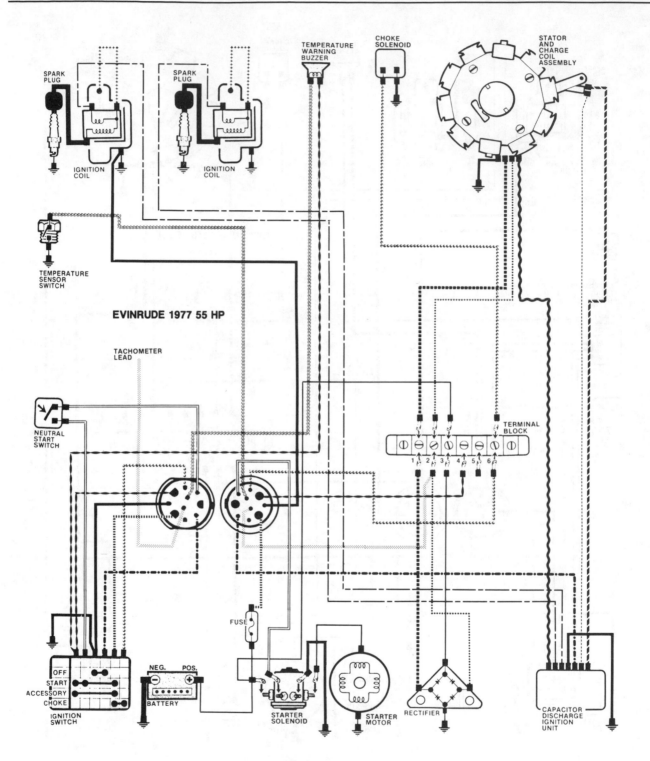

Evinrude 1977 55 HP

DIAGRAM KEY

BLACK	RED	PURPLE
BLACK AND WHITE	ORANGE	PURPLE AND RED
BLACK AND ORANGE	ORANGE AND BLUE	PURPLE AND WHITE
BLACK AND BROWN	ORANGE AND GREEN	BROWN
BLACK AND YELLOW	YELLOW	BROWN AND YELLOW
WHITE	YELLOW AND RED	BROWN AND WHITE
WHITE AND BLACK	YELLOW AND PURPLE	TAN
GRAY	GREEN	
GRAY AND YELLOW	BLUE	

GROUND

CONNECTION

NO CONNECTION

EVINRUDE 1978-1979 55 HP

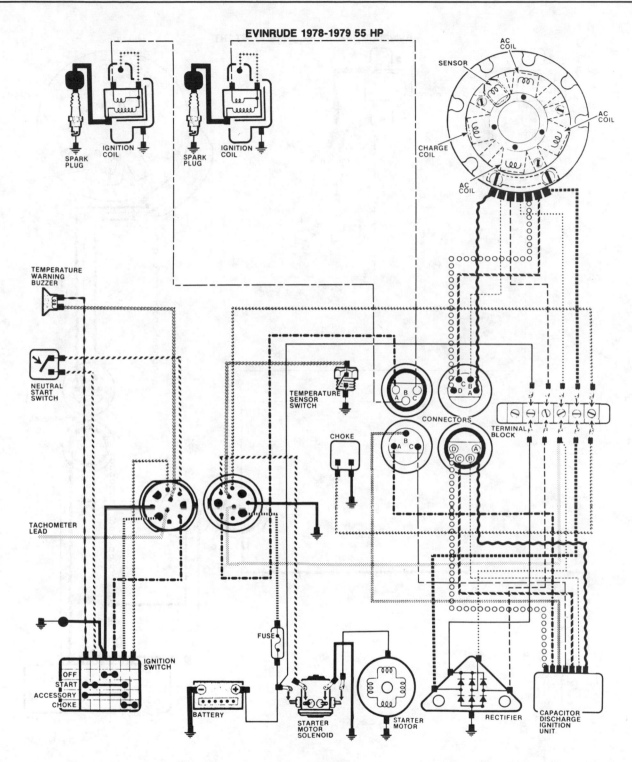

DIAGRAM KEY

———— BLACK	———— RED	············ PURPLE
━•━•━ BLACK AND WHITE	– – – ORANGE	············ PURPLE AND RED
++++++ BLACK AND ORANGE	········· ORANGE AND BLUE	············ PURPLE AND WHITE
———— BLACK AND BROWN	∿∿∿∿ ORANGE AND GREEN	∿∿∿∿ BROWN
━━━━ BLACK AND YELLOW	■■■■■ YELLOW	oooooo BROWN AND YELLOW
———— WHITE	━━━━ YELLOW AND RED	━━━━ BROWN AND WHITE
– – – – WHITE AND BLACK	∿∿∿∿ YELLOW AND PURPLE	×××××× TAN
░░░░░ GRAY	– – – BLUE AND YELLOW	
·········· GRAY AND YELLOW	●●●●●● BLUE	

GROUND

CONNECTION

NO CONNECTION

4

EVINRUDE 1980 55 HP, MANUAL START

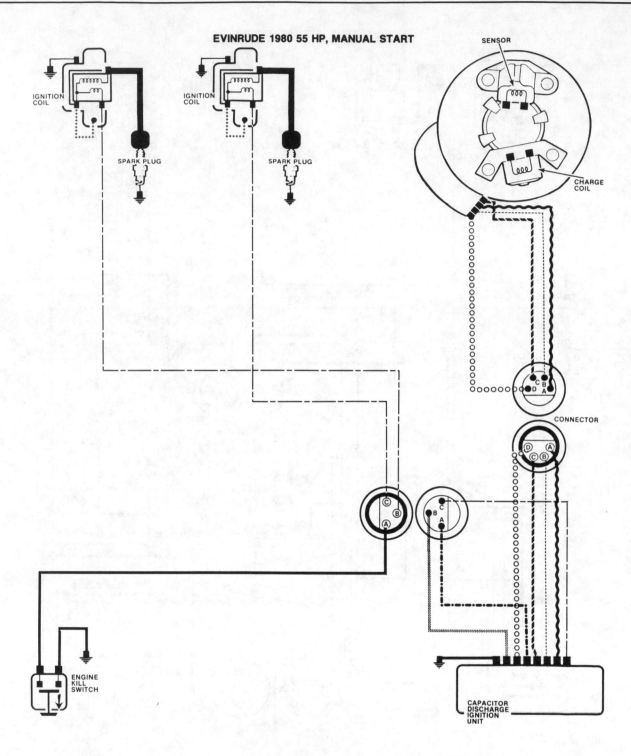

IGNITION COIL

SPARK PLUG

IGNITION COIL

SPARK PLUG

SENSOR

CHARGE COIL

CONNECTOR

C B
D A

D A
C B

C
B
A

C
B
A

ENGINE KILL SWITCH

CAPACITOR DISCHARGE IGNITION UNIT

DIAGRAM KEY

BLACK	RED	PURPLE
BLACK AND WHITE	ORANGE	PURPLE AND RED
BLACK AND ORANGE	ORANGE AND BLUE	PURPLE AND WHITE
BLACK AND BROWN	ORANGE AND GREEN	BROWN
BLACK AND YELLOW	YELLOW	BROWN AND YELLOW
WHITE	YELLOW AND RED	BROWN AND WHITE
WHITE AND BLACK	YELLOW AND PURPLE	TAN
GRAY	GREEN	GROUND
GRAY AND YELLOW	BLUE	CONNECTION
		NO CONNECTION

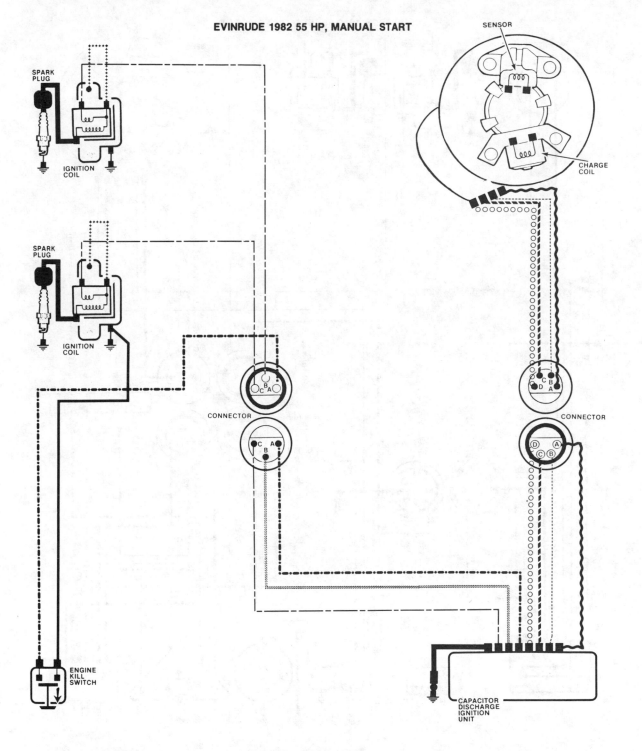

EVINRUDE 1982 55 HP, MANUAL START

DIAGRAM KEY

BLACK	RED
BLACK AND WHITE	ORANGE
BLACK AND ORANGE	ORANGE AND BLUE
BLACK AND BROWN	ORANGE AND GREEN
BLACK AND YELLOW	YELLOW
WHITE	YELLOW AND RED
WHITE AND BLACK	YELLOW AND PURPLE
GRAY	GREEN
GRAY AND YELLOW	BLUE

PURPLE	GROUND
PURPLE AND RED	CONNECTION
PURPLE AND WHITE	NO CONNECTION
BROWN	
BROWN AND YELLOW	
BROWN AND WHITE	
TAN	

EVINRUDE 1980 60 HP & 1981 50/60 HP

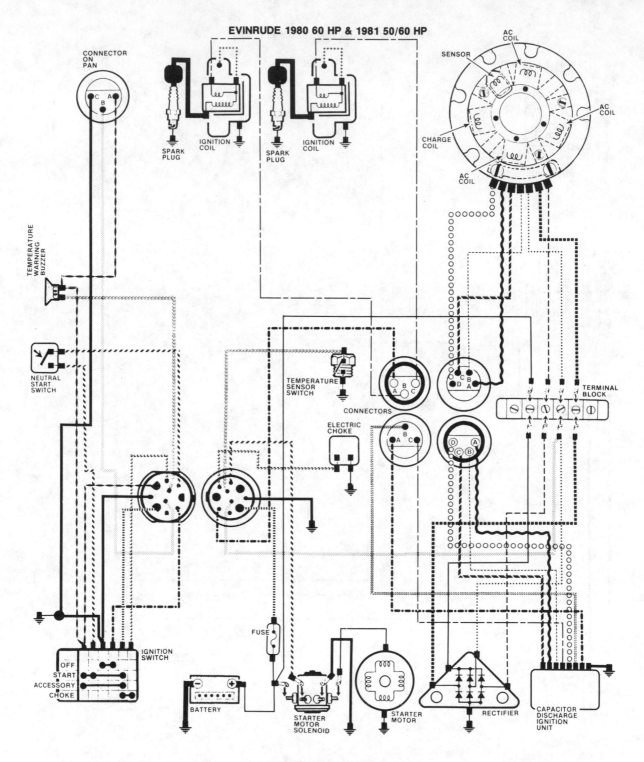

CONNECTOR ON PAN

SENSOR

AC COIL

AC COIL

CHARGE COIL

AC COIL

SPARK PLUG

IGNITION COIL

SPARK PLUG

IGNITION COIL

TEMPERATURE WARNING BUZZER

NEUTRAL START SWITCH

TEMPERATURE SENSOR SWITCH

CONNECTORS

ELECTRIC CHOKE

TERMINAL BLOCK

IGNITION SWITCH

OFF
START
ACCESSORY
CHOKE

FUSE

BATTERY

STARTER MOTOR SOLENOID

STARTER MOTOR

RECTIFIER

CAPACITOR DISCHARGE IGNITION UNIT

DIAGRAM KEY

BLACK	RED	PURPLE	GROUND
BLACK AND WHITE	ORANGE	PURPLE AND RED	CONNECTION
BLACK AND ORANGE	ORANGE AND BLUE	PURPLE AND WHITE	NO CONNECTION
BLACK AND BROWN	ORANGE AND GREEN	BROWN	
BLACK AND YELLOW	YELLOW	BROWN AND YELLOW	
WHITE	YELLOW AND RED	BROWN AND WHITE	
WHITE AND BLACK	YELLOW AND PURPLE	TAN	
GRAY	BLUE AND YELLOW		
GRAY AND YELLOW	BLUE		

EVINRUDE 1982-1984 50 & 60 HP, REMOTE ELECTRIC START

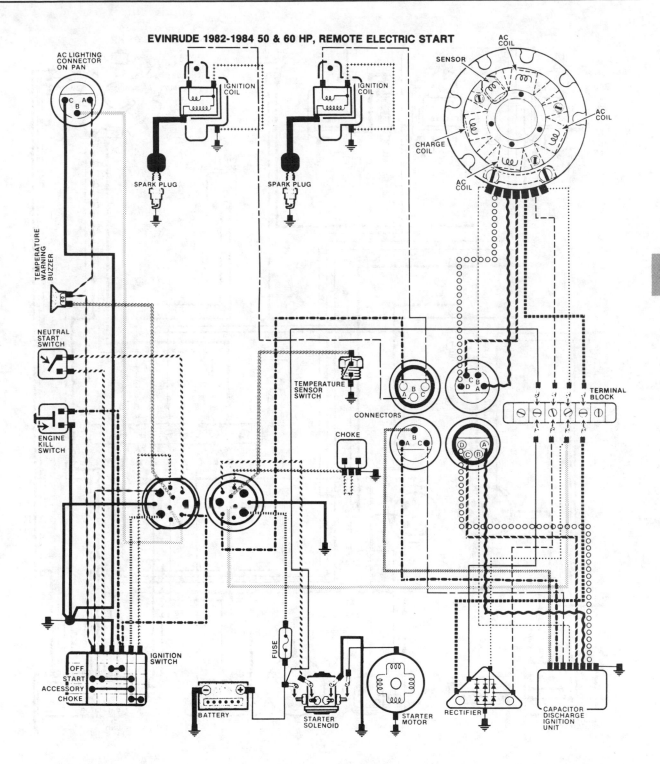

DIAGRAM KEY

——— BLACK	——— RED	∿∿∿ PURPLE	⬛ GROUND
⌄⌄⌄⌄ BLACK AND WHITE	– – – ORANGE	·∥∥∥∥ PURPLE AND RED	
·········· BLACK AND ORANGE	░░░░░ ORANGE AND BLUE	∿∿∿ PURPLE AND WHITE	✦ CONNECTION
·–·–·– BLACK AND BROWN	∿∿∿ ORANGE AND GREEN	∿∿∿ BROWN	
·–··–·· BLACK AND YELLOW	▪▪▪▪▪ YELLOW	∘∘∘∘∘∘ BROWN AND YELLOW	┴ NO CONNECTION
——— WHITE	⁄⁄⁄⁄⁄ YELLOW AND RED	▪–▪–▪ BROWN AND WHITE	
– – – WHITE AND BLACK	∿∿∿ YELLOW AND PURPLE	✕✕✕✕ TAN	
······ GRAY	– – – BLUE AND YELLOW		
········ GRAY AND YELLOW	•••••• BLUE		

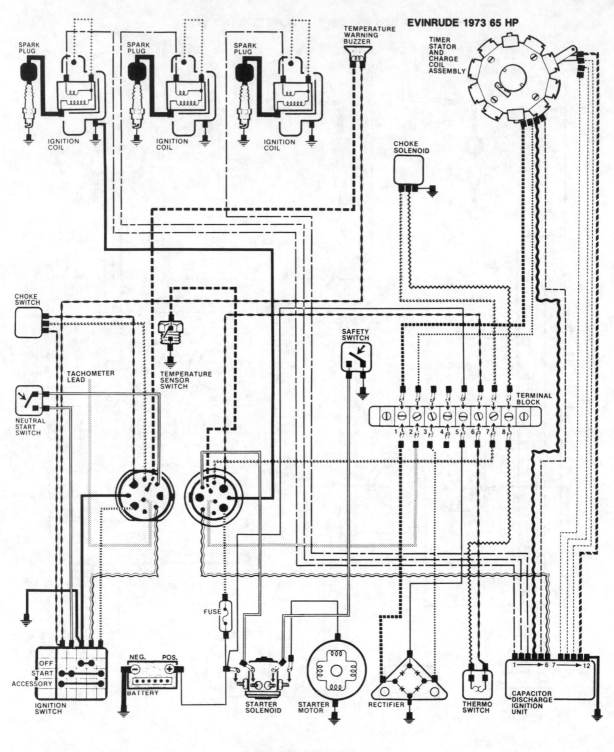

EVINRUDE 1973 65 HP

SPARK PLUG

IGNITION COIL

TEMPERATURE WARNING BUZZER

TIMER STATOR AND CHARGE COIL ASSEMBLY

CHOKE SOLENOID

CHOKE SWITCH

TACHOMETER LEAD

TEMPERATURE SENSOR SWITCH

NEUTRAL START SWITCH

SAFETY SWITCH

TERMINAL BLOCK

OFF START ACCESSORY

IGNITION SWITCH

NEG. POS.

BATTERY

FUSE

STARTER SOLENOID

STARTER MOTOR

RECTIFIER

THERMO SWITCH

CAPACITOR DISCHARGE IGNITION UNIT

DIAGRAM KEY

BLACK	RED	PURPLE
BLACK AND WHITE	ORANGE	PURPLE AND RED
BLACK AND ORANGE	ORANGE AND BLUE	PURPLE AND WHITE
BLACK AND BROWN	BLACK AND YELLOW	BROWN
WHITE	YELLOW	BROWN AND YELLOW
WHITE AND BLACK	YELLOW AND RED	TAN
GRAY	YELLOW AND PURPLE	
GRAY AND YELLOW	BROWN AND ORANGE	
	BLUE	

GROUND

CONNECTION

NO CONNECTION

EVINRUDE 1974-1976 70 & 75 HP

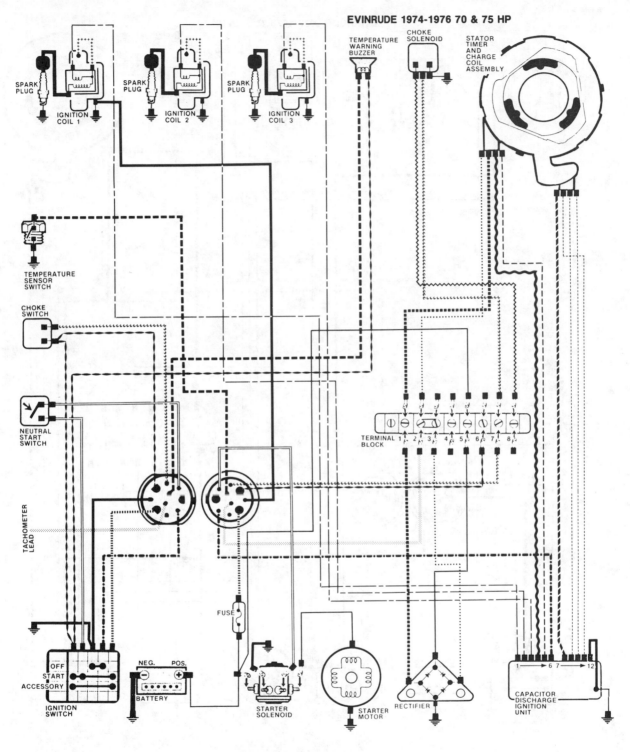

4

DIAGRAM KEY

————————	BLACK
—·—·—·—·—	BLACK AND WHITE
+++++++++	BLACK AND ORANGE
————————	BLACK AND BROWN
————————	BLACK AND YELLOW
——————	WHITE
- - - - - -	WHITE AND BLACK
~~	GRAY
············	GRAY AND YELLOW
————————	RED
— — — —	ORANGE
:::::::::::::	ORANGE AND BLUE
∿∿∿∿∿∿	ORANGE AND GREEN
▪▪▪▪▪▪▪▪	YELLOW
/////////	YELLOW AND RED
vvvvvvvv	YELLOW AND PURPLE
— — — —	BROWN AND ORANGE
••••••••	BLUE
·············	PURPLE
:::::::::::::	PURPLE AND RED
⌐⌐⌐⌐⌐⌐	PURPLE AND WHITE
∿∿∿∿∿∿	BROWN
○○○○○○○	BROWN AND YELLOW
- - - - -	TAN

▪	GROUND
╂	CONNECTION
╀	NO CONNECTION

EVINRUDE 1977-1978 70 & 75 HP

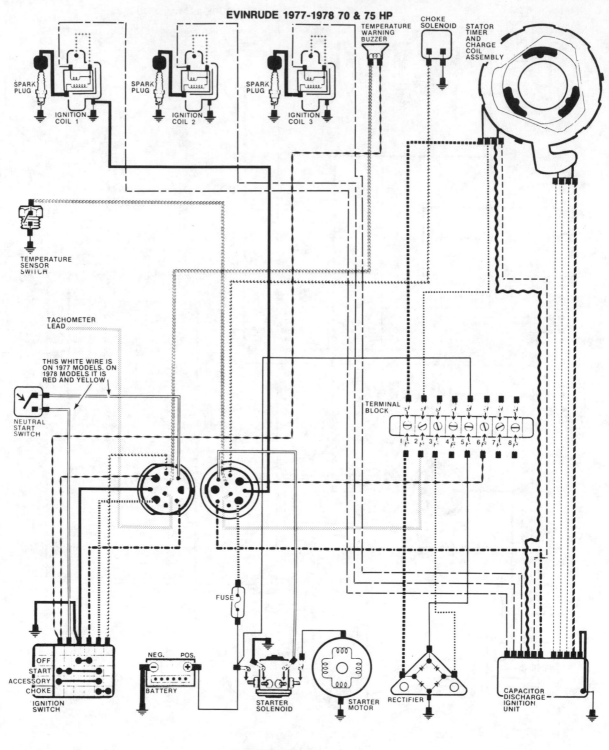

DIAGRAM KEY

BLACK	RED	PURPLE	GROUND
BLACK AND WHITE	ORANGE	PURPLE AND RED	CONNECTION
BLACK AND ORANGE	ORANGE AND BLUE	PURPLE AND WHITE	NO CONNECTION
BLACK AND BROWN	ORANGE AND GREEN	BROWN	
BLACK AND YELLOW	YELLOW	BROWN AND YELLOW	
WHITE	YELLOW AND RED	TAN	
WHITE AND BLACK	YELLOW AND PURPLE		
GRAY	BROWN AND ORANGE		
GRAY AND YELLOW	BLUE		

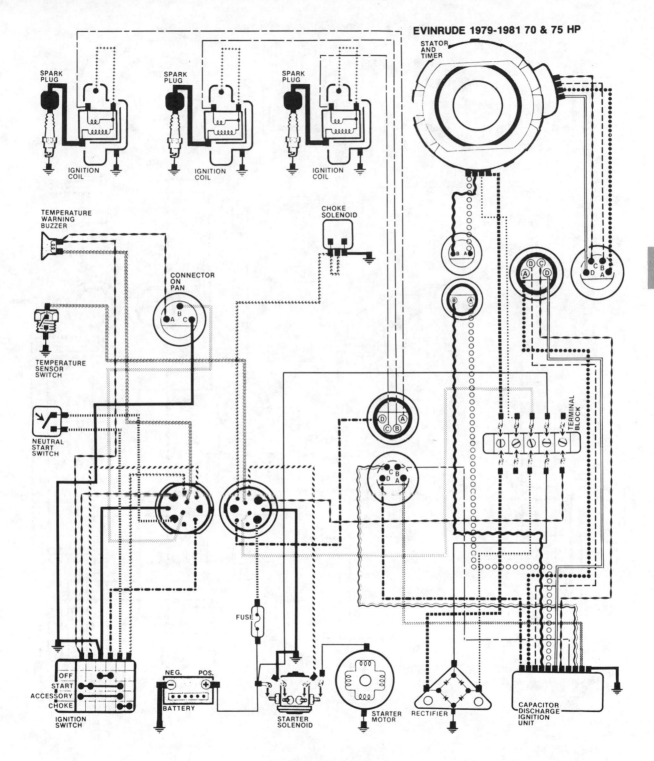

EVINRUDE 1979-1981 70 & 75 HP

SPARK PLUG

IGNITION COIL

TEMPERATURE WARNING BUZZER

CHOKE SOLENOID

STATOR AND TIMER

CONNECTOR ON PAN

TEMPERATURE SENSOR SWITCH

NEUTRAL START SWITCH

TERMINAL BLOCK

FUSE

OFF
START
ACCESSORY
CHOKE

IGNITION SWITCH

NEG. POS.

BATTERY

STARTER SOLENOID

STARTER MOTOR

RECTIFIER

CAPACITOR DISCHARGE IGNITION UNIT

DIAGRAM KEY

BLACK	RED	PURPLE
BLACK AND WHITE	ORANGE	PURPLE AND RED
BLACK AND ORANGE	ORANGE AND BLUE	PURPLE AND WHITE
BLACK AND BROWN	ORANGE AND GREEN	BROWN
BLACK AND YELLOW	YELLOW	BROWN AND YELLOW
WHITE	YELLOW AND RED	BROWN AND WHITE
WHITE AND BLACK	YELLOW AND PURPLE	TAN
GRAY	GREEN	
GRAY AND YELLOW	BLUE	

GROUND

CONNECTION

NO CONNECTION

EVINRUDE 1982-1984 70 & 75 HP

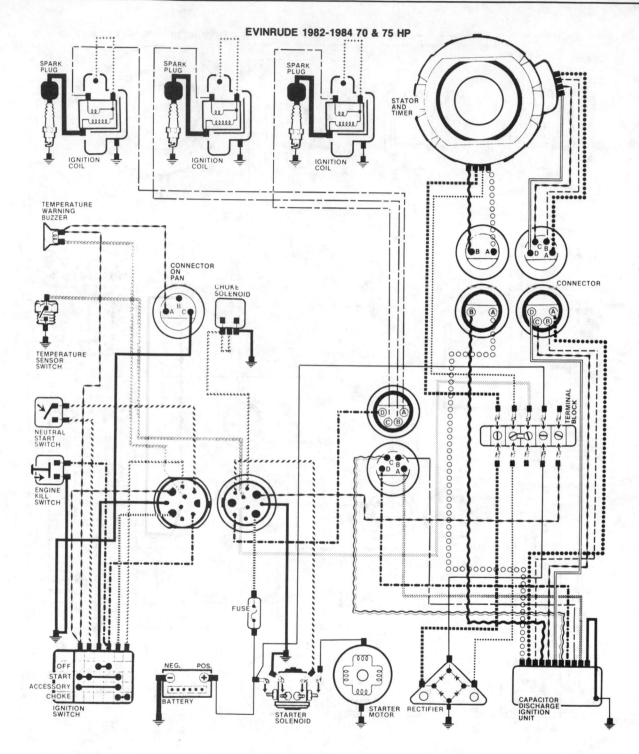

DIAGRAM KEY

BLACK		RED		PURPLE	
BLACK AND WHITE		ORANGE		PURPLE AND RED	
BLACK AND ORANGE		ORANGE AND BLUE		PURPLE AND WHITE	
BLACK AND BROWN		ORANGE AND GREEN		BROWN	
BLACK AND YELLOW		YELLOW		BROWN AND YELLOW	
WHITE		YELLOW AND RED		BROWN AND WHITE	
WHITE AND BLACK		YELLOW AND PURPLE		TAN	
GRAY		GREEN			
GRAY AND YELLOW		BLUE			

GROUND

CONNECTION

NO CONNECTION

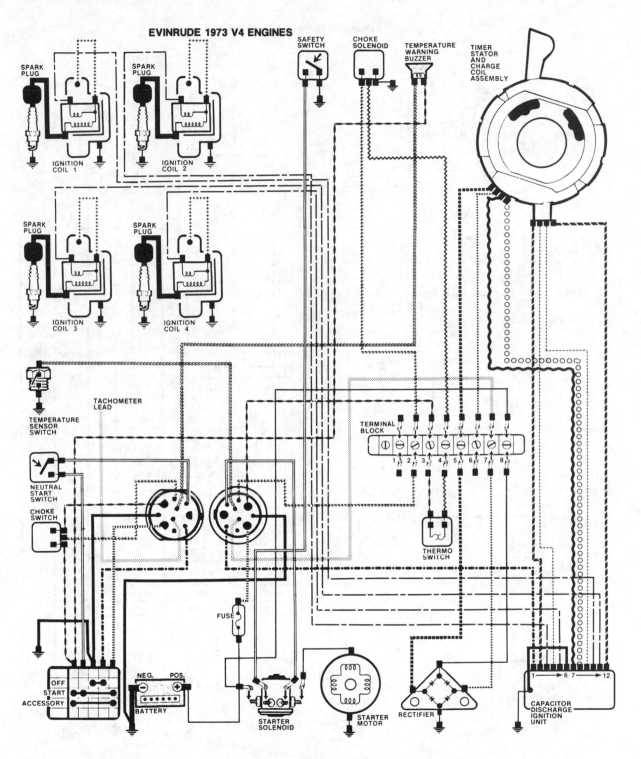

EVINRUDE 1973 V4 ENGINES

SPARK PLUG — IGNITION COIL 1

SPARK PLUG — IGNITION COIL 2

SPARK PLUG — IGNITION COIL 3

SPARK PLUG — IGNITION COIL 4

SAFETY SWITCH

CHOKE SOLENOID

TEMPERATURE WARNING BUZZER

TIMER STATOR AND CHARGE COIL ASSEMBLY

4

TEMPERATURE SENSOR SWITCH

TACHOMETER LEAD

NEUTRAL START SWITCH

CHOKE SWITCH

TERMINAL BLOCK

1 2 3 4 5 6 7 8

THERMO SWITCH

OFF START ACCESSORY

NEG. POS.

BATTERY

FUSE

STARTER SOLENOID

STARTER MOTOR

RECTIFIER

CAPACITOR DISCHARGE IGNITION UNIT

1 6 7 12

DIAGRAM KEY

———— BLACK	———— RED	—•—•— PURPLE
—••—••— BLACK AND WHITE	— — — ORANGE	•••••••• PURPLE AND RED
+++++++ BLACK AND ORANGE	～～～～ ORANGE AND BLUE	～～～～ PURPLE AND WHITE
—•—•— BLACK AND BROWN	～～～～ ORANGE AND GREEN	～～～～ BROWN
—•—•— BLACK AND YELLOW	■■■■■ YELLOW	○○○○○ BROWN AND YELLOW
———— WHITE	///// YELLOW AND RED	■■■■■ BROWN AND WHITE
- - - - WHITE AND BLACK	∧∧∧∧ YELLOW AND PURPLE	～～～～ TAN
░░░░░ GRAY	- - - - GREEN	
•••••••• GRAY AND YELLOW	●●●●● BLUE	

 GROUND

┼ CONNECTION

┼ NO CONNECTION

EVINRUDE 1974-1976 V4 ENGINES

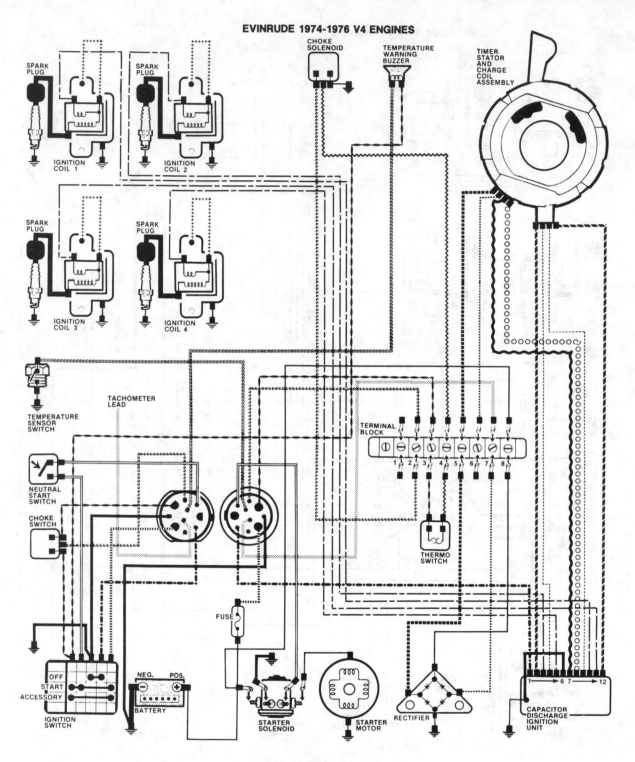

SPARK PLUG

IGNITION COIL 1

SPARK PLUG

IGNITION COIL 2

SPARK PLUG

IGNITION COIL 3

SPARK PLUG

IGNITION COIL 4

CHOKE SOLENOID

TEMPERATURE WARNING BUZZER

TIMER STATOR AND CHARGE COIL ASSEMBLY

TEMPERATURE SENSOR SWITCH

TACHOMETER LEAD

TERMINAL BLOCK

NEUTRAL START SWITCH

CHOKE SWITCH

THERMO SWITCH

FUSE

OFF
START
ACCESSORY

IGNITION SWITCH

NEG. POS.

BATTERY

STARTER SOLENOID

STARTER MOTOR

RECTIFIER

CAPACITOR DISCHARGE IGNITION UNIT

DIAGRAM KEY

BLACK	RED	PURPLE
BLACK AND WHITE	ORANGE	PURPLE AND RED
BLACK AND ORANGE	ORANGE AND BLUE	PURPLE AND WHITE
BLACK AND BROWN	ORANGE AND GREEN	BROWN
BLACK AND YELLOW	YELLOW	BROWN AND YELLOW
WHITE	YELLOW AND RED	BROWN AND WHITE
WHITE AND BLACK	YELLOW AND PURPLE	TAN
GRAY	GREEN	
GRAY AND YELLOW	BLUE	

GROUND

CONNECTION

NO CONNECTION

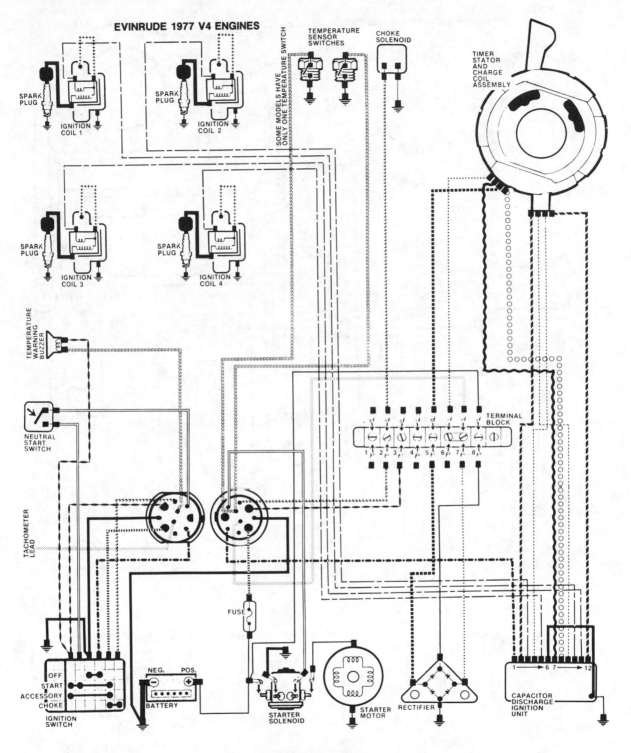

EVINRUDE 1977 V4 ENGINES

DIAGRAM KEY

BLACK	RED	PURPLE	GROUND
BLACK AND WHITE	ORANGE	PURPLE AND RED	CONNECTION
BLACK AND ORANGE	ORANGE AND BLUE	PURPLE AND WHITE	NO CONNECTION
BLACK AND BROWN	ORANGE AND GREEN	BROWN	
BLACK AND YELLOW	YELLOW	BROWN AND YELLOW	
WHITE	YELLOW AND RED	BROWN AND WHITE	
WHITE AND BLACK	YELLOW AND PURPLE	TAN	
GRAY	GREEN		
GRAY AND YELLOW	BLUE		

EVINRUDE 1978-1979 V4 ENGINES

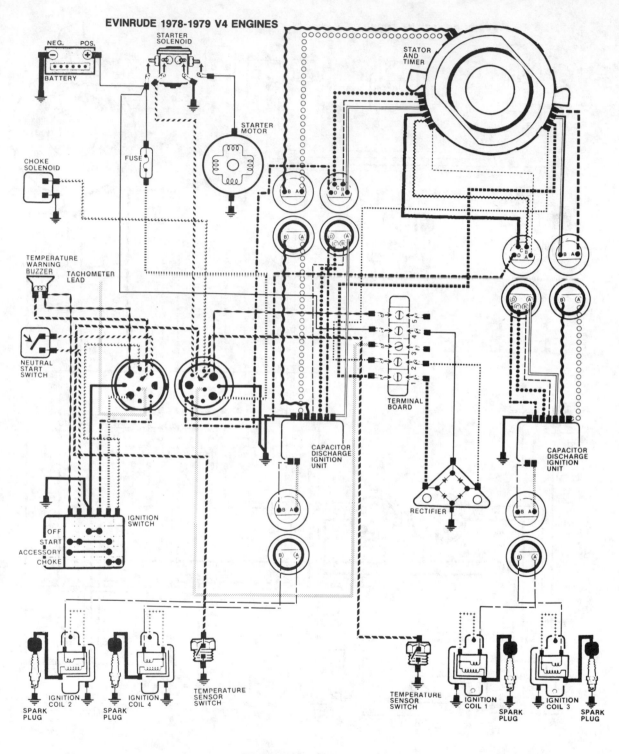

DIAGRAM KEY

BLACK	RED	PURPLE
TAN	ORANGE	PURPLE AND RED
BLACK AND ORANGE	ORANGE AND BLUE	PURPLE AND WHITE
BLACK AND BROWN	ORANGE AND GREEN	BROWN
BLACK AND YELLOW	YELLOW	BROWN AND YELLOW
WHITE	YELLOW AND RED	BROWN AND WHITE
WHITE AND BLACK	GREEN AND WHITE	BLUE AND WHITE
GRAY	GREEN	
GRAY AND YELLOW	BLUE	

GROUND

CONNECTION

NO CONNECTION

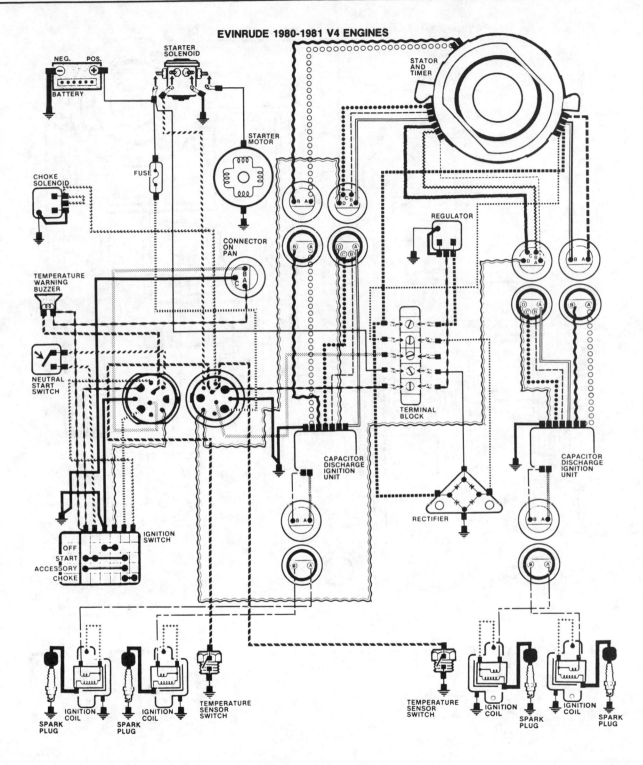

EVINRUDE 1980-1981 V4 ENGINES

4

DIAGRAM KEY

	BLACK		RED		PURPLE	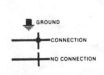 GROUND
	BLACK AND WHITE		ORANGE		PURPLE AND RED	CONNECTION
	BLACK AND ORANGE		ORANGE AND BLUE		PURPLE AND WHITE	
	BLACK AND BROWN		BLACK AND YELLOW		BROWN	
	BLACK AND YELLOW		YELLOW		BROWN AND YELLOW	NO CONNECTION
	WHITE		YELLOW AND RED		BROWN AND WHITE	
	WHITE AND BLACK		YELLOW AND PURPLE		TAN	
	GRAY		GREEN			
	GRAY AND YELLOW		BLUE			

EVINRUDE 1982-1984 V4 ENGINES, MANUAL TRIM AND TILT

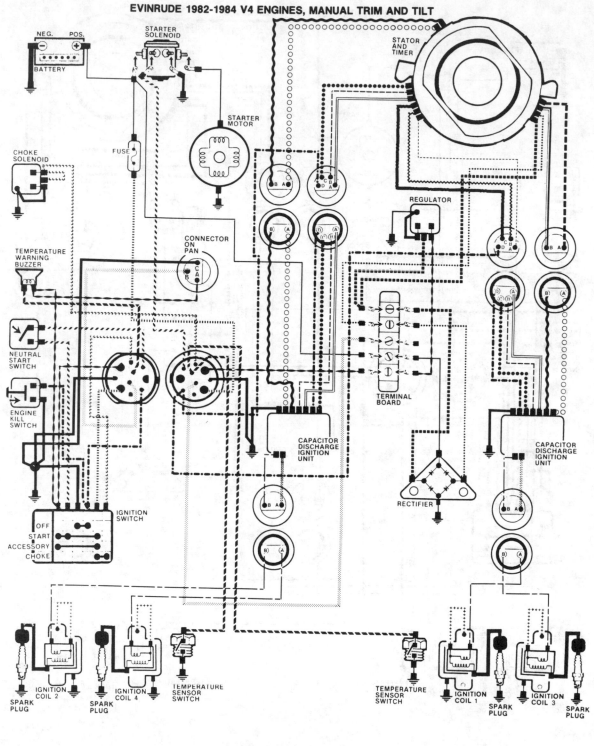

DIAGRAM KEY

BLACK	RED	PURPLE	GROUND
TAN	ORANGE	PURPLE AND RED	
BLACK AND ORANGE	ORANGE AND BLUE	PURPLE AND WHITE	CONNECTION
BLACK AND BROWN	ORANGE AND GREEN	BROWN	
BLACK AND YELLOW	YELLOW	BROWN AND YELLOW	NO CONNECTION
WHITE	YELLOW AND RED	BROWN AND WHITE	
WHITE AND BLACK	GREEN AND WHITE	BLUE AND WHITE	
GRAY	GREEN		
GRAY AND YELLOW	BLUE		

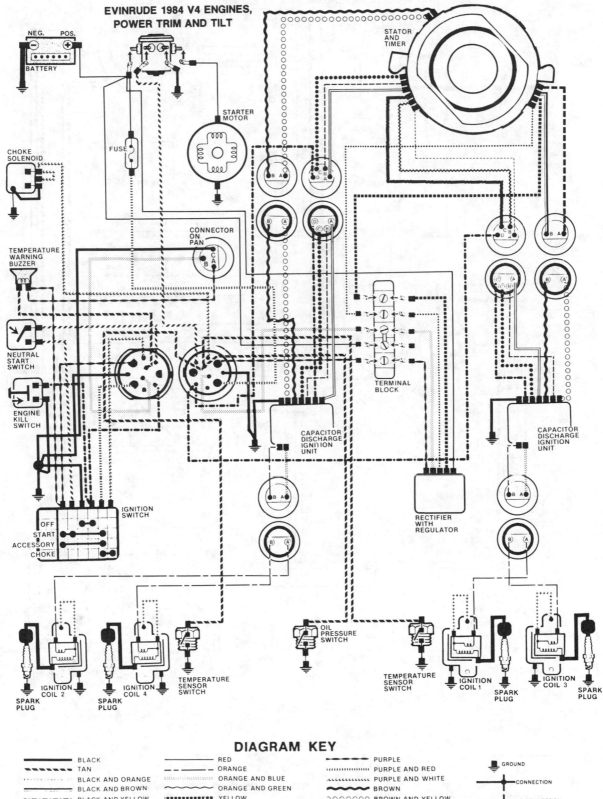

EVINRUDE 1984 V4 ENGINES, POWER TRIM AND TILT

4

DIAGRAM KEY

▬▬▬ BLACK	▬▬▬ RED	▬•▬•▬ PURPLE	◼ GROUND
▬ ▬ ▬ TAN	▬ ▬ ▬ ORANGE	•••••••• PURPLE AND RED	┼ CONNECTION
▬•▬•▬ BLACK AND ORANGE	∷∷∷∷∷ ORANGE AND BLUE	≈≈≈≈≈ PURPLE AND WHITE	
▬⋯▬⋯ BLACK AND BROWN	∿∿∿∿∿ ORANGE AND GREEN	∿∿∿∿ BROWN	┼ NO CONNECTION
▬•••▬ BLACK AND YELLOW	▬▬▬ YELLOW	○○○○○○ BROWN AND YELLOW	
━━━ WHITE	∿∿∿∿ YELLOW AND RED	▬ ▬ ▬ BROWN AND WHITE	
▬ ▬ ▬ WHITE AND BLACK	∿∿∿∿ GREEN AND WHITE	▬▬▬ BLUE AND WHITE	
▬▬▬ GRAY	▬ ▬ ▬ GREEN		
∷∷∷∷ GRAY AND YELLOW	•••••••• BLUE		

EVINRUDE 1976 V6 ENGINES

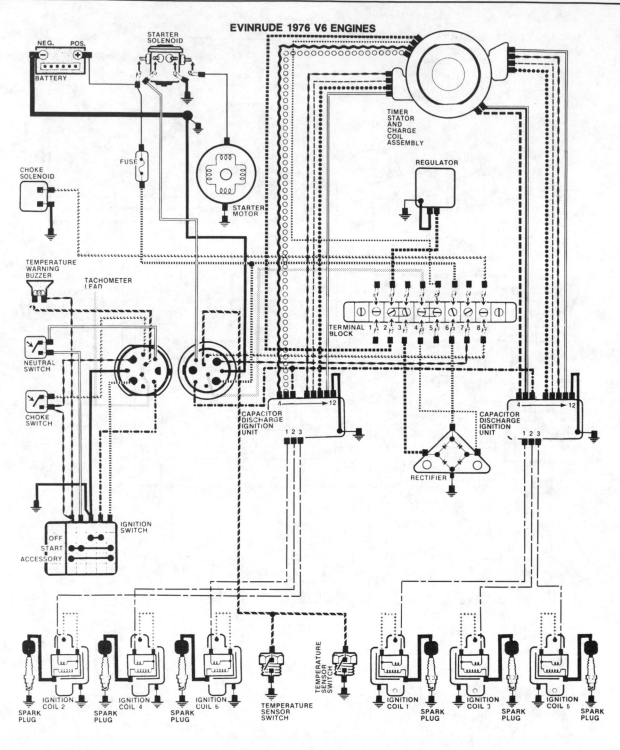

DIAGRAM KEY

					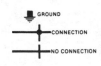
————	BLACK	————	RED	············	PURPLE	GROUND
—·—·—	TAN	— — —	ORANGE	··············	PURPLE AND RED	
+·+·+·+	BLACK AND ORANGE	············	ORANGE AND BLUE	‹‹‹‹‹‹‹	PURPLE AND WHITE	CONNECTION
————	BLACK AND BROWN	∿∿∿∿	ORANGE AND GREEN	∿∿∿∿	BROWN	
—●—●—	BLACK AND YELLOW	▬▬▬▬	YELLOW	○○○○○	BROWN AND YELLOW	NO CONNECTION
————	WHITE	▪▪▪▪▪	YELLOW AND RED	— — —	BROWN AND WHITE	
– – –	BLACK AND YELLOW	∿∿∿∿	YELLOW AND PURPLE	————	RED AND WHITE	
············	GRAY	————	GREEN			
············	GRAY AND YELLOW	●●●●●	BLUE			

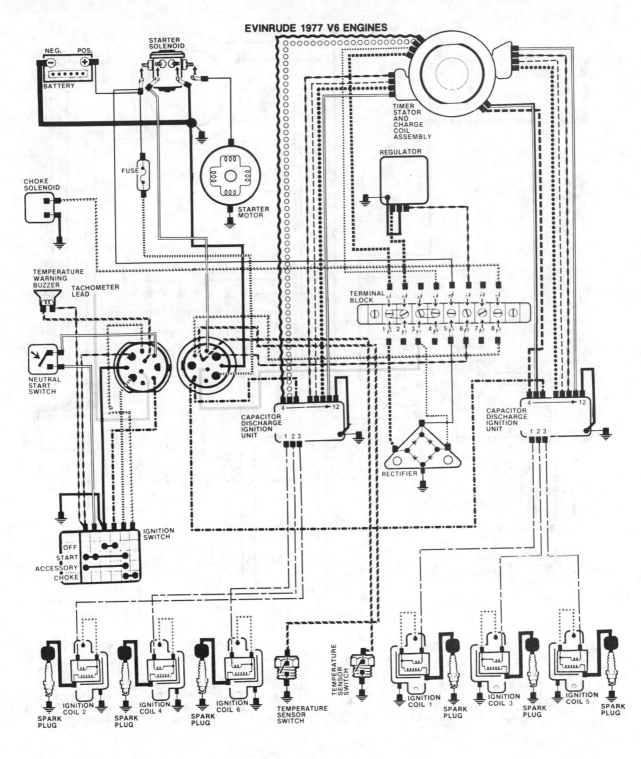

EVINRUDE 1977 V6 ENGINES

4

DIAGRAM KEY

▬▬▬ BLACK	───── RED	∿∿∿ PURPLE	GROUND
▰▰▰ TAN	─ ─ ─ ORANGE	⋯⋯⋯ PURPLE AND RED	
┼┼┼ BLACK AND ORANGE	∿∿∿ ORANGE AND BLUE	⋯⋯⋯ PURPLE AND WHITE	─┼─ CONNECTION
─··─ BLACK AND BROWN	∿∿∿ ORANGE AND GREEN	∿∿∿ BROWN	
─·─·─ BLACK AND YELLOW	▮▮▮ YELLOW	○○○○○ BROWN AND YELLOW	─┼─ NO CONNECTION
───── WHITE	⫽⫽⫽ YELLOW AND RED	▬ ▬ ▬ BROWN AND WHITE	
─ ─ ─ BLACK AND YELLOW	∿∿∿ YELLOW AND PURPLE	▬▬▬ RED AND WHITE	
∿∿∿ GRAY	───── GREEN		
┄┄┄ GRAY AND YELLOW	•••• BLUE		

EVINRUDE 1978 V6 ENGINES

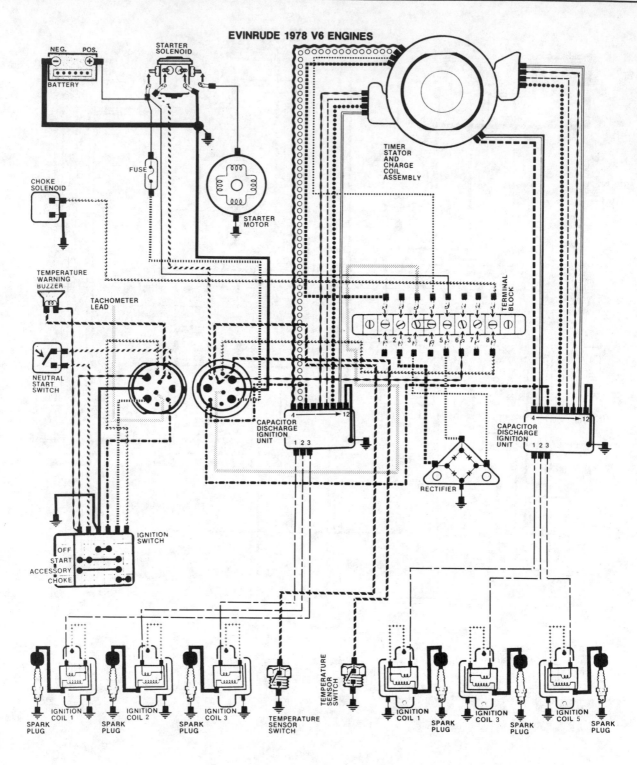

DIAGRAM KEY

BLACK	RED	PURPLE		GROUND
TAN	ORANGE	PURPLE AND RED		
BLACK AND ORANGE	ORANGE AND BLUE	PURPLE AND WHITE		CONNECTION
BLACK AND BROWN	ORANGE AND GREEN	BROWN		
BLACK AND YELLOW	YELLOW	BROWN AND YELLOW		NO CONNECTION
WHITE	YELLOW AND RED	BROWN AND WHITE		
BLACK AND YELLOW	YELLOW AND PURPLE	RED AND WHITE		
GRAY	GREEN			
GRAY AND YELLOW	BLUE			

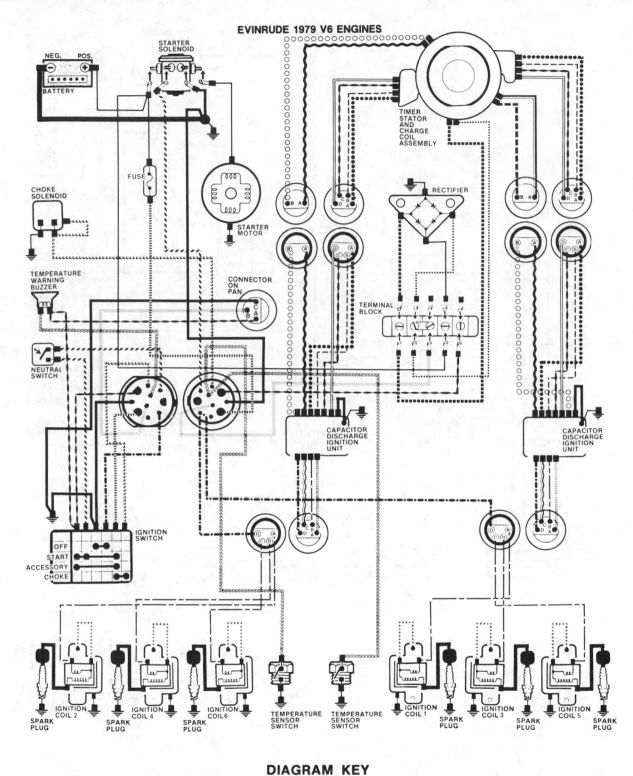

EVINRUDE 1979 V6 ENGINES

DIAGRAM KEY

BLACK	RED	PURPLE	GROUND
BLACK AND WHITE	ORANGE	PURPLE AND RED	CONNECTION
BLACK AND ORANGE	ORANGE AND BLUE	PURPLE AND WHITE	NO CONNECTION
BLACK AND BROWN	ORANGE AND GREEN	BROWN	
BLACK AND YELLOW	YELLOW	BROWN AND YELLOW	
WHITE	YELLOW AND RED	BROWN AND WHITE	
WHITE AND BLACK	YELLOW AND PURPLE	TAN	
GRAY	GREEN		
GRAY AND YELLOW	BLUE		

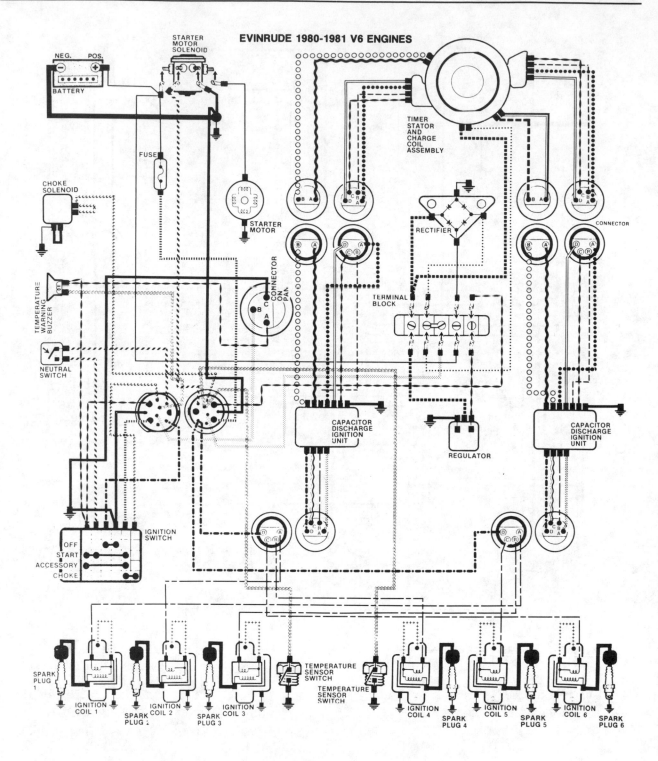

EVINRUDE 1980-1981 V6 ENGINES

DIAGRAM KEY

BLACK	RED	PURPLE	GROUND
BLACK AND WHITE	ORANGE	PURPLE AND RED	CONNECTION
BLACK AND ORANGE	ORANGE AND BLUE	PURPLE AND WHITE	NO CONNECTION
BLACK AND BROWN	ORANGE AND GREEN	BROWN	
BLACK AND YELLOW	YELLOW	BROWN AND YELLOW	
WHITE	YELLOW AND RED	BROWN AND WHITE	
WHITE AND BLACK	YELLOW AND PURPLE	TAN	
GRAY	GREEN		
GRAY AND YELLOW	BLUE		

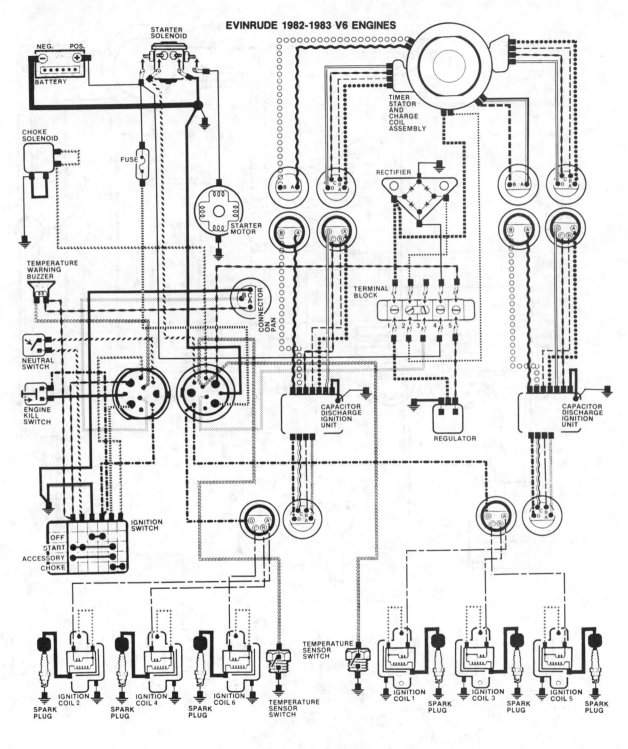

EVINRUDE 1982-1983 V6 ENGINES

DIAGRAM KEY

BLACK	RED	PURPLE
BLACK AND WHITE	ORANGE	PURPLE AND RED
BLACK AND ORANGE	ORANGE AND BLUE	PURPLE AND WHITE
BLACK AND BROWN	ORANGE AND GREEN	BROWN
BLACK AND YELLOW	YELLOW	BROWN AND YELLOW
WHITE	YELLOW AND RED	BROWN AND WHITE
WHITE AND BLACK	YELLOW AND PURPLE	TAN
GRAY	GREEN	
GRAY AND YELLOW	BLUE	

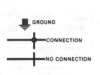

GROUND

CONNECTION

NO CONNECTION

4

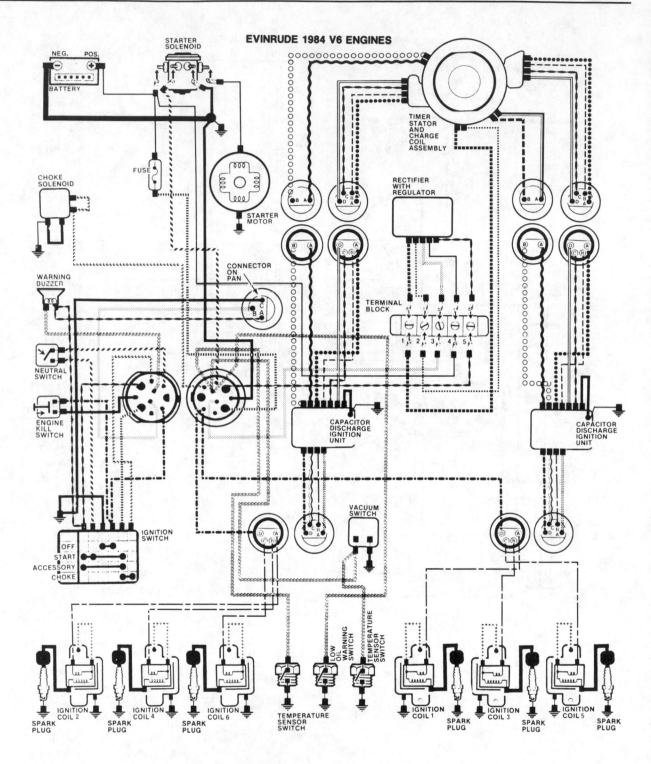

EVINRUDE 1984 V6 ENGINES

DIAGRAM KEY

▬▬▬ BLACK	——— RED	▬▬▬ PURPLE
⟋⟋⟋ BLACK AND WHITE	– – – ORANGE	∙∙∙∙∙∙∙∙ PURPLE AND RED
+++++++ BLACK AND ORANGE	≋≋≋ ORANGE AND BLUE	⟨⟨⟨⟨⟨ PURPLE AND WHITE
▬▬ BLACK AND BROWN	⌇⌇⌇ ORANGE AND GREEN	⌒⌒⌒ BROWN
∙━∙━∙ BLACK AND YELLOW	▰▰▰ YELLOW	○○○○○ BROWN AND YELLOW
——— WHITE	⟋⟋⟋ YELLOW AND RED	▬ ▬ ▬ BROWN AND WHITE
∙∙∙∙∙∙∙ WHITE AND BLACK	⋀⋀⋀ YELLOW AND PURPLE	≈≈≈≈≈ TAN
░░░ GRAY	——— GREEN	
∙∙∙∙∙∙∙ GRAY AND YELLOW	●●●●● BLUE	

GROUND

CONNECTION

NO CONNECTION

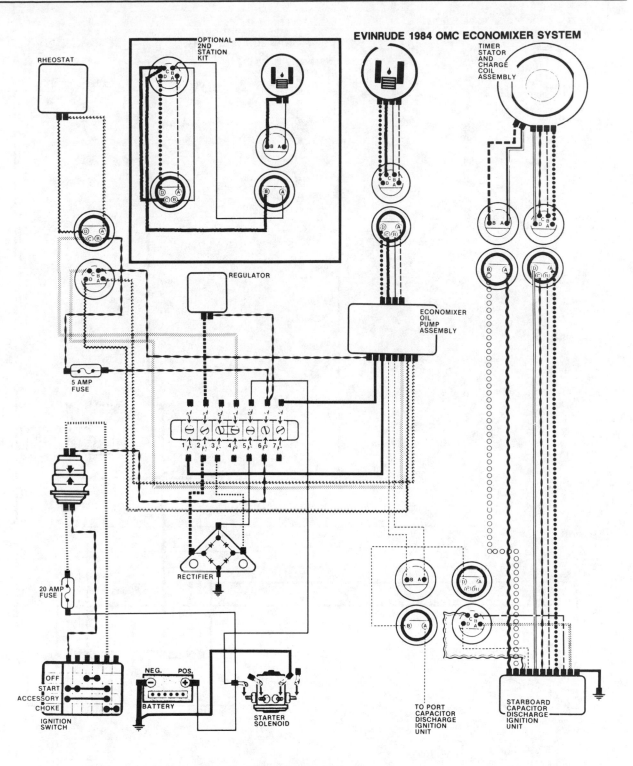

EVINRUDE 1984 OMC ECONOMIXER SYSTEM

4

DIAGRAM KEY

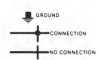

BLACK	RED	PURPLE
TAN	ORANGE	PURPLE AND RED
BLACK AND ORANGE	ORANGE AND BLUE	PURPLE AND WHITE
BLACK AND BROWN	ORANGE AND GREEN	BROWN
BLACK AND YELLOW	YELLOW	BROWN AND YELLOW
WHITE	YELLOW AND RED	BROWN AND WHITE
BLACK AND YELLOW	YELLOW AND PURPLE	RED AND WHITE
GRAY	GREEN	
GRAY AND YELLOW	BLUE	

GROUND

CONNECTION

NO CONNECTION

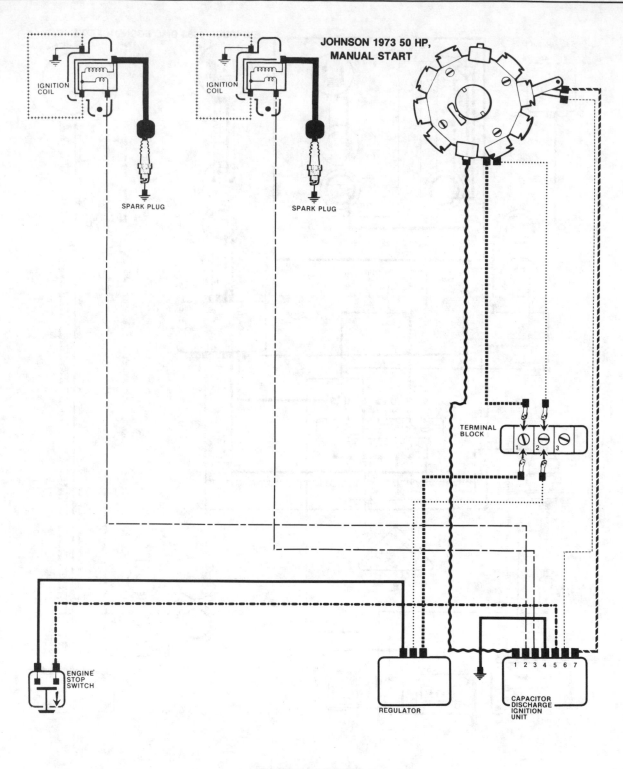

JOHNSON 1973 50 HP, MANUAL START

IGNITION COIL

IGNITION COIL

SPARK PLUG

SPARK PLUG

TERMINAL BLOCK

ENGINE STOP SWITCH

REGULATOR

CAPACITOR DISCHARGE IGNITION UNIT

DIAGRAM KEY

BLACK	RED	PURPLE
BLACK AND WHITE	ORANGE	PURPLE AND RED
BLACK AND ORANGE	ORANGE AND BLUE	PURPLE AND WHITE
BLACK AND BROWN	ORANGE AND GREEN	BROWN
BLACK AND YELLOW	YELLOW	BROWN AND YELLOW
WHITE	YELLOW AND RED	BROWN AND WHITE
WHITE AND BLACK	YELLOW AND PURPLE	TAN
GRAY	GREEN	
GRAY AND YELLOW	BLUE	

GROUND

CONNECTION

NO CONNECTION

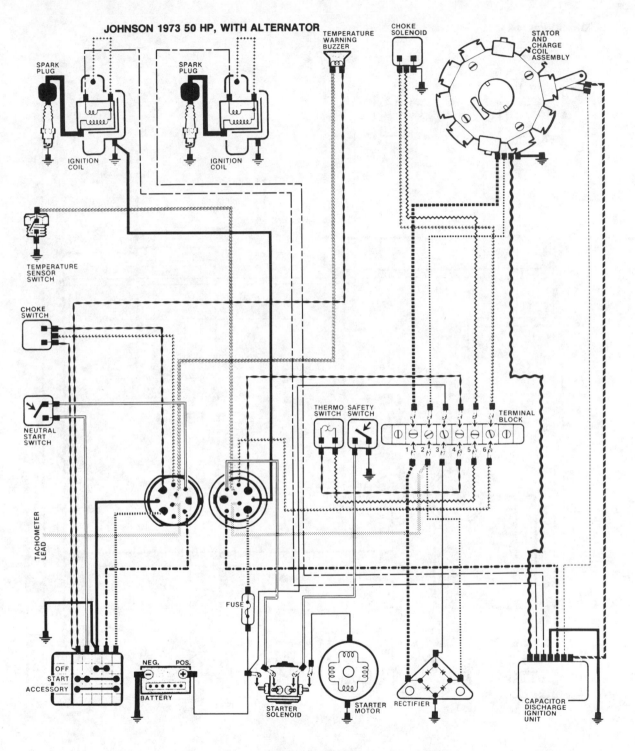

JOHNSON 1973 50 HP, WITH ALTERNATOR

SPARK PLUG

IGNITION COIL

SPARK PLUG

IGNITION COIL

TEMPERATURE WARNING BUZZER

CHOKE SOLENOID

STATOR AND CHARGE COIL ASSEMBLY

TEMPERATURE SENSOR SWITCH

CHOKE SWITCH

NEUTRAL START SWITCH

THERMO SWITCH

SAFETY SWITCH

TERMINAL BLOCK

1 2 3 4 5 6

TACHOMETER LEAD

FUSE

OFF START ACCESSORY

NEG. POS.

BATTERY

STARTER SOLENOID

STARTER MOTOR

RECTIFIER

CAPACITOR DISCHARGE IGNITION UNIT

DIAGRAM KEY

BLACK	RED	PURPLE
BLACK AND WHITE	ORANGE	PURPLE AND RED
BLACK AND ORANGE	ORANGE AND BLUE	PURPLE AND WHITE
BLACK AND BROWN	ORANGE AND GREEN	BROWN
BLACK AND YELLOW	YELLOW	BROWN AND YELLOW
WHITE	YELLOW AND RED	BROWN AND WHITE
WHITE AND BLACK	YELLOW AND PURPLE	TAN
GRAY	GREEN	
GRAY AND YELLOW	BLUE	

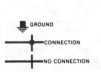

GROUND

CONNECTION

NO CONNECTION

JOHNSON 1974-1975 50 HP, WITH ALTERNATOR

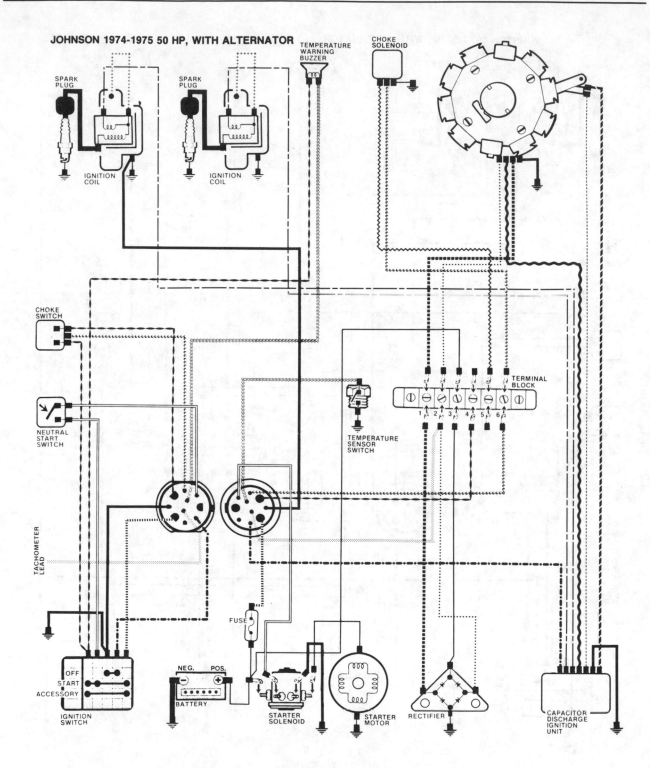

DIAGRAM KEY

—— BLACK	—— RED	—— PURPLE
BLACK AND WHITE	ORANGE	PURPLE AND RED
BLACK AND ORANGE	ORANGE AND BLUE	PURPLE AND WHITE
BLACK AND BROWN	ORANGE AND GREEN	BROWN
BLACK AND YELLOW	YELLOW	BROWN AND YELLOW
WHITE	YELLOW AND RED	BROWN AND WHITE
WHITE AND BLACK	YELLOW AND PURPLE	TAN
GRAY	GREEN	
GRAY AND YELLOW	BLUE	

GROUND

CONNECTION

NO CONNECTION

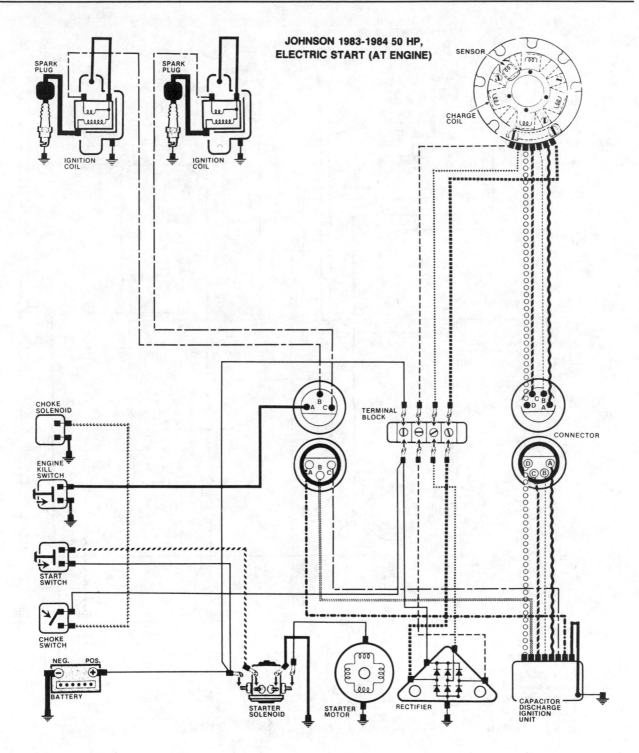

JOHNSON 1983-1984 50 HP, ELECTRIC START (AT ENGINE)

DIAGRAM KEY

—————— BLACK	—————— RED	∿∿∿∿∿ PURPLE
▪▪▪▪▪▪ BLACK AND WHITE	– – – – ORANGE	∷∷∷∷∷ PURPLE AND RED
+++++++ BLACK AND ORANGE	∷∷∷∷∷ ORANGE AND BLUE	⟨⟨⟨⟨⟨ PURPLE AND WHITE
═══════ BLACK AND BROWN	∿∿∿∿∿ ORANGE AND GREEN	∿∿∿∿∿ BROWN
—————— BLACK AND YELLOW	▬▬▬▬▬ YELLOW	⟨○○○○○ BROWN AND YELLOW
—————— WHITE	⁄⁄⁄⁄⁄ YELLOW AND RED	▬ ▬ ▬ BROWN AND WHITE
- - - - - WHITE AND BLACK	∿∿∿∿∿ YELLOW AND PURPLE	⋉⋉⋉⋉⋉ TAN
—————— GRAY	– – – – BLUE AND YELLOW	
———— GRAY AND YELLOW	●●●●●● BLUE	

GROUND

CONNECTION

NO CONNECTION

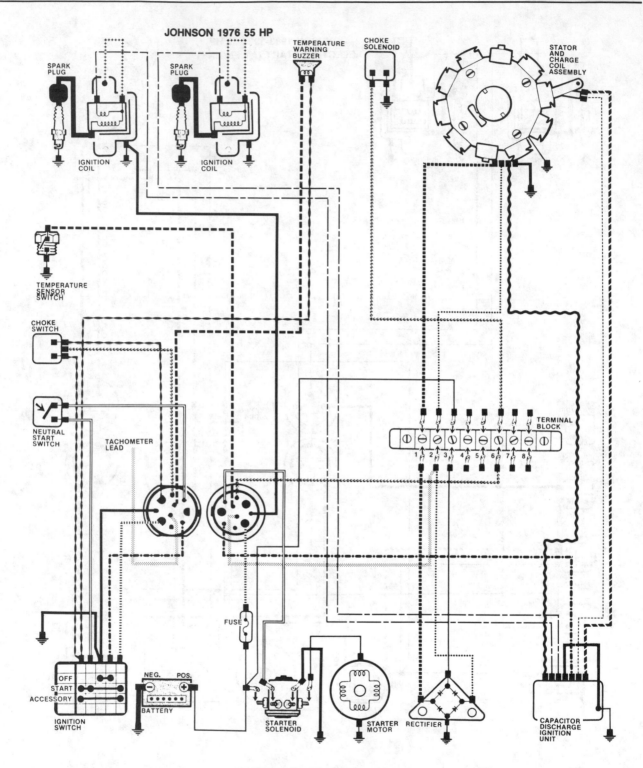

JOHNSON 1976 55 HP

DIAGRAM KEY

▬▬▬	BLACK	————	RED	▬▬▬▬	PURPLE	◼ GROUND
▬▬▬	BLACK AND WHITE	– – – –	ORANGE	··········	PURPLE AND RED	
+++++++	BLACK AND ORANGE	▨▨▨▨	ORANGE AND BLUE	‹‹‹‹‹‹‹	PURPLE AND WHITE	✚ CONNECTION
══════	BLACK AND BROWN	∿∿∿∿	ORANGE AND GREEN	～～～	BROWN	
·–·–·–	BLACK AND YELLOW	▬▬▬▬	YELLOW	○○○○○	BROWN AND YELLOW	╪ NO CONNECTION
════	WHITE	⁄⁄⁄⁄⁄⁄	YELLOW AND RED	▬ ▬ ▬	TAN	
- - - - -	WHITE AND BLACK	∧∧∧∧∧	YELLOW AND PURPLE			
∶∶∶∶∶∶	GRAY	– – – –	BROWN AND ORANGE			
········	GRAY AND YELLOW	●●●●●●	BLUE			

4

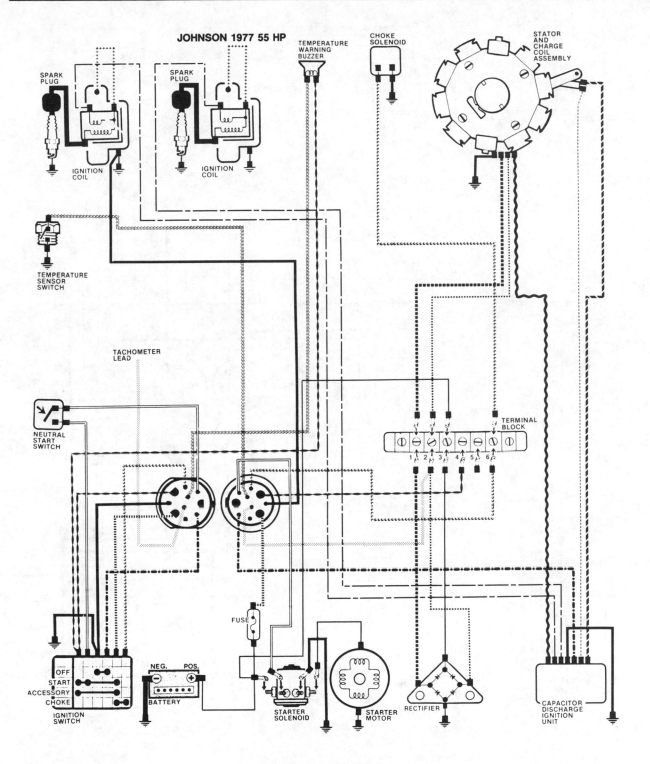

JOHNSON 1977 55 HP

DIAGRAM KEY

BLACK	RED	PURPLE
BLACK AND WHITE	ORANGE	PURPLE AND RED
BLACK AND ORANGE	ORANGE AND BLUE	PURPLE AND WHITE
BLACK AND BROWN	ORANGE AND GREEN	BROWN
BLACK AND YELLOW	YELLOW	BROWN AND YELLOW
WHITE	YELLOW AND RED	BROWN AND WHITE
WHITE AND BLACK	YELLOW AND PURPLE	TAN
GRAY	GREEN	
GRAY AND YELLOW	BLUE	

GROUND

CONNECTION

NO CONNECTION

JOHNSON 1978-1979 55 HP

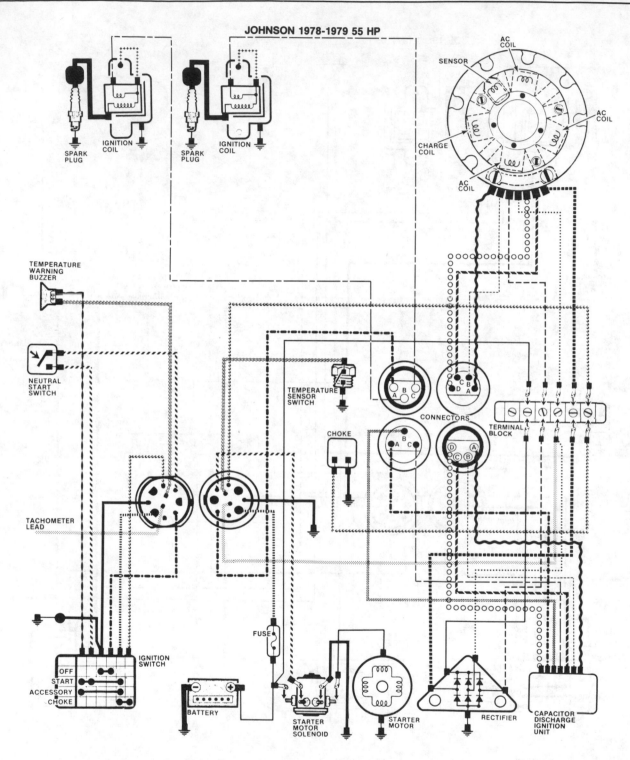

DIAGRAM KEY

BLACK	RED	PURPLE	GROUND
BLACK AND WHITE	ORANGE	PURPLE AND RED	
BLACK AND ORANGE	ORANGE AND BLUE	PURPLE AND WHITE	CONNECTION
BLACK AND BROWN	ORANGE AND GREEN	BROWN	
BLACK AND YELLOW	YELLOW	BROWN AND YELLOW	NO CONNECTION
WHITE	YELLOW AND RED	BROWN AND WHITE	
WHITE AND BLACK	YELLOW AND PURPLE	TAN	
GRAY	GREEN		
GRAY AND YELLOW	BLUE		

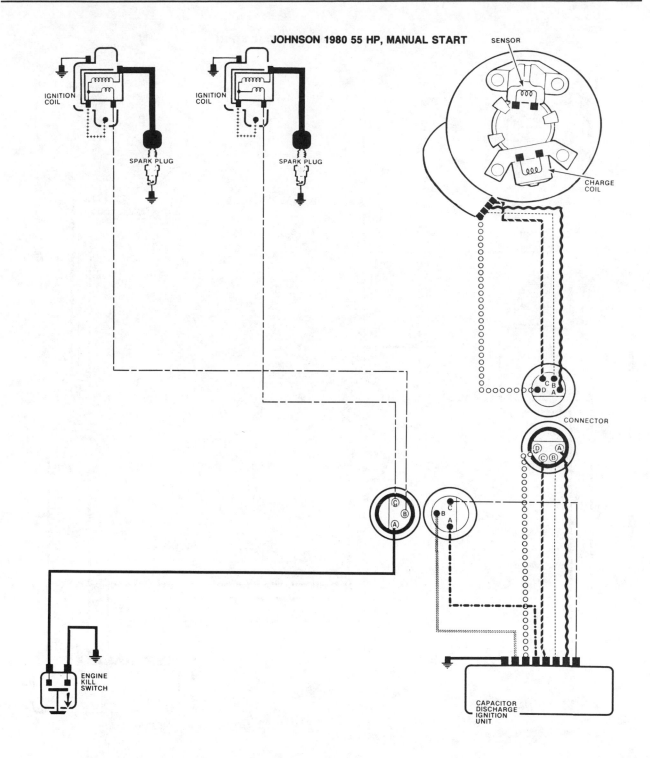

JOHNSON 1980 55 HP, MANUAL START

IGNITION COIL

SPARK PLUG

SENSOR

CHARGE COIL

CONNECTOR

ENGINE KILL SWITCH

CAPACITOR DISCHARGE IGNITION UNIT

4

DIAGRAM KEY

BLACK	RED	PURPLE
BLACK AND WHITE	ORANGE	PURPLE AND RED
BLACK AND ORANGE	ORANGE AND BLUE	PURPLE AND WHITE
BLACK AND BROWN	ORANGE AND GREEN	BROWN
BLACK AND YELLOW	YELLOW	BROWN AND YELLOW
WHITE	YELLOW AND RED	BROWN AND WHITE
WHITE AND BLACK	YELLOW AND PURPLE	TAN
GRAY	GREEN	
GRAY AND YELLOW	BLUE	

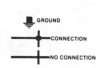

GROUND

CONNECTION

NO CONNECTION

JOHNSON 1982 55 HP, MANUAL START

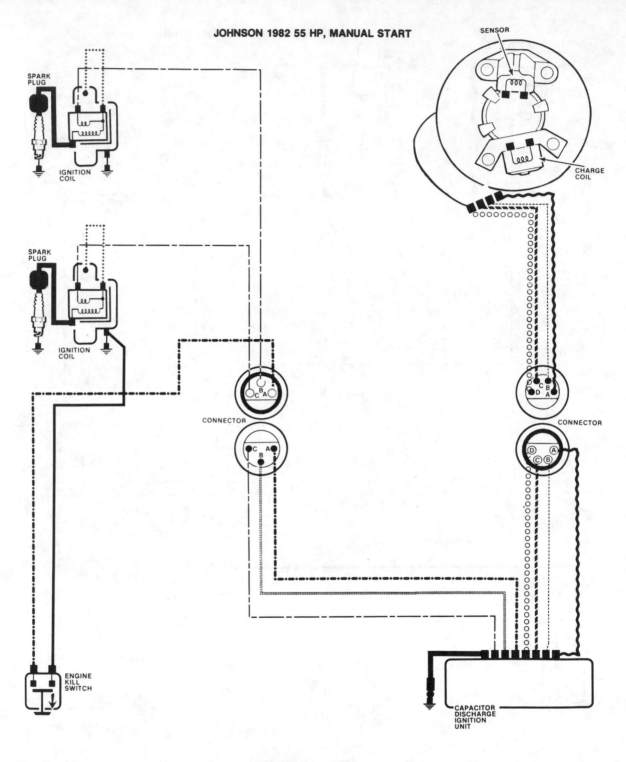

SPARK PLUG

IGNITION COIL

SPARK PLUG

IGNITION COIL

ENGINE KILL SWITCH

CONNECTOR

CONNECTOR

SENSOR

CHARGE COIL

CONNECTOR

CONNECTOR

CAPACITOR DISCHARGE IGNITION UNIT

DIAGRAM KEY

BLACK	RED	PURPLE
BLACK AND WHITE	ORANGE	PURPLE AND RED
BLACK AND ORANGE	ORANGE AND BLUE	PURPLE AND WHITE
BLACK AND BROWN	ORANGE AND GREEN	BROWN
BLACK AND YELLOW	YELLOW	BROWN AND YELLOW
WHITE	YELLOW AND RED	BROWN AND WHITE
WHITE AND BLACK	YELLOW AND PURPLE	TAN
GRAY	GREEN	
GRAY AND YELLOW	BLUE	

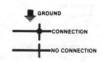

GROUND

CONNECTION

NO CONNECTION

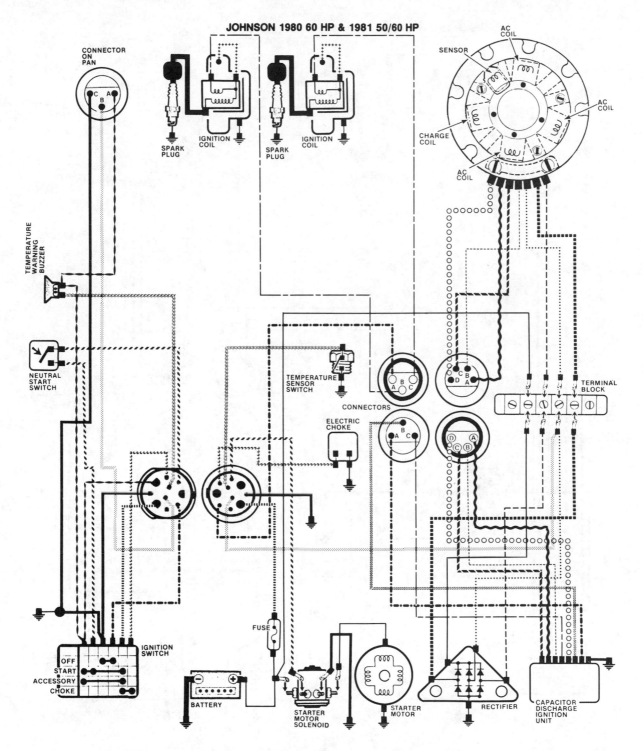

JOHNSON 1980 60 HP & 1981 50/60 HP

DIAGRAM KEY

BLACK	RED	PURPLE
BLACK AND WHITE	ORANGE	PURPLE AND RED
BLACK AND ORANGE	ORANGE AND BLUE	PURPLE AND WHITE
BLACK AND BROWN	ORANGE AND GREEN	BROWN
BLACK AND YELLOW	YELLOW	BROWN AND YELLOW
WHITE	YELLOW AND RED	BROWN AND WHITE
WHITE AND BLACK	YELLOW AND PURPLE	TAN
GRAY	BLUE AND YELLOW	
GRAY AND YELLOW	BLUE	

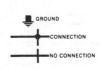

GROUND

CONNECTION

NO CONNECTION

JOHNSON 1982-1984 50 & 60 HP, REMOTE ELECTRIC START

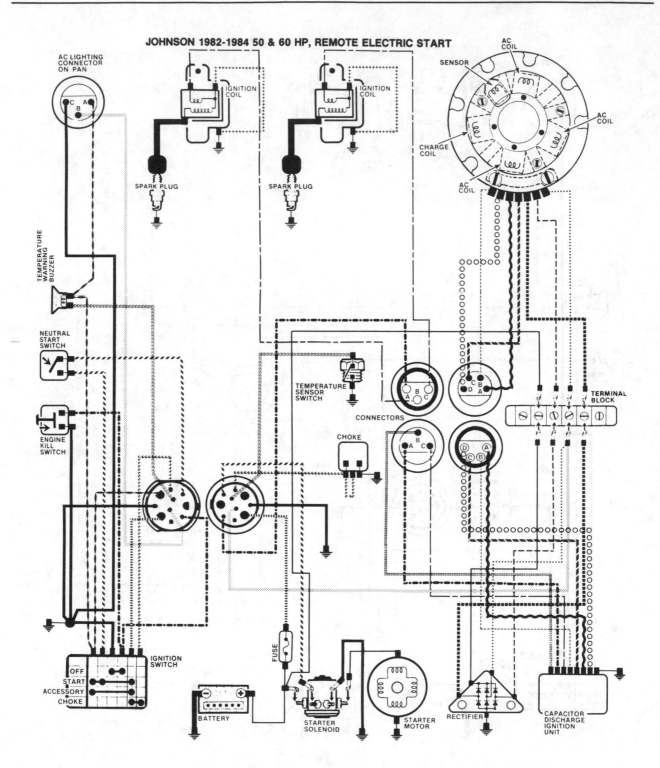

DIAGRAM KEY

BLACK	RED	PURPLE
BLACK AND WHITE	ORANGE	PURPLE AND RED
BLACK AND ORANGE	ORANGE AND BLUE	PURPLE AND WHITE
BLACK AND BROWN	ORANGE AND GREEN	BROWN
BLACK AND YELLOW	YELLOW	BROWN AND YELLOW
WHITE	YELLOW AND RED	BROWN AND WHITE
WHITE AND BLACK	YELLOW AND PURPLE	TAN
GRAY	BLUE AND YELLOW	GROUND
GRAY AND YELLOW	BLUE	CONNECTION
		NO CONNECTION

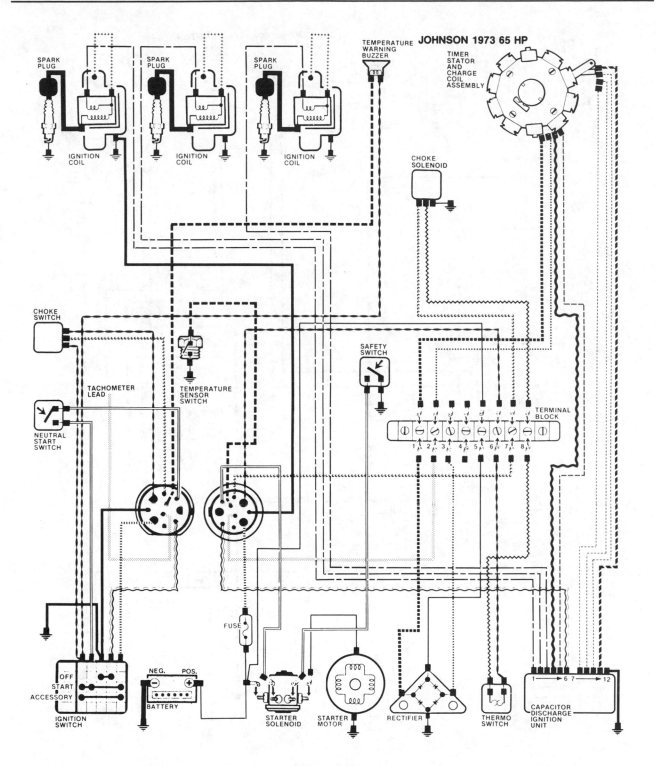

JOHNSON 1973 65 HP

SPARK PLUG

IGNITION COIL

SPARK PLUG

IGNITION COIL

SPARK PLUG

IGNITION COIL

TEMPERATURE WARNING BUZZER

TIMER STATOR AND CHARGE COIL ASSEMBLY

CHOKE SOLENOID

CHOKE SWITCH

TACHOMETER LEAD

TEMPERATURE SENSOR SWITCH

SAFETY SWITCH

TERMINAL BLOCK

1 2 3 4 5 6 7 8

NEUTRAL START SWITCH

OFF
START
ACCESSORY

IGNITION SWITCH

NEG. POS.

BATTERY

FUSE

STARTER SOLENOID

STARTER MOTOR

RECTIFIER

THERMO SWITCH

1   6 7   12

CAPACITOR DISCHARGE IGNITION UNIT

DIAGRAM KEY

▬▬▬▬ BLACK	─ ─ ─ RED	⌒⌒⌒ PURPLE
▬ ▬ ▬ BLACK AND WHITE	─ ─ ─ ORANGE	∙∙∙∙∙∙∙ PURPLE AND RED
✛✛✛✛ BLACK AND ORANGE	∷∷∷∷ ORANGE AND BLUE	∿∿∿∿ PURPLE AND WHITE
▬▬▬ BLACK AND BROWN	⌒⌒⌒ BLACK AND YELLOW	∿∿∿∿ BROWN
▬▬▬ WHITE	▬▬▬ YELLOW	○○○○○ BROWN AND YELLOW
─ ─ ─ WHITE AND BLACK	▬▬▬ YELLOW AND RED	▬ ▬ ▬ TAN
▬▬▬ GRAY	∿∿∿ YELLOW AND PURPLE	
∙∙∙∙∙∙ GRAY AND YELLOW	─ ─ ─ BROWN AND ORANGE	
●●●●● BLUE		

⏚ GROUND

╋ CONNECTION

╋ NO CONNECTION

4

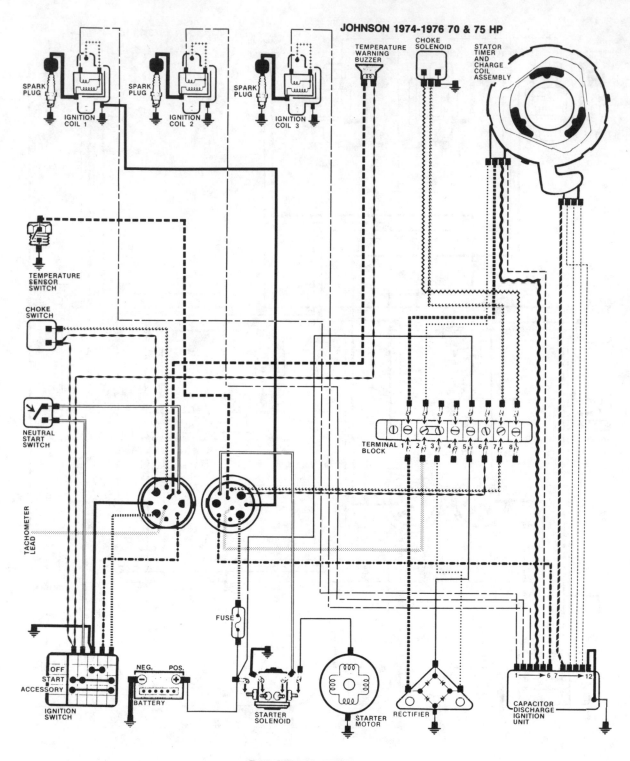

JOHNSON 1974-1976 70 & 75 HP

SPARK PLUG
IGNITION COIL 1
SPARK PLUG
IGNITION COIL 2
SPARK PLUG
IGNITION COIL 3
TEMPERATURE WARNING BUZZER
CHOKE SOLENOID
STATOR TIMER AND CHARGE COIL ASSEMBLY

TEMPERATURE SENSOR SWITCH

CHOKE SWITCH

NEUTRAL START SWITCH

TERMINAL BLOCK 1 2 3 4 5 6 7 8

TACHOMETER LEAD

OFF START ACCESSORY
IGNITION SWITCH

NEG. POS.
BATTERY

FUSE

STARTER SOLENOID

STARTER MOTOR

RECTIFIER

1 6 7 12
CAPACITOR DISCHARGE IGNITION UNIT

DIAGRAM KEY

BLACK	RED	PURPLE	GROUND
BLACK AND WHITE	ORANGE	PURPLE AND RED	
BLACK AND ORANGE	ORANGE AND BLUE	PURPLE AND WHITE	CONNECTION
BLACK AND BROWN	ORANGE AND GREEN	BROWN	
BLACK AND YELLOW	YELLOW	BROWN AND YELLOW	NO CONNECTION
WHITE	YELLOW AND RED	TAN	
WHITE AND BLACK	YELLOW AND PURPLE		
GRAY	BROWN AND ORANGE		
GRAY AND YELLOW	BLUE		

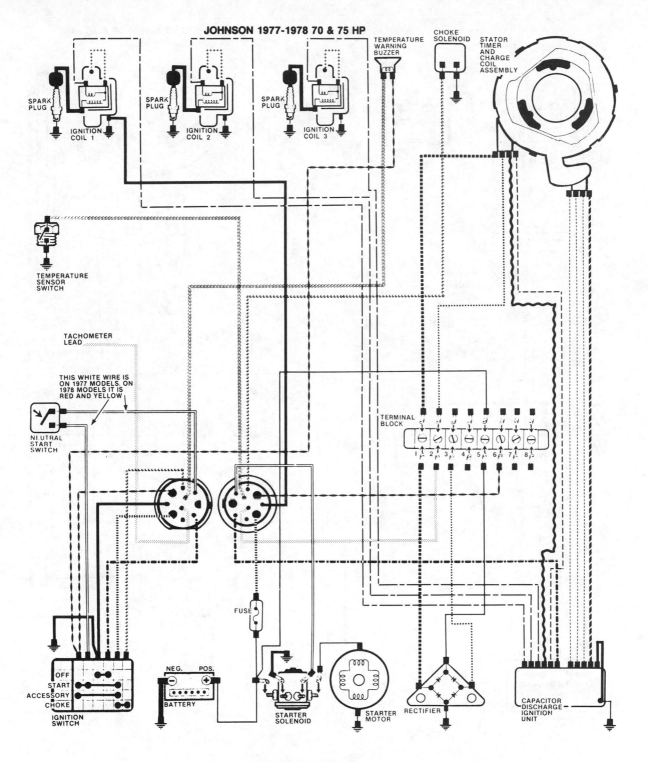

JOHNSON 1977-1978 70 & 75 HP

DIAGRAM KEY

——— BLACK	——— RED	⌒⌒⌒ PURPLE
—▬—▬— BLACK AND WHITE	– – – ORANGE	⋯⋯⋯ PURPLE AND RED
+++++ BLACK AND ORANGE	⋮⋮⋮⋮ ORANGE AND BLUE	⋯⋯⋯ PURPLE AND WHITE
——— BLACK AND BROWN	∿∿∿ ORANGE AND GREEN	∿∿∿ BROWN
●–●–● BLACK AND YELLOW	▬▬▬ YELLOW	○○○○ BROWN AND YELLOW
——— WHITE	▬▬▬ YELLOW AND RED	▬ ▬ ▬ TAN
– – – WHITE AND BLACK	∿∿∿ YELLOW AND PURPLE	
⋯⋯⋯ GRAY	– – – BROWN AND ORANGE	
⋯⋯⋯ GRAY AND YELLOW	●●●● BLUE	

GROUND

CONNECTION

NO CONNECTION

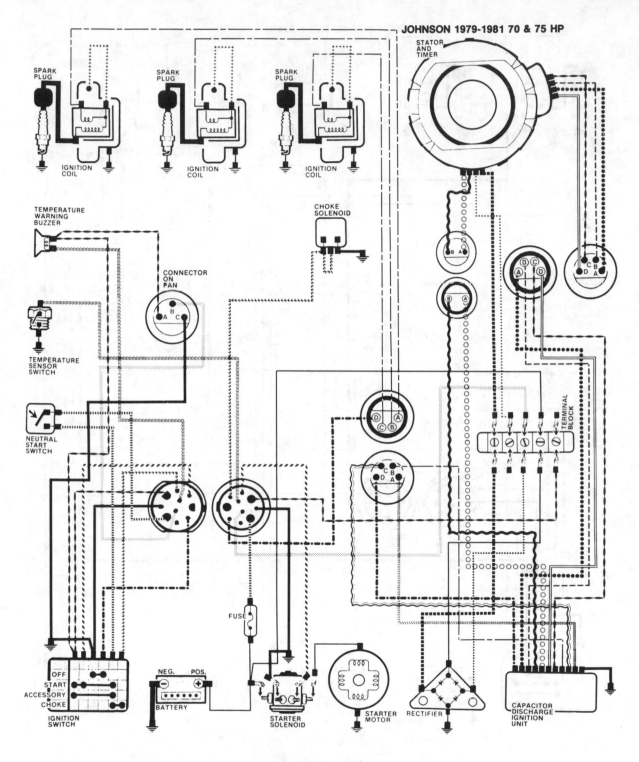

JOHNSON 1979-1981 70 & 75 HP

STATOR AND TIMER

SPARK PLUG

IGNITION COIL

SPARK PLUG

IGNITION COIL

SPARK PLUG

IGNITION COIL

TEMPERATURE WARNING BUZZER

CHOKE SOLENOID

CONNECTOR ON PAN

TEMPERATURE SENSOR SWITCH

NEUTRAL START SWITCH

TERMINAL BLOCK

OFF
START
ACCESSORY
CHOKE

IGNITION SWITCH

NEG. POS.

BATTERY

FUSE

STARTER SOLENOID

STARTER MOTOR

RECTIFIER

CAPACITOR DISCHARGE IGNITION UNIT

DIAGRAM KEY

BLACK	RED	PURPLE	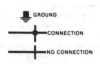 GROUND
BLACK AND WHITE	ORANGE	PURPLE AND RED	
BLACK AND ORANGE	ORANGE AND BLUE	PURPLE AND WHITE	CONNECTION
BLACK AND BROWN	ORANGE AND GREEN	BROWN	
BLACK AND YELLOW	YELLOW	BROWN AND YELLOW	NO CONNECTION
WHITE	YELLOW AND RED	BROWN AND WHITE	
WHITE AND BLACK	YELLOW AND PURPLE	TAN	
GRAY	GREEN		
GRAY AND YELLOW	BLUE		

JOHNSON 1982-1984 70 & 75 HP

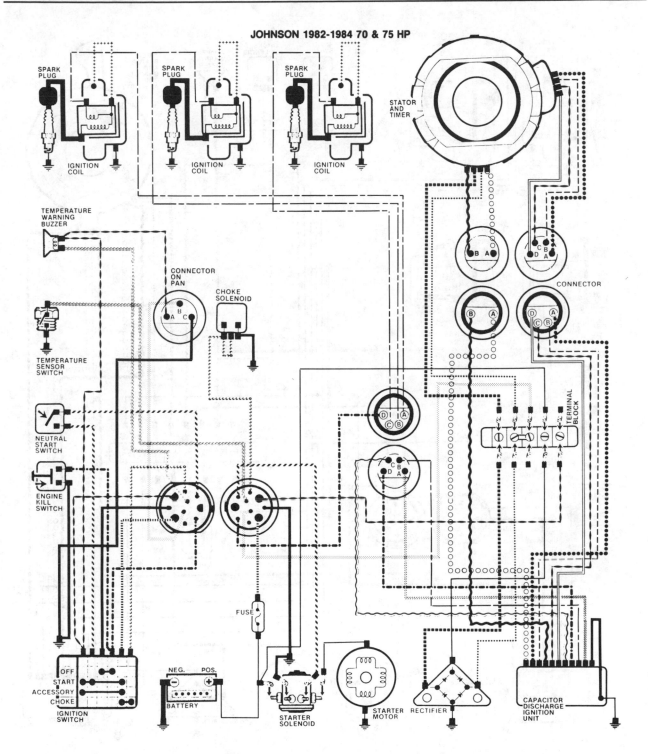

4

DIAGRAM KEY

BLACK	RED	PURPLE
BLACK AND WHITE	ORANGE	PURPLE AND RED
BLACK AND ORANGE	ORANGE AND BLUE	PURPLE AND WHITE
BLACK AND BROWN	ORANGE AND GREEN	BROWN
BLACK AND YELLOW	YELLOW	BROWN AND YELLOW
WHITE	YELLOW AND RED	BROWN AND WHITE
WHITE AND BLACK	YELLOW AND PURPLE	TAN
GRAY	GREEN	
GRAY AND YELLOW	BLUE	

GROUND

CONNECTION

NO CONNECTION

JOHNSON 1973 V4 ENGINES

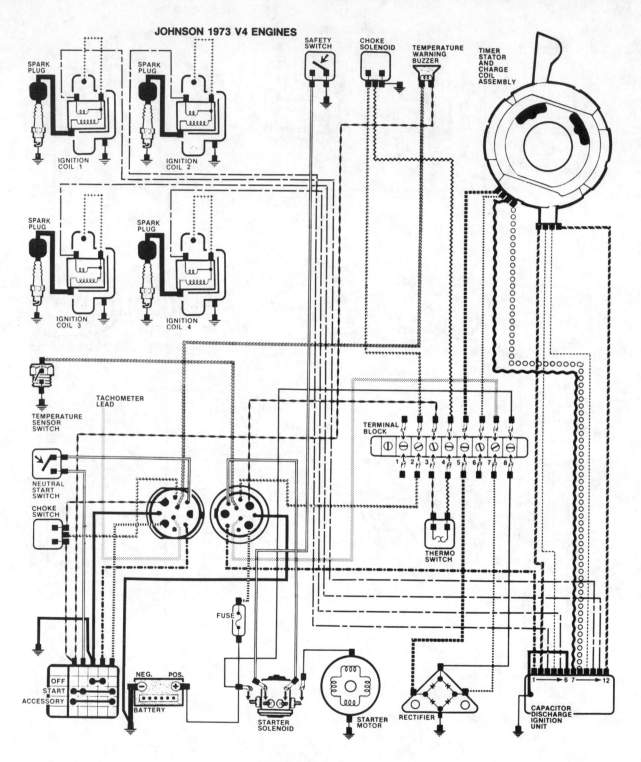

SPARK PLUG

IGNITION COIL 1

SPARK PLUG

IGNITION COIL 2

SPARK PLUG

IGNITION COIL 3

SPARK PLUG

IGNITION COIL 4

SAFETY SWITCH

CHOKE SOLENOID

TEMPERATURE WARNING BUZZER

TIMER STATOR AND CHARGE COIL ASSEMBLY

TEMPERATURE SENSOR SWITCH

TACHOMETER LEAD

NEUTRAL START SWITCH

CHOKE SWITCH

TERMINAL BLOCK

THERMO SWITCH

FUSE

OFF
START
ACCESSORY

NEG. POS.

BATTERY

STARTER SOLENOID

STARTER MOTOR

RECTIFIER

CAPACITOR DISCHARGE IGNITION UNIT

DIAGRAM KEY

BLACK	RED	PURPLE	GROUND
BLACK AND WHITE	ORANGE	PURPLE AND RED	
BLACK AND ORANGE	ORANGE AND BLUE	PURPLE AND WHITE	CONNECTION
BLACK AND BROWN	ORANGE AND GREEN	BROWN	
BLACK AND YELLOW	YELLOW	BROWN AND YELLOW	NO CONNECTION
WHITE	YELLOW AND RED	BROWN AND WHITE	
WHITE AND BLACK	YELLOW AND PURPLE	TAN	
GRAY	GREEN		
GRAY AND YELLOW	BLUE		

JOHNSON 1974-1976 V4 ENGINES

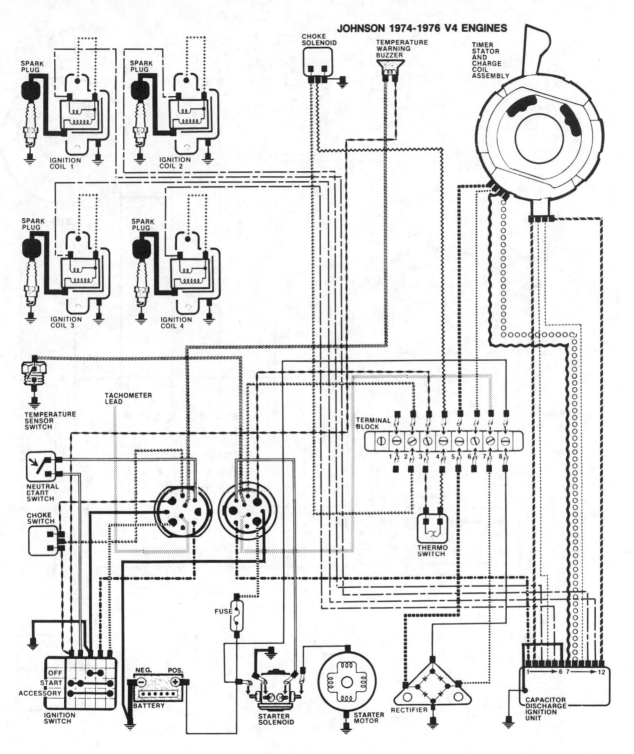

DIAGRAM KEY

━━━━ BLACK	───── RED	∿∿∿ PURPLE
⟋⟋⟋⟋ BLACK AND WHITE	─ ─ ─ ORANGE	∙∙∙∙∙∙∙∙ PURPLE AND RED
++++++++ BLACK AND ORANGE	∿∿∿∿∿ ORANGE AND BLUE	∴∴∴∴∴∴ PURPLE AND WHITE
──── BLACK AND BROWN	∿∿∿∿ ORANGE AND GREEN	∿∿∿ BROWN
─∙─∙─ BLACK AND YELLOW	∎∎∎∎∎ YELLOW	⟋⟋⟋⟋⟋ BROWN AND YELLOW
───── WHITE	⟋⟋⟋⟋⟋ YELLOW AND RED	■ ■ ■ TAN
─ ─ ─ WHITE AND BLACK	∿∿∿∿∿ YELLOW AND PURPLE	
∷∷∷∷∷ GRAY	─ ─ ─ BROWN AND ORANGE	
∙∙∙∙∙∙∙ GRAY AND YELLOW	●●●●●● BLUE	

⏚ GROUND

┿ CONNECTION

─┼─ NO CONNECTION

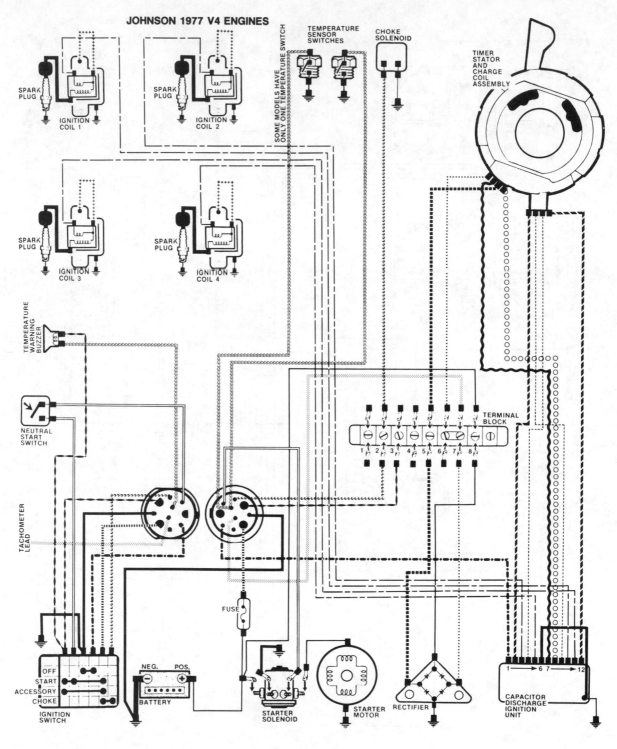

JOHNSON 1977 V4 ENGINES

DIAGRAM KEY

BLACK	RED	PURPLE
BLACK AND WHITE	ORANGE	PURPLE AND RED
BLACK AND ORANGE	ORANGE AND BLUE	PURPLE AND WHITE
BLACK AND BROWN	ORANGE AND GREEN	BROWN
BLACK AND YELLOW	YELLOW	BROWN AND YELLOW
WHITE	YELLOW AND RED	BROWN AND WHITE
WHITE AND BLACK	YELLOW AND PURPLE	TAN
GRAY	GREEN	
GRAY AND YELLOW	BLUE	

GROUND

CONNECTION

NO CONNECTION

JOHNSON 1978-1979 V4 ENGINES

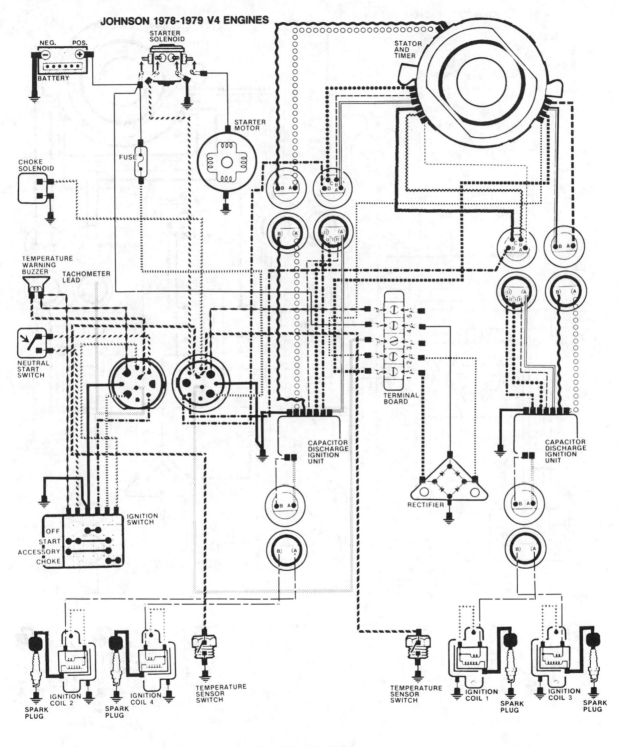

DIAGRAM KEY

BLACK	RED	PURPLE	GROUND
TAN	ORANGE	PURPLE AND RED	
BLACK AND ORANGE	ORANGE AND BLUE	PURPLE AND WHITE	CONNECTION
BLACK AND BROWN	ORANGE AND GREEN	BROWN	
BLACK AND YELLOW	YELLOW	BROWN AND YELLOW	NO CONNECTION
WHITE	YELLOW AND RED	BROWN AND WHITE	
WHITE AND BLACK	GREEN AND WHITE	BLUE AND WHITE	
GRAY	GREEN		
GRAY AND YELLOW	BLUE		

4

JOHNSON 1980-1981 V4 ENGINES

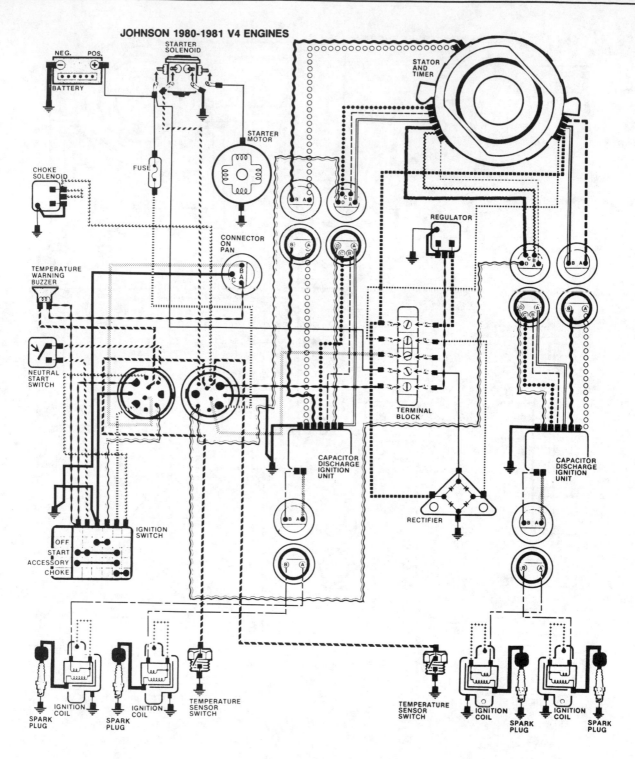

DIAGRAM KEY

BLACK	RED	PURPLE	GROUND
BLACK AND WHITE	ORANGE	PURPLE AND RED	CONNECTION
BLACK AND ORANGE	ORANGE AND BLUE	PURPLE AND WHITE	NO CONNECTION
BLACK AND BROWN	BLACK AND YELLOW	BROWN	
BLACK AND YELLOW	YELLOW	BROWN AND YELLOW	
WHITE	YELLOW AND RED	BROWN AND WHITE	
WHITE AND BLACK	YELLOW AND PURPLE	TAN	
GRAY	GREEN		
GRAY AND YELLOW	BLUE		

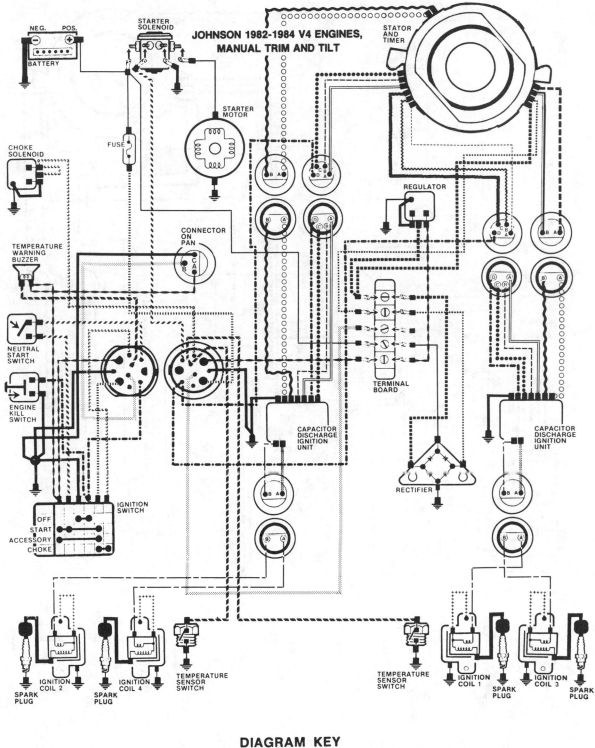

JOHNSON 1982-1984 V4 ENGINES, MANUAL TRIM AND TILT

DIAGRAM KEY

BLACK	RED	PURPLE
TAN	ORANGE	PURPLE AND RED
BLACK AND ORANGE	ORANGE AND BLUE	PURPLE AND WHITE
BLACK AND BROWN	ORANGE AND GREEN	BROWN
BLACK AND YELLOW	YELLOW	BROWN AND YELLOW
WHITE	YELLOW AND RED	BROWN AND WHITE
WHITE AND BLACK	GREEN AND WHITE	BLUE AND WHITE
GRAY	GREEN	
GRAY AND YELLOW	BLUE	

GROUND

CONNECTION

NO CONNECTION

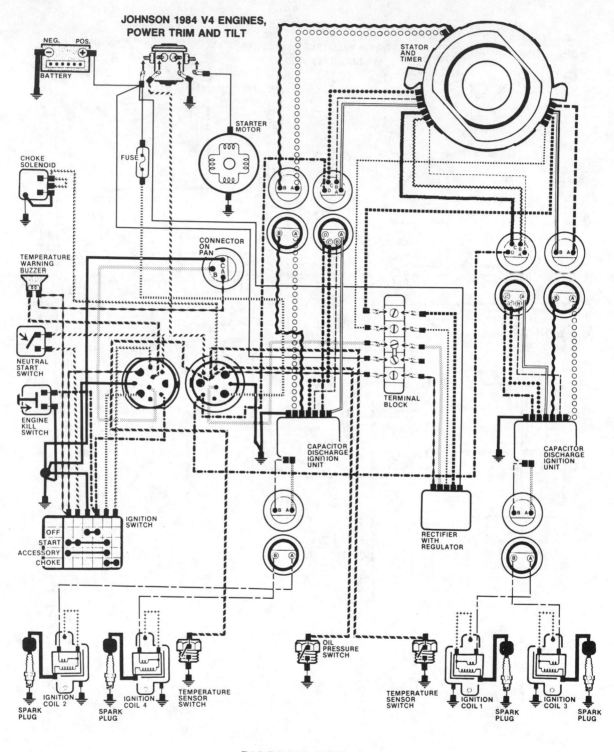

JOHNSON 1984 V4 ENGINES,
POWER TRIM AND TILT

NEG. POS.
BATTERY

CHOKE SOLENOID

FUSE

STARTER MOTOR

STATOR AND TIMER

TEMPERATURE WARNING BUZZER

CONNECTOR ON PAN

NEUTRAL START SWITCH

ENGINE KILL SWITCH

TERMINAL BLOCK

CAPACITOR DISCHARGE IGNITION UNIT

CAPACITOR DISCHARGE IGNITION UNIT

RECTIFIER WITH REGULATOR

IGNITION SWITCH
OFF
START
ACCESSORY
CHOKE

OIL PRESSURE SWITCH

SPARK PLUG
IGNITION COIL 2

SPARK PLUG
IGNITION COIL 4

TEMPERATURE SENSOR SWITCH

TEMPERATURE SENSOR SWITCH

IGNITION COIL 1
SPARK PLUG

IGNITION COIL 3
SPARK PLUG

DIAGRAM KEY

BLACK	RED	PURPLE
TAN	ORANGE	PURPLE AND RED
BLACK AND ORANGE	ORANGE AND BLUE	PURPLE AND WHITE
BLACK AND BROWN	ORANGE AND GREEN	BROWN
BLACK AND YELLOW	YELLOW	BROWN AND YELLOW
WHITE	YELLOW AND RED	BROWN AND WHITE
WHITE AND BLACK	GREEN AND WHITE	BLUE AND WHITE
GRAY	GREEN	
GRAY AND YELLOW	BLUE	

GROUND
CONNECTION
NO CONNECTION

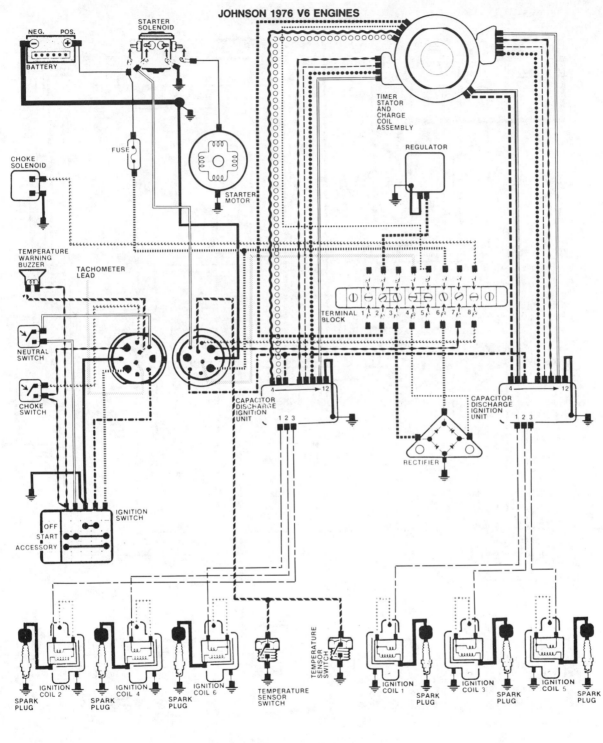

JOHNSON 1976 V6 ENGINES

DIAGRAM KEY

BLACK	RED	PURPLE
TAN	ORANGE	PURPLE AND RED
BLACK AND ORANGE	ORANGE AND BLUE	PURPLE AND WHITE
BLACK AND BROWN	ORANGE AND GREEN	BROWN
BLACK AND YELLOW	YELLOW	BROWN AND YELLOW
WHITE	YELLOW AND RED	BROWN AND WHITE
BLACK AND YELLOW	YELLOW AND PURPLE	RED AND WHITE
GRAY	GREEN	
GRAY AND YELLOW	BLUE	

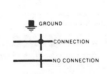

GROUND

CONNECTION

NO CONNECTION

JOHNSON 1977 V6 ENGINES

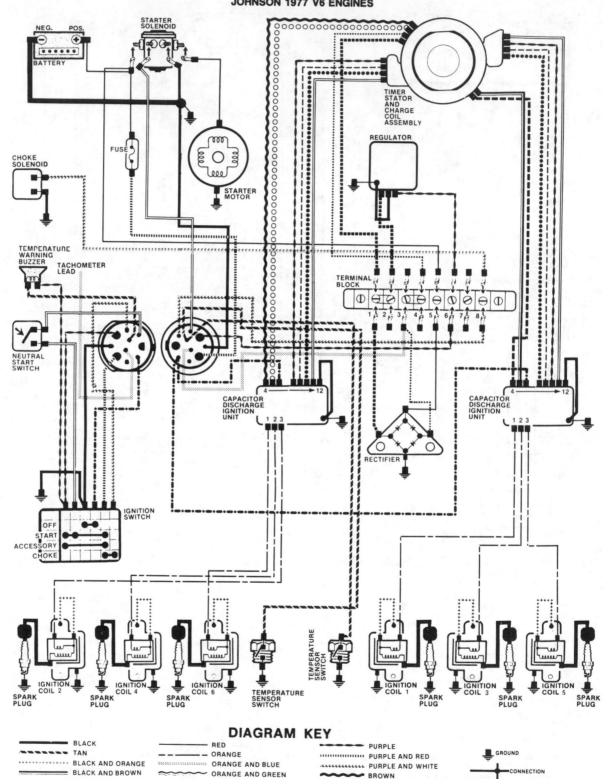

DIAGRAM KEY

BLACK	RED	PURPLE	GROUND
TAN	ORANGE	PURPLE AND RED	
BLACK AND ORANGE	ORANGE AND BLUE	PURPLE AND WHITE	CONNECTION
BLACK AND BROWN	ORANGE AND GREEN	BROWN	
BLACK AND YELLOW	YELLOW	BROWN AND YELLOW	NO CONNECTION
WHITE	YELLOW AND RED	BROWN AND WHITE	
BLACK AND YELLOW	YELLOW AND PURPLE	RED AND WHITE	
GRAY	GREEN		
GRAY AND YELLOW	BLUE		

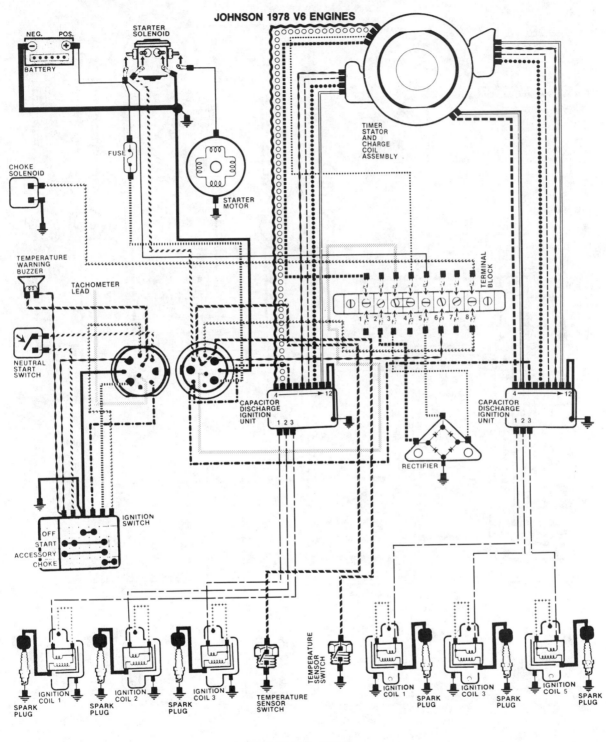

JOHNSON 1978 V6 ENGINES

DIAGRAM KEY

BLACK	RED	PURPLE
TAN	ORANGE	PURPLE AND RED
BLACK AND ORANGE	ORANGE AND BLUE	PURPLE AND WHITE
BLACK AND BROWN	ORANGE AND GREEN	BROWN
BLACK AND YELLOW	YELLOW	BROWN AND YELLOW
WHITE	YELLOW AND RED	BROWN AND WHITE
BLACK AND YELLOW	YELLOW AND PURPLE	RED AND WHITE
GRAY	GREEN	
GRAY AND YELLOW	BLUE	

GROUND

CONNECTION

NO CONNECTION

JOHNSON 1979 V6 ENGINES

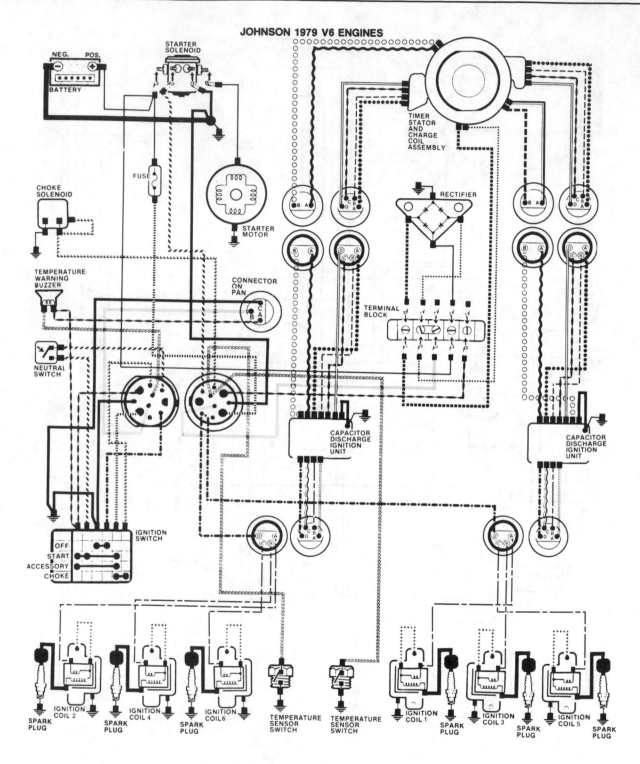

NEG. POS.

STARTER
SOLENOID

BATTERY

TIMER
STATOR
AND
CHARGE
COIL
ASSEMBLY

CHOKE
SOLENOID

FUSE

STARTER
MOTOR

RECTIFIER

TEMPERATURE
WARNING
BUZZER

CONNECTOR
ON
PAN

TERMINAL
BLOCK

NEUTRAL
SWITCH

CAPACITOR
DISCHARGE
IGNITION
UNIT

CAPACITOR
DISCHARGE
IGNITION
UNIT

IGNITION
SWITCH

OFF
START
ACCESSORY
CHOKE

SPARK
PLUG
IGNITION
COIL 2

SPARK
PLUG
IGNITION
COIL 4

SPARK
PLUG
IGNITION
COIL 6

TEMPERATURE
SENSOR
SWITCH

TEMPERATURE
SENSOR
SWITCH

IGNITION
COIL 1
SPARK
PLUG

IGNITION
COIL 3
SPARK
PLUG

IGNITION
COIL 5
SPARK
PLUG

DIAGRAM KEY

BLACK	RED	PURPLE
BLACK AND WHITE	ORANGE	PURPLE AND RED
BLACK AND ORANGE	ORANGE AND BLUE	PURPLE AND WHITE
BLACK AND BROWN	ORANGE AND GREEN	BROWN
BLACK AND YELLOW	YELLOW	BROWN AND YELLOW
WHITE	YELLOW AND RED	BROWN AND WHITE
WHITE AND BLACK	YELLOW AND PURPLE	TAN
GRAY	GREEN	
GRAY AND YELLOW	BLUE	

GROUND

CONNECTION

NO CONNECTION

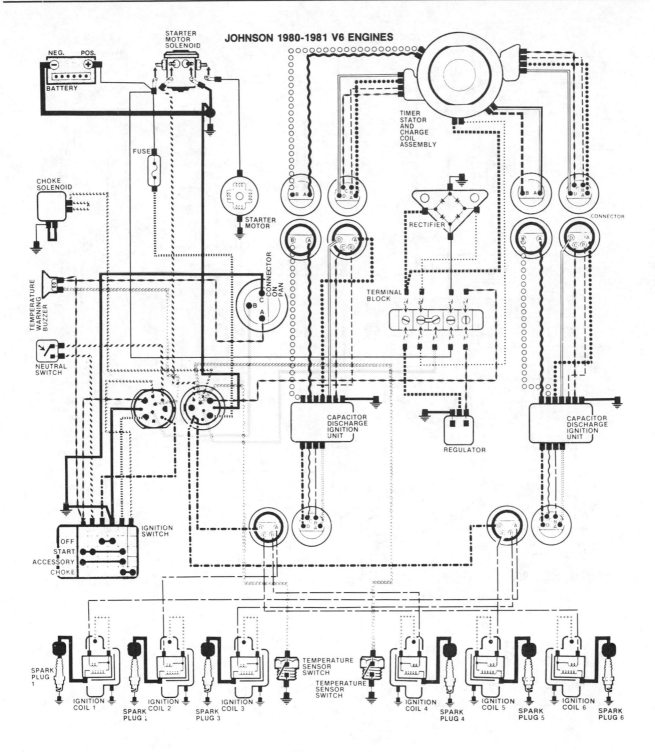

JOHNSON 1980-1981 V6 ENGINES

DIAGRAM KEY

────────	BLACK	──────	RED	∿∿∿∿∿	PURPLE	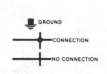 GROUND
─ ─ ─ ─	BLACK AND WHITE	─ ─ ─ ─	ORANGE	··············	PURPLE AND RED	CONNECTION
+++++++++	BLACK AND ORANGE	∿∿∿∿∿	ORANGE AND BLUE	∿∿∿∿∿	PURPLE AND WHITE	NO CONNECTION
─··─··─	BLACK AND BROWN	∿∿∿∿∿	ORANGE AND GREEN	∿∿∿∿∿	BROWN	
─·─·─·─	BLACK AND YELLOW	▬▬▬▬▬	YELLOW	oooooooo	BROWN AND YELLOW	
────────	WHITE	⁄⁄⁄⁄⁄	YELLOW AND RED	▬ ▬ ▬ ▬	BROWN AND WHITE	
────────	WHITE AND BLACK	─ ─ ─ ─	YELLOW AND PURPLE	∿∿∿∿∿	TAN	
▒▒▒▒▒	GRAY	─ ─ ─ ─	GREEN			
············	GRAY AND YELLOW	●●●●●●●	BLUE			

SPARK PLUG 1 — IGNITION COIL 1 — SPARK PLUG 2 — IGNITION COIL 2 — SPARK PLUG 3 — IGNITION COIL 3 — TEMPERATURE SENSOR SWITCH — TEMPERATURE SENSOR SWITCH — IGNITION COIL 4 — SPARK PLUG 4 — IGNITION COIL 5 — SPARK PLUG 5 — IGNITION COIL 6 — SPARK PLUG 6

BATTERY — CHOKE SOLENOID — FUSE — STARTER MOTOR SOLENOID — STARTER MOTOR — TIMER STATOR AND CHARGE COIL ASSEMBLY — RECTIFIER — CONNECTOR — TERMINAL BLOCK — CAPACITOR DISCHARGE IGNITION UNIT — REGULATOR — CAPACITOR DISCHARGE IGNITION UNIT — TEMPERATURE WARNING BUZZER — NEUTRAL SWITCH — CONNECTOR ON PAN — IGNITION SWITCH — OFF — START — ACCESSORY — CHOKE

4

JOHNSON 1982-1983 V6 ENGINES

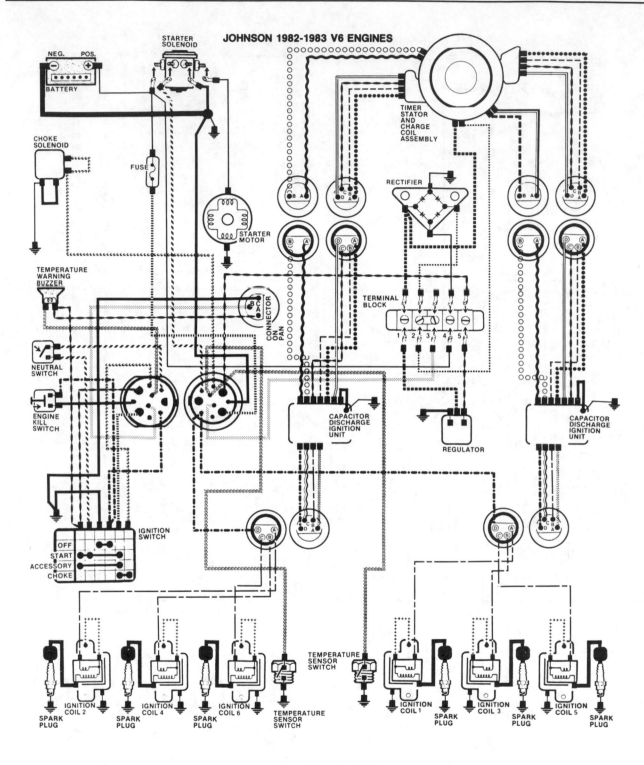

DIAGRAM KEY

———— BLACK	– – – RED	⌒⌒ PURPLE
◣◣◣ BLACK AND WHITE	– – – ORANGE	‖‖‖‖ PURPLE AND RED
+++++++ BLACK AND ORANGE	⁓⁓⁓⁓ ORANGE AND BLUE	◦◦◦◦ PURPLE AND WHITE
═══════ BLACK AND BROWN	⌇⌇⌇⌇ ORANGE AND GREEN	∿∿∿ BROWN
•–•–•– BLACK AND YELLOW	▮▮▮▮ YELLOW	◯◯◯◯ BROWN AND YELLOW
———— WHITE	⌁⌁⌁ YELLOW AND RED	– ■ – ■ BROWN AND WHITE
– – – – WHITE AND BLACK	∿∿∿ YELLOW AND PURPLE	≈≈≈ TAN
▦▦▦ GRAY	– – – – GREEN	
•••••• GRAY AND YELLOW	●●●●●● BLUE	

GROUND
CONNECTION
NO CONNECTION

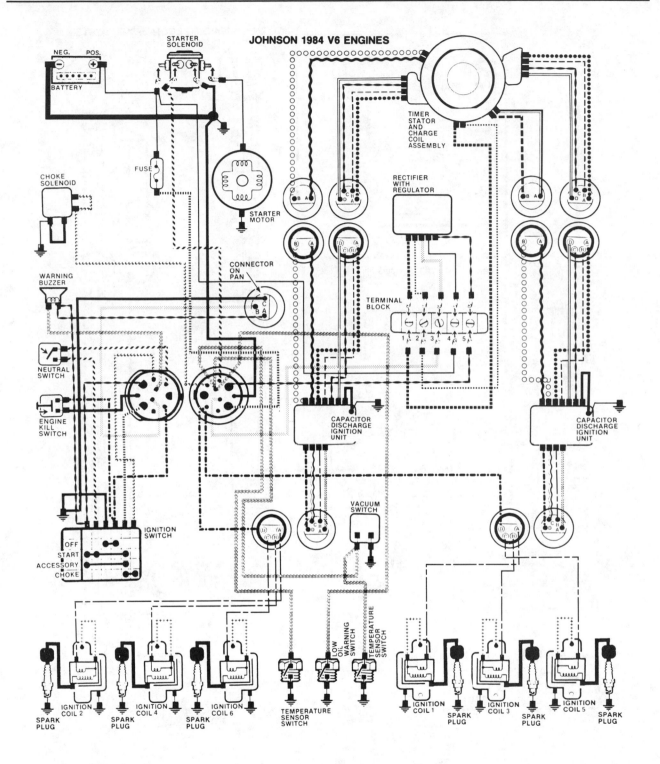

JOHNSON 1984 V6 ENGINES

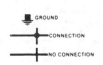

DIAGRAM KEY

BLACK	RED	PURPLE
BLACK AND WHITE	ORANGE	PURPLE AND RED
BLACK AND ORANGE	ORANGE AND BLUE	PURPLE AND WHITE
BLACK AND BROWN	ORANGE AND GREEN	BROWN
BLACK AND YELLOW	YELLOW	BROWN AND YELLOW
WHITE	YELLOW AND RED	BROWN AND WHITE
WHITE AND BLACK	YELLOW AND PURPLE	TAN
GRAY	GREEN	
GRAY AND YELLOW	BLUE	

GROUND

CONNECTION

NO CONNECTION

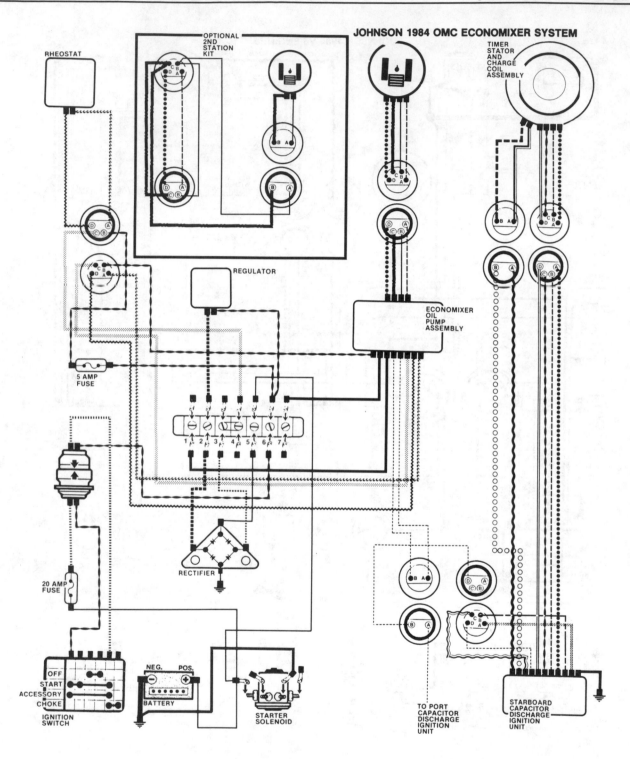

JOHNSON 1984 OMC ECONOMIXER SYSTEM

DIAGRAM KEY

BLACK	RED	PURPLE	GROUND
TAN	ORANGE	PURPLE AND RED	
BLACK AND ORANGE	ORANGE AND BLUE	PURPLE AND WHITE	CONNECTION
BLACK AND BROWN	ORANGE AND GREEN	BROWN	
BLACK AND YELLOW	YELLOW	BROWN AND YELLOW	NO CONNECTION
WHITE	YELLOW AND RED	BROWN AND WHITE	
BLACK AND YELLOW	YELLOW AND PURPLE	RED AND WHITE	
GRAY	GREEN		
GRAY AND YELLOW	BLUE		

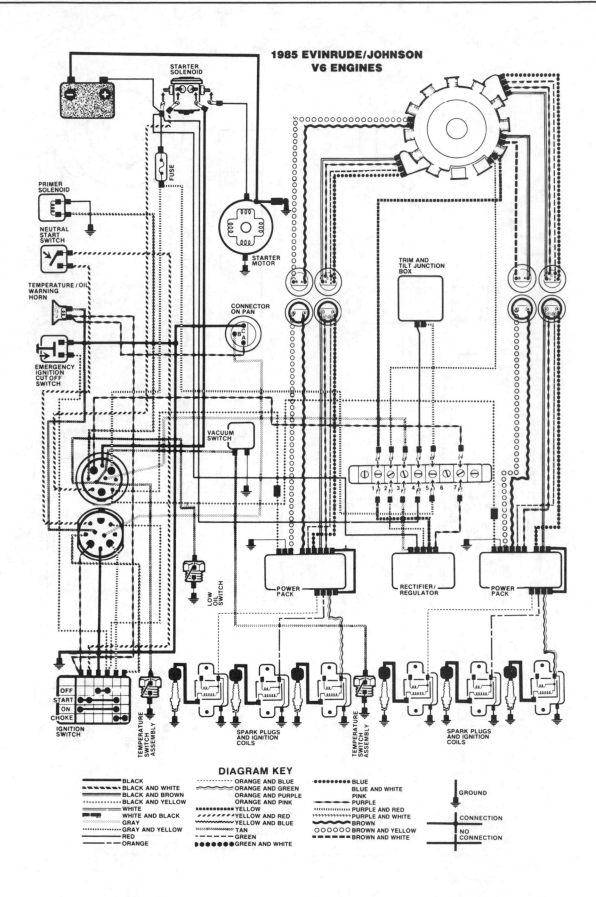

1985 EVINRUDE/JOHNSON V6 ENGINES

4

STARTER SOLENOID

PRIMER SOLENOID

NEUTRAL START SWITCH

TEMPERATURE/OIL WARNING HORN

EMERGENCY IGNITION CUT OFF SWITCH

FUSE

STARTER MOTOR

CONNECTOR ON PAN

TRIM AND TILT JUNCTION BOX

VACUUM SWITCH

POWER PACK

RECTIFIER/ REGULATOR

POWER PACK

LOW OIL SWITCH

OFF
START
ON
CHOKE

IGNITION SWITCH

TEMPERATURE SWITCH ASSEMBLY

SPARK PLUGS AND IGNITION COILS

TEMPERATURE SWITCH ASSEMBLY

SPARK PLUGS AND IGNITION COILS

DIAGRAM KEY

BLACK	ORANGE AND BLUE	BLUE
BLACK AND WHITE	ORANGE AND GREEN	BLUE AND WHITE
BLACK AND BROWN	ORANGE AND PURPLE	PINK
BLACK AND YELLOW	ORANGE AND PINK	PURPLE
WHITE	YELLOW	PURPLE AND RED
WHITE AND BLACK	YELLOW AND RED	PURPLE AND WHITE
GRAY	YELLOW AND BLUE	BROWN
GRAY AND YELLOW	TAN	BROWN AND YELLOW
RED	GREEN	BROWN AND WHITE
ORANGE	GREEN AND WHITE	

GROUND

CONNECTION

NO CONNECTION

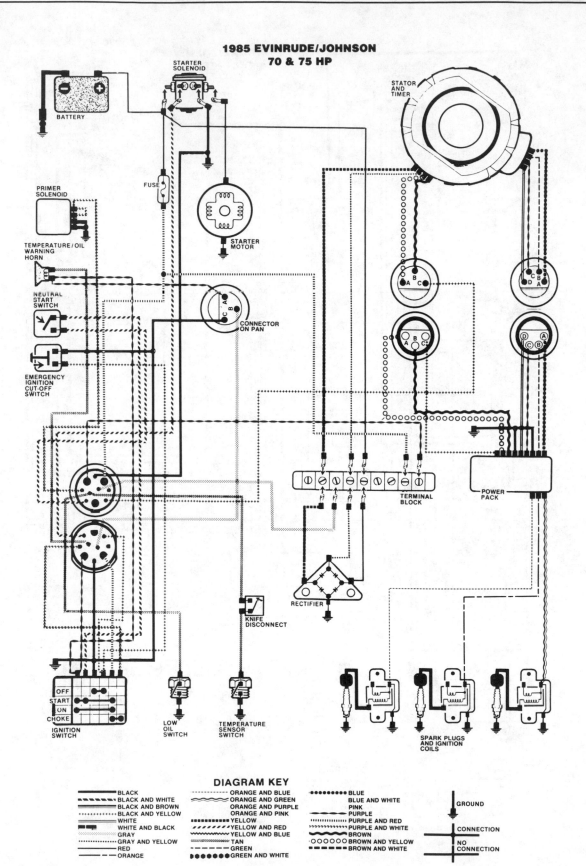

1985 EVINRUDE/JOHNSON 70 & 75 HP

BATTERY

STARTER SOLENOID

FUSE

STARTER MOTOR

STATOR AND TIMER

PRIMER SOLENOID

TEMPERATURE/OIL WARNING HORN

NEUTRAL START SWITCH

CONNECTOR ON PAN

EMERGENCY IGNITION CUT-OFF SWITCH

TERMINAL BLOCK

POWER PACK

RECTIFIER

KNIFE DISCONNECT

OFF
START
ON
CHOKE
IGNITION SWITCH

LOW OIL SWITCH

TEMPERATURE SENSOR SWITCH

SPARK PLUGS AND IGNITION COILS

DIAGRAM KEY

BLACK	ORANGE AND BLUE	BLUE
BLACK AND WHITE	ORANGE AND GREEN	BLUE AND WHITE
BLACK AND BROWN	ORANGE AND PURPLE	PINK
BLACK AND YELLOW	ORANGE AND PINK	PURPLE
WHITE	YELLOW	PURPLE AND RED
WHITE AND BLACK	YELLOW AND RED	PURPLE AND WHITE
GRAY	YELLOW AND BLUE	BROWN
GRAY AND YELLOW	TAN	BROWN AND YELLOW
RED	GREEN	BROWN AND WHITE
ORANGE	GREEN AND WHITE	

GROUND

CONNECTION

NO CONNECTION

1985 EVINRUDE/JOHNSON 90 & 115 HP WITH MANUAL TILT

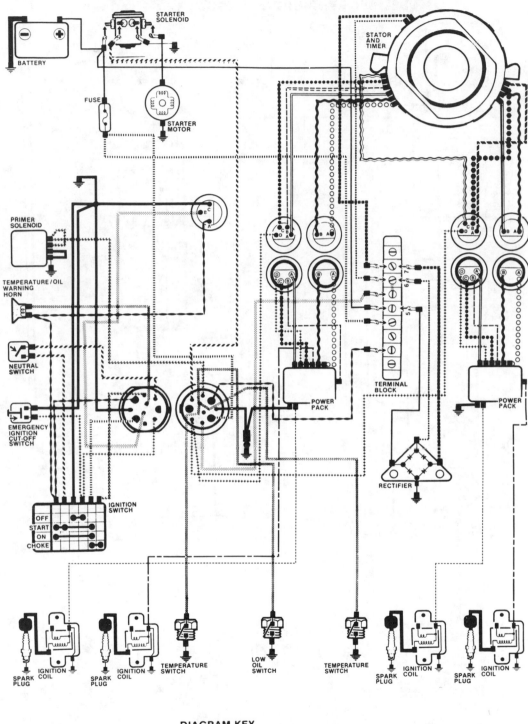

DIAGRAM KEY

BLACK	ORANGE AND BLUE	BLUE	
BLACK AND WHITE	ORANGE AND GREEN	BLUE AND WHITE	GROUND
BLACK AND BROWN	ORANGE AND PURPLE	PINK	
BLACK AND YELLOW	ORANGE AND PINK	PURPLE	
WHITE	YELLOW	PURPLE AND RED	CONNECTION
WHITE AND BLACK	YELLOW AND RED	PURPLE AND WHITE	
GRAY	YELLOW AND BLUE	BROWN	NO
GRAY AND YELLOW	TAN	BROWN AND YELLOW	CONNECTION
RED	GREEN	BROWN AND WHITE	
ORANGE	GREEN AND WHITE		

1985-1986 EVINRUDE/JOHNSON 120 & 140 HP

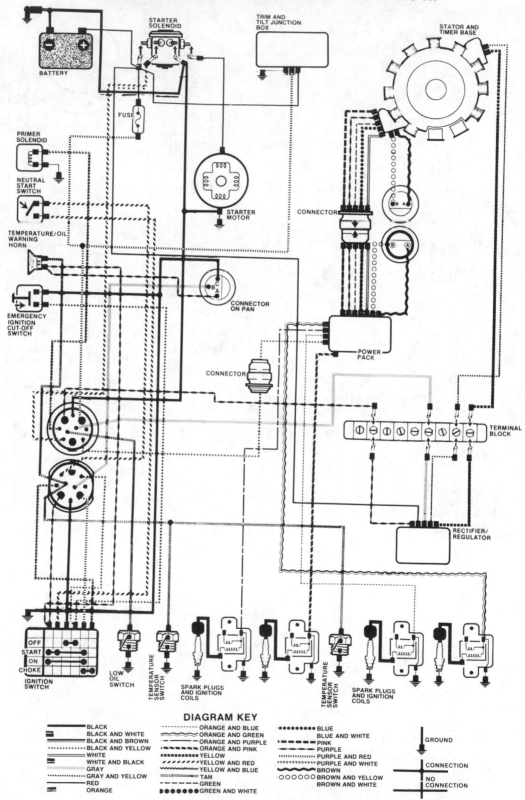

DIAGRAM KEY

BLACK	ORANGE AND BLUE	BLUE	GROUND
BLACK AND WHITE	ORANGE AND GREEN	BLUE AND WHITE	
BLACK AND BROWN	ORANGE AND PURPLE	PINK	
BLACK AND YELLOW	ORANGE AND PINK	PURPLE	CONNECTION
WHITE	YELLOW	PURPLE AND RED	
WHITE AND BLACK	YELLOW AND RED	PURPLE AND WHITE	NO
GRAY	YELLOW AND BLUE	BROWN	CONNECTION
GRAY AND YELLOW	TAN	BROWN AND YELLOW	
RED	GREEN	BROWN AND WHITE	
ORANGE	GREEN AND WHITE		

1985 EVINRUDE/JOHNSON 90 & 115 HP WITH POWER TRIM & TILT

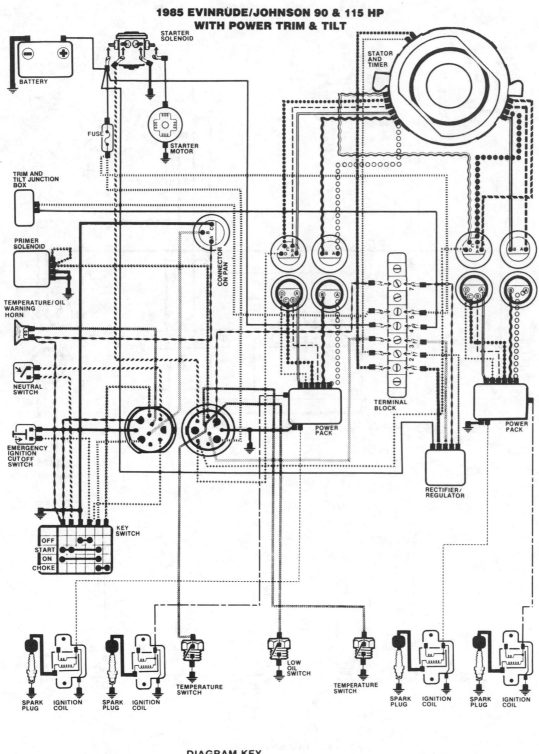

DIAGRAM KEY

BLACK	ORANGE AND BLUE	BLUE
BLACK AND WHITE	ORANGE AND GREEN	BLUE AND WHITE
BLACK AND BROWN	ORANGE AND PURPLE	PINK
BLACK AND YELLOW	ORANGE AND PINK	PURPLE
WHITE	YELLOW	PURPLE AND RED
WHITE AND BLACK	YELLOW AND RED	PURPLE AND WHITE
GRAY	YELLOW AND BLUE	BROWN
GRAY AND YELLOW	TAN	BROWN AND YELLOW
RED	GREEN	BROWN AND WHITE
ORANGE	GREEN AND WHITE	

GROUND

CONNECTION

NO CONNECTION

1985 EVINRUDE/JOHNSON 40 & 50 HP

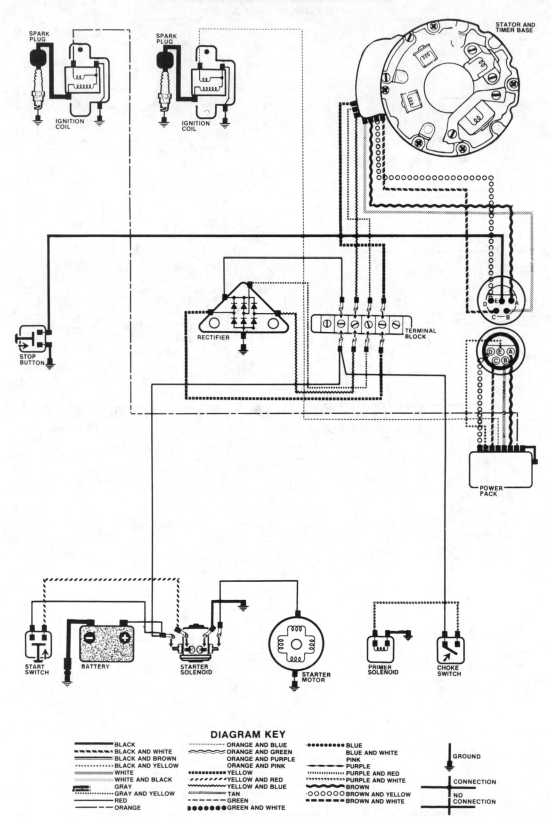

DIAGRAM KEY

BLACK	BLUE
BLACK AND WHITE	BLUE AND WHITE
BLACK AND BROWN	PINK
BLACK AND YELLOW	PURPLE
WHITE	PURPLE AND RED
WHITE AND BLACK	PURPLE AND WHITE
GRAY	BROWN
GRAY AND YELLOW	BROWN AND YELLOW
RED	BROWN AND WHITE
ORANGE	

ORANGE AND BLUE	
ORANGE AND GREEN	
ORANGE AND PURPLE	
ORANGE AND PINK	
YELLOW	GROUND
YELLOW AND RED	
YELLOW AND BLUE	CONNECTION
TAN	
GREEN	NO
GREEN AND WHITE	CONNECTION

Labels in diagram: SPARK PLUG, IGNITION COIL, STATOR AND TIMER BASE, STOP BUTTON, RECTIFIER, TERMINAL BLOCK, POWER PACK, START SWITCH, BATTERY, STARTER SOLENOID, STARTER MOTOR, PRIMER SOLENOID, CHOKE SWITCH

1986 60-75 HP WITH REMOTE ELECTRIC START

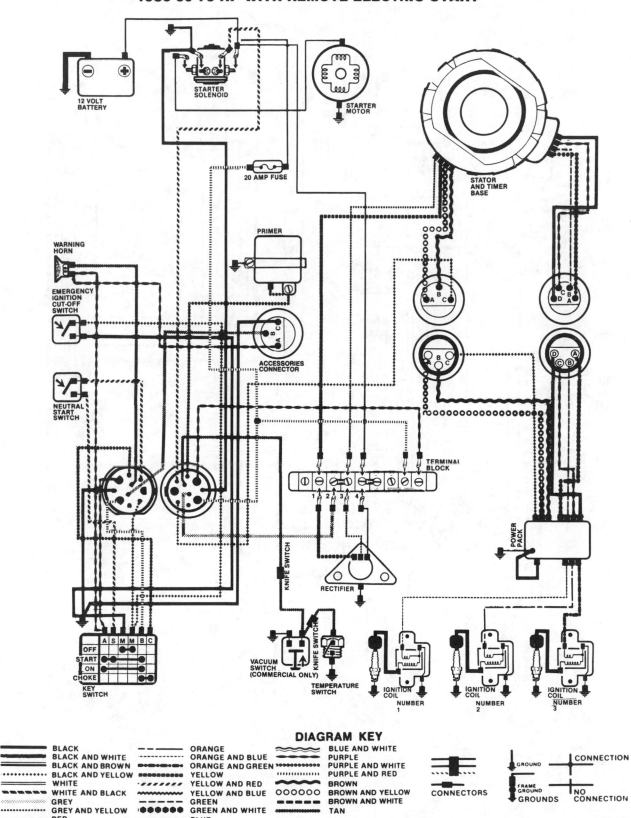

DIAGRAM KEY

BLACK	ORANGE	BLUE AND WHITE		CONNECTION
BLACK AND WHITE	ORANGE AND BLUE	PURPLE		
BLACK AND BROWN	ORANGE AND GREEN	PURPLE AND WHITE	GROUND	
BLACK AND YELLOW	YELLOW	PURPLE AND RED		
WHITE	YELLOW AND RED	BROWN	CONNECTORS	NO
WHITE AND BLACK	YELLOW AND BLUE	BROWN AND YELLOW	FRAME GROUND	CONNECTION
GREY	GREEN	BROWN AND WHITE		
GREY AND YELLOW	GREEN AND WHITE	TAN	GROUNDS	
RED	BLUE			

1986 90-110 WITH MANUAL TILT

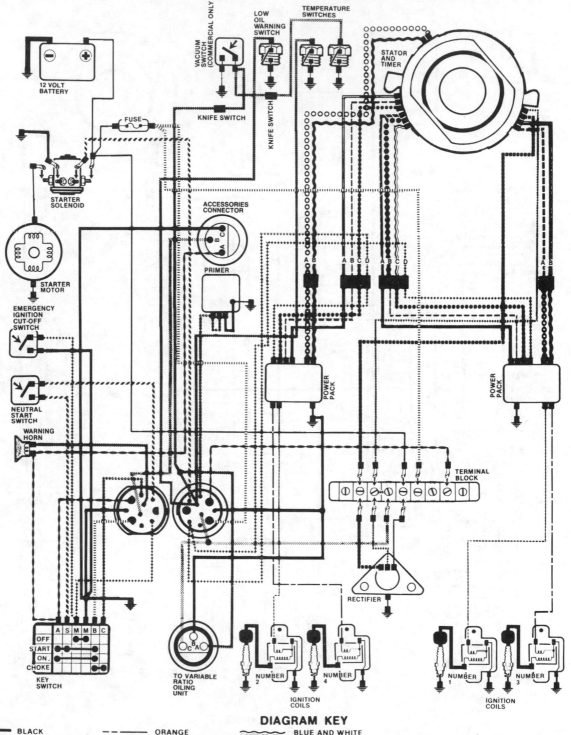

DIAGRAM KEY

BLACK	ORANGE	BLUE AND WHITE
BLACK AND WHITE	ORANGE AND BLUE	PURPLE
BLACK AND BROWN	ORANGE AND GREEN	PURPLE AND WHITE
BLACK AND YELLOW	YELLOW	PURPLE AND RED
WHITE	YELLOW AND RED	BROWN
WHITE AND BLACK	YELLOW AND BLUE	BROWN AND YELLOW
GREY	GREEN	BROWN AND WHITE
GREY AND YELLOW	GREEN AND WHITE	TAN
RED	BLUE	

CONNECTORS

GROUND · CONNECTION

FRAME GROUND

GROUNDS · NO CONNECTION

1986 90-110 HP WITH REMOTE ELECTRIC START

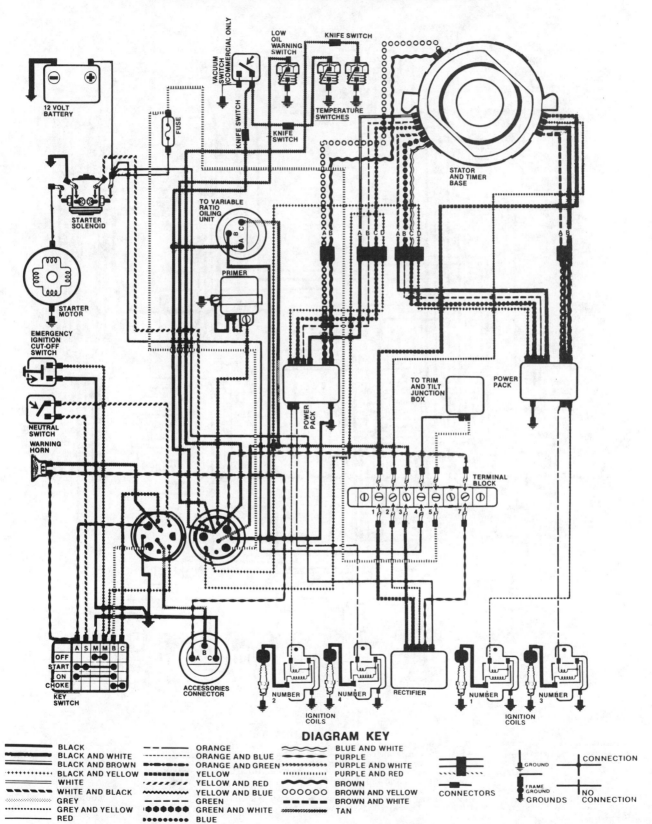

4

DIAGRAM KEY

BLACK	ORANGE	BLUE AND WHITE
BLACK AND WHITE	ORANGE AND BLUE	PURPLE
BLACK AND BROWN	ORANGE AND GREEN	PURPLE AND WHITE
BLACK AND YELLOW	YELLOW	PURPLE AND RED
WHITE	YELLOW AND RED	BROWN
WHITE AND BLACK	YELLOW AND BLUE	BROWN AND YELLOW
GREY	GREEN	BROWN AND WHITE
GREY AND YELLOW	GREEN AND WHITE	TAN
RED	BLUE	

CONNECTORS

GROUND
FRAME GROUND
GROUNDS

CONNECTION

NO CONNECTION

1986 150-175 HP

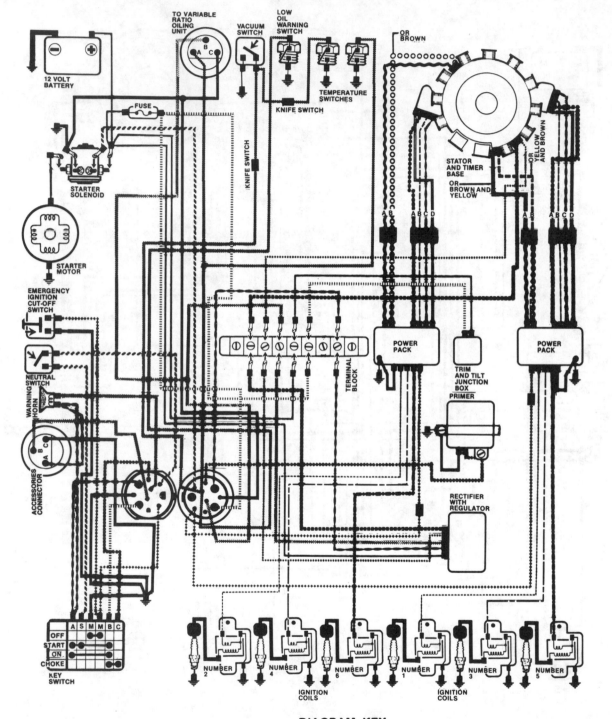

DIAGRAM KEY

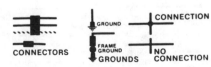

BLACK	ORANGE	BLUE AND WHITE
BLACK AND WHITE	ORANGE AND BLUE	PURPLE
BLACK AND BROWN	ORANGE AND GREEN	PURPLE AND WHITE
BLACK AND YELLOW	YELLOW	PURPLE AND RED
WHITE	YELLOW AND RED	BROWN
WHITE AND BLACK	YELLOW AND BLUE	BROWN AND YELLOW
GREY	GREEN	BROWN AND WHITE
GREY AND YELLOW	GREEN AND WHITE	TAN
RED	BLUE	

CONNECTORS

GROUND / FRAME GROUND / GROUNDS

CONNECTION / NO CONNECTION

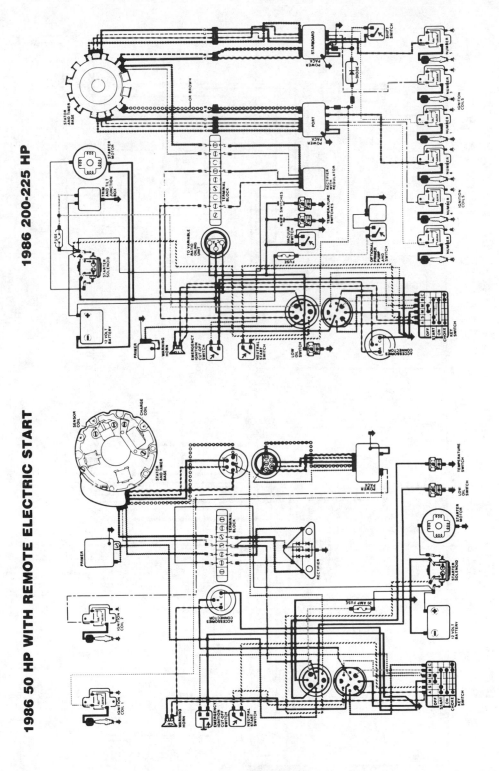

1986 200-225 HP

1986 50 HP WITH REMOTE ELECTRIC START

DIAGRAM KEY

BLACK	ORANGE	BLUE AND WHITE	CONNECTION
BLACK AND WHITE	ORANGE AND BLUE	PURPLE	
BLACK AND BROWN	ORANGE AND GREEN	PURPLE AND WHITE	GROUND
BLACK AND YELLOW	YELLOW	PURPLE AND RED	
WHITE	YELLOW AND RED	BROWN	FRAME GROUND
WHITE AND BLACK	YELLOW AND BLUE	BROWN AND YELLOW	NO CONNECTION
GREY	GREEN	BROWN AND WHITE	CONNECTORS
GREY AND YELLOW	GREEN AND WHITE	TAN	GROUNDS
RED	BLUE		

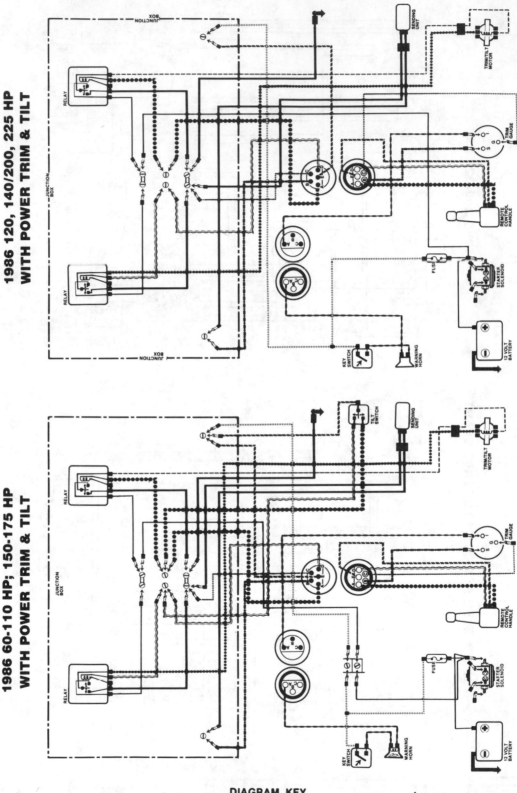

1986 120, 140/200, 225 HP WITH POWER TRIM & TILT

1986 60-110 HP; 150-175 HP WITH POWER TRIM & TILT

DIAGRAM KEY

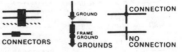

——— BLACK	•••••• GREEN AND WHITE	⋯⋯⋯ PURPLE AND RED
——— RED	•••••• BLUE	▬▬▬ TAN AND WHITE
⟋⟋⟋ RED AND WHITE	∿∿∿ BLUE AND WHITE	▬▬▬ TAN AND BLACK
– – – GREEN	∿∿∿ PURPLE	

CONNECTORS

GROUND

FRAME GROUND

GROUNDS

CONNECTION

NO CONNECTION

1987-1989 POWER TRIM/TILT

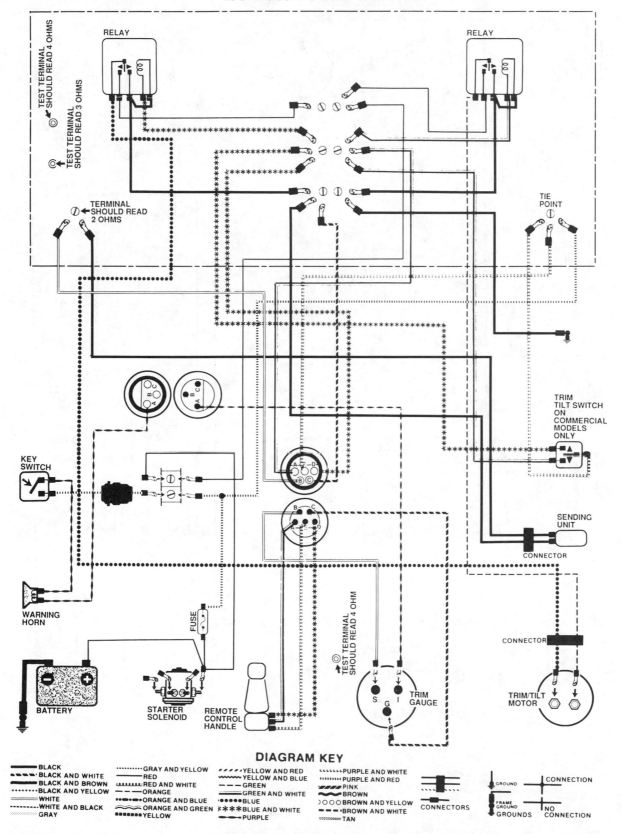

DIAGRAM KEY

━━ BLACK	⋯⋯ GRAY AND YELLOW	⫽⫽⫽ YELLOW AND RED	⌣⌣⌣ PURPLE AND WHITE
◢◢ BLACK AND WHITE	� RED	⩗⩗ YELLOW AND BLUE	⎺⎺ PURPLE AND RED
━━ BLACK AND BROWN	⟋⟋ RED AND WHITE	━ ━ GREEN	≈≈ PINK
⋯⋯ BLACK AND YELLOW	─ ─ ORANGE	━━ GREEN AND WHITE	∿∿ BROWN
─── WHITE	∿∿ ORANGE AND BLUE	●●● BLUE	)─(BROWN AND YELLOW
─ ─ WHITE AND BLACK	∿∿ ORANGE AND GREEN	★★★★ BLUE AND WHITE	⊃─⊂ BROWN AND WHITE
⋯⋯ GRAY	▪▪▪ YELLOW	►─► PURPLE	∿∿∿ TAN

CONNECTORS

GROUND   CONNECTION
FRAME GROUND   NO CONNECTION
GROUNDS

4

1987-1988 48-50 REMOTE START

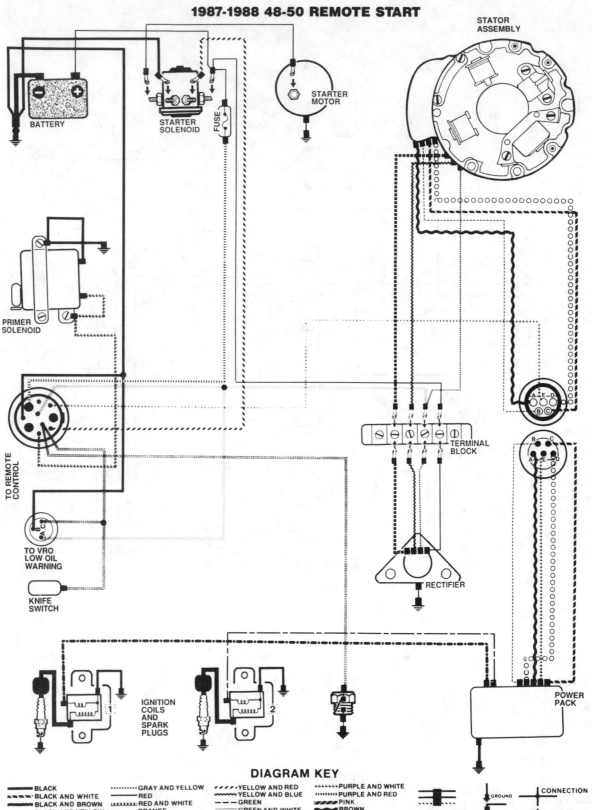

DIAGRAM KEY

BLACK	GRAY AND YELLOW	YELLOW AND RED	PURPLE AND WHITE	
BLACK AND WHITE	RED	YELLOW AND BLUE	PURPLE AND RED	CONNECTION
BLACK AND BROWN	RED AND WHITE	GREEN	PINK	
BLACK AND YELLOW	ORANGE	GREEN AND WHITE	BROWN	
WHITE	ORANGE AND BLUE	BLUE	BROWN AND YELLOW	
WHITE AND BLACK	ORANGE AND GREEN	BLUE AND WHITE	BROWN AND WHITE	
GRAY	YELLOW	PURPLE	TAN	NO CONNECTION

CONNECTORS

GROUND
FRAME GROUND
GROUNDS

1987 90-110 Power Tilt

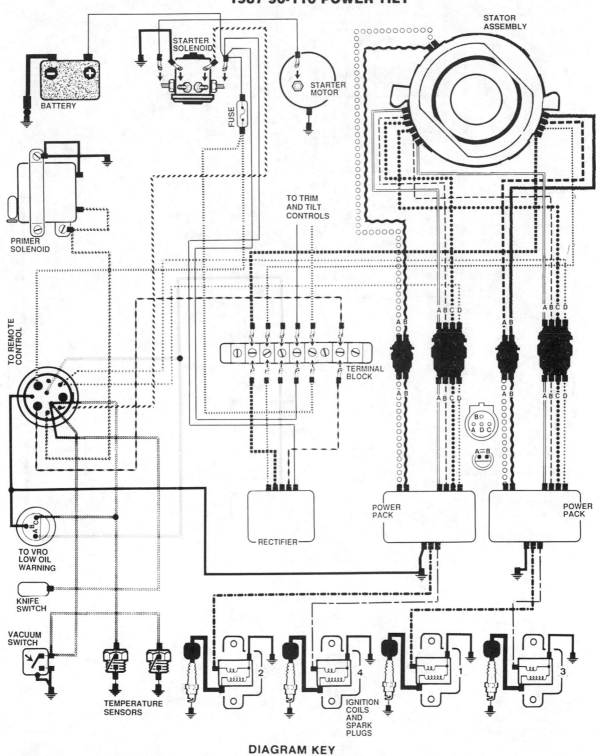

STATOR ASSEMBLY

STARTER SOLENOID

STARTER MOTOR

BATTERY

FUSE

PRIMER SOLENOID

TO TRIM AND TILT CONTROLS

TO REMOTE CONTROL

TERMINAL BLOCK

POWER PACK

POWER PACK

RECTIFIER

TO VRO LOW OIL WARNING

KNIFE SWITCH

VACUUM SWITCH

TEMPERATURE SENSORS

IGNITION COILS AND SPARK PLUGS

DIAGRAM KEY

BLACK	GRAY AND YELLOW	YELLOW AND RED
BLACK AND WHITE	RED	YELLOW AND BLUE
BLACK AND BROWN	RED AND WHITE	GREEN
BLACK AND YELLOW	ORANGE	GREEN AND WHITE
WHITE	ORANGE AND BLUE	BLUE
WHITE AND BLACK	ORANGE AND GREEN	BLUE AND WHITE
GRAY	YELLOW	PURPLE

PURPLE AND WHITE	
PURPLE AND RED	
PINK	
BROWN	
BROWN AND YELLOW	CONNECTORS
BROWN AND WHITE	

GROUND — CONNECTION

FRAME GROUND — NO CONNECTION

GROUNDS

1987 120, 140

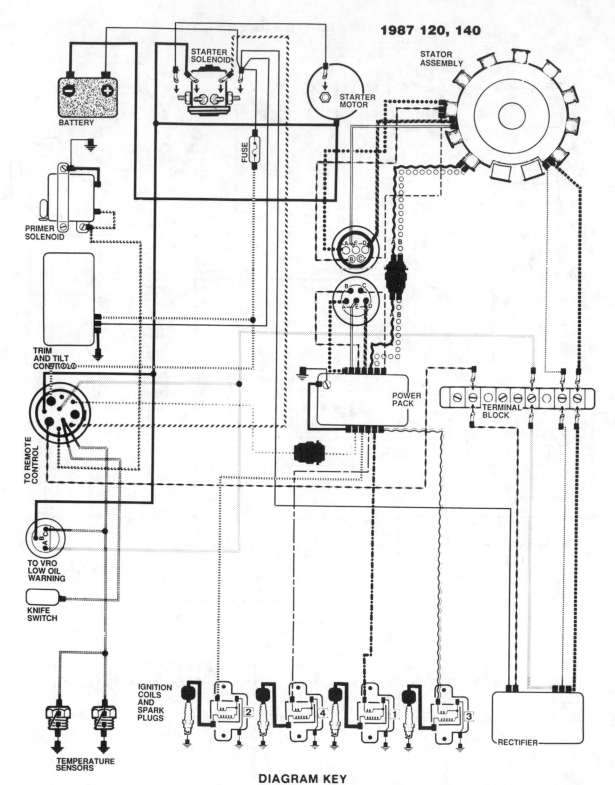

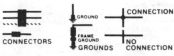

DIAGRAM KEY

▬▬ BLACK	∙∙∙∙∙∙ GRAY AND YELLOW	⁄⁄⁄⁄ YELLOW AND RED	⁛⁛⁛⁛ PURPLE AND WHITE
▬▬ BLACK AND WHITE	───── RED	⁓⁓⁓⁓ YELLOW AND BLUE	⁛⁛⁛⁛ PURPLE AND RED
▬▬ BLACK AND BROWN	⁛⁛⁛⁛⁛ RED AND WHITE	── ── GREEN	⁓⁓⁓⁓ PINK
∙∙∙∙∙∙ BLACK AND YELLOW	── ── ORANGE	════ GREEN AND WHITE	▬▬ BROWN
───── WHITE	⦁⦁⦁⦁ ORANGE AND BLUE	∙∙∙∙∙ BLUE	)))) BROWN AND YELLOW
── ── WHITE AND BLACK	⌇⌇⌇⌇ ORANGE AND GREEN	✱✱✱ BLUE AND WHITE	▬▬ BROWN AND WHITE
⁛⁛⁛⁛ GRAY	▬▬▬ YELLOW	▬▬▬ PURPLE	── ── TAN

▬▬ CONNECTORS	GROUND ⁄⁄⁄ FRAME GROUND GROUNDS	── CONNECTION ── NO CONNECTION

1987-1988 150-175

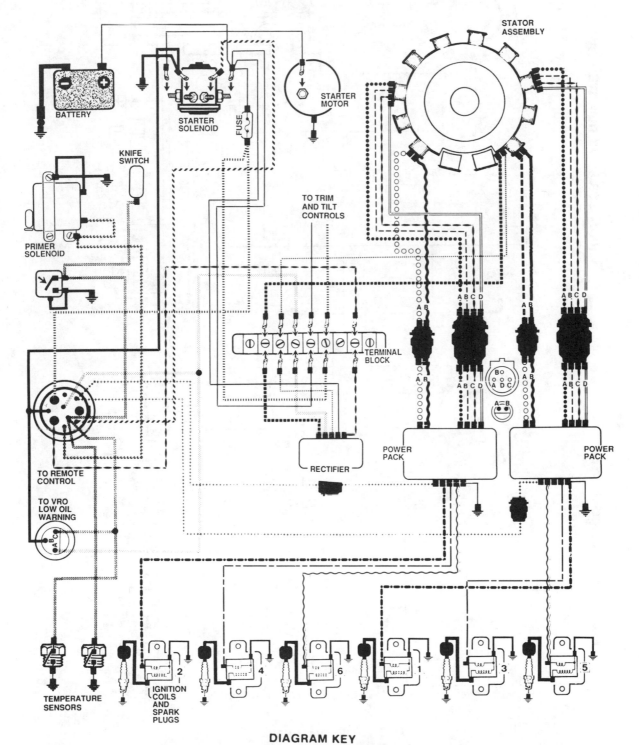

STATOR
ASSEMBLY

BATTERY

STARTER
SOLENOID

FUSE

STARTER
MOTOR

KNIFE
SWITCH

PRIMER
SOLENOID

TO TRIM
AND TILT
CONTROLS

TERMINAL
BLOCK

POWER
PACK

POWER
PACK

TO REMOTE
CONTROL

TO VRO
LOW OIL
WARNING

RECTIFIER

TEMPERATURE
SENSORS

IGNITION
COILS
AND
SPARK
PLUGS

DIAGRAM KEY

BLACK	GRAY AND YELLOW	YELLOW AND RED
BLACK AND WHITE	RED	YELLOW AND BLUE
BLACK AND BROWN	RED AND WHITE	GREEN
BLACK AND YELLOW	ORANGE	GREEN AND WHITE
WHITE	ORANGE AND BLUE	BLUE
WHITE AND BLACK	ORANGE AND GREEN	BLUE AND WHITE
GRAY	YELLOW	PURPLE

PURPLE AND WHITE
PURPLE AND RED
PINK
BROWN
BROWN AND YELLOW
BROWN AND WHITE
TAN

CONNECTORS

GROUND

FRAME
GROUND

GROUNDS

CONNECTION

NO
CONNECTION

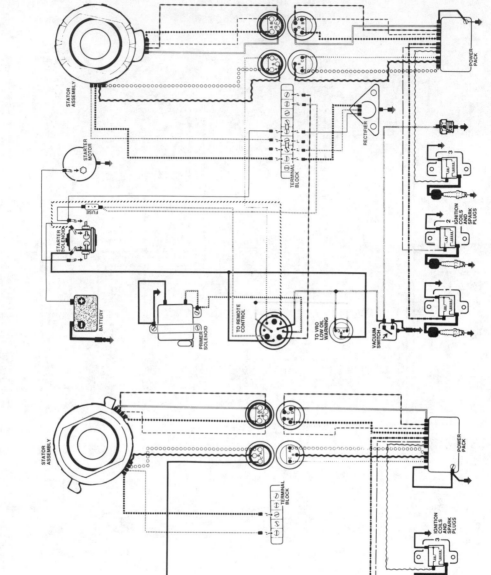

1987-1988 60-75 REMOTE START

1987-1988 65 MANUAL START

DIAGRAM KEY

BLACK	GRAY AND YELLOW	YELLOW AND RED	PURPLE AND WHITE
BLACK AND WHITE	RED	YELLOW AND BLUE	PURPLE AND RED
BLACK AND BROWN	RED AND WHITE	GREEN	PINK
BLACK AND YELLOW	ORANGE	GREEN AND WHITE	BROWN
WHITE	ORANGE AND BLUE	BLUE	BROWN AND YELLOW
WHITE AND BLACK	ORANGE AND GREEN	BLUE AND WHITE	BROWN AND WHITE
GRAY	YELLOW	PURPLE	TAN

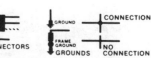

GROUND
FRAME GROUND
GROUNDS

CONNECTION
NO CONNECTION

CONNECTORS

1987 200, 225

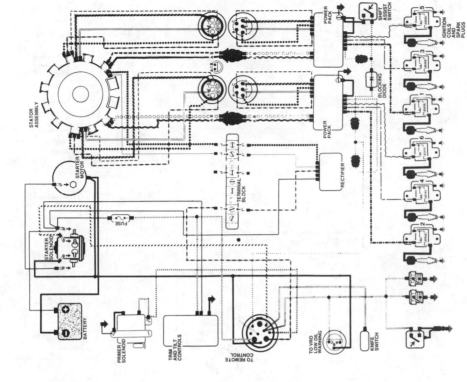

1987-1988 48-50 TILLER ELECTRIC

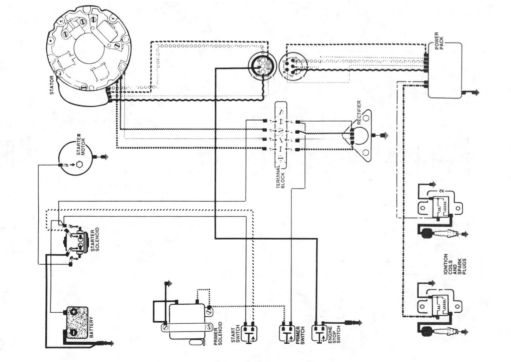

4

DIAGRAM KEY

BLACK	GRAY AND YELLOW	YELLOW AND RED	PURPLE AND WHITE
BLACK AND WHITE	RED	YELLOW AND BLUE	PURPLE AND RED
BLACK AND BROWN	RED AND WHITE	GREEN	PINK
BLACK AND YELLOW	ORANGE	GREEN AND WHITE	BROWN
WHITE	ORANGE AND BLUE	BLUE	BROWN AND YELLOW
WHITE AND BLACK	ORANGE AND GREEN	BLUE AND WHITE	BROWN AND WHITE
GRAY	YELLOW	PURPLE	TAN

CONNECTORS

GROUND
FRAME GROUND
GROUNDS

CONNECTION
NO CONNECTION

1987 88-110 MANUAL TILT

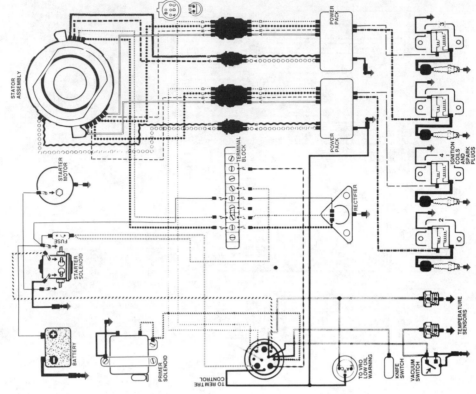

STATOR ASSEMBLY

POWER PACK

POWER PACK

TERMINAL BLOCK

RECTIFIER

IGNITION COILS AND SPARK PLUGS

STARTER MOTOR

FUSE

STARTER SOLENOID

BATTERY

PRIMER SOLENOID

TO REMTRE CONTROL

TO VRO LOW OIL WARNING

KNIFE SWITCH

VACUUM SWITCH

TEMPERATURE SENSORS

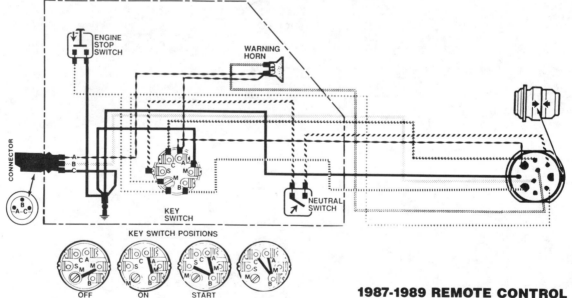

ENGINE STOP SWITCH

WARNING HORN

CONNECTOR

KEY SWITCH

NEUTRAL SWITCH

KEY SWITCH POSITIONS

OFF   ON   START

 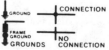

1987-1989 REMOTE CONTROL

DIAGRAM KEY

——— BLACK	········· GRAY AND YELLOW	⁄⁄⁄⁄ YELLOW AND RED	ᴸᴸᴸᴸ PURPLE AND WHITE
- - - BLACK AND WHITE	——— RED	∿∿∿ YELLOW AND BLUE	⁝⁝⁝⁝ PURPLE AND RED
━━ BLACK AND BROWN	⸱⸱⸱⸱⸱ RED AND WHITE	— — GREEN	∿∿∿ PINK
⋯⋯ BLACK AND YELLOW	— ORANGE	——— GREEN AND WHITE	∿∿∿ BROWN
——— WHITE	⬝⬝⬝ ORANGE AND BLUE	●●●● BLUE	○○○○ BROWN AND YELLOW
- - - WHITE AND BLACK	⬝⬝⬝ ORANGE AND GREEN	✱✱✱ BLUE AND WHITE	- - - BROWN AND WHITE
∷∷∷ GRAY	▪▪▪▪ YELLOW	——— PURPLE	⸱⸱⸱⸱ TAN

CONNECTORS

GROUND

FRAME GROUND

GROUNDS

CONNECTION

NO CONNECTION

1988-1989 88-110 HP

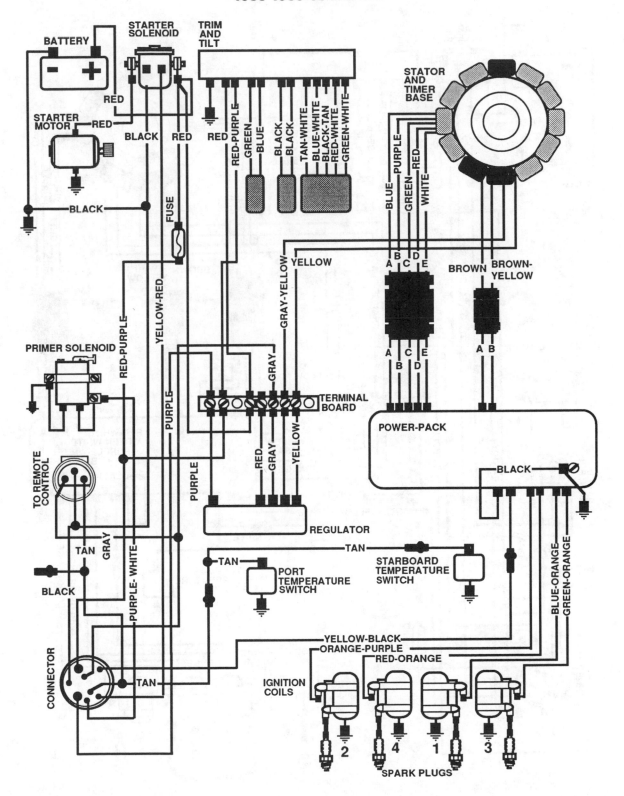

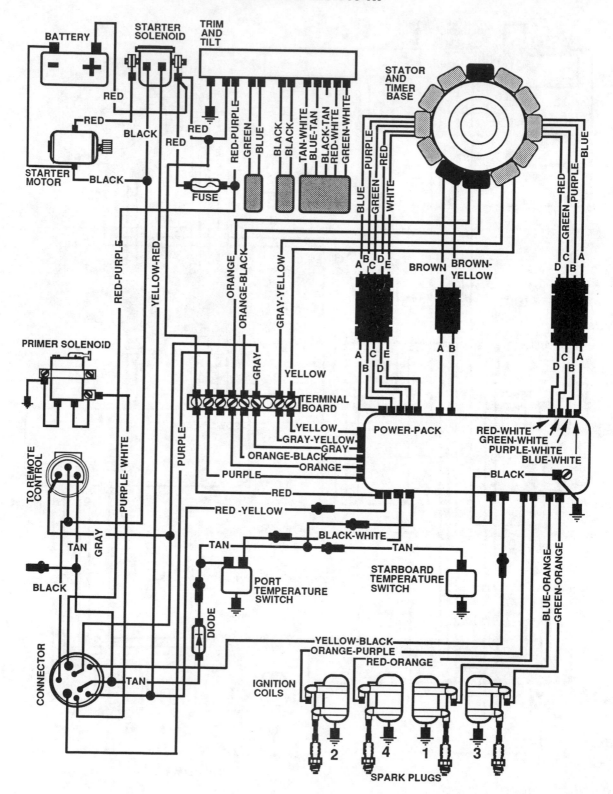

1988-1989 120-140 HP

1988-1989 200-225 HP

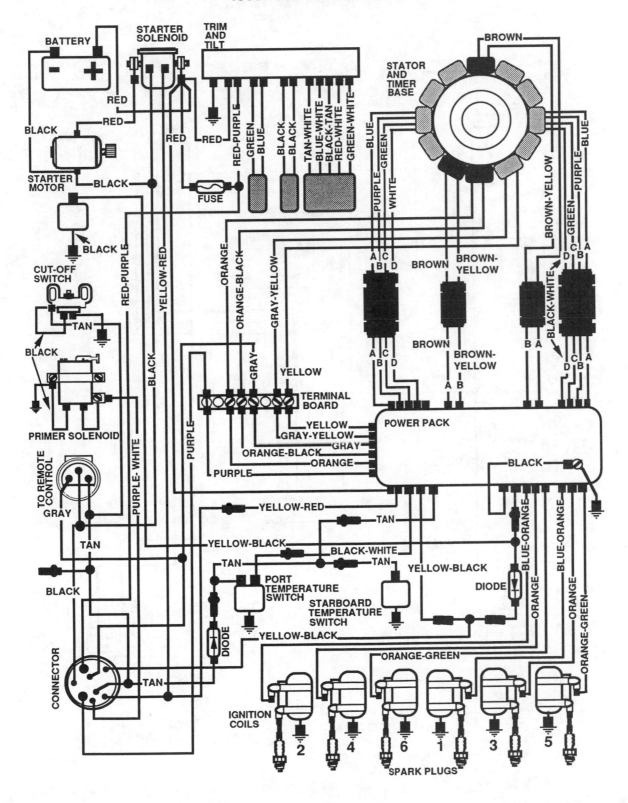

1989 48-50 HP REMOTE START

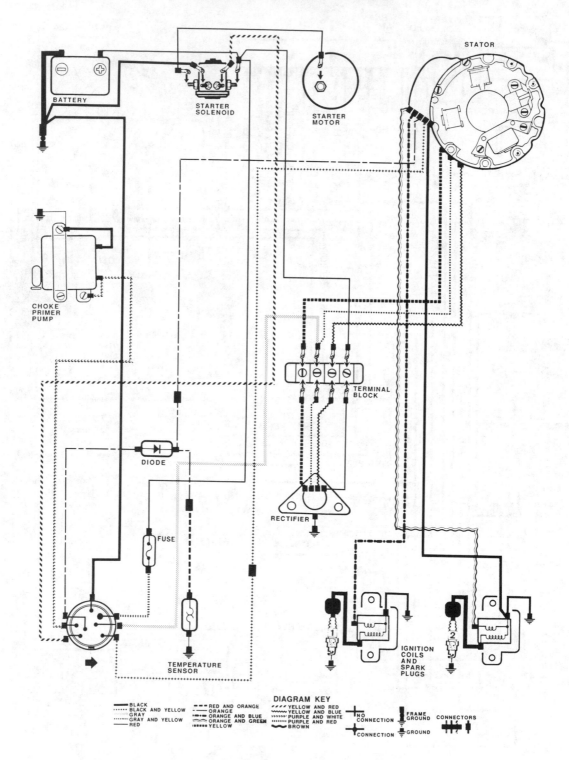

STATOR

BATTERY

STARTER
SOLENOID

STARTER
MOTOR

CHOKE
PRIMER
PUMP

DIODE

FUSE

TERMINAL
BLOCK

RECTIFIER

IGNITION
COILS
AND
SPARK
PLUGS

TEMPERATURE
SENSOR

DIAGRAM KEY

BLACK
BLACK AND YELLOW
GRAY
GRAY AND YELLOW
RED

RED AND ORANGE
ORANGE
ORANGE AND BLUE
ORANGE AND GREEN
YELLOW

YELLOW AND RED
YELLOW AND BLUE
PURPLE AND WHITE
PURPLE AND RED
BROWN

NO
CONNECTION

CONNECTION

FRAME
GROUND

GROUND

CONNECTORS

1989 60-70 HP REMOTE START

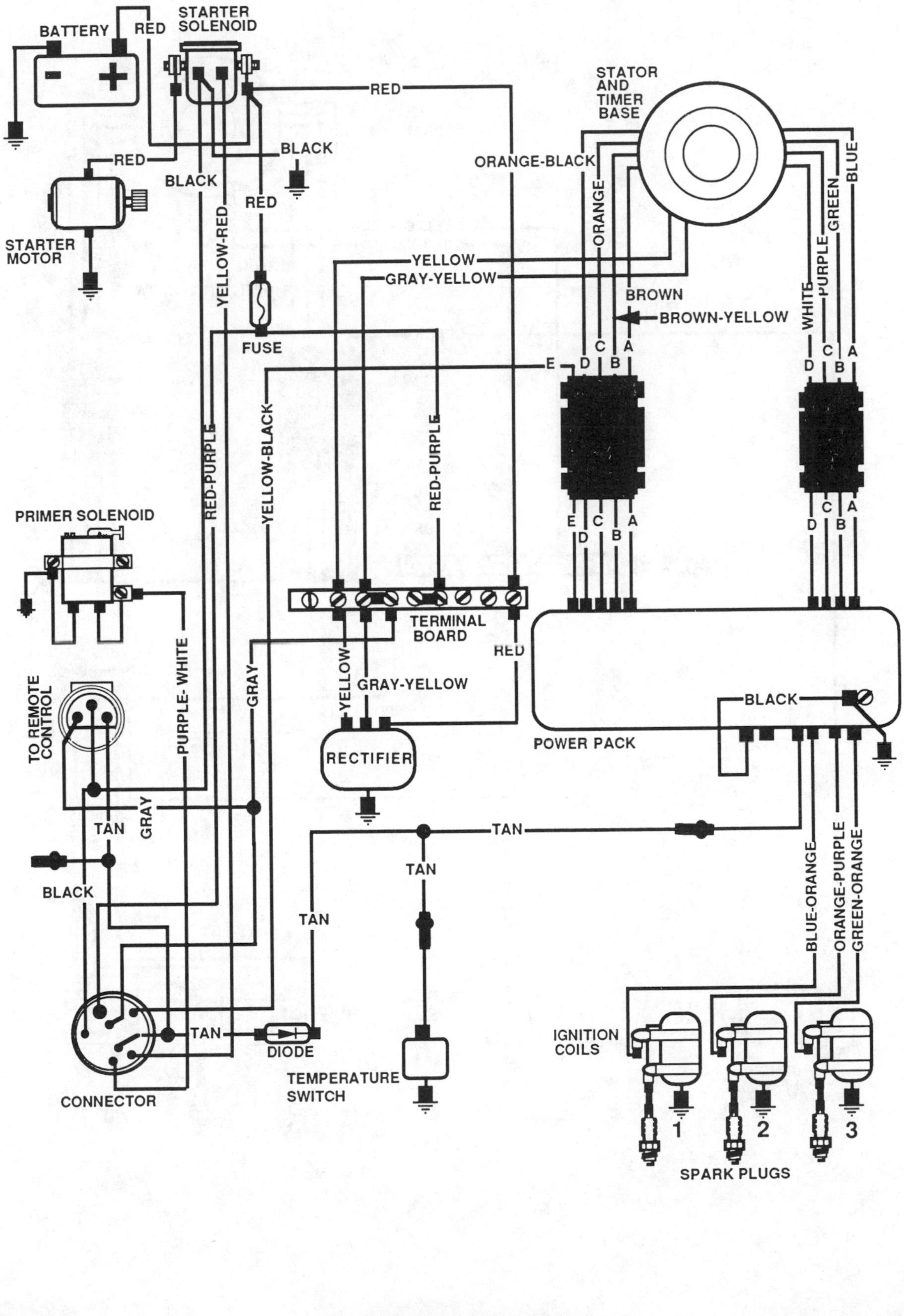

1989 65 HP MANUAL START

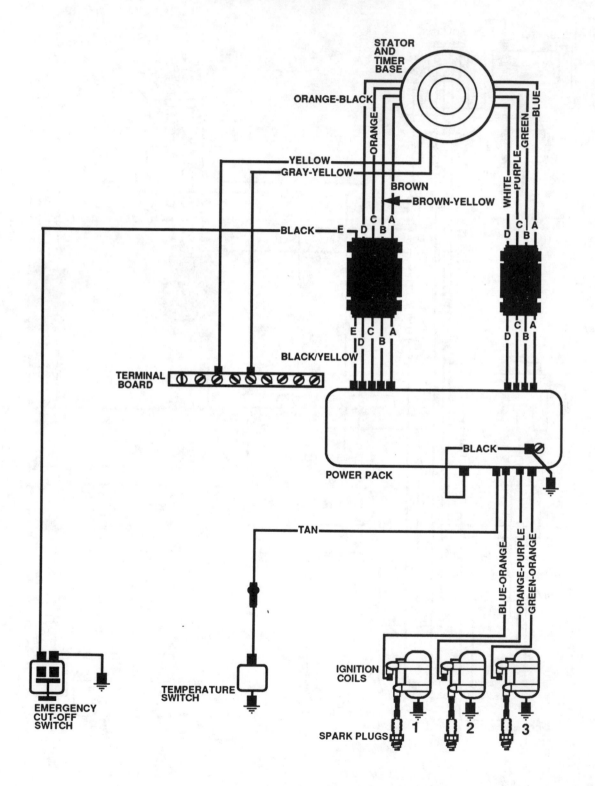

1989 150-175 HP (9 AMP)

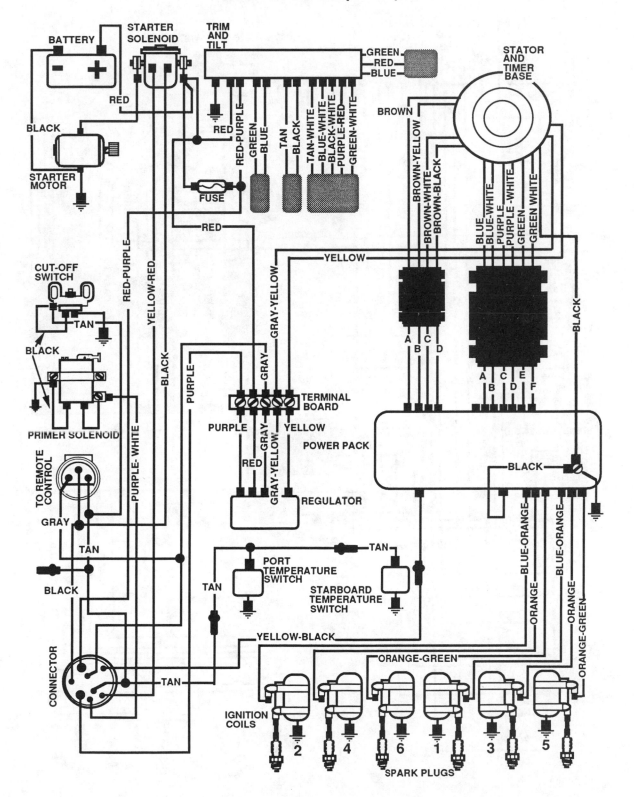

4

1989 150-175 HP (35 AMP)

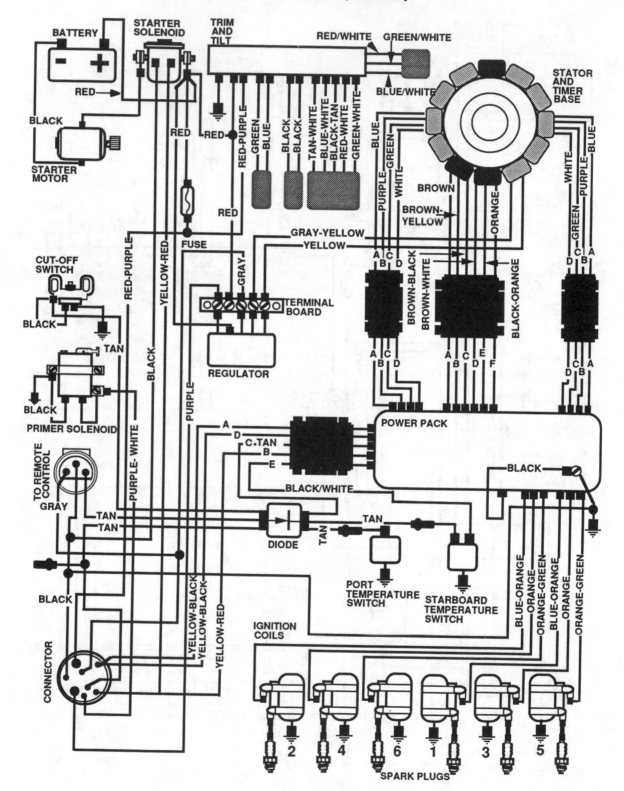

SEA DRIVE SELECTRIM/TILT

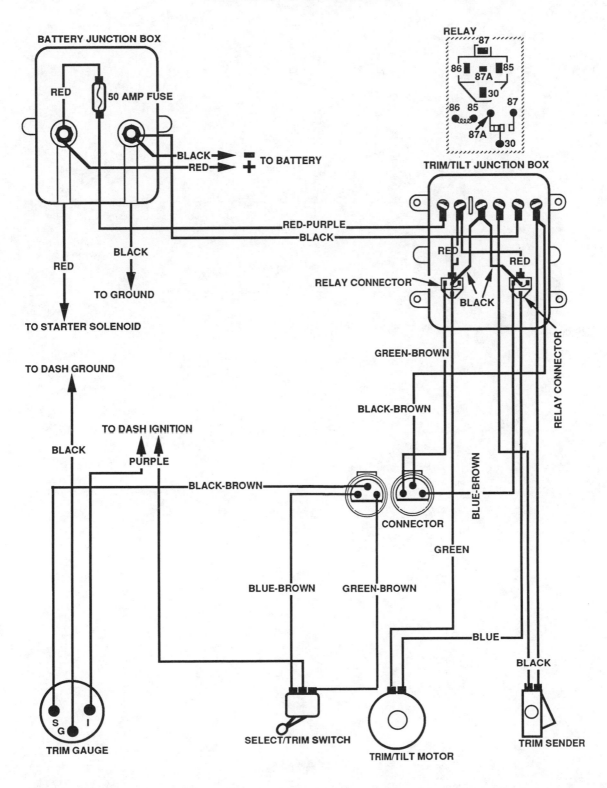

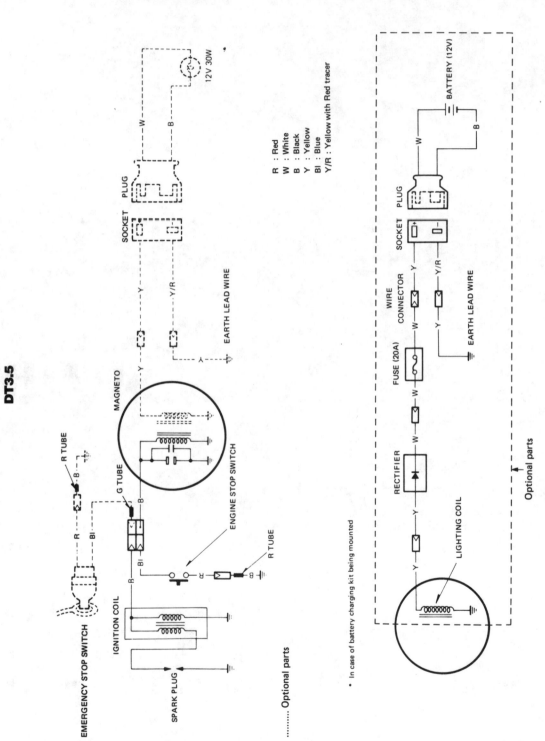

DT3.5

R : Red
W : White
B : Black
Y : Yellow
Bl : Blue
Y/R : Yellow with Red tracer

12V 30W

PLUG

SOCKET

EARTH LEAD WIRE

MAGNETO

ENGINE STOP SWITCH

EMERGENCY STOP SWITCH

R TUBE

G TUBE

R TUBE

IGNITION COIL

SPARK PLUG

.... Optional parts

BATTERY (12V)

PLUG

SOCKET

WIRE
CONNECTOR

FUSE (20A)

RECTIFIER

EARTH LEAD WIRE

LIGHTING COIL

Optional parts

* In case of battery charging kit being mounted

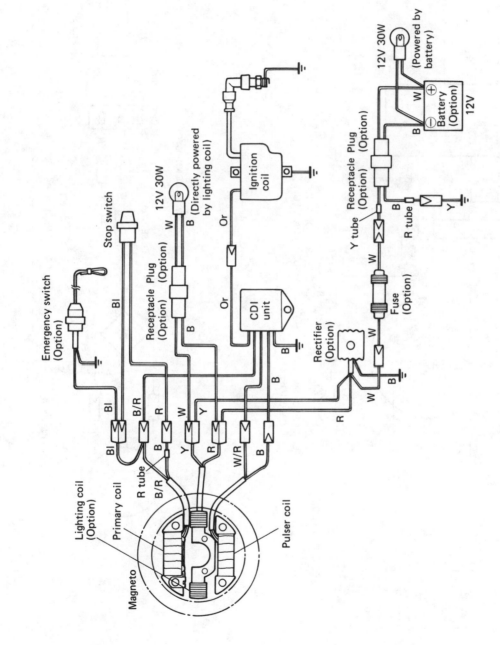

DT4

Emergency switch (Option)

Stop switch

Receptacle Plug (Option)

12V 30W

B (Directly powered by lighting coil)

Ignition coil

CDI unit

Rectifier (Option)

Y tube

Receptacle Plug (Option)

Fuse (Option)

Battery (Option)

12V

12V 30W

(Powered by battery)

R tube

Lighting coil (Option)

Primary coil

R tube

Magneto

Pulser coil

5

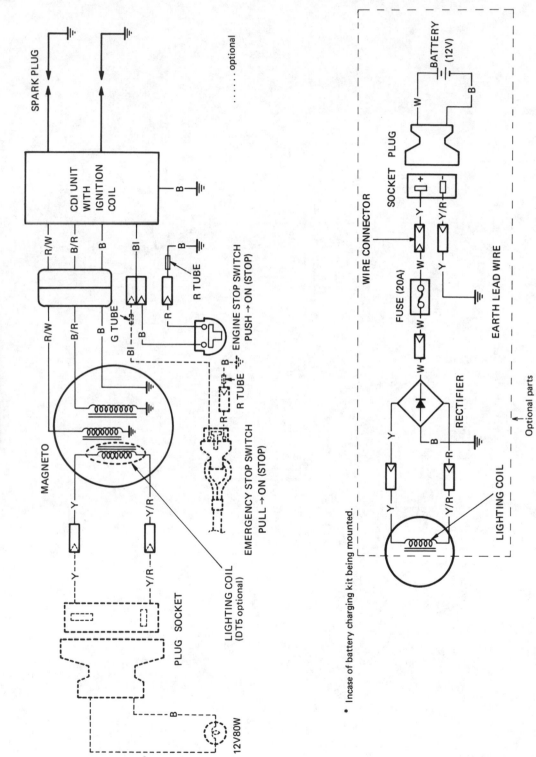

1982-1986 DT5/DT8

SPARK PLUG

CDI UNIT WITH IGNITION COIL

MAGNETO

LIGHTING COIL (DT5 optional)

ENGINE STOP SWITCH PUSH → ON (STOP)

EMERGENCY STOP SWITCH PULL → ON (STOP)

PLUG SOCKET

12V80W

...... optional

BATTERY (12V)

SOCKET PLUG

WIRE CONNECTOR

FUSE (20A)

EARTH LEAD WIRE

RECTIFIER

LIGHTING COIL

Optional parts

* Incase of battery charging kit being mounted.

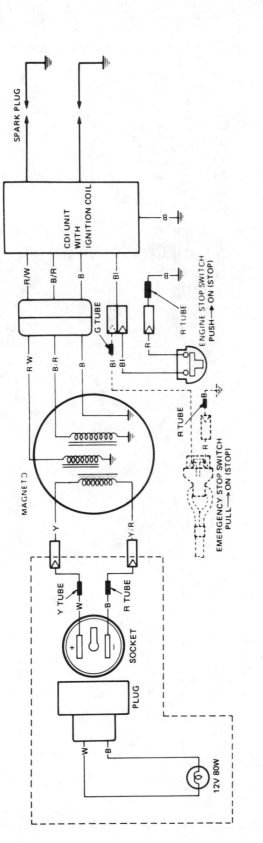

1984-1986 DT6

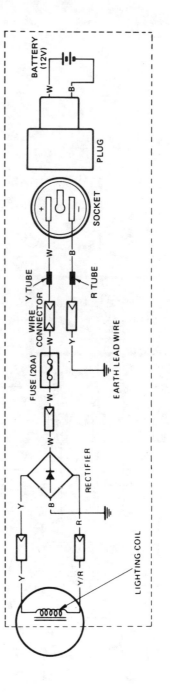

* In case of battery charging kit being mounted.

- - - - - - **optional**

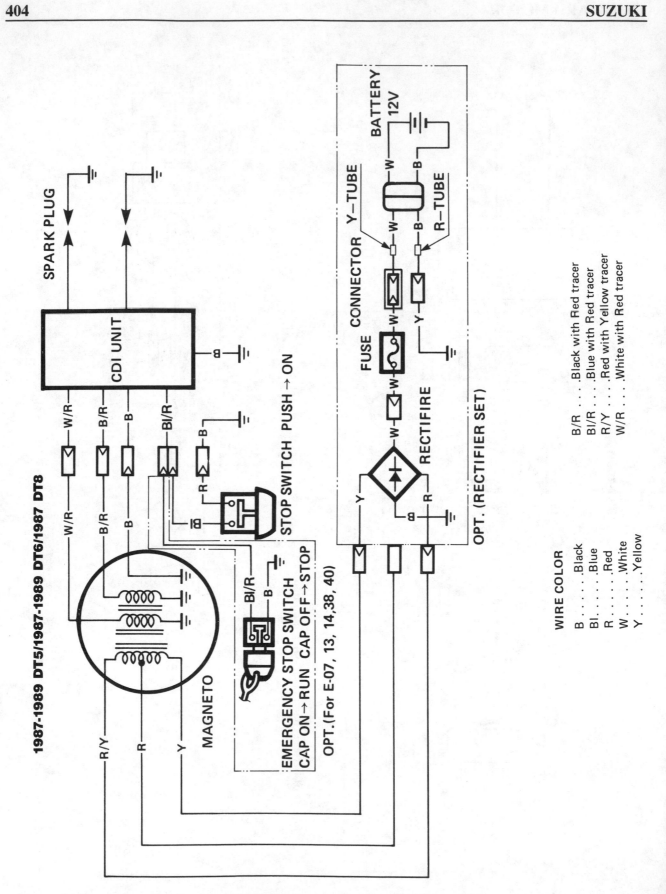

1987-1989 DT5/1987-1989 DT6/1987 DT8

SPARK PLUG

CDI UNIT

STOP SWITCH PUSH → ON

MAGNETO

EMERGENCY STOP SWITCH
CAP ON → RUN CAP OFF → STOP
OPT.(For E-07, 13, 14,38, 40)

BATTERY 12V

CONNECTOR Y–TUBE

R–TUBE

FUSE

RECTIFIRE

OPT. (RECTIFIER SET)

WIRE COLOR

B . . . . . . .Black
Bl. . . . . . .Blue
R . . . . . .Red
W . . . . . .White
Y . . . . . . .Yellow

B/R . . . .Black with Red tracer
Bl/R . . . .Blue with Red tracer
R/Y . . . .Red with Yellow tracer
W/R . . . .White with Red tracer

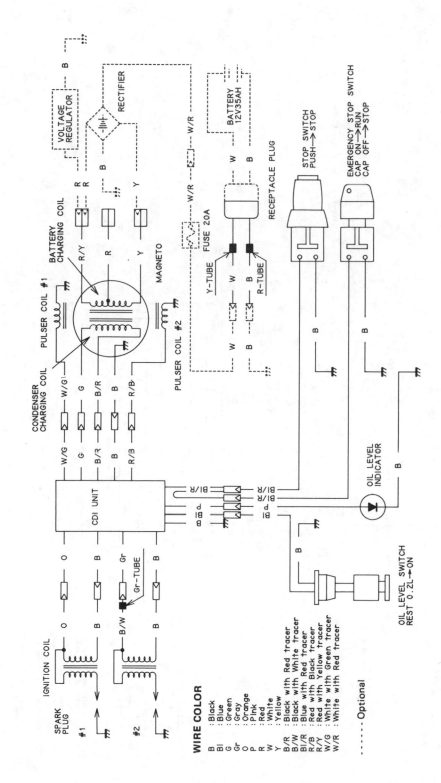

1988 DT8C/DT9.9MC

WIRE COLOR

B : Black
Bl : Blue
G : Green
Gr : Gray
O : Orange
P : Pink
R : Red
W : White
Y : Yellow
B/R : Black with Red tracer
B/W : Black with White tracer
Bl/R : Blue with Red tracer
R/B : Red with Black tracer
R/Y : Red with Yellow tracer
W/G : White with Green tracer
W/R : White with Red tracer

- - - - - : Optional

5

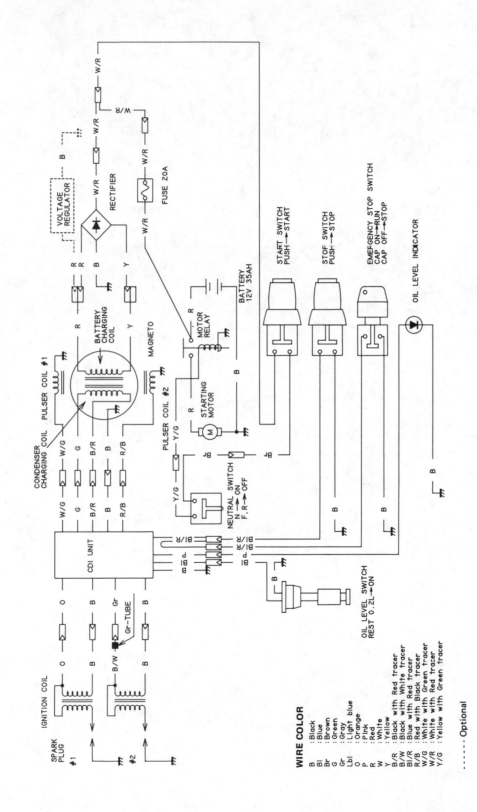

1988 DT9.9CE

WIRE COLOR

B   : Black
Bl   : Blue
Br   : Brown
G   : Green
Gr   : Gray
Lbl : Light blue
O   : Orange
P   : Pink
R   : Red
W   : White
Y   : Yellow
B/R : Black with Red tracer
B/W : Black with White tracer
Bl/R : Blue with Red tracer
R/B : Red with Black tracer
W/G : White with Green tracer
W/R : White with Red tracer
Y/G : Yellow with Green tracer

------ Optional

1988 DT9.9CN

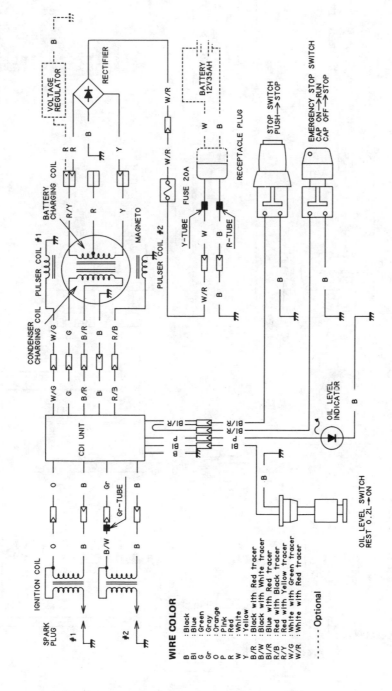

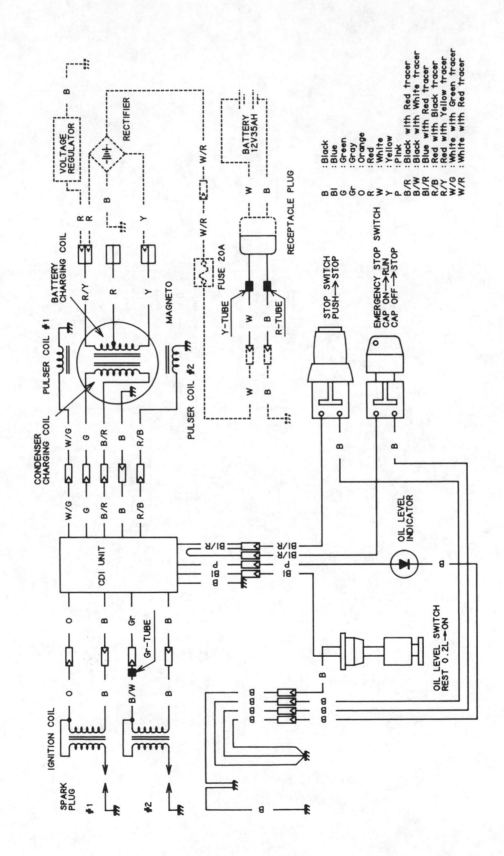

1989 DT8C/DT9.9MC

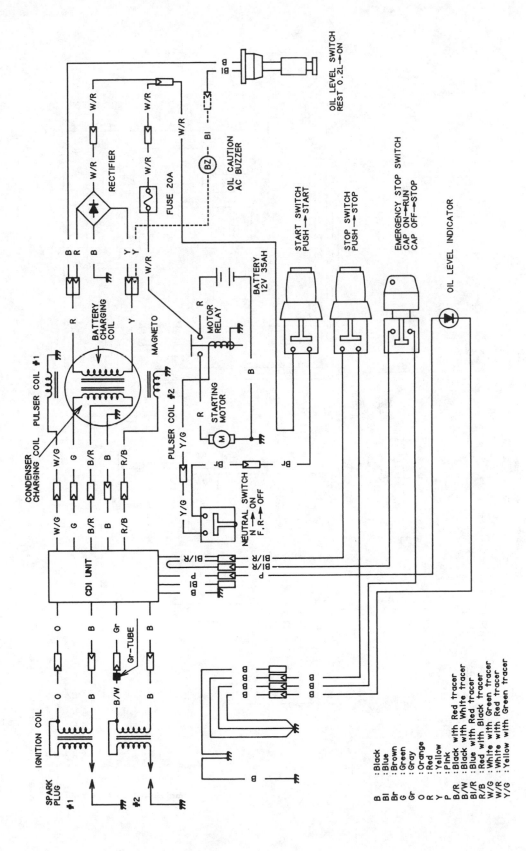

1989 DT9.9CE/DT9.9CEN WITH AC BUZZER

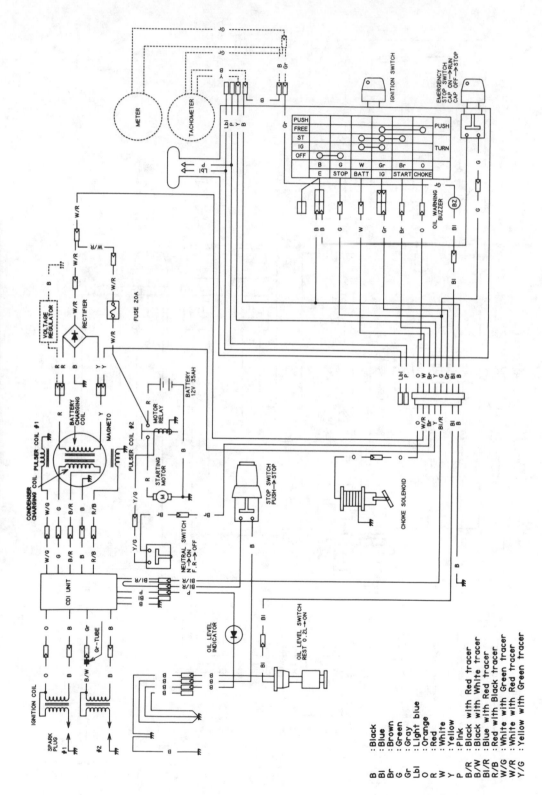

1989 DT9.9CE/DT9.9CEN WITH REMOTE CONTROL

PUSH						PUSH
FREE						
ST						
IG						TURN
OFF						
	B	G	W	Gr	Br	O
	E	STOP	BATT	IG	START	CHOKE

B : Black
Bl : Blue
Br : Brown
G : Green
Gr : Gray
Lbl : Light blue
O : Orange
R : Red
W : White
Y : Yellow
P : Pink
B/R : Black with Red tracer
B/W : Black with White tracer
Bl/R : Blue with Red tracer
R/B : Red with Black tracer
W/G : White with Green tracer
W/R : White with Red tracer
Y/G : Yellow with Green tracer

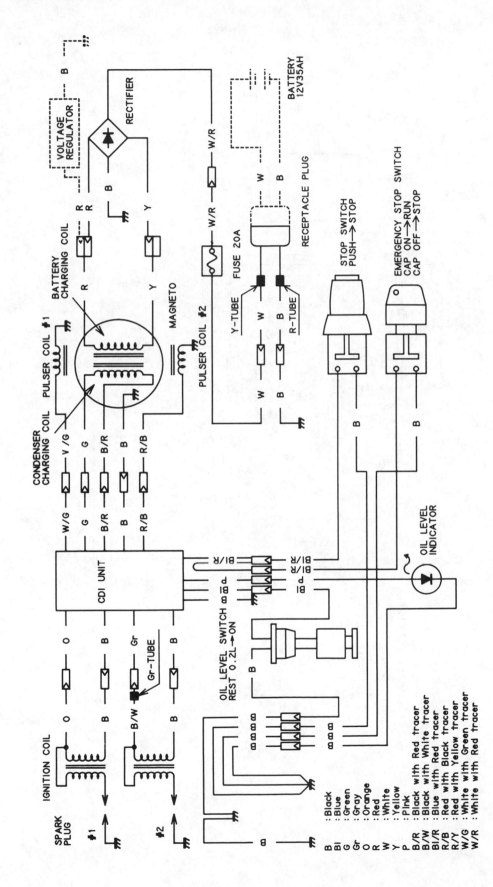

1989 DT9.9CN

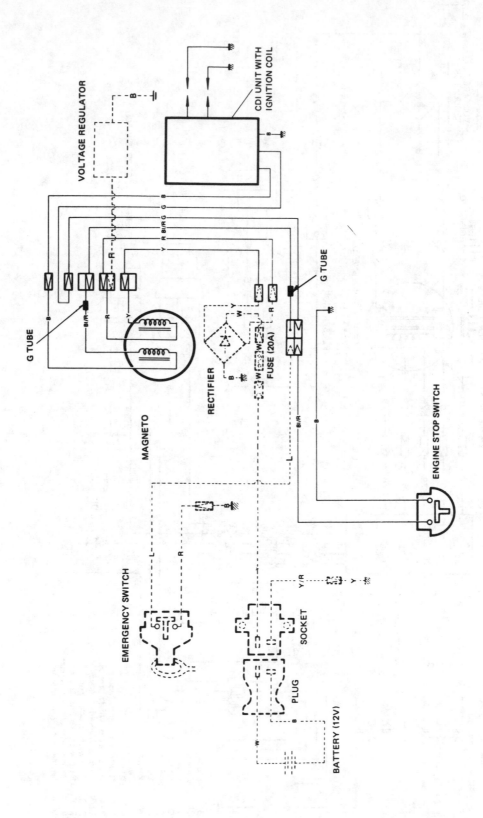

1977-1982 DT9.9/DT16

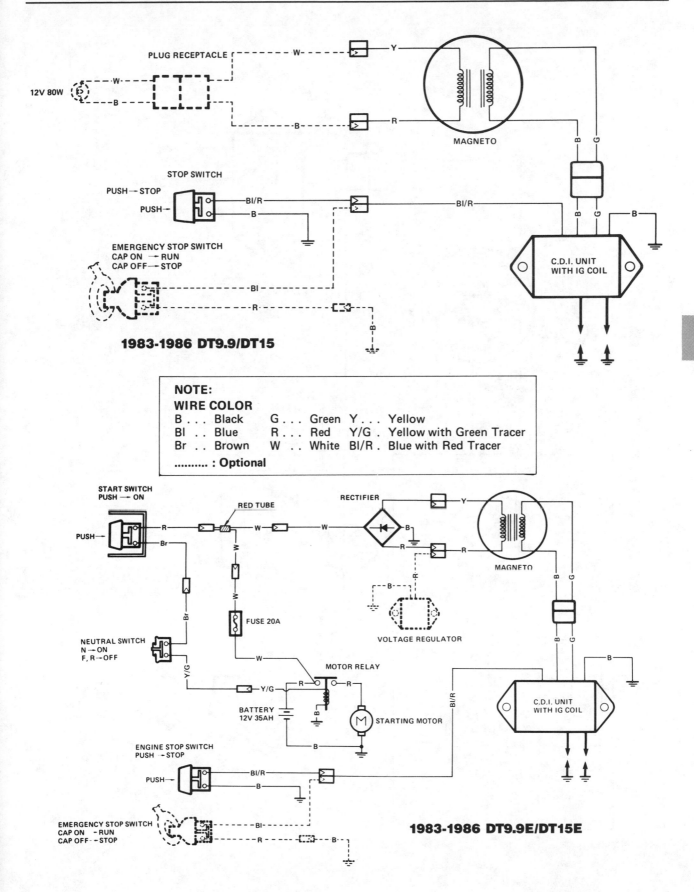

NOTE:
WIRE COLOR
B . . . Black	G . . . Green	Y . . . Yellow	
Bl . . Blue	R . . . Red	Y/G .	Yellow with Green Tracer
Br . . Brown	W . . White	Bl/R .	Blue with Red Tracer

.... : Optional

1983-1986 DT9.9/DT15

1983-1986 DT9.9E/DT15E

5

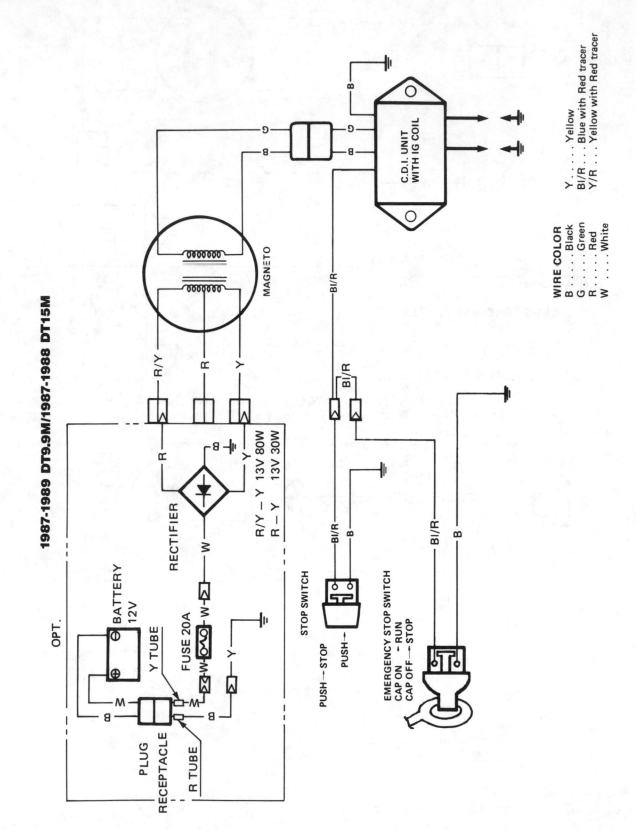

1987-1989 DT9.9M/1987-1988 DT15M

MAGNETO

C.D.I. UNIT WITH IG COIL

RECTIFIER

R/Y – Y 13V 80W
R – Y 13V 30W

BATTERY 12V

FUSE 20A

PLUG RECEPTACLE

Y TUBE

R TUBE

OPT.

STOP SWITCH

PUSH→STOP

EMERGENCY STOP SWITCH
CAP ON → RUN
CAP OFF → STOP

PUSH→

WIRE COLOR

B . . . . . Black
G . . . . . Green
R . . . . . Red
W . . . . . White

Y . . . . . Yellow
Bl/R . . . Blue with Red tracer
Y/R . . . Yellow with Red tracer

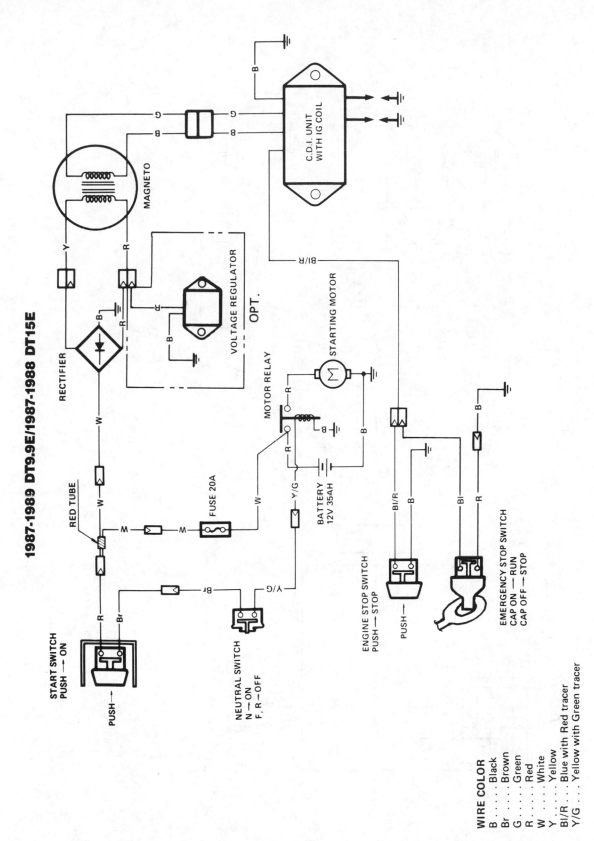

1987-1989 DT9.9E/1987-1988 DT15E

MAGNETO

C.D.I. UNIT WITH IG COIL

VOLTAGE REGULATOR
OPT.

RECTIFIER

STARTING MOTOR

MOTOR RELAY

BATTERY 12V 35AH

FUSE 20A

RED TUBE

START SWITCH
PUSH → ON

PUSH

NEUTRAL SWITCH
N → ON
F, R → OFF

ENGINE STOP SWITCH
PUSH → STOP

PUSH

EMERGENCY STOP SWITCH
CAP ON → RUN
CAP OFF → STOP

WIRE COLOR
B . . . . . Black
Br . . . . Brown
G . . . . . Green
R . . . . . Red
W . . . . White
Y . . . . . Yellow
Bl/R . . . Blue with Red tracer
Y/G . . . Yellow with Green tracer

5

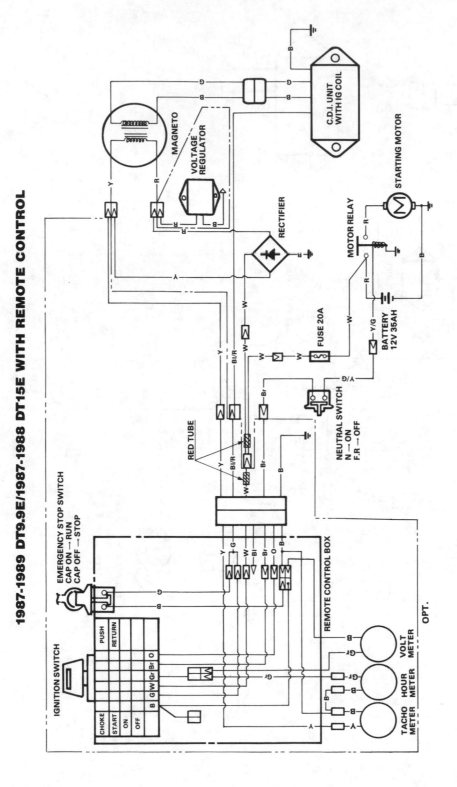

1987-1989 DT9.9E/1987-1988 DT15E WITH REMOTE CONTROL

WIRE COLOR

B . . . . . Black	W . . . . . White
Bl . . . . Blue	Y . . . . . Yellow
Br . . . . Brown	Bl/R . . . Blue with Red tracer
G . . . . . Green	Y/G . . . Yellow with Green tracer
Gr . . . . Gray	
O . . . . . Orange	
R . . . . . Red	

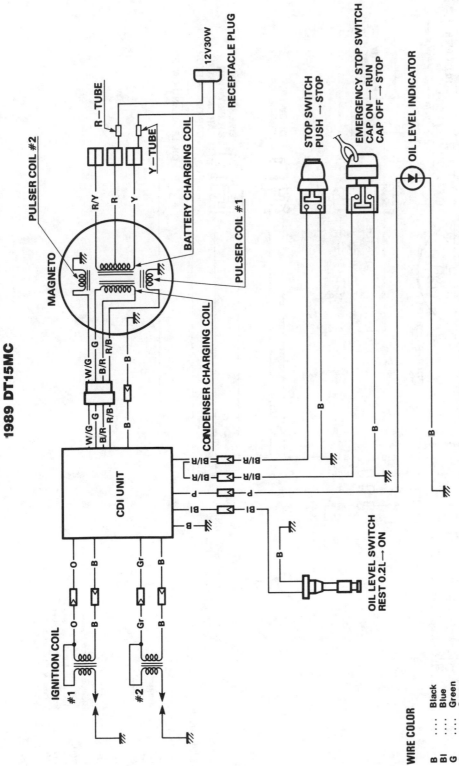

1989 DT15MC

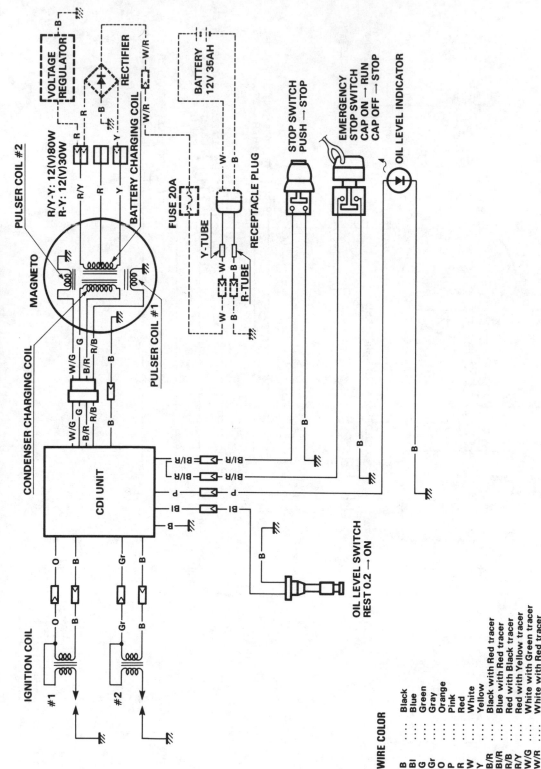

1989 DT15MC WITH RECTIFIER AND BATTERY

VOLTAGE REGULATOR

RECTIFIER

BATTERY 12V 35AH

PULSER COIL #2

R/Y-Y: 12(V)80W
R-Y: 12(V)30W

FUSE 20A

STOP SWITCH
PUSH → STOP

EMERGENCY
STOP SWITCH
CAP ON → RUN
CAP OFF → STOP

OIL LEVEL INDICATOR

MAGNETO

BATTERY CHARGING COIL

Y-TUBE

R-TUBE

RECEPTACLE PLUG

CONDENSER CHARGING COIL

PULSER COIL #1

CDI UNIT

OIL LEVEL SWITCH
REST 0.2 → ON

IGNITION COIL

#1

#2

WIRE COLOR

B	......	Black
Bl	......	Blue
G	......	Green
Gr	......	Gray
O	......	Orange
P	......	Pink
R	......	Red
W	......	White
Y	......	Yellow
B/R	......	Black with Red tracer
Bl/R	......	Blue with Red tracer
R/B	......	Red with Black tracer
R/Y	......	Red with Yellow tracer
W/G	......	White with Green tracer
W/R	......	White with Red tracer

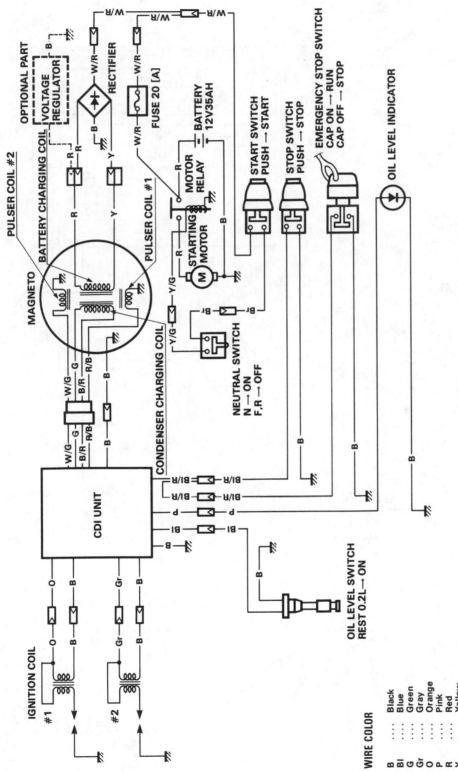

1989 DT15CE

WIRE COLOR

B	...	Black
Bl	...	Blue
G	...	Green
Gr	...	Gray
O	...	Orange
P	...	Pink
R	...	Red
Y	...	Yellow
B/R	...	Black with Red tracer
Bl/R	...	Blue with Red tracer
R/B	...	Red with Black tracer
R/Y	...	Red with Yellow tracer
W/G	...	White with Green tracer
W/R	...	White with Red tracer
Y/G	...	Yellow with Green tracer

5

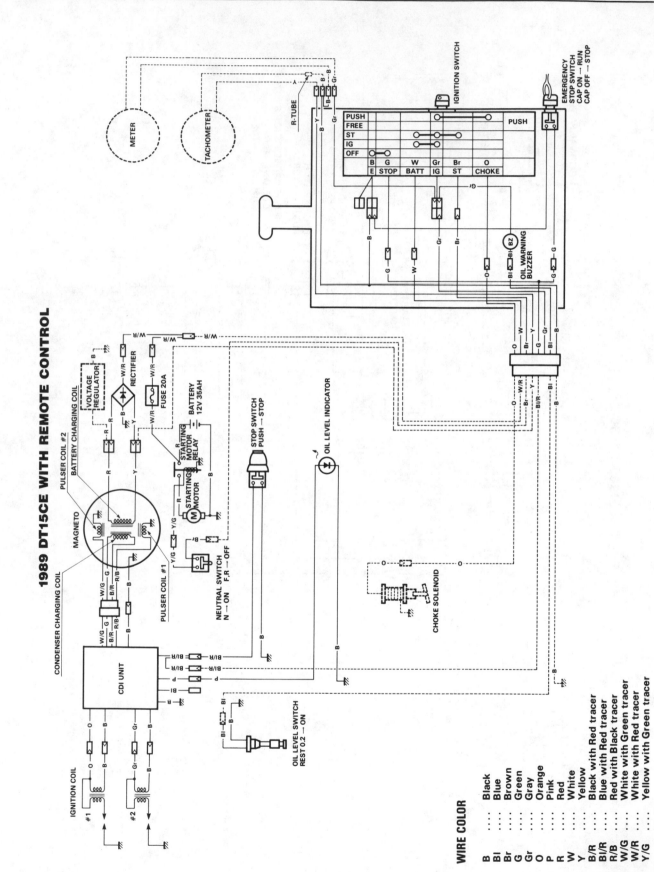

1989 DT15CE WITH REMOTE CONTROL

WIRE COLOR

B	.....	Black
Bl	.....	Blue
Br	.....	Brown
G	.....	Green
Gr	.....	Gray
O	.....	Orange
P	.....	Pink
R	.....	Red
W	.....	White
Y	.....	Yellow
B/R	.....	Black with Red tracer
Bl/R	.....	Blue with Red tracer
R/B	.....	Red with Black tracer
W/G	.....	White with Green tracer
W/R	.....	White with Red tracer
Y/G	.....	Yellow with Green tracer

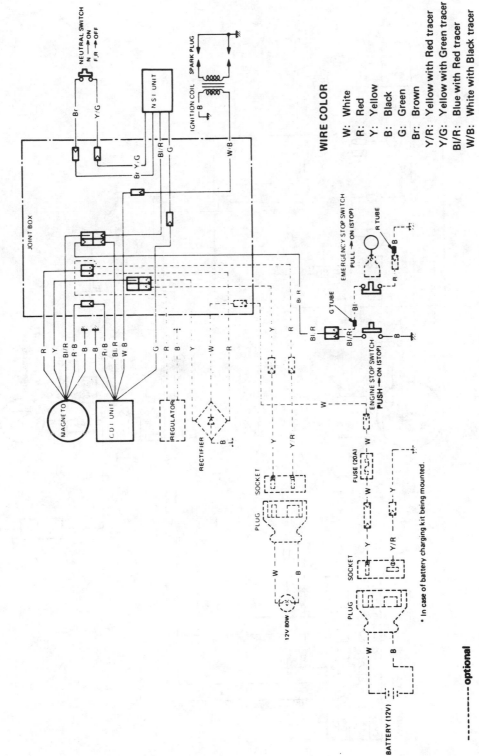

1981-1982 DT20P/DT25/DT25P/DT28

WIRE COLOR

W: White
R: Red
Y: Yellow
B: Black
G: Green
Br: Brown
Y/R: Yellow with Red tracer
Y/G: Yellow with Green tracer
Bl/R: Blue with Red tracer
W/B: White with Black tracer

----- **optional**

* In case of battery charging kit being mounted.

5

1981-1982 DT25PE/DT28PE

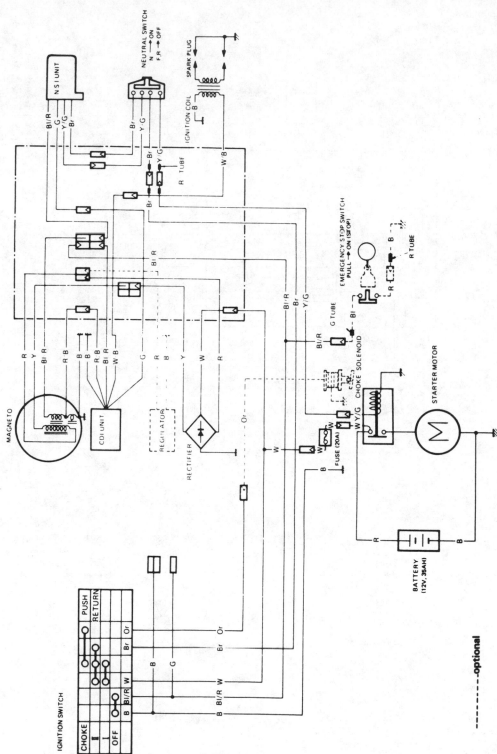

- - - - - - - - optional

1986-1988 DT20/1985-1988 DT25/1983-1988 DT30

[Electric starter type]

[Manual starter type]

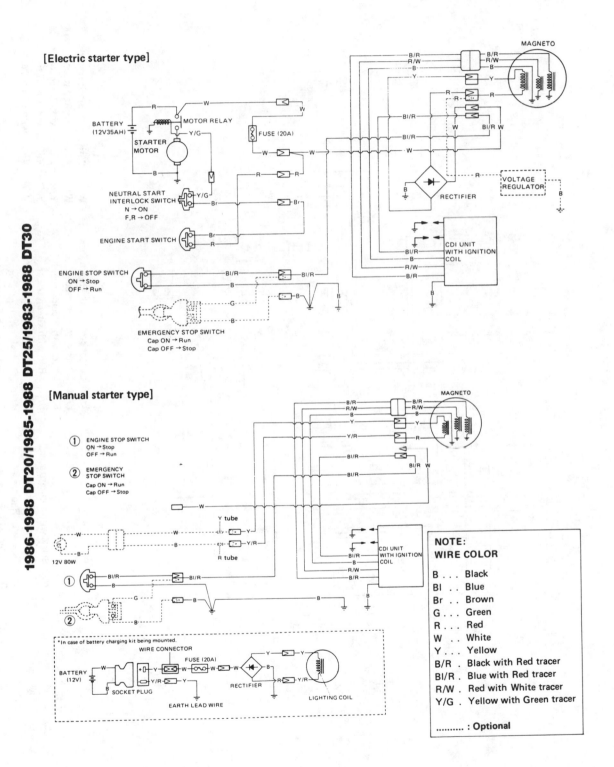

NOTE:
WIRE COLOR

B . . .	Black
Bl . .	Blue
Br . .	Brown
G . . .	Green
R . . .	Red
W . . .	White
Y . . .	Yellow
B/R .	Black with Red tracer
Bl/R .	Blue with Red tracer
R/W .	Red with White tracer
Y/G .	Yellow with Green tracer
.... :	Optional

5

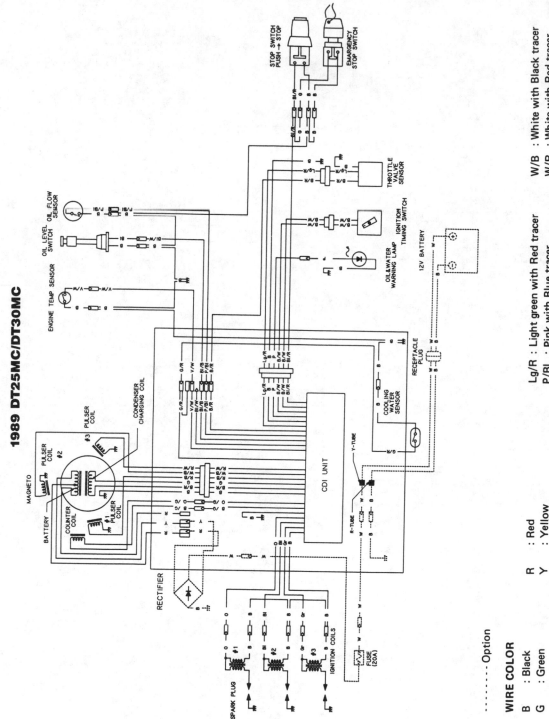

1989 DT25MC/DT30MC

STOP SWITCH PUSH → STOP

EMARGENCY STOP SWITCH

THROTTLE VALVE SENSOR

IGNITIOM TIMING SWITCH

OIL&WATER WARNING LAMP

12V BATTERY

OIL FLOW SENSOR

OIL LEVEL SWITCH

ENGINE TEMP SENSOR

RECEPTACLE PLUG

COOLING WATER SENSOR

CDI UNIT

MAGNETO

PULSER COIL #2

PULSER COIL #3

CONDENSER CHARGING COIL

BATTERY

COUNTER COIL

PULSER COIL #1

RECTIFIER

SPARK PLUG

IGNITION COILS

FUSE (20A)

------- Option

WIRE COLOR

B : Black
G : Green
Gr : Gray
Lbl : Light blue
Lg : Light green
O : Orange
P : Pink

R : Red
Y : Yellow
W : White
B/W : Black with White tracer
B/R : Black with Red tracer
Bl/R : Blue with Red tracer
G/R : Green with Red tracer

Lg/R : Light green with Red tracer
P/Bl : Pink with Blue tracer
R/B : Red with Black tracer
R/G : Red with Green tracer
R/Y : Red with Yellow tracer
R/W : Red with White tracer
O/G : Orange with Green tracer

W/B : White with Black tracer
W/R : White with Red tracer
Y/B : Yellow with Black tracer
Y/G : Yellow with Green tracer
V/W : Violet with White tracer

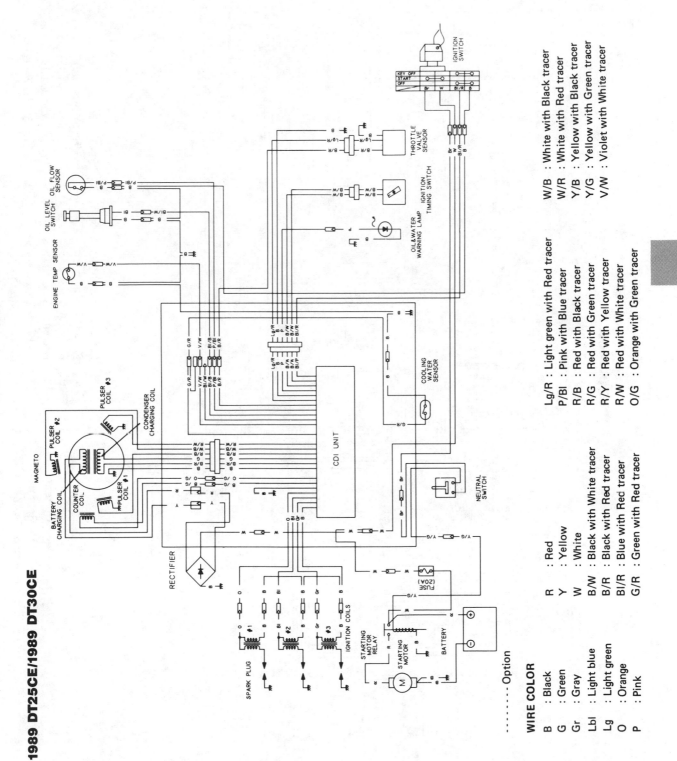

1989 DT25CE/1989 DT30CE

------- Option

WIRE COLOR

B	: Black
G	: Green
Gr	: Gray
Lbl	: Light blue
Lg	: Light green
O	: Orange
P	: Pink

R	: Red
Y	: Yellow
W	: White
B/W	: Black with White tracer
B/R	: Black with Red tracer
Bl/R	: Blue with Red tracer
G/R	: Green with Red tracer

Lg/R	: Light green with Red tracer
P/Bl	: Pink with Blue tracer
R/B	: Red with Black tracer
R/G	: Red with Green tracer
R/Y	: Red with Yellow tracer
R/W	: Red with White tracer
O/G	: Orange with Green tracer

W/B	: White with Black tracer
W/R	: White with Red tracer
Y/B	: Yellow with Black tracer
Y/G	: Yellow with Green tracer
V/W	: Violet with White tracer

5

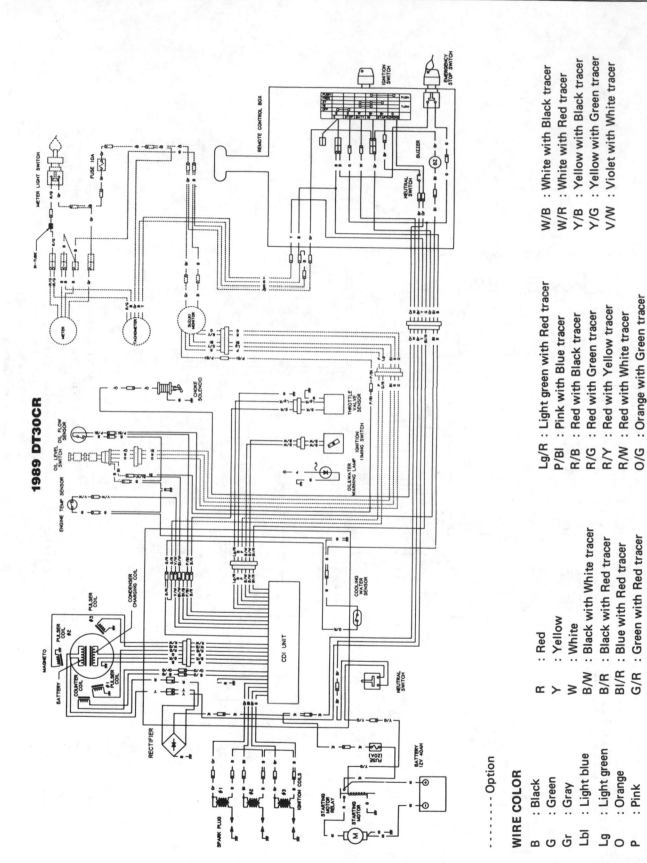

1989 DT30CR

------- Option

WIRE COLOR

B	: Black
G	: Green
Gr	: Gray
Lbl	: Light blue
Lg	: Light green
O	: Orange
P	: Pink

R	: Red
Y	: Yellow
W	: White
B/W	: Black with White tracer
B/R	: Black with Red tracer
Bl/R	: Blue with Red tracer
G/R	: Green with Red tracer

Lg/R	: Light green with Red tracer
P/Bl	: Pink with Blue tracer
R/B	: Red with Black tracer
R/G	: Red with Green tracer
R/Y	: Red with Yellow tracer
R/W	: Red with White tracer
O/G	: Orange with Green tracer

W/B	: White with Black tracer
W/R	: White with Red tracer
Y/B	: Yellow with Black tracer
Y/G	: Yellow with Green tracer
V/W	: Violet with White tracer

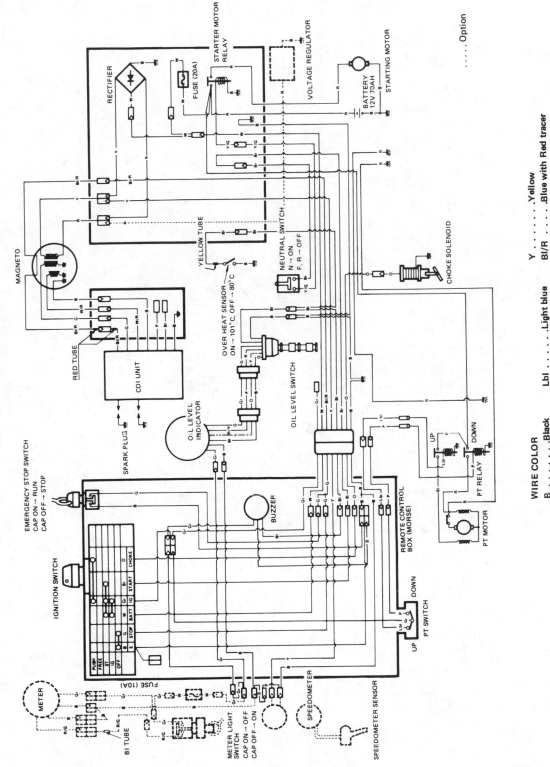

1987-1989 DT35TC

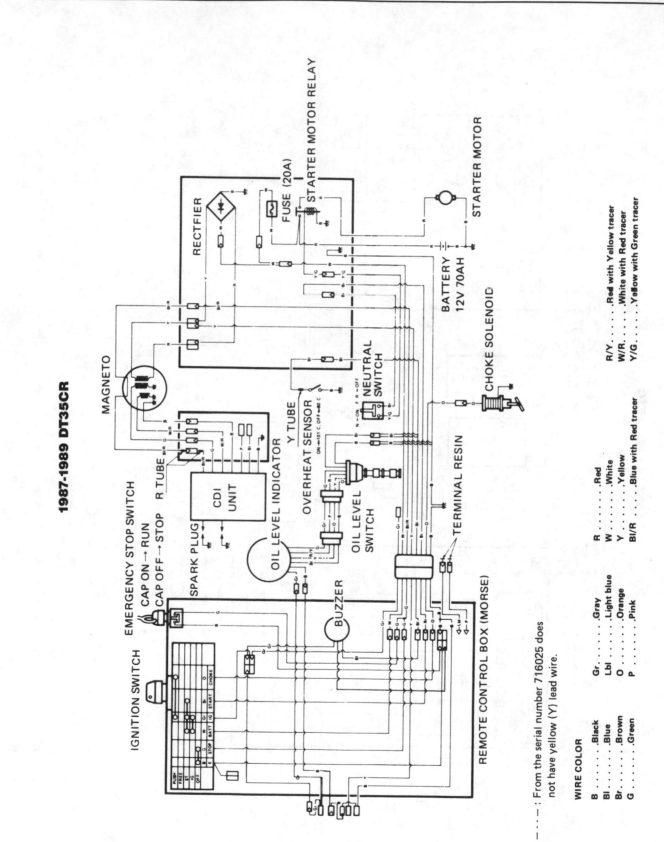

1987-1989 DT35CR

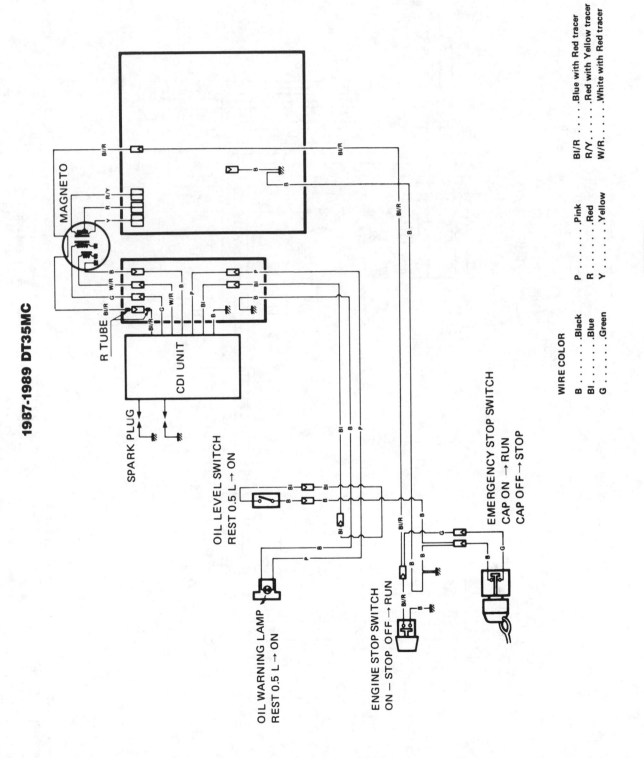

1987-1989 DT35MC

MAGNETO

R TUBE

CDI UNIT

SPARK PLUG

OIL LEVEL SWITCH
REST 0.5 L → ON

OIL WARNING LAMP
REST 0.5 L → ON

ENGINE STOP SWITCH
ON – STOP OFF → RUN

EMERGENCY STOP SWITCH
CAP ON → RUN
CAP OFF → STOP

WIRE COLOR

B . . . . .Black
Bl . . . . . . .Blue
G . . . . . . .Green

P . . . . . . .Pink
R . . . . . . .Red
Y . . . . . . .Yellow

Bl/R . . . . . .Blue with Red tracer
R/Y . . . . . .Red with Yellow tracer
W/R. . . . . .White with Red tracer

5

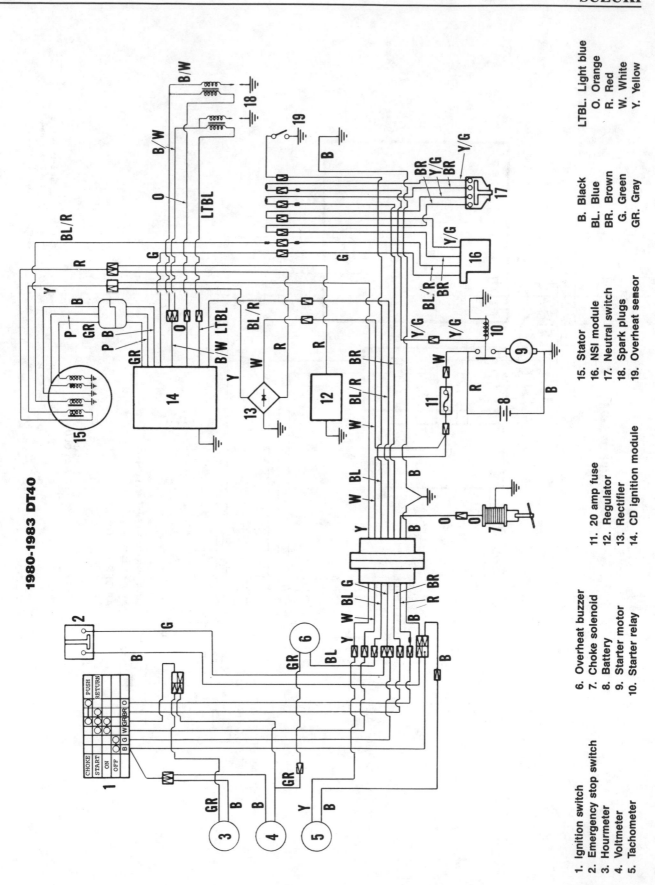

1980-1983 DT40

LTBL. Light blue
O. Orange
R. Red
W. White
Y. Yellow

B. Black
BL. Blue
BR. Brown
G. Green
GR. Gray

15. Stator
16. NSI module
17. Neutral switch
18. Spark plugs
19. Overheat sensor

11. 20 amp fuse
12. Regulator
13. Rectifier
14. CD Ignition module

6. Overheat buzzer
7. Choke solenoid
8. Battery
9. Starter motor
10. Starter relay

1. Ignition switch
2. Emergency stop switch
3. Hourmeter
4. Voltmeter
5. Tachometer

1984-1986 DT40M

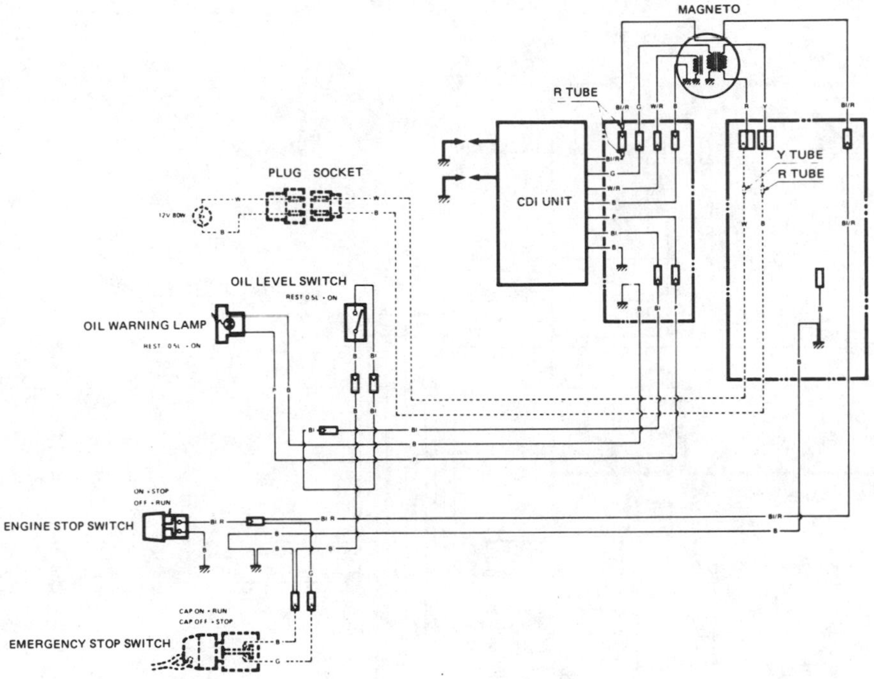

1984-1986 DT40E

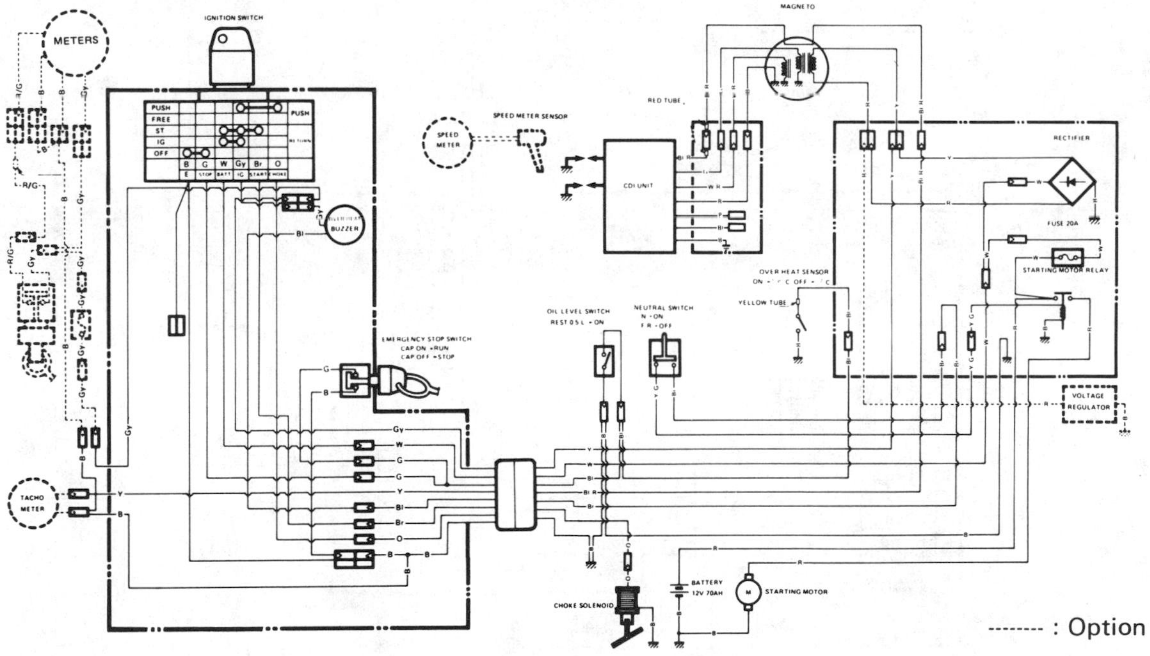

-------- : Option

WIRE COLOR								
B . . .	Black	O . . .	Orange	W . .	White	Br . . .	Brown	W/R . . . White with Red tracer
G . . .	Green	P . . .	Pink	Y . . .	Yellow	G/Y . .	Green with Yellow tracer	Bl/R . . Blue with Red tracer
Gy . .	Grey	R . . .	Red	Bl . .	Blue	O/R . .	Orange with Red tracer	Y/G . . Yellow with Green tracer

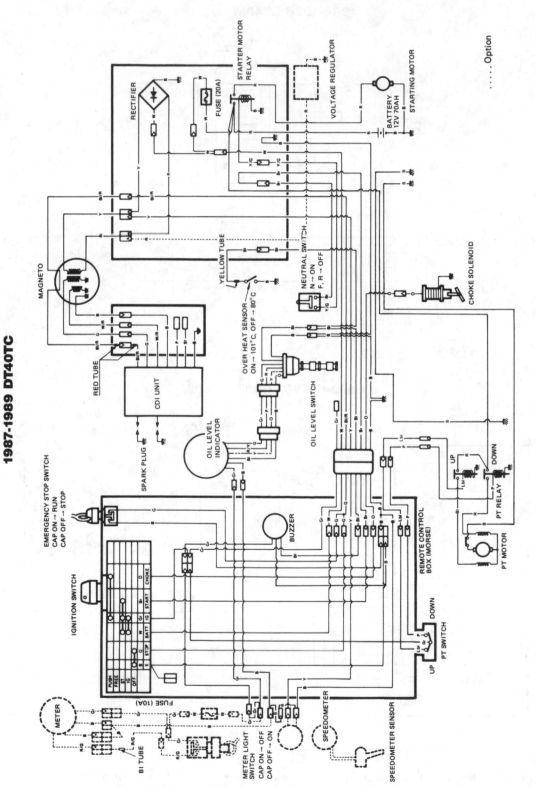

1987-1989 DT40TC

EMERGENCY STOP SWITCH
CAP ON → RUN
CAP OFF → STOP

IGNITION SWITCH

METER LIGHT SWITCH
CAP ON → OFF
CAP OFF → ON

METER

SPEEDOMETER SENSOR

SPEEDOMETER

PT SWITCH

SPARK PLUG

CDI UNIT

RED TUBE

MAGNETO

OIL LEVEL INDICATOR

OVER HEAT SENSOR
ON → 101°C, OFF → 80°C

YELLOW TUBE

OIL LEVEL SWITCH

NEUTRAL SWITCH
N → ON
F, R → OFF

BUZZER

REMOTE CONTROL BOX (MORSE)

PT RELAY

PT MOTOR

CHOKE SOLENOID

RECTIFIER

FUSE (20A)

STARTER MOTOR RELAY

VOLTAGE REGULATOR

BATTERY 12V 70AH

STARTING MOTOR

...... Option

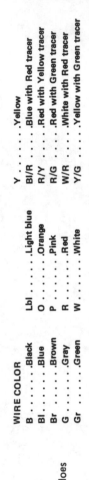

WIRE COLOR

B	Black	Lbl	Light blue
Bl	Blue	O	Orange
Br	Brown	P	Pink
G	Gray	R	Red
Gr	Green	W	White

Y	Yellow
Bl/R	Blue with Red tracer
R/Y	Red with Yellow tracer
R/G	Red with Green tracer
W/R	White with Red tracer
Y/G	Yellow with Green tracer

- - - : From the serial number 716025 does not have yellow (Y) lead wire.

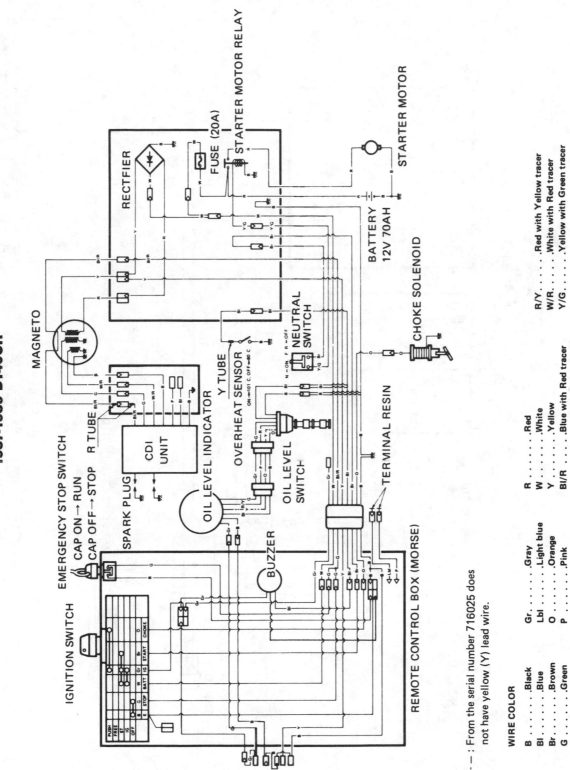

1987-1989 DT40CR

5

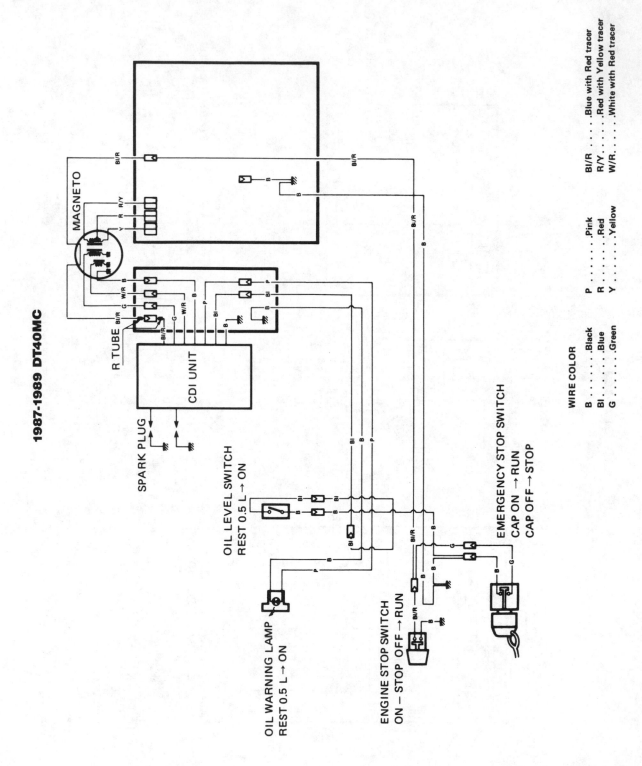

1987-1989 DT40MC

MAGNETO

CDI UNIT

R TUBE

SPARK PLUG

OIL WARNING LAMP
REST 0.5 L → ON

OIL LEVEL SWITCH
REST 0.5 L → ON

ENGINE STOP SWITCH
ON – STOP OFF → RUN

EMERGENCY STOP SWITCH
CAP ON → RUN
CAP OFF → STOP

WIRE COLOR

B . . . . .Black
Bl . . . . .Blue
G . . . . .Green

P . . . . .Pink
R . . . . .Red
Y . . . . . . .Yellow

Bl/R . . . . .Blue with Red tracer
R/Y . . . . .Red with Yellow tracer
W/R . . . . .White with Red tracer

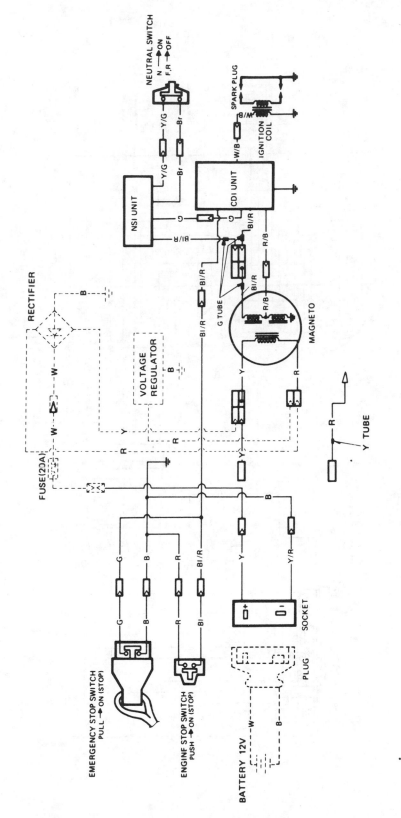

1977-1983 DT50M

.... : Option

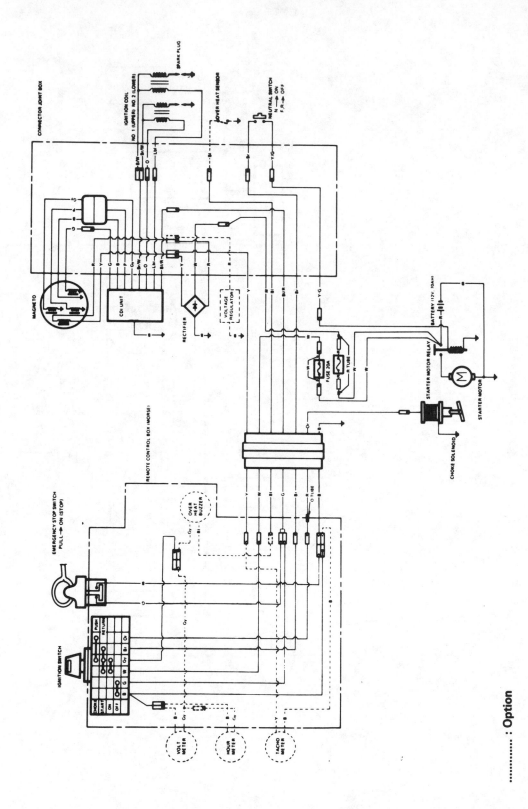

1977-1983 DT50/DT50W

: Option

1977-1983 DT50T

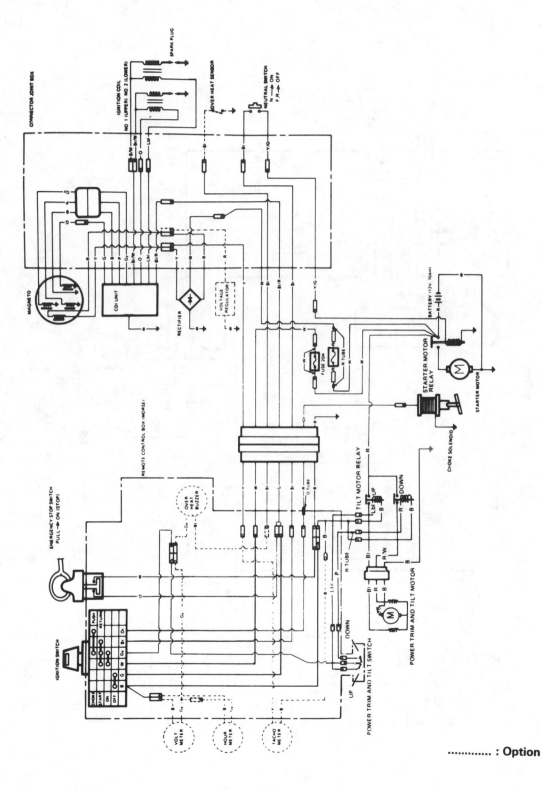

.... : Option

5

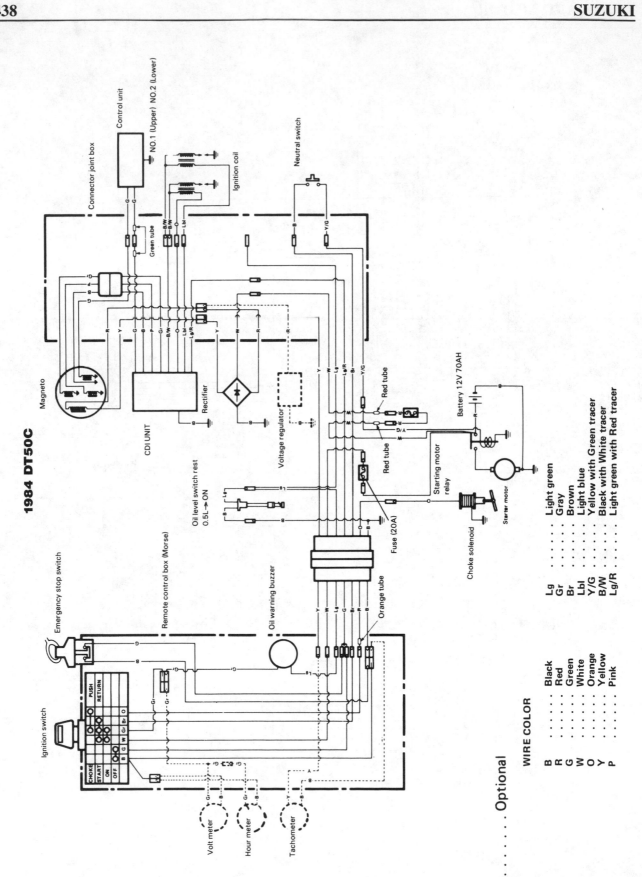

1984 DT50C

WIRE COLOR

B			Black
R			Red
G			Green
W			White
O			Orange
Y			Yellow
P			Pink

Lg			Light green
Gr			Gray
Br			Brown
Lbl			Light blue
Y/G			Yellow with Green tracer
B/W			Black with White tracer
Lg/R			Light green with Red tracer

. . . . **Optional**

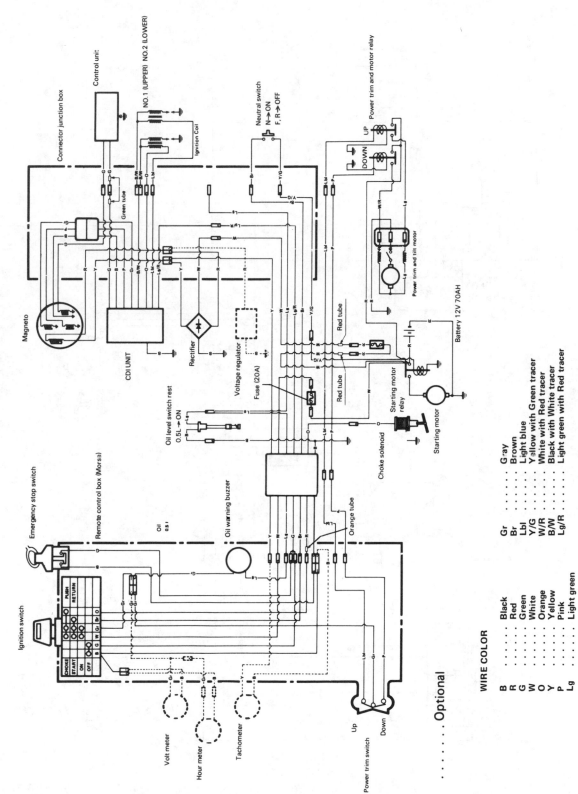

1984 DT50TC

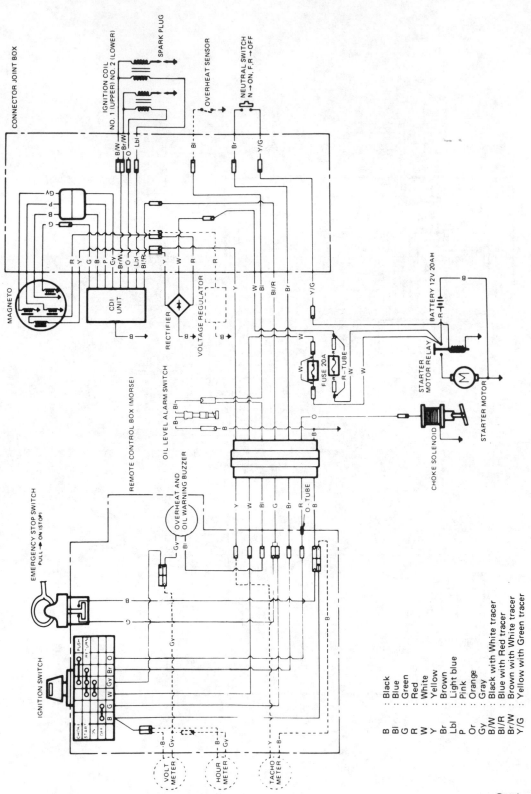

1983-1984 DT60C

.... : Option

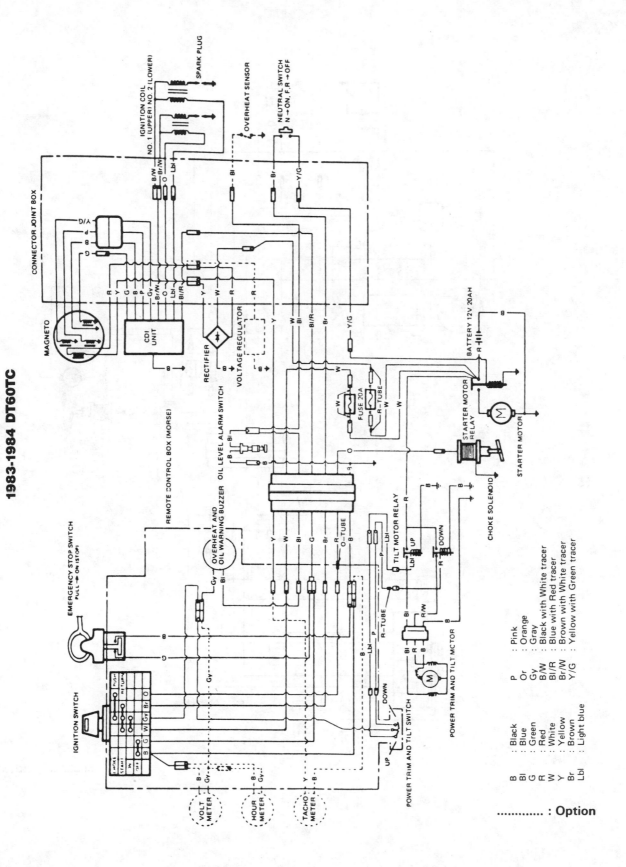

1983-1984 DT60TC

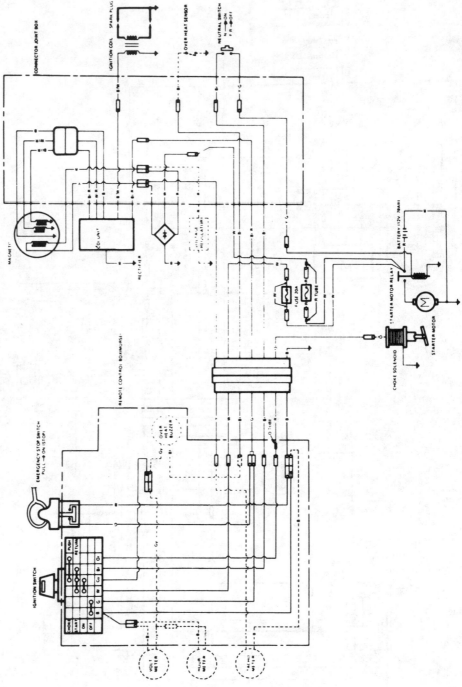

1978-1982 DT65

.... : Option

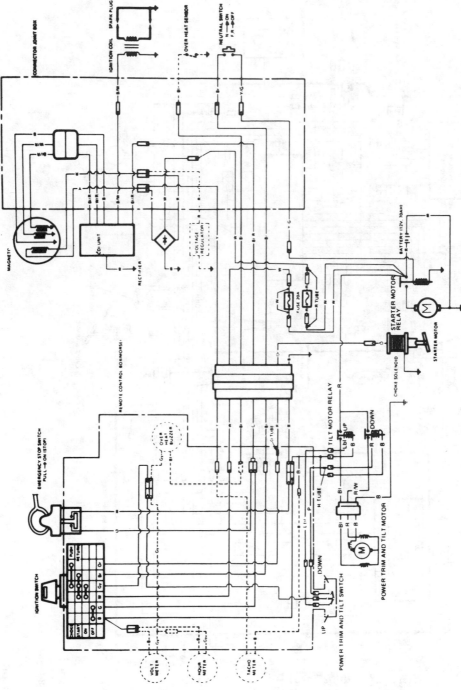

1978-1982 DT65T

.... : **Option**

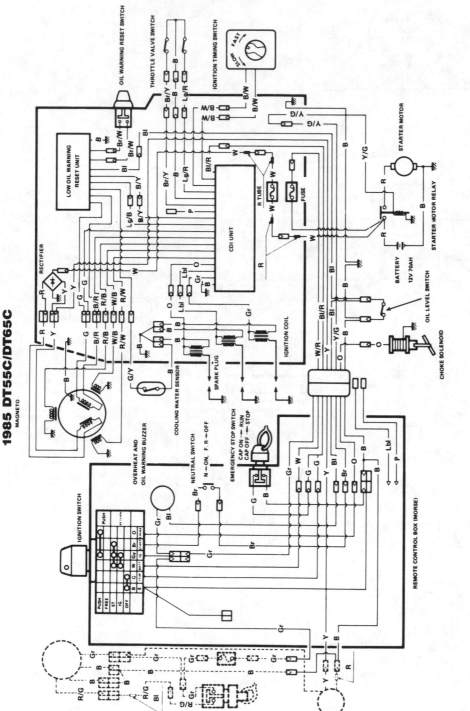

1985 DT55C/DT65C

WIRE COLOR

B	. . . . Black
Bl	. . . . Blue
Br	. . . . Brown
G	. . . . Green
Gr	. . . . Gray
Lbl	. . . . Light blue
O	. . . . Orange

P	. . . . . Pink
R	. . . . Red
W	. . . . White
Y	. . . . . Yellow
B/R	. . . Black with Red tracer
B/W	. . . Black with White tracer
B/Y	. . . Black with Yellow tracer

Bl/R	. . Blue with Red tracer
Br/W	. . Brown with White tracer
Br/Y	. . Brown with Yellow tracer
Lg/B	. . Light green with Black tracer
Lg/R	. . Light green with Red tracer
R/B	. . . Red with Black tracer
R/G	. . . Red with Green tracer

R/W	. . . Red with White tracer
W/B	. . . White with Black tracer
W/R	. . . White with Red tracer
Y/R	. . . Yellow with Red tracer

- - - - - **optional**

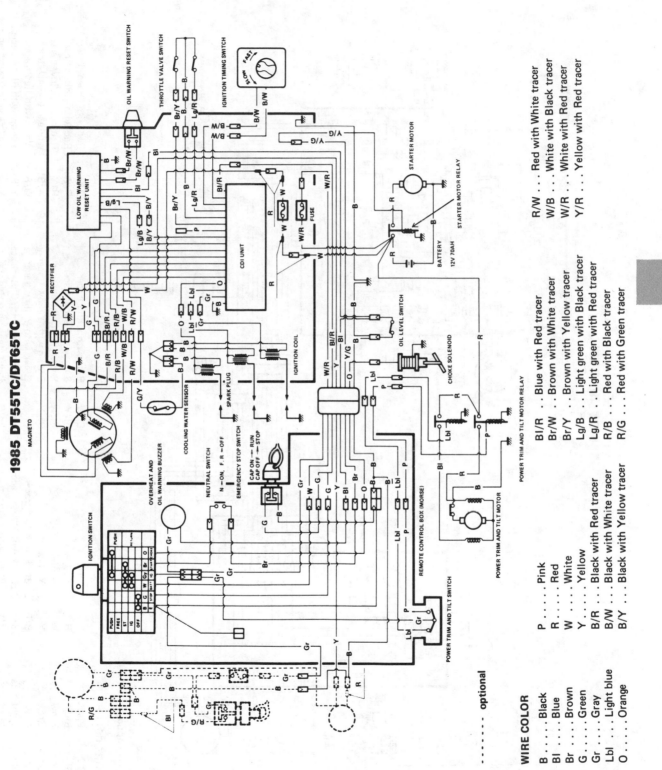

1985 DT55TC/DT65TC

WIRE COLOR

B . . . . . Black
Bl . . . . Blue
Br . . . . Brown
G . . . . Green
Gr . . . . Gray
Lbl . . . . Light blue
O . . . . . Orange

P . . . . . Pink
R . . . . . Red
W . . . . White
Y . . . . Yellow
B/R . . . Black with Red tracer
B/W . . . Black with White tracer
B/Y . . . Black with Yellow tracer

Bl/R . . Blue with Red tracer
Br/W . . Brown with White tracer
Br/Y . . Brown with Yellow tracer
Lg/B . . Light green with Black tracer
Lg/R . . Light green with Red tracer
R/B . . . Red with Black tracer
R/G . . . Red with Green tracer

R/W . . . Red with White tracer
W/B . . . White with Black tracer
W/R . . . White with Red tracer
Y/R . . . Yellow with Red tracer

- - - - - - optional

5

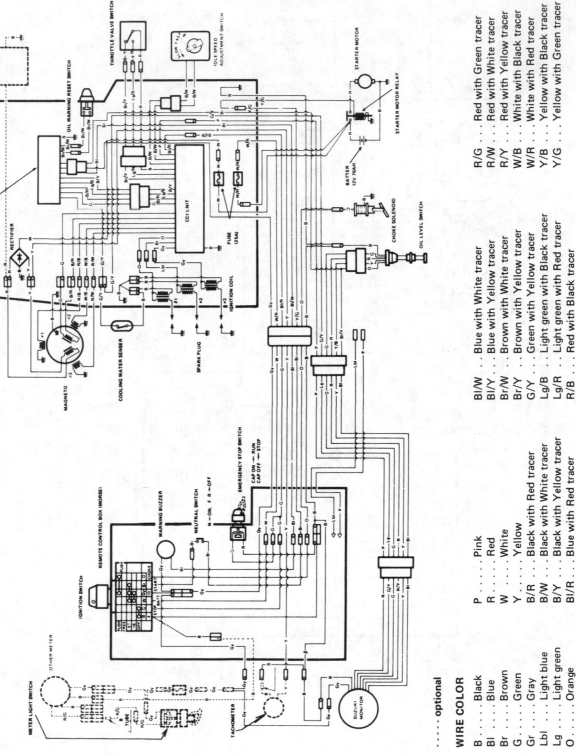

1986 DT55C/DT65C

WIRE COLOR

B . . . . . Black	P . . . . . Pink	Bl/W . . Blue with White tracer	R/G . . . Red with Green tracer
Bl . . . . . Blue	R . . . . . Red	Bl/Y . . . Blue with Yellow tracer	R/W . . . Red with White tracer
Br . . . . . Brown	W . . . . . White	Br/W . . Brown with White tracer	R/Y . . . Red with Yellow tracer
G . . . . . Green	Y . . . . . Yellow	Br/Y . . . Brown with Yellow tracer	W/B . . . White with Black tracer
Gr . . . . . Gray	B/R . . . Black with Red tracer	G/Y . . . Green with Yellow tracer	W/R . . . White with Red tracer
Lbl . . . . Light blue	B/W . . . Black with White tracer	Lg/B . . . Light green with Black tracer	Y/B . . . Yellow with Black tracer
Lg . . . . Light green	B/Y . . . Black with Yellow tracer	Lg/R . . . Light green with Red tracer	Y/G . . . Yellow with Green tracer
O . . . . . Orange	Bl/R . . . Blue with Red tracer	R/B . . . Red with Black tracer	

optional

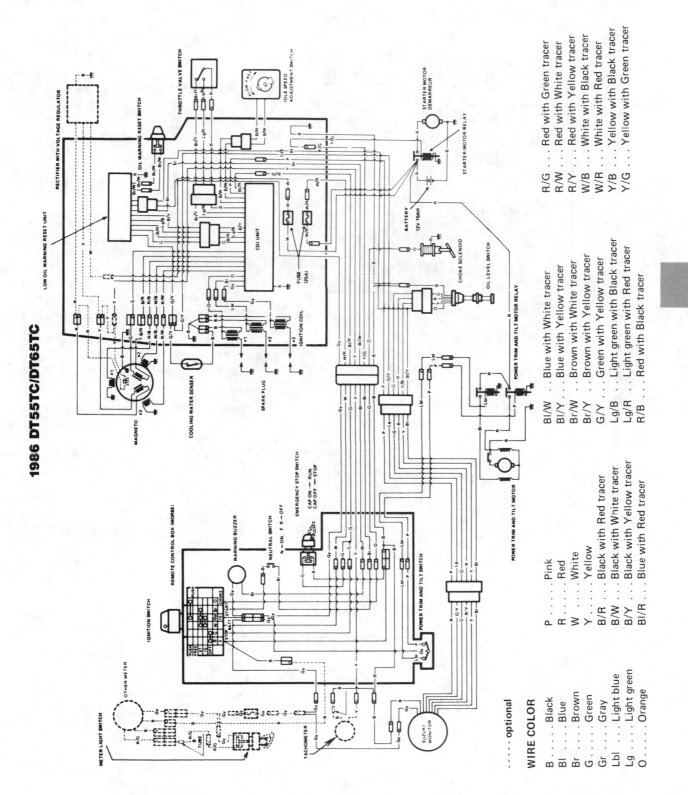

1986 DT55TC/DT65TC

WIRE COLOR

R/G	. .	Red with Green tracer
R/W	. .	Red with White tracer
R/Y	. .	Red with Yellow tracer
W/B	. .	White with Black tracer
W/R	. .	White with Red tracer
Y/B	. .	Yellow with Black tracer
Y/G	. .	Yellow with Green tracer

Bl/W	. .	Blue with White tracer
Bl/Y	. .	Blue with Yellow tracer
Br/W	. .	Brown with White tracer
Br/Y	. .	Brown with Yellow tracer
G/Y	. .	Green with Yellow tracer
Lg/B	. .	Light green with Black tracer
Lg/R	. .	Light green with Red tracer
R/B	. .	Red with Black tracer

- - - - - optional

P	. . . . .	Pink
R	. . . . .	Red
W	. . . . .	White
Y	. . . . .	Yellow
B/R	. . .	Black with Red tracer
B/W	. . .	Black with White tracer
B/Y	. . .	Black with Yellow tracer
Bl/R	. . .	Blue with Red tracer

B	. . . .	Black
Bl	. . .	Blue
Br	. . .	Brown
G	. . . .	Green
Gr	. . .	Gray
Lbl	. . .	Light blue
Lg	. . .	Light green
O	. . . .	Orange

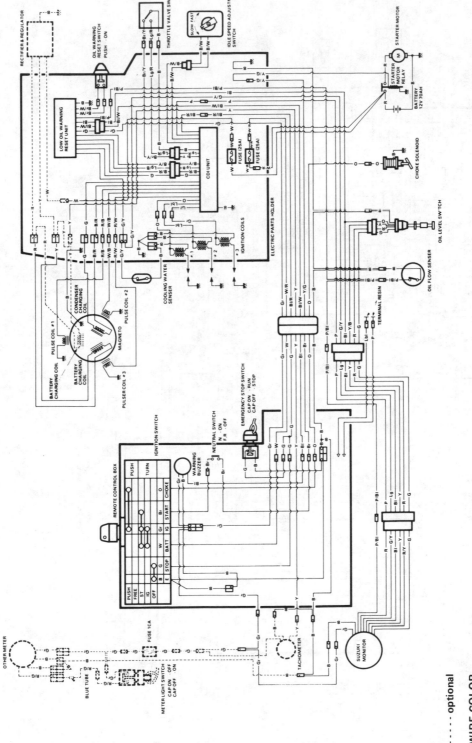

1987-1988 DT55C/DT65C

- - - - optional

WIRE COLOR

B . . . . . Black	P . . . . . Pink	Bl/W . . Blue with White tracer	R/W . . . Red with White tracer
Bl . . . . Blue	R . . . . . Red	Br/W . . Brown with White tracer	R/Y . . . Red with Yellow tracer
Br . . . . Brown	W . . . White	Br/Y . . Brown with Yellow tracer	W/B . . . White with Black tracer
G . . . . . Green	Y . . . . Yellow	G/Y . . . Green with Yellow tracer	W/R . . . White with Red tracer
Gr . . . . Gray	B/R . . . Black with Red tracer	Lg/B . . . Light green with Black tracer	Y/B . . . Yellow with Black tracer
Lbl . . . . Light blue	B/W . . . Black with White tracer	Lg/R . . . Light green with Red tracer	Y/G . . . Yellow with Green tracer
Lg . . . . Light green	B/Y . . . Black with Yellow tracer	P/Bl . . . Pink with Blue tracer	
O . . . . . Orange	Bl/R . . . Blue with Red tracer	R/G . . . Red with Green tracer	

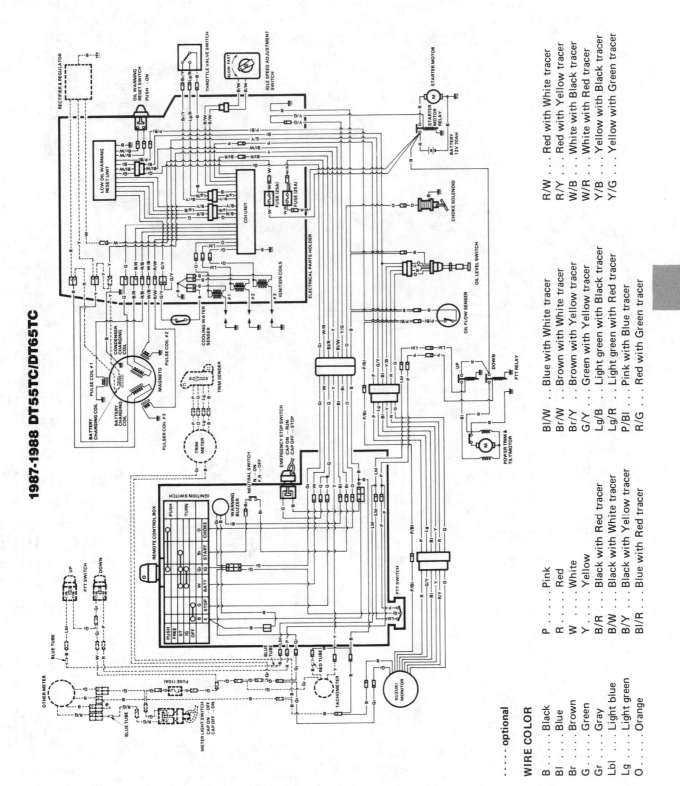

1987-1988 DT55TC/DT65TC

5

- - - - - optional

WIRE COLOR

B . . . . . Black	P . . . . . Pink
Bl . . . . . Blue	R . . . . . Red
Br . . . . . Brown	W . . . . . White
G . . . . . Green	Y . . . . . Yellow
Gr . . . . . Gray	B/R . . Black with Red tracer
Lbl . . . Light blue	B/W . . Black with White tracer
Lg . . . Light green	B/Y . . Black with Yellow tracer
O . . . . . Orange	Bl/R . . Blue with Red tracer

Bl/W . . Blue with White tracer	R/W . . Red with White tracer
Br/W . . Brown with White tracer	R/Y . . Red with Yellow tracer
Br/Y . . Brown with Yellow tracer	W/B . . White with Black tracer
G/Y . . Green with Yellow tracer	W/R . . White with Red tracer
Lg/B . . Light green with Black tracer	Y/B . . Yellow with Black tracer
Lg/R . . Light green with Red tracer	Y/G . . Yellow with Green tracer
P/Bl . . Pink with Blue tracer	
R/G . . Red with Green tracer	

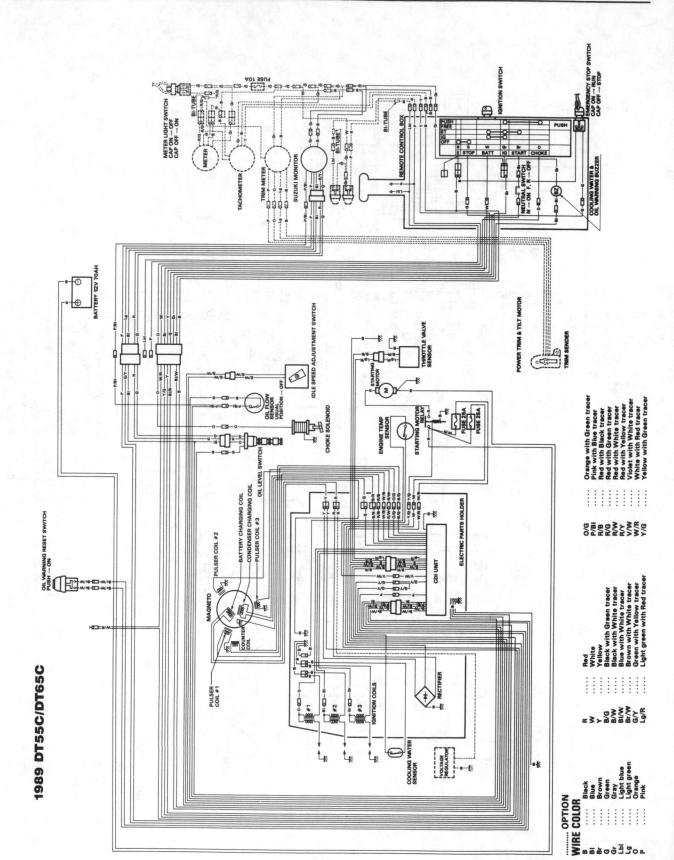

1989 DT55C/DT65C

OPTION
WIRE COLOR

B	:	Black
Bl	:	Blue
Br	:	Brown
Gr	:	Gray
Lbl	:	Light blue
Lg	:	Light green
O	:	Orange
P	:	Pink

R	:	Red
W	:	White
Y	:	Yellow
B/G	:	Black with Green tracer
B/W	:	Black with White tracer
Bl/W	:	Blue with White tracer
Br/W	:	Brown with White tracer
G/Y	:	Green with Yellow tracer
Lg/R	:	Light green with Red tracer

O/G	:	Orange with Green tracer
P/Bl	:	Pink with Blue tracer
R/B	:	Red with Black tracer
R/G	:	Red with Green tracer
R/W	:	Red with White tracer
R/Y	:	Red with Yellow tracer
V/W	:	Violet with White tracer
W/R	:	White with Red tracer
Y/G	:	Yellow with Green tracer

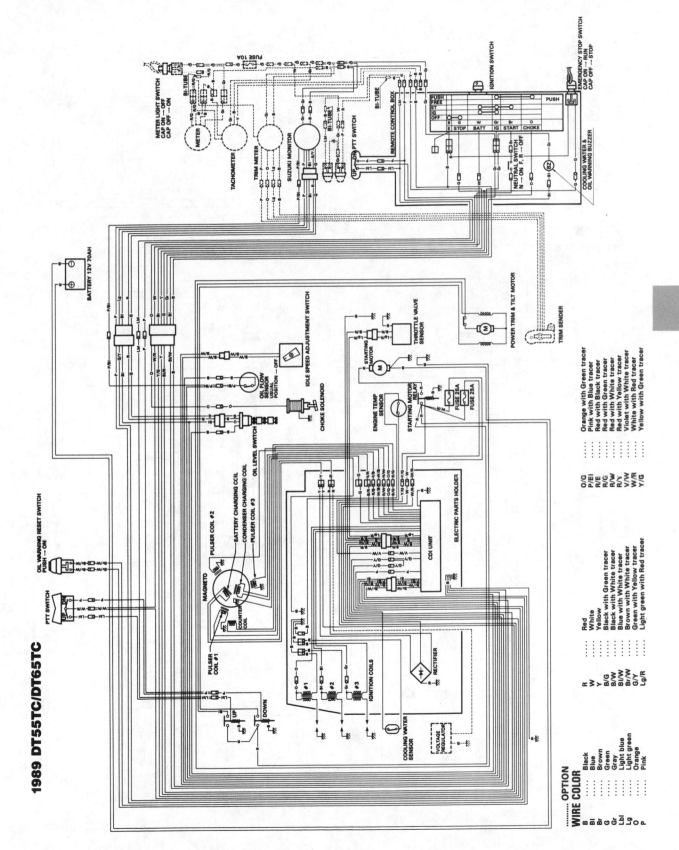

1989 DT55TC/DT65TC

OPTION
WIRE COLOR

B	......	Black
Bl	......	Blue
Br	......	Brown
Gr	......	Gray
Lbl	......	Light blue
Lg	......	Light green
O	......	Orange
P	......	Pink

R	......	Red
W	......	White
Y	......	Yellow
B/G	......	Black with Green tracer
B/W	......	Black with White tracer
Bl/W	......	Blue with White tracer
Br/W	......	Brown with White tracer
G/Y	......	Green with Yellow tracer
Lg/R	......	Light green with Red tracer

O/G	......	Orange with Green tracer
P/Bl	......	Pink with Blue tracer
R/E	......	Red with Black tracer
R/G	......	Red with Green tracer
R/W	......	Red with White tracer
R/Y	......	Red with Yellow tracer
V/W	......	Violet with White tracer
W/R	......	White with Red tracer
Y/G	......	Yellow with Green tracer

5

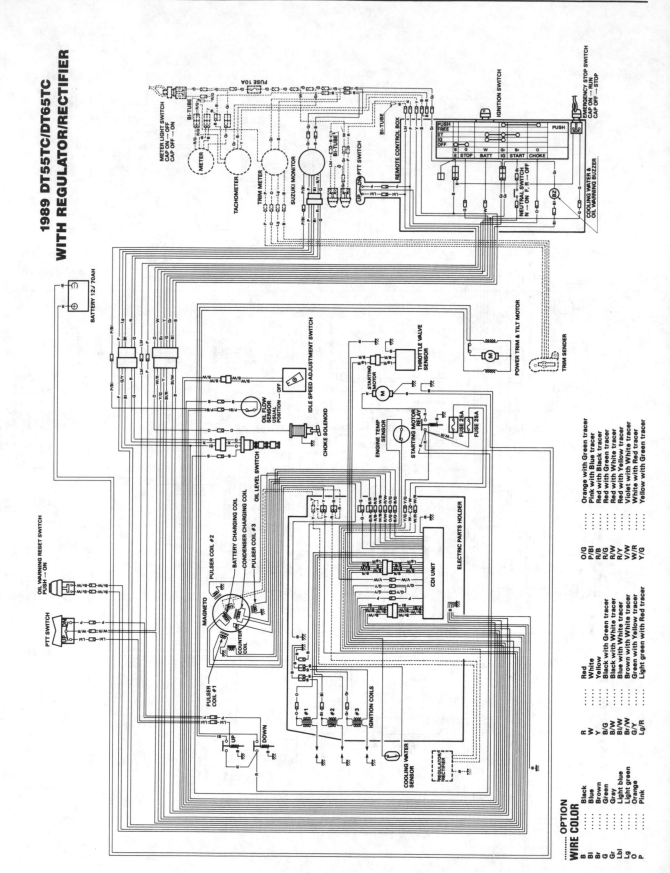

1989 DT55TC/DT65TC WITH REGULATOR/RECTIFIER

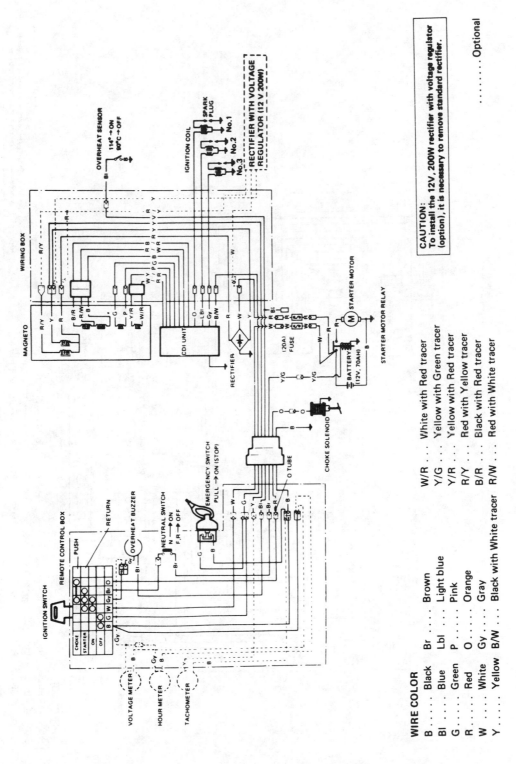

1981-1982 DT85

CAUTION:
To install the 12V, 200W rectifier with voltage regulator (option), it is necessary to remove standard rectifier.

.... Optional

WIRE COLOR

B	..... Black	Br	..... Brown	W/R ... White with Red tracer
Bl	..... Blue	Lbl	..... Light blue	Y/G ... Yellow with Green tracer
G	..... Green	P	..... Pink	Y/R ... Yellow with Red tracer
R	..... Red	O	..... Orange	R/Y ... Red with Yellow tracer
W	..... White	Gy	..... Gray	B/R ... Black with Red tracer
Y	..... Yellow	B/W ... Black with White tracer		R/W ... Red with White tracer

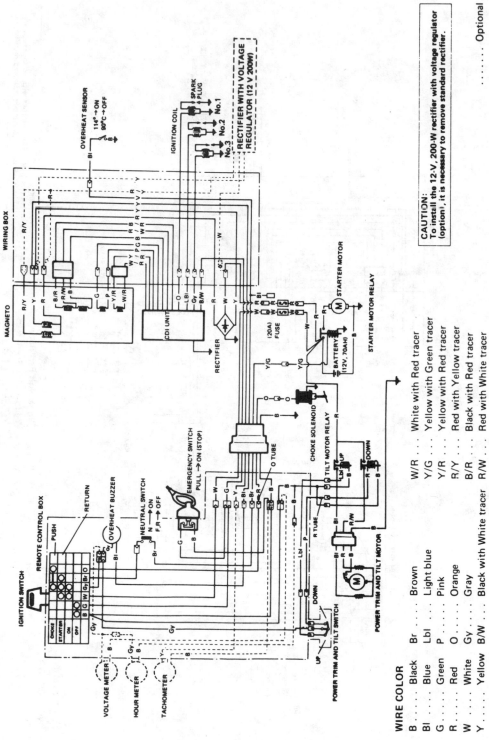

1981-1982 DT85T

WIRE COLOR

B	. . . . . .	Black	Br	. . . . . .	Brown	
Bl	. . . . . .	Blue	Lbl	. . . .	Light blue	
G	. . . . . .	Green	P	. . . . .	Pink	
R	. . . . . .	Red	O	. . . . . .	Orange	
W	. . . . . .	White	Gy	. . . . .	Gray	
Y	. . . . . .	Yellow	B/W	. . .	Black with White tracer	

W/R . . .	White with Red tracer
Y/G . . .	Yellow with Green tracer
Y/R . . .	Yellow with Red tracer
R/Y . . .	Red with Yellow tracer
B/R . . .	Black with Red tracer
R/W . . .	Red with White tracer

. . . . Optional

CAUTION:
To install the 12-V, 200-W rectifier with voltage regulator (option), it is necessary to remove standard rectifier.

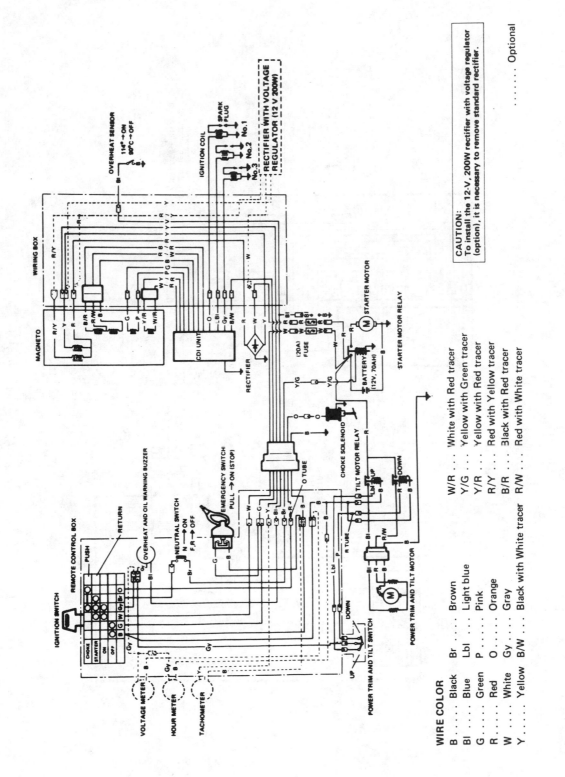

1981-1982 DT85TC

WIRE COLOR

B	Black	Br	Brown
Bl	Blue	Lbl	Light blue
G	Green	P	Pink
R	Red	O	Orange
W	White	Gy	Gray
Y	Yellow	B/W	Black with White tracer

W/R	...	White with Red tracer
Y/G	...	Yellow with Green tracer
Y/R	...	Yellow with Red tracer
R/Y	...	Red with Yellow tracer
B/R	...	Black with Red tracer
R/W	...	Red with White tracer

CAUTION:
To install the 12-V, 200W rectifier with voltage regulator (option), it is necessary to remove standard rectifier.

.... Optional

5

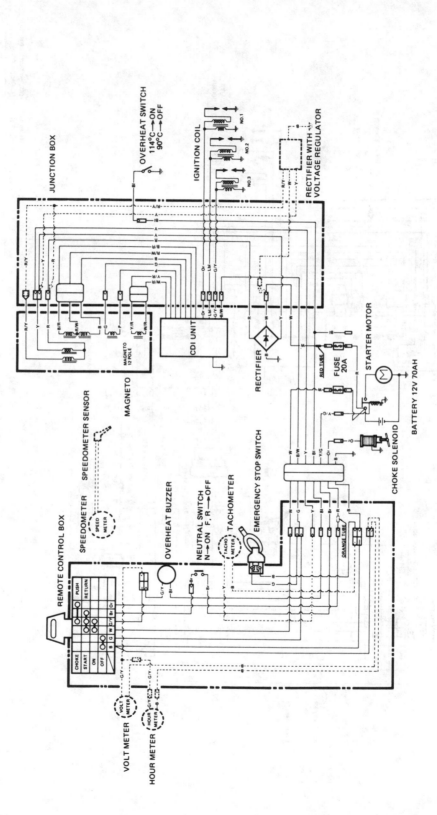

1983-1986 DT75

JUNCTION BOX

OVERHEAT SWITCH
114°C → ON
90°C → OFF

IGNITION COIL

NO.1
NO.2
NO.3

RECTIFIER WITH VOLTAGE REGULATOR

SPEEDOMETER SENSOR

SPEEDOMETER

MAGNETO 12 POLE

MAGNETO

CDI UNIT

RECTIFIER

STARTER MOTOR

FUSE 20A

BATTERY 12V 70AH

CHOKE SOLENOID

REMOTE CONTROL BOX

OVERHEAT BUZZER

NEUTRAL SWITCH
N → ON F, R → OFF

TACHOMETER

EMERGENCY STOP SWITCH

VOLT METER

HOUR METER

| CHOKE | START | ON | OFF | | | | | | | |

PUSH   RETURN

SPEED METER

TACHO METER

ORANGE TUBE

RED TUBE

CAUTION:
To install the 12V, 200W rectifier with voltage regulator (option), it is necessary to remove standard rectifier.

.... Optional

WIRE COLOR

B	....	Black
Bl	....	Blue
G	....	Green
R	....	Red
W	....	White
Y	....	Yellow

Br	....	Brown
Lbl	....	Light blue
P	....	Pink
Or	....	Orange
Gy	....	Gray
B/W	....	Black with White tracer

W/R	....	White with Red tracer
Y/G	....	Yellow with Green tracer
Y/R	....	Yellow with Red tracer
R/Y	....	Red with Yellow tracer
B/R	....	Black with Red tracer
R/W	....	Red with White tracer

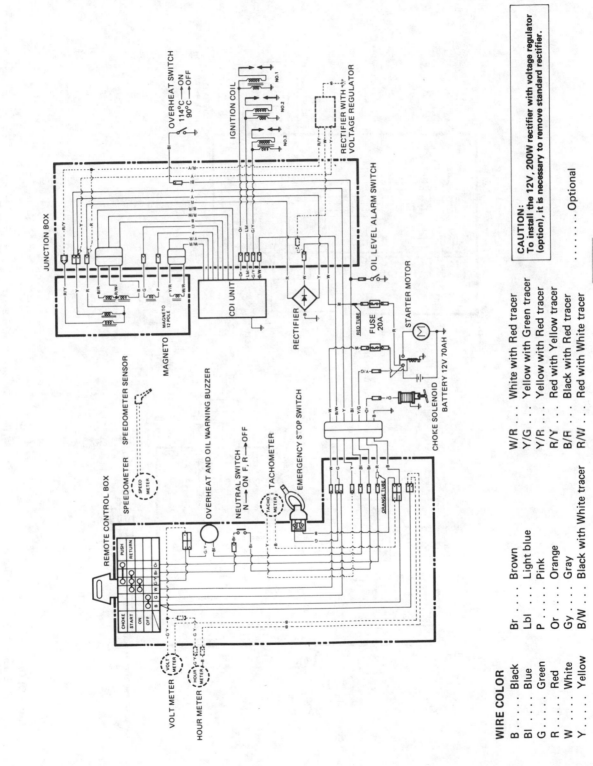

1983-1986 DT75C

REMOTE CONTROL BOX

SPEEDOMETER

SPEEDOMETER SENSOR

OVERHEAT AND OIL WARNING BUZZER

NEUTRAL SWITCH
N → ON F, R → OFF

TACHOMETER

EMERGENCY STOP SWITCH

JUNCTION BOX

MAGNETO 12 POLE

MAGNETO

CDI UNIT

RECTIFIER

OIL LEVEL ALARM SWITCH

FUSE 20A

RED TUBE

STARTER MOTOR

BATTERY 12V 70AH

CHOKE SOLENOID

OVERHEAT SWITCH
114°C → ON
90°C → OFF

IGNITION COIL
NO.1
NO.2
NO.3

RECTIFIER WITH VOLTAGE REGULATOR

VOLT METER

HOUR METER

CHOKE
START
ON
OFF

PUSH
RETURN

ORANGE TUBE

CAUTION:
To install the 12V, 200W rectifier with voltage regulator (option), it is necessary to remove standard rectifier.

.... Optional

5

WIRE COLOR

B	Black	Br	Brown
Bl	Blue	Lbl	Light blue
G	Green	P	Pink
R	Red	Or	Orange
W	White	Gy	Gray
Y	Yellow	B/W	Black with White tracer

W/R	White with Red tracer
Y/G	Yellow with Green tracer
Y/R	Yellow with Red tracer
R/Y	Red with Yellow tracer
B/R	Black with Red tracer
R/W	Red with White tracer

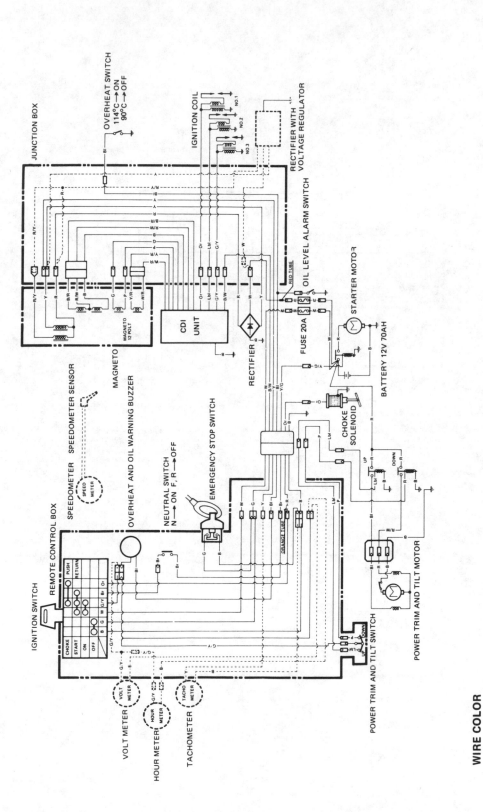

1983-1986 DT75TC

JUNCTION BOX

OVERHEAT SWITCH
114°C → ON
90°C → OFF

IGNITION COIL
NO.1
NO.2
NO.3

RECTIFIER WITH
VOLTAGE REGULATOR

OIL LEVEL ALARM SWITCH

STARTER MOTOR

RED TUBE

FUSE 20A

BATTERY 12V 70AH

RECTIFIER

MAGNETO
12 POLY

CDI
UNIT

SPEEDOMETER SENSOR

SPEEDOMETER

SPEED
METER

MAGNETO

OVERHEAT AND OIL WARNING BUZZER

NEUTRAL SWITCH
N → ON, F, R → OFF

EMERGENCY STOP SWITCH

ORANGE TUBE

CHOKE
SOLENOID

POWER TRIM AND TILT MOTOR

UP   DOWN

REMOTE CONTROL BOX

IGNITION SWITCH

	CHOKE	START	ON	OFF
PUSH				
RETURN				

B G W G/Y Br Or

POWER TRIM AND TILT SWITCH
UP   DOWN

VOLT METER

VOLT
METER

HOUR METER

HOUR
METER

TACHOMETER

TACHO
METER

WIRE COLOR

B	. . . .	Black	Br	. . . . Brown
Bl	. . . .	Blue	Lbl	. . . Light blue
G	. . . .	Green	P	. . . . Pink
R	. . . .	Red	Or	. . . . Orange
W	. . . .	White	Gy	. . . . Gray
Y	. . . .	Yellow	B/W	. . . . Black with White tracer

W/R . . .	White with Red tracer
Y/G . . .	Yellow with Green tracer
Y/R . . .	Yellow with Red tracer
R/Y . . .	Red with Yellow tracer
B/R . . .	Black with Red tracer
R/W . . .	Red with White tracer

CAUTION:
To install the 12V, 200W rectifier with voltage regulator (option), it is necessary to remove standard rectifier.

. . . . Optional

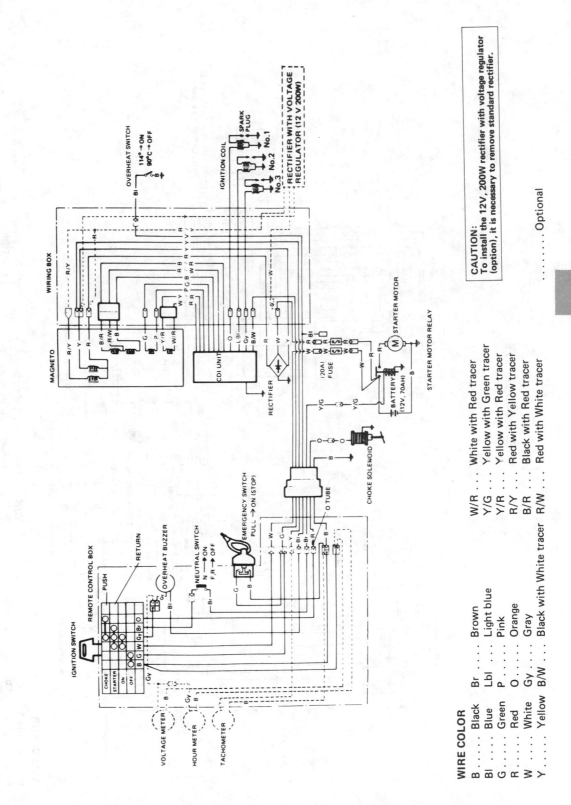

1983-1986 DT85

OVERHEAT SWITCH
114° → ON
90°C → OFF

SPARK PLUG
IGNITION COIL
No.1
No.2
No.3

RECTIFIER WITH VOLTAGE REGULATOR (12 V 200W)

WIRING BOX

MAGNETO

CDI UNIT

RECTIFIER

(20A) FUSE

STARTER MOTOR
M
STARTER MOTOR RELAY

BATTERY (12V, 70AH)

CHOKE SOLENOID

O TUBE

EMERGENCY SWITCH
PULL → ON (STOP)

REMOTE CONTROL BOX

IGNITION SWITCH

PUSH
RETURN

OVERHEAT BUZZER

NEUTRAL SWITCH
N → ON
F.R → OFF

CHOKE
STARTER
ON
OFF

VOLTAGE METER
HOUR METER
TACHOMETER

CAUTION:
To install the 12V, 200W rectifier with voltage regulator (option), it is necessary to remove standard rectifier.

.... Optional

5

WIRE COLOR

B	Black	Br	Brown
Bl	Blue	Lbl	Light blue
G	Green	P	Pink
R	Red	O	Orange
W	White	Gy	Gray
Y	Yellow	B/W	Black with White tracer

W/R	White with Red tracer
Y/G	Yellow with Green tracer
Y/R	Yellow with Red tracer
R/Y	Red with Yellow tracer
B/R	Black with Red tracer
R/W	Red with White tracer

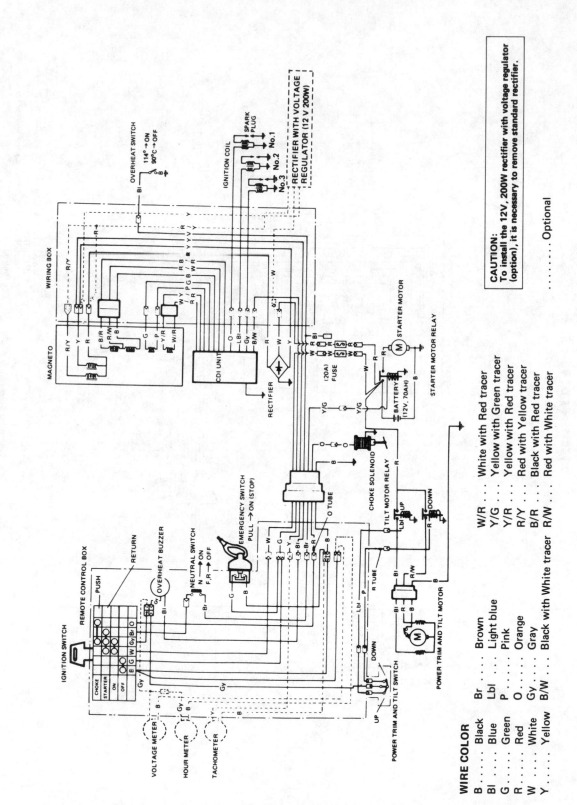

1983-1986 DT85T

WIRE COLOR

B	Black	Br	Brown	W/R . . .	White with Red tracer
Bl	Blue	Lbl . . .	Light blue	Y/G . . .	Yellow with Green tracer
G	Green	P	Pink	Y/R . . .	Yellow with Red tracer
R	Red	O	Orange	R/Y . . .	Red with Yellow tracer
W	White	Gy . . .	Gray	B/R . . .	Black with Red tracer
Y	Yellow	B/W . . .	Black with White tracer	R/W . . .	Red with White tracer

CAUTION:
To install the 12 V. 200W rectifier with voltage regulator (option), it is necessary to remove standard rectifier.

. . . . Optional

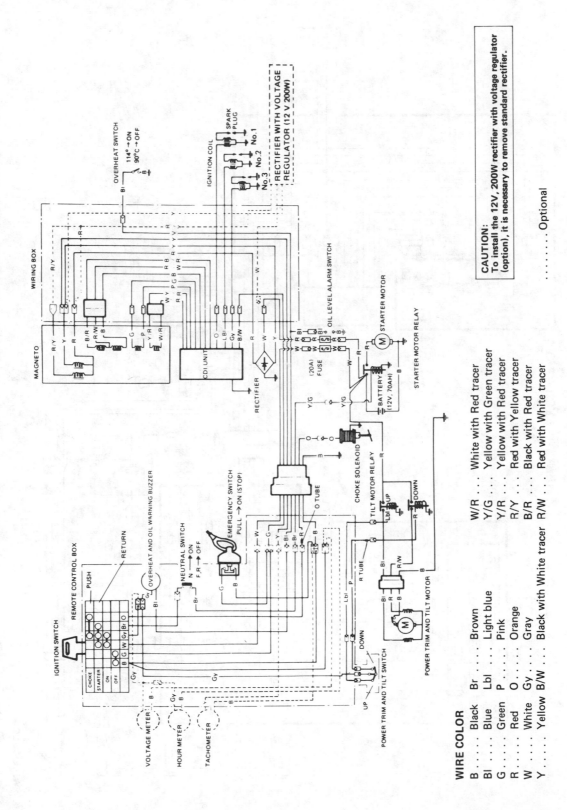

1983-1986 DT85TC

WIRE COLOR

B	. . . .	Black	Br	. . . .	Brown	W/R	. . .	White with Red tracer
Bl	. . . .	Blue	Lbl	. . .	Light blue	Y/G	. . .	Yellow with Green tracer
G	. . . .	Green	P	. . . .	Pink	Y/R	. . .	Yellow with Red tracer
R	. . . .	Red	O	. . . .	Orange	R/Y	. . .	Red with Yellow tracer
W	. . . .	White	Gy	. . . .	Gray	B/R	. . .	Black with Red tracer
Y	. . . .	Yellow	B/W	. . .	Black with White tracer	R/W	. . .	Red with White tracer

CAUTION:
To install the 12V, 200W rectifier with voltage regulator (option), it is necessary to remove standard rectifier.

. . . . Optional

5

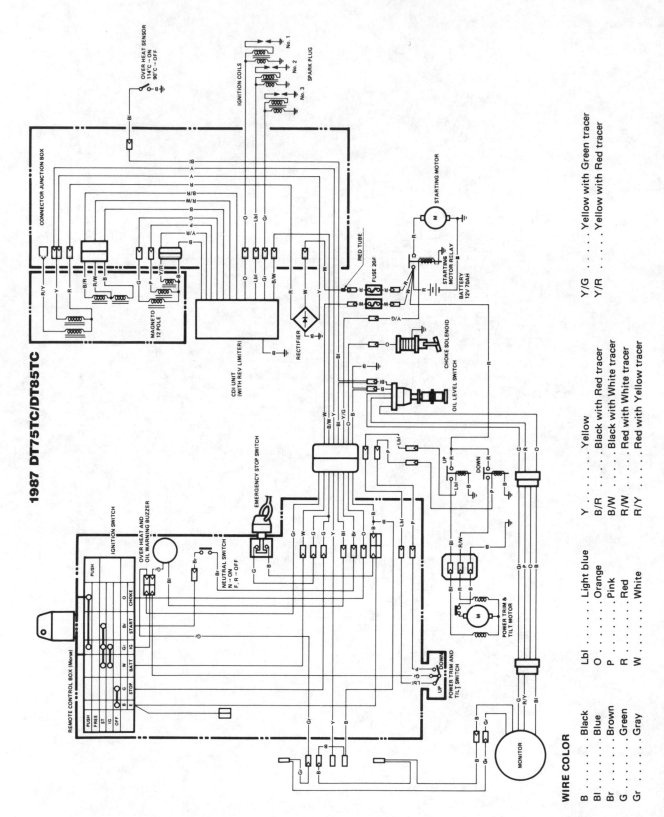

1987 DT75TC/DT85TC

WIRE COLOR

B . . . . Black
Bl . . . . . . Blue
Br . . . . . . Brown
G . . . . . . Green
Gr . . . . . . Gray

Lbl . . . . . . Light blue
O . . . . . . Orange
P . . . . . . Pink
R . . . . . . Red
W . . . . . . White

Y . . . . . . Yellow
B/R . . . . Black with Red tracer
B/W . . . . Black with White tracer
R/W . . . . Red with White tracer
R/Y . . . . Red with Yellow tracer

Y/G . . . . . Yellow with Green tracer
Y/R . . . . . Yellow with Red tracer

5

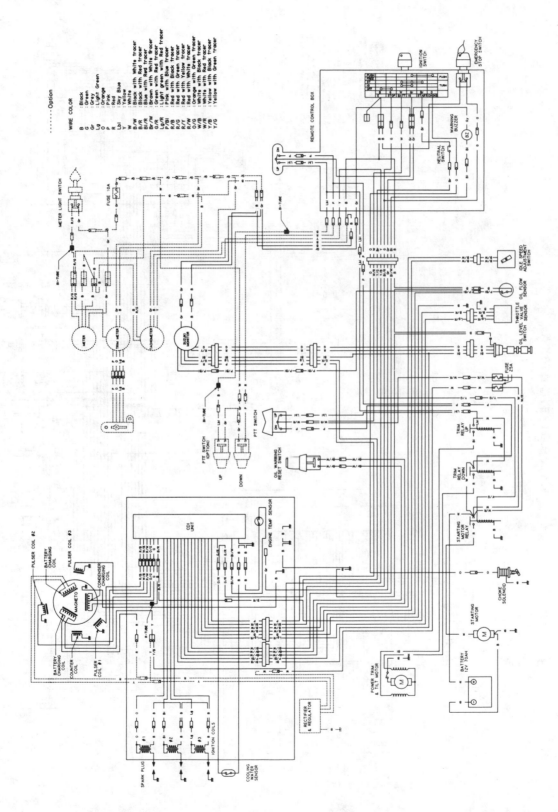

1988 DT75TC/DT85TC WITH BATTERY CHARGING COIL

1988 DT75TC/DT85TC

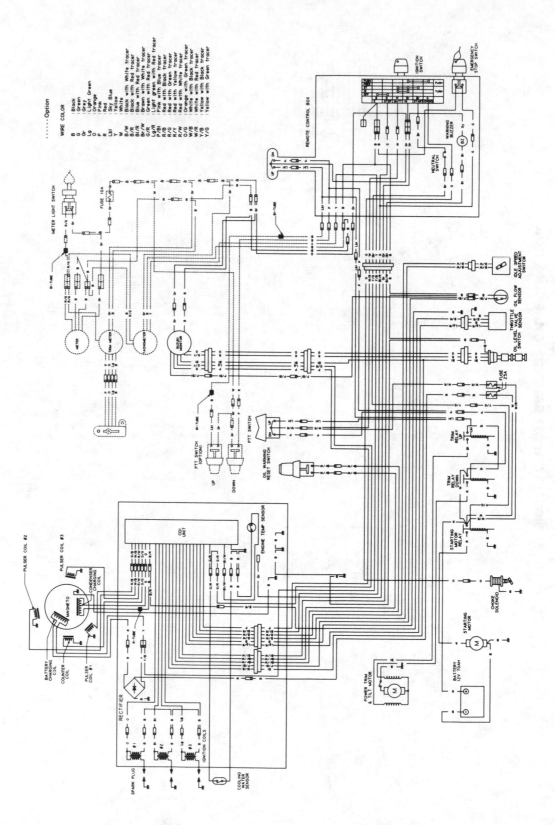

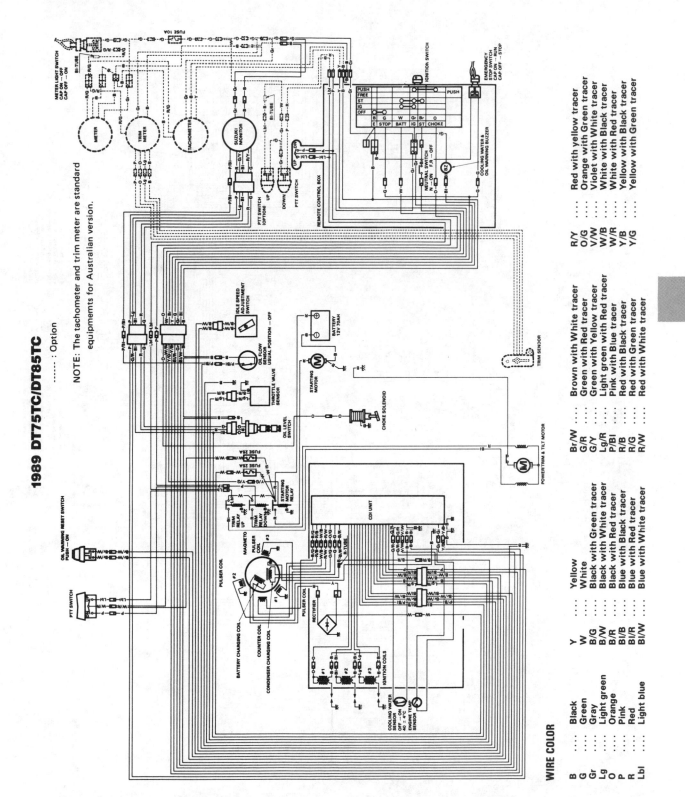

1989 DT75TC/DT85TC

----- : Option

NOTE: The tachometer and trim meter are standard equipments for Australian version.

WIRE COLOR

B	:	Black	Y	:	Yellow	Br/W	:	Brown with White tracer	R/Y	:	Red with yellow tracer
G	:	Green	W	:	White	G/R	:	Green with Red tracer	O/G	:	Orange with Green tracer
Gr	:	Gray	B/G	:	Black with Green tracer	G/Y	:	Green with Yellow tracer	V/W	:	Violet with White tracer
Lg	:	Light green	B/W	:	Black with White tracer	Lg/R	:	Light green with Red tracer	W/B	:	White with Black tracer
O	:	Orange	B/R	:	Black with Red tracer	P/Bl	:	Pink with Blue tracer	W/R	:	White with Red tracer
P	:	Pink	Bl/B	:	Blue with Black tracer	R/B	:	Red with Black tracer	Y/B	:	Yellow with Black tracer
R	:	Red	Bl/R	:	Blue with Red tracer	R/G	:	Red with Green tracer	Y/G	:	Yellow with Green tracer
Lbl	:	Light blue	Bl/W	:	Blue with White tracer	R/W	:	Red with White tracer			

5

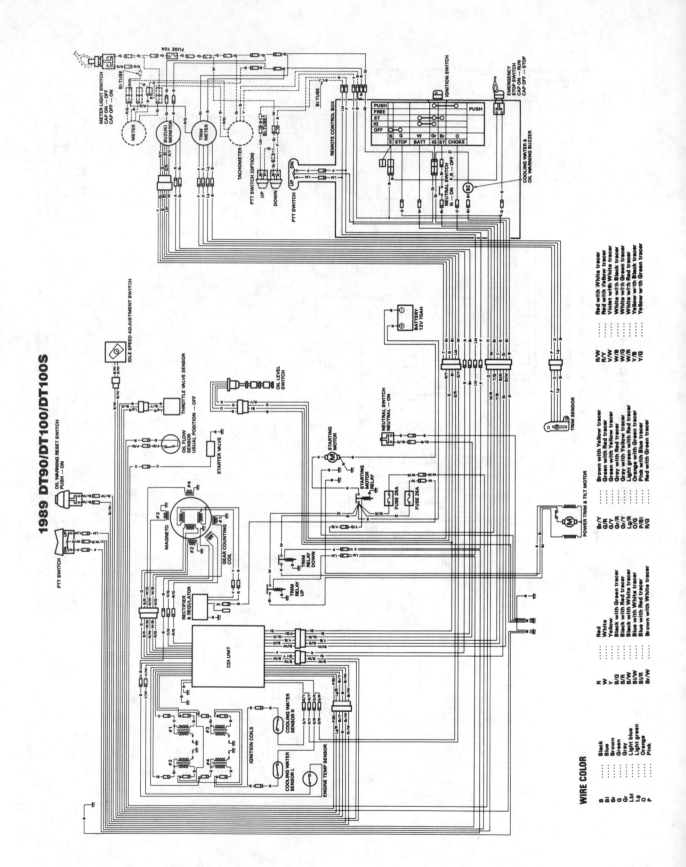

1989 DT90/DT100/DT100S

WIRE COLOR

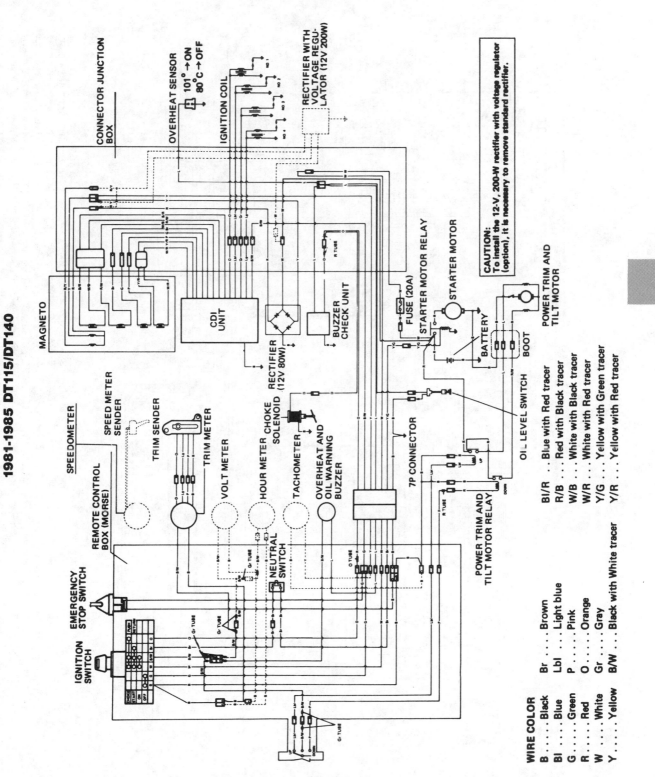

1981-1985 DT115/DT140

CONNECTOR JUNCTION BOX

OVERHEAT SENSOR 101° → ON 80°C → OFF

IGNITION COIL

RECTIFIER WITH VOLTAGE REGU- LATOR (12V 200W)

CAUTION:
To install the 12-V, 200-W rectifier with voltage regulator (option), it is necessary to remove standard rectifier.

5

MAGNETO

CDI UNIT

RECTIFIER (12V 80W)

BUZZER CHECK UNIT

FUSE (20A)

STARTER MOTOR RELAY

STARTER MOTOR

BATTERY

BOOT

POWER TRIM AND TILT MOTOR

SPEEDOMETER

SPEED METER SENDER

TRIM SENDER

TRIM METER

VOLT METER

HOUR METER

CHOKE SOLENOID

TACHOMETER

OVERHEAT AND OIL WARNING BUZZER

7P CONNECTOR

OIL LEVEL SWITCH

POWER TRIM AND TILT MOTOR RELAY

REMOTE CONTROL BOX (MORSE)

EMERGENCY STOP SWITCH

NEUTRAL SWITCH

IGNITION SWITCH

Gr-TUBE

WIRE COLOR

B	.... Black	Br	.... Brown	Bl/R .. Blue with Red tracer
Bl	.... Blue	Lbl	.. Light blue	R/B .. Red with Black tracer
G	.... Green	P	.... Pink	W/B .. White with Black tracer
R	.... Red	O	.... Orange	W/R .. White with Red tracer
W	.... White	Gr	.... Gray	Y/G ... Yellow with Green tracer
Y	.... Yellow	B/W .. Black with White tracer		Y/R ... Yellow with Red tracer

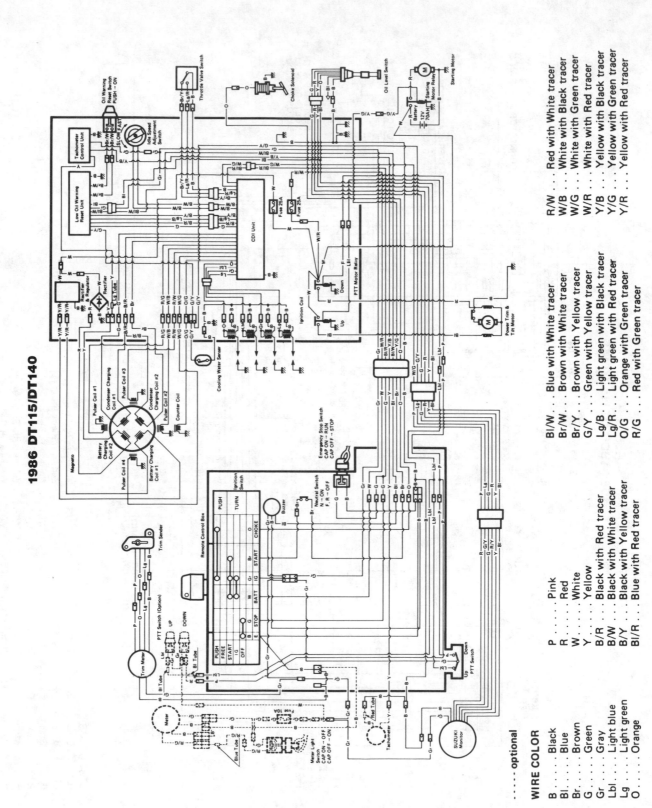

1986 DT115/DT140

WIRE COLOR

B . . . . . . Black	P . . . . . . Pink	R/W . . . Red with White tracer
Bl . . . . . Blue	R . . . . . Red	W/B . . . White with Black tracer
Br . . . . . Brown	W . . . . . White	W/G . . . White with Green tracer
G . . . . . Green	Y . . . . . Yellow	W/R . . . White with Red tracer
Gr . . . . . Gray	B/R . . . Black with Red tracer	Y/B . . . Yellow with Black tracer
Lbl . . . . Light blue	B/W . . . Black with White tracer	Y/G . . . Yellow with Green tracer
Lg . . . . Light green	B/Y . . . Black with Yellow tracer	Y/R . . . Yellow with Red tracer
O . . . . . Orange	Bl/R . . . Blue with Red tracer	

Bl/W . . . Blue with White tracer	
Br/W . . . Brown with White tracer	
Br/Y . . . Brown with Yellow tracer	
G/Y . . . Green with Yellow tracer	
Lg/B . . . Light green with Black tracer	
Lg/R . . . Light green with Red tracer	
O/G . . . Orange with Green tracer	
R/G . . . Red with Green tracer	

- - - - - optional

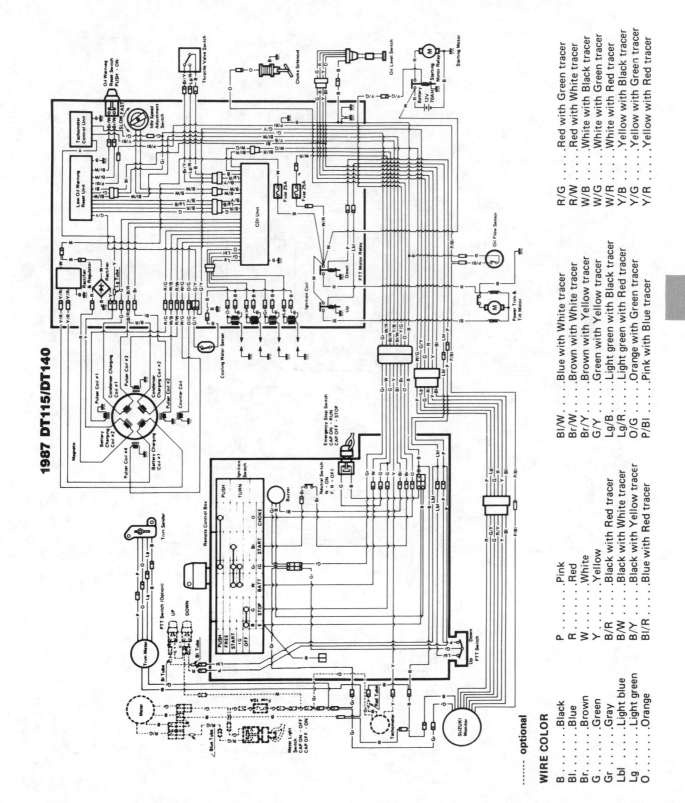

1987 DT115/DT140

optional

WIRE COLOR

B	. . . .	Black
Bl	. . . .	Blue
Br	. . . . . .	Brown
G	. . . . . .	Green
Gr	. . . . . .	Gray
Lbl	. . . .	Light blue
Lg	. . . . .	Light green
O	. . . . . .	Orange

P	. . . .	Pink
R	. . . .	Red
W	. . . . . .	White
Y	. . . . . .	Yellow
B/R	. . . .	Black with Red tracer
B/W	. . . .	Black with White tracer
B/Y	. . .	Black with Yellow tracer
Bl/R	. .	Blue with Red tracer

Bl/W	. . .	Blue with White tracer
Br/W	. . .	Brown with White tracer
Br/Y	. . .	Brown with Yellow tracer
G/Y	. . . .	Green with Yellow tracer
Lg/B	. . .	Light green with Black tracer
Lg/R	. . .	Light green with Red tracer
O/G	. . .	Orange with Green tracer
P/Bl	. . .	Pink with Blue tracer

R/G	. . . .	Red with Green tracer
R/W	. . .	Red with White tracer
W/B	. . .	White with Black tracer
W/G	. . .	White with Green tracer
W/R	. . .	White with Red tracer
Y/B	. . .	Yellow with Black tracer
Y/G	. . .	Yellow with Green tracer
Y/R	. . .	Yellow with Red tracer

5

1988 DT115/DT140

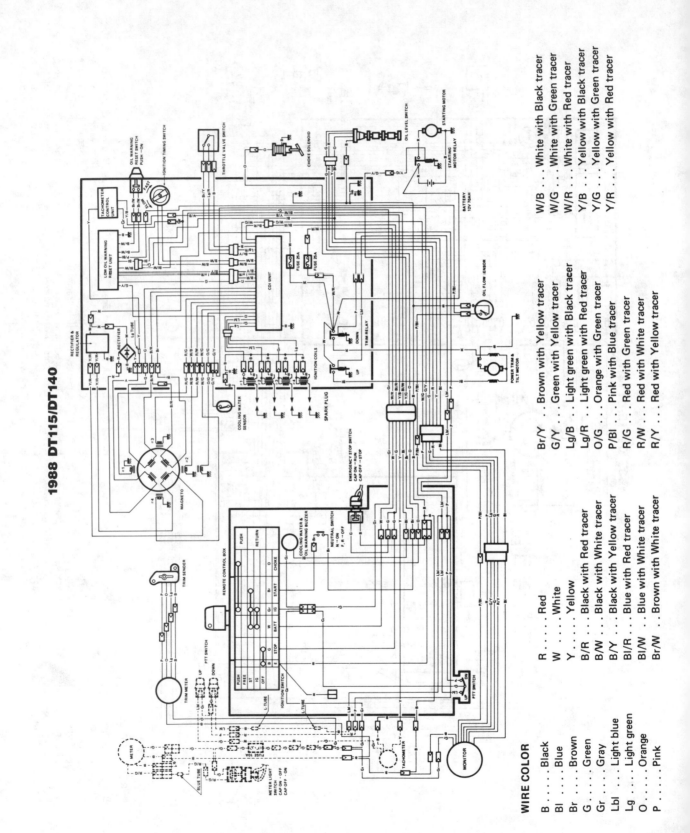

WIRE COLOR

B	. . . .	Black	Br/Y	. . Brown with Yellow tracer
Bl	. . . .	Blue	G/Y	. . Green with Yellow tracer
Br	. . . .	Brown	Lg/B	. . Light green with Black tracer
G	. . . .	Green	Lg/R	. . Light green with Red tracer
Gr	. . . .	Gray	O/G	. . Orange with Green tracer
Lbl	. .	Light blue	P/Bl	. . Pink with Blue tracer
Lg	. .	Light green	R/G	. . Red with Green tracer
O	. . . .	Orange	R/W	. . Red with White tracer
P	. . . .	Pink	R/Y	. . Red with Yellow tracer
R	. . . .	Red	W/B	. . White with Black tracer
W	. . .	White	W/G	. . White with Green tracer
Y	. . .	Yellow	W/R	. . White with Red tracer
B/R	. .	Black with Red tracer	Y/B	. . Yellow with Black tracer
B/W	. .	Black with White tracer	Y/G	. . Yellow with Green tracer
B/Y	. .	Black with Yellow tracer	Y/R	. . Yellow with Red tracer
Bl/R	. .	Blue with Red tracer		
Bl/W	. .	Blue with White tracer		
Br/W	. .	Brown with White tracer		

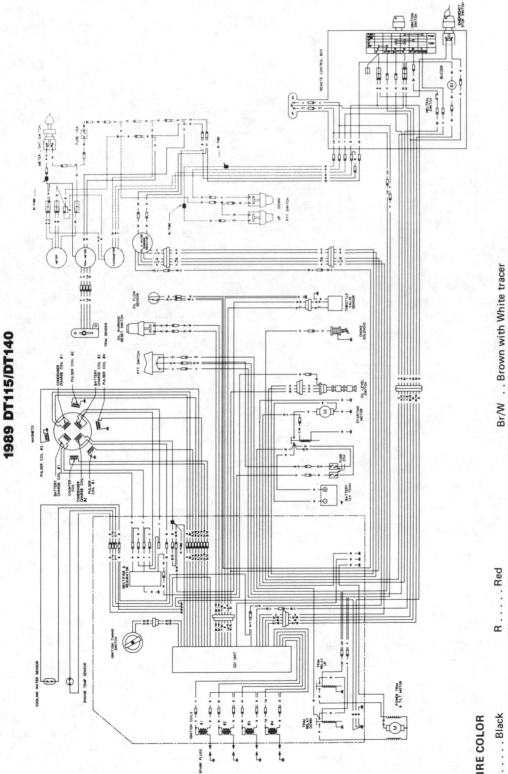

1989 DT115/DT140

WIRE COLOR

B	. . . .	Black
Bl	. . . .	Blue
Br	. . . .	Brown
G	. . . .	Green
Gr	. . . .	Gray
Lbl	. . .	Light blue
Lg	. . .	Light green
O	. . . .	Orange
P	. . . .	Pink

R	. . . . .	Red
W	. . . . .	White
Y	. . . . .	Yellow
B/G	. . .	Black with Green tracer
B/R	. . .	Black with Red tracer
B/W	. . .	Black with White tracer
Bl/B	. . .	Blue with Black tracer
Bl/R	. . .	Blue with Red tracer
Bl/W	. .	Blue with White tracer

Br/W	. .	Brown with White tracer
G/Y	. . .	Green with Yellow tracer
Gr/Y	. . .	Gray with Yellow tracer
Lg/R	. . .	Light green with Red tracer
O/G	. . .	Orange with Green tracer
P/Bl	. . .	Pink with Blue tracer
R/G	. . .	Red with Green tracer
R/W	. . .	Red with White tracer
R/Y	. . .	Red with Yellow tracer

V/W	. . .	Violet with White tracer
W/B	. . .	White with Black tracer
W/G	. . .	White with Green tracer
W/R	. . .	White with Red tracer
Y/B	. . .	Yellow with Black tracer
Y/G	. . .	Yellow with Green tracer

5

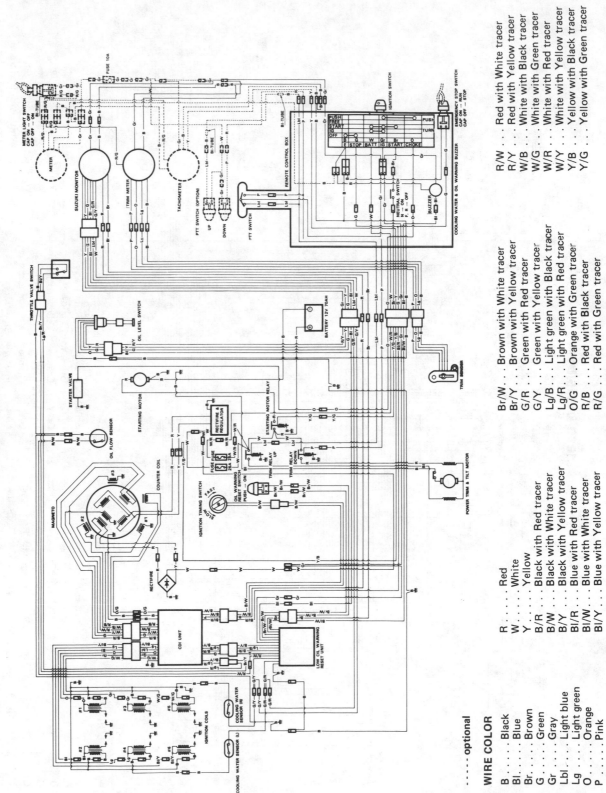

1986 DT150/DT200

WIRE COLOR

B	. . . . .	Black
Bl	. . . . .	Blue
Br	. . . . .	Brown
G	. . . . .	Green
Gr	. . . . .	Gray
Lbl	. . . .	Light blue
Lg	. . . .	Light green
O	. . . . .	Orange
P	. . . . .	Pink

R	. . . . .	Red
W	. . . . .	White
Y	. . . . .	Yellow
B/R	. . .	Black with Red tracer
B/W	. . .	Black with White tracer
B/Y	. . .	Black with Yellow tracer
Bl/R	. . .	Blue with Red tracer
Bl/W	. . .	Blue with White tracer
Bl/Y	. . .	Blue with Yellow tracer

Br/W	. . .	Brown with White tracer
Br/Y	. . .	Brown with Yellow tracer
G/R	. . .	Green with Red tracer
G/Y	. . .	Green with Yellow tracer
Lg/B	. . .	Light green with Black tracer
Lg/R	. . .	Light green with Red tracer
O/G	. . .	Orange with Green tracer
R/B	. . .	Red with Black tracer
R/G	. . .	Red with Green tracer

R/W	. . .	Red with White tracer
R/Y	. . .	Red with Yellow tracer
W/B	. . .	White with Black tracer
W/G	. . .	White with Green tracer
W/R	. . .	White with Red tracer
W/Y	. . .	White with Yellow tracer
Y/B	. . .	Yellow with Black tracer
Y/G	. . .	Yellow with Green tracer

- - - - optional

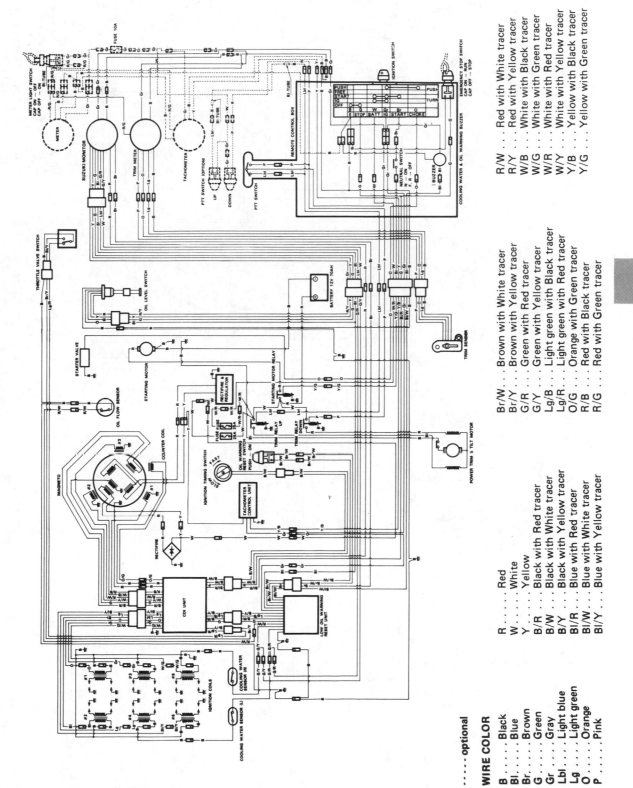

1986 DT150SS

- - - - optional

WIRE COLOR

B	. . . . .	Black
Bl	. . . . .	Blue
Br	. . . . .	Brown
G	. . . . .	Green
Gr	. . . . .	Gray
Lbl	. . . . .	Light blue
Lg	. . . . .	Light green
O	. . . . .	Orange
P	. . . . .	Pink

R	. . . . .	Red
W	. . . . .	White
Y	. . . . .	Yellow
B/R	. . .	Black with Red tracer
B/W	. . .	Black with White tracer
B/Y	. . .	Black with Yellow tracer
Bl/R	. . .	Blue with Red tracer
Bl/W	. . .	Blue with White tracer
Bl/Y	. . .	Blue with Yellow tracer

Br/W	. . .	Brown with White tracer
Br/Y	. . .	Brown with Yellow tracer
G/R	. . .	Green with Red tracer
G/Y	. . .	Green with Yellow tracer
Lg/B	. . .	Light green with Black tracer
Lg/R	. . .	Light green with Red tracer
O/G	. . .	Orange with Green tracer
R/B	. . .	Red with Black tracer
R/G	. . .	Red with Green tracer

R/W	. . .	Red with White tracer
R/Y	. . .	Red with Yellow tracer
W/B	. . .	White with Black tracer
W/G	. . .	White with Green tracer
W/R	. . .	White with Red tracer
W/Y	. . .	White with Yellow tracer
Y/B	. . .	Yellow with Black tracer
Y/G	. . .	Yellow with Green tracer

5

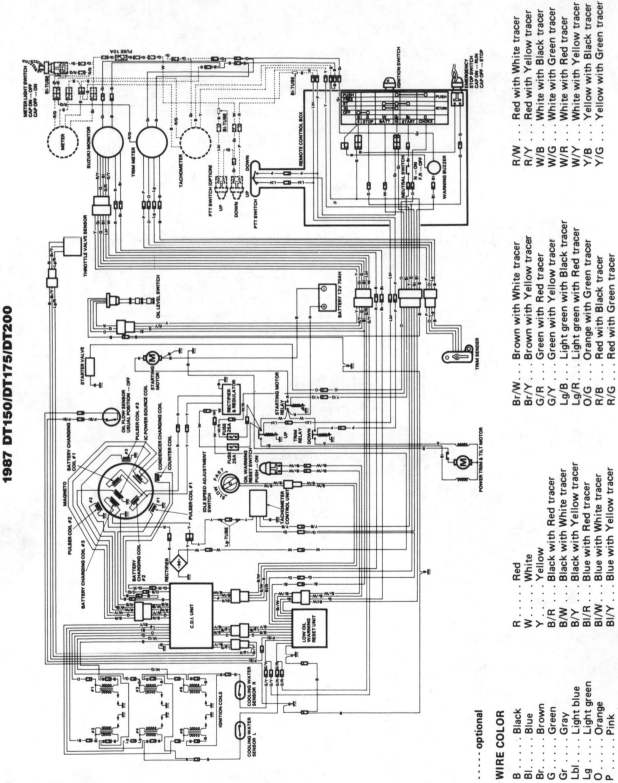

1987 DT150/DT175/DT200

WIRE COLOR

B . . . . . Black
Bl . . . . . Blue
Br . . . . . Brown
G . . . . . Green
Gr . . . . . Gray
Lbl . . . . . Light blue
Lg . . . . . Light green
O . . . . . Orange
P . . . . . Pink

R . . . . . Red
W . . . . . White
Y . . . . . Yellow
B/R . . . . . Black with Red tracer
B/W . . . . . Black with White tracer
B/Y . . . . . Black with Yellow tracer
Bl/R . . . . . Blue with Red tracer
Bl/W . . . . . Blue with White tracer
Bl/Y . . . . . Blue with Yellow tracer

Br/W . . . Brown with White tracer
Br/Y . . . Brown with Yellow tracer
G/R . . . Green with Red tracer
G/Y . . . Green with Yellow tracer
Lg/B . . . Light green with Black tracer
Lg/R . . . Light green with Red tracer
O/G . . . Orange with Green tracer
R/B . . . Red with Black tracer
R/G . . . Red with Green tracer

R/W . . . Red with White tracer
R/Y . . . Red with Yellow tracer
W/B . . . White with Black tracer
W/G . . . White with Green tracer
W/R . . . White with Red tracer
W/Y . . . White with Yellow tracer
Y/B . . . Yellow with Black tracer
Y/G . . . Yellow with Green tracer

- - - - optional

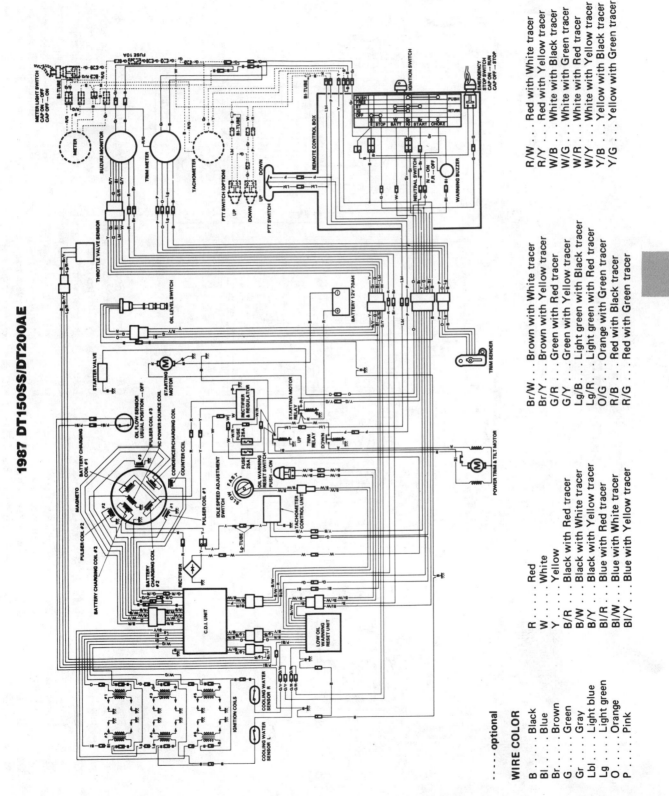

1987 DT150SS/DT200AE

5

WIRE COLOR

B	. . . . . Black	R/W	. . . Red with White tracer
Bl	. . . . Blue	R/Y	. . . Red with Yellow tracer
Br	. . . . Brown	W/B	. . . White with Black tracer
G	. . . . . Green	W/G	. . . White with Green tracer
Gr	. . . . Gray	W/R	. . . White with Red tracer
Lbl	. . . Light blue	W/Y	. . . White with Yellow tracer
Lg	. . . . Light green	Y/B	. . . Yellow with Black tracer
O	. . . . Orange	Y/G	. . . Yellow with Green tracer
P	. . . . . Pink		

Br/W	. . Brown with White tracer		
Br/Y	. . Brown with Yellow tracer		
G/R	. . . Green with Red tracer		
G/Y	. . . Green with Yellow tracer		
Lg/B	. . . Light green with Black tracer		
Lg/R	. . . Light green with Red tracer		
O/G	. . . Orange with Green tracer		
R/B	. . . Red with Black tracer		
R/G	. . . Red with Green tracer		

R	. . . . . Red	
W	. . . . . White	
Y	. . . . . Yellow	
B/R	. . . . Black with Red tracer	
B/W	. . . . Black with White tracer	
B/Y	. . . . Black with Yellow tracer	
Bl/R	. . . . Blue with Red tracer	
Bl/W	. . . Blue with White tracer	
Bl/Y	. . . Blue with Yellow tracer	

- - - - - optional

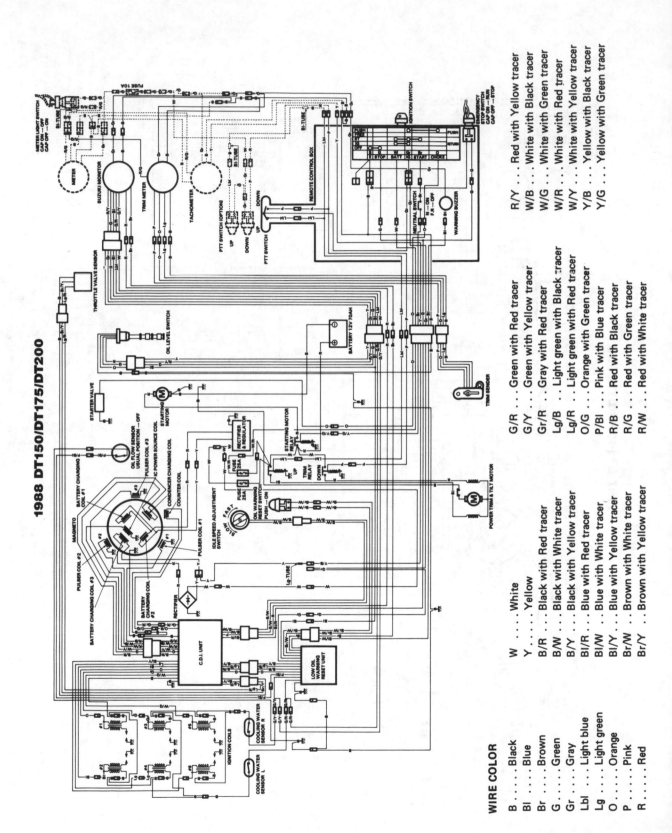

1988 DT150/DT175/DT200

WIRE COLOR

B	Black	W	White	G/R	Green with Red tracer
Bl	Blue	Y	Yellow	G/Y	Green with Yellow tracer
Br	Brown	B/R	Black with Red tracer	Gr/R	Gray with Red tracer
G	Green	B/W	Black with White tracer	Lg/B	Light green with Black tracer
Gr	Gray	B/Y	Black with Yellow tracer	Lg/R	Light green with Red tracer
Lbl	Light blue	Bl/R	Blue with Red tracer	O/G	Orange with Green tracer
Lg	Light green	Bl/W	Blue with White tracer	P/Bl	Pink with Blue tracer
O	Orange	Bl/Y	Blue with Yellow tracer	R/B	Red with Black tracer
P	Pink	Br/W	Brown with White tracer	R/G	Red with Green tracer
R	Red	Br/Y	Brown with Yellow tracer	R/W	Red with White tracer
				R/Y	Red with Yellow tracer
				W/B	White with Black tracer
				W/G	White with Green tracer
				W/R	White with Red tracer
				W/Y	White with Yellow tracer
				Y/B	Yellow with Black tracer
				Y/G	Yellow with Green tracer

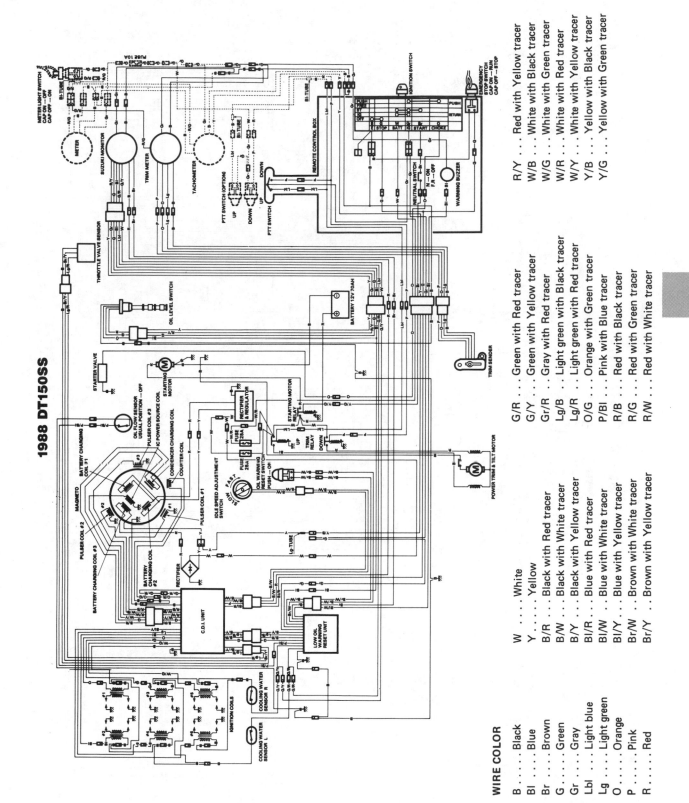

1988 DT150SS

WIRE COLOR

B	. . . . . .	Black
Bl	. . . . . .	Blue
Br	. . . . . .	Brown
G	. . . . . .	Green
Gr	. . . . . .	Gray
Lbl	. . . . . .	Light blue
Lg	. . . . . .	Light green
O	. . . . . .	Orange
P	. . . . . .	Pink
R	. . . . . .	Red

W	. . . . . .	White
Y	. . . . . .	Yellow
B/R	. . . . . .	Black with Red tracer
B/W	. . . . . .	Black with White tracer
B/Y	. . . . . .	Black with Yellow tracer
Bl/R	. . . . . .	Blue with Red tracer
Bl/W	. . . . . .	Blue with White tracer
Bl/Y	. . . . . .	Blue with Yellow tracer
Br/W	. . . . . .	Brown with White tracer
Br/Y	. . . . . .	Brown with Yellow tracer

G/R	. .	Green with Red tracer
G/Y	. .	Green with Yellow tracer
Gr/R	. .	Gray with Red tracer
Lg/B	. .	Light green with Black tracer
Lg/R	. .	Light green with Red tracer
O/G	. .	Orange with Green tracer
P/Bl	. .	Pink with Blue tracer
R/B	. .	Red with Black tracer
R/G	. .	Red with Green tracer
R/W	. .	Red with White tracer

R/Y	. . .	Red with Yellow tracer
W/B	. . .	White with Black tracer
W/G	. . .	White with Green tracer
W/R	. . .	White with Red tracer
W/Y	. . .	White with Yellow tracer
Y/B	. . .	Yellow with Black tracer
Y/G	. . .	Yellow with Green tracer

5

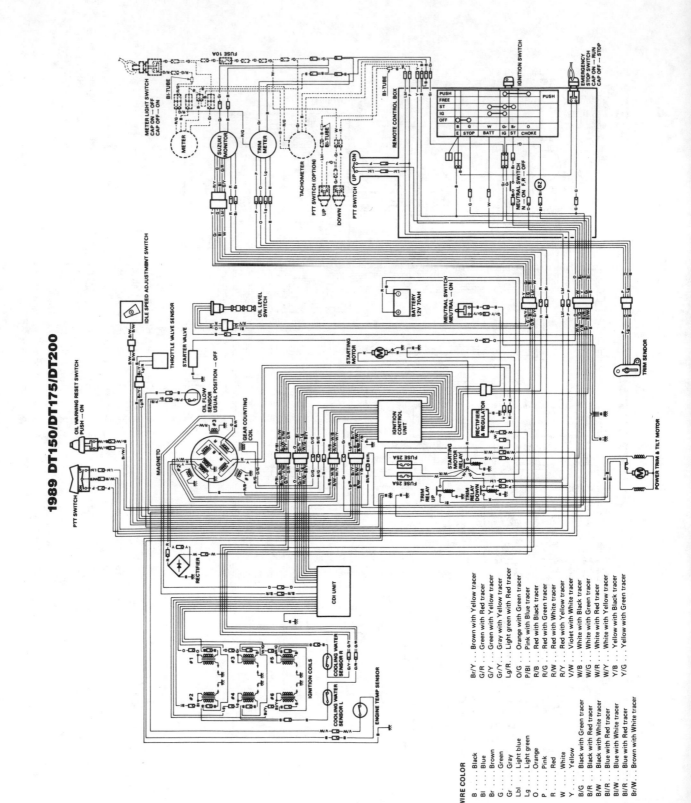

1989 DT150/DT175/DT200

WIRE COLOR

B	. . . . .	Black
Bl	. . . . .	Blue
Br	. . . . .	Brown
G	. . . . .	Green
Gr	. . . . .	Gray
Lbl	. . . . .	Light blue
Lg	. . . . .	Light green
O	. . . . .	Orange
P	. . . . .	Pink
R	. . . . .	Red
W	. . . . .	White
Y	. . . . .	Yellow

B/G	. . . . .	Black with Green tracer
B/R	. . . . .	Black with Red tracer
B/W	. . . . .	Black with White tracer
Bl/R	. . . . .	Blue with Red tracer
Bl/W	. . . . .	Blue with White tracer
Br/R	. . . . .	Blue with Red tracer
Br/W	. . . . .	Brown with White tracer

Br/Y	. . . . .	Brown with Yellow tracer
G/R	. . . . .	Green with Red tracer
G/Y	. . . . .	Green with Yellow tracer
Gr/Y	. . . . .	Gray with Yellow tracer
Lg/R	. . . . .	Light green with Red tracer
O/G	. . . . .	Orange with Green tracer
P/Bl	. . . . .	Pink with Blue tracer
R/B	. . . . .	Red with Black tracer
R/G	. . . . .	Red with Green tracer
R/W	. . . . .	Red with White tracer
R/Y	. . . . .	Red with Yellow tracer
V/W	. . . . .	Violet with White tracer
W/B	. . . . .	White with Black tracer
W/G	. . . . .	White with Green tracer
W/R	. . . . .	White with Red tracer
W/Y	. . . . .	White with Yellow tracer
Y/B	. . . . .	Yellow with Black tracer
Y/R	. . . . .	Yellow with Red tracer
Y/G	. . . . .	Yellow with Green tracer

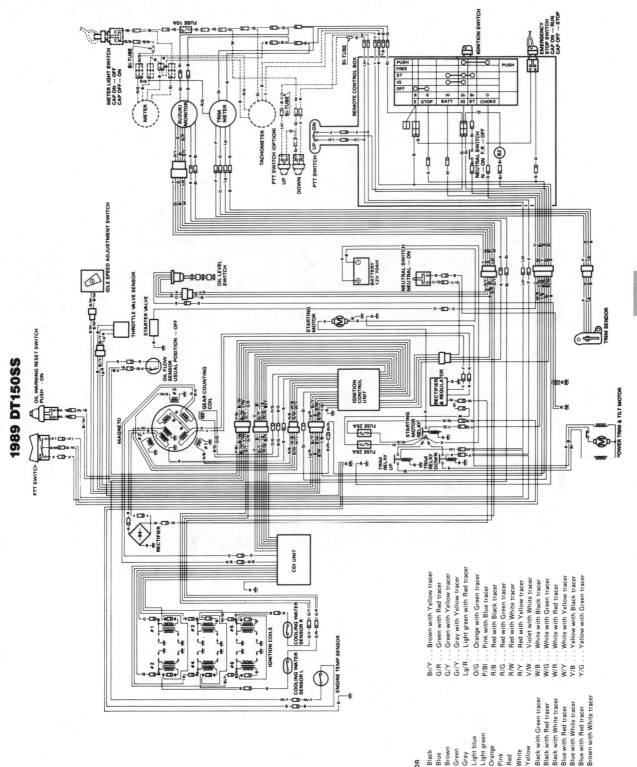

1989 DT150SS

5

WIRE COLOR

B	. . . .	Black
Bl	. . . .	Blue
Br	. . . .	Brown
G	. . . .	Green
Gr	. . . .	Gray
Lbl	. . . .	Light blue
Lg	. . . .	Light green
O	. . . .	Orange
P	. . . .	Pink
R	. . . .	Red
W	. . . .	White
Y	. . . .	Yellow
B/G	. . . .	Black with Green tracer
B/R	. . . .	Black with Red tracer
B/W	. . . .	Black with White tracer
Bl/R	. . . .	Blue with Red tracer
Bl/W	. . . .	Blue with White tracer
Bl/R	. . . .	Blue with Red tracer
Br/W	. . . .	Brown with White tracer

Br/Y	. . . .	Brown with Yellow tracer
G/R	. . . .	Green with Red tracer
G/Y	. . . .	Green with Yellow tracer
Gr/Y	. . . .	Gray with Yellow tracer
Lg/R	. . . .	Light green with Red tracer
O/G	. . . .	Orange with Green tracer
P/Bl	. . . .	Pink with Blue tracer
R/B	. . . .	Red with Black tracer
R/G	. . . .	Red with Green tracer
R/W	. . . .	Red with White tracer
R/Y	. . . .	Red with Yellow tracer
V/W	. . . .	Violet with White tracer
W/B	. . . .	White with Black tracer
W/G	. . . .	White with Green tracer
W/R	. . . .	White with Red tracer
W/Y	. . . .	White with Yellow tracer
Y/B	. . . .	Yellow with Black tracer
Y/R	. . . .	Yellow with Red tracer
Y/G	. . . .	Yellow with Green tracer

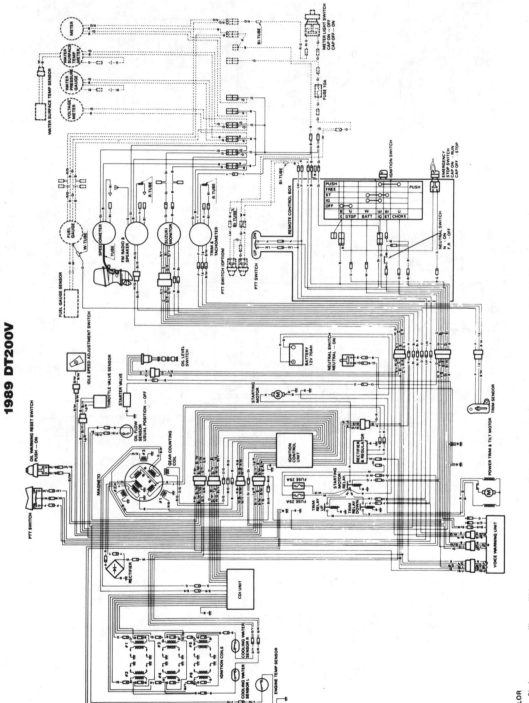

1989 DT200V

WIRE COLOR

B	Black	W	White	G/R	Green with Red tracer	V/W	Violet with White tracer
Bl	Blue	Y	Yellow	G/Y	Green with Yellow tracer	W/B	White with Black tracer
Br	Brown	B/G	Black with Green tracer	Gr/Y	Gray with Yellow tracer	W/G	White with Green tracer
G	Green	B/R	Black with Red tracer	Lg/R	Light green with Red tracer	W/R	White with Red tracer
Gr	Gray	B/W	Black with White tracer	O/G	Orange with Green tracer	W/Y	White with Yellow tracer
Lbl	Light blue	Bl/R	Blue with Red tracer	P/Bl	Pink with Blue tracer	Y/B	Yellow with Black tracer
Lg	Light green	Bl/W	Blue with White tracer	R/B	Red with Black tracer	Y/G	Yellow with Green tracer
O	Orange	Bl/Y	Blue with Red tracer	R/G	Red with Green tracer		
P	Pink	Br/W	Brown with White tracer	R/W	Red with White tracer		
R	Red	Br/Y	Brown with Yellow tracer	R/Y	Red with Yellow tracer		

TOHATSU

M5B(S)

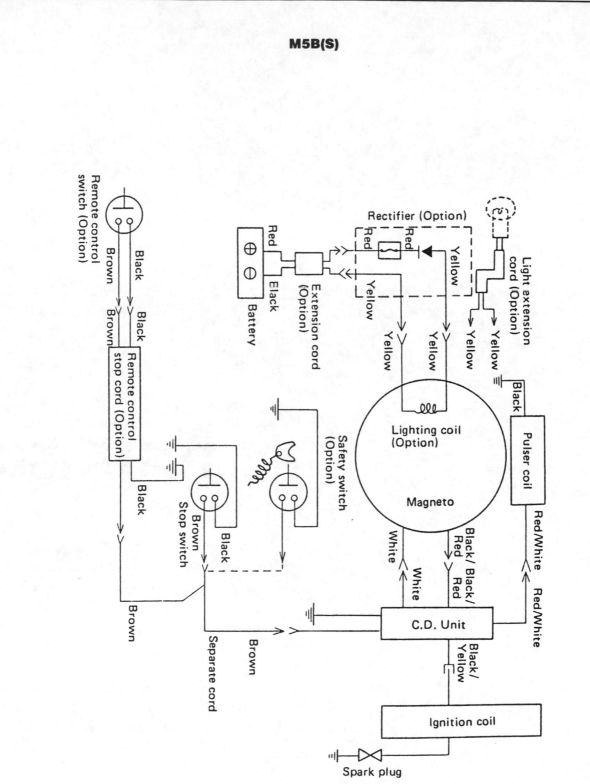

M8A

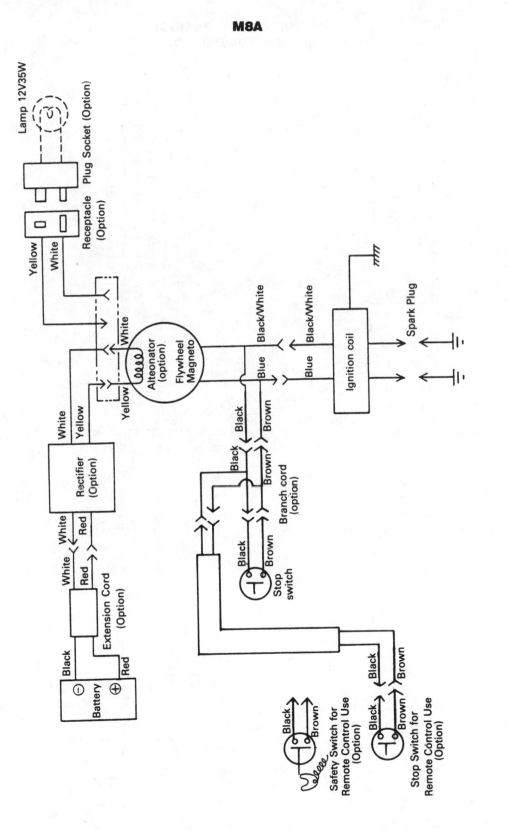

M9.9B/M12C/M15B/M18C/
M25C/M30A2/M40C

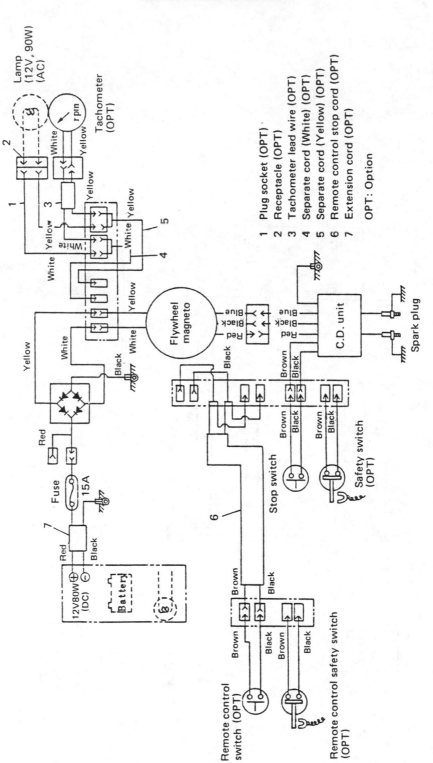

M9.9BEF/M12CEF/M15BEF/M18CEF/
M25CEF/M30A2EF/M40CEF

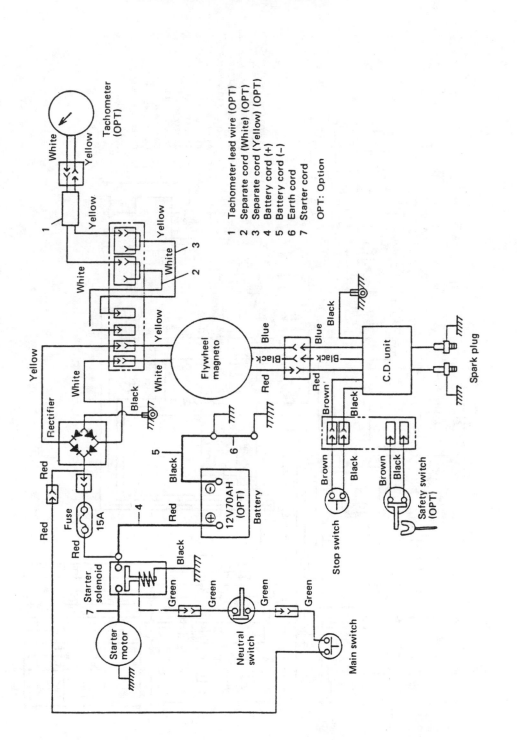

1 Tachometer lead wire (OPT)
2 Separate cord (White) (OPT)
3 Separate cord (Yellow) (OPT)
4 Battery cord (+)
5 Battery cord (−)
6 Earth cord
7 Starter cord

OPT: Option

6

M9.9BEF/M12CEP/M15BEP/M18CEP/ M25CEP/M30A2EP/M40CEP

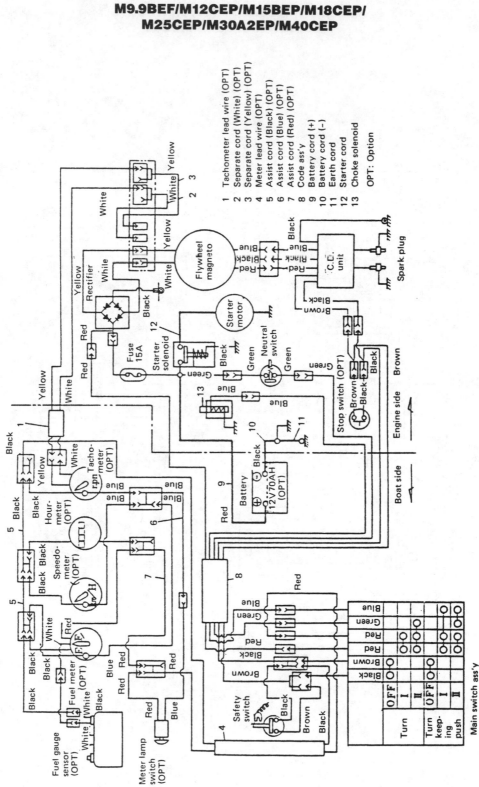

1 Tachometer lead wire (OPT)
2 Separate cord (White) (OPT)
3 Separate cord (Yellow) (OPT)
4 Meter lead wire (OPT)
5 Assist cord (Black) (OPT)
6 Assist cord (Blue) (OPT)
7 Assist cord (Red) (OPT)
8 Code ass'y
9 Battery cord (+)
10 Battery cord (−)
11 Earth cord
12 Starter cord
13 Choke solenoid

OPT: Option

M35A

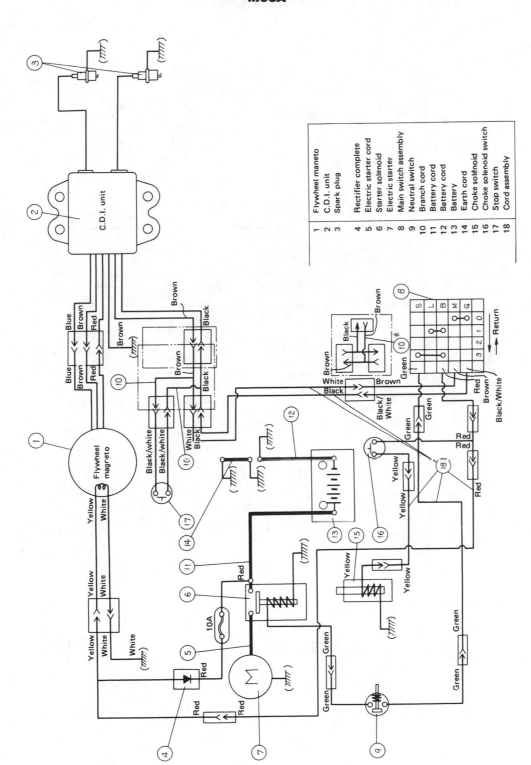

1	Flywheel maneto
2	C.D.I. unit
3	Spark plug
4	Rectifier complete
5	Electric starter cord
6	Starter solenoid
7	Electric starter
8	Main switch assembly
9	Neutral switch
10	Branch cord
11	Battery cord
12	Battery cord
13	Battery
14	Earth cord
15	Choke solenoid
16	Choke solenoid switch
17	Stop switch
18	Cord assembly

6

M55BEP/M70AEP

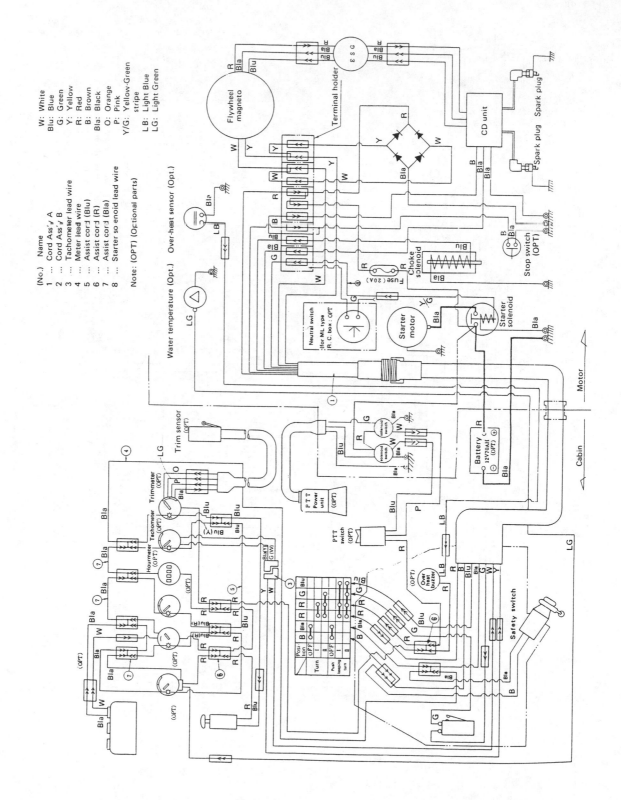

M90A

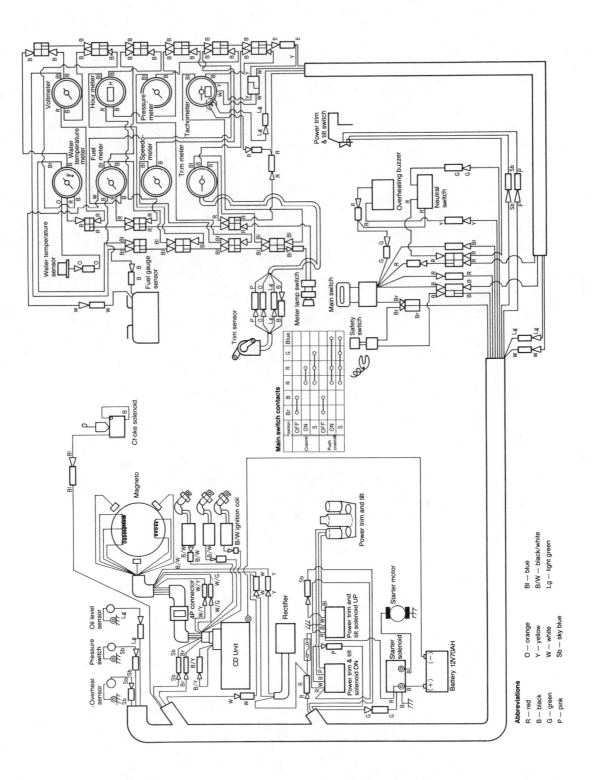

YAMAHA 7

8N

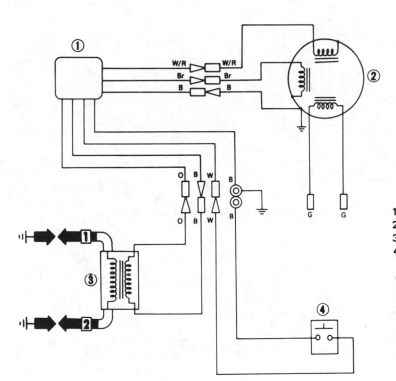

1. CDI unit
2. CDI magneto
3. Ignition coil
4. Engine stop button

W/R	:	White/Red
Br	:	Brown
B	:	Black
O	:	Orange
W	:	White
G	:	Green
R	:	Red

7

9.9N

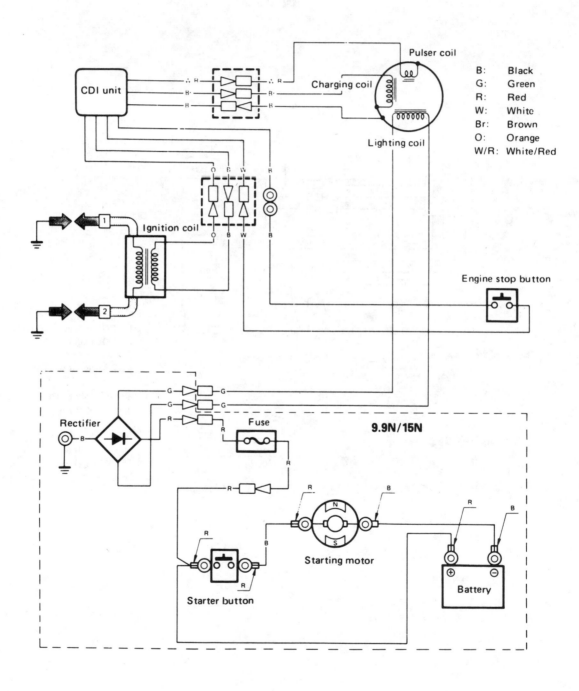

B: Black
G: Green
R: Red
W: White
Br: Brown
O: Orange
W/R: White/Red

Pulser coil

Charging coil

Lighting coil

CDI unit

Ignition coil

Engine stop button

Rectifier

Fuse

9.9N/15N

Starter button

Starting motor

Battery

15N

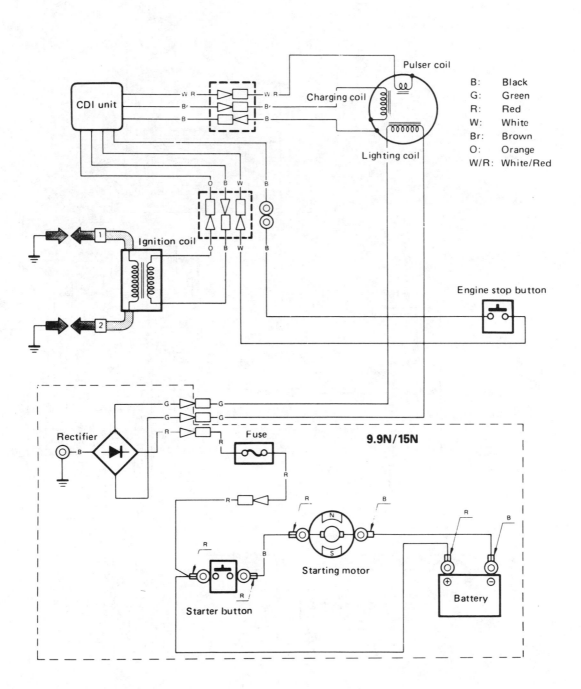

B:	Black
G:	Green
R:	Red
W:	White
Br:	Brown
O:	Orange
W/R:	White/Red

30EN

W/R. . . . . White/Red
Br . . . . . Brown
B . . . . . Black
O . . . . . Orange
W . . . . . White
G . . . . . Green
R . . . . . Red
L . . . . . Blue
P . . . . . Pink
Y . . . . . Yellow
Sb. . . . . Sky blue

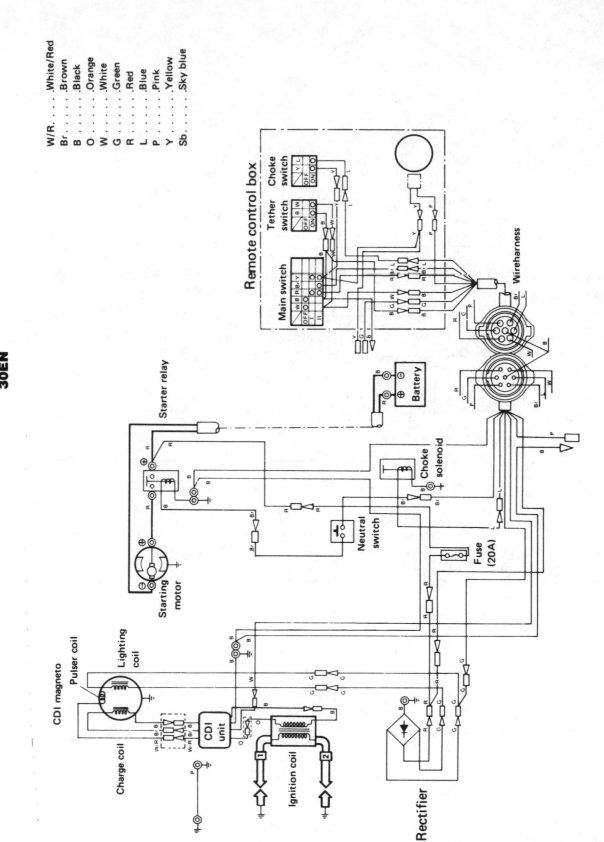

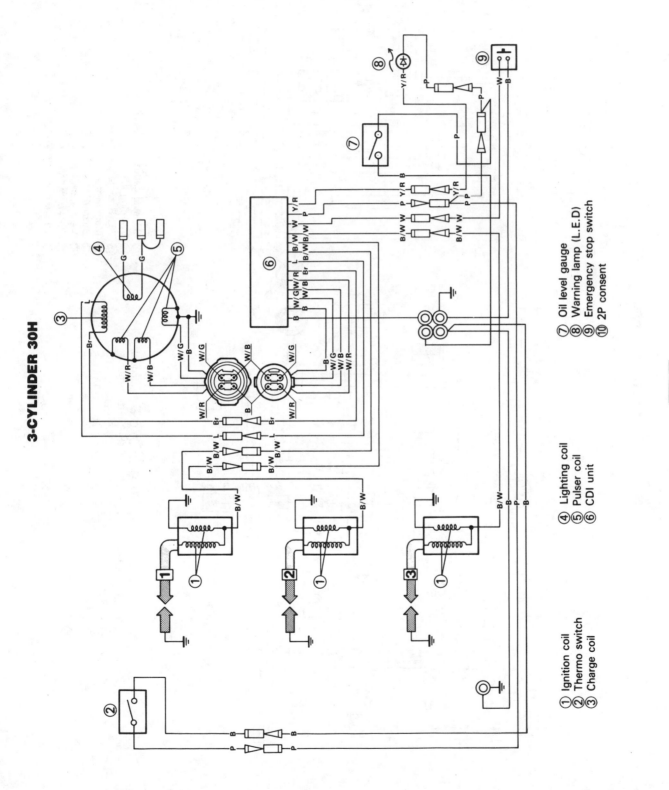

3-CYLINDER 30H

① Ignition coil
② Thermo switch
③ Charge coil

④ Lighting coil
⑤ Pulser coil
⑥ CDI unit

⑦ Oil level gauge
⑧ Warning lamp (L.E.D)
⑨ Emergency stop switch
⑩ 2P consent

7

3-CYLINDER 30EH

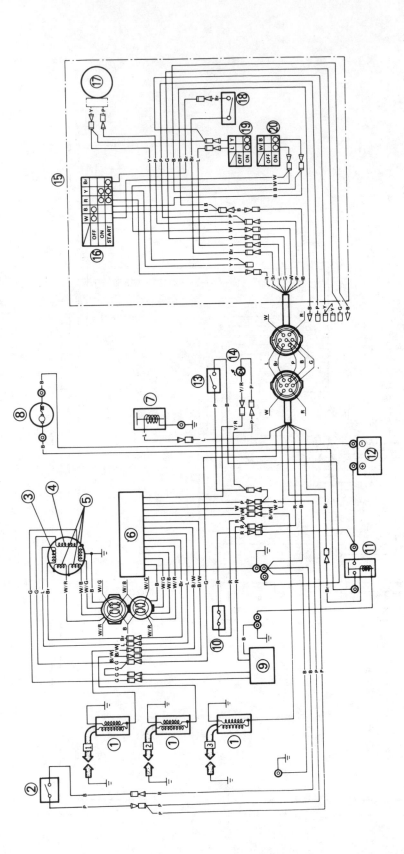

⑬ Oil level gauge
⑭ Warning light
⑮ 703 Remote control box
⑯ Main switch
⑰ Buzzer
⑱ Neutral switch
⑲ Choke switch
⑳ Emergency stop switch

⑦ Choke solenoid
⑧ Starting motor
⑨ Rectifier
⑩ Fuse (10A)
⑪ Starter relay
⑫ Battery

① Ignition coil
② Thermo switch
③ Charge coil
④ Lighting coil
⑤ Pulser coil
⑥ C.D.I. unit

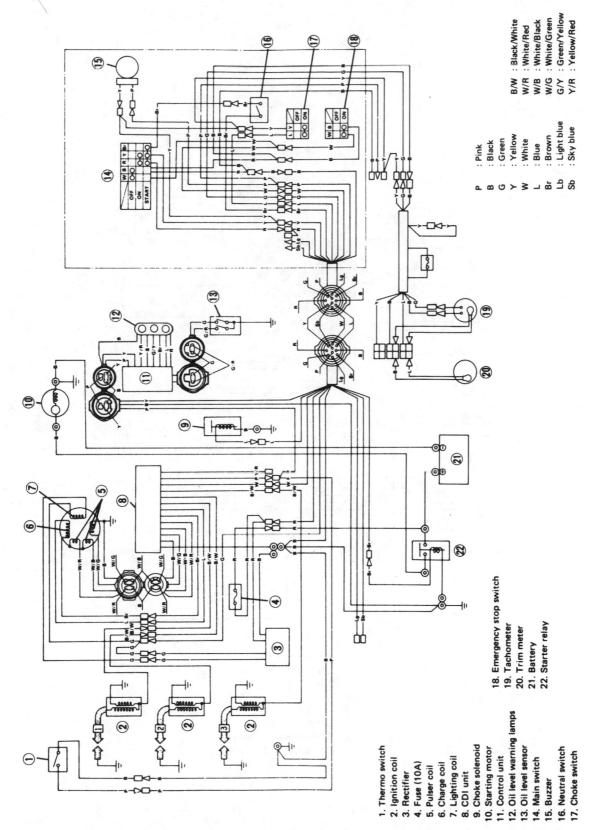

40EJ

1. Thermo switch
2. Ignition coil
3. Rectifier
4. Fuse (10A)
5. Pulser coil
6. Charge coil
7. Lighting coil
8. CDI unit
9. Choke solenoid
10. Starting motor
11. Control unit
12. Oil level warning lamps
13. Oil level sensor
14. Main switch
15. Buzzer
16. Neutral switch
17. Choke switch
18. Emergency stop switch
19. Tachometer
20. Trim meter
21. Battery
22. Starter relay

P : Pink
B : Black
G : Green
Y : Yellow
W : White
L : Blue
Br : Brown
Lb : Light blue
Sb : Sky blue

B/W : Black/White
W/R : White/Red
W/B : White/Black
W/G : White/Green
G/Y : Green/Yellow
Y/R : Yellow/Red

7

40N

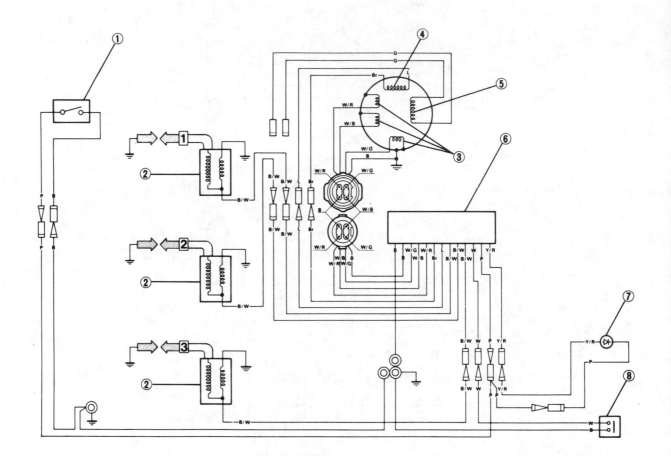

B	Black	L	Blue	Sb	Sky blue
Br	Brown	O	Orange	W	White
G	Green	P	Pink	Y	Yellow
Gy	Gray	R	Red	Lg	Light green

① Thermo switch
② Ignition coil
③ Pulser coil
④ Charge coil
⑤ Lighting coil
⑥ CDI unit
⑦ Overheat warning lamp
⑧ Emergency stop switch

40EN

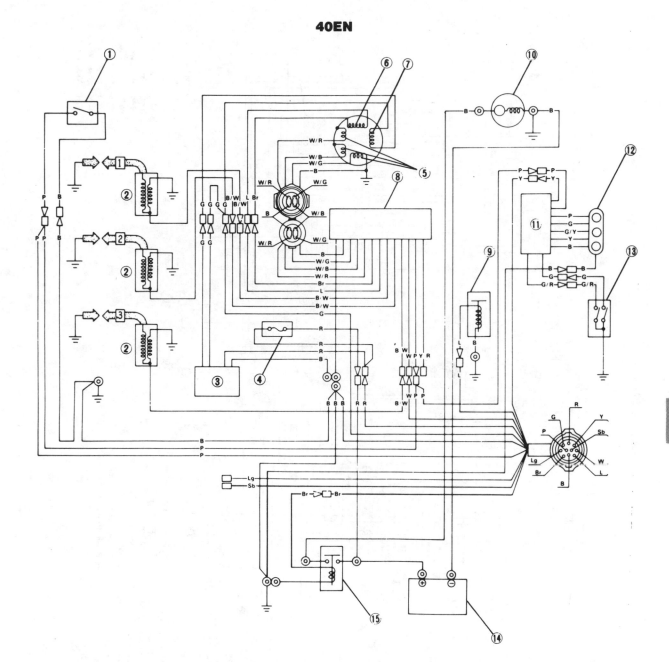

B	Black	L	Blue	Sb	Sky blue
Br	Brown	O	Orange	W	White
G	Green	P	Pink	Y	Yellow
Gy	Gray	R	Red	Lg	Light green

1. Thermo switch
2. Ignition coil
3. Rectifier
4. Fuse (10A)
5. Pulser coil
6. Charge coil
7. Lighting coil
8. CDI unit
9. Choke solenoid
10. Starting motor
11. Control unit
12. Oil level warning lamps
13. Oil level sensor
14. Battery
15. Starter relay

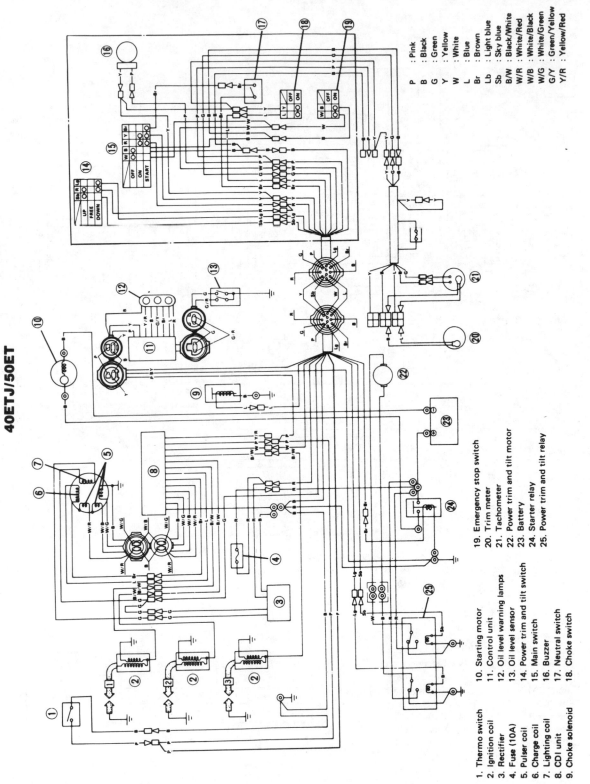

40ETJ/50ET

P : Pink	
B : Black	
G : Green	
Y : Yellow	
W : White	
L : Blue	
Br : Brown	
Lb : Light blue	
Sb : Sky blue	
B/W : Black/White	
W/R : White/Red	
W/B : White/Black	
W/G : White/Green	
G/Y : Green/Yellow	
Y/R : Yellow/Red	

1. Thermo switch
2. Ignition coil
3. Rectifier
4. Fuse (10A)
5. Pulser coil
6. Charge coil
7. Lighting coil
8. CDI unit
9. Choke solenoid
10. Starting motor
11. Control unit
12. Oil level warning lamps
13. Oil level sensor
14. Power trim and tilt switch
15. Main switch
16. Buzzer
17. Neutral switch
18. Choke switch
19. Emergency stop switch
20. Trim meter
21. Tachometer
22. Power trim and tilt motor
23. Battery
24. Starter relay
25. Power trim and tilt relay

50ETN

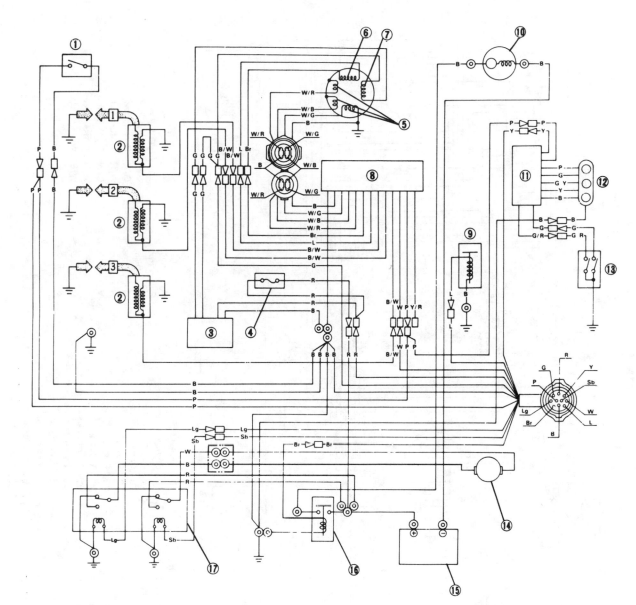

B	Black	L	Blue	Sb	Sky blue
Br	Brown	O	Orange	W	White
G	Green	P	Pink	Y	Yellow
Gy	Gray	R	Red	Lg	Light green

① Thermo switch
② Ignition coil
③ Rectifier
④ Fuse (10A)
⑤ Pulser coil
⑥ Charge coil
⑦ Lighting coil
⑧ CDI unit
⑨ Choke solenoid
⑩ Starting motor
⑪ Control unit
⑫ Oil level warning lamps
⑬ Oil level sensor
⑭ Power tilt motor
⑮ Battery
⑯ Starter relay
⑰ Power tilt relay

7

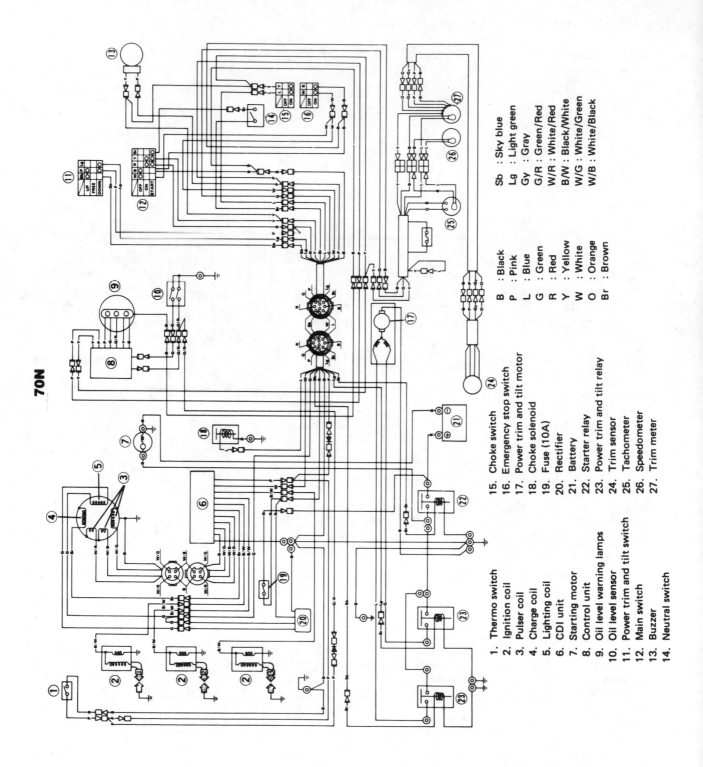

70N

Sb : Sky blue
Lg : Light green
Gy : Gray
G/R : Green/Red
W/R : White/Red
B/W : Black/White
W/G : White/Green
W/B : White/Black

B : Black
P : Pink
L : Blue
G : Green
R : Red
Y : Yellow
W : White
O : Orange
Br : Brown

1. Thermo switch
2. Ignition coil
3. Pulser coil
4. Charge coil
5. Lighting coil
6. CDI unit
7. Starting motor
8. Control unit
9. Oil level warning lamps
10. Oil level sensor
11. Power trim and tilt switch
12. Main switch
13. Buzzer
14. Neutral switch
15. Choke switch
16. Emergency stop switch
17. Power trim and tilt motor
18. Choke solenoid
19. Fuse (10A)
20. Rectifier
21. Battery
22. Starter relay
23. Power trim and tilt relay
24. Trim sensor
25. Tachometer
26. Speedometer
27. Trim meter

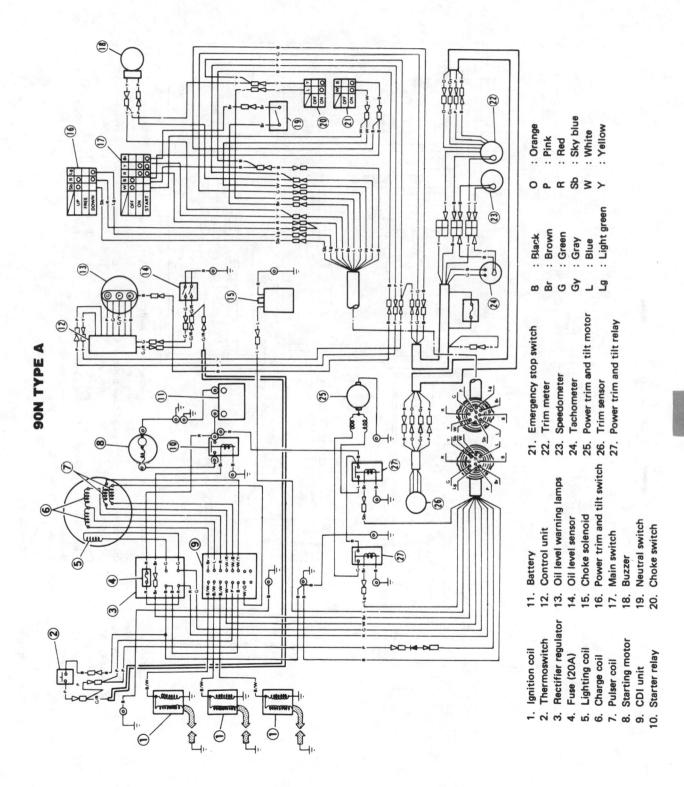

90N TYPE A

B	:	Black
Br	:	Brown
G	:	Green
Gy	:	Gray
L	:	Blue
Lg	:	Light green

O	:	Orange
P	:	Pink
R	:	Red
Sb	:	Sky blue
W	:	White
Y	:	Yellow

1. Ignition coil
2. Thermoswitch
3. Rectifier regulator
4. Fuse (20A)
5. Lighting coil
6. Charge coil
7. Pulser coil
8. Starting motor
9. CDI unit
10. Starter relay
11. Battery
12. Control unit
13. Oil level warning lamps
14. Oil level sensor
15. Choke solenoid
16. Power trim and tilt switch
17. Main switch
18. Buzzer
19. Neutral switch
20. Choke switch
21. Emergency stop switch
22. Trim meter
23. Speedometer
24. Tachometer
25. Power trim and tilt motor
26. Trim sensor
27. Power trim and tilt relay

7

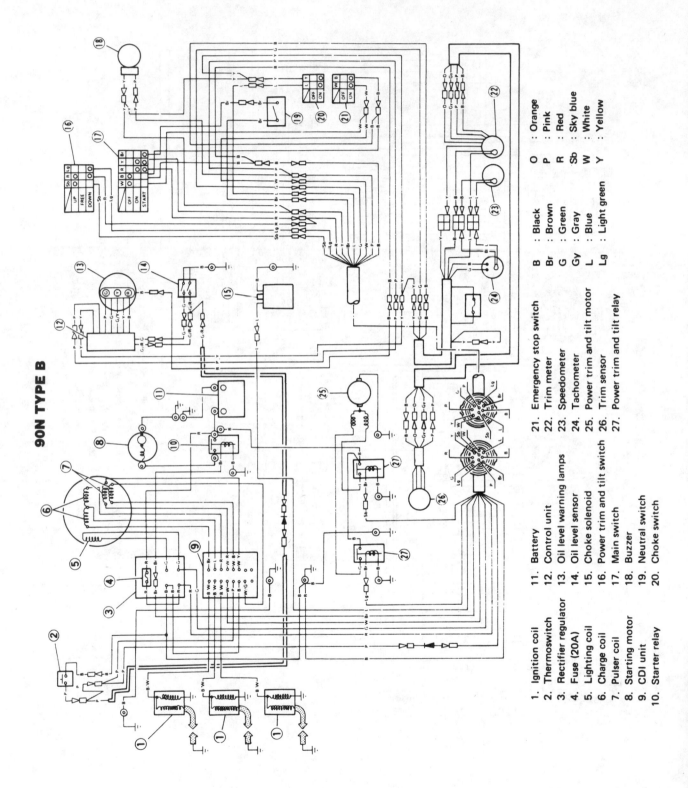

90N TYPE B

1.	Ignition coil	11.	Battery	21.	Emergency stop switch
2.	Thermoswitch	12.	Control unit	22.	Trim meter
3.	Rectifier regulator	13.	Oil level warning lamps	23.	Speedometer
4.	Fuse (20A)	14.	Oil level sensor	24.	Tachometer
5.	Lighting coil	15.	Choke solenoid	25.	Power trim and tilt motor
6.	Charge coil	16.	Power trim and tilt switch	26.	Trim sensor
7.	Pulser coil	17.	Main switch	27.	Power trim and tilt relay
8.	Starting motor	18.	Buzzer		
9.	CDI unit	19.	Neutral switch		
10.	Starter relay	20.	Choke switch		

B	: Black	O	: Orange
Br	: Brown	P	: Pink
G	: Green	R	: Red
Gy	: Gray	Sb	: Sky blue
L	: Blue	W	: White
Lg	: Light green	Y	: Yellow

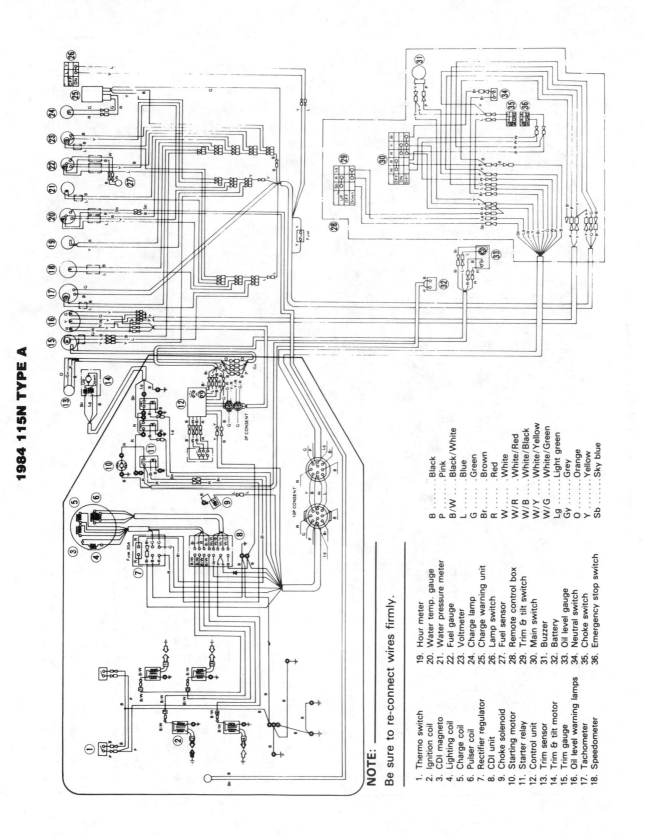

1984 115N TYPE A

NOTE:

Be sure to re-connect wires firmly.

1. Thermo switch	19. Hour meter	B ...... Black
2. Ignition coil	20. Water temp. gauge	P ...... Pink
3. CDI magneto	21. Water pressure meter	B/W .... Black/White
4. Lighting coil	22. Fuel gauge	L ...... Blue
5. Charge coil	23. Voltmeter	G ...... Green
6. Pulser coil	24. Charge lamp	Br ..... Brown
7. Rectifier regulator	25. Charge warning unit	R ...... Red
8. CDI unit	26. Lamp switch	W ...... White
9. Choke solenoid	27. Fuel sensor	W/R .... White/Red
10. Starting motor	28. Remote control box	W/B .... White/Black
11. Starter relay	29. Trim & tilt switch	W/Y .... White/Yellow
12. Control unit	30. Main switch	W/G .... White/Green
13. Trim sensor	31. Buzzer	Lg ..... Light green
14. Trim & tilt motor	32. Battery	Gy ..... Grey
15. Trim gauge	33. Oil level gauge	O ...... Orange
16. Oil level warning lamps	34. Neutral switch	Y ...... Yellow
17. Tachometer	35. Choke switch	Sb ..... Sky blue
18. Speedometer	36. Emergency stop switch	

7

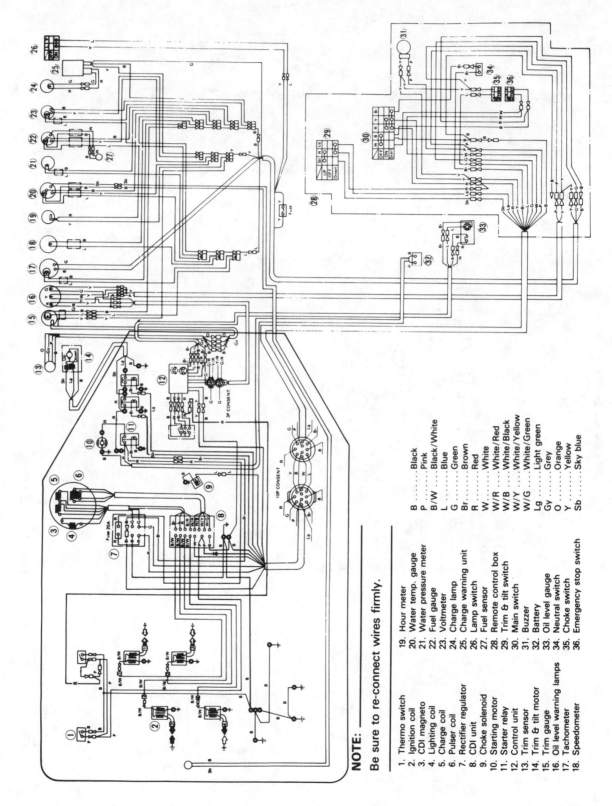

1984 115N TYPE B

NOTE:

Be sure to re-connect wires firmly.

1. Thermo switch
2. Ignition coil
3. CDI magneto
4. Lighting coil
5. Charge coil
6. Pulser coil
7. Rectifier regulator
8. CDI unit
9. Choke solenoid
10. Starting motor
11. Starter relay
12. Control unit
13. Trim sensor
14. Trim & tilt motor
15. Trim gauge
16. Oil level warning lamps
17. Tachometer
18. Speedometer
19. Hour meter
20. Water temp. gauge
21. Water pressure meter
22. Fuel gauge
23. Voltmeter
24. Charge lamp
25. Charge warning unit
26. Lamp switch
27. Fuel sensor
28. Remote control box
29. Trim & tilt switch
30. Main switch
31. Buzzer
32. Battery
33. Oil level gauge
34. Neutral switch
35. Choke switch
36. Emergency stop switch

B .... Black
P .... Pink
B/W .... Black/White
L .... Blue
G .... Green
Br .... Brown
R .... Red
W .... White
W/R ...... White/Red
W/B ...... White/Black
W/Y ...... White/Yellow
W/G ...... White/Green
Lg .... Light green
Gy .... Grey
O .... Orange
Y .... Yellow
Sb .... Sky blue

1985 115 HP

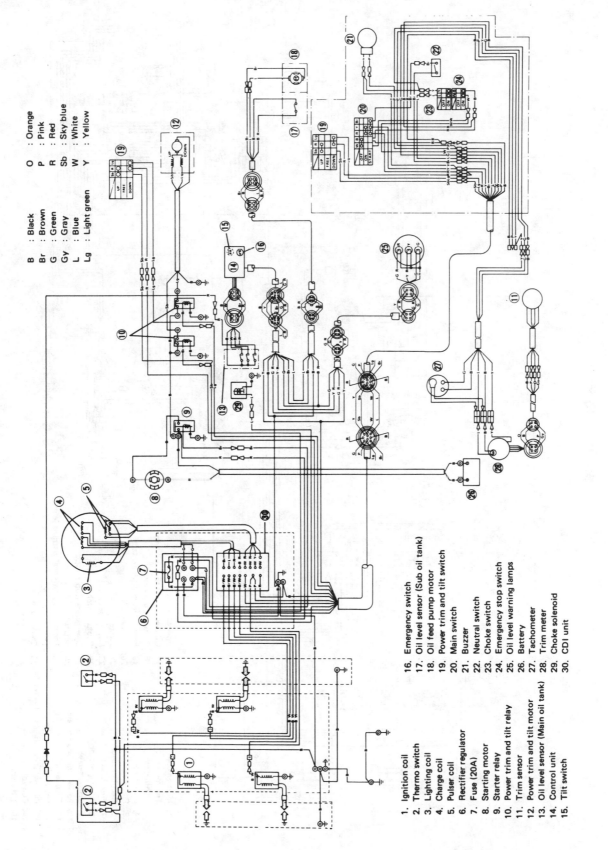

Color code:

B : Black
Br : Brown
G : Green
Gy : Gray
L : Blue
Lg : Light green

O : Orange
P : Pink
R : Red
Sb : Sky blue
W : White
Y : Yellow

1. Ignition coil
2. Thermo switch
3. Lighting coil
4. Charge coil
5. Pulser coil
6. Rectifier regulator
7. Fuse (20A)
8. Starting motor
9. Starter relay
10. Power trim and tilt relay
11. Trim sensor
12. Power trim and tilt motor
13. Oil level sensor (Main oil tank)
14. Control unit
15. Tilt switch

16. Emergency switch
17. Oil level sensor (Sub oil tank)
18. Oil feed pump motor
19. Power trim and tilt switch
20. Main switch
21. Buzzer
22. Neutral switch
23. Choke switch
24. Emergency stop switch
25. Oil level warning lamps
26. Battery
27. Tachometer
28. Trim meter
29. Choke solenoid
30. CDI unit

7

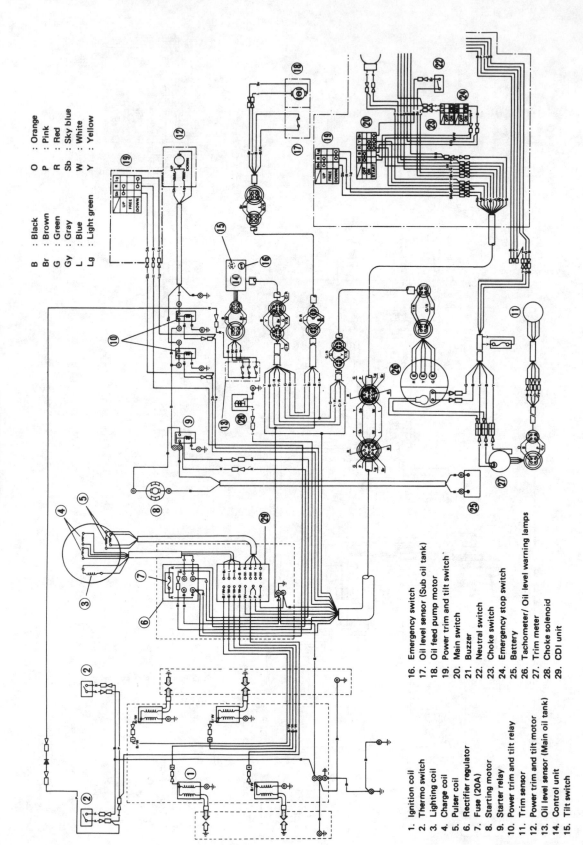

1986-ON 115 HP

B : Black
Br : Brown
G : Green
Gy : Gray
L : Blue
Lg : Light green

O : Orange
P : Pink
R : Red
Sb : Sky blue
W : White
Y : Yellow

1. Ignition coil
2. Thermo switch
3. Lighting coil
4. Charge coil
5. Pulser coil
6. Rectifier regulator
7. Fuse (20A)
8. Starting motor
9. Starter relay
10. Power trim and tilt relay
11. Trim sensor
12. Power trim and tilt motor
13. Oil level sensor (Main oil tank)
14. Control unit
15. Tilt switch
16. Emergency switch
17. Oil level sensor (Sub oil tank)
18. Oil feed pump motor
19. Power trim and tilt switch
20. Main switch
21. Buzzer
22. Neutral switch
23. Choke switch
24. Emergency stop switch
25. Battery
26. Tachometer/ Oil level warning lamps
27. Trim meter
28. Choke solenoid
29. CDI unit

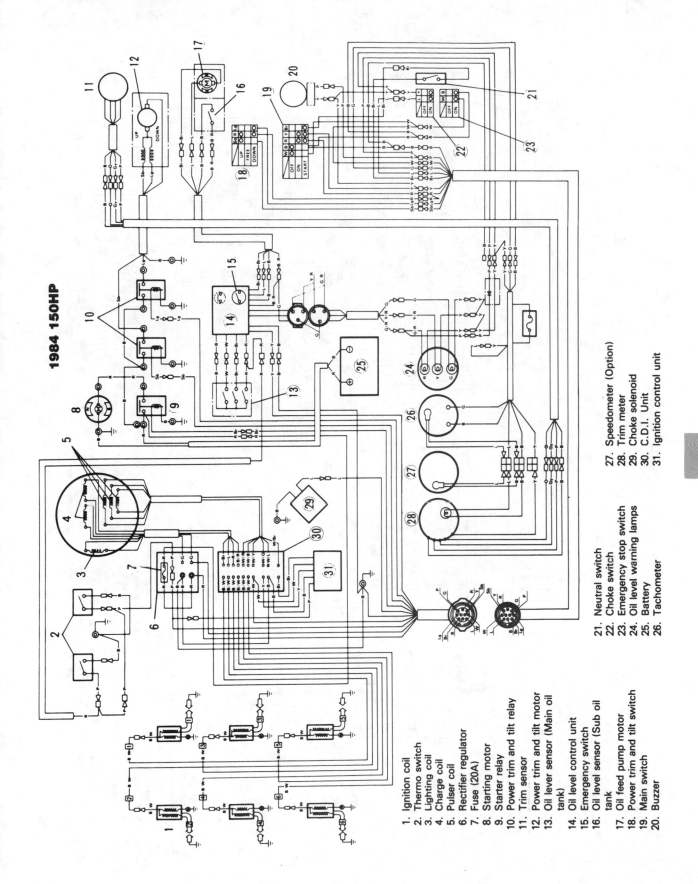

1984 150HP

1. Ignition coil
2. Thermo switch
3. Lighting coil
4. Charge coil
5. Pulser coil
6. Rectifier regulator
7. Fuse (20A)
8. Starting motor
9. Starter relay
10. Power trim and tilt relay
11. Trim sensor
12. Power trim and tilt motor
13. Oil lever sensor (Main oil tank)
14. Oil level control unit
15. Emergency switch
16. Oil level sensor (Sub oil tank)
17. Oil feed pump motor
18. Power trim and tilt switch
19. Main switch
20. Buzzer
21. Neutral switch
22. Choke switch
23. Emergency stop switch
24. Oil level warning lamps
25. Battery
26. Tachometer
27. Speedometer (Option)
28. Trim meter
29. Choke solenoid
30. C.D.I. Unit
31. Ignition control unit

7

1985-ON 150HP

B : Black   O : Orange
Br : Brown   P : Pink
G : Green   R : Red
Gy : Gray   Sb : Sky blue
L : Blue   W : White
Lg : Light green Y : Yellow

1. Ignition coil
2. Thermo switch
3. Lighting coil
4. Charge coil
5. Pulser coil
6. Rectifier regulator
7. Fuse (20A)
8. Starting motor
9. Starter relay
10. Power trim and tilt relay
11. Trim sensor
12. Power trim and tilt motor
13. Oil level sensor (Main oil tank)
14. Control unit
15. Tilt switch
16. Emergency switch
17. Oil level sensor (Sub oil tank)
18. Oil feed pump motor
19. Power trim and tilt switch
20. Main switch
21. Buzzer
22. Neutral switch
23. Choke switch
24. Emergency stop switch
25. Oil level warning lamps
26. Battery
27. Tachometer
28. Trim meter
29. Choke solenoid
30. CDI unit
31. Control unit

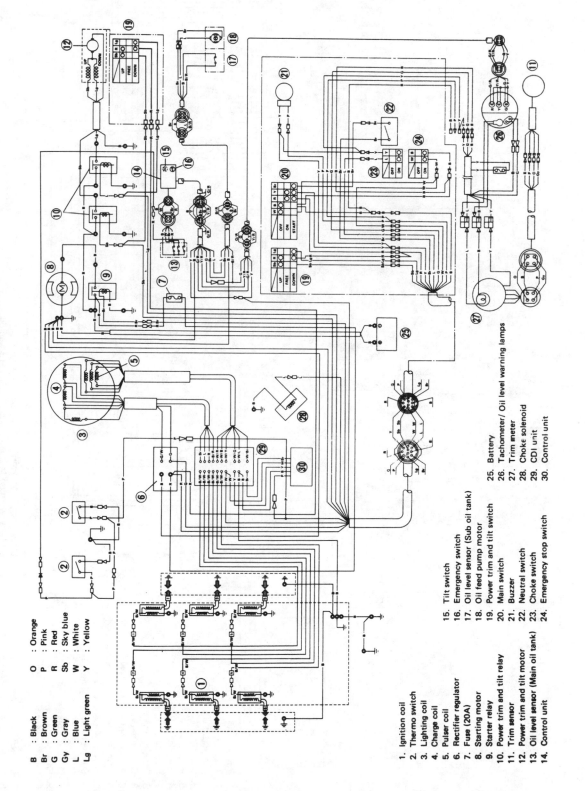

1986-ON 150/175/200 HP

B : Black
Br : Brown
G : Green
Gy : Gray
L : Blue
Lg : Light green

O : Orange
P : Pink
R : Red
Sb : Sky blue
W : White
Y : Yellow

1. Ignition coil
2. Thermo switch
3. Lighting coil
4. Charge coil
5. Pulser coil
6. Rectifier regulator
7. Fuse (20A)
8. Starting motor
9. Starter relay
10. Power trim and tilt relay
11. Trim sensor
12. Power trim and tilt motor
13. Oil level sensor (Main oil tank)
14. Control unit

15. Tilt switch
16. Emergency switch
17. Oil level sensor (Sub oil tank)
18. Oil feed pump motor
19. Power trim and tilt switch
20. Main switch
21. Buzzer
22. Neutral switch
23. Choke switch
24. Emergency stop switch

25. Battery
26. Tachometer / Oil level warning lamps
27. Trim meter
28. Choke solenoid
29. CDI unit
30. Control unit

7

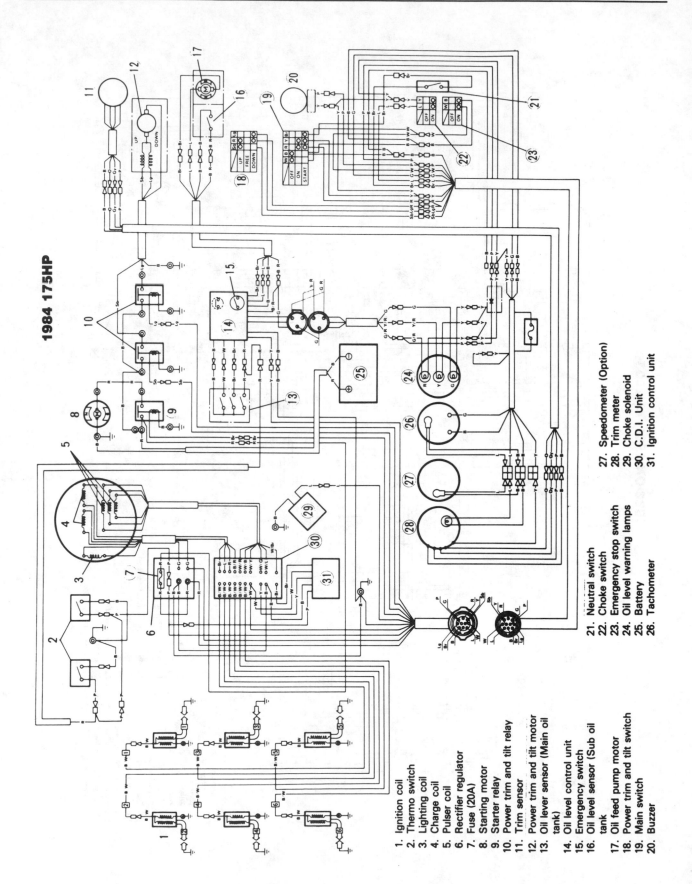

1984 175HP

1. Ignition coil
2. Thermo switch
3. Lighting coil
4. Charge coil
5. Pulser coil
6. Rectifier regulator
7. Fuse (20A)
8. Starting motor
9. Starter relay
10. Power trim and tilt relay
11. Trim sensor
12. Power trim and tilt motor
13. Oil lever sensor (Main oil tank)
14. Oil level control unit
15. Emergency switch
16. Oil level sensor (Sub oil tank)
17. Oil feed pump motor
18. Power trim and tilt switch
19. Main switch
20. Buzzer

21. Neutral switch
22. Choke switch
23. Emergency stop switch
24. Oil level warning lamps
25. Battery
26. Tachometer
27. Speedometer (Option)
28. Trim meter
29. Choke solenoid
30. C.D.I. Unit
31. Ignition control unit

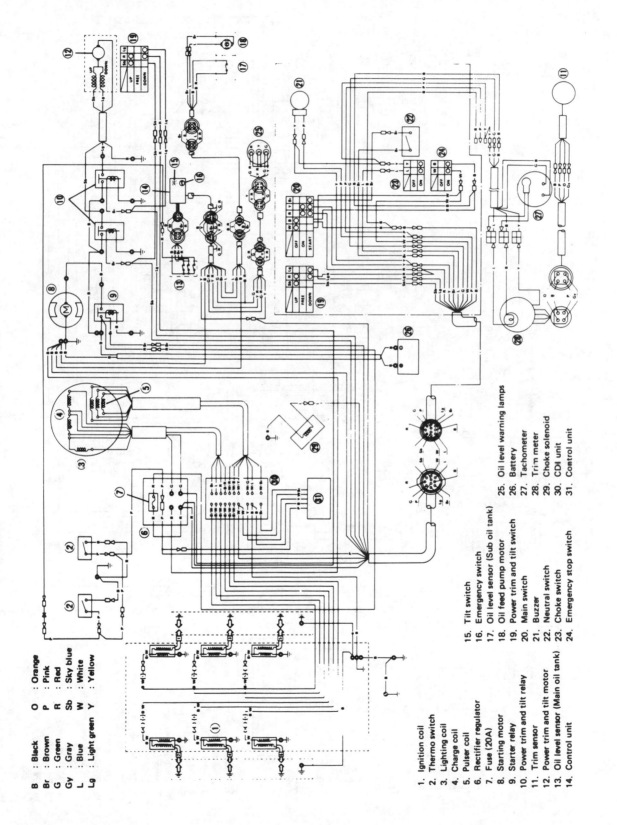

1985 175 HP

B : Black   O : Orange
Br : Brown   P : Pink
G : Green   R : Red
Gy : Gray   Sb : Sky blue
L : Blue   W : White
Lg : Light green   Y : Yellow

1. Ignition coil
2. Thermo switch
3. Lighting coil
4. Charge coil
5. Pulser coil
6. Rectifier regulator
7. Fuse (20A)
8. Starting motor
9. Starter relay
10. Power trim and tilt relay
11. Trim sensor
12. Power trim and tilt motor
13. Oil level sensor (Main oil tank)
14. Control unit
15. Tilt switch
16. Emergency switch
17. Oil level sensor (Sub oil tank)
18. Oil feed pump motor
19. Power trim and tilt switch
20. Main switch
21. Buzzer
22. Neutral switch
23. Choke switch
24. Emergency stop switch
25. Oil level warning lamps
26. Battery
27. Tachometer
28. Trim meter
29. Choke solenoid
30. CDI unit
31. Control unit

7

1984 200HP

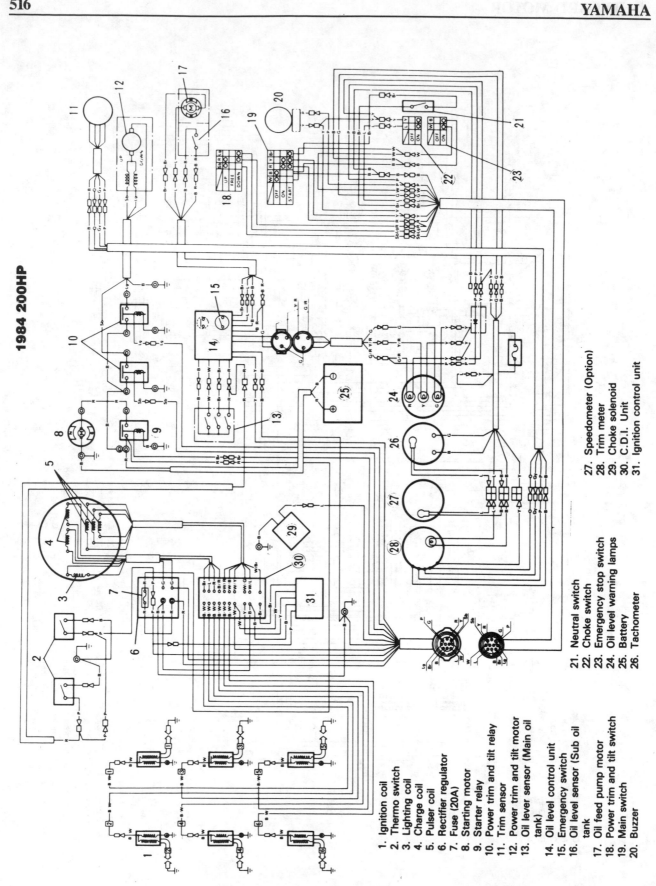

1. Ignition coil
2. Thermo switch
3. Lighting coil
4. Charge coil
5. Pulser coil
6. Rectifier regulator
7. Fuse (20A)
8. Starting motor
9. Starter relay
10. Power trim and tilt relay
11. Trim sensor
12. Power trim and tilt motor
13. Oil lever sensor (Main oil tank)
14. Oil level control unit
15. Emergency switch
16. Oil level sensor (Sub oil tank)
17. Oil feed pump motor
18. Power trim and tilt switch
19. Main switch
20. Buzzer
21. Neutral switch
22. Choke switch
23. Emergency stop switch
24. Oil level warning lamps
25. Battery
26. Tachometer
27. Speedometer (Option)
28. Trim meter
29. Choke solenoid
30. C.D.I. Unit
31. Ignition control unit

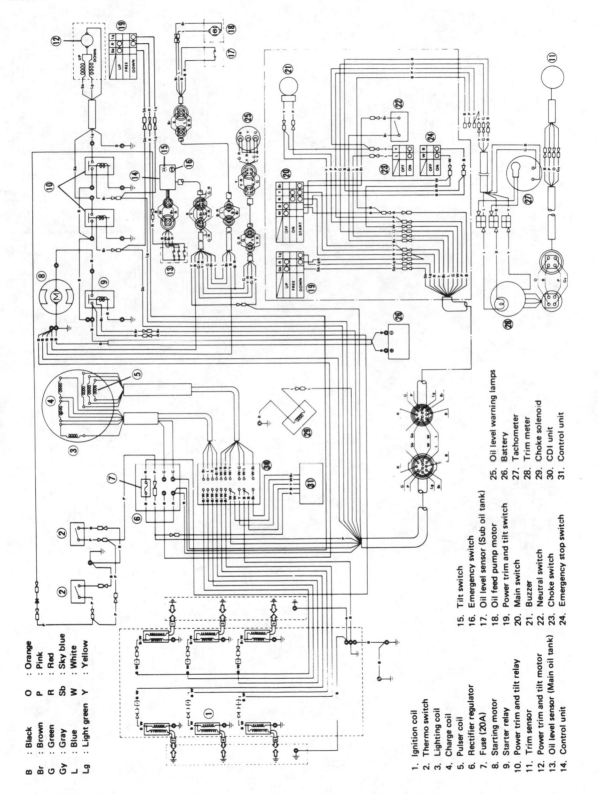

1985 200 HP

B : Black
Br : Brown
G : Green
Gy : Gray
L : Blue
Lg : Light green

O : Orange
P : Pink
R : Red
Sb : Sky blue
W : White
Y : Yellow

1. Ignition coil
2. Thermo switch
3. Lighting coil
4. Charge coil
5. Pulser coil
6. Rectifier regulator
7. Fuse (20A)
8. Starting motor
9. Starter relay
10. Power trim and tilt relay
11. Trim sensor
12. Power trim and tilt motor
13. Oil level sensor (Main oil tank)
14. Control unit

15. Tilt switch
16. Emergency switch
17. Oil level sensor (Sub oil tank)
18. Oil feed pump motor
19. Power trim and tilt switch
20. Main switch
21. Buzzer
22. Neutral switch
23. Choke switch
24. Emergency stop switch

25. Oil level warning lamps
26. Battery
27. Tachometer
28. Trim meter
29. Choke solenoid
30. CDI unit
31. Control unit

7

1984 220HP

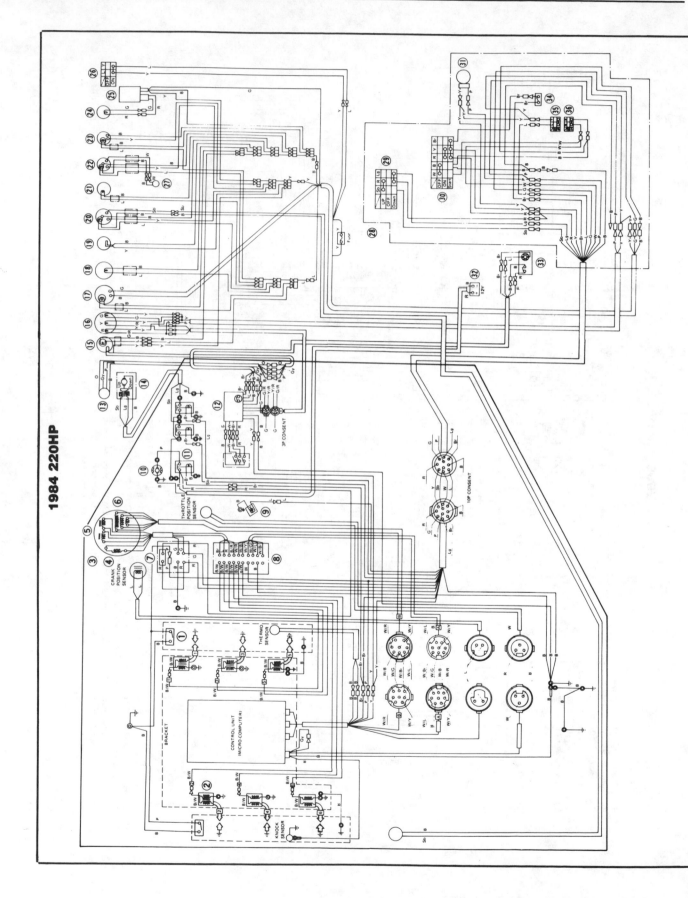

Equipment

1. Thermo switch	13. Trim sensor	25. Charge warning unit
2. Ignition coil	14. Trim & tilt motor	26. Lamp switch
3. CDI magneto	15. Trim gauge	27. Fuel sensor
4. Lighting coil	16. Oil level lamp	28. Remote control box
5. Charge coil	17. Tachometer	29. Trim & tilt switch
6. Pulser coil	18. Speed meter	30. Main switch
7. Rectifier regulator	19. Hourmeter	31. Buzzer
8. CDI unit	20. Water temp. gauge	32. Battery
9. Choke solenoid	21. Water pressure meter	33. Sub oil tank
10. Starting motor	22. Fuel gauge	34. Neutral switch
11. Starter relay	23. Voltmeter	35. Choke switch
12. Control unit	24. Charge lamp	36. Emergency stop switch
(Oil injection)		

7

Wiring color

B : Black	L : Blue	R : Red	W/B : White/Black
P : Pink	G : Green	W : White	W/Y : White/Yellow
B/W : Black/White	Br : Brown	W/R : White/Red	W/G : White/Green
Lg : Light green	Gy : Grey	O : Orange	Y : Yellow
Sb : Sky blue			

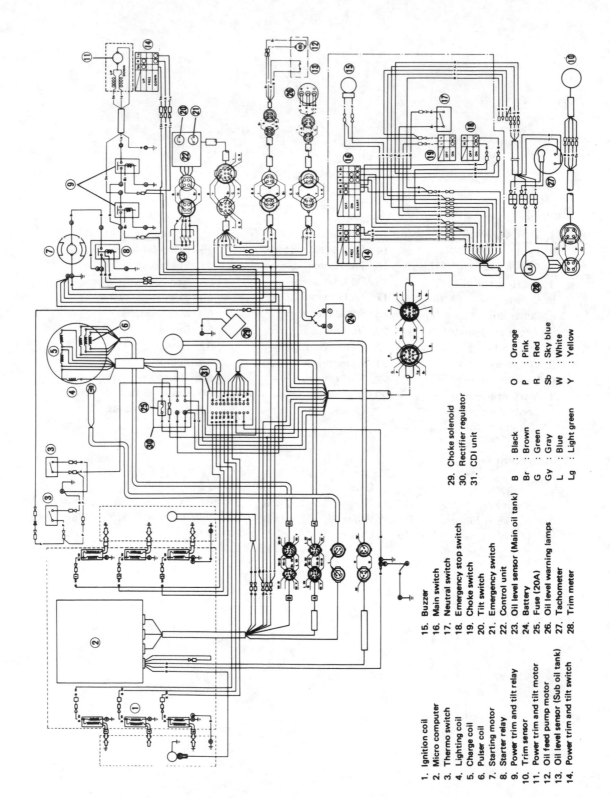

1985 220 HP V6 SPECIAL

1. Ignition coil
2. Micro computer
3. Thermo switch
4. Lighting coil
5. Charge coil
6. Pulser coil
7. Starting motor
8. Starter relay
9. Power trim and tilt relay
10. Trim sensor
11. Power trim and tilt motor
12. Oil feed pump motor
13. Oil level sensor (Sub oil tank)
14. Power trim and tilt switch

15. Buzzer
16. Main switch
17. Neutral switch
18. Emergency stop switch
19. Choke switch
20. Tilt switch
21. Emergency switch
22. Control unit
23. Oil level sensor (Main oil tank)
24. Battery
25. Fuse (20A)
26. Oil level warning lamps
27. Tachometer
28. Trim meter

29. Choke solenoid
30. Rectifier regulator
31. CDI unit

B   : Black
Br : Brown
G   : Green
Gy : Gray
L   : Blue
Lg : Light green

O   : Orange
P   : Pink
R   : Red
Sb : Sky blue
W   : White
Y   : Yellow

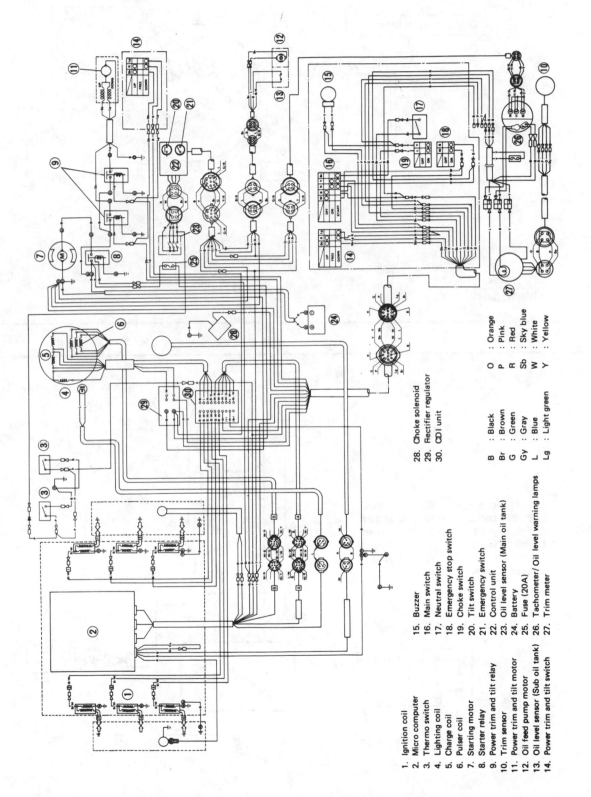

1986 220 HP V6 SPECIAL

1. Ignition coil
2. Micro computer
3. Thermo switch
4. Lighting coil
5. Charge coil
6. Pulser coil
7. Starting motor
8. Starter relay
9. Power trim and tilt relay
10. Trim sensor
11. Power trim and tilt motor
12. Oil feed pump motor
13. Oil level sensor (Sub oil tank)
14. Power trim and tilt switch

15. Buzzer
16. Main switch
17. Neutral switch
18. Emergency stop switch
19. Choke switch
20. Tilt switch
21. Emergency switch
22. Control unit
23. Oil level sensor (Main oil tank)
24. Battery
25. Fuse (20A)
26. Tachometer/ Oil level warning lamps
27. Trim meter

28. Choke solenoid
29. Rectifier regulator
30. CDI unit

B : Black	O : Orange	
Br : Brown	P : Pink	
G : Green	R : Red	
Gy : Gray	Sb : Sky blue	
L : Blue	W : White	
Lg : Light green	Y : Yellow	

7

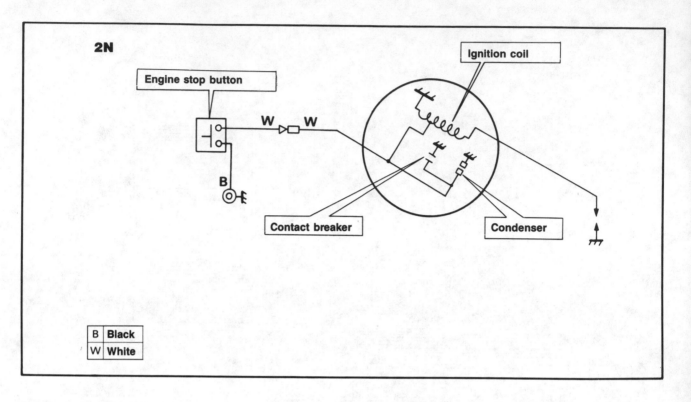

2N

Engine stop button

Ignition coil

Contact breaker

Condenser

B	Black
W	White

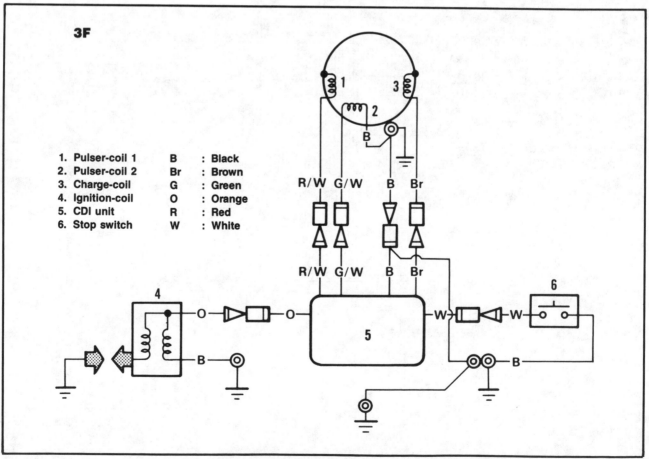

3F

1. Pulser-coil 1
2. Pulser-coil 2
3. Charge-coil
4. Ignition-coil
5. CDI unit
6. Stop switch

B : Black
Br : Brown
G : Green
O : Orange
R : Red
W : White

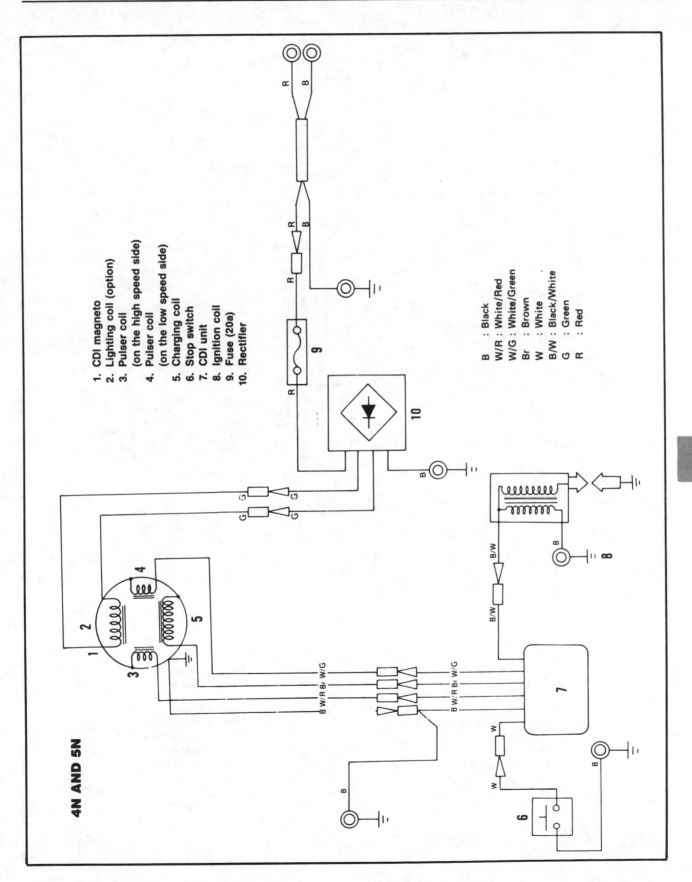

4N AND 5N

1. CDI magneto
2. Lighting coil (option)
3. Pulser coil (on the high speed side)
4. Pulser coil (on the low speed side)
5. Charging coil
6. Stop switch
7. CDI unit
8. Ignition coil
9. Fuse (20a)
10. Rectifier

B : Black
W/R : White/Red
W/G : White/Green
Br : Brown
W : White
B/W : Black/White
G : Green
R : Red

25G

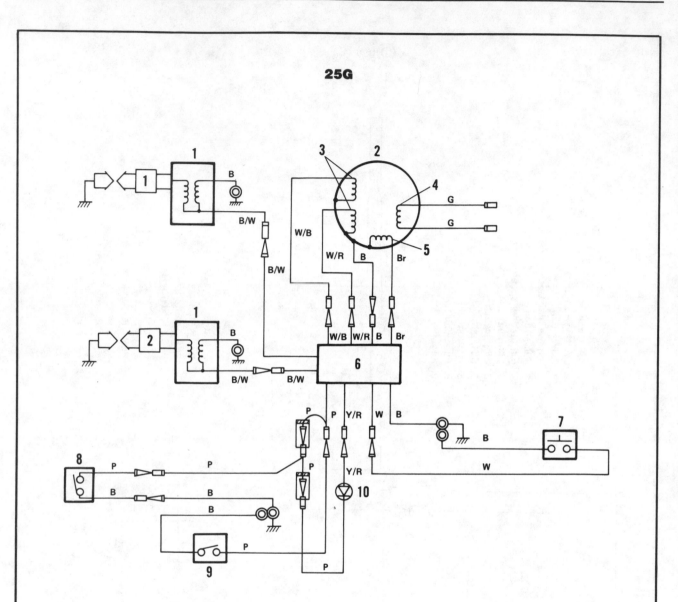

1. Ignition coil
2. C.D.I. magneto
3. Pulser coil
4. Lighting coil
5. Charge coil
6. C.D.I. unit
7. Emergency stop switch
8. Thermo switch
9. Oil level sensor
10. Warning lamp

B	: Black
Br	: Brown
G	: Green
P	: Pink
W	: White
B/W	: Black/white
W/B	: White/black
Y/R	: Yellow/red
W/R	: White/red

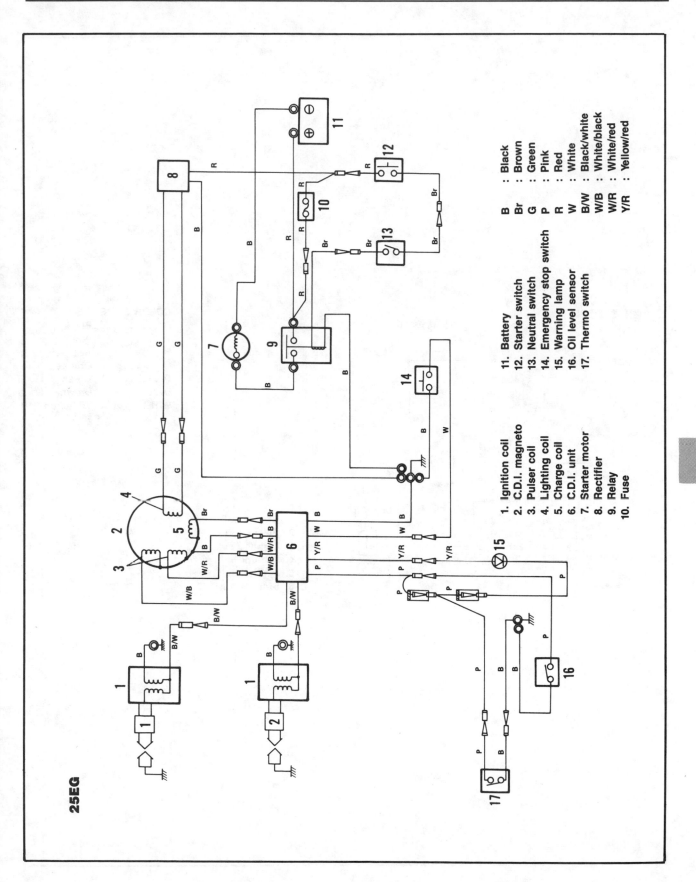

1. Ignition coil
2. C.D.I. magneto
3. Pulser coil
4. Lighting coil
5. Charge coil
6. C.D.I. unit
7. Starter motor
8. Rectifier
9. Relay
10. Fuse

11. Battery
12. Starter switch
13. Neutral switch
14. Emergency stop switch
15. Warning lamp
16. Oil level sensor
17. Thermo switch

B   : Black
Br : Brown
G   : Green
P   : Pink
R   : Red
W   : White
B/W : Black/white
W/B : White/black
W/R : White/red
Y/R : Yellow/red

25EG

7

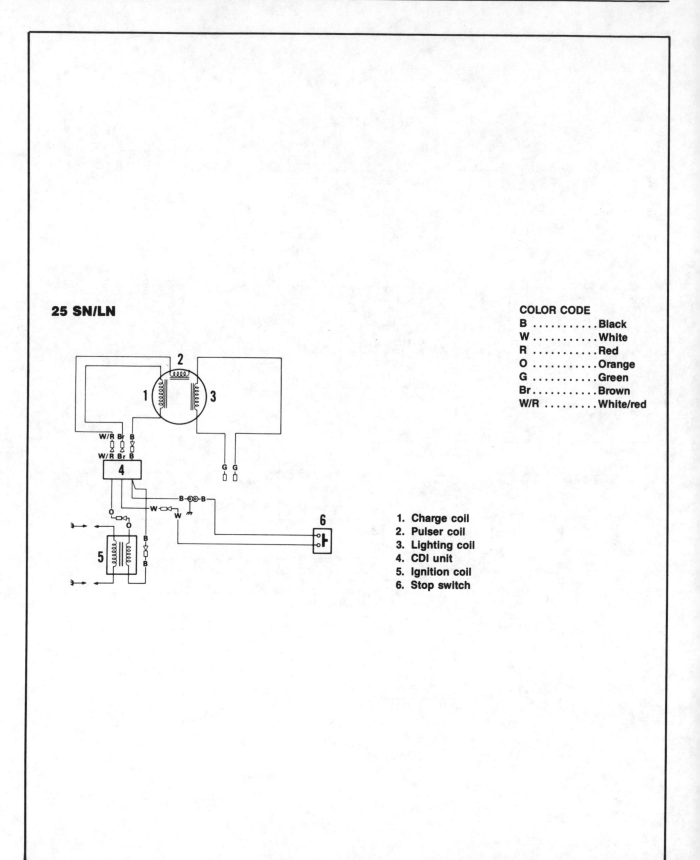

25 SN/LN

COLOR CODE
B . . . . Black
W . . . . White
R . . . . Red
O . . . . Orange
G . . . . Green
Br . . . . Brown
W/R . . . . White/red

1. Charge coil
2. Pulser coil
3. Lighting coil
4. CDI unit
5. Ignition coil
6. Stop switch

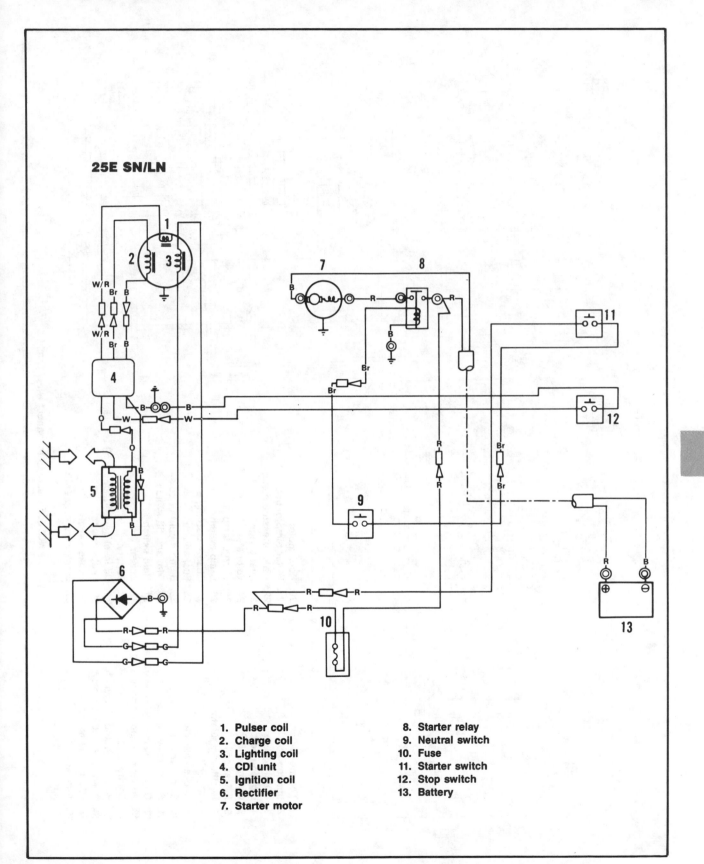

25E SN/LN

1. Pulser coil
2. Charge coil
3. Lighting coil
4. CDI unit
5. Ignition coil
6. Rectifier
7. Starter motor
8. Starter relay
9. Neutral switch
10. Fuse
11. Starter switch
12. Stop switch
13. Battery

7

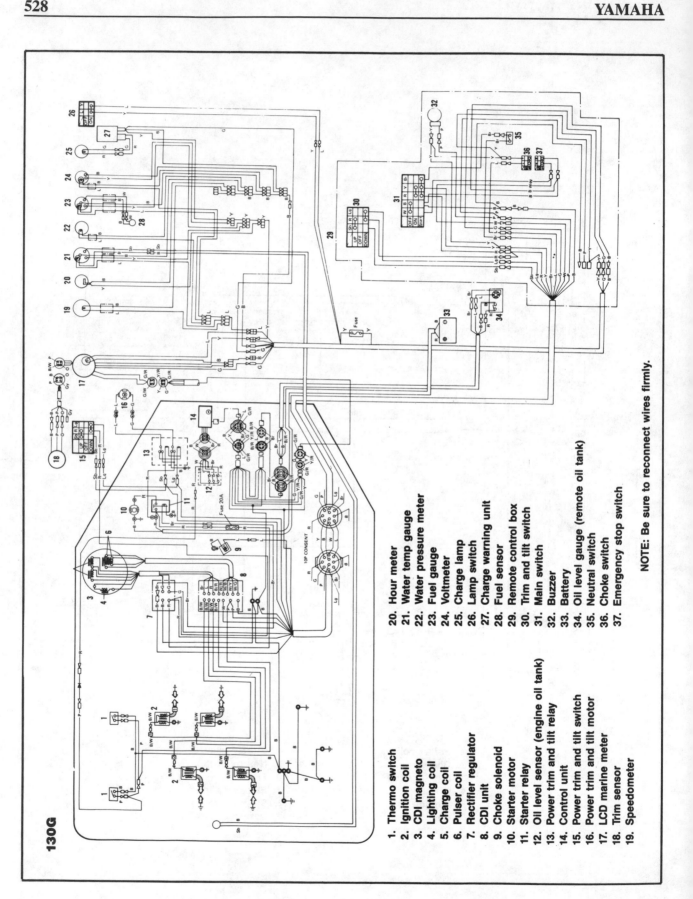

130G

1. Thermo switch
2. Ignition coil
3. CDI magneto
4. Lighting coil
5. Charge coil
6. Pulser coil
7. Rectifier regulator
8. CDI unit
9. Choke solenoid
10. Starter motor
11. Starter relay
12. Oil level sensor (engine oil tank)
13. Power trim and tilt relay
14. Control unit
15. Power trim and tilt switch
16. Power trim and tilt motor
17. LCD marine meter
18. Trim sensor
19. Speedometer

20. Hour meter
21. Water temp gauge
22. Water pressure meter
23. Fuel gauge
24. Voltmeter
25. Charge lamp
26. Lamp switch
27. Charge warning unit
28. Fuel sensor
29. Remote control box
30. Trim and tilt switch
31. Main switch
32. Buzzer
33. Battery
34. Oil level gauge (remote oil tank)
35. Neutral switch
36. Choke switch
37. Emergency stop switch

NOTE: Be sure to reconnect wires firmly.

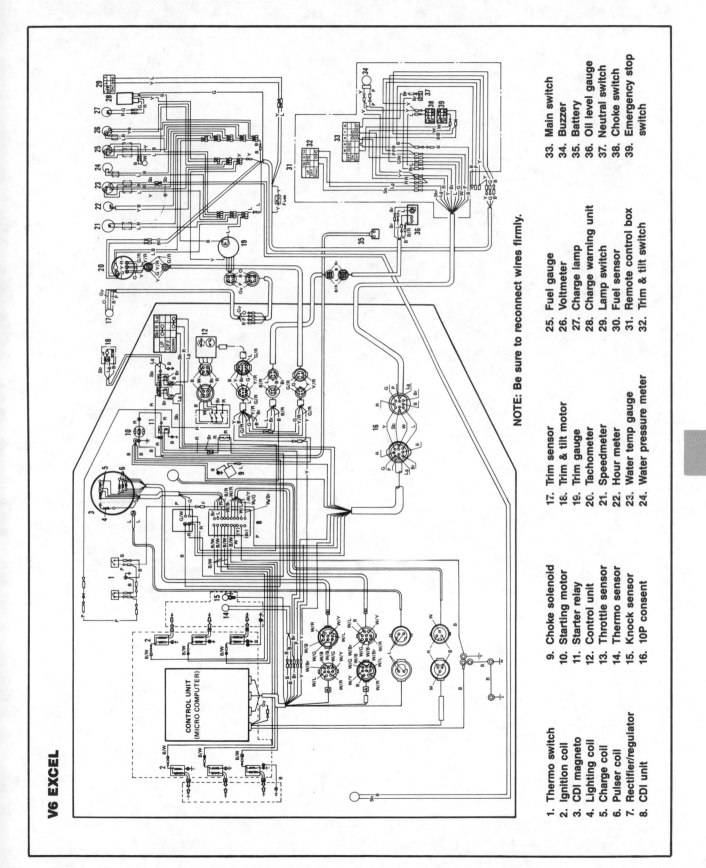

V6 EXCEL

CONTROL UNIT (MICRO COMPUTER)

NOTE: Be sure to reconnect wires firmly.

1. Thermo switch
2. Ignition coil
3. CDI magneto
4. Lighting coil
5. Charge coil
6. Pulser coil
7. Rectifier/regulator
8. CDI unit
9. Choke solenoid
10. Starting motor
11. Starter relay
12. Control unit
13. Throttle sensor
14. Thermo sensor
15. Knock sensor
16. 10P consent
17. Trim sensor
18. Trim & tilt motor
19. Trim gauge
20. Tachometer
21. Speedmeter
22. Hour meter
23. Water temp gauge
24. Water pressure meter
25. Fuel gauge
26. Voltmeter
27. Charge lamp
28. Charge warning unit
29. Lamp switch
30. Fuel sensor
31. Remote control box
32. Trim & tilt switch
33. Main switch
34. Buzzer
35. Battery
36. Oil level gauge
37. Neutral switch
38. Choke switch
39. Emergency stop switch

7

INBOARD/OUTDRIVE

MERCRUISER

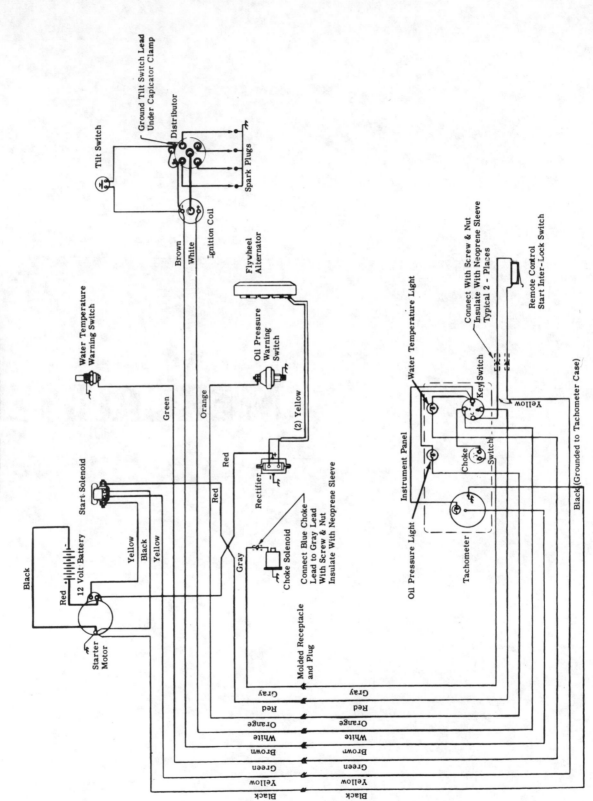

ENGINE—MERCRUISER 60

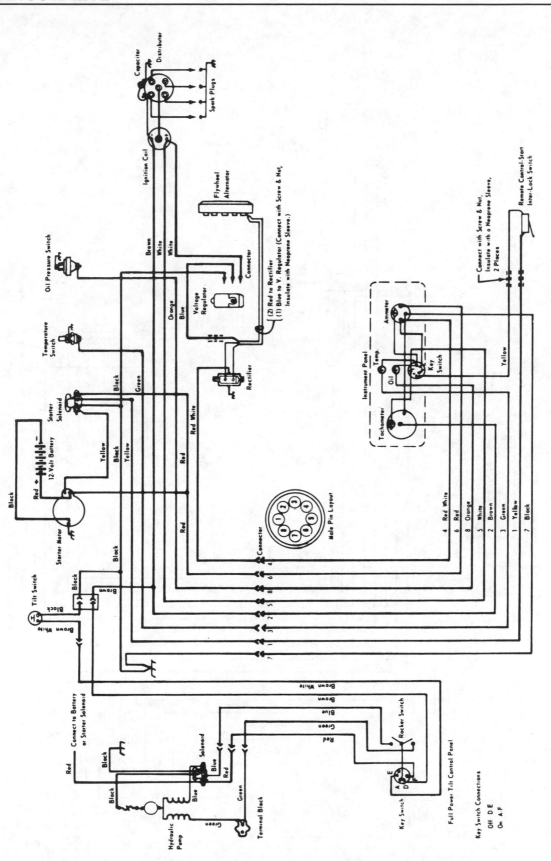

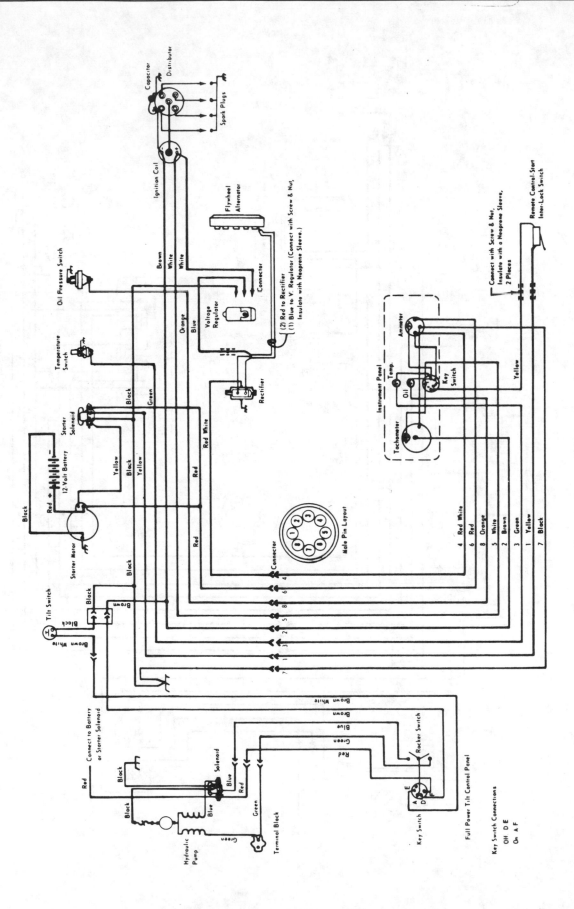

ENGINE—MERCRUISER 90

ENGINE—MERCRUISER 110 AND 140 (6-CYL.) WITH INDICATOR LIGHT

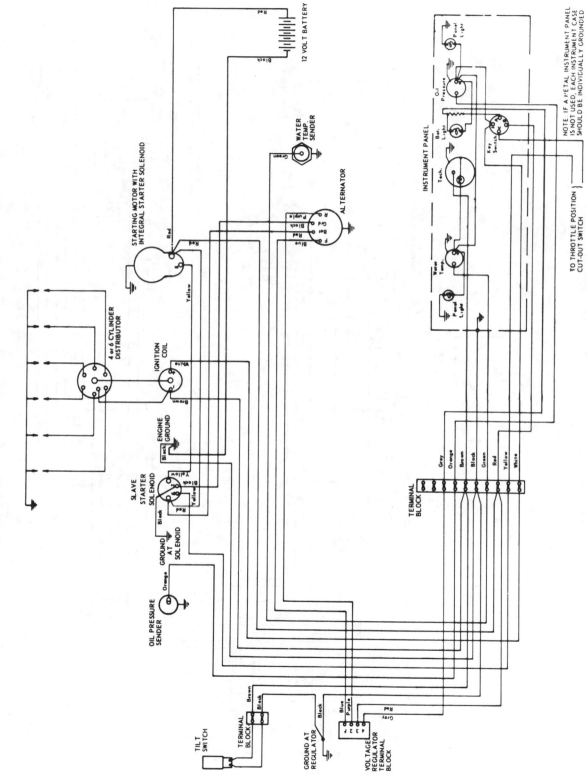

ENGINE—MERCRUISER 110, 120, 140 (4-CYL.) AND 150 WITH AMMETER AND ELECTROMECHANICAL REGULATOR

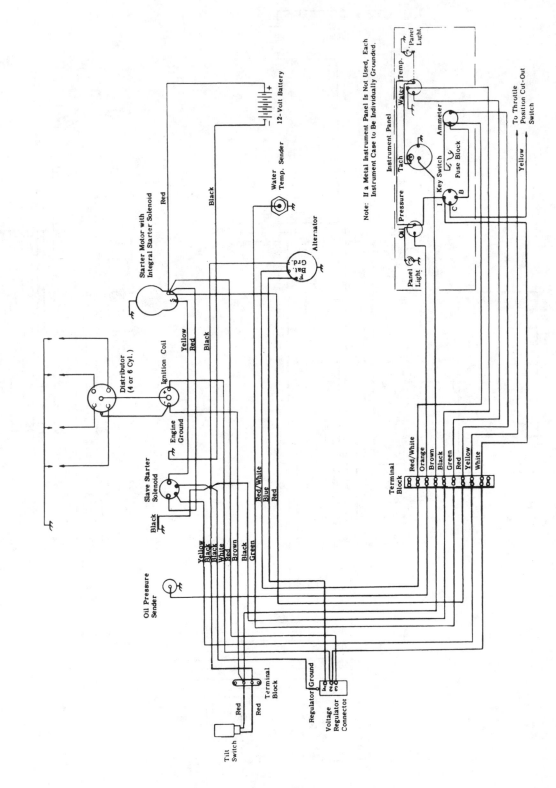

ENGINE—MERCRUISER 110, 120 AND 150 WITH AMMETER AND TRANSISTOR REGULATOR

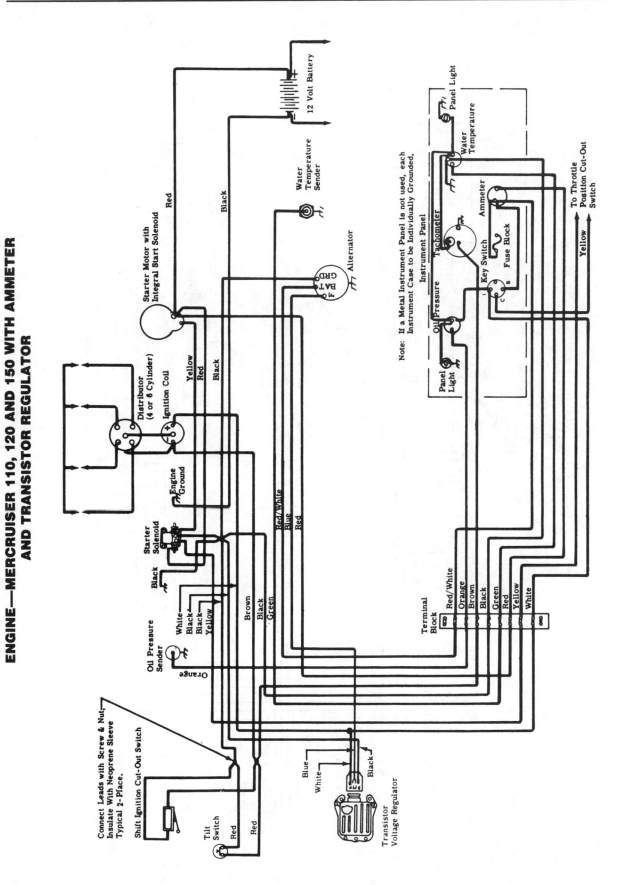

ENGINE—MERCRUISER 110, 140 (4-CYL.) AND 150 WITH AMMETER, TRANSISTOR REGULATOR AND BALLAST RESISTORS

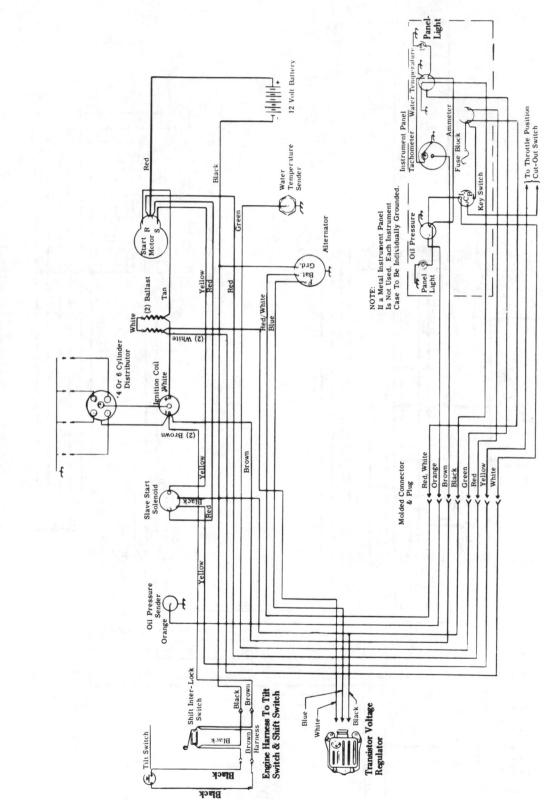

NOTE:
If a Metal Instrument Panel
Is Not Used. Each Instrument
Case To Be Individually Grounded.

ENGINE—MERCRUISER 120, 140 and 165 WITH CIRCUIT BREAKER AND VACUUM GAUGE

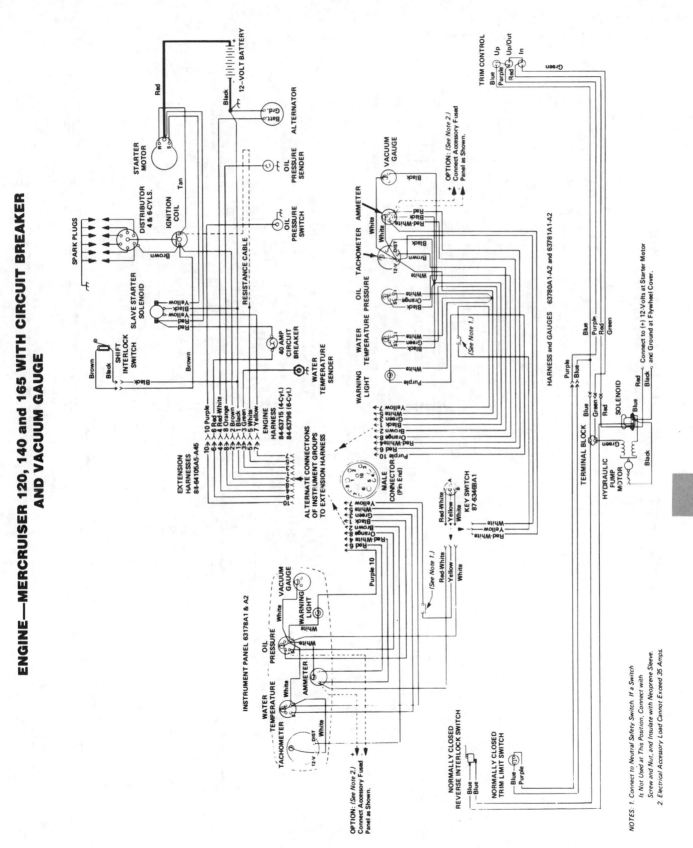

NOTES: 1. Connect to Neutral Safety Switch. If a Switch Is Not Used at This Position, Connect with Screw and Nut, and Insulate with Neoprene Sleeve.

2. Electrical Accessory Load Cannot Exceed 35 Amps.

8

ENGINE—MERCRUISER 120 (SERIAL NO. 3770650 AND UP), 140 (3771645 AND UP) AND 165 (3774865 AND UP)

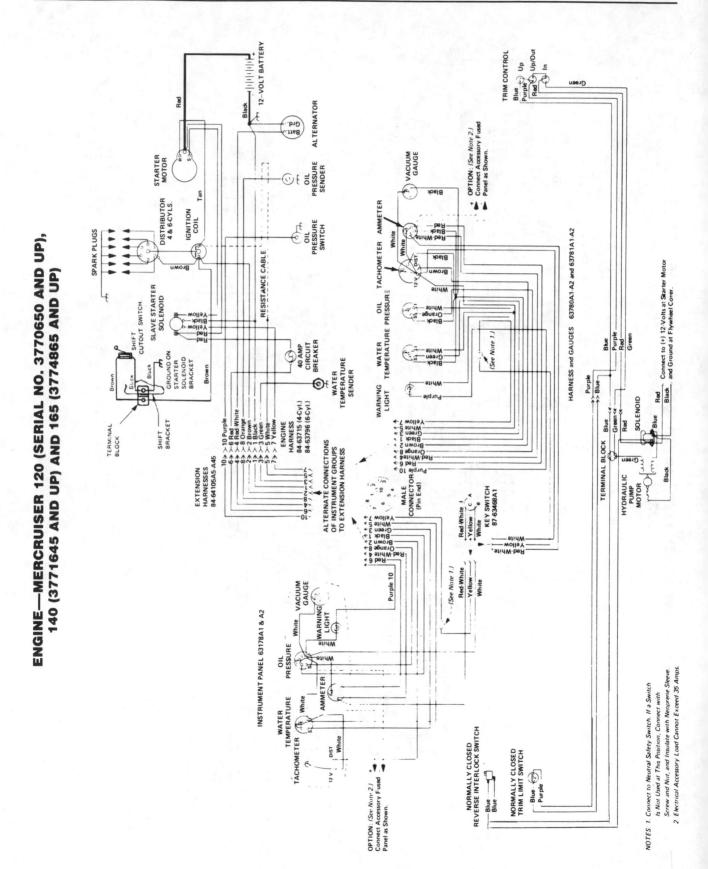

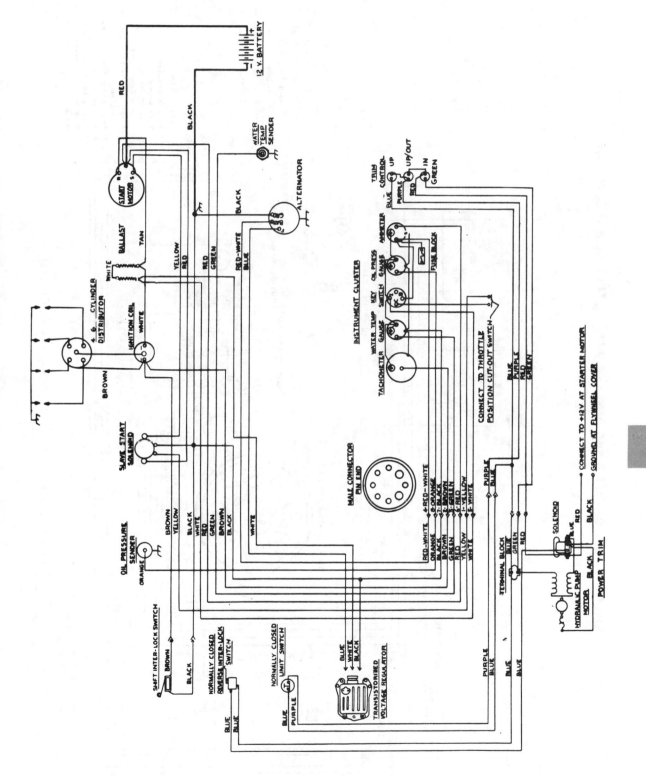

ENGINE—MERCRUISER 140 WITH AMMETER AND TRANSISTOR REGULATOR

8

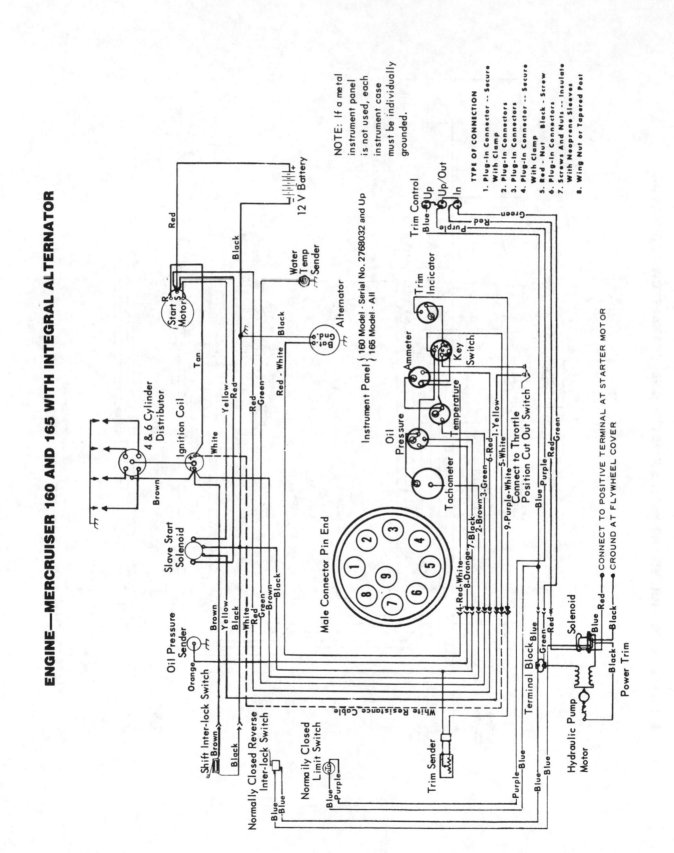

ENGINE—MERCRUISER 160 AND 165 WITH INTEGRAL ALTERNATOR

NOTE: If a metal instrument panel is not used, each instrument case must be individually grounded.

Instrument Panel { 160 Model - Serial No. 2768032 and Up
165 Model - All

TYPE OF CONNECTION
1. Plug-In Connector -- Secure With Clamp
2. Plug-In Connectors
3. Plug-In Connectors
4. Plug-In Connector -- Secure With Clamp
5. Red - Nut   Black - Screw
6. Plug-In Connectors
7. Screws And Nuts --- Insulate With Neoprene Sleeves
8. Wing Nut or Tapered Post

12 V Battery

Water Temp Sender

Start Motor

Alternator

Bat. Gnd.

4 & 6 Cylinder Distributor

Ignition Coil

Slave Start Solenoid

Oil Pressure Sender

Shift Inter-lock Switch

Inter-lock Switch

Normally Closed Reverse

Normally Closed Limit Switch

Trim Sender

White Resistance Cable

Male Connector Pin End

Trim Control

Trim Incicator

Ammeter

Key Switch

Oil Pressure

Temperature

Tachometer

Connect to Throttle Position Cut Out Switch

Terminal Block

Hydraulic Pump Motor

Solenoid

Power Trim

CONNECT TO POSITIVE TERMINAL AT STARTER MOTOR

GROUND AT FLYWHEEL COVER

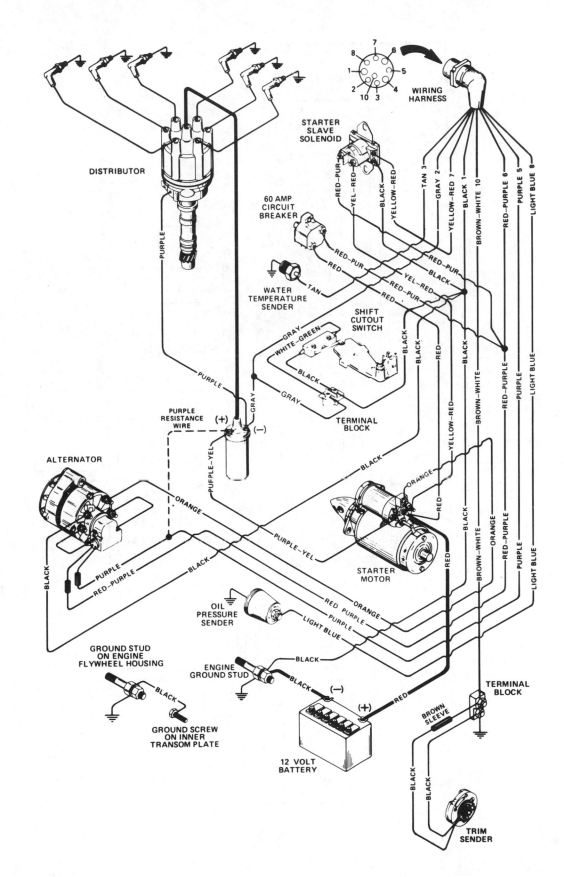

ENGINE—MERCRUISER 185 (V6)

7
8
6
1
5
2
4
10 3

WIRING HARNESS

DISTRIBUTOR

STARTER SLAVE SOLENOID

60 AMP CIRCUIT BREAKER

WATER TEMPERATURE SENDER

SHIFT CUTOUT SWITCH

TERMINAL BLOCK

PURPLE RESISTANCE WIRE

ALTERNATOR

STARTER MOTOR

OIL PRESSURE SENDER

GROUND STUD ON ENGINE FLYWHEEL HOUSING

GROUND SCREW ON INNER TRANSOM PLATE

ENGINE GROUND STUD

12 VOLT BATTERY

TERMINAL BLOCK

BROWN SLEEVE

TRIM SENDER

RED–PUR
YEL–RED
BLACK
YELLOW–RED
TAN 3
GRAY 2
YELLOW–RED 7
BLACK 1
BROWN–WHITE 10
RED–PURPLE 6
PURPLE 5
LIGHT BLUE 8

PURPLE
GRAY
GRAY
PURPLE–YEL
ORANGE
BLACK
PURPLE
RED
RED–PUR
RED
RED–PUR
YEL–RED
RED
WHITE–GREEN
BLACK
ORANGE
RED
RED
PURPLE
LIGHT BLUE
BLACK
BLACK
RED
RED
BLACK
BLACK
YELLOW–RED
BROWN–WHITE
RED–PURPLE
LIGHT BLUE
BLACK
ORANGE
RED–PURPLE
PURPLE
LIGHT BLUE
BLACK
(+)
(−)
(+)
(−)

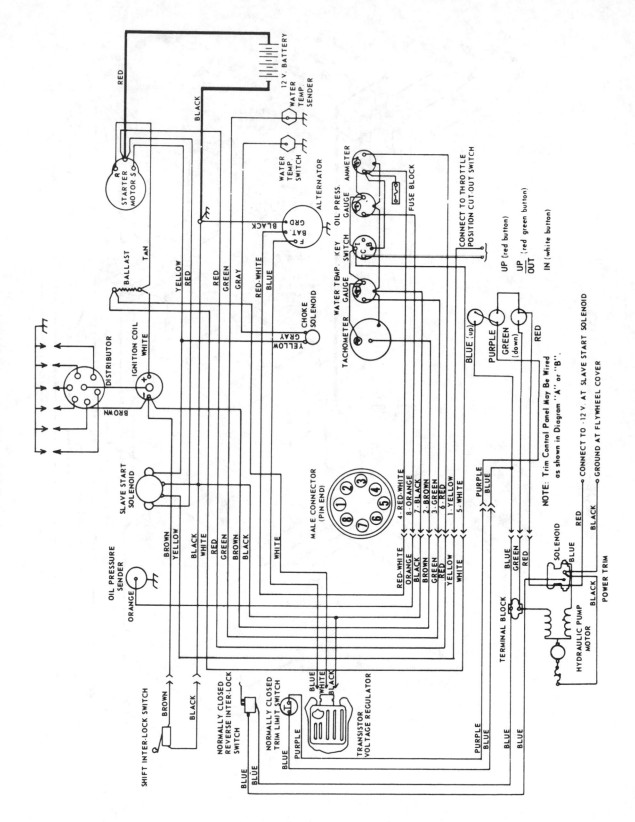

ENGINE—MERCRUISER 200

ENGINE—MERCRUISER 215-E

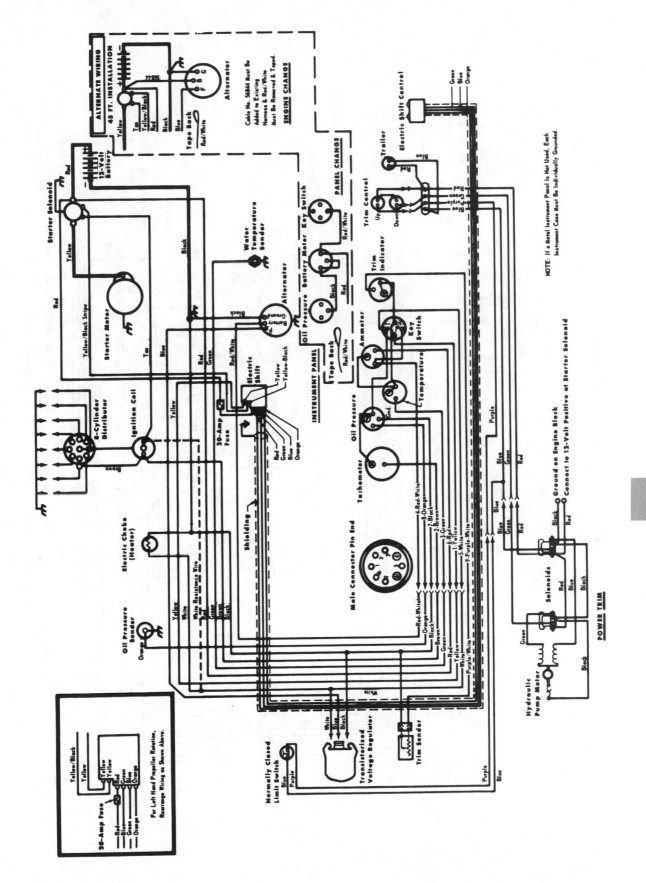

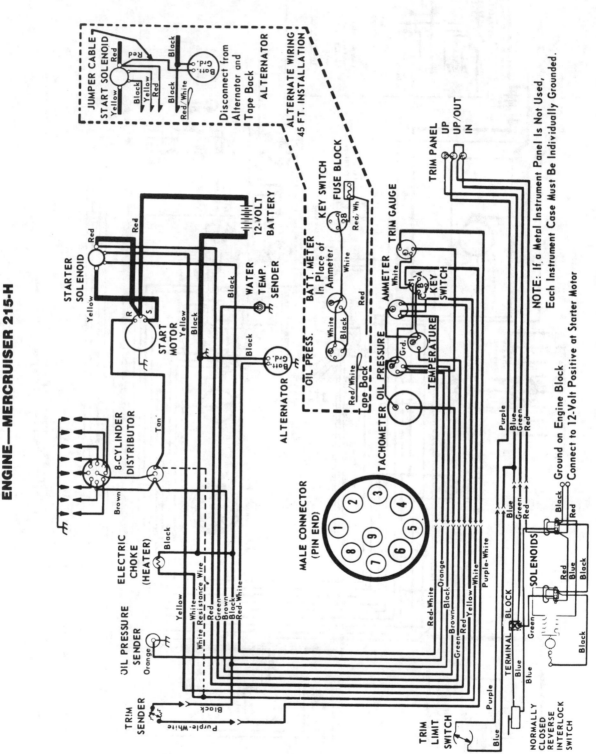

ENGINE—MERCRUISER 215-H

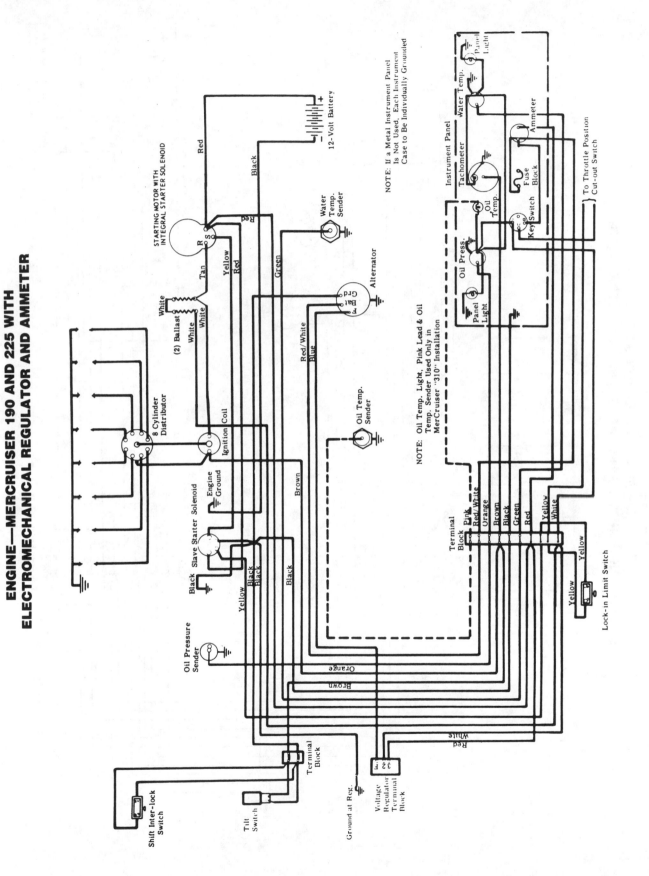

ENGINE—MERCRUISER 190 AND 225 WITH ELECTROMECHANICAL REGULATOR AND AMMETER

ENGINE—MERCRUISER 225 WITH ELECTROMECHANICAL REGULATOR AND INDICATOR LIGHT

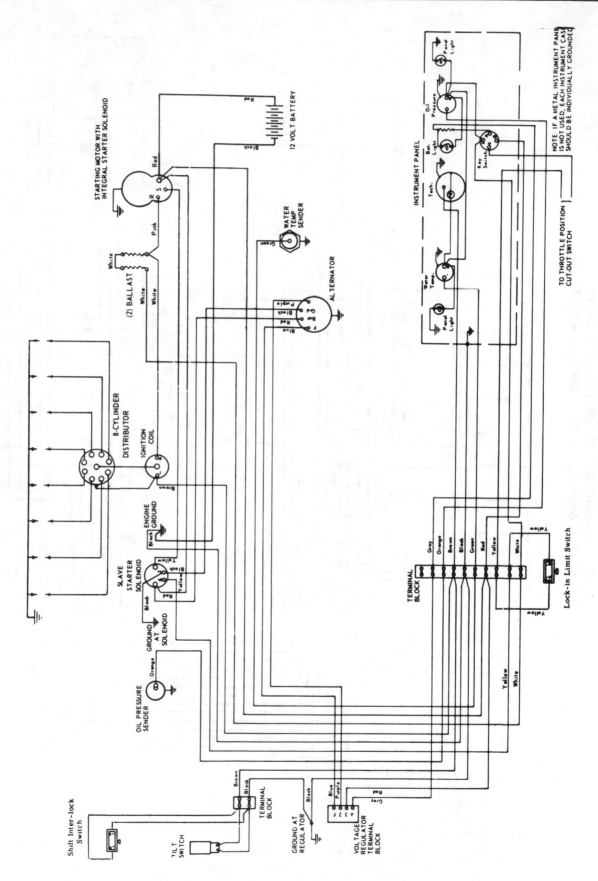

ENGINE—MERCRUISER 225 WITH TRANSISTOR REGULATOR

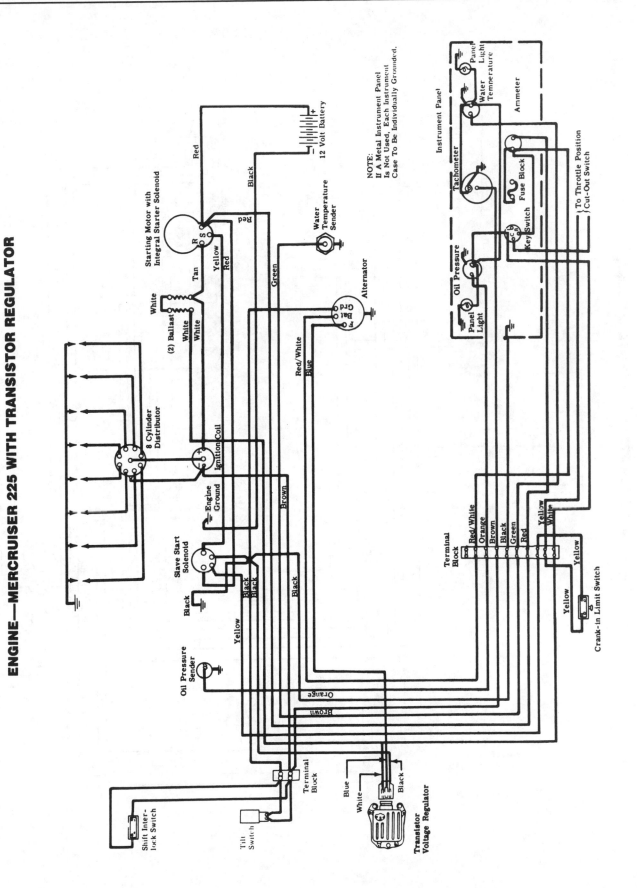

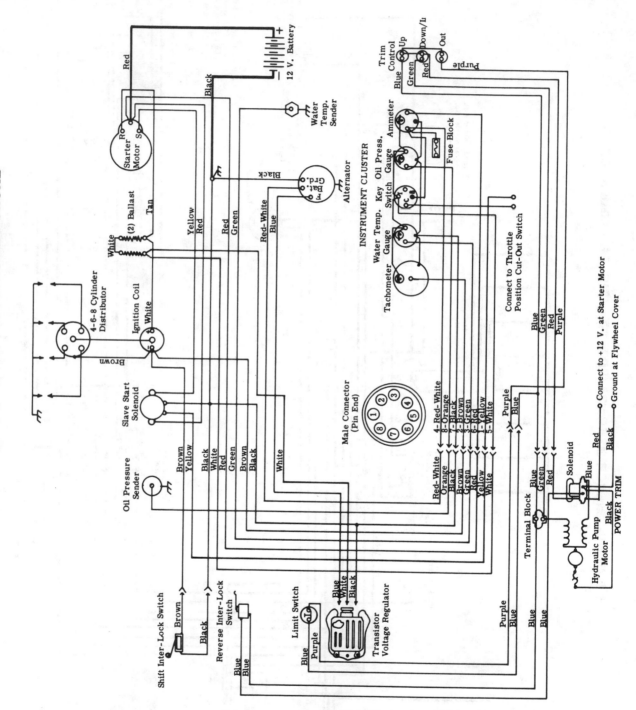

ENGINE—MERCRUISER 225 WITH ELECTRIC CHOKE

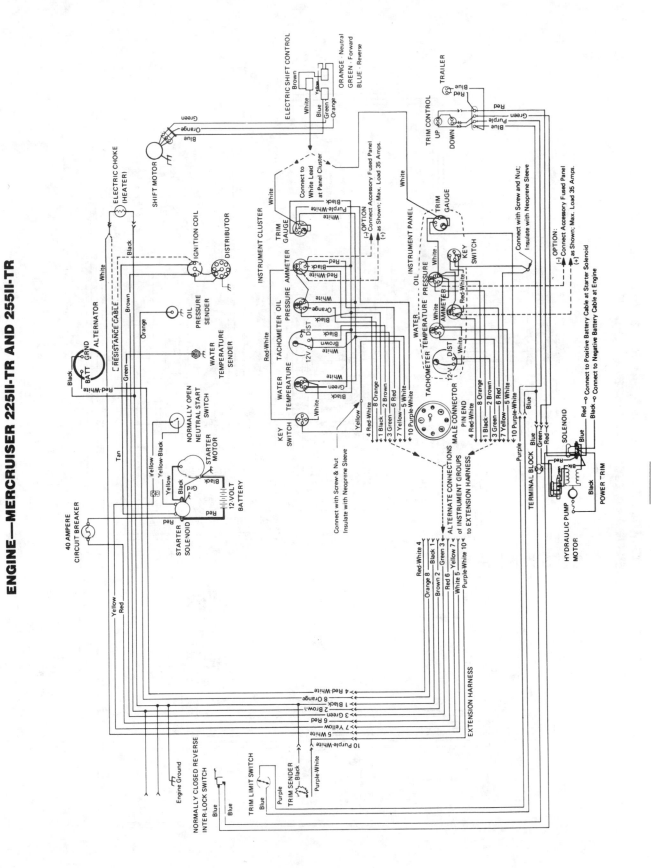

ENGINE—MERCRUISER 225II-TR AND 255II-TR

ENGINE—MERCRUISER 225II-TR (SERIAL NO. 3779775 AND UP),
255IITR AND 255II-TRS (3838788 AND UP)

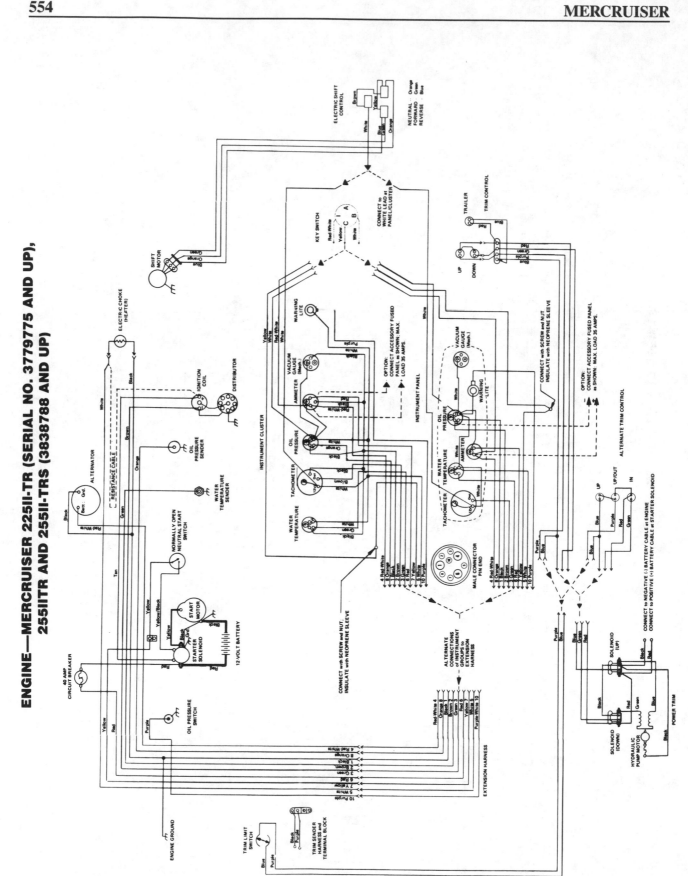

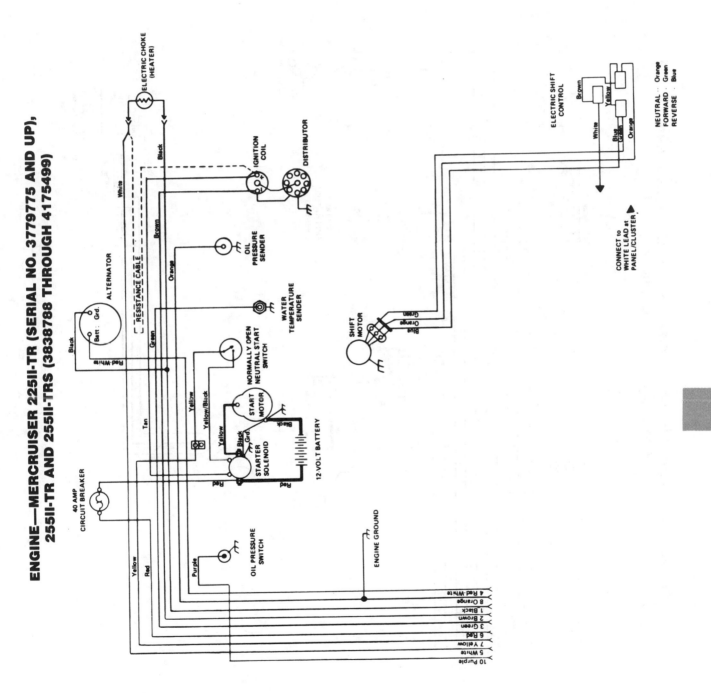

ENGINE—MERCRUISER 225II-TR (SERIAL NO. 3779775 AND UP), 255II-TR AND 255II-TRS (3838788 THROUGH 4175499)

ELECTRIC CHOKE (HEATER)

IGNITION COIL

DISTRIBUTOR

White

Black

Brown

Orange

OIL PRESSURE SENDER

WATER TEMPERATURE SENDER

ALTERNATOR

RESISTANCE CABLE

Bat.   Grd.

Black

Red-White

Green

Ten

Yellow/Black

Yellow

NORMALLY OPEN NEUTRAL START SWITCH

START MOTOR

STARTER SOLENOID

Black   Grd.

Black

Red

Red

12-VOLT BATTERY

40 AMP CIRCUIT BREAKER

Yellow

Red

Purple

OIL PRESSURE SWITCH

ENGINE GROUND

SHIFT MOTOR

Green

Orange

Blue

ELECTRIC SHIFT CONTROL

Brown

Yellow

White

Blue

Green

Orange

NEUTRAL · Orange
FORWARD · Green
REVERSE · Blue

CONNECT to WHITE LEAD at PANEL/CLUSTER

4 Red-White
8 Orange
1 Black
2 Brown
3 Green
6 Red
7 Yellow
5 White
10 Purple

8

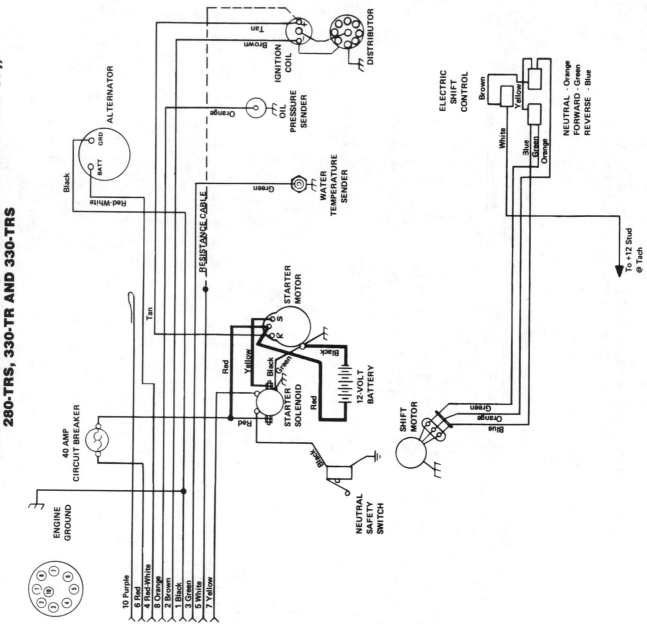

ENGINE—MERCRUISER 228-TR, 255-TR (SERIAL NO. 4175500 AND UP), 280-TRS, 330-TR AND 330-TRS

ENGINE GROUND

40 AMP CIRCUIT BREAKER

10 Purple
6 Red
4 Red-White
8 Orange
2 Brown
1 Black
3 Green
5 White
7 Yellow

ALTERNATOR
GRD
BATT
Black
Red-White

Tan

IGNITION COIL
Tan
Brown
DISTRIBUTOR

OIL PRESSURE SENDER
Orange

WATER TEMPERATURE SENDER
Green

RESISTANCE CABLE

STARTER MOTOR
R S

STARTER SOLENOID
Red
Yellow
Black
Green
Red

Black
12-VOLT BATTERY

NEUTRAL SAFETY SWITCH
Black

SHIFT MOTOR
Green
Orange
Blue

ELECTRIC SHIFT CONTROL
Brown
Yellow
White
Blue
Green
Orange

NEUTRAL - Orange
FORWARD - Green
REVERSE - Blue

To +12 Stud
@ Tach

ENGINE—MERCRUISER 228 AND 250 (SERIAL NO. 4657551 AND UP)

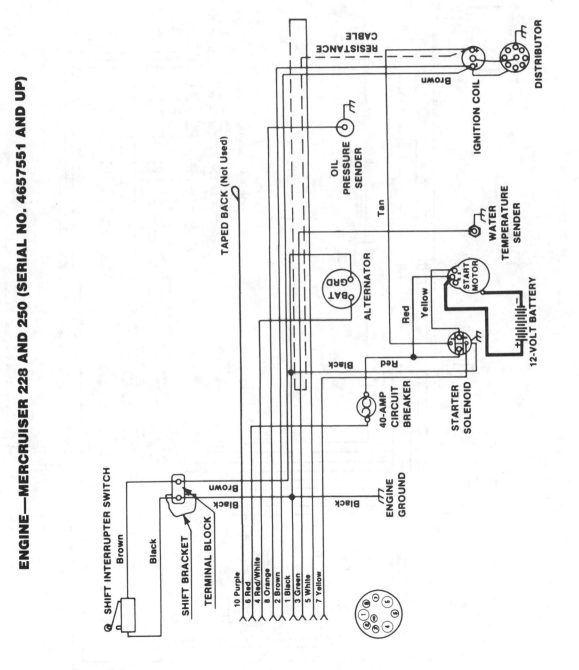

8

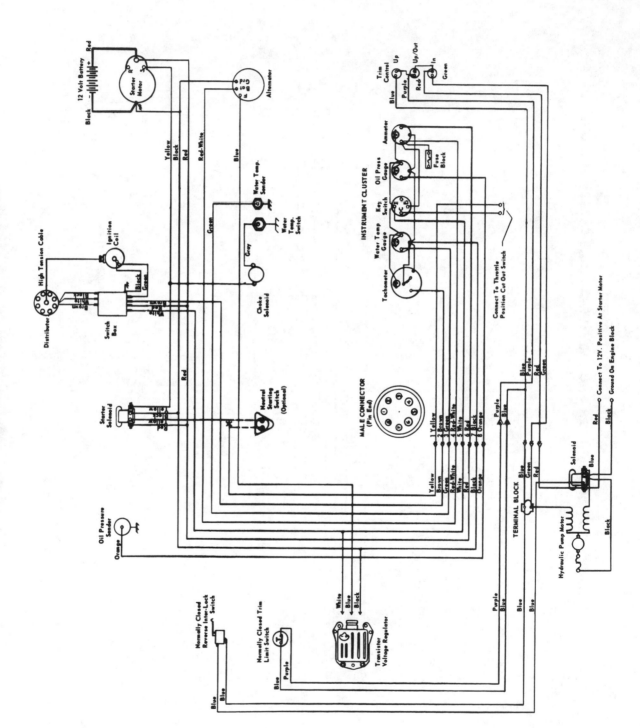

ENGINE—MERCRUISER 250 AND 325 WITH SWITCH BOX

ENGINE—MERCRUISER 250 AND 325 WITH WATER TEMPERATURE SWITCH

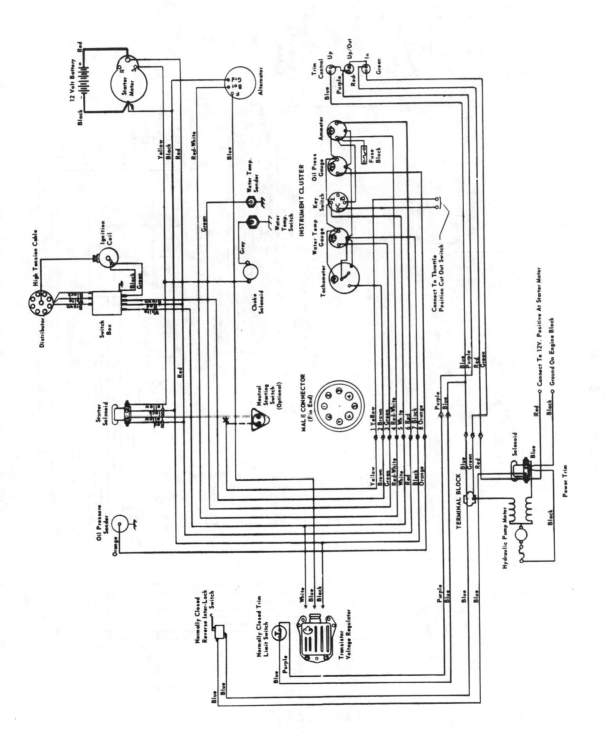

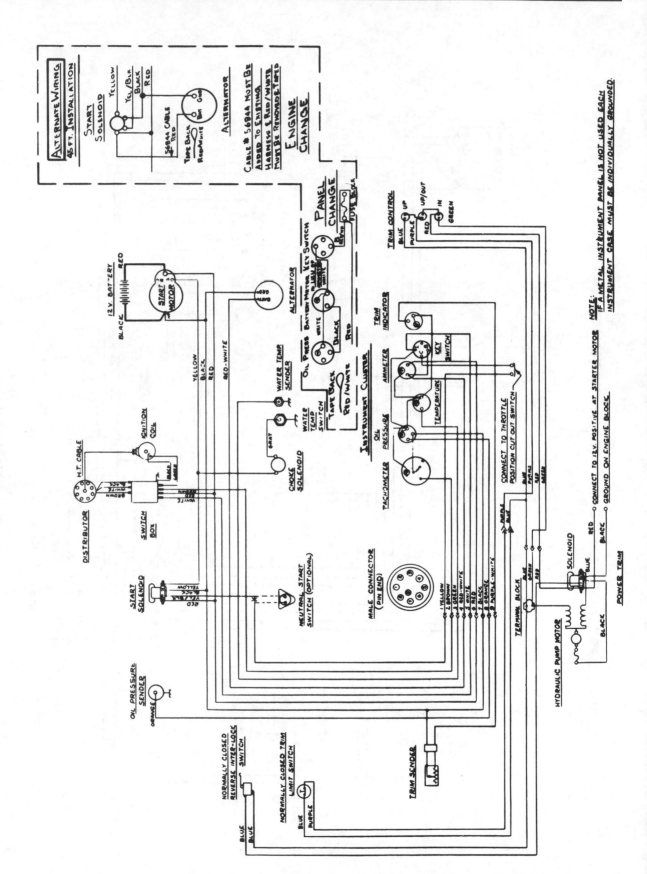

ENGINE—MERCRUISER 270

ENGINE—MERCRUISER 325 WITH WATER TEMPERATURE SWITCH AND TRIM SENDER

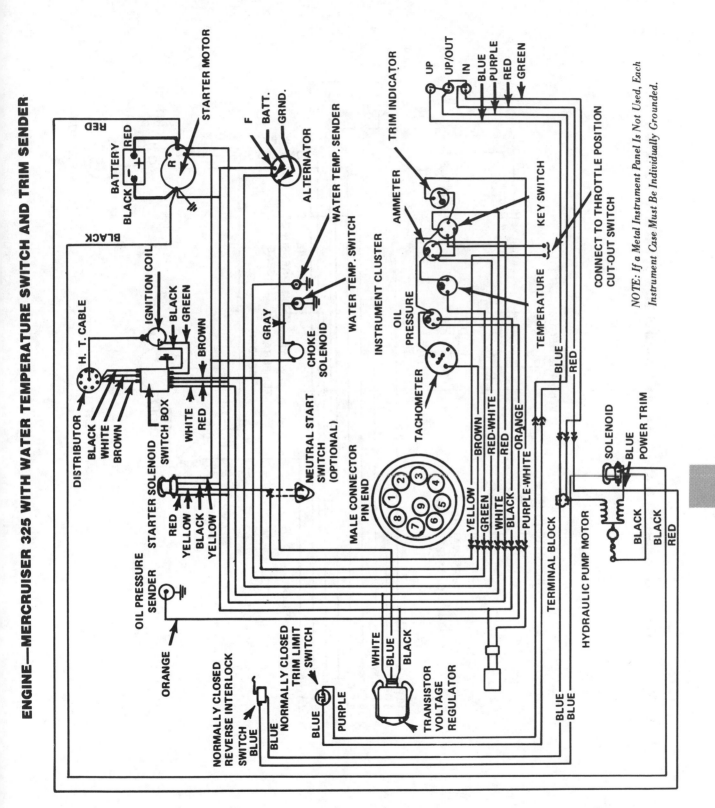

NOTE: *If a Metal Instrument Panel Is Not Used, Each Instrument Case Must Be Individually Grounded.*

8

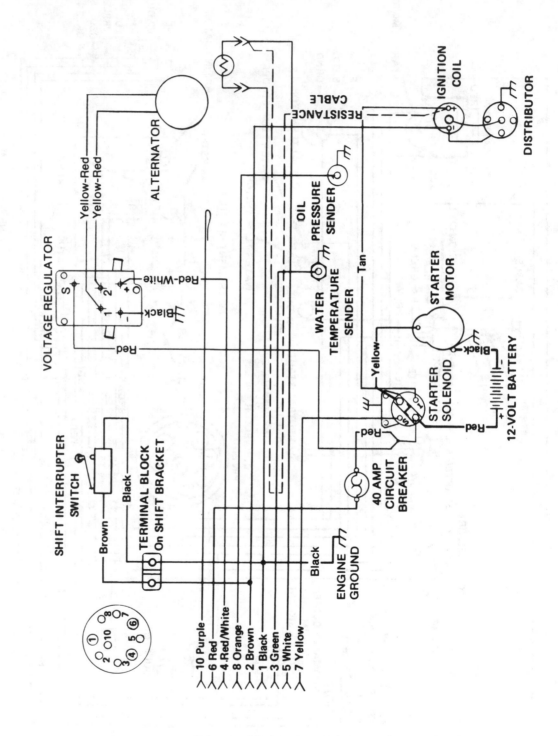

ENGINE—MERCRUISER 470 WITH WATER-COOLED VOLTAGE REGULATOR

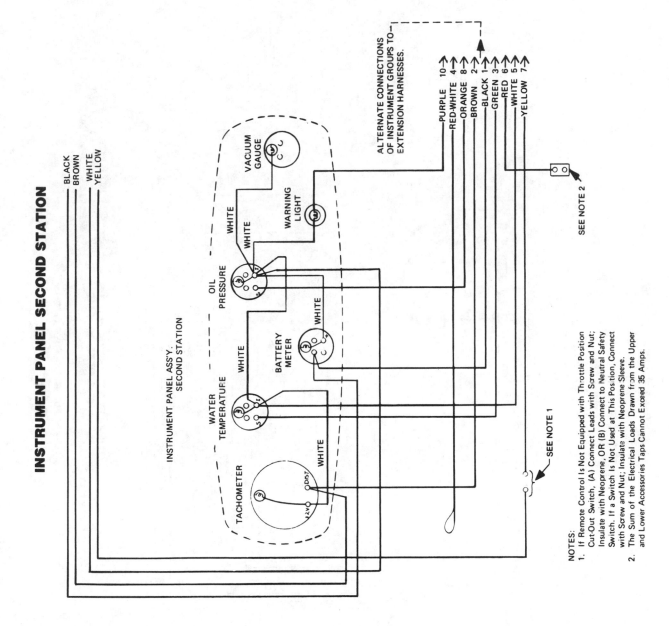

INSTRUMENT PANEL SECOND STATION

BLACK
BROWN
WHITE
YELLOW

INSTRUMENT PANEL ASS'Y.
SECOND STATION

TACHOMETER

WATER
TEMPERATURE

WHITE

BATTERY
METER

WHITE

OIL
PRESSURE

WHITE
WHITE

WARNING
LIGHT

VACUUM
GAUGE

WHITE

ALTERNATE CONNECTIONS
OF INSTRUMENT GROUPS TO
EXTENSION HARNESSES.

PURPLE 10
RED-WHITE 4
ORANGE 8
BROWN 2
BLACK 1
GREEN 3
RED 6
WHITE 5
YELLOW 7

SEE NOTE 2

SEE NOTE 1

NOTES:
1. If Remote Control Is Not Equipped with Throttle Position Cut-Out Switch, (A) Connect Leads with Screw and Nut; Insulate with Neoprene, OR (B) Connect to Neutral Safety Switch. If a Switch Is Not Used at This Position, Connect with Screw and Nut; Insulate with Neoprene Sleeve.
2. The Sum of the Electrical Loads Drawn from the Upper and Lower Accessories Taps Cannot Exceed 35 Amps.

8

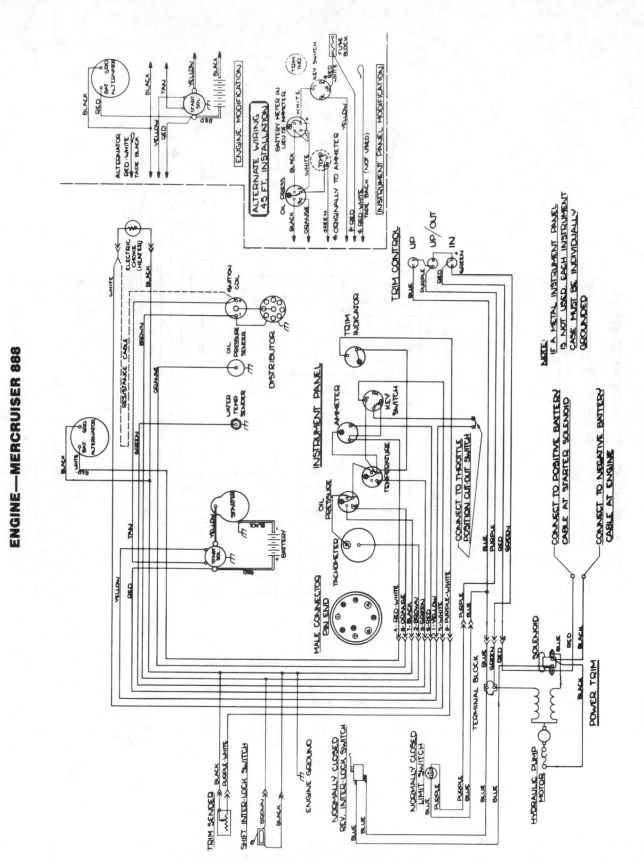

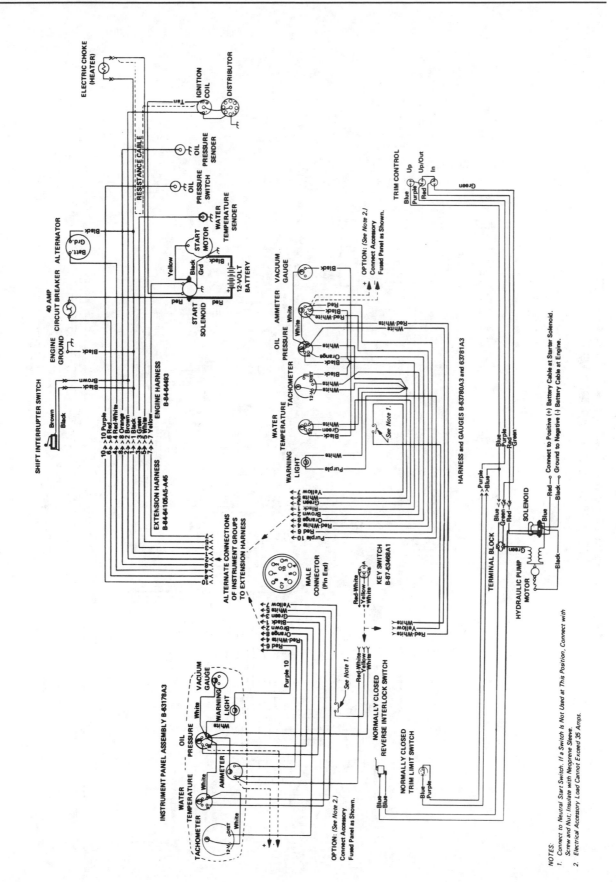

ENGINE—MERCRUISER 888 WITH CIRCUIT BREAKER AND VACUUM GAUGE

8

NOTES:
1. Connect to Neutral Start Switch. If a Switch Is Not Used at This Position, Connect with Screw and Nut; Insulate with Neoprene Sleeve.
2. Electrical Accessory Load Cannot Exceed 35 Amps.

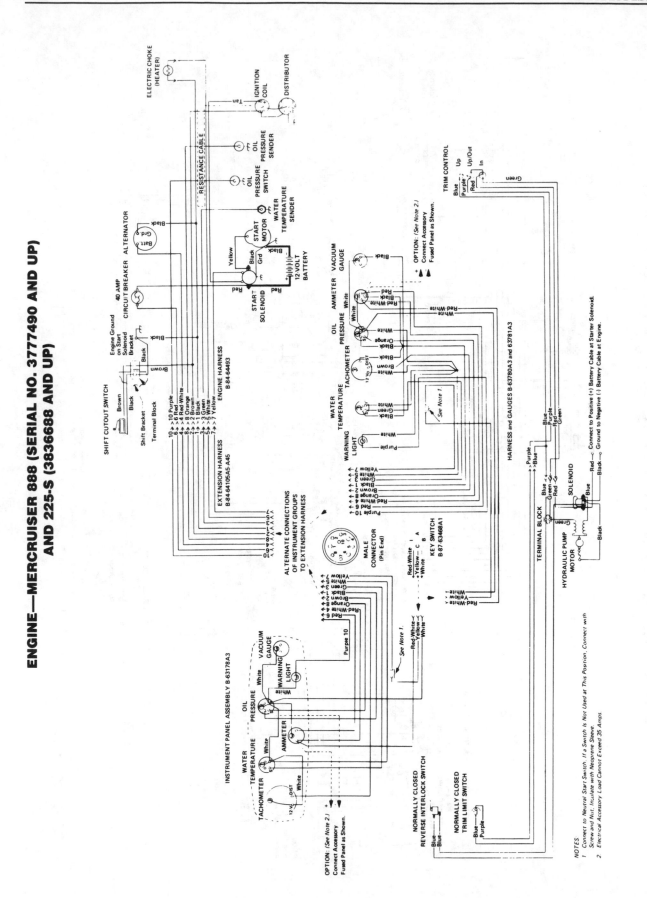

ENGINE—MERCRUISER 888 (SERIAL NO. 3777490 AND UP) AND 225-S (3836688 AND UP)

NOTES

1 Connect to Neutral Start Switch. If a Switch Is Not Used at This Position, Connect with Screw and Nut. Insulate with Neoprene Sleeve.

2 Electrical Accessory Load Cannot Exceed 35 Amps.

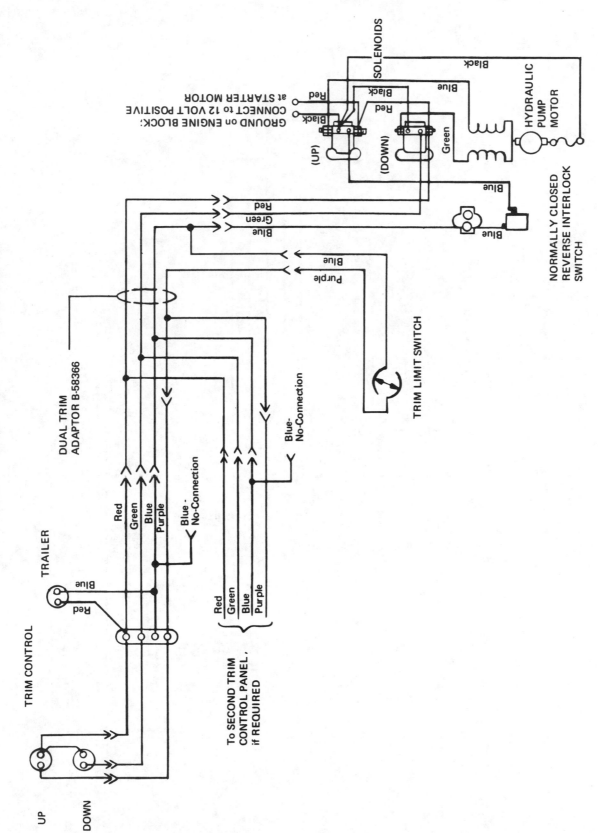

POWER TRIM—MERCRUISER 215, 225II-TR AND 255II-TR

TRIM CONTROL

TRAILER

DUAL TRIM ADAPTOR B-58366

Red

Blue

UP

DOWN

Red
Green
Blue
Purple

Blue - No-Connection

Red
Green
Blue
Purple

To SECOND TRIM CONTROL PANEL, if REQUIRED

Blue - No-Connection

TRIM LIMIT SWITCH

Purple

Blue

Blue

Red

Green

Blue

SOLENOIDS

Red

Black

(UP)

Red

Black

(DOWN)

Green

Blue

Black

HYDRAULIC PUMP MOTOR

GROUND on ENGINE BLOCK;
CONNECT to 12 VOLT POSITIVE
at STARTER MOTOR

Blue

Blue

NORMALLY CLOSED
REVERSE INTERLOCK
SWITCH

8

POWER TILT

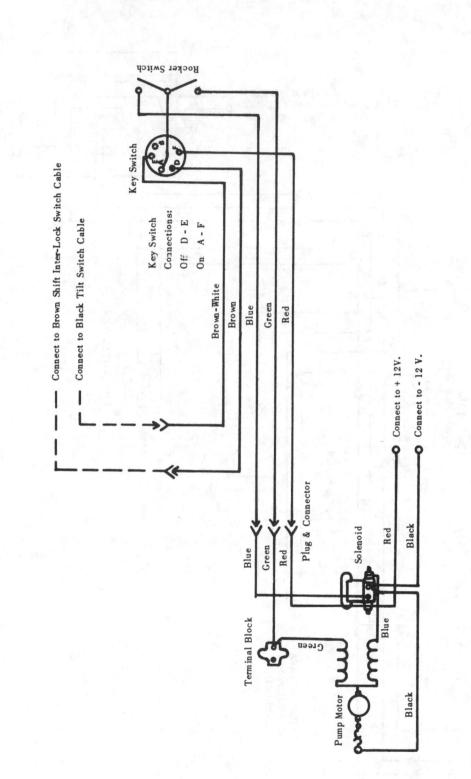

Connect to Brown Shift Inter-Lock Switch Cable

Connect to Black Tilt Switch Cable

Rocker Switch

Key Switch

Key Switch
Connections:
Off D - E
On A - F

Brown-White

Brown

Blue

Green

Red

Blue

Green

Red

Plug & Connector

Solenoid

Red

Black

Connect to + 12V.

Connect to - 12 V.

Terminal Block

Green

Blue

Pump Motor

Black

Black

ENGINE—MERCRUISER 898

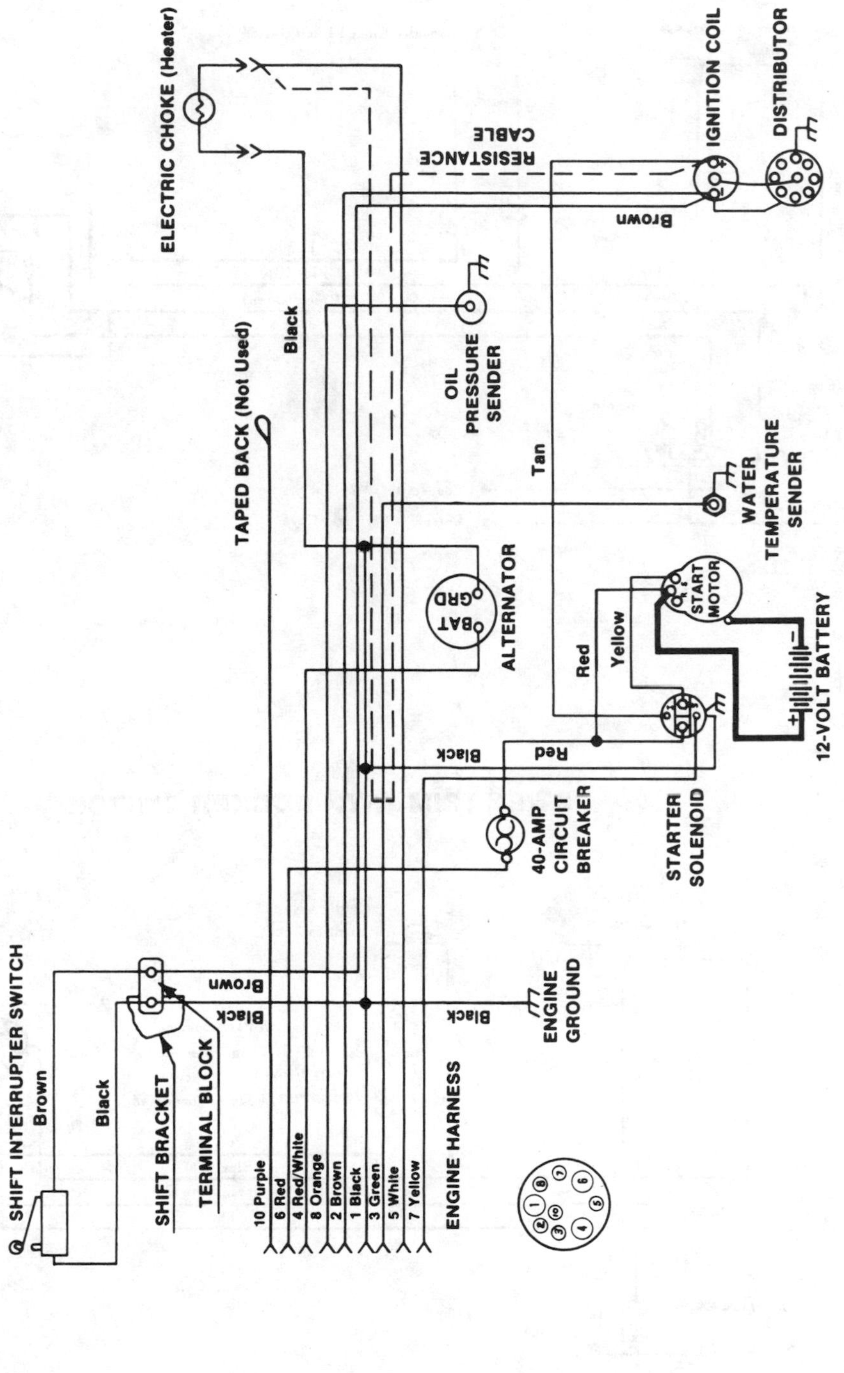

ELECTRIC CHOKE (Heater)

IGNITION COIL

DISTRIBUTOR

RESISTANCE CABLE

Brown

Black

OIL PRESSURE SENDER

TAPED BACK (Not Used)

Tan

WATER TEMPERATURE SENDER

BAT

GRD

ALTERNATOR

Red

Yellow

START MOTOR

12-VOLT BATTERY

Red

Black

40-AMP CIRCUIT BREAKER

STARTER SOLENOID

SHIFT INTERRUPTER SWITCH

Brown

Black

SHIFT BRACKET

TERMINAL BLOCK

Brown

Black

ENGINE GROUND

Black

ENGINE HARNESS

10 Purple
6 Red
4 Red/White
8 Orange
2 Brown
1 Black
3 Green
5 White
7 Yellow

8

POWER TRIM WITH PUSH BUTTON (EARLY)

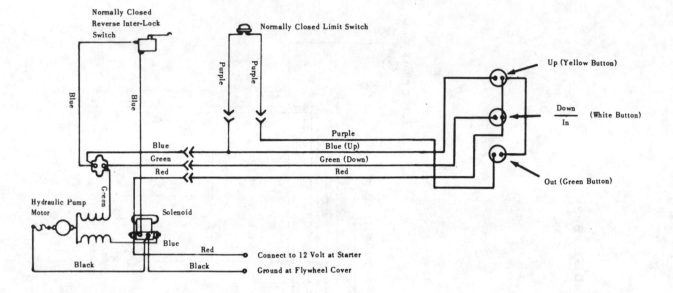

POWER TRIM WITH ROCKER SWITCH

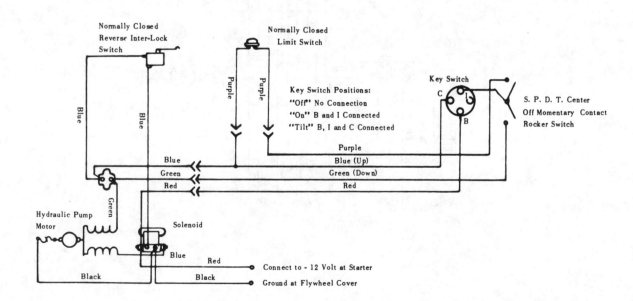

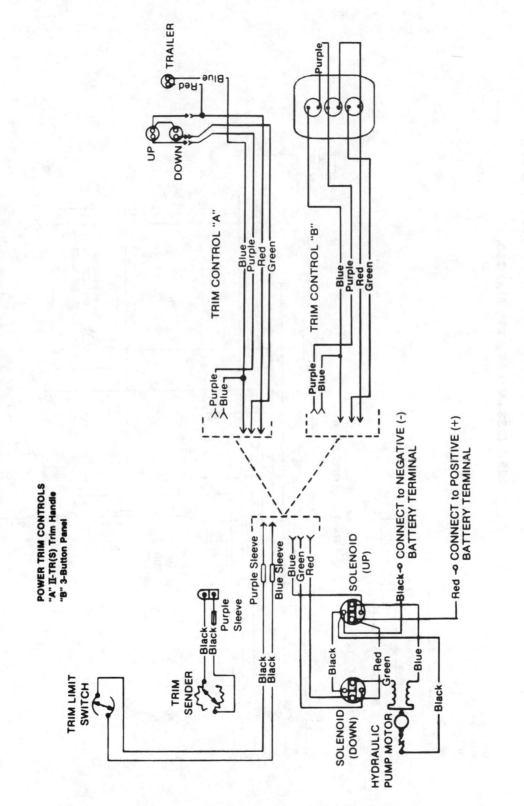

POWER TRIM WITH TRIM SENDER (DOUBLE SOLENOID SYSTEM)

POWER TRIM CONTROLS
"A" II-TR(S) Trim Handle
"B" 3-Button Panel

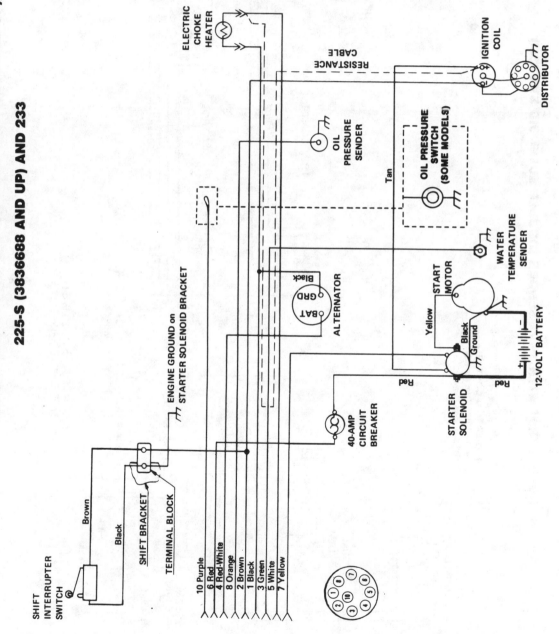

ENGINE—MERCRUISER 888 (SERIAL NO. 3777490 AND UP), 225-S (3836688 AND UP) AND 233

ELECTRIC CHOKE HEATER

IGNITION COIL

DISTRIBUTOR

RESISTANCE CABLE

OIL PRESSURE SENDER

OIL PRESSURE SWITCH (SOME MODELS)

Tan

WATER TEMPERATURE SENDER

ENGINE GROUND on STARTER SOLENOID BRACKET

Black

BAT

GRD

ALTERNATOR

START MOTOR

Yellow

Black

Ground

12-VOLT BATTERY

40-AMP CIRCUIT BREAKER

Red

STARTER SOLENOID

Red

SHIFT BRACKET

TERMINAL BLOCK

Brown

Black

SHIFT INTERRUPTER SWITCH

10 Purple
6 Red
4 Red-White
8 Orange
2 Brown
1 Black
3 Green
5 White
7 Yellow

INSTRUMENT PANEL

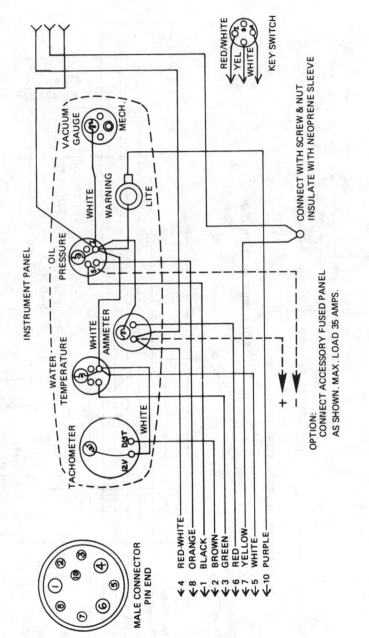

8

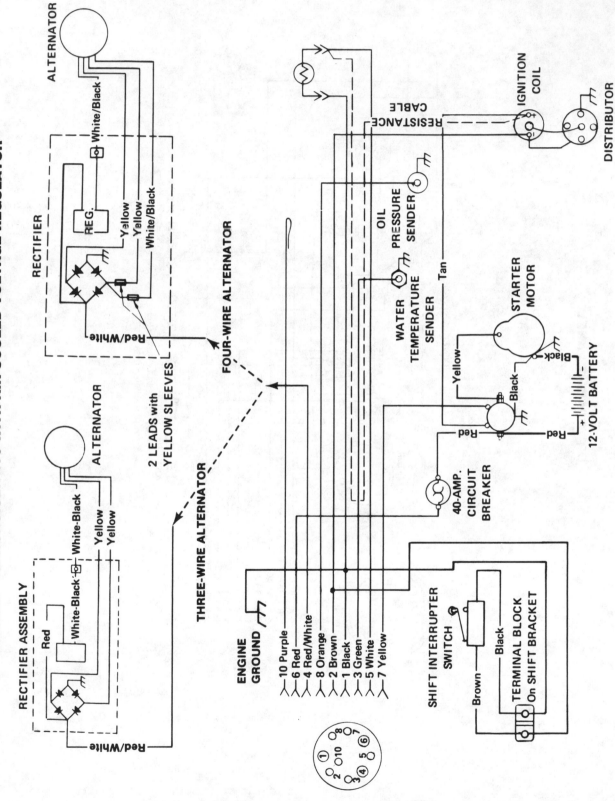

ENGINE—MERCRUISER 470 WITH AIR-COOLED VOLTAGE REGULATOR

INSTRUMENT CLUSTER WITH WARNING LIGHT (THUNDERBOLT IGNITION)

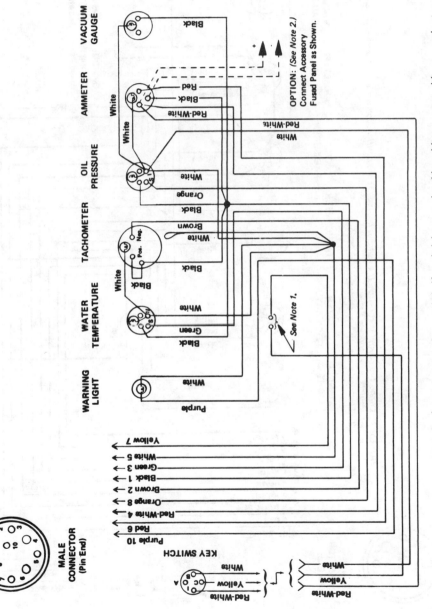

NOTES: 1. Connect to neutral start switch. If a switch is not used at this position, connect with screw and nut and insulate with neoprene sleeve.

2. Electrical accessory load cannot exceed 35 amps.

MALE CONNECTOR
(Pin End)

8

INSTRUMENT CLUSTER WITH WARNING LIGHT (BREAKER POINT)

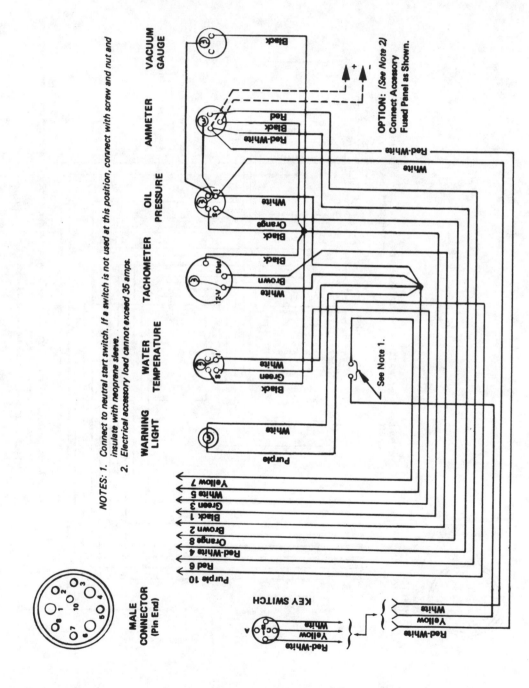

NOTES: 1. Connect to neutral start switch. If a switch is not used at this position, connect with screw and nut and insulate with neoprene sleeve.

2. Electrical accessory load cannot exceed 35 amps.

OPTION: (See Note 2) Connect Accessory Fused Panel as Shown.

VACUUM GAUGE

AMMETER

OIL PRESSURE

TACHOMETER

WATER TEMPERATURE

WARNING LIGHT

Yellow 7
White 5
Green 3
Black 1
Brown 2
Orange 8
Red-White 4
Red 6
Purple 10

MALE CONNECTOR (Pin End)

KEY SWITCH

Red-White
Yellow
White

INSTRUMENT CLUSTER WITHOUT WARNING LIGHT (BREAKER POINT)

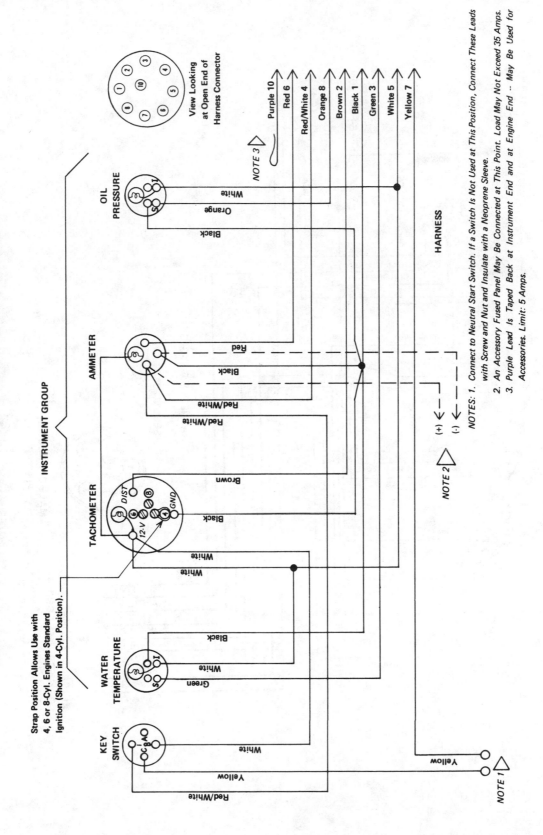

View Looking
at Open End of
Harness Connector

Strap Position Allows Use with
4, 6 or 8-Cyl. Engines Standard
Ignition (Shown in 4-Cyl. Position).

INSTRUMENT GROUP

OIL PRESSURE

AMMETER

TACHOMETER

WATER TEMPERATURE

KEY SWITCH

HARNESS

Purple 10
Red 6
Red/White 4
Orange 8
Brown 2
Black 1
Green 3
White 5
Yellow 7

NOTE 3

NOTE 2

(+)
(−)

NOTE 1

NOTES: 1. Connect to Neutral Start Switch. If a Switch Is Not Used at This Position, Connect These Leads
with Screw and Nut and Insulate with a Neoprene Sleeve.

2. An Accessory Fused Panel May Be Connected at This Point. Load May Not Exceed 35 Amps.

3. Purple Lead Is Taped Back at Instrument End and at Engine End -- May Be Used for
Accessories. Limit: 5 Amps.

8

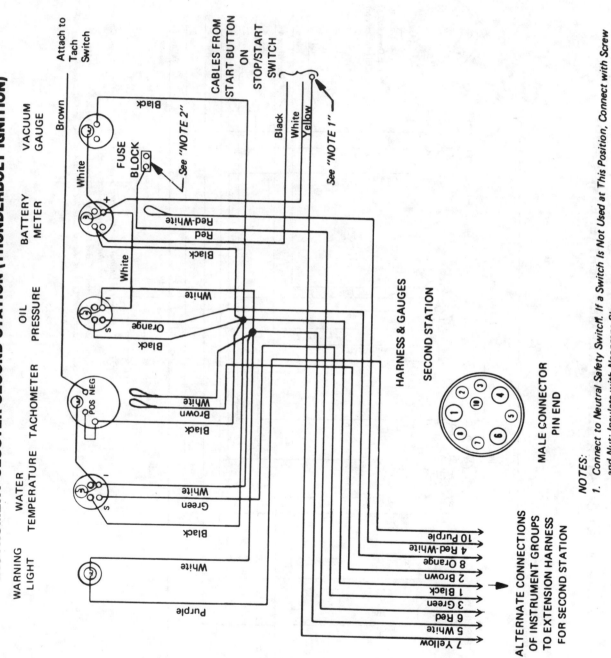

INSTRUMENT CLUSTER SECOND STATION (THUNDERBOLT IGNITION)

WARNING LIGHT · WATER TEMPERATURE · TACHOMETER · OIL PRESSURE · BATTERY METER · VACUUM GAUGE

Attach to Tach Switch

Brown

Black

CABLES FROM START BUTTON ON STOP/START SWITCH

White

FUSE BLOCK

See "NOTE 2"

Black
White
Yellow

See "NOTE 1"

+
Red-White
Red
Black
White

White
Orange
Black

POS NEG
Brown
White
Black

HARNESS & GAUGES

SECOND STATION

Green
White
Black

White

Purple

10 Purple
4 Red-White
8 Orange
2 Brown
1 Black
3 Green
6 Red
5 White
7 Yellow

ALTERNATE CONNECTIONS OF INSTRUMENT GROUPS TO EXTENSION HARNESS FOR SECOND STATION

MALE CONNECTOR PIN END

NOTES:

1. Connect to Neutral Safety Switch. If a Switch Is Not Used at This Position, Connect with Screw and Nut; Insulate with Neoprene Sleeve.

2. The Sum of the Electrical Loads (Drawn from the Upper and Lower Accessories Taps) Cannot Exceed 35 Amps.

INSTRUMENT CLUSTER SECOND STATION (BREAKER POINT)

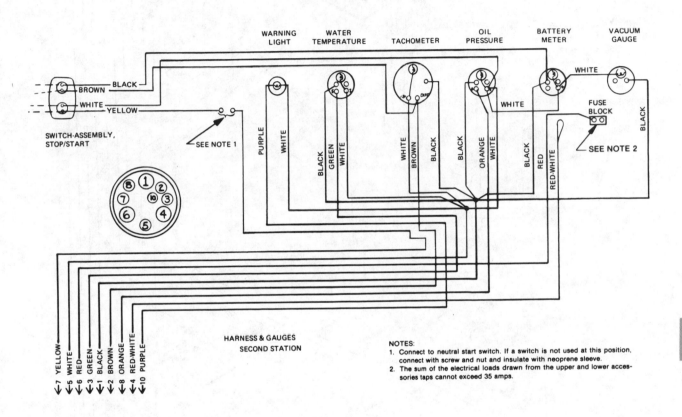

WARNING LIGHT WATER TEMPERATURE TACHOMETER OIL PRESSURE BATTERY METER VACUUM GAUGE

BROWN BLACK
WHITE YELLOW

SWITCH-ASSEMBLY, STOP/START

SEE NOTE 1

PURPLE WHITE BLACK GREEN WHITE WHITE BROWN BLACK BLACK ORANGE WHITE BLACK RED RED-WHITE WHITE FUSE BLOCK BLACK SEE NOTE 2

7 YELLOW
5 WHITE
6 RED
3 GREEN
1 BLACK
2 BROWN
8 ORANGE
4 RED-WHITE
10 PURPLE

HARNESS & GAUGES SECOND STATION

NOTES:
1. Connect to neutral start switch. If a switch is not used at this position, connect with screw and nut and insulate with neoprene sleeve.
2. The sum of the electrical loads drawn from the upper and lower accessories taps cannot exceed 35 amps.

8

BLK = Black
BLU = Blue
BRN = Brown
GRY = Gray
GRN = Green
ORN = Orange
PNK = Pink
PUR = Purple
RED = Red
TAN = Tan
WHT = White
YEL = Yellow
LIT = Light
DRK = Dark

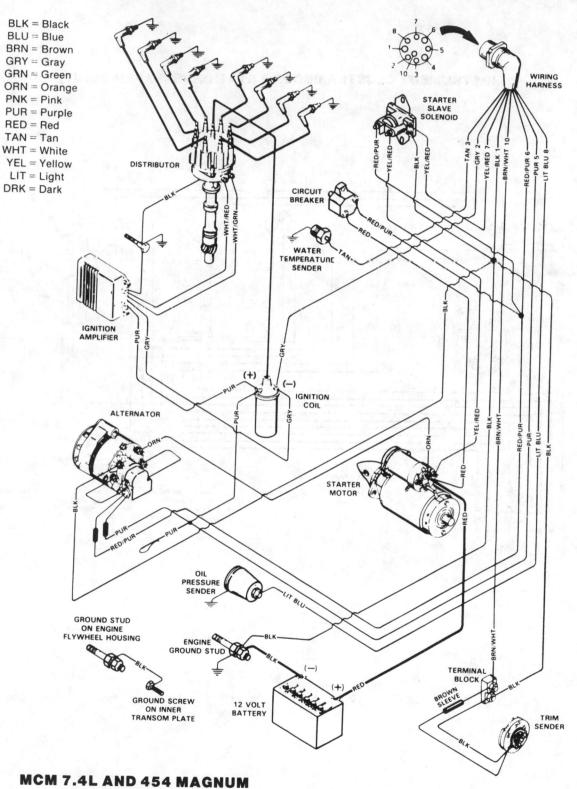

**MCM 7.4L AND 454 MAGNUM
(BRAVO ONE DRIVE)**

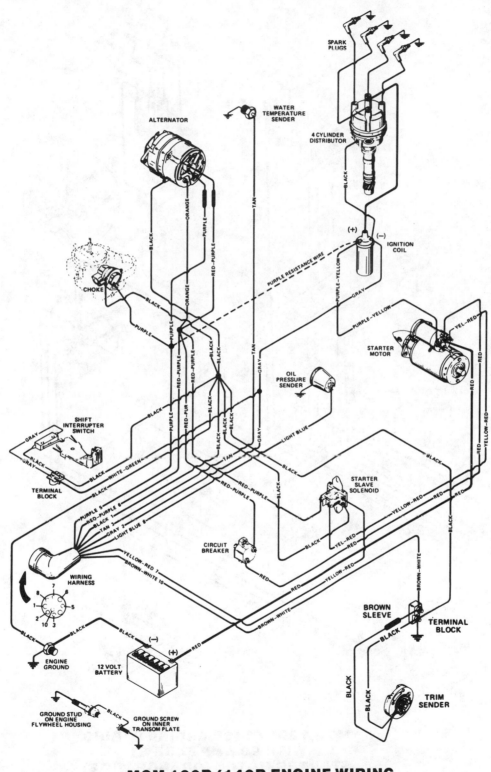

SPARK PLUGS

WATER TEMPERATURE SENDER

ALTERNATOR

4 CYLINDER DISTRIBUTOR

BLACK

ORANGE

PURPLE

RED–PURPLE

TAN

PURPLE RESISTANCE WIRE

(+) (−) IGNITION COIL

CHOKE

BLACK

PURPLE

PURPLE–YELLOW

GRAY

PURPLE–YELLOW

YEL–RED

STARTER MOTOR

RED

BLACK

PURPLE

RED–PUR

RED–PURPLE

BLACK

BLACK

BLACK

TAN

GRAY

OIL PRESSURE SENDER

RED

YELLOW–RED

SHIFT INTERRUPTER SWITCH

GRAY

GRAY

BLACK

BLACK–WHITE–GREEN

LIGHT BLUE

BLACK

BLACK

TERMINAL BLOCK

PURPLE 5

RED–PURPLE 6

BLACK 1

TAN 3

GRAY 2

LIGHT BLUE 8

RED–PUR

RED–PURPLE

BLACK

STARTER SLAVE SOLENOID

YELLOW–RED

RED

BLACK

YEL–RED

BLACK

YELLOW–RED

YELLOW–RED 7

BROWN–WHITE 10

CIRCUIT BREAKER

RED

WIRING HARNESS

7 8

1

9

10 3

BROWN–WHITE

BROWN SLEEVE

BLACK

TERMINAL BLOCK

BLACK

BLACK

RED

ENGINE GROUND

12 VOLT BATTERY

(−) (+)

BLACK

BLACK

BLACK

TRIM SENDER

GROUND STUD ON ENGINE FLYWHEEL HOUSING

BLACK

GROUND SCREW ON INNER TRANSOM PLATE

8

**MCM 120R/140R ENGINE WIRING
(BATTERY METER CIRCUIT)**

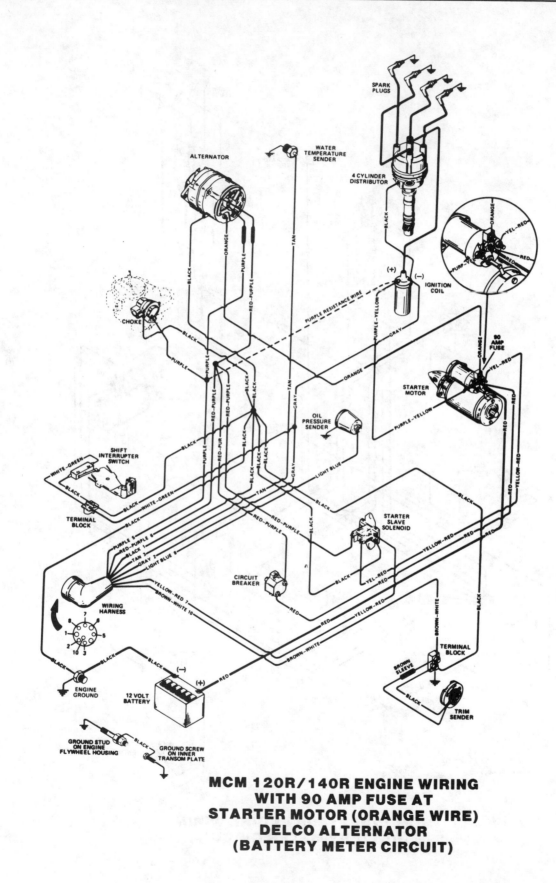

**MCM 120R/140R ENGINE WIRING
WITH 90 AMP FUSE AT
STARTER MOTOR (ORANGE WIRE)
DELCO ALTERNATOR
(BATTERY METER CIRCUIT)**

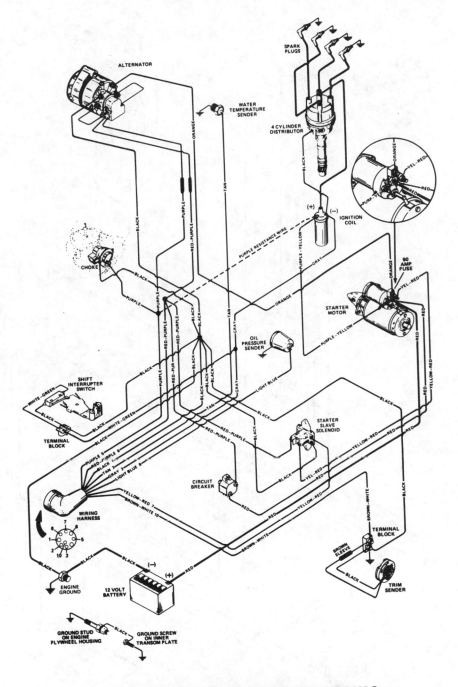

**MCM 120R/140R ENGINE WIRING
WITH 90 AMP FUSE AT
STARTER MOTOR (ORANGE WIRE)
MANDO ALTERNATOR
(BATTERY METER CIRCUIT)**

8

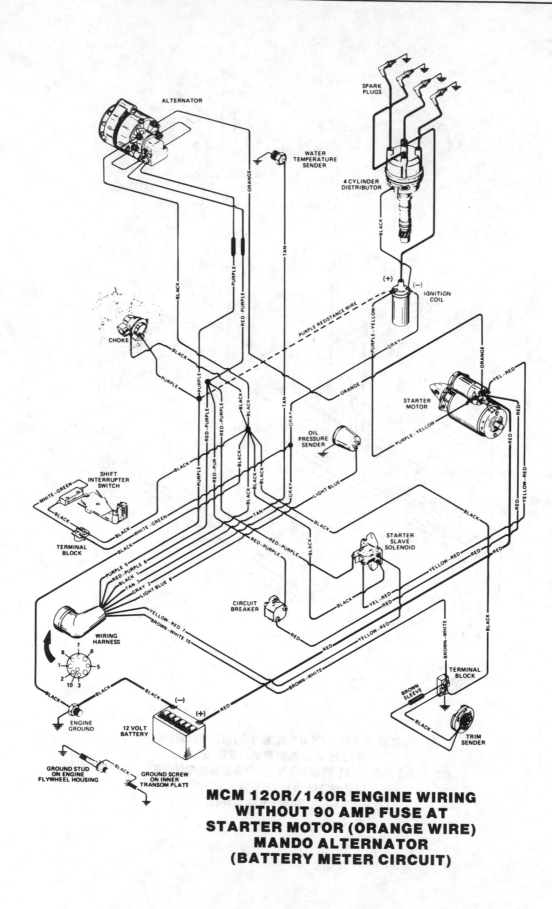

**MCM 120R/140R ENGINE WIRING
WITHOUT 90 AMP FUSE AT
STARTER MOTOR (ORANGE WIRE)
MANDO ALTERNATOR
(BATTERY METER CIRCUIT)**

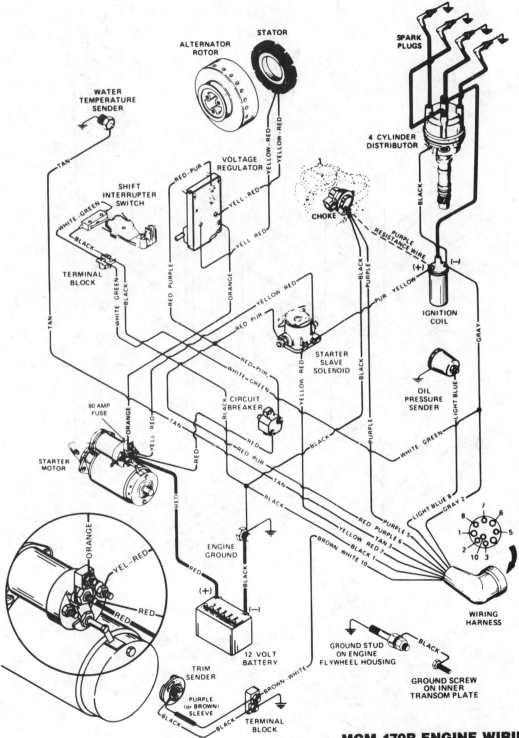

**MCM 170R ENGINE WIRING
WITH 90 AMP FUSE AT DELCO
STARTER MOTOR (ORANGE WIRE)
(BATTERY METER CIRCUIT)**

8

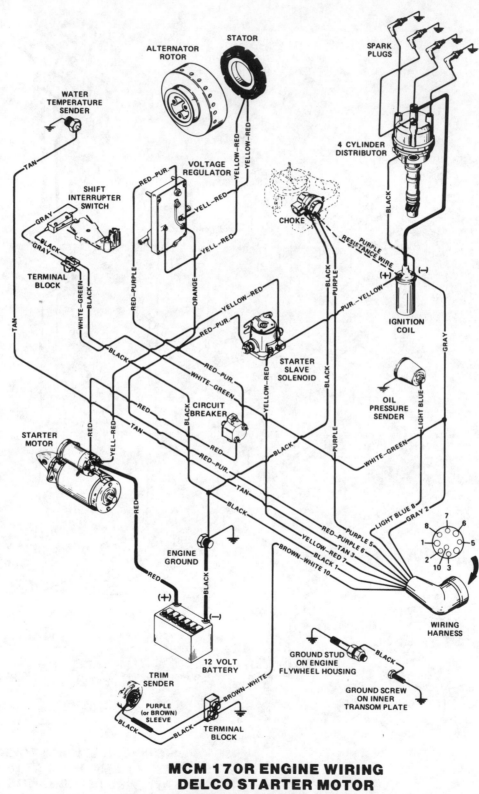

**MCM 170R ENGINE WIRING
DELCO STARTER MOTOR
(BATTERY METER CIRCUIT)**

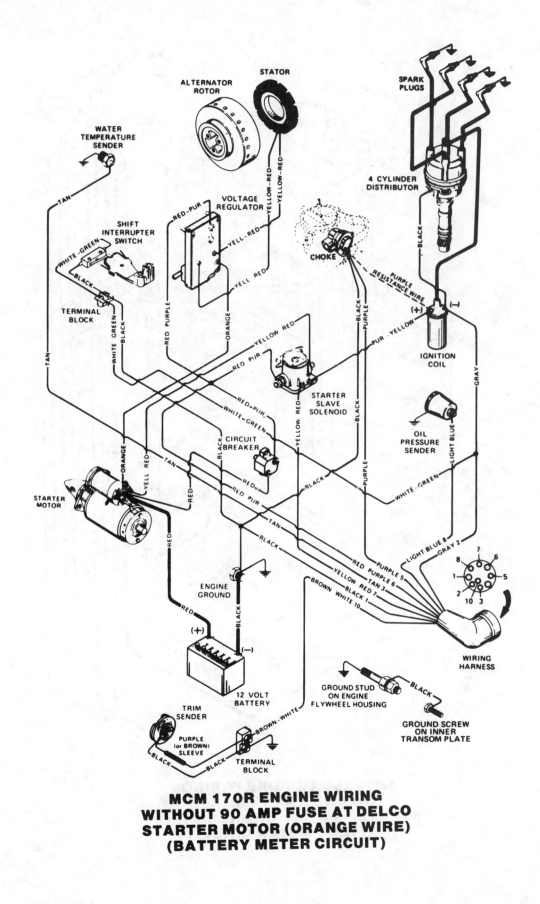

MCM 170R ENGINE WIRING WITHOUT 90 AMP FUSE AT DELCO STARTER MOTOR (ORANGE WIRE) (BATTERY METER CIRCUIT)

8

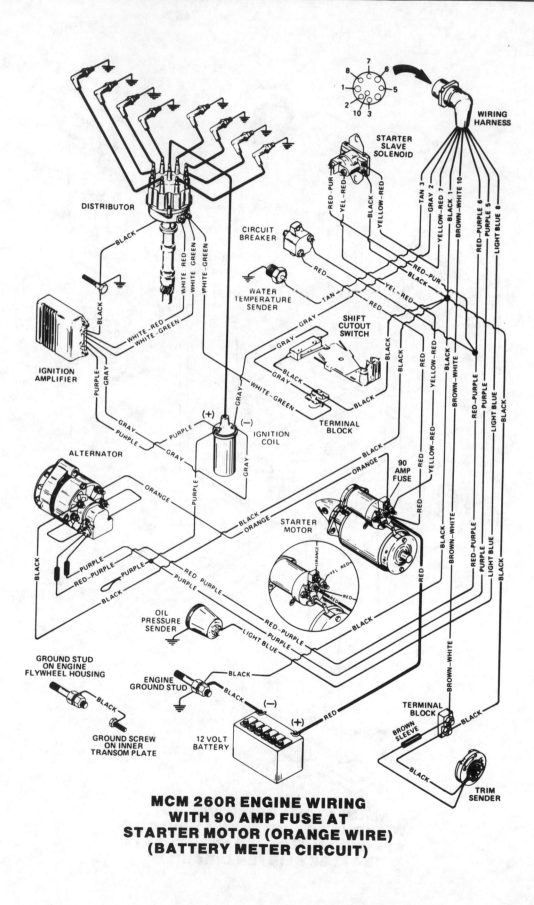

**MCM 260R ENGINE WIRING
WITH 90 AMP FUSE AT
STARTER MOTOR (ORANGE WIRE)
(BATTERY METER CIRCUIT)**

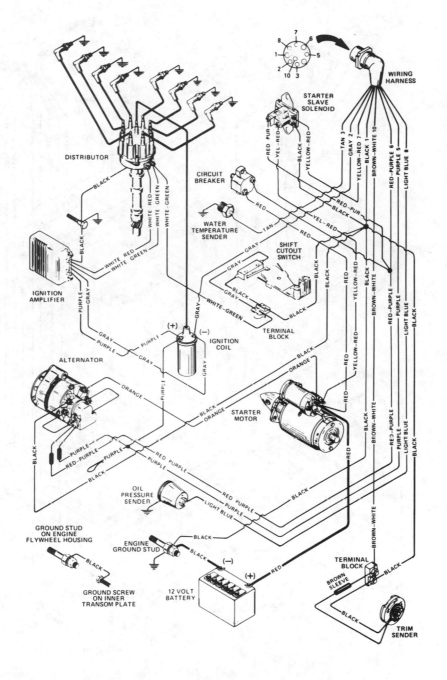

**MCM 260R ENGINE WIRING
WITHOUT 90 AMP FUSE AT
STARTER MOTOR (ORANGE WIRE)
(BATTERY METER CIRCUIT)**

8

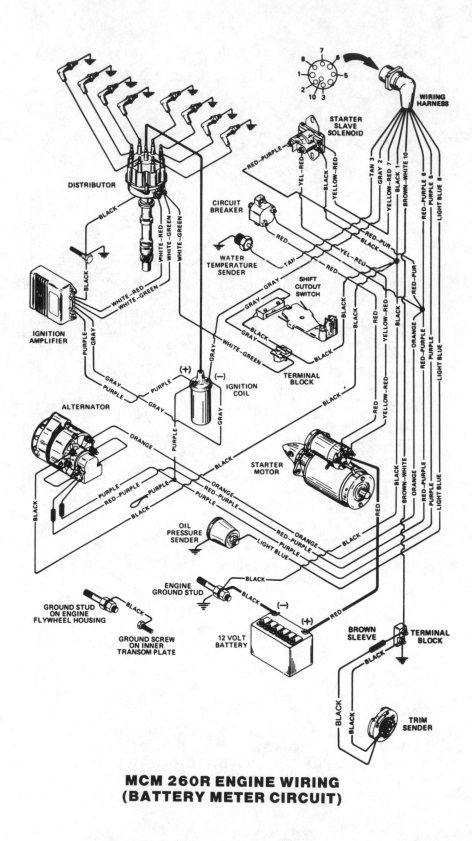

**MCM 260R ENGINE WIRING
(BATTERY METER CIRCUIT)**

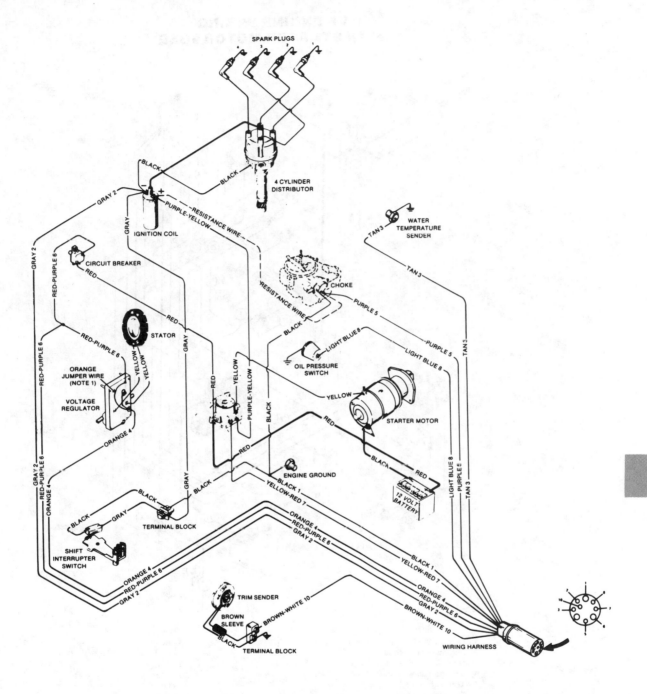

NOTE 1: Remove this wire if ammeter is to be used. Jumper must be left connected if Battery Meter is used.

MCM 485 ENGINE WIRING
(AMMETER CIRCUIT)

V6 ENGINE WIRING
WITH STARTER MOTOR FUSE

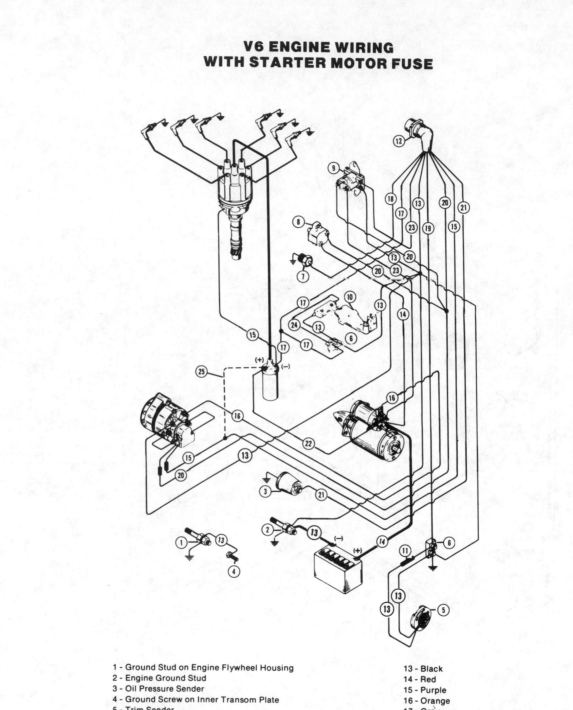

1 - Ground Stud on Engine Flywheel Housing
2 - Engine Ground Stud
3 - Oil Pressure Sender
4 - Ground Screw on Inner Transom Plate
5 - Trim Sender
6 - Terminal Block
7 - Water Temperature Sender
8 - Circuit Breaker
9 - Starter Slave Solenoid
10 - Shift Cutout Switch
11 - Brown Sleeve
12 - Wiring Harness

13 - Black
14 - Red
15 - Purple
16 - Orange
17 - Gray
18 - Tan
19 - Brown/White
20 - Red/Purple
21 - Light Blue
22 - Purple/Yellow
23 - Yellow/Red
24 - White/Green
25 - Purple Resistance Wire

V6 ENGINE WIRING WITHOUT STARTER MOTOR FUSE

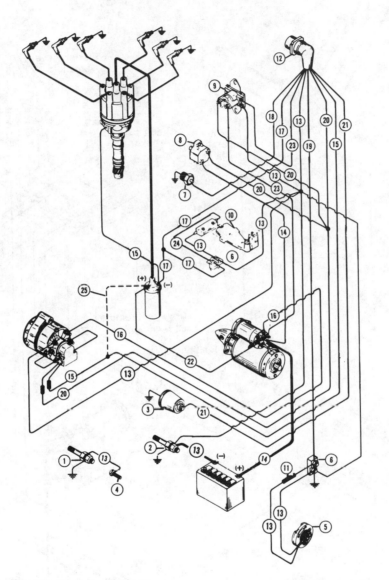

1 - Ground Stud on Engine Flywheel Housing
2 - Engine Ground Stud
3 - Oil Pressure Sender
4 - Ground Screw on Inner Transom Plate
5 - Trim Sender
6 - Terminal Block
7 - Water Temperature Sender
8 - Circuit Breaker
9 - Starter Slave Solenoid
10 - Shift Cutout Switch
11 - Brown Sleeve
12 - Wiring Harness

13 - Black
14 - Red
15 - Purple
16 - Orange
17 - Gray
18 - Tan
19 - Brown/White
20 - Red/Purple
21 - Light Blue
22 - Purple/Yellow
23 - Yellow/Red
24 - White/Green
25 - Purple Resistance Wire

8

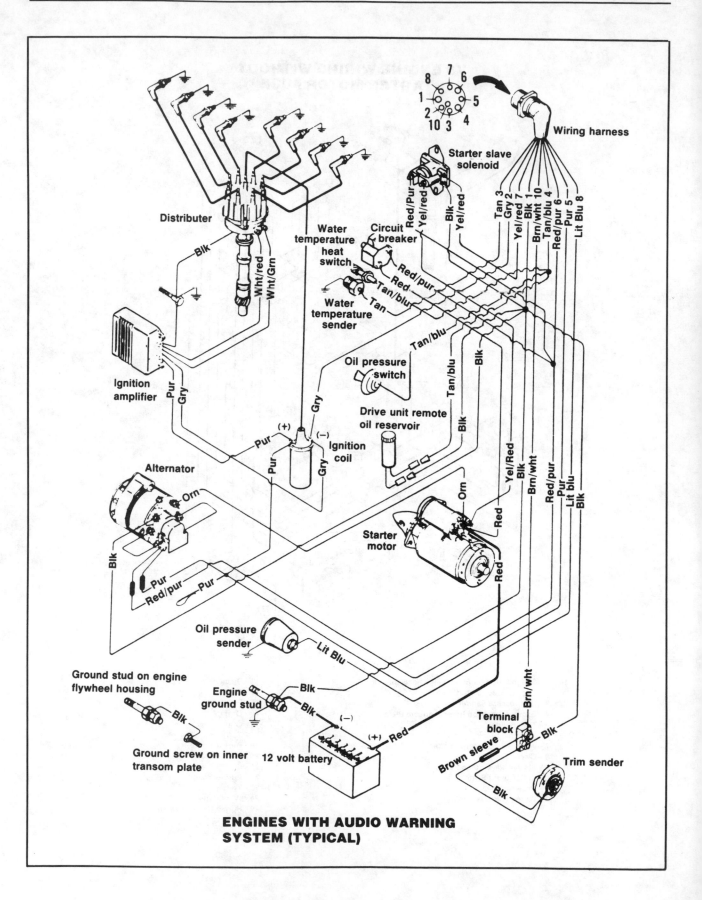

**ENGINES WITH AUDIO WARNING
SYSTEM (TYPICAL)**

INSTRUMENTATION (WITH CONNECTOR PLUG)

1 - Key Switch
2 - Water Temperature
3 - Oil Pressure
4 - Tachometer
5 - Battery Meter
6 - Trim
7 - Fuse
8 - Red/Purple
9 - Yellow/Red
10 - Orange
11 - Purple
12 - Black
13 - Tan
14 - Light Blue
15 - Gray
16 - Brown/White

INSTRUMENTATION (WITH RING TERMINALS)

1 - Black
2 - Purple
3 - Gray
4 - Orange
5 - Light Blue
6 - Tan

7 - Red/Purple
8 - Yellow/Red
9 - Brown/White
10 - Tachometer
11 - Oil Pressure
12 - Water Temperature

13 - Battery Meter
14 - Ignition Switch
15 - Fuse
16 - Trim Indicator
17 - Shift Throttle Control

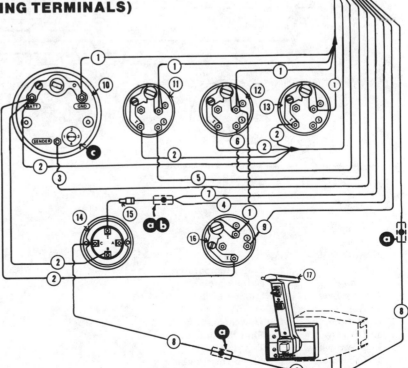

8

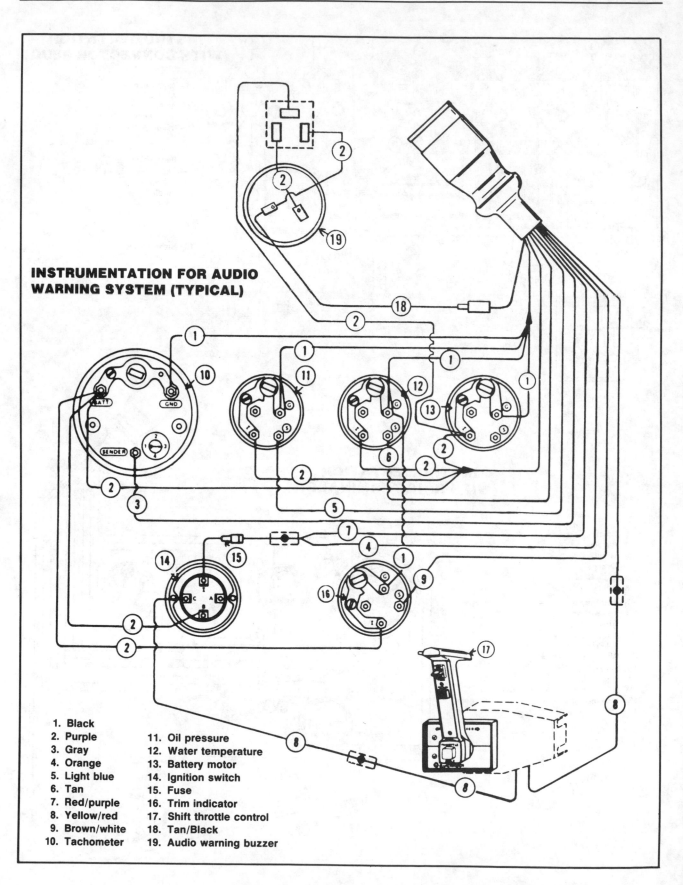

INSTRUMENTATION FOR AUDIO WARNING SYSTEM (TYPICAL)

1. Black
2. Purple
3. Gray
4. Orange
5. Light blue
6. Tan
7. Red/purple
8. Yellow/red
9. Brown/white
10. Tachometer
11. Oil pressure
12. Water temperature
13. Battery motor
14. Ignition switch
15. Fuse
16. Trim indicator
17. Shift throttle control
18. Tan/Black
19. Audio warning buzzer

DUAL STATION
(NEUTRAL SAFETY SWITCH
IN ONE REMOTE CONTROL)

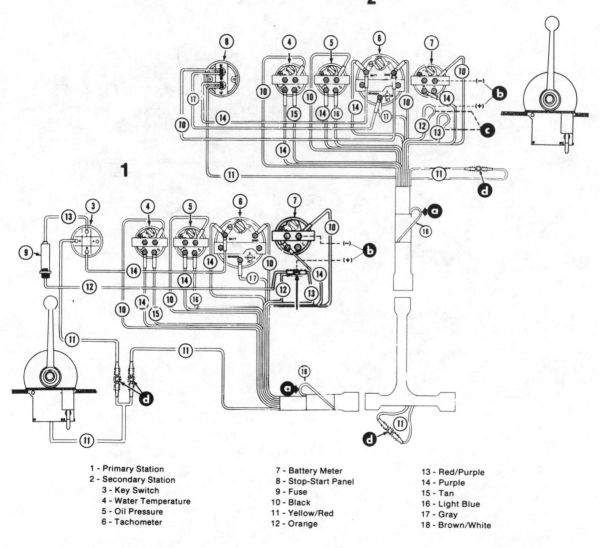

1 - Primary Station	7 - Battery Meter	13 - Red/Purple
2 - Secondary Station	8 - Stop-Start Panel	14 - Purple
3 - Key Switch	9 - Fuse	15 - Tan
4 - Water Temperature	10 - Black	16 - Light Blue
5 - Oil Pressure	11 - Yellow/Red	17 - Gray
6 - Tachometer	12 - Orange	18 - Brown/White

DUAL STATION
(NEUTRAL SAFETY SWITCH
IN BOTH REMOTE CONTROLS)

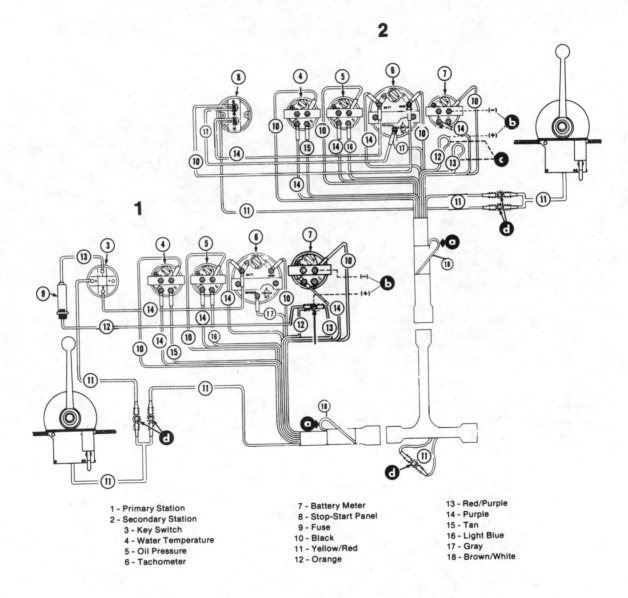

1 - Primary Station	7 - Battery Meter	13 - Red/Purple
2 - Secondary Station	8 - Stop-Start Panel	14 - Purple
3 - Key Switch	9 - Fuse	15 - Tan
4 - Water Temperature	10 - Black	16 - Light Blue
5 - Oil Pressure	11 - Yellow/Red	17 - Gray
6 - Tachometer	12 - Orange	18 - Brown/White

OMC

9

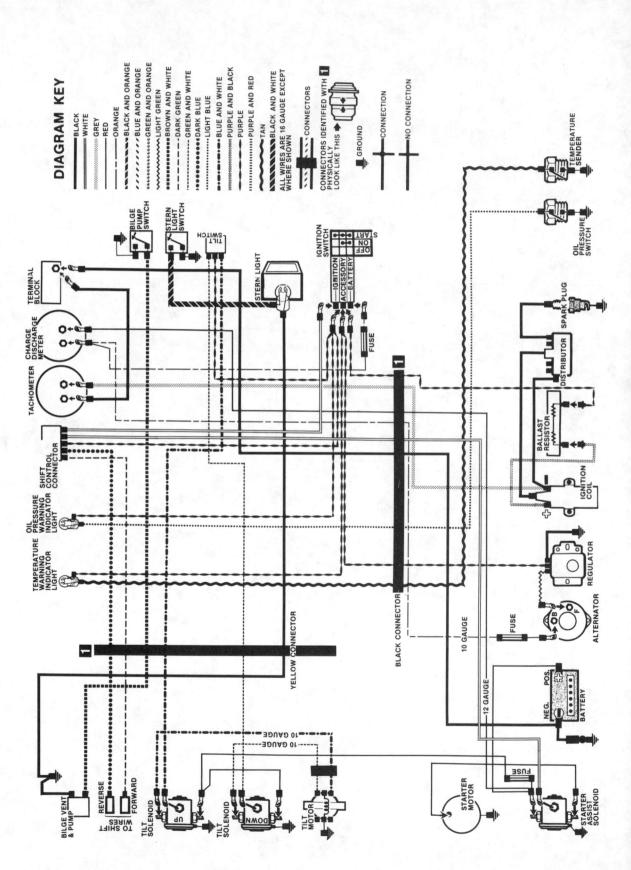

1964-1971 FIXED MOUNT, SINGLE STATION

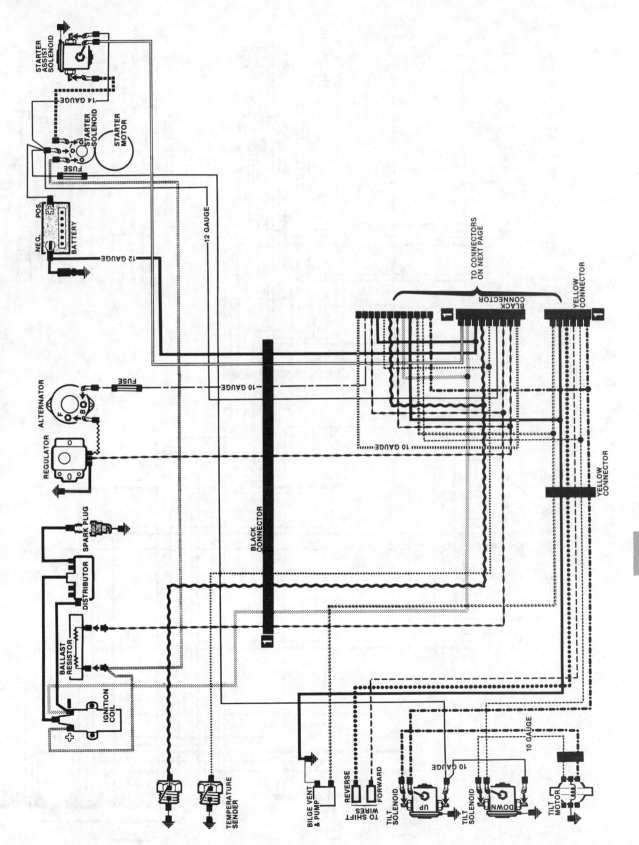

1964-1971 FIXED MOUNTS, DUAL STATION

9

1964-1971 FIXED MOUNTS, DUAL STATION

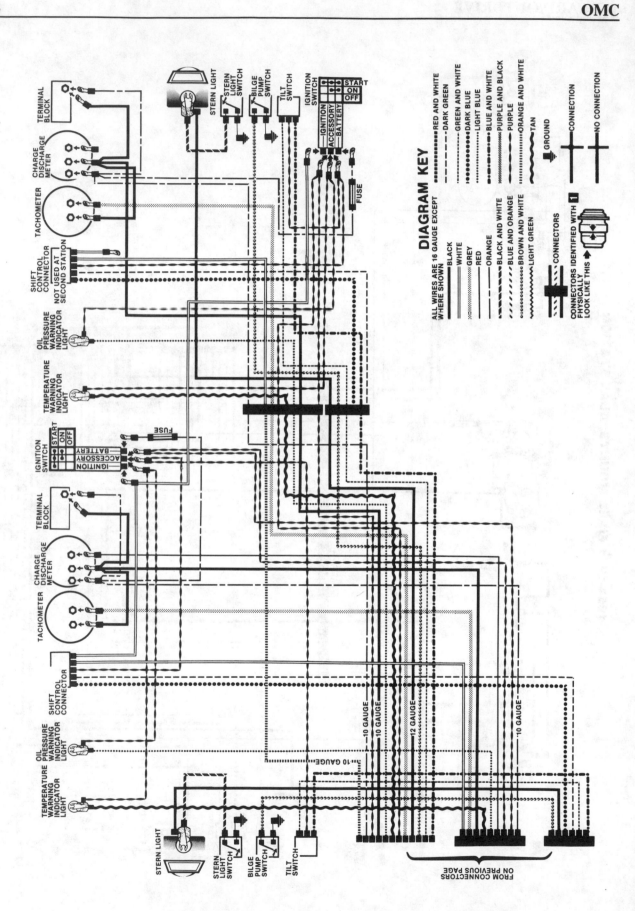

FROM CONNECTORS ON PREVIOUS PAGE

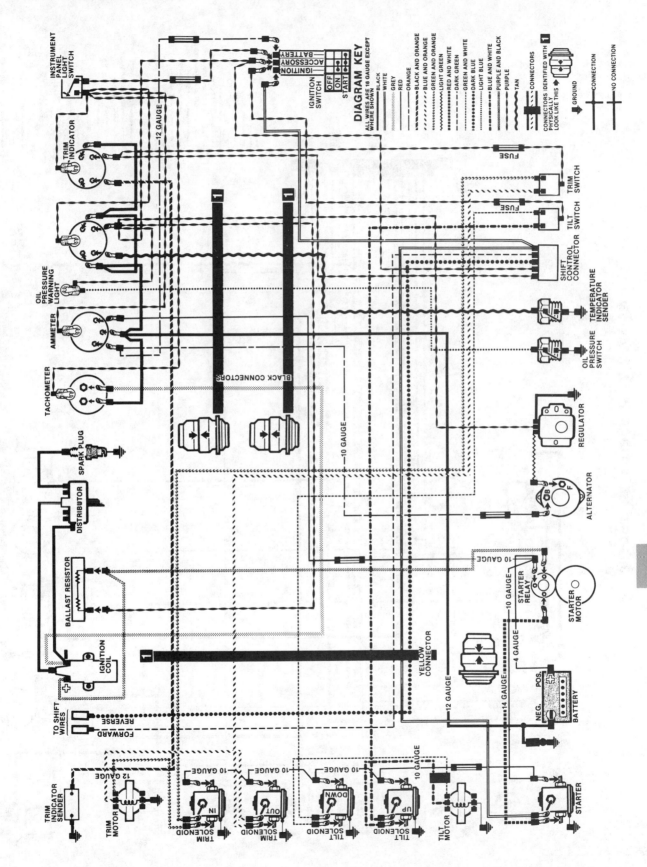

1964-1971 SELECTRIM, SINGLE STATION

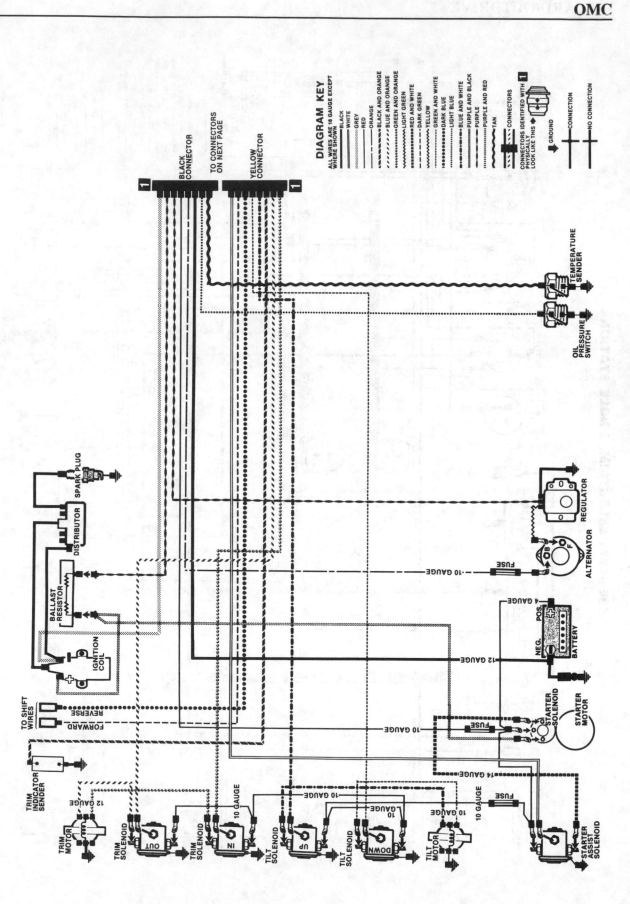

1964-1971 SELECTRIM, DUAL STATION

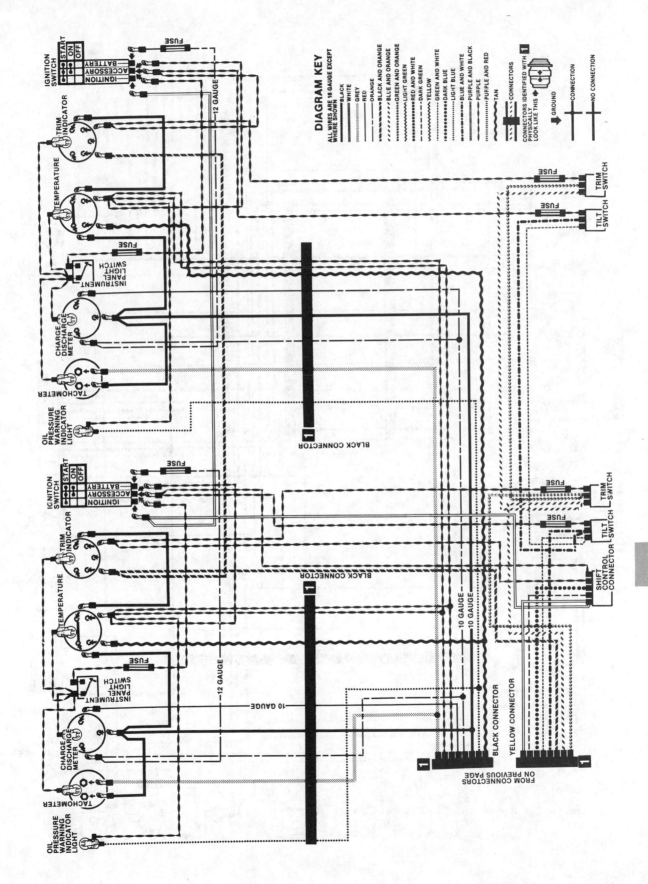

1964-1971 SELECTRIM, DUAL STATION

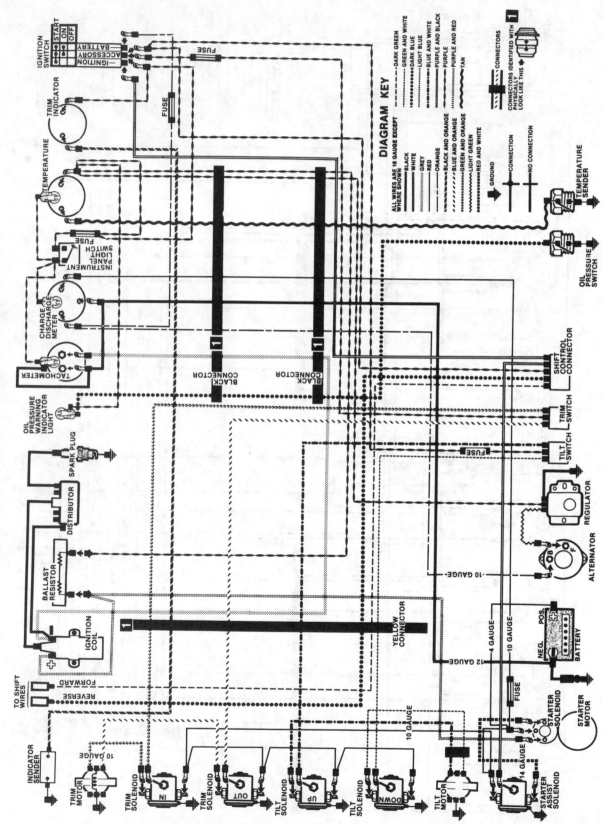

1974-1976 140 HP SELECTRIM

1972 100 HP

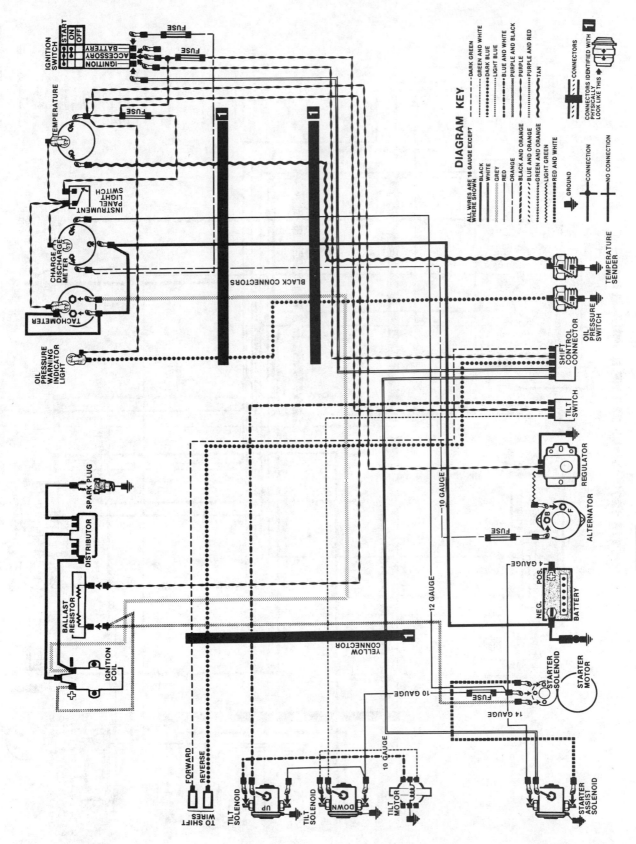

DIAGRAM KEY

ALL WIRES ARE 16 GAUGE EXCEPT WHERE SHOWN

- ———— DARK GREEN
- ———— GREEN AND WHITE
- ———— DARK BLUE
- ———— LIGHT BLUE
- ———— BLUE AND WHITE
- ———— PURPLE AND BLACK
- ———— PURPLE
- ———— PURPLE AND RED
- ———— TAN
- ———— BLACK
- ———— WHITE
- ———— GREY
- ———— RED
- ———— ORANGE
- ———— BLACK AND ORANGE
- ———— BLUE AND ORANGE
- ———— GREEN AND ORANGE
- ———— LIGHT GREEN
- ———— RED AND WHITE

GROUND

CONNECTION

NO CONNECTION

CONNECTORS IDENTIFIED WITH PHYSICALLY LOOK LIKE THIS

CONNECTORS

9

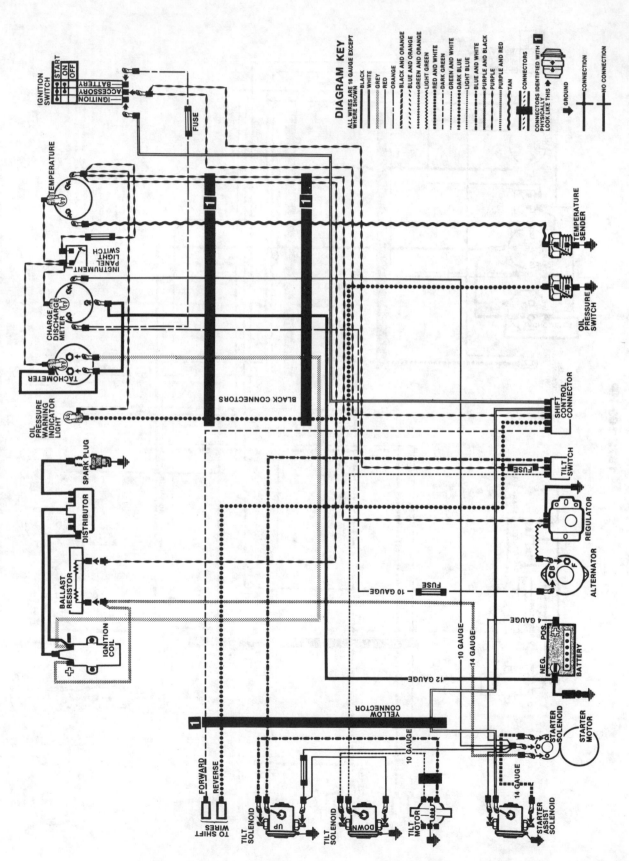

1974-1976 120/140/165/225 HP MANUAL TRIM

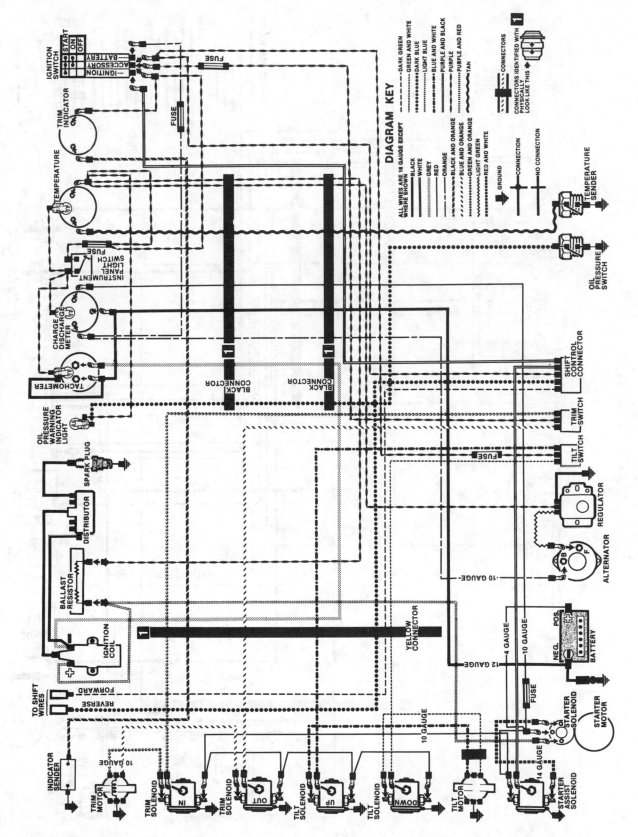

1972 120/165 HP SELECTRIM

1972 140/225/245 HP

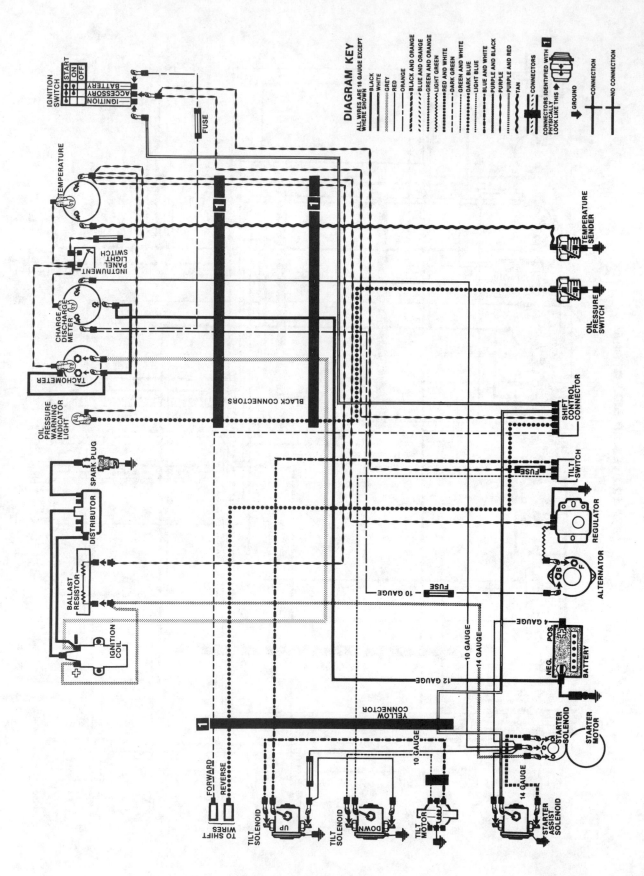

DIAGRAM KEY

ALL WIRES ARE 16 GAUGE EXCEPT
WHERE SHOWN

BLACK
WHITE
GREY
RED
ORANGE
BLACK AND ORANGE
BLUE AND ORANGE
LIGHT GREEN
GREEN AND ORANGE
RED AND WHITE
DARK GREEN
GREEN AND WHITE
DARK BLUE
LIGHT BLUE
BLUE AND WHITE
PURPLE AND BLACK
PURPLE
PURPLE AND RED
TAN
CONNECTORS

CONNECTORS IDENTIFIED WITH ▮1
PHYSICALLY
LOOK LIKE THIS ▶

GROUND
CONNECTION
NO CONNECTION

IGNITION SWITCH

START
ON
OFF

BATTERY
ACCESSORY
IGNITION

FUSE

TEMPERATURE

INSTRUMENT PANEL LIGHT SWITCH

CHARGE & DISCHARGE METER

TACHOMETER

OIL PRESSURE WARNING INDICATOR LIGHT

SPARK PLUG

DISTRIBUTOR

BALLAST RESISTOR

IGNITION COIL

BLACK CONNECTORS

TEMPERATURE SENDER

OIL PRESSURE SWITCH

SHIFT CONTROL CONNECTOR

TILT SWITCH

FUSE

REGULATOR

ALTERNATOR

10 GAUGE FUSE

BATTERY

NEG. POS.

4 GAUGE

12 GAUGE

10 GAUGE

14 GAUGE

STARTER SOLENOID

STARTER MOTOR

YELLOW CONNECTOR

FORWARD
REVERSE

TO SHIFT WIRES

TILT SOLENOID UP

TILT SOLENOID DOWN

TILT MOTOR

10 GAUGE

14 GAUGE

STARTER ASSIST SOLENOID

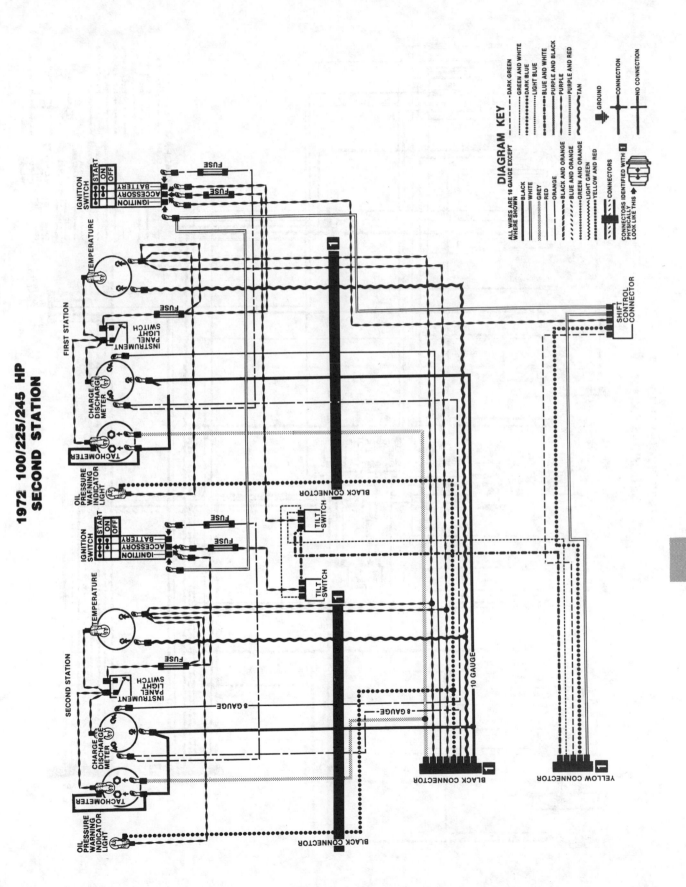

1972 100/225/245 HP
SECOND STATION

DIAGRAM KEY

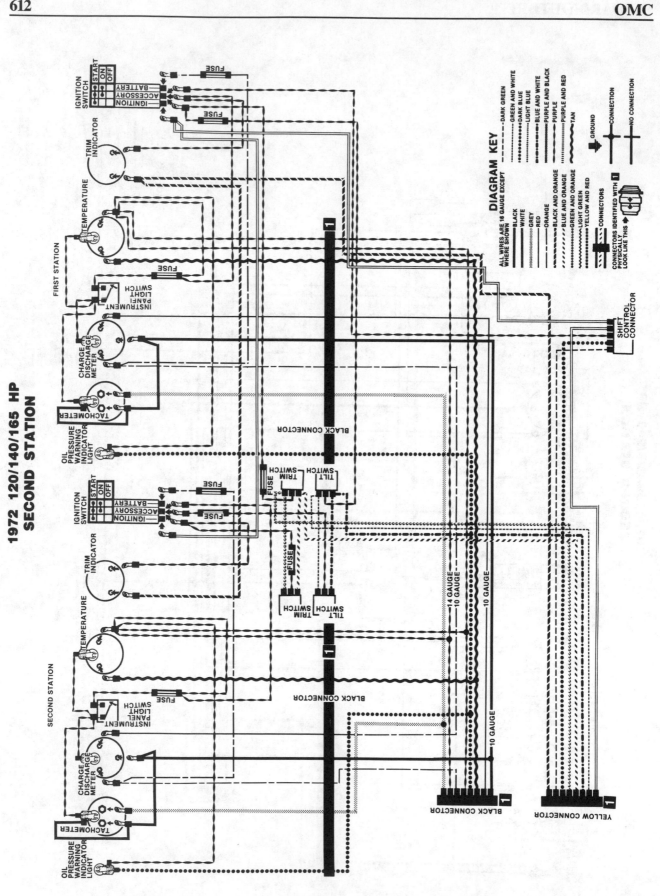

1972 120/140/165 HP
SECOND STATION

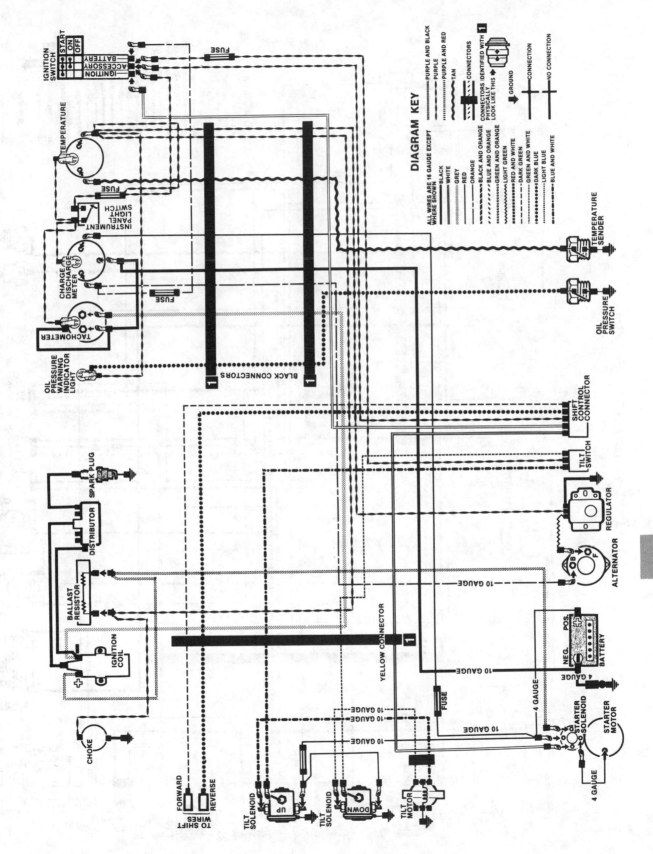

1973 175/190/235 HP FIXED MOUNT

9

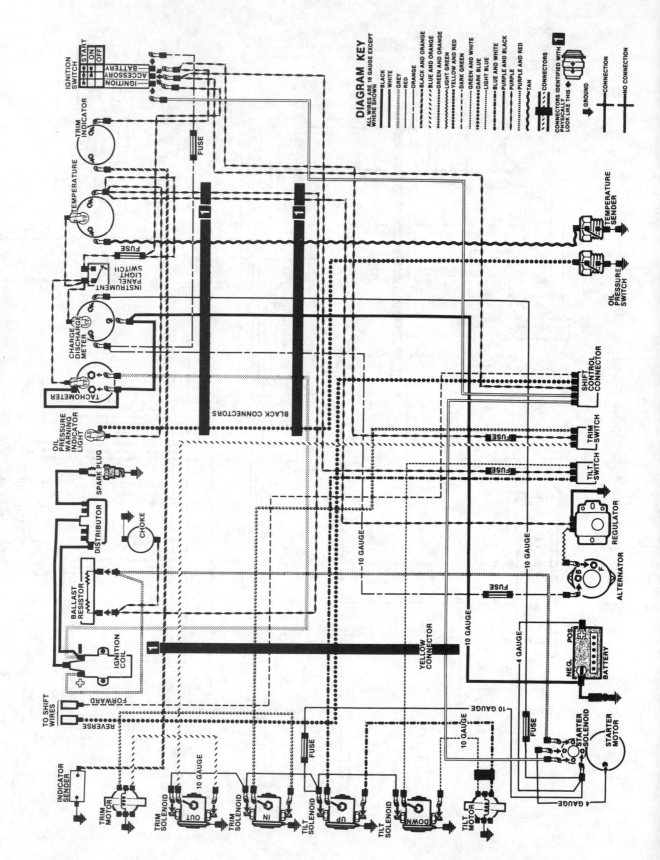

1973 175/190/235 HP SELECTRIM

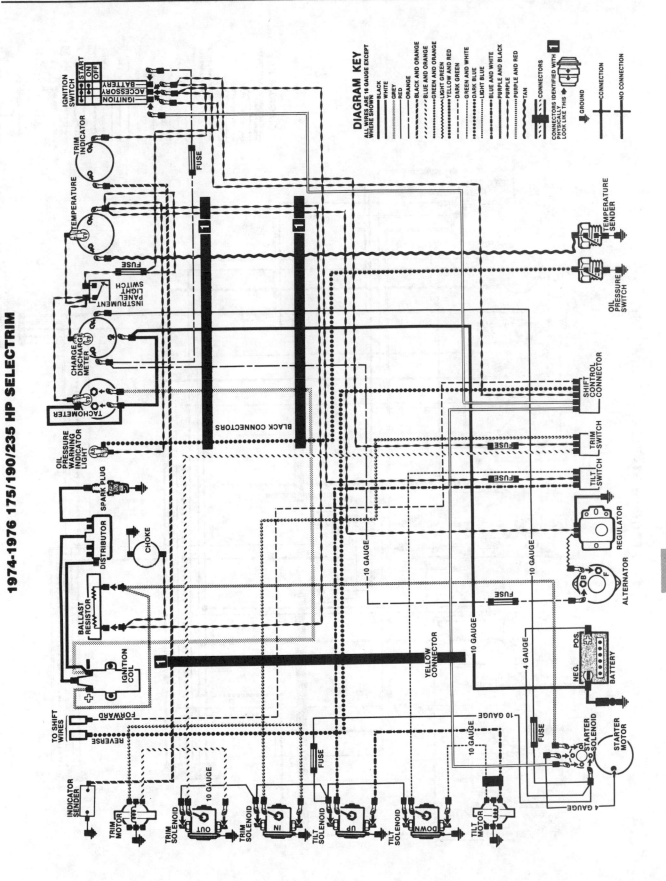

1974-1976 175/190/235 HP SELECTRIM

DIAGRAM KEY
ALL WIRES ARE 16 GAUGE EXCEPT WHERE SHOWN

BLACK
WHITE
GREY
RED
ORANGE
BLACK AND ORANGE
BLUE AND ORANGE
GREEN AND ORANGE
LIGHT GREEN
YELLOW AND RED
GREEN AND WHITE
DARK GREEN
LIGHT BLUE
BLUE AND WHITE
PURPLE AND BLACK
PURPLE
PURPLE AND RED
TAN

CONNECTORS IDENTIFIED WITH [1]
CONNECTORS IDENTIFIED WITH
PHYSICALLY LOOK LIKE THIS ►

GROUND
CONNECTION
NO CONNECTION

9

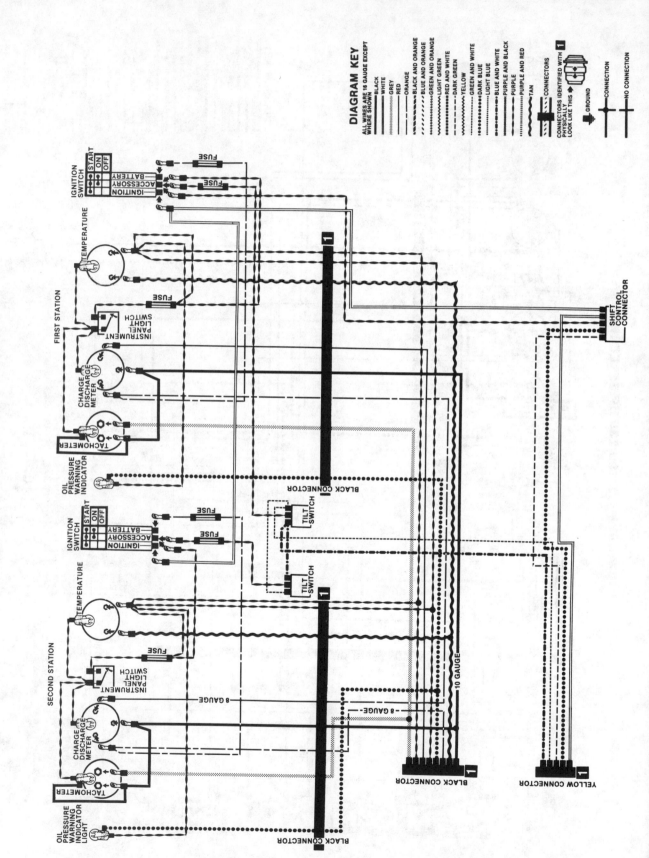

1973 SECOND STATION (FIXED MOUNT)

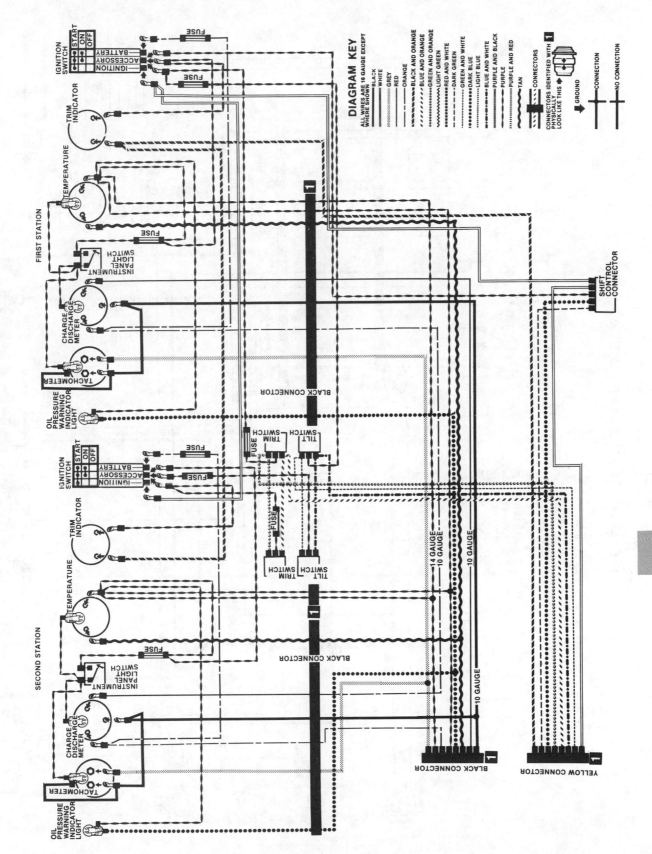

1973 SECOND STATION (SELECTRIM)

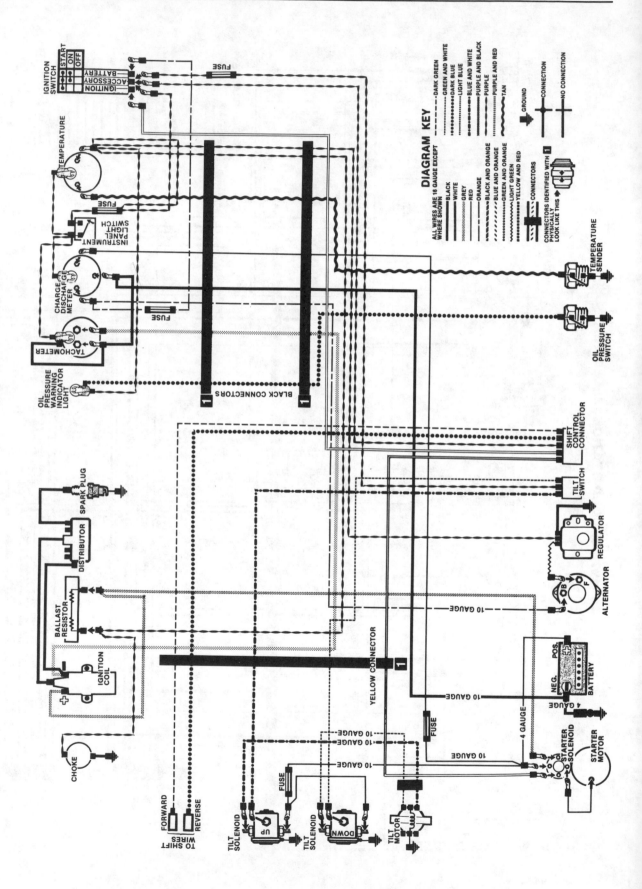

1974-1976 175/190/235 HP FIXED MOUNT

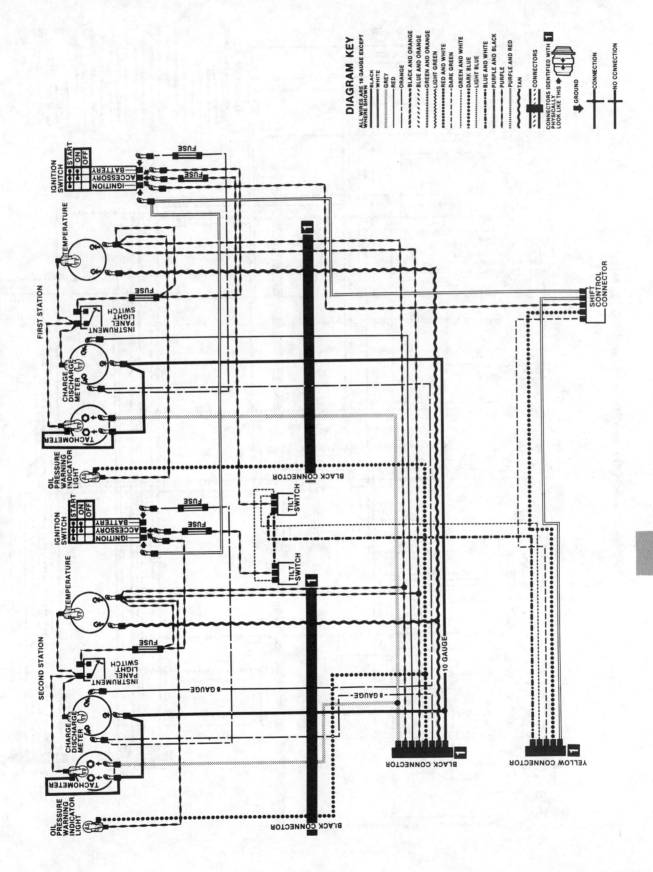

1974-1976 SECOND STATION (FIXED MOUNT)

9

1974-1976 SECOND STATION (SELECTRIM)

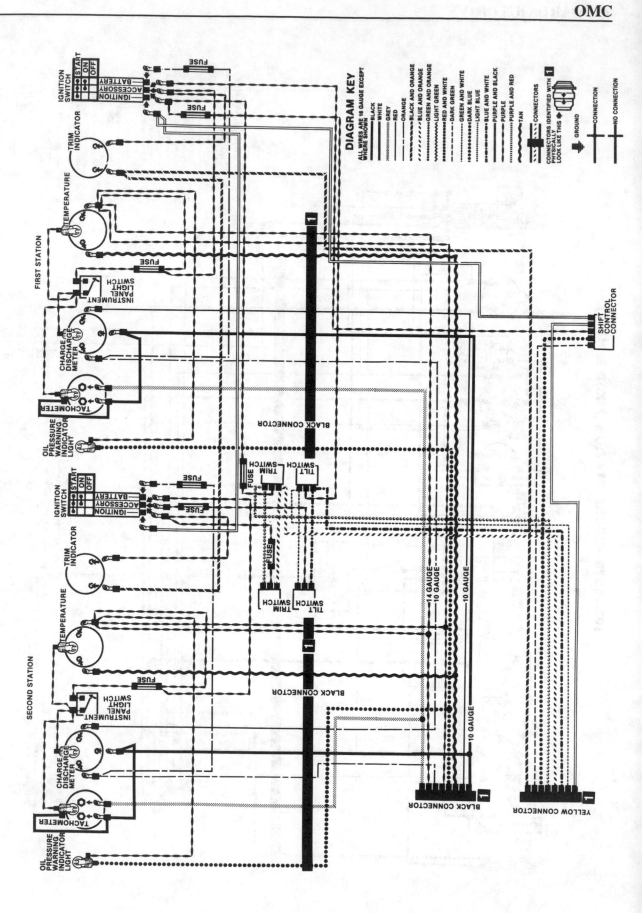

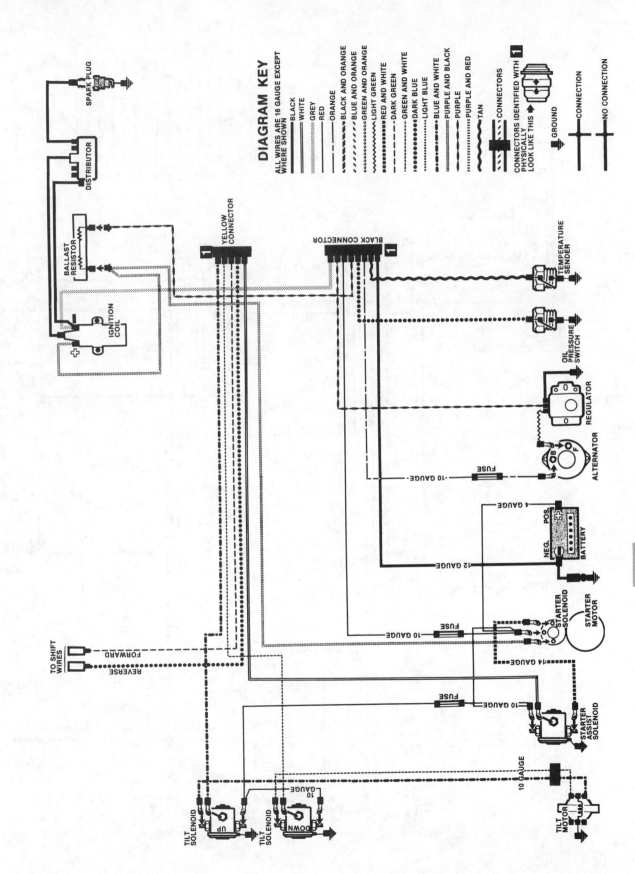

DIAGRAM KEY

ALL WIRES ARE 16 GAUGE EXCEPT WHERE SHOWN

- BLACK
- WHITE
- GREY
- RED
- ORANGE
- BLACK AND ORANGE
- BLUE AND ORANGE
- GREEN AND ORANGE
- LIGHT GREEN
- RED AND WHITE
- DARK GREEN
- GREEN AND WHITE
- DARK BLUE
- LIGHT BLUE
- BLUE AND WHITE
- PURPLE AND BLACK
- PURPLE
- PURPLE AND RED
- TAN
- CONNECTORS

CONNECTORS IDENTIFIED WITH **1** PHYSICALLY LOOK LIKE THIS

GROUND

CONNECTION

NO CONNECTION

1977 120/140 HP MANUAL TRIM

SPARK PLUG

DISTRIBUTOR

BALLAST RESISTOR

IGNITION COIL

YELLOW CONNECTOR

BLACK CONNECTOR

TEMPERATURE SENDER

OIL PRESSURE SWITCH

REGULATOR

ALTERNATOR

10 GAUGE

FUSE

4 GAUGE

BATTERY

POS.

NEG.

12 GAUGE

STARTER SOLENOID

STARTER MOTOR

10 GAUGE

FUSE

14 GAUGE

10 GAUGE

FUSE

STARTER ASSIST SOLENOID

TO SHIFT WIRES

FORWARD

REVERSE

TILT SOLENOID

UP

TILT SOLENOID

DOWN

10 GAUGE

10 GAUGE

TILT MOTOR

9

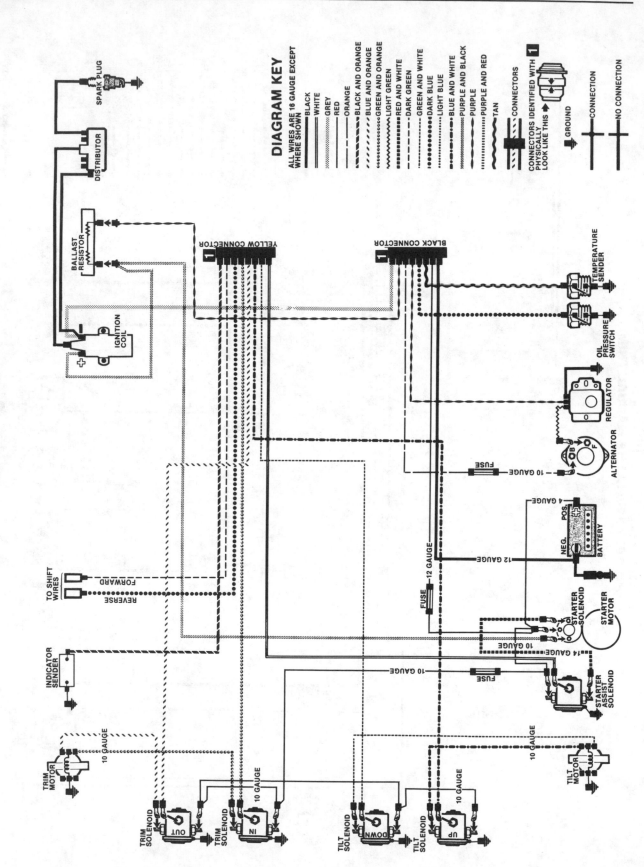

1977 120/140 HP SELECTRIM

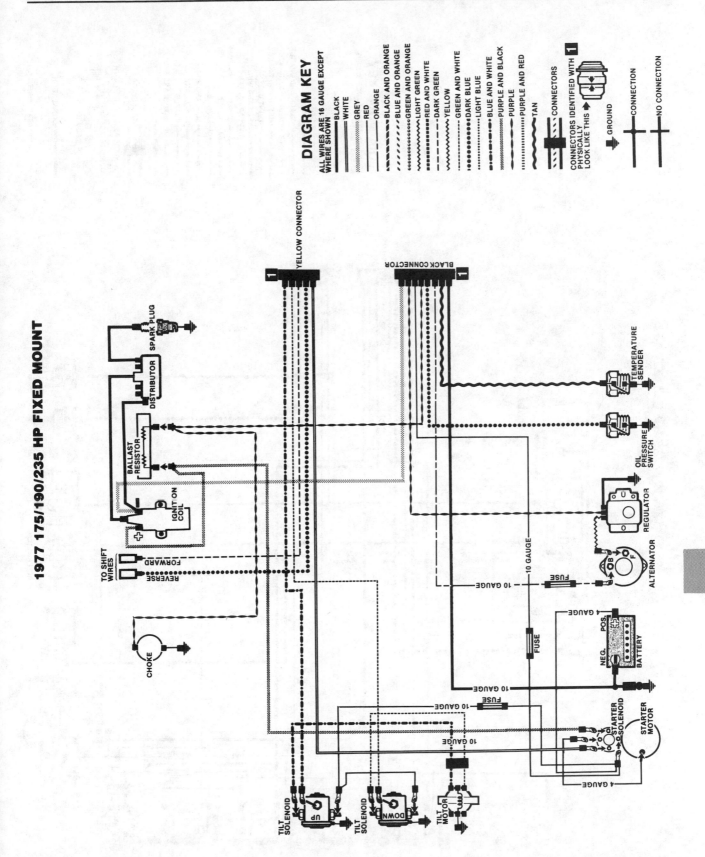

DIAGRAM KEY

ALL WIRES ARE 16 GAUGE EXCEPT WHERE SHOWN

BLACK
WHITE
GREY
RED
ORANGE
BLACK AND ORANGE
BLUE AND ORANGE
GREEN AND ORANGE
LIGHT GREEN
RED AND WHITE
DARK GREEN
YELLOW
GREEN AND WHITE
DARK BLUE
LIGHT BLUE
BLUE AND WHITE
PURPLE AND BLACK
PURPLE
PURPLE AND RED
TAN

CONNECTORS
CONNECTORS IDENTIFIED WITH THIS PHYSICALLY LOOK LIKE THIS
GROUND
CONNECTION
NO CONNECTION

1977 175/190/235 HP FIXED MOUNT

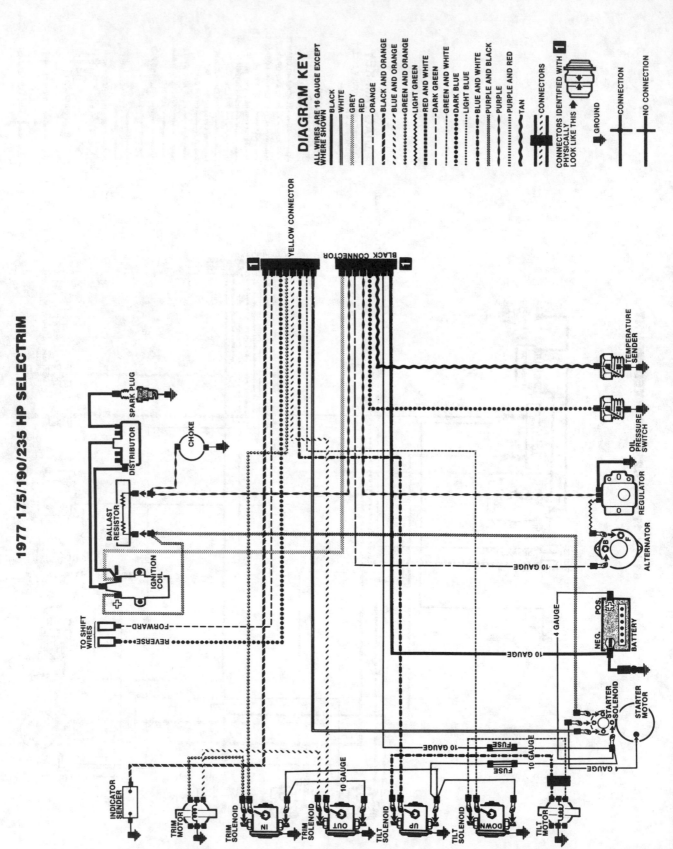

DIAGRAM KEY

ALL WIRES ARE 16 GAUGE EXCEPT WHERE SHOWN

BLACK
WHITE
GREY
RED
ORANGE
BLACK AND ORANGE
BLUE AND ORANGE
GREEN AND ORANGE
LIGHT GREEN
RED AND WHITE
DARK GREEN
GREEN AND WHITE
DARK BLUE
LIGHT BLUE
BLUE AND WHITE
PURPLE AND BLACK
PURPLE
PURPLE AND RED
TAN
CONNECTORS

CONNECTORS IDENTIFIED WITH 1 PHYSICALLY LOOK LIKE THIS

GROUND
CONNECTION
NO CONNECTION

1977 175/190/235 HP SELECTRIM

YELLOW CONNECTOR

BLACK CONNECTOR

SPARK PLUG

DISTRIBUTOR

CHOKE

BALLAST RESISTOR

IGNITION COIL

TO SHIFT WIRES

FORWARD

REVERSE

TEMPERATURE SENDER

OIL PRESSURE SWITCH

REGULATOR

ALTERNATOR

10 GAUGE

10 GAUGE

4 GAUGE

BATTERY

NEG. POS.

STARTER SOLENOID

STARTER MOTOR

INDICATOR SENDER

TRIM MOTOR

TRIM SOLENOID IN

TRIM SOLENOID OUT

10 GAUGE

TILT SOLENOID UP

FUSE

10 GAUGE

TILT SOLENOID DOWN

FUSE

10 GAUGE

10 GAUGE

GAUGE

TILT MOTOR

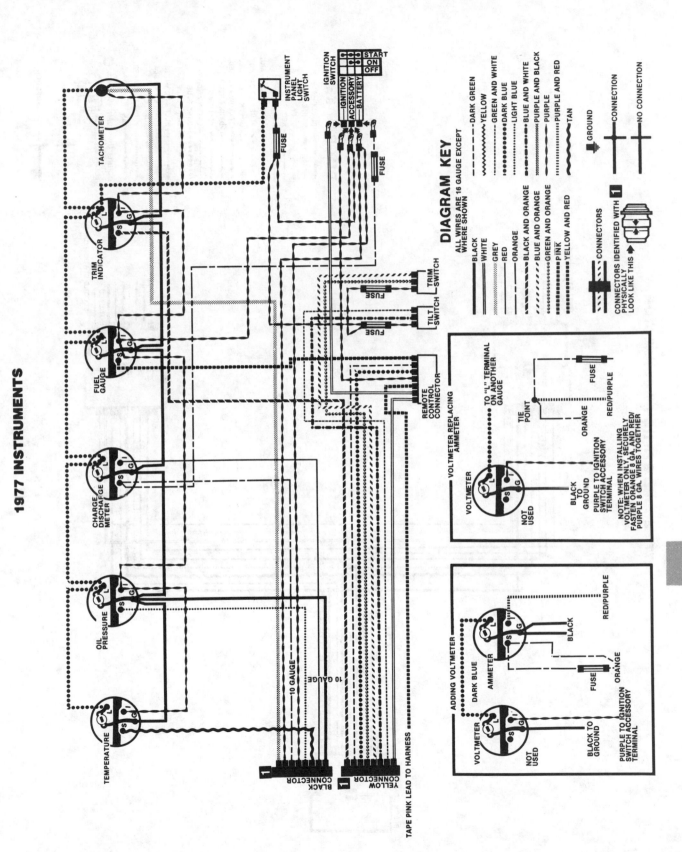

1977 INSTRUMENTS

DIAGRAM KEY

ALL WIRES ARE 16 GAUGE EXCEPT WHERE SHOWN

BLACK
WHITE
GREY
RED
ORANGE
BLUE AND ORANGE
BLUE AND ORANGE
GREEN AND ORANGE
PINK
YELLOW AND RED

DARK GREEN
YELLOW
GREEN AND WHITE
DARK BLUE
LIGHT BLUE
BLUE AND WHITE
PURPLE AND BLACK
PURPLE
PURPLE AND RED
TAN

GROUND
CONNECTION
NO CONNECTION

CONNECTORS IDENTIFIED WITH ☐1

CONNECTORS IDENTIFIED WITH 1 PHYSICALLY LOOK LIKE THIS

TACHOMETER

INSTRUMENT PANEL LIGHT SWITCH

FUSE

IGNITION SWITCH

	START	ON	OFF
IGNITION			
ACCESSORY			
BATTERY			

TRIM INDICATOR

FUEL GAUGE

CHARGE DISCHARGE METER

OIL PRESSURE

TEMPERATURE

FUSE

TRIM SWITCH
FUSE
TILT SWITCH

REMOTE CONTROL CONNECTOR

VOLTMETER REPLACING AMMETER

TO "I" TERMINAL ON ANOTHER GAUGE

TIE POINT

FUSE

ORANGE

RED/PURPLE

VOLTMETER

BLACK TO GROUND

PURPLE TO IGNITION SWITCH ACCESSORY TERMINAL

NOT USED

NOTE: WHEN INSTALLING VOLTMETER ONLY, SECURELY FASTEN ORANGE 8 GA. AND RED/ PURPLE 8 GA. WIRES TOGETHER

ADDING VOLTMETER

DARK BLUE

AMMETER

RED/PURPLE

BLACK

VOLTMETER

FUSE

ORANGE

BLACK TO GROUND

PURPLE TO IGNITION SWITCH ACCESSORY TERMINAL.

NOT USED

10 GAUGE

BLACK CONNECTOR ☐1

YELLOW CONNECTOR ☐1

TAPE PINK LEAD TO HARNESS

9

DIAGRAM KEY

BLACK
WHITE
GREY
RED
ORANGE
BLACK AND ORANGE
BLUE AND ORANGE
GREEN AND ORANGE
YELLOW AND RED
DARK GREEN
YELLOW
GREEN AND WHITE
DARK BLUE
LIGHT BLUE
BLUE AND WHITE
PURPLE AND BLACK
PURPLE
PURPLE AND RED
TAN

CONNECTORS IDENTIFIED WITH
PHYSICALLY
LOOK LIKE THIS

CONNECTION   NO CONNECTION

1977 SECOND STATION Y CONNECTOR

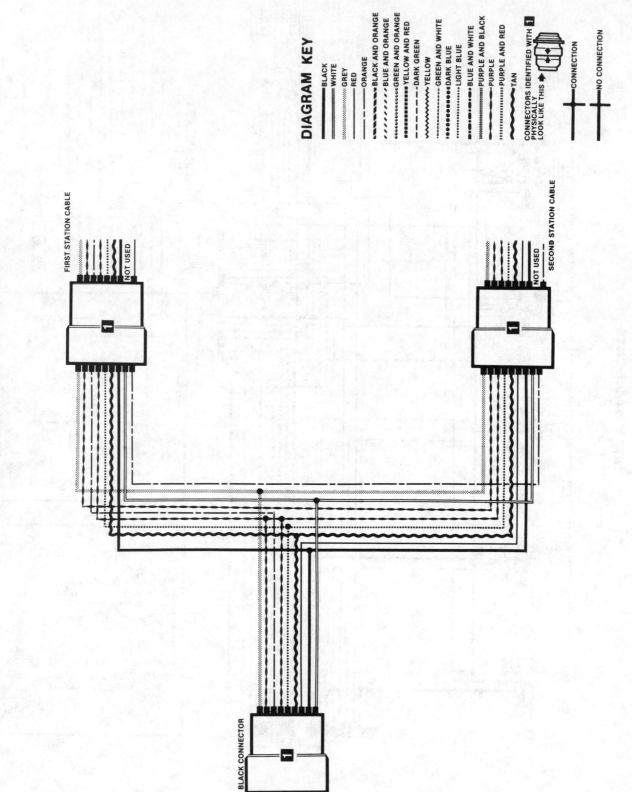

FIRST STATION CABLE

NOT USED

SECOND STATION CABLE

NOT USED

BLACK CONNECTOR

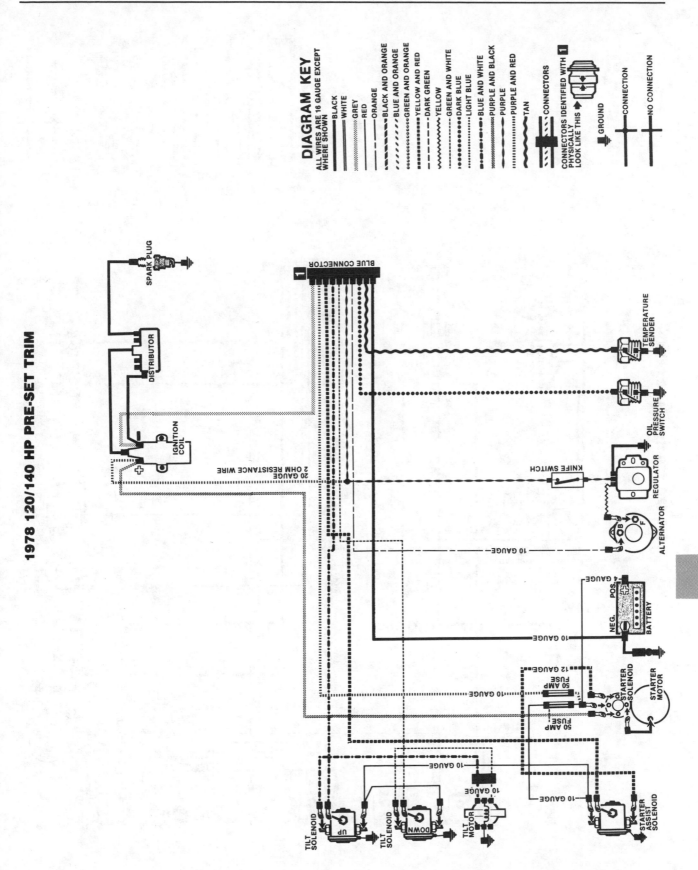

1978 120/140 HP PRE-SET TRIM

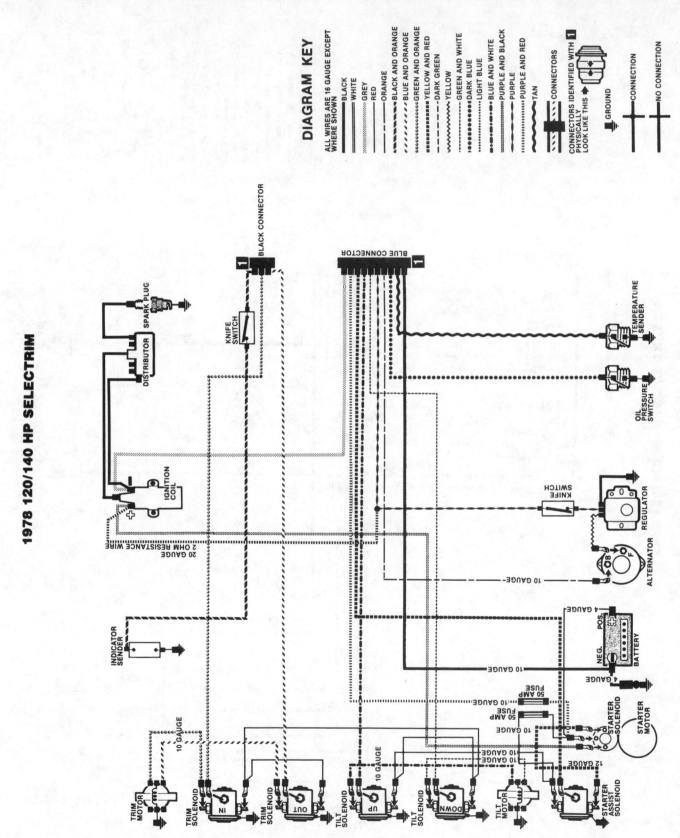

1978 120/140 HP SELECTRIM

DIAGRAM KEY

ALL WIRES ARE 16 GAUGE EXCEPT
WHERE SHOWN

BLACK
WHITE
GREY
RED
ORANGE
BLACK AND ORANGE
BLUE AND ORANGE
GREEN AND ORANGE
YELLOW AND RED
DARK GREEN
YELLOW
GREEN AND WHITE
DARK BLUE
LIGHT BLUE
BLUE AND WHITE
PURPLE
PURPLE AND BLACK
PURPLE AND RED
TAN
CONNECTORS

CONNECTORS IDENTIFIED WITH
PHYSICALLY
LOOK LIKE THIS

GROUND

CONNECTION

NO CONNECTION

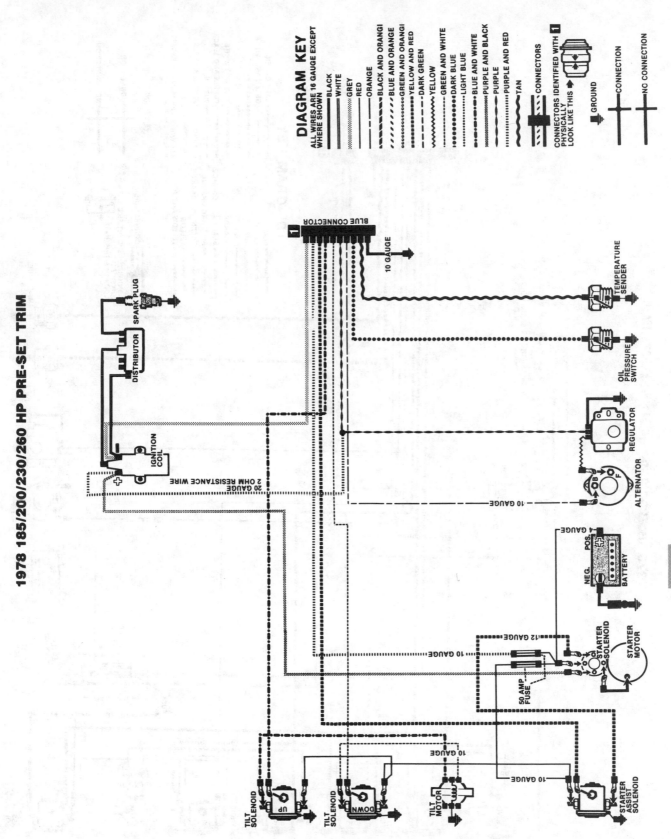

1978 185/200/230/260 HP PRE-SET TRIM

9

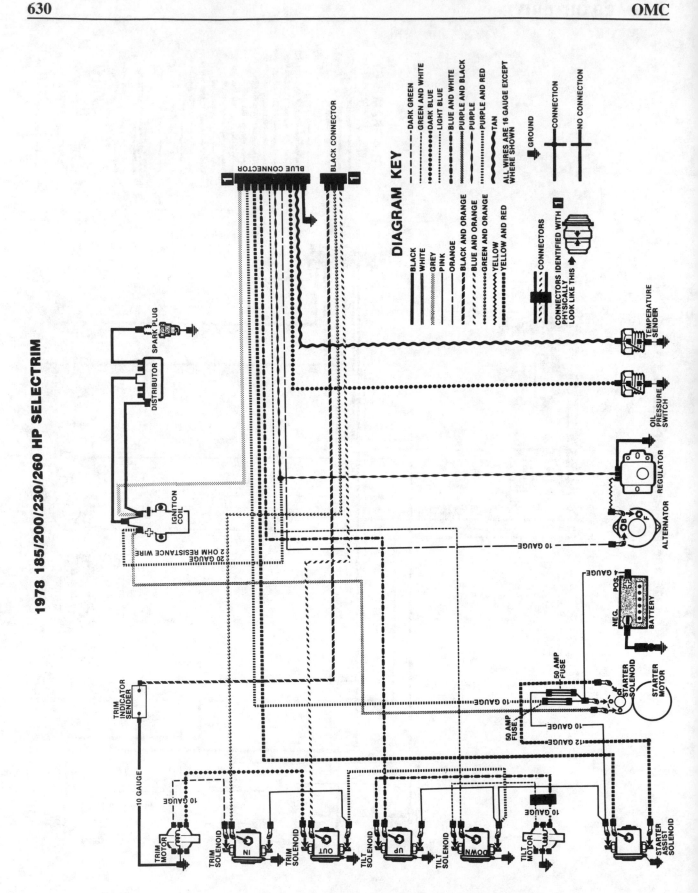

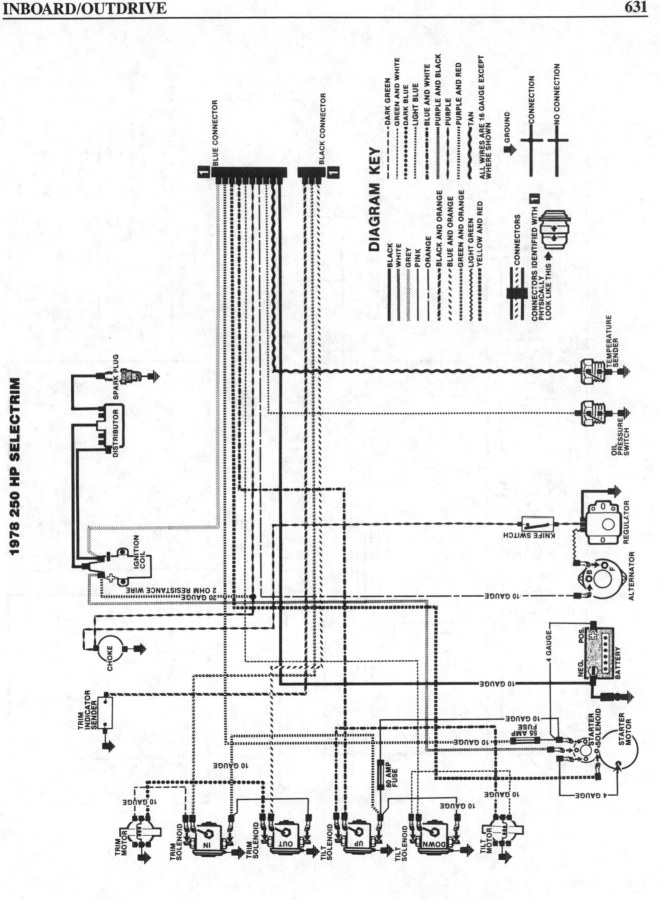

1978 250 HP SELECTRIM

DIAGRAM KEY

BLACK	DARK GREEN
WHITE	GREEN AND WHITE
GREY	DARK BLUE
PINK	LIGHT BLUE
ORANGE	BLUE AND WHITE
BLACK AND ORANGE	PURPLE AND BLACK
BLUE AND ORANGE	PURPLE
GREEN AND ORANGE	PURPLE AND RED
LIGHT GREEN	TAN
YELLOW AND RED	

ALL WIRES ARE 16 GAUGE EXCEPT WHERE SHOWN

GROUND

CONNECTION

NO CONNECTION

CONNECTORS

CONNECTORS IDENTIFIED WITH 1 PHYSICALLY LOOK LIKE THIS

BLUE CONNECTOR

BLACK CONNECTOR

SPARK PLUG

DISTRIBUTOR

IGNITION COIL

2 OHM RESISTANCE WIRE

20 GAUGE

CHOKE

TEMPERATURE SENDER

OIL PRESSURE SWITCH

KNIFE SWITCH

REGULATOR

ALTERNATOR

10 GAUGE

BATTERY

NEG. POS.

4 GAUGE

10 GAUGE

TRIM INDICATOR SENDER

STARTER SOLENOID

STARTER MOTOR

55 AMP FUSE

10 GAUGE

80 AMP FUSE

4 GAUGE

10 GAUGE

10 GAUGE

10 GAUGE

TRIM MOTOR

TRIM SOLENOID IN

TRIM SOLENOID OUT

TILT SOLENOID

TILT SOLENOID UP

TILT SOLENOID DOWN

TILT MOTOR

9

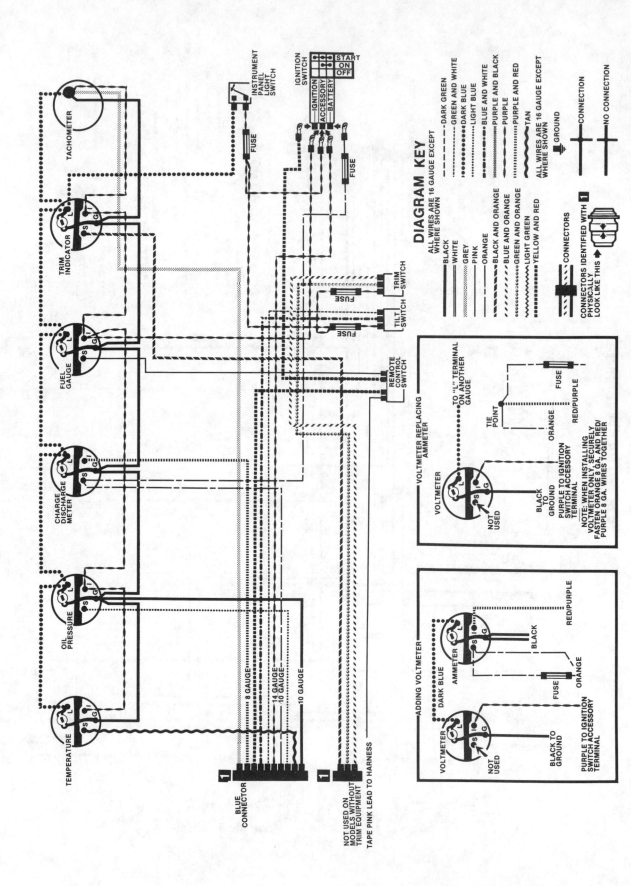

1978 INSTRUMENTS

TACHOMETER

TRIM INDICATOR

FUEL GAUGE

CHARGE DISCHARGE METER

OIL PRESSURE

TEMPERATURE

INSTRUMENT PANEL LIGHT SWITCH

IGNITION SWITCH

START
ON
OFF

IGNITION
ACCESSORY
BATTERY

FUSE

FUSE

TRIM SWITCH

TILT SWITCH

FUSE

FUSE

REMOTE CONTROL SWITCH

8 GAUGE
14 GAUGE
10 GAUGE
10 GAUGE

BLUE CONNECTOR

NOT USED ON MODELS WITHOUT TRIM EQUIPMENT

TAPE PINK LEAD TO HARNESS

DIAGRAM KEY

ALL WIRES ARE 16 GAUGE EXCEPT WHERE SHOWN

BLACK
WHITE
GREY
PINK
ORANGE
BLACK AND ORANGE
BLUE AND ORANGE
GREEN AND ORANGE
LIGHT GREEN
YELLOW AND RED

DARK GREEN
GREEN AND WHITE
DARK BLUE
LIGHT BLUE
BLUE AND WHITE
PURPLE AND BLACK
PURPLE
PURPLE AND RED
TAN

ALL WIRES ARE 16 GAUGE EXCEPT WHERE SHOWN

GROUND

CONNECTION

NO CONNECTION

CONNECTORS

CONNECTORS IDENTIFIED WITH 1 PHYSICALLY LOOK LIKE THIS

VOLTMETER REPLACING AMMETER

TO "L" TERMINAL ON ANOTHER GAUGE

TIE POINT

FUSE

ORANGE

RED/PURPLE

VOLTMETER

NOT USED

BLACK TO GROUND

PURPLE TO IGNITION SWITCH ACCESSORY TERMINAL

NOTE: WHEN INSTALLING VOLTMETER ONLY, SECURELY FASTEN ORANGE 8 GA. AND RED/PURPLE 8 GA. WIRES TOGETHER

ADDING VOLTMETER

DARK BLUE

AMMETER

BLACK

RED/PURPLE

ORANGE

FUSE

VOLTMETER

NOT USED

BLACK TO GROUND

PURPLE TO IGNITION SWITCH ACCESSORY TERMINAL

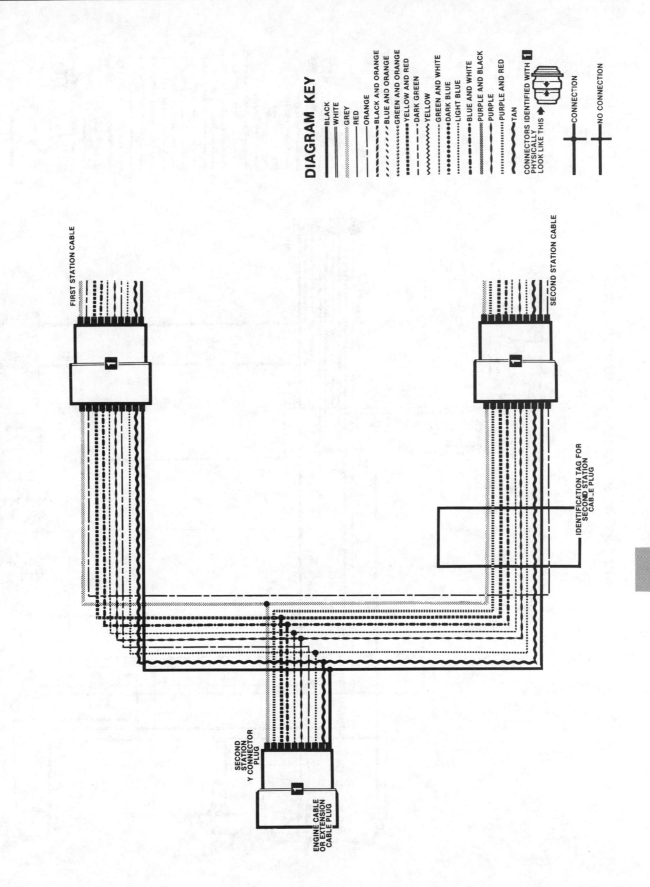

1978 SECOND STATION Y CONNECTOR

FIRST STATION CABLE

SECOND STATION CABLE

SECOND STATION Y CONNECTOR PLUG

ENGINE CABLE OR EXTENSION CABLE PLUG

IDENTIFICATION TAG FOR SECOND STATION CAB_E PLUG

DIAGRAM KEY

BLACK
WHITE
GREY
RED
ORANGE
BLACK AND ORANGE
BLUE AND ORANGE
GREEN AND ORANGE
YELLOW AND RED
DARK GREEN
YELLOW
GREEN AND WHITE
DARK BLUE
LIGHT BLUE
BLUE AND WHITE
PURPLE AND BLACK
PURPLE
PURPLE AND RED
TAN

CONNECTORS IDENTIFIED WITH **1**
PHYSICALLY
LOOK LIKE THIS

CONNECTION

NO CONNECTION

9

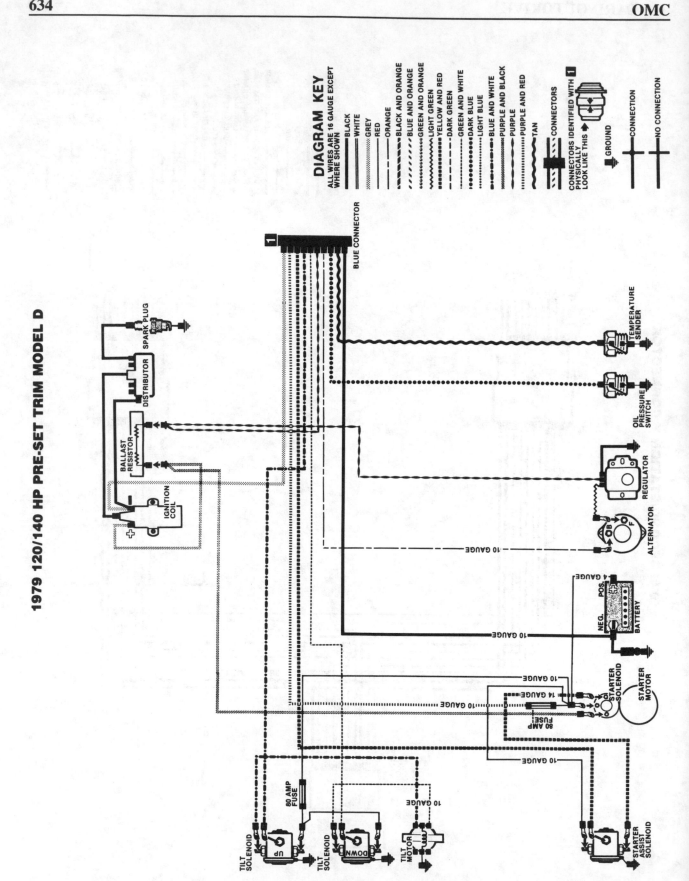

1979 120/140 HP PRE-SET TRIM MODEL D

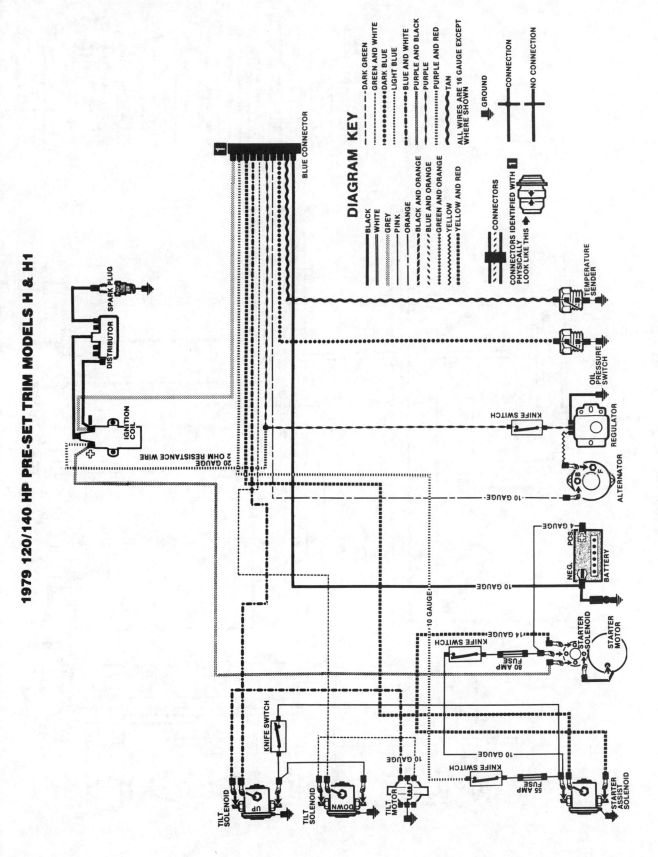

1979 120/140 HP PRE-SET TRIM MODELS H & H1

9

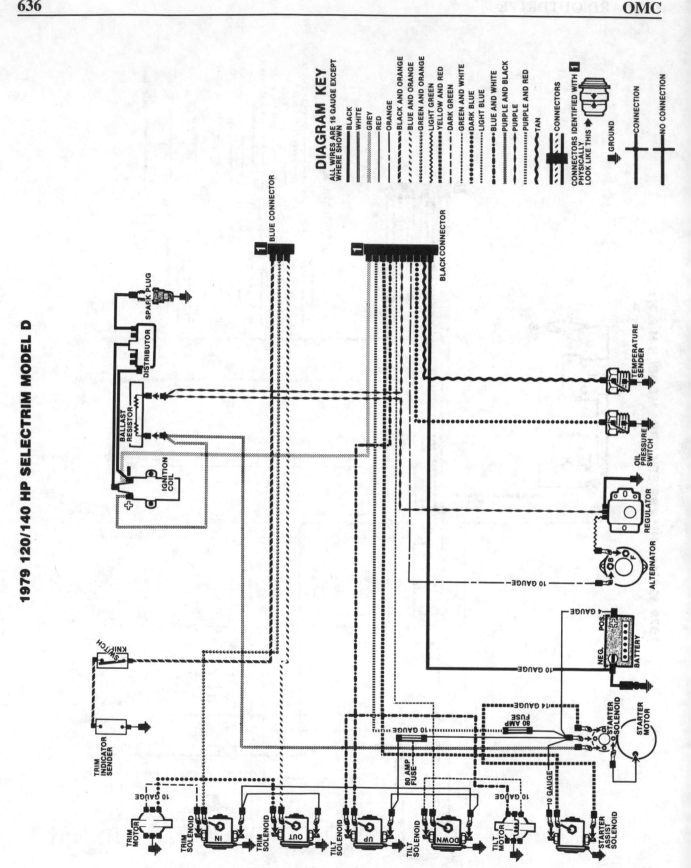

1979 120/140 HP SELECTRIM MODEL D

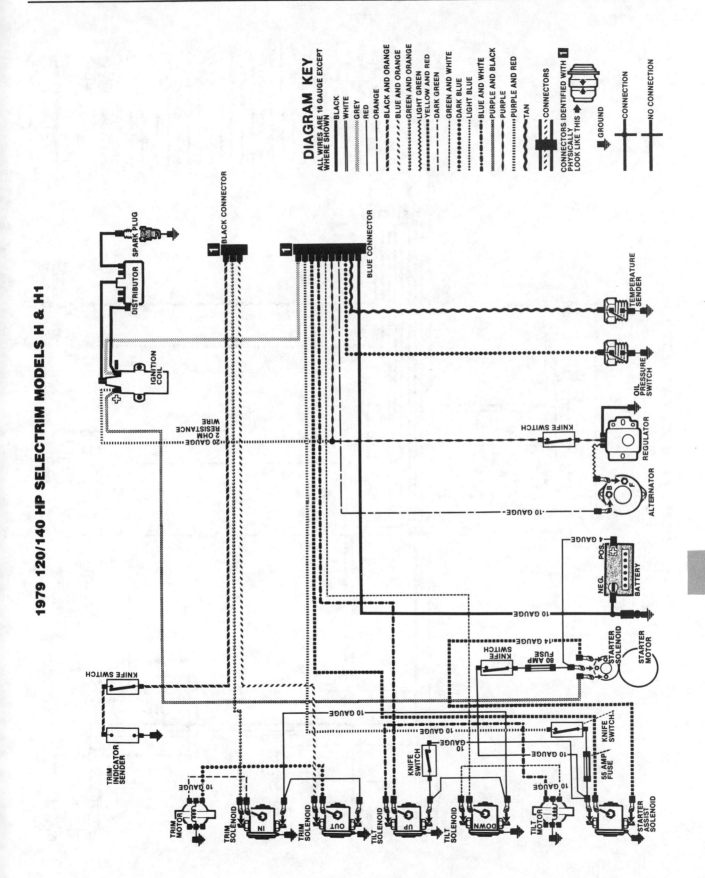

DIAGRAM KEY

ALL WIRES ARE 16 GAUGE EXCEPT WHERE SHOWN

BLACK
WHITE
GREY
RED
ORANGE
BLACK AND ORANGE
BLUE AND ORANGE
GREEN AND ORANGE
LIGHT GREEN
YELLOW AND RED
DARK GREEN
GREEN AND WHITE
DARK BLUE
LIGHT BLUE
BLUE AND WHITE
PURPLE
PURPLE AND BLACK
PURPLE AND RED
TAN
CONNECTORS

CONNECTORS IDENTIFIED WITH 1 PHYSICALLY LOOK LIKE THIS

GROUND
CONNECTION
NO CONNECTION

1979 120/140 HP SELECTRIM MODELS H & H1

SPARK PLUG

DISTRIBUTOR

IGNITION COIL

BLACK CONNECTOR

BLACK CONNECTOR

BLUE CONNECTOR

2 OHM RESISTANCE WIRE

20 GAUGE

TEMPERATURE SENDER

OIL PRESSURE SWITCH

KNIFE SWITCH

REGULATOR

ALTERNATOR

10 GAUGE

4 GAUGE

POS.

NEG.

BATTERY

10 GAUGE

14 GAUGE

STARTER SOLENOID

STARTER MOTOR

KNIFE SWITCH

80 AMP FUSE

KNIFE SWITCH

10 GAUGE

10 GAUGE

KNIFE SWITCH

10 GAUGE

10 GAUGE

KNIFE SWITCH

55 AMP FUSE

TRIM INDICATOR SENDER

10 GAUGE

TRIM MOTOR

TRIM SOLENOID

IN

TRIM SOLENOID

OUT

TILT SOLENOID

UP

TILT SOLENOID

DOWN

TILT MOTOR

STARTER ASSIST SOLENOID

10 GAUGE

9

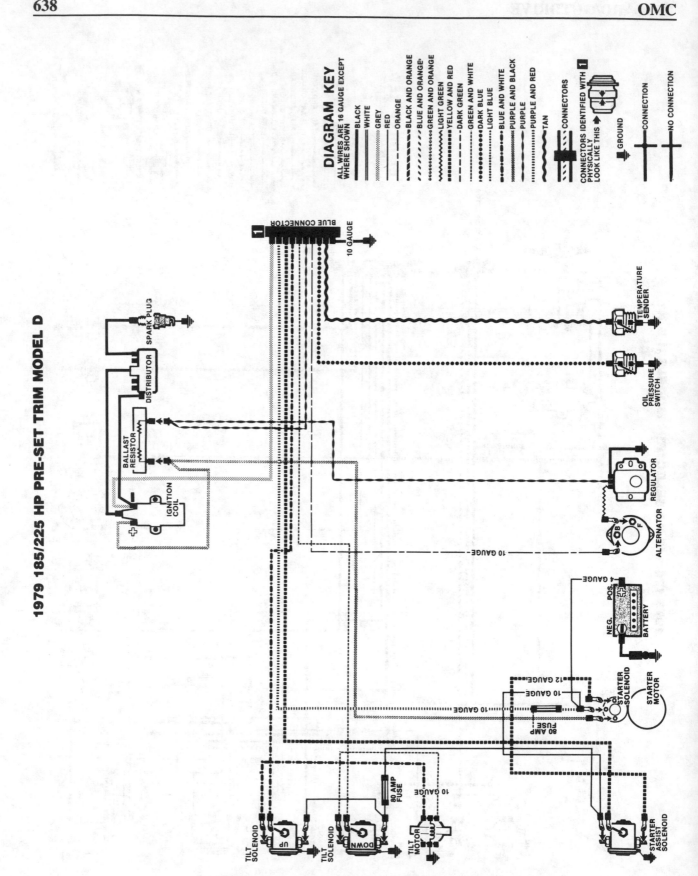

1979 185/225 HP PRE-SET TRIM MODEL D

DIAGRAM KEY

ALL WIRES ARE 16 GAUGE EXCEPT WHERE SHOWN

BLACK
WHITE
GREY
RED
ORANGE
BLACK AND ORANGE
BLUE AND ORANGE
GREEN AND ORANGE
LIGHT GREEN
YELLOW AND RED
DARK GREEN
GREEN AND WHITE
DARK BLUE
LIGHT BLUE
BLUE AND WHITE
PURPLE AND BLACK
PURPLE
PURPLE AND RED
TAN

CONNECTORS

CONNECTORS IDENTIFIED WITH 1

CONNECTORS PHYSICALLY LOOK LIKE THIS

GROUND
CONNECTION
NO CONNECTION

BLUE CONNECTOR

10 GAUGE

TEMPERATURE SENDER

OIL PRESSURE SWITCH

SPARK PLUG

DISTRIBUTOR

BALLAST RESISTOR

IGNITION COIL

REGULATOR

ALTERNATOR

10 GAUGE

4 GAUGE

NEG.   POS.

BATTERY

STARTER SOLENOID

STARTER MOTOR

12 GAUGE

10 GAUGE

80 AMP FUSE

TILT SOLENOID   UP

TILT SOLENOID   DOWN

TILT MOTOR

80 AMP FUSE

10 GAUGE

STARTER ASSIST SOLENOID

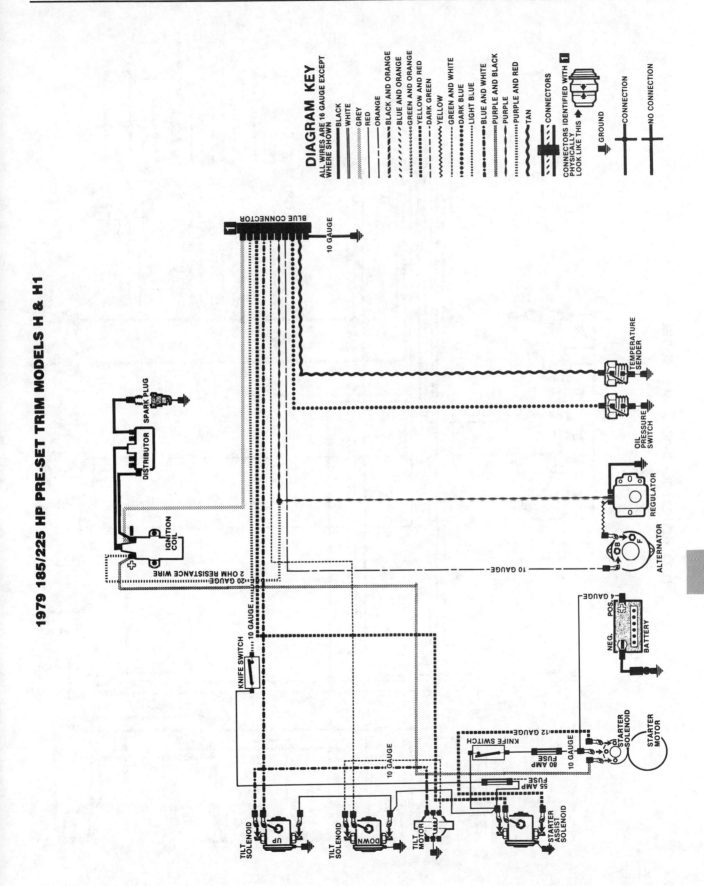

DIAGRAM KEY

ALL WIRES ARE 16 GAUGE EXCEPT WHERE SHOWN

- BLACK
- WHITE
- GREY
- RED
- ORANGE
- BLACK AND ORANGE
- BLUE AND ORANGE
- GREEN AND ORANGE
- YELLOW AND RED
- DARK GREEN
- YELLOW
- GREEN AND WHITE
- DARK BLUE
- LIGHT BLUE
- BLUE AND WHITE
- PURPLE AND BLACK
- PURPLE
- PURPLE AND RED
- TAN
- CONNECTORS
- CONNECTORS IDENTIFIED WITH PHYSICALLY LOOK LIKE THIS
- GROUND
- CONNECTION
- NO CONNECTION

1979 185/225 HP PRE-SET TRIM MODELS H & H1

9

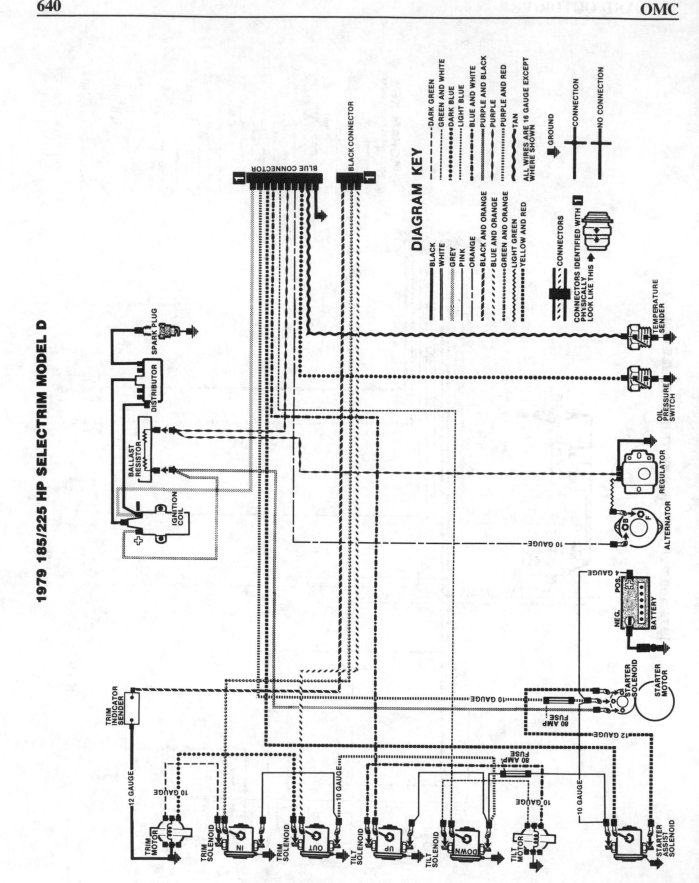

1979 185/225 HP SELECTRIM MODEL D

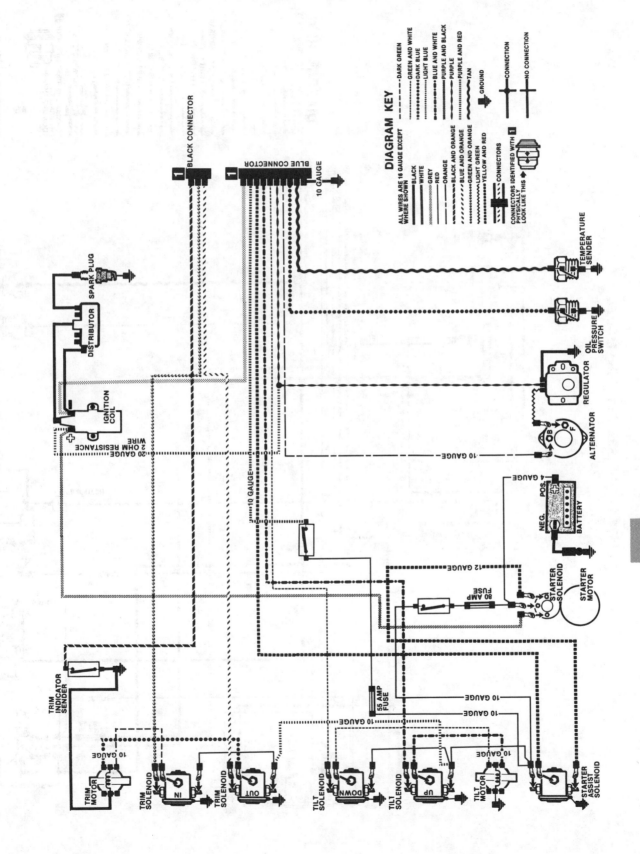

1979 185/225 HP SELECTRIM MODELS H & J

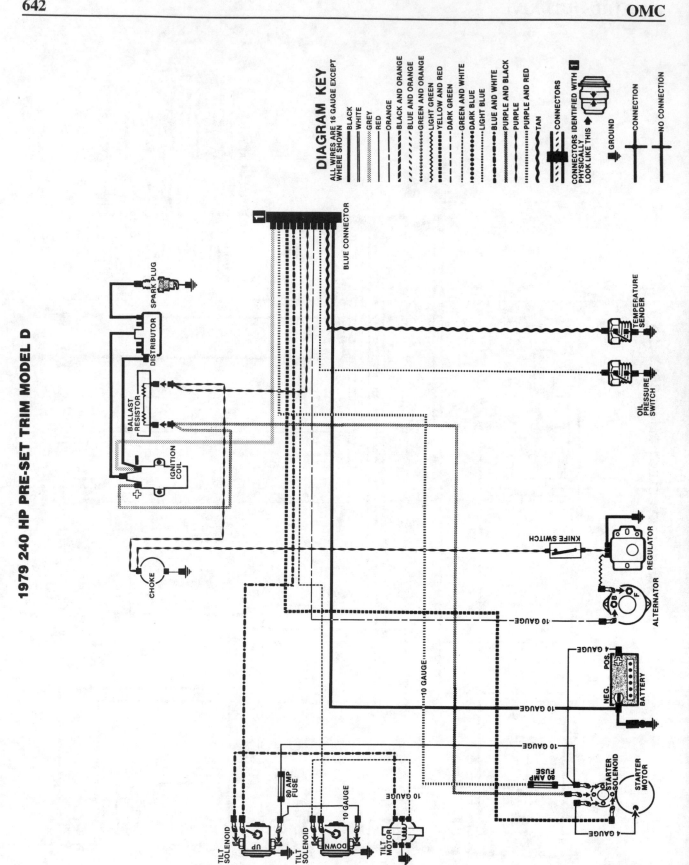

1979 240 HP PRE-SET TRIM MODEL D

DIAGRAM KEY

ALL WIRES ARE 16 GAUGE EXCEPT WHERE SHOWN

BLACK
WHITE
GREY
RED
ORANGE
BLACK AND ORANGE
BLUE AND ORANGE
GREEN AND ORANGE
LIGHT GREEN
YELLOW AND RED
DARK GREEN
GREEN AND WHITE
DARK BLUE
LIGHT BLUE
BLUE AND WHITE
PURPLE AND BLACK
PURPLE
PURPLE AND RED
TAN
CONNECTORS
CONNECTORS IDENTIFIED WITH 1 LOOK LIKE THIS
GROUND
CONNECTION
NO CONNECTION

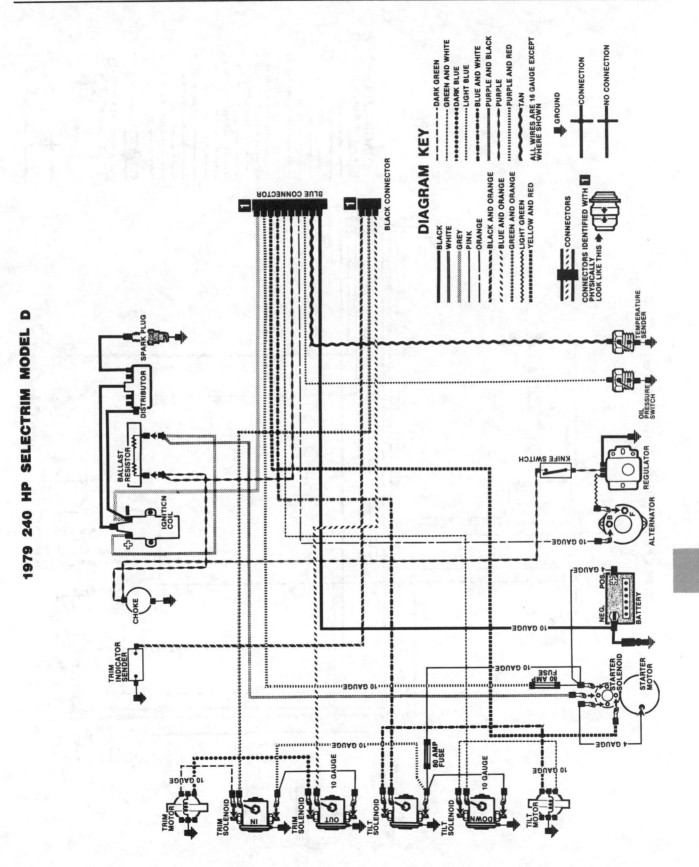

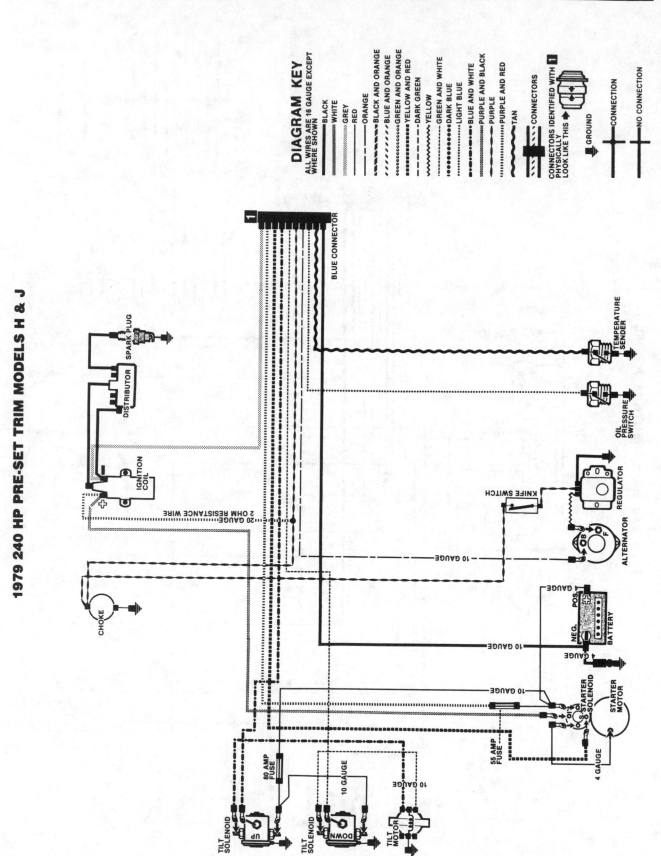

1979 240 HP PRE-SET TRIM MODELS H & J

DIAGRAM KEY

ALL WIRES ARE 16 GAUGE EXCEPT WHERE SHOWN

Black
White
Grey
Red
Orange
Black and Orange
Blue and Orange
Green and Orange
Yellow and Red
Dark Green
Yellow
Green and White
Dark Blue
Light Blue
Blue and White
Purple and Black
Purple
Purple and Red
Tan

CONNECTORS

CONNECTORS IDENTIFIED WITH [1] PHYSICALLY LOOK LIKE THIS

GROUND

CONNECTION

NO CONNECTION

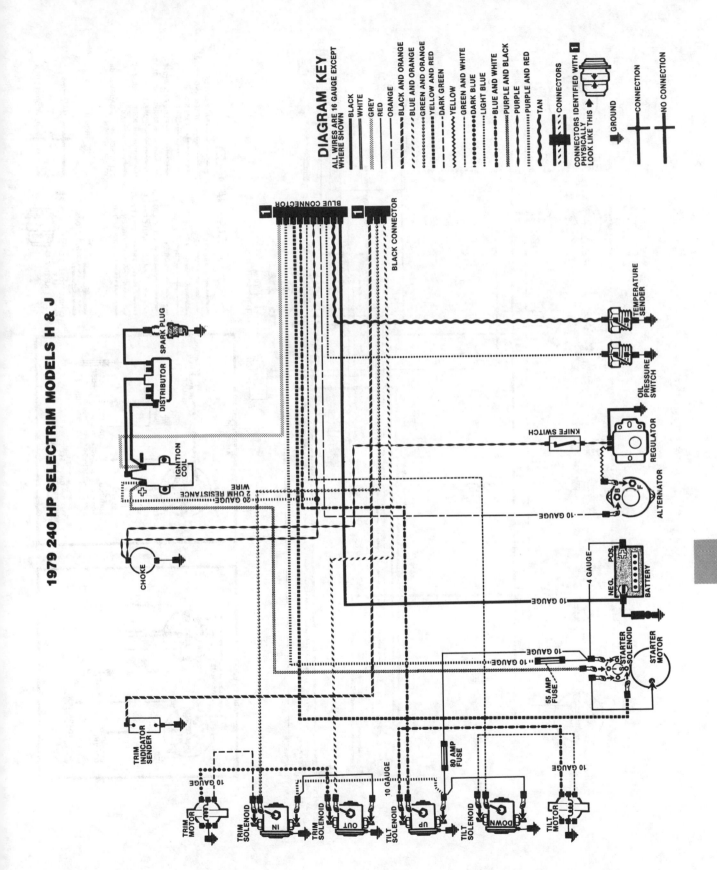

1979 240 HP SELECTRIM MODELS H & J

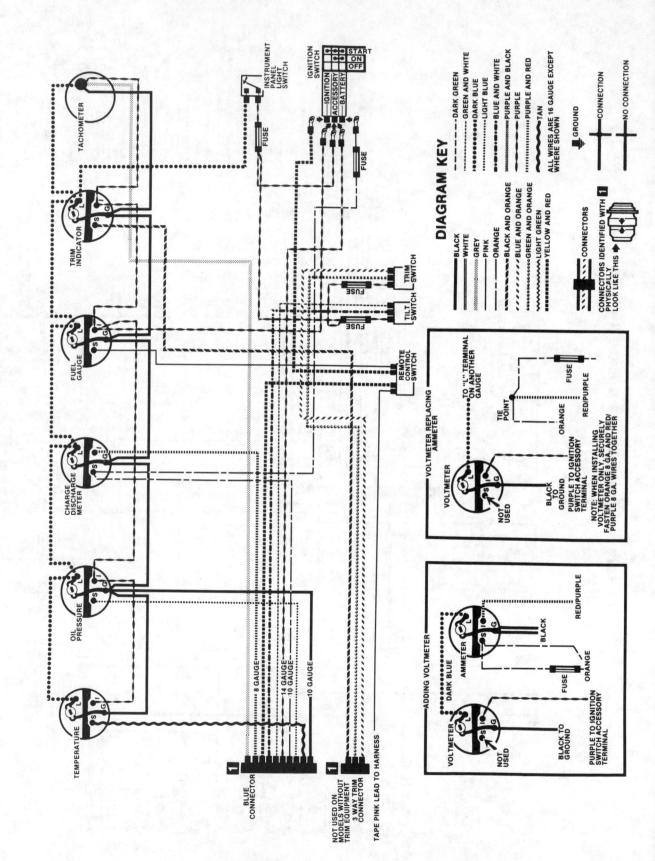

1979-ON INSTRUMENTS

TACHOMETER

TRIM INDICATOR

FUEL GAUGE

CHARGE DISCHARGE METER

OIL PRESSURE

TEMPERATURE

INSTRUMENT PANEL LIGHT SWITCH

IGNITION SWITCH

FUSE

FUSE

TRIM SWITCH

TILT SWITCH

FUSE

FUSE

REMOTE CONTROL SWITCH

8 GAUGE
14 GAUGE
10 GAUGE
10 GAUGE

BLUE CONNECTOR

NOT USED ON MODELS WITHOUT TRIM EQUIPMENT
3 WAY TRIM CONNECTOR

TAPE PINK LEAD TO HARNESS

DIAGRAM KEY

BLACK
WHITE
GREY
PINK
ORANGE
BLACK AND ORANGE
BLUE AND ORANGE
GREEN AND ORANGE
LIGHT GREEN
YELLOW AND RED

DARK GREEN
GREEN AND WHITE
DARK BLUE
LIGHT BLUE
BLUE AND WHITE
PURPLE AND BLACK
PURPLE
PURPLE AND RED
TAN

ALL WIRES ARE 16 GAUGE EXCEPT WHERE SHOWN

GROUND

CONNECTION

NO CONNECTION

CONNECTORS

CONNECTORS IDENTIFIED WITH [1] LOOK LIKE THIS

VOLTMETER REPLACING AMMETER

VOLTMETER

TO "L" TERMINAL ON ANOTHER GAUGE

FUSE

TIE POINT

ORANGE

RED/PURPLE

NOT USED

BLACK TO GROUND

PURPLE TO IGNITION SWITCH ACCESSORY TERMINAL

NOTE: WHEN INSTALLING VOLTMETER, FASTEN ORANGE 8 GA. AND RED/PURPLE 8 GA. WIRES TOGETHER

ADDING VOLTMETER

VOLTMETER

DARK BLUE

AMMETER

BLACK

RED/PURPLE

FUSE

ORANGE

NOT USED

BLACK TO GROUND

PURPLE TO IGNITION SWITCH ACCESSORY TERMINAL

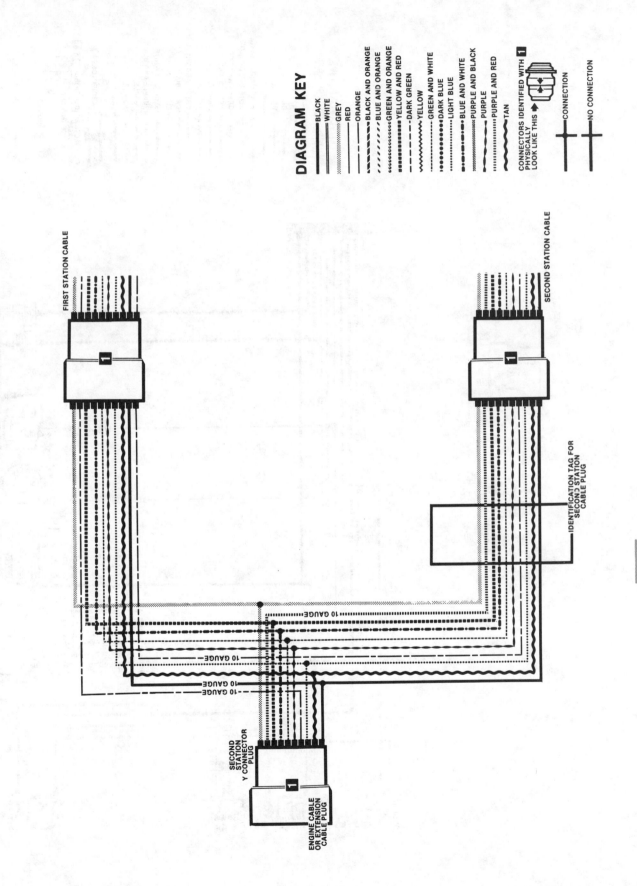

1979 SECOND STATION Y CONNECTOR

DIAGRAM KEY

BLACK
WHITE
GREY
RED
ORANGE
BLACK AND ORANGE
BLUE AND ORANGE
GREEN AND ORANGE
YELLOW AND RED
DARK GREEN
YELLOW
GREEN AND WHITE
DARK BLUE
LIGHT BLUE
BLUE AND WHITE
PURPLE AND BLACK
PURPLE
PURPLE AND RED
TAN

CONNECTORS IDENTIFIED WITH
PHYSICALLY
LOOK LIKE THIS

CONNECTION

NO CONNECTION

FIRST STATION CABLE

SECOND STATION CABLE

IDENTIFICATION TAG FOR
SECOND STATION
CABLE PLUG

10 GAUGE
10 GAUGE
10 GAUGE
10 GAUGE

SECOND
STATION
Y CONNECTOR PLUG

ENGINE CABLE
OR EXTENSION
CABLE PLUG

9

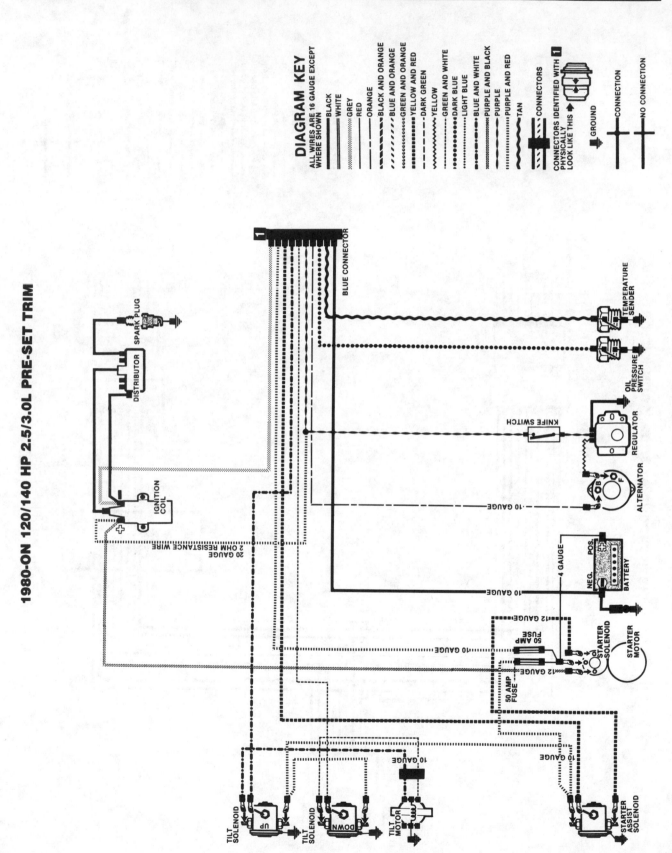

1980-ON 120/140 HP 2.5/3.0L PRE-SET TRIM

DIAGRAM KEY

ALL WIRES ARE 16 GAUGE EXCEPT
WHERE SHOWN

BLACK
WHITE
GREY
RED
ORANGE
BLACK AND ORANGE
BLUE AND ORANGE
GREEN AND ORANGE
YELLOW AND RED
DARK GREEN
YELLOW
GREEN AND WHITE
DARK BLUE
LIGHT BLUE
BLUE AND WHITE
PURPLE AND BLACK
PURPLE
PURPLE AND RED
TAN
CONNECTORS

CONNECTORS IDENTIFIED WITH 1

CONNECTORS
PHYSICALLY
LOOK LIKE THIS

GROUND

CONNECTION

NO CONNECTION

1980-ON 120/140 HP 2.5/3.0L SELECTRIM

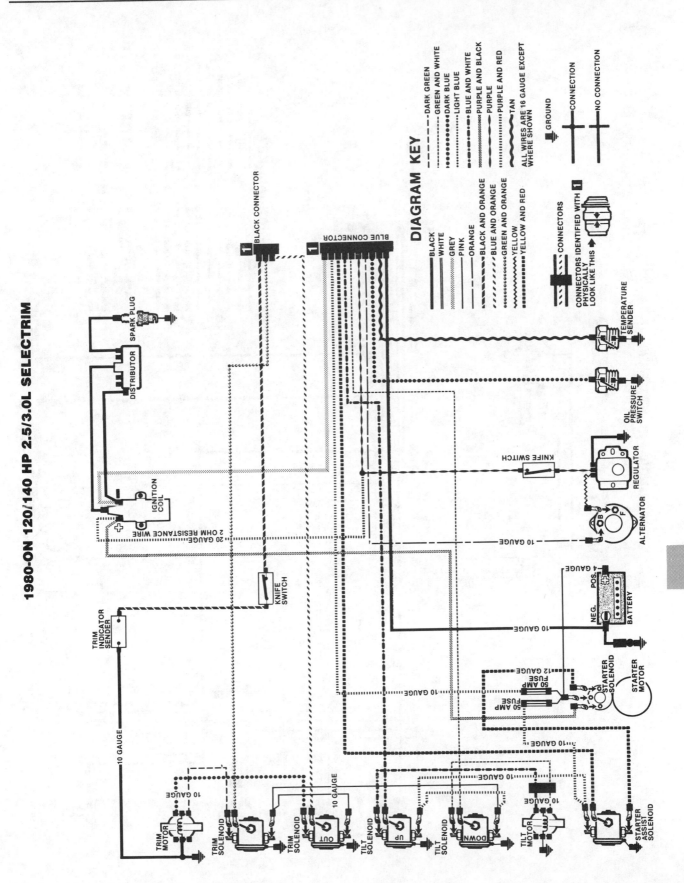

DIAGRAM KEY

————————	BLACK
····················	WHITE
— — — —	GREY
— ·· — ·· —	PINK
– · – · – ·	ORANGE
–··–··–··–	BLACK AND ORANGE
∿∿∿∿∿∿	BLUE AND WHITE
········	GREEN AND ORANGE
∿∿∿∿∿∿	YELLOW
–·–·–·–	YELLOW AND RED

— — — —	DARK GREEN
·····	GREEN AND WHITE
–·–·–	DARK BLUE
∿∿∿∿	LIGHT BLUE
∿∿∿∿	BLUE AND WHITE
········	PURPLE AND BLACK
— — —	PURPLE
∿∿∿∿	PURPLE AND RED
–·–·–	TAN

ALL WIRES ARE 16 GAUGE EXCEPT WHERE SHOWN

⏚ GROUND
┼ CONNECTION
┼ NO CONNECTION

CONNECTORS IDENTIFIED WITH **1**

CONNECTORS PHYSICALLY LOOK LIKE THIS

9

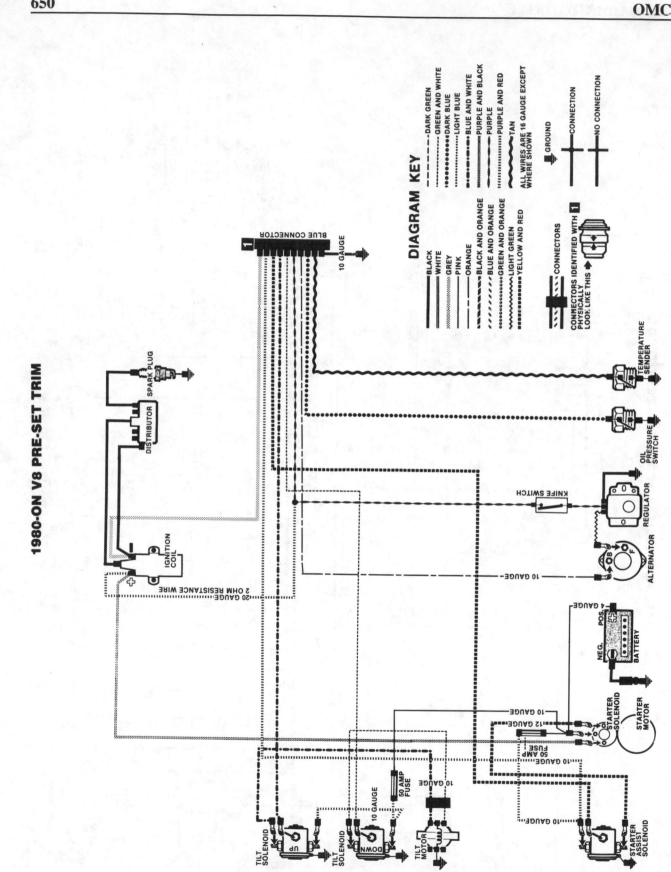

DIAGRAM KEY

BLACK	DARK GREEN
WHITE	GREEN AND WHITE
GREY	DARK BLUE
PINK	LIGHT BLUE
ORANGE	BLUE AND WHITE
BLACK AND ORANGE	PURPLE AND BLACK
BLUE AND ORANGE	PURPLE
GREEN AND ORANGE	PURPLE AND RED
LIGHT GREEN	TAN
YELLOW AND RED	

ALL WIRES ARE 16 GAUGE EXCEPT WHERE SHOWN

GROUND

CONNECTION

NO CONNECTION

CONNECTORS

CONNECTORS IDENTIFIED WITH ▮

CONNECTORS IDENTIFIED WITH ▮ PHYSICALLY LOOK LIKE THIS

1980-ON V8 PRE-SET TRIM

BLUE CONNECTOR

10 GAUGE

SPARK PLUG

DISTRIBUTOR

IGNITION COIL

2 OHM RESISTANCE WIRE

20 GAUGE

TEMPERATURE SENDER

OIL PRESSURE SWITCH

KNIFE SWITCH

REGULATOR

ALTERNATOR

10 GAUGE

NEG. POS.

BATTERY

4 GAUGE

STARTER SOLENOID

STARTER MOTOR

10 GAUGE

12 GAUGE

50 AMP FUSE

10 GAUGE

TILT SOLENOID

UP

TILT SOLENOID

DOWN

10 GAUGE

50 AMP FUSE

10 GAUGE

TILT MOTOR

10 GAUGE

STARTER ASSIST SOLENOID

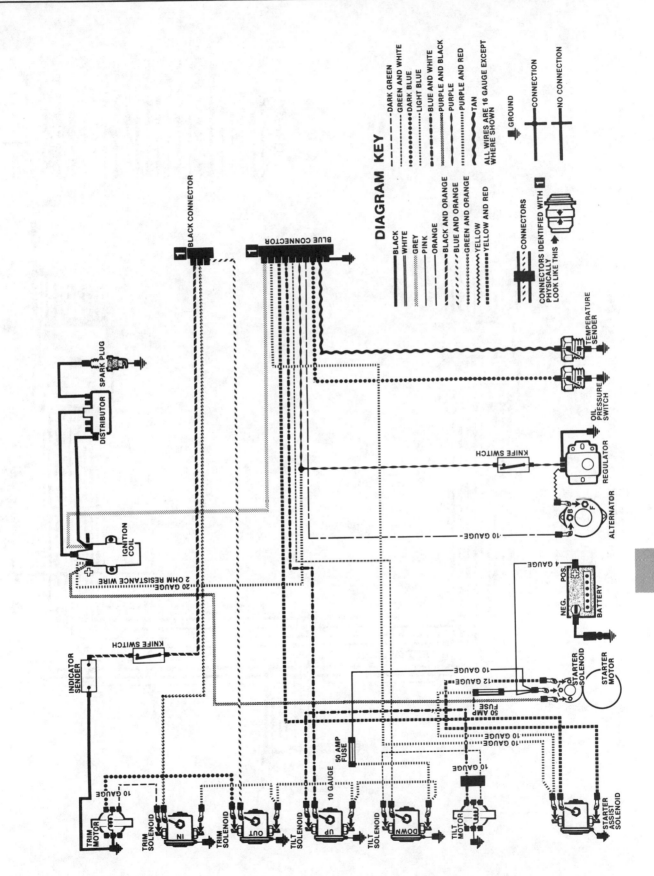

1980-ON V8 SELECTRIM

DIAGRAM KEY

BLACK
WHITE
GREY
PINK
ORANGE
BLACK AND ORANGE
BLUE AND ORANGE
GREEN AND ORANGE
YELLOW
YELLOW AND RED

DARK GREEN
GREEN AND WHITE
DARK BLUE
LIGHT BLUE
BLUE AND WHITE
PURPLE AND BLACK
PURPLE
PURPLE AND RED
TAN

ALL WIRES ARE 16 GAUGE EXCEPT WHERE SHOWN

GROUND
CONNECTION
NO CONNECTION

CONNECTORS

CONNECTORS IDENTIFIED WITH 1 PHYSICALLY LOOK LIKE THIS

SPARK PLUG
DISTRIBUTOR
IGNITION COIL
2 OHM RESISTANCE WIRE
20 GAUGE

BLACK CONNECTOR
BLUE CONNECTOR

TEMPERATURE SENDER
OIL PRESSURE SWITCH
KNIFE SWITCH
REGULATOR
ALTERNATOR
10 GAUGE

BATTERY
POS.
NEG.
4 GAUGE

INDICATOR SENDER
KNIFE SWITCH

STARTER SOLENOID
STARTER MOTOR
10 GAUGE
12 GAUGE
50 AMP FUSE
10 GAUGE
50 AMP FUSE

TRIM MOTOR
10 GAUGE
TRIM SOLENOID IN
TRIM SOLENOID OUT
TILT SOLENOID UP
10 GAUGE
TILT SOLENOID DOWN
TILT MOTOR
10 GAUGE
STARTER ASSIST SOLENOID

9

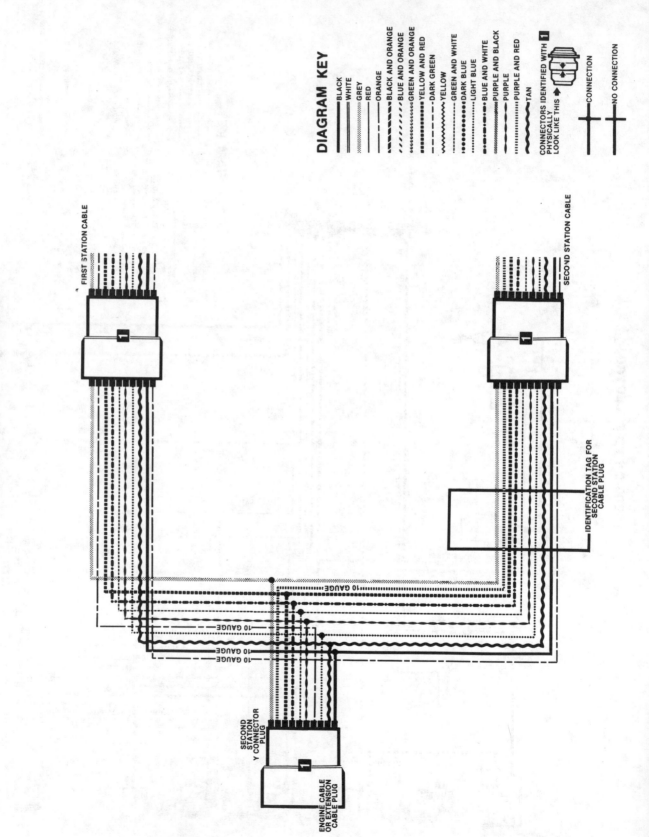

1980-ON SECOND STATION Y CONNECTOR

DIAGRAM KEY

BLACK
WHITE
GREY
RED
ORANGE
BLACK AND ORANGE
BLUE AND ORANGE
GREEN AND ORANGE
YELLOW AND RED
DARK GREEN
YELLOW
GREEN AND WHITE
DARK BLUE
LIGHT BLUE
BLUE AND WHITE
PURPLE AND BLACK
PURPLE
PURPLE AND RED
TAN

CONNECTORS IDENTIFIED WITH **1**
PHYSICALLY
LOOK LIKE THIS

CONNECTION

NO CONNECTION

FIRST STATION CABLE

SECOND STATION CABLE

IDENTIFICATION TAG FOR
SECOND STATION
CABLE PLUG

10 GAUGE
10 GAUGE
10 GAUGE
10 GAUGE

SECOND
STATION
Y CONNECTOR
PLUG

ENGINE CABLE
OR EXTENSION
CABLE PLUG

1986 OMC COBRA ENGINE CABLE

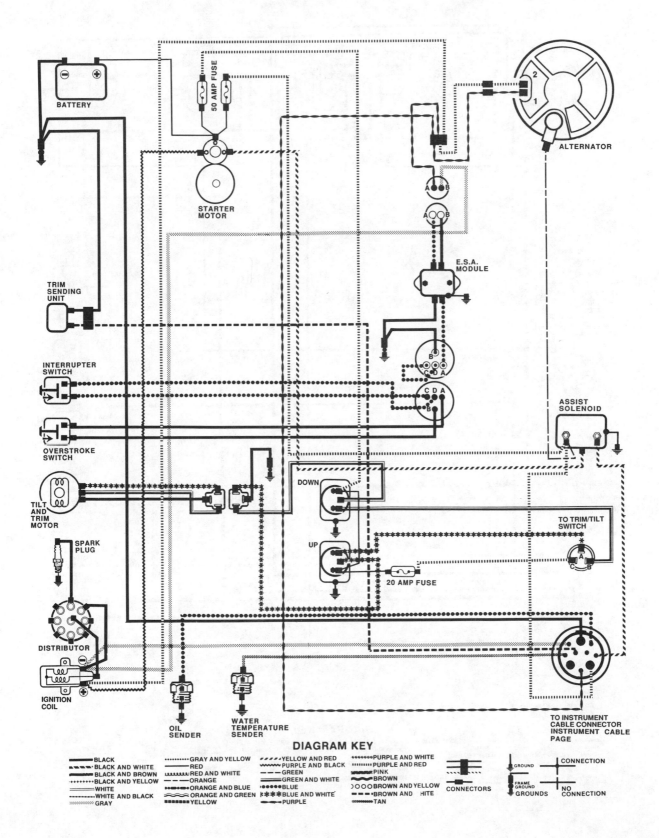

9

DIAGRAM KEY

▬▬▬ BLACK	⋯⋯⋯ GRAY AND YELLOW	⫸⫸ YELLOW AND RED	●●●● PURPLE AND WHITE
━━━ BLACK AND WHITE	▬▬▬ RED	∿∿∿ PURPLE AND BLACK	⋯⋯ PURPLE AND RED
━━━ BLACK AND BROWN	⊔⊔⊔ RED AND WHITE	─ ─ ─ GREEN	∿∿∿ PINK
⋯⋯⋯ BLACK AND YELLOW	▬▬▬ ORANGE	═══ GREEN AND WHITE	▬▬▬ BROWN
▬▬▬ WHITE	●●● ORANGE AND BLUE	●●●● BLUE	⟩⟩⟩⟩ BROWN AND YELLOW
─ ─ ─ WHITE AND BLACK	∿∿∿ ORANGE AND GREEN	✳✳✳ BLUE AND WHITE	▬ ▬ BROWN AND WHITE
▭▭▭ GRAY	▬▬▬ YELLOW	▬▬ PURPLE	∿∿∿ TAN

CONNECTORS — GROUND — CONNECTION

FRAME GROUND — NO CONNECTION

GROUNDS

1986 OMC COBRA INSTRUMENT CABLE

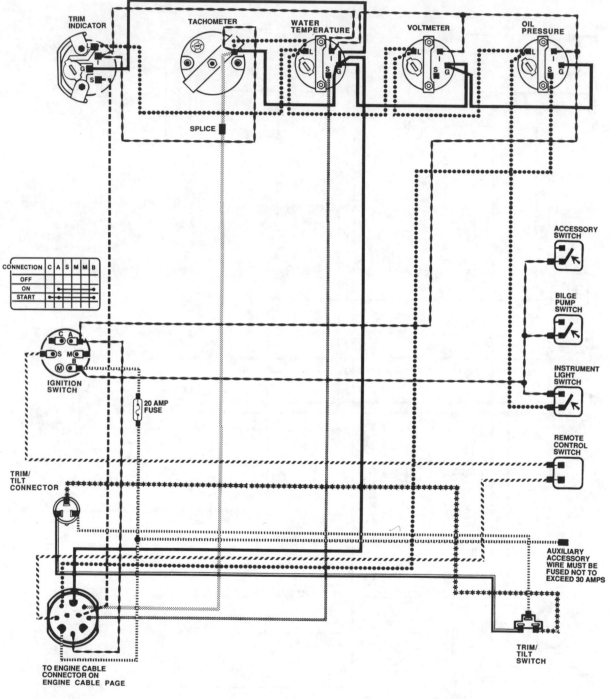

CONNECTION	C	A	S	M	M	B
OFF						
ON						
START						

IGNITION
SWITCH

20 AMP
FUSE

TRIM INDICATOR

TACHOMETER

WATER TEMPERATURE

VOLTMETER

OIL PRESSURE

SPLICE

ACCESSORY SWITCH

BILGE PUMP SWITCH

INSTRUMENT LIGHT SWITCH

REMOTE CONTROL SWITCH

TRIM/TILT CONNECTOR

AUXILIARY ACCESSORY WIRE MUST BE FUSED NOT TO EXCEED 30 AMPS

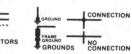

TRIM/TILT SWITCH

TO ENGINE CABLE CONNECTOR ON ENGINE CABLE PAGE

DIAGRAM KEY

BLACK	GRAY AND YELLOW	YELLOW AND RED	PURPLE AND WHITE		GROUND	CONNECTION
BLACK AND WHITE	RED	PURPLE AND BLACK	PURPLE AND RED			
BLACK AND BROWN	RED AND WHITE	GREEN	PINK			
BLACK AND YELLOW	ORANGE	GREEN AND WHITE	BROWN			
WHITE	ORANGE AND BLUE	BLUE	BROWN AND YELLOW	CONNECTORS	FRAME GROUND	NO
WHITE AND BLACK	ORANGE AND GREEN	BLUE AND WHITE	BROWN AND WHITE		GROUNDS	CONNECTION
GRAY	YELLOW	PURPLE	TAN			

1987 OMC ENGINE CABLE 2.3 & 7.5

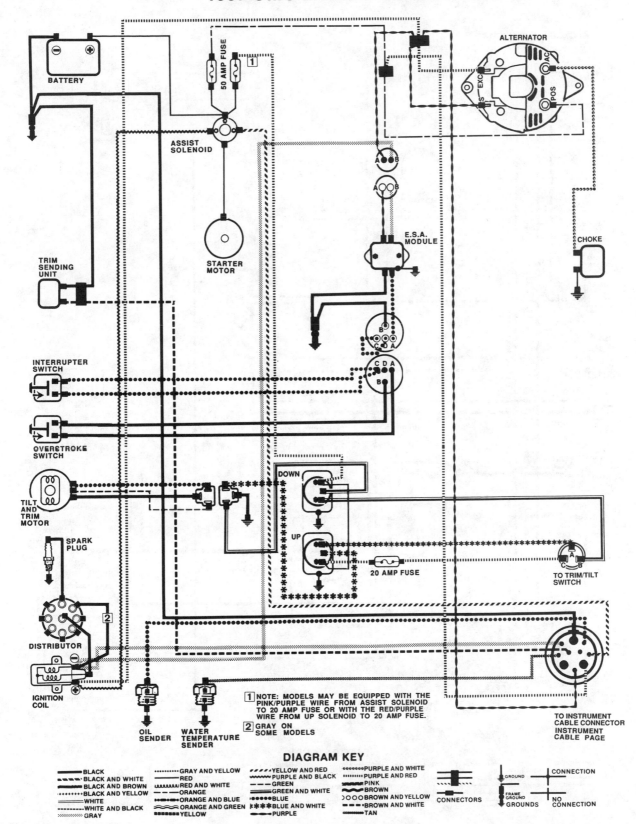

1 NOTE: MODELS MAY BE EQUIPPED WITH THE PINK/PURPLE WIRE FROM ASSIST SOLENOID TO 20 AMP FUSE OR WITH THE RED/PURPLE WIRE FROM UP SOLENOID TO 20 AMP FUSE.

2 GRAY ON SOME MODELS

DIAGRAM KEY

BLACK	GRAY AND YELLOW	YELLOW AND RED	PURPLE AND WHITE
BLACK AND WHITE	RED	PURPLE AND BLACK	PURPLE AND RED
BLACK AND BROWN	RED AND WHITE	GREEN	PINK
BLACK AND YELLOW	ORANGE	GREEN AND WHITE	BROWN
WHITE	ORANGE AND BLUE	BLUE	BROWN AND YELLOW
WHITE AND BLACK	ORANGE AND GREEN	BLUE AND WHITE	BROWN AND WHITE
GRAY	YELLOW	PURPLE	TAN

CONNECTORS

GROUND   CONNECTION

FRAME GROUND

GROUNDS   NO CONNECTION

1987 OMC ENGINE CABLE 3.0, 4.3, 5.0, 5.7

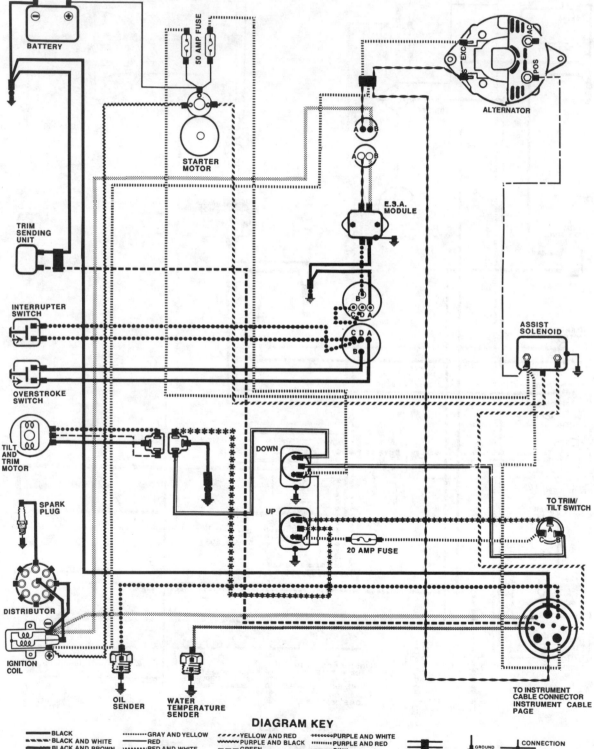

DIAGRAM KEY

BLACK	GRAY AND YELLOW	YELLOW AND RED	PURPLE AND WHITE
BLACK AND WHITE	RED	PURPLE AND BLACK	PURPLE AND RED
BLACK AND BROWN	RED AND WHITE	GREEN	PINK
BLACK AND YELLOW	ORANGE	GREEN AND WHITE	BROWN
WHITE	ORANGE AND BLUE	BLUE	BROWN AND YELLOW
WHITE AND BLACK	ORANGE AND GREEN	BLUE AND WHITE	BROWN AND WHITE
GRAY	YELLOW	PURPLE	TAN

GROUND — CONNECTION
FRAME GROUND — GROUNDS — NO CONNECTION
CONNECTORS

1987 OMC Cobra Instrument Cable

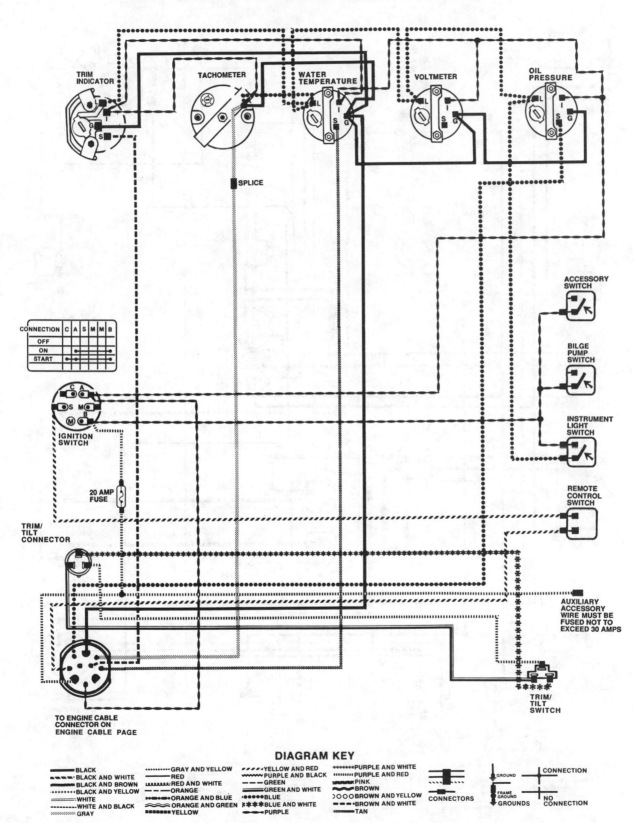

DIAGRAM KEY

BLACK	GRAY AND YELLOW	YELLOW AND RED
BLACK AND WHITE	RED	PURPLE AND BLACK
BLACK AND BROWN	RED AND WHITE	GREEN
BLACK AND YELLOW	ORANGE	GREEN AND WHITE
WHITE	ORANGE AND BLUE	BLUE
WHITE AND BLACK	ORANGE AND GREEN	BLUE AND WHITE
GRAY	YELLOW	PURPLE

PURPLE AND WHITE
PURPLE AND RED
PINK
BROWN
BROWN AND YELLOW
BROWN AND WHITE
TAN

CONNECTORS

GROUND
FRAME GROUND
GROUNDS

CONNECTION

NO CONNECTION

1988 OMC ENGINE CABLE 2.3 & 460 KING COBRA

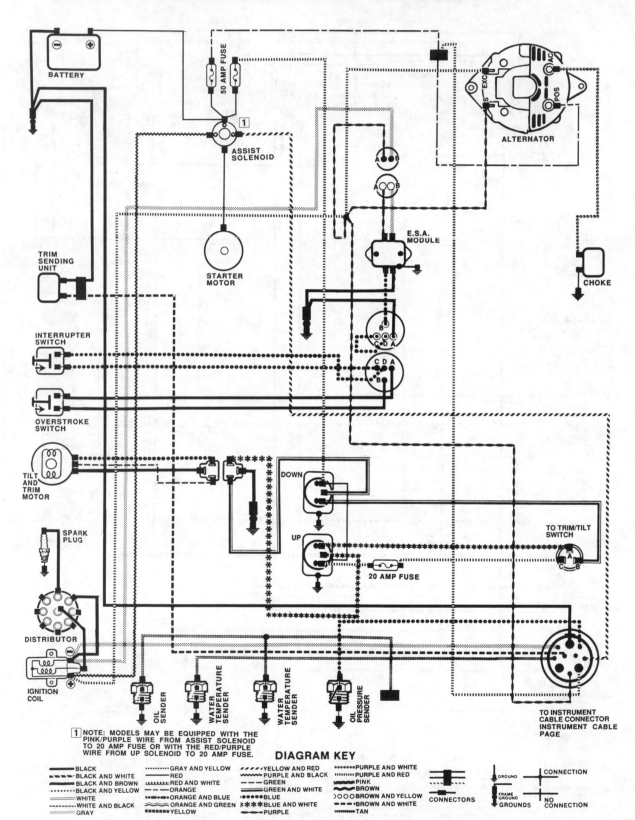

NOTE: MODELS MAY BE EQUIPPED WITH THE
PINK/PURPLE WIRE FROM ASSIST SOLENOID
TO 20 AMP FUSE OR WITH THE RED/PURPLE
WIRE FROM UP SOLENOID TO 20 AMP FUSE.

DIAGRAM KEY

BLACK	GRAY AND YELLOW	YELLOW AND RED	PURPLE AND WHITE	GROUND	CONNECTION
BLACK AND WHITE	RED	PURPLE AND BLACK	PURPLE AND RED		
BLACK AND BROWN	RED AND WHITE	GREEN	PINK		
BLACK AND YELLOW	ORANGE	GREEN AND WHITE	BROWN	FRAME GROUND	NO
WHITE	ORANGE AND BLUE	BLUE	BROWN AND YELLOW	CONNECTORS	CONNECTION
WHITE AND BLACK	ORANGE AND GREEN	BLUE AND WHITE	BROWN AND WHITE	GROUNDS	
GRAY	YELLOW	PURPLE	TAN		

1988 OMC ENGINE CABLE 3.0, 4.3, 5.0, 5.7 & 350 COBRA

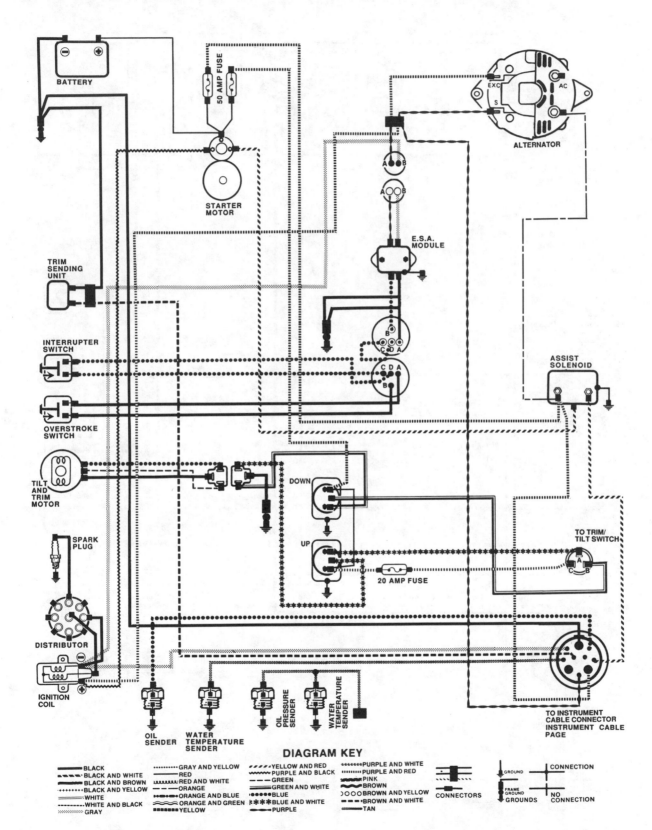

DIAGRAM KEY

▬▬ BLACK	▪▪▪▪ GRAY AND YELLOW	╱╱╱ YELLOW AND RED	◦◦◦◦ PURPLE AND WHITE
▬ ▬ BLACK AND WHITE	▬ RED	⌇⌇ PURPLE AND BLACK	▪▪▪▪ PURPLE AND RED
▬▬ BLACK AND BROWN	⌇⌇⌇ RED AND WHITE	▬ ▬ GREEN	⌇⌇⌇ PINK
▪▪▪▪ BLACK AND YELLOW	▬ ▬ ORANGE	▬▬ GREEN AND WHITE	▬▬ BROWN
▬▬ WHITE	⌇⌇ ORANGE AND BLUE	●●●● BLUE	◌◌◌◌ BROWN AND YELLOW
▬ ▬ WHITE AND BLACK	⌇⌇⌇ ORANGE AND GREEN	✳✳✳ BLUE AND WHITE	▬ ▬ BROWN AND WHITE
▒▒▒ GRAY	▬▬ YELLOW	⌇⌇ PURPLE	▬▬ TAN

CONNECTORS · **GROUNDS** · **CONNECTION** · **NO CONNECTION**

GROUND — FRAME GROUND

9

1988 OMC COBRA INSTRUMENT CABLE

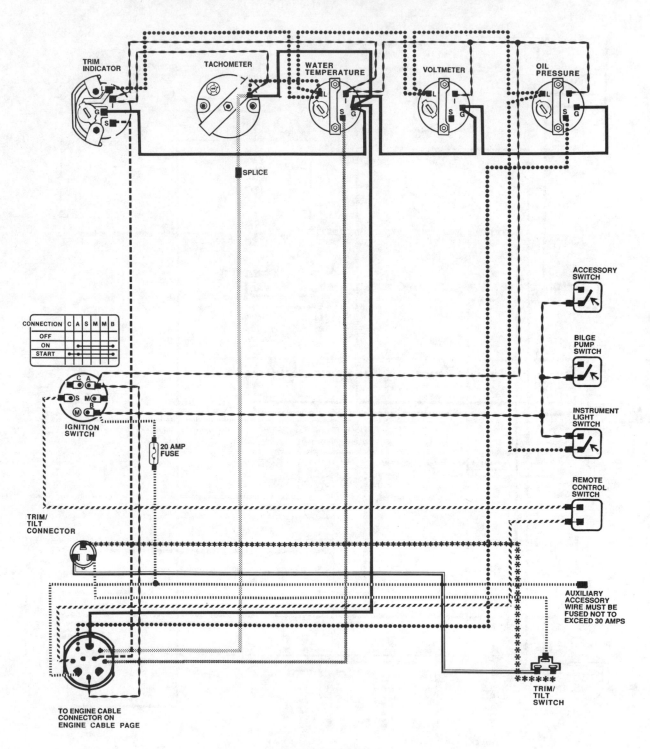

1989 OMC ENGINE CABLE 2.3, 5.0, 5.8 & 7.5

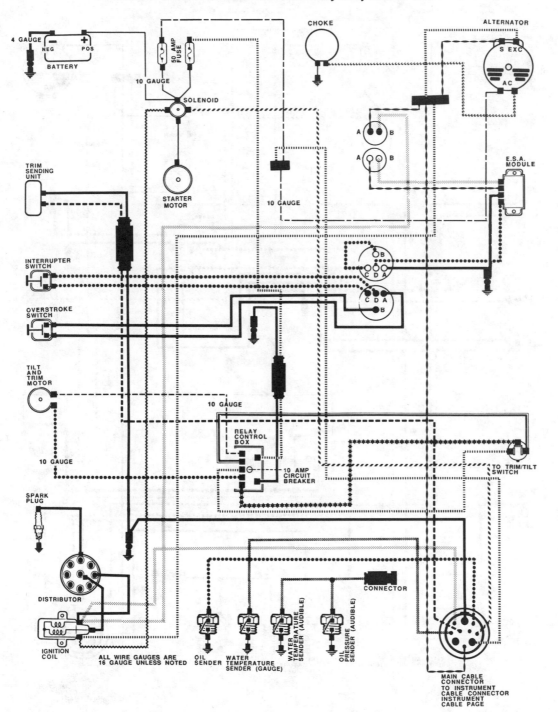

9

DIAGRAM KEY

BLACK	GRAY AND YELLOW	YELLOW AND RED	PURPLE AND WHITE
BLACK AND WHITE	RED	PURPLE AND BLACK	PURPLE AND RED
BLACK AND BROWN	RED AND WHITE	GREEN	PINK
BLACK AND YELLOW	ORANGE	GREEN AND WHITE	BROWN
WHITE	ORANGE AND BLUE	BLUE	BROWN AND YELLOW
WHITE AND BLACK	ORANGE AND GREEN	BLUE AND WHITE	BROWN AND WHITE
GRAY	YELLOW	PURPLE	TAN

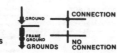

CONNECTORS

GROUND

FRAME GROUND

GROUNDS

CONNECTION

NO CONNECTION

1989 OMC ENGINE CABLE 3.0, 4.3 & 5.7

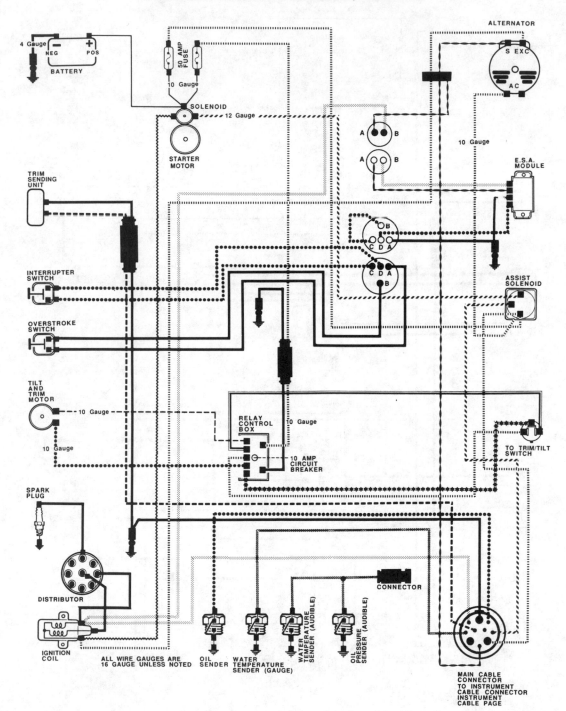

DIAGRAM KEY

BLACK	GRAY AND YELLOW	YELLOW AND RED	PURPLE AND WHITE
BLACK AND WHITE	RED	PURPLE AND BLACK	PURPLE AND RED
BLACK AND BROWN	RED AND WHITE	GREEN	PINK
BLACK AND YELLOW	ORANGE	GREEN AND WHITE	BROWN
WHITE	ORANGE AND BLUE	BLUE	BROWN AND YELLOW
WHITE AND BLACK	ORANGE AND GREEN	BLUE AND WHITE	BROWN AND WHITE
GRAY	YELLOW	PURPLE	TAN

CONNECTORS   GROUND   CONNECTION

FRAME GROUND   GROUNDS   NO CONNECTION

1989 OMC COBRA INSTRUMENT CABLE

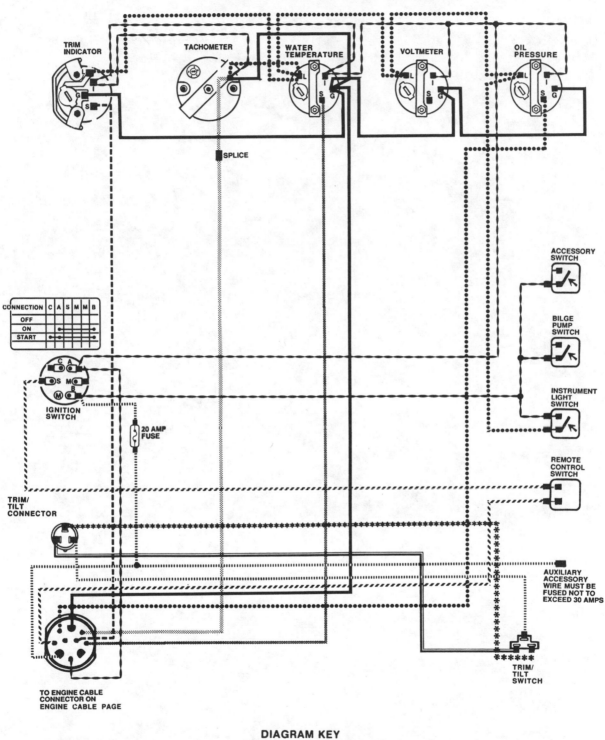

DIAGRAM KEY

————BLACK	·········GRAY AND YELLOW	////YELLOW AND RED	∘∘∘∘∘∘PURPLE AND WHITE
——— BLACK AND WHITE	——— RED	∿∿∿∿PURPLE AND BLACK	∷∷∷∷PURPLE AND RED
▬▬▬BLACK AND BROWN	⊔⊔⊔⊔RED AND WHITE	— — GREEN	▬▬PINK
·····BLACK AND YELLOW	——— ORANGE	══════GREEN AND WHITE	·······BROWN
————WHITE	⋈⋈⋈ORANGE AND BLUE	•••••BLUE	∘∘∘∘BROWN AND YELLOW
——— WHITE AND BLACK	▭▭▭ORANGE AND GREEN	✳✳✳BLUE AND WHITE	— — BROWN AND WHITE
▓▓▓▓GRAY	▬▬▬YELLOW	——— PURPLE	∿∿∿TAN

CONNECTORS / GROUNDS / CONNECTION / NO CONNECTION

9

MODELS AQ200C, 225C, 255A WITH AMMETER

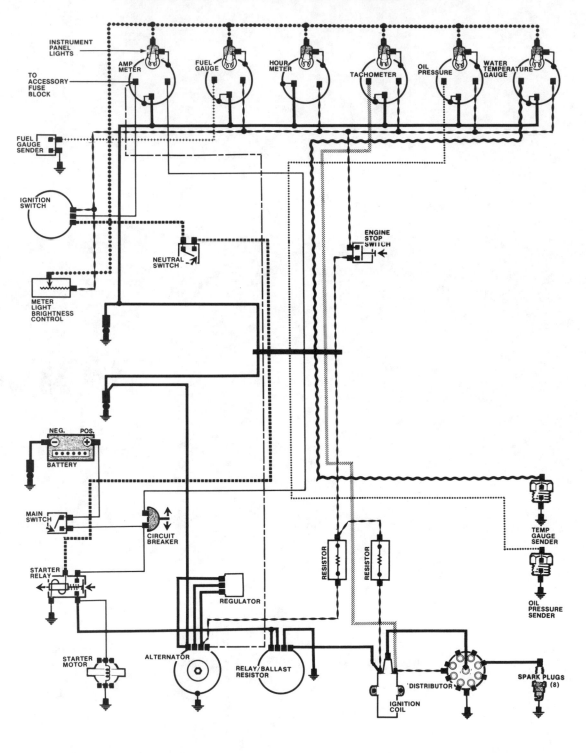

DIAGRAM KEY

BLACK	DARK BLUE	PURPLE
WHITE	LIGHT BLUE	YELLOW
GREY	TAN	PINK
GREEN	ORANGE	YELLOW AND RED
RED		

CONNECTORS

GROUND · FRAME GROUND · GROUNDS · CONNECTION · NO CONNECTION

MODELS AQ200C, 225C, 255A WITH VOLTMETER

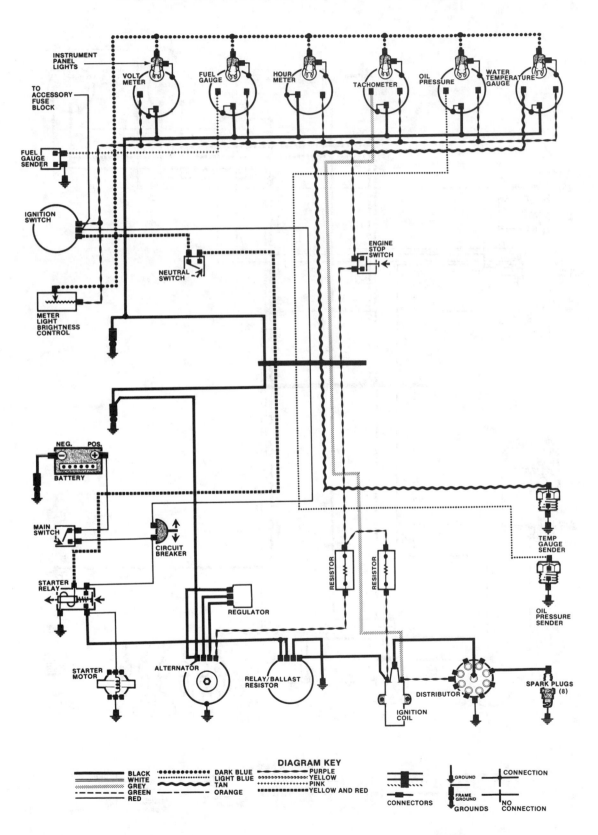

INSTRUMENT PANEL LIGHTS

TO ACCESSORY FUSE BLOCK

VOLT METER

FUEL GAUGE

HOUR METER

TACHOMETER

OIL PRESSURE

WATER TEMPERATURE GAUGE

FUEL GAUGE SENDER

IGNITION SWITCH

ENGINE STOP SWITCH

NEUTRAL SWITCH

METER LIGHT BRIGHTNESS CONTROL

NEG. POS.

BATTERY

MAIN SWITCH

CIRCUIT BREAKER

RESISTOR

RESISTOR

TEMP GAUGE SENDER

OIL PRESSURE SENDER

STARTER RELAY

REGULATOR

STARTER MOTOR

ALTERNATOR

RELAY/BALLAST RESISTOR

IGNITION COIL

DISTRIBUTOR

SPARK PLUGS (8)

DIAGRAM KEY

BLACK	DARK BLUE	PURPLE
WHITE	LIGHT BLUE	YELLOW
GREY	TAN	PINK
GREEN	ORANGE	YELLOW AND RED
RED		

CONNECTORS

GROUND

FRAME GROUND

GROUNDS

CONNECTION

NO CONNECTION

10

MODEL AQD21

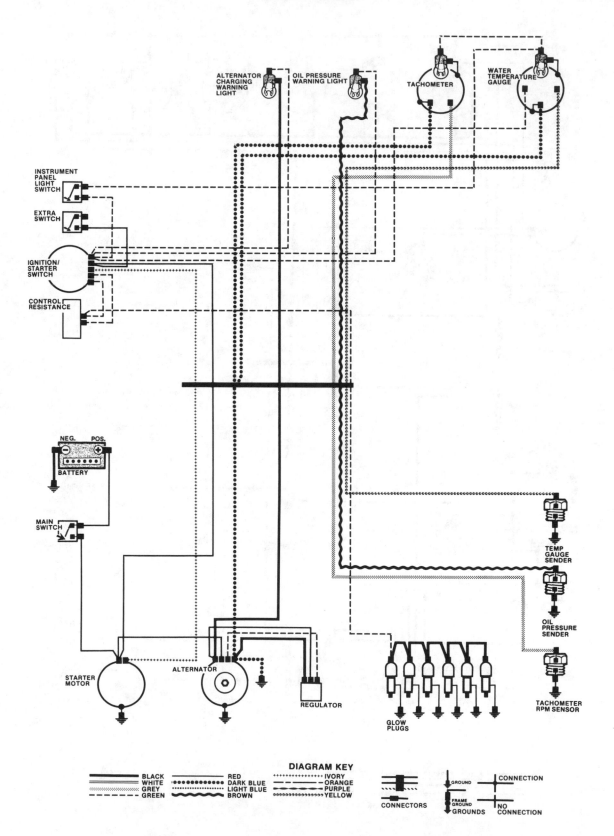

MODEL AQ140

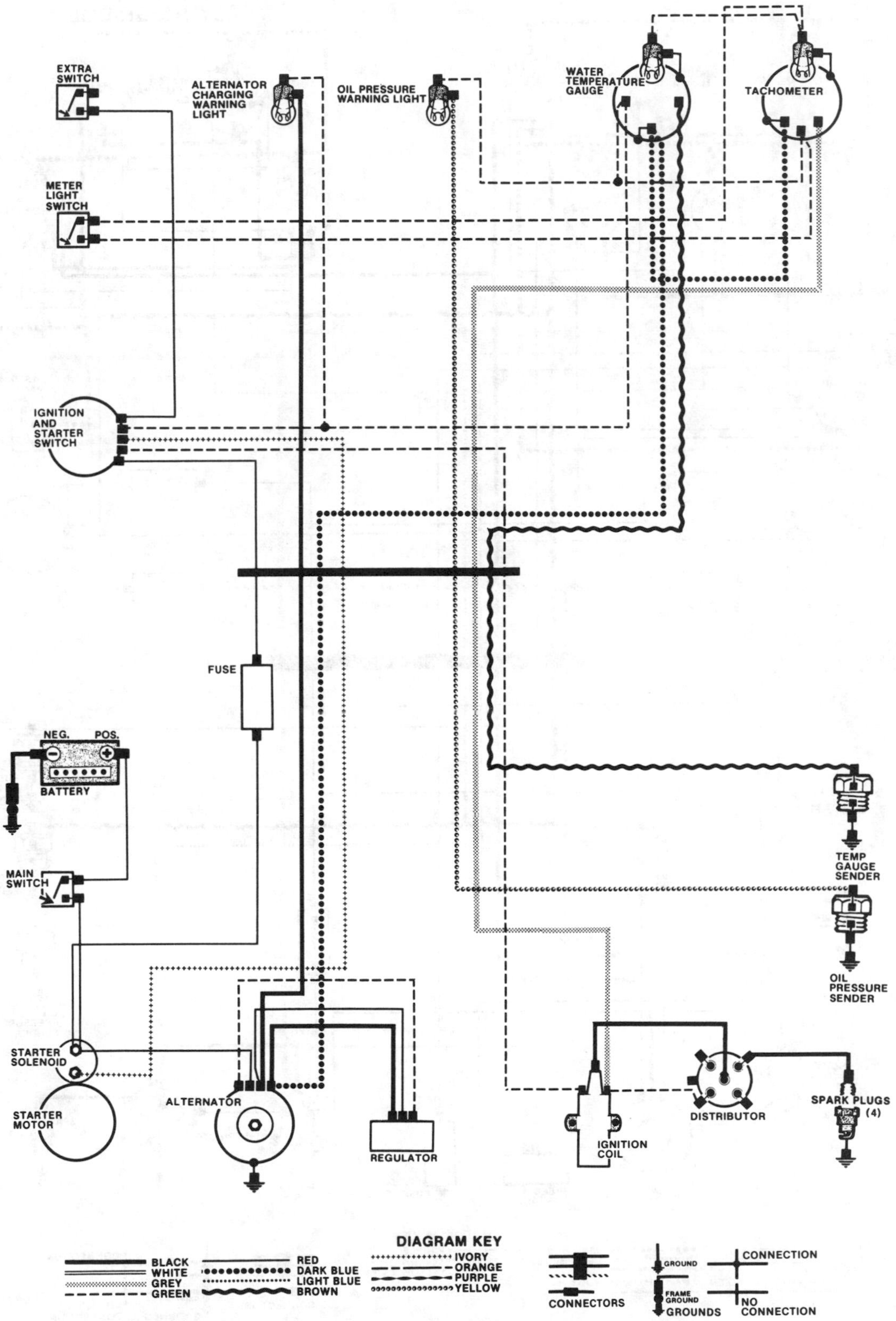

EXTRA SWITCH
ALTERNATOR CHARGING WARNING LIGHT
OIL PRESSURE WARNING LIGHT
WATER TEMPERATURE GAUGE
TACHOMETER
METER LIGHT SWITCH
IGNITION AND STARTER SWITCH
FUSE
NEG.
POS.
BATTERY
MAIN SWITCH
TEMP GAUGE SENDER
OIL PRESSURE SENDER
STARTER SOLENOID
STARTER MOTOR
ALTERNATOR
REGULATOR
IGNITION COIL
DISTRIBUTOR
SPARK PLUGS (4)
DIAGRAM KEY
BLACK
WHITE
GREY
GREEN
RED
DARK BLUE
LIGHT BLUE
BROWN
IVORY
ORANGE
PURPLE
YELLOW
CONNECTORS
GROUND
FRAME GROUND
GROUNDS
CONNECTION
NO CONNECTION

MODELS AQ200, 225, 260, 290 WITH AMMETER

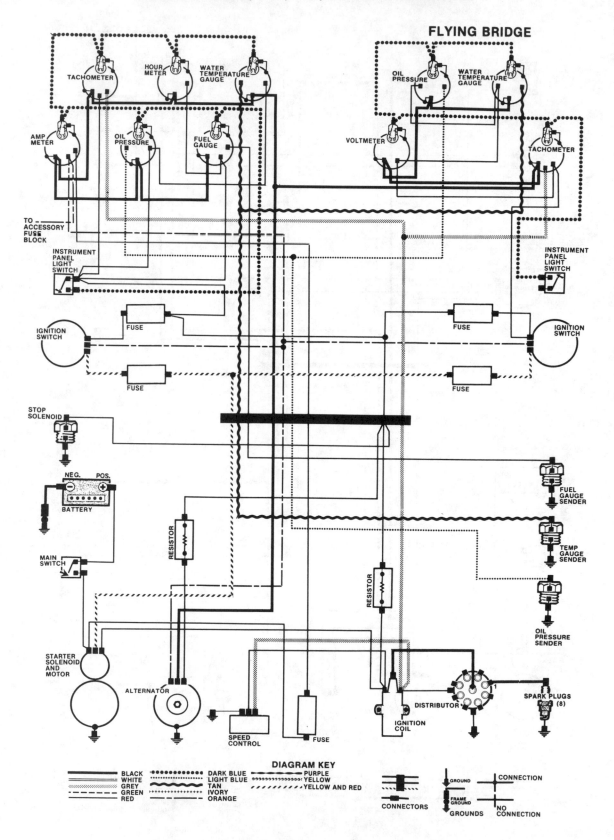

MODELS AQ200, 225, 260, 290 WITH VOLTMETER

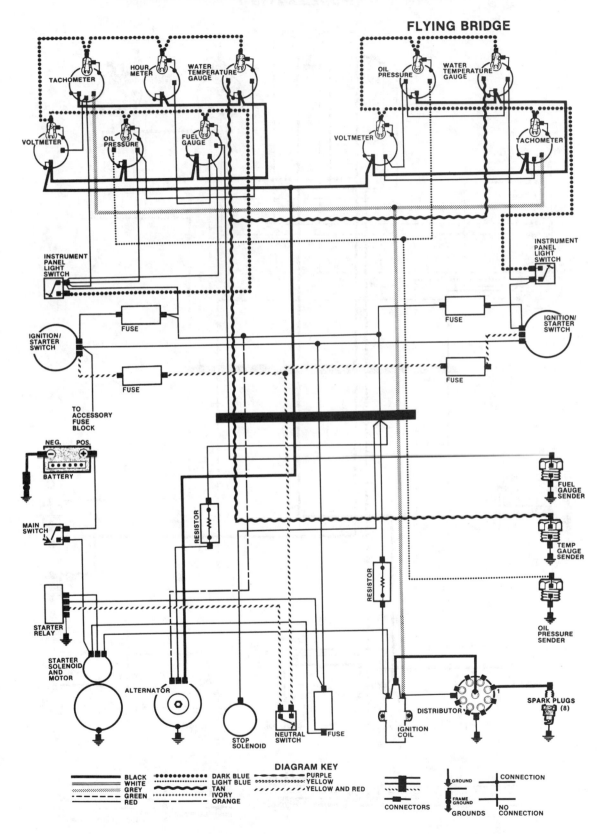

MODEL AQ115

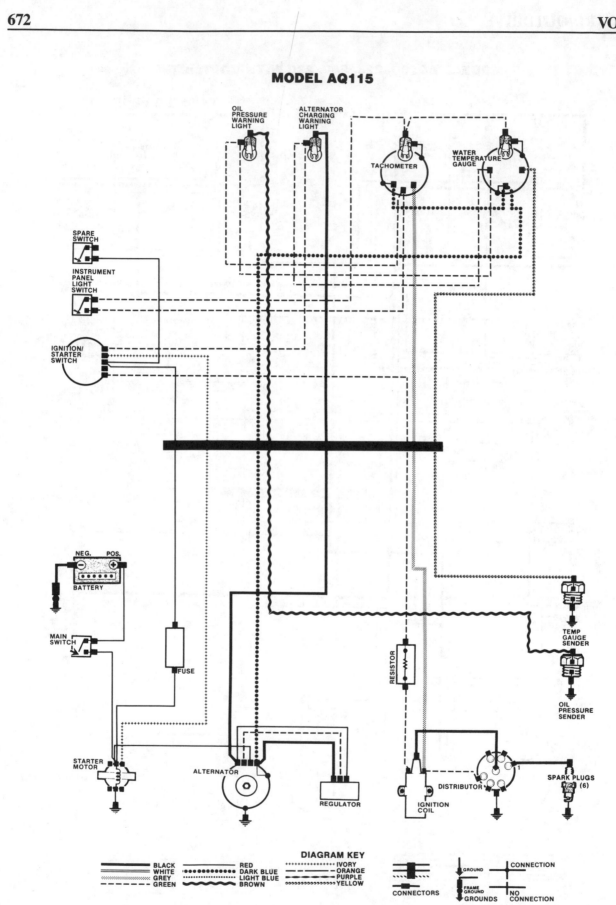

OIL
PRESSURE
WARNING
LIGHT

ALTERNATOR
CHARGING
WARNING
LIGHT

TACHOMETER

WATER
TEMPERATURE
GAUGE

SPARE
SWITCH

INSTRUMENT
PANEL
LIGHT
SWITCH

IGNITION/
STARTER
SWITCH

NEG.   POS.

BATTERY

TEMP
GAUGE
SENDER

MAIN
SWITCH

RESISTOR

OIL
PRESSURE
SENDER

FUSE

STARTER
MOTOR

ALTERNATOR

REGULATOR

IGNITION
COIL

DISTRIBUTOR

SPARK PLUGS
(6)

DIAGRAM KEY

BLACK	RED	IVORY
WHITE	DARK BLUE	ORANGE
GREY	LIGHT BLUE	PURPLE
GREEN	BROWN	YELLOW

CONNECTORS

GROUND

FRAME
GROUND
GROUNDS

CONNECTION

NO
CONNECTION

MODELS AQ130, 170C

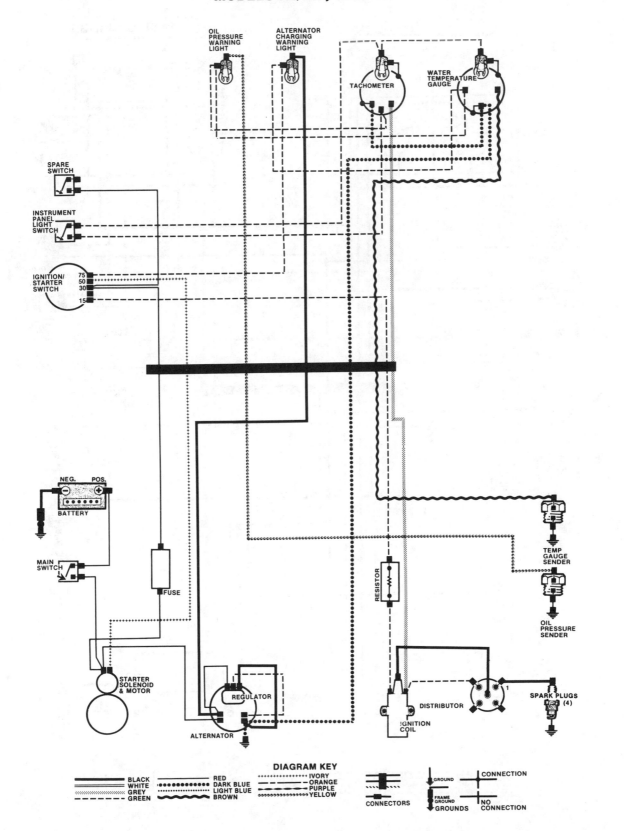

DIAGRAM KEY

BLACK	RED	IVORY	
WHITE	DARK BLUE	ORANGE	
GREY	LIGHT BLUE	PURPLE	CONNECTORS
GREEN	BROWN	YELLOW	

GROUND
FRAME GROUND
GROUNDS

CONNECTION
NO CONNECTION

10

MODELS AQ190, 240

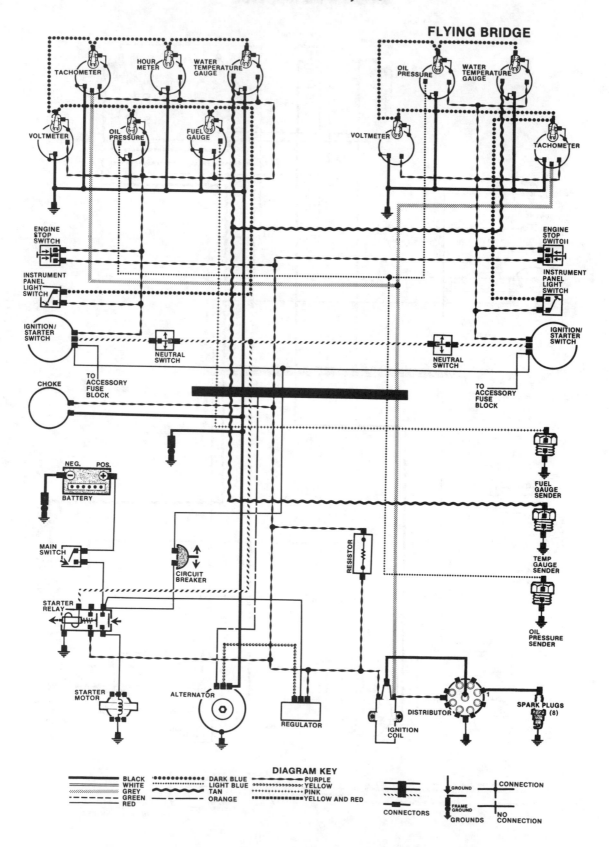

FLYING BRIDGE

TACHOMETER HOUR METER WATER TEMPERATURE GAUGE

OIL PRESSURE WATER TEMPERATURE GAUGE

VOLTMETER OIL PRESSURE FUEL GAUGE

VOLTMETER TACHOMETER

ENGINE STOP SWITCH

ENGINE STOP SWITCH

INSTRUMENT PANEL LIGHT SWITCH

INSTRUMENT PANEL LIGHT SWITCH

IGNITION/ STARTER SWITCH

IGNITION/ STARTER SWITCH

NEUTRAL SWITCH

NEUTRAL SWITCH

CHOKE

TO ACCESSORY FUSE BLOCK

TO ACCESSORY FUSE BLOCK

FUEL GAUGE SENDER

NEG. POS.

BATTERY

TEMP GAUGE SENDER

MAIN SWITCH

CIRCUIT BREAKER

RESISTOR

OIL PRESSURE SENDER

STARTER RELAY

STARTER MOTOR ALTERNATOR REGULATOR IGNITION COIL DISTRIBUTOR SPARK PLUGS (8)

DIAGRAM KEY

BLACK
WHITE
GREY
GREEN
RED

DARK BLUE
LIGHT BLUE
TAN
ORANGE

PURPLE
YELLOW
PINK
YELLOW AND RED

CONNECTORS

GROUND

FRAME GROUND

GROUNDS

CONNECTION

NO CONNECTION

MODEL AQ280

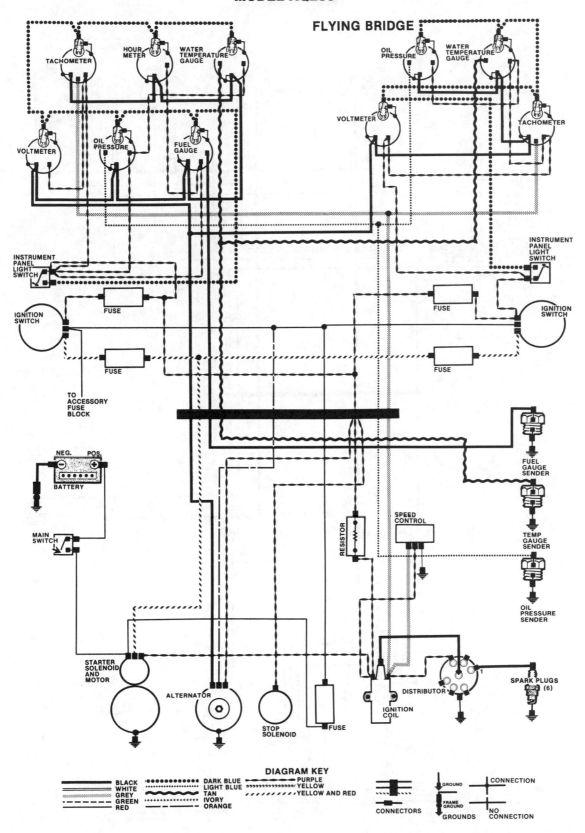

FLYING BRIDGE

DIAGRAM KEY

BLACK	DARK BLUE	PURPLE	
WHITE	LIGHT BLUE	YELLOW	
GREY	TAN	YELLOW AND RED	
GREEN	IVORY		
RED	ORANGE		

CONNECTORS

GROUND
FRAME GROUND
GROUNDS

CONNECTION
NO CONNECTION

10

MODEL AQ120

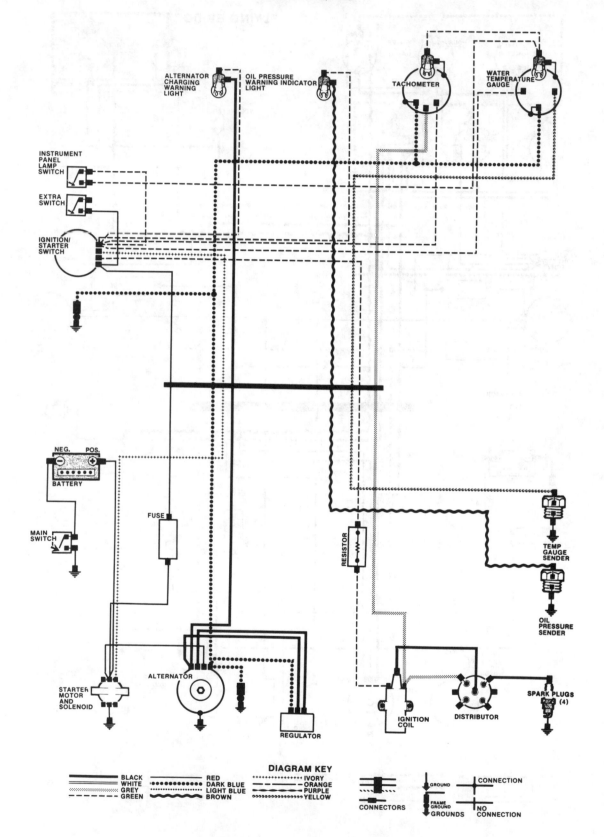

MODEL AQAD30A

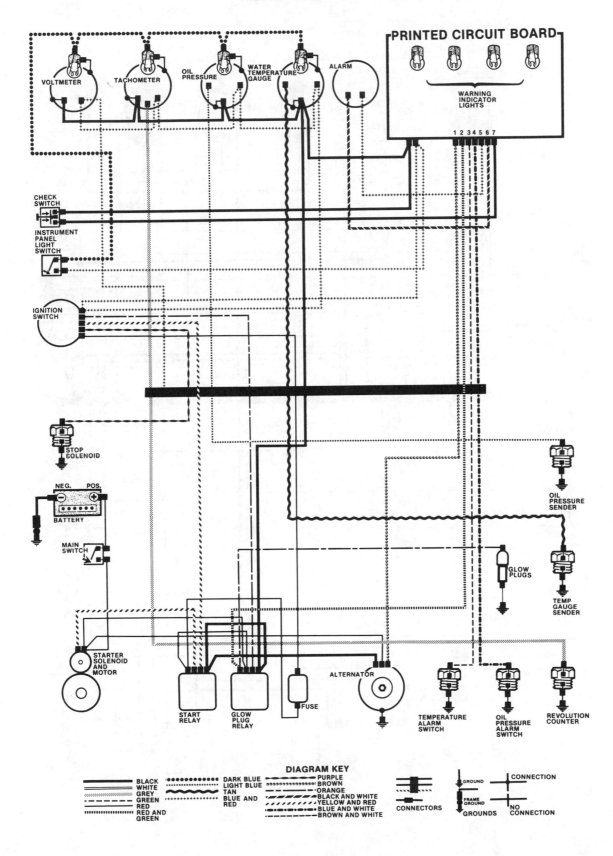

PRINTED CIRCUIT BOARD

VOLTMETER

TACHOMETER

OIL PRESSURE

WATER TEMPERATURE GAUGE

ALARM

WARNING INDICATOR LIGHTS

1 2 3 4 5 6 7

CHECK SWITCH

INSTRUMENT PANEL LIGHT SWITCH

IGNITION SWITCH

STOP SOLENOID

OIL PRESSURE SENDER

NEG. POS.

BATTERY

GLOW PLUGS

TEMP GAUGE SENDER

MAIN SWITCH

STARTER SOLENOID AND MOTOR

ALTERNATOR

START RELAY

GLOW PLUG RELAY

FUSE

TEMPERATURE ALARM SWITCH

OIL PRESSURE ALARM SWITCH

REVOLUTION COUNTER

10

DIAGRAM KEY

BLACK	DARK BLUE	PURPLE
WHITE	LIGHT BLUE	BROWN
GREY	TAN	ORANGE
GREEN	BLUE AND RED	BLACK AND WHITE
RED		YELLOW AND RED
RED AND GREEN		BLUE AND WHITE
		BROWN AND WHITE

CONNECTORS

GROUND

FRAME GROUND

GROUNDS

CONNECTION

NO CONNECTION

MODEL AQD40A
1 of 2

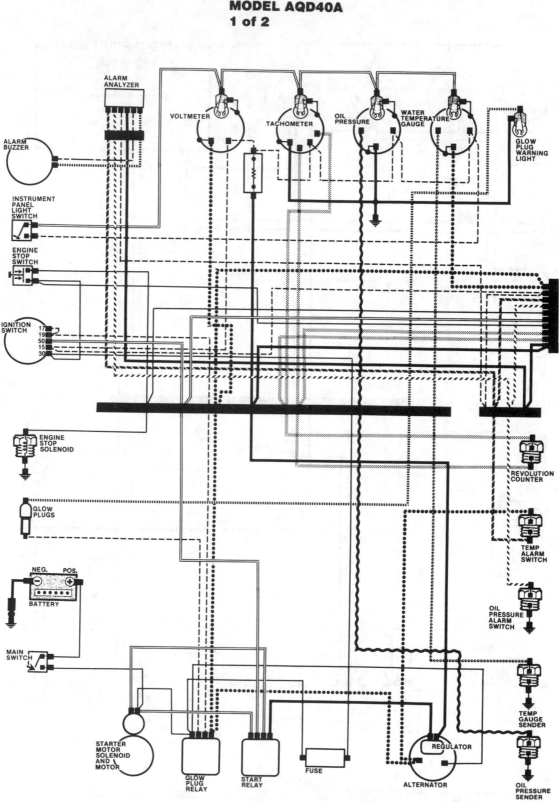

MODEL AQD40A
2 of 2

FLYING BRIDGE

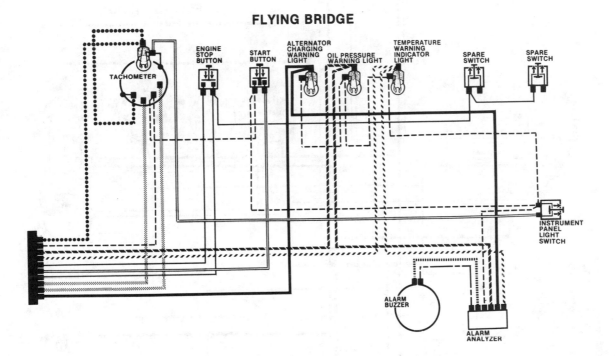

DIAGRAM KEY

BLACK	DARK BLUE	RED AND GREEN
WHITE	LIGHT BLUE	WHITE AND RED
GREY	BROWN	YELLOW AND BLUE
GREEN	YELLOW	BLUE AND RED
RED	IVORY	

CONNECTORS

GROUND
FRAME GROUND
GROUNDS

CONNECTION
NO CONNECTION

10

MODEL AQ175

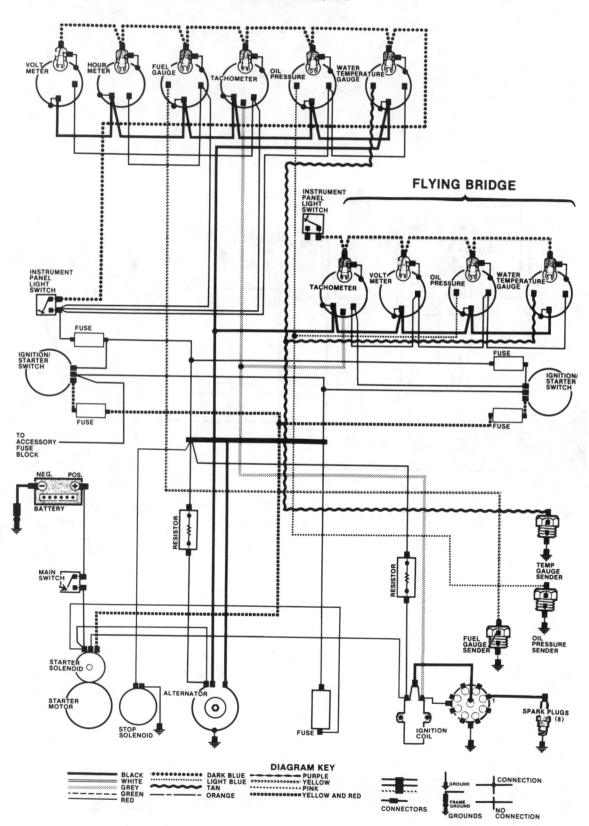

FLYING BRIDGE

DIAGRAM KEY

BLACK	DARK BLUE	PURPLE	
WHITE	LIGHT BLUE	YELLOW	
GREY	TAN	PINK	
GREEN	ORANGE	YELLOW AND RED	
RED			

CONNECTORS

GROUND
FRAME GROUND
GROUNDS

CONNECTION
NO CONNECTION

MODELS AQ165, 170

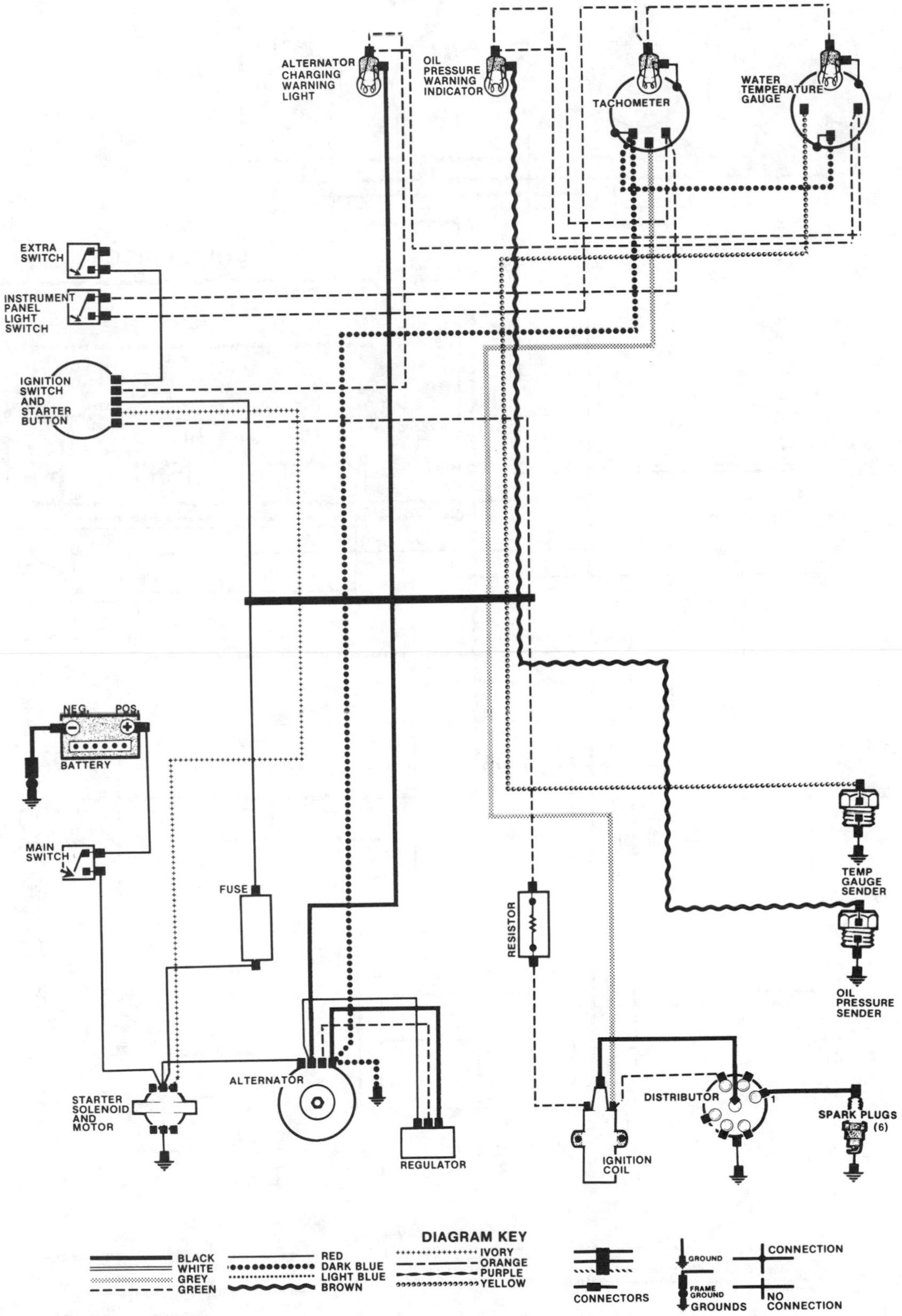

DIAGRAM KEY

BLACK	RED	IVORY
WHITE	DARK BLUE	ORANGE
GREY	LIGHT BLUE	PURPLE
GREEN	BROWN	YELLOW

CONNECTORS

GROUND

FRAME GROUND

GROUNDS

CONNECTION

NO CONNECTION

10

MODELS AQ125, 145

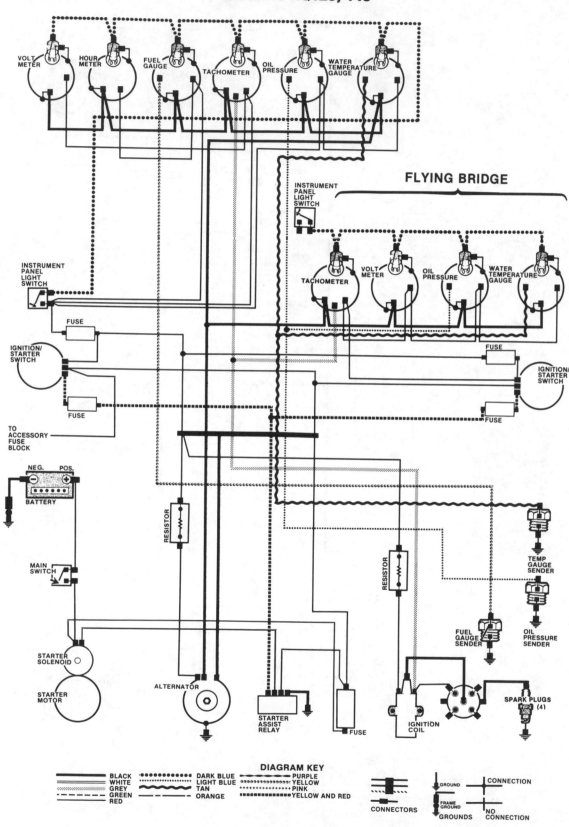

FLYING BRIDGE

DIAGRAM KEY

BLACK	DARK BLUE		
WHITE	LIGHT BLUE		CONNECTION
GREY	YELLOW		
GREEN	PINK		
RED	ORANGE	YELLOW AND RED	

CONNECTORS

GROUND

FRAME GROUND

GROUNDS

NO CONNECTION

MODEL AQD32A

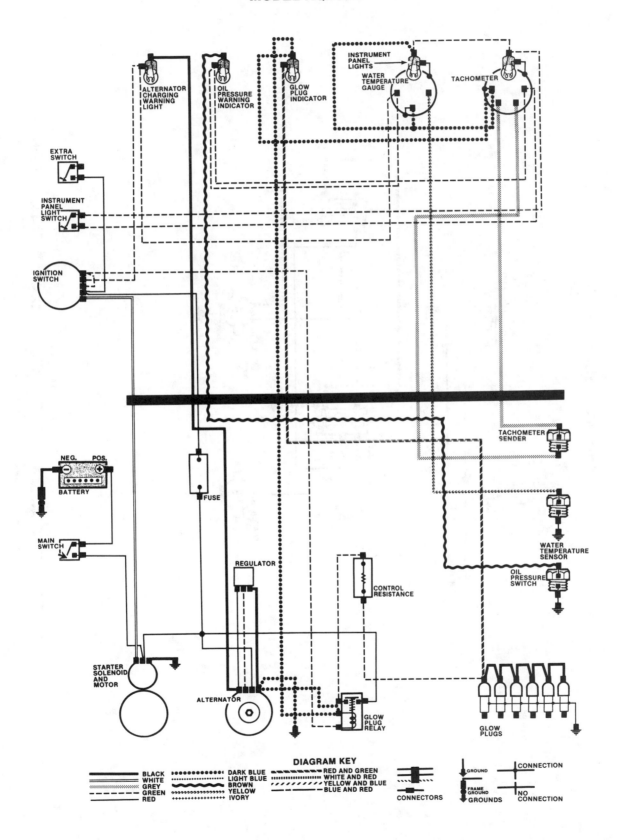

MODEL 100B DRIVE

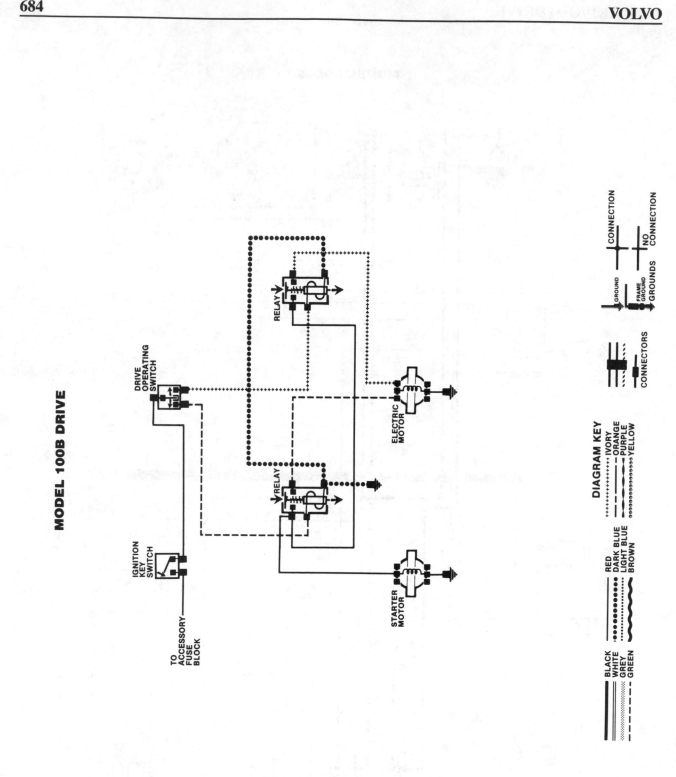

IGNITION KEY SWITCH

TO ACCESSORY FUSE BLOCK

DRIVE OPERATING SWITCH

RELAY

RELAY

ELECTRIC MOTOR

STARTER MOTOR

DIAGRAM KEY

BLACK
WHITE
GREY
GREEN
RED
DARK BLUE
LIGHT BLUE
BROWN
IVORY
ORANGE
PURPLE
YELLOW

CONNECTION

NO CONNECTION

GROUND

FRAME GROUND

GROUNDS

CONNECTORS

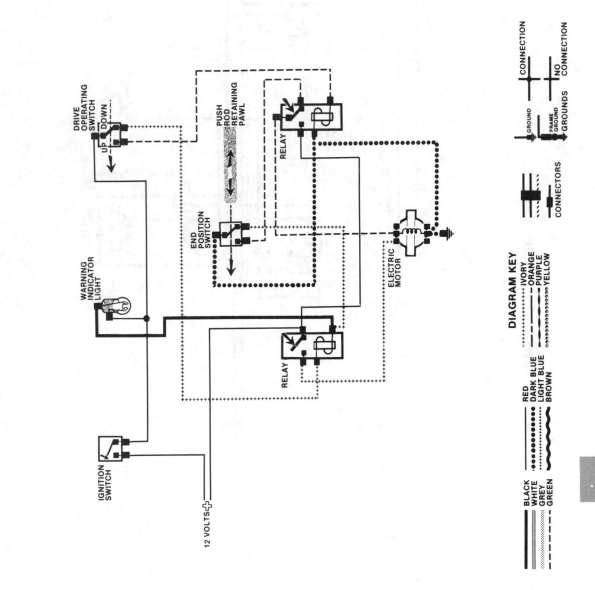

MODEL 250 DRIVE

DIAGRAM KEY

CONNECTION

NO CONNECTION

GROUND

FRAME GROUND

GROUNDS

CONNECTORS

BLACK
WHITE
GREY
GREEN

RED
DARK BLUE
LIGHT BLUE
BROWN

IVORY
ORANGE
PURPLE
YELLOW

DRIVE OPERATING SWITCH

UP   DOWN

PUSH ROD RETAINING PAWL

RELAY

END POSITION SWITCH

ELECTRIC MOTOR

WARNING INDICATOR LIGHT

RELAY

IGNITION SWITCH

12 VOLTS

10

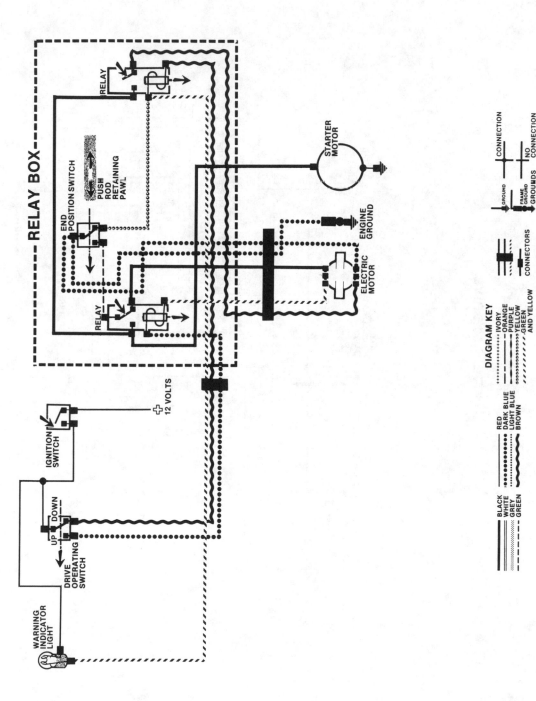

MODELS 270 AND 280 DRIVE (4-WIRE)

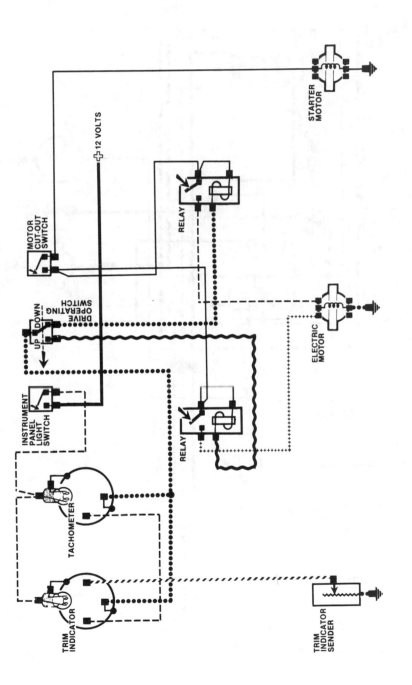

MODEL 270T DRIVE

10

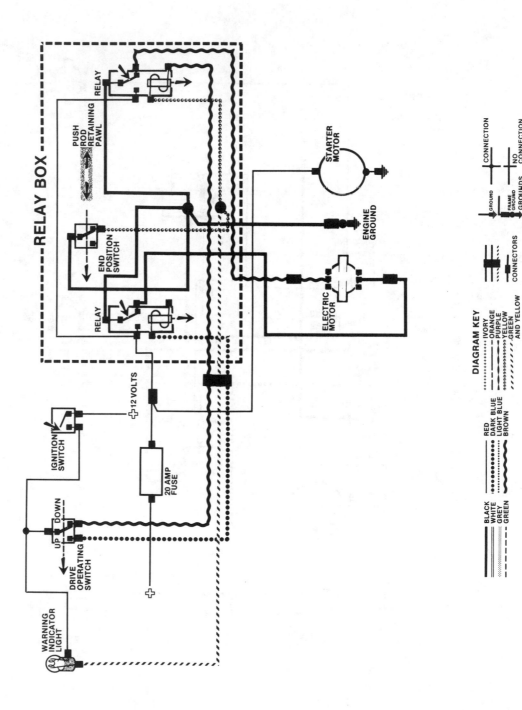

MODEL 280 DRIVE (2-WIRE)

RELAY BOX

RELAY

PUSH
ROD
RETAINING
PAWL

END
POSITION
SWITCH

RELAY

STARTER
MOTOR

ENGINE
GROUND

ELECTRIC
MOTOR

12 VOLTS

IGNITION
SWITCH

20 AMP
FUSE

UP   DOWN

DRIVE
OPERATING
SWITCH

WARNING
INDICATOR
LIGHT

DIAGRAM KEY

CONNECTION

NO
CONNECTION

GROUND

FRAME
GROUND

GROUNDS

CONNECTORS

IVORY
ORANGE
PURPLE
YELLOW
GREEN
AND YELLOW

RED
DARK BLUE
LIGHT BLUE
BROWN

BLACK
WHITE
GREY
GREEN

MODEL 270E, C & D DRIVE

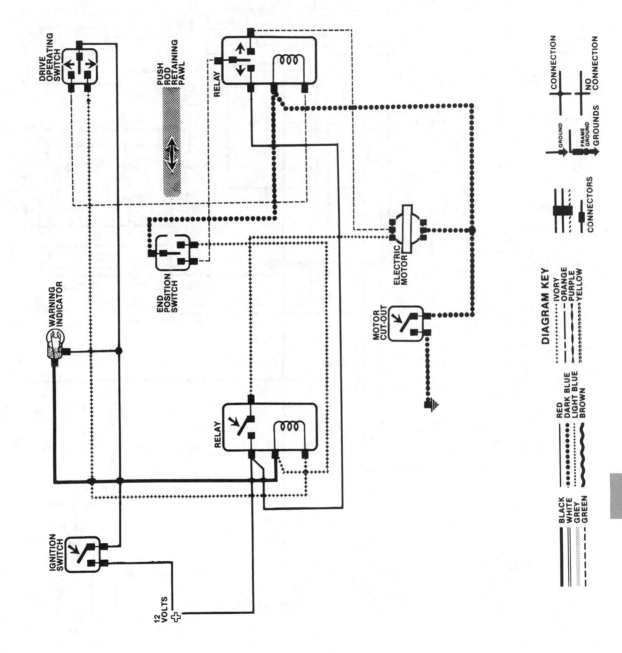

DIAGRAM KEY

BLACK	RED
WHITE	DARK BLUE
GREY	LIGHT BLUE
GREEN	BROWN
IVORY	
ORANGE	
PURPLE	
YELLOW	

DRIVE OPERATING SWITCH

PUSH ROD RETAINING PAWL

RELAY

WARNING INDICATOR

END POSITION SWITCH

ELECTRIC MOTOR

MOTOR CUT-OUT

RELAY

IGNITION SWITCH

12 VOLTS

CONNECTION

NO CONNECTION

GROUND

FRAME GROUND

GROUNDS

CONNECTORS

10

MODELS AQ131A, AQ151B

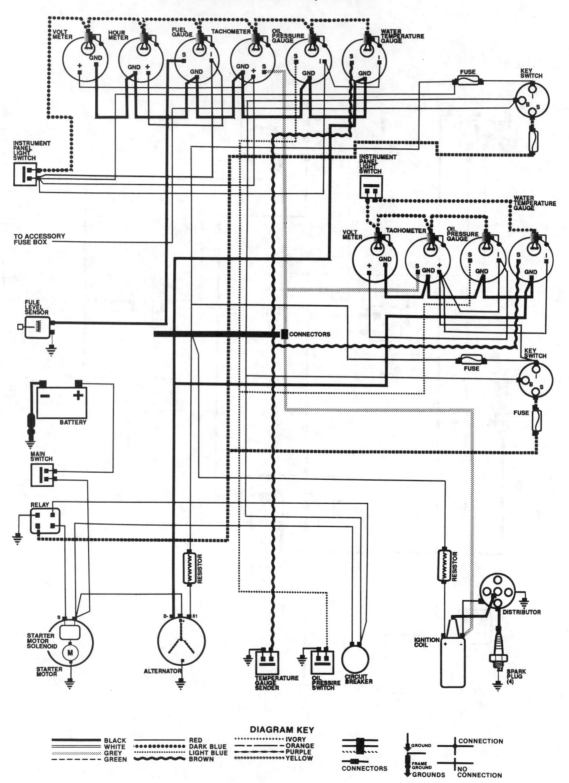

AQ171

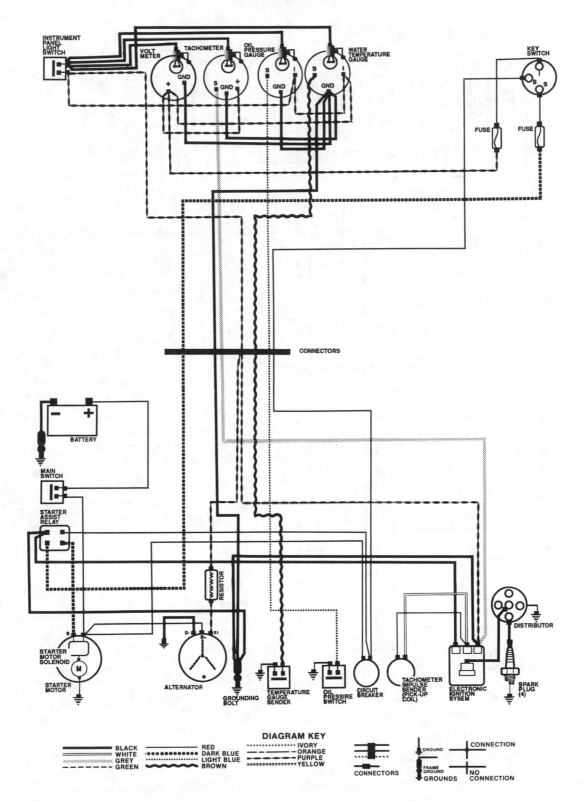

INSTRUMENT PANEL LIGHT SWITCH

VOLT METER

TACHOMETER

OIL PRESSURE GAUGE

WATER TEMPERATURE GAUGE

KEY SWITCH

FUSE

FUSE

CONNECTORS

BATTERY

MAIN SWITCH

STARTER ASSIST RELAY

RESISTOR

DISTRIBUTOR

STARTER MOTOR SOLENOID

STARTER MOTOR

ALTERNATOR

GROUNDING BOLT

TEMPERATURE GAUGE SENDER

OIL PRESSURE SWITCH

CIRCUIT BREAKER

TACHOMETER IMPULSE SENDER (PICK-UP COIL)

ELECTRONIC IGNITION SYSEM

SPARK PLUG (4)

10

DIAGRAM KEY

BLACK	RED	IVORY
WHITE	DARK BLUE	ORANGE
GREY	LIGHT BLUE	PURPLE
GREEN	BROWN	YELLOW

CONNECTORS

GROUND

FRAME GROUND

GROUNDS

CONNECTION

NO CONNECTION

MODELS AQ205, AQ211, AQ231, AQ271C, AQ311B

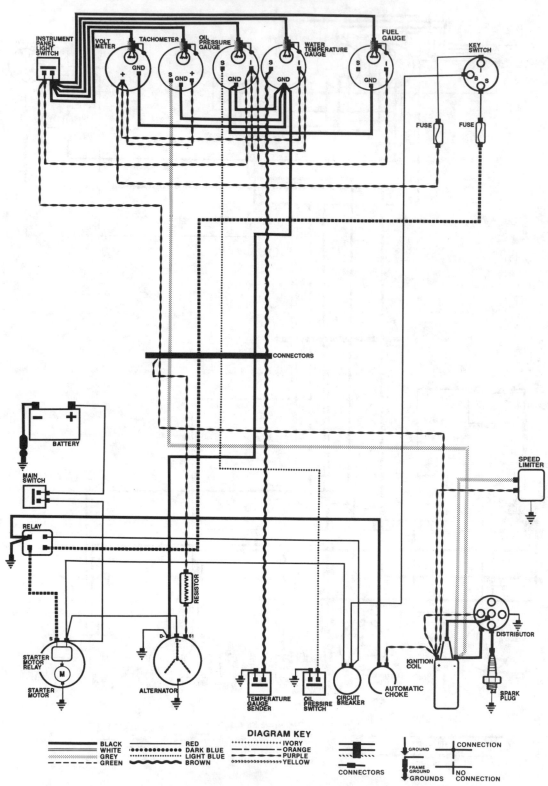

DIAGRAM KEY

WIRING COLOR CODE

The American Boat and Yacht Council (ABYC) offers a wiring color code as a voluntary standard to be used as a guide to aid the manufacturer, consumer and general public in the design, construction, equipage and maintenance of small crafts. The voluntary standard is directed toward small crafts using a direct current (DC) system under 50 volts. Wiring color codes, circuits and routings are as follows:

COLOR	CIRCUIT	ROUTING
Brown	Generator Armature Alternator Charge Light	Generator Armature to Regulator Generator Terminal/Alternator Auxiliary Terminal to Light to Regulator
Dark Blue	Cabin and Instruments Lights	Fuse or Switch to Lights
Dark Gray	Navigation Lights Tachometer	Fuse or Switch to Lights Tachometer Sender to Guage
Green	—	Bonding
Light Blue	Oil Pressure	Oil Pressure Sender to Gauge
Orange	Accessory Feed	Ammeter to Alternator or Generator Output and Accessory Fuses or Switches
Pink	Fuel Gauge	Fuel Gauge Sender to Gauge
Purple	Ignition Instrument Feed	Ignition Switch to Coil and Electrical Instruments Distribution Panel to Electric Instruments
Red	—	Positive Mains, Particulary Unfused
Tan	Water Temperature	Water Temperature Sender to Gauge
White or Black*	—	Return, Negative Main
Yellow	Generator or Alternator Field	Generator or Alternator Field to Regulator Field Terminal
Yellow/Red	Starting	Starting Switch to Solenoid

*Either white or black should be used consistantly throughout the entire wiring system.

INDEX

OUTBOARD MOTOR

12

12

INBOARD/OUTDRIVE

Volvo

12

NOTES

NOTES

NOTES

NOTES

NOTES